TECHNOLOGY

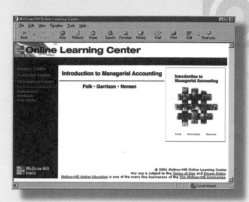

Online Learning Center

More and more students are studying online, and more and more instructors rely on the Internet to present and manage course material. That's why the **Introduction to Managerial Accounting** team has provided the most complete and up-to-date collection of Web resources—whether it be alternate problems and solutions, an online tutorial, or links to professional resources. Whether you're an instructor building a lesson plan or a student preparing for an exam, the **Introduction to Managerial Accounting OLC** is the perfect one-stop resource.

PowerWeb

Keeping your accounting course timely can be a job in itself, and now McGraw-Hill does that job for you. PowerWeb is a site from which you can

access all the latest news and developments pertinent to your course, without all the clutter and dead links of a typical online search. Students can visit PowerWeb to take a self-grading quiz or check a daily news feed analyzed by an expert in management accounting.

Course Management

The **Introduction to Managerial Accounting OLC** is even better used in conjunction with a course management system, such as BlackBoard or WebCT. Our Instructor Advantage service is ready to help you integrate your McGraw-Hill text and supplements into any 3rd-party course management platform; contact your McGraw-Hill representative for details.

If you're new to course management, we'd like to recommend PageOut, McGraw-Hill's course management system. With PageOut, you can construct a personalized course Website in a matter of minutes—you don't even need to know a word of HTML. Better still, PageOut is FREE for all McGraw-Hill adopters. To learn how to use it in your accounting course, call one of our PageOut specialists at 1-800-541-7145.

Online Information Center
Overview
Table of Contents
Author Biographies
Preface
Print and Electronic Supplements
Link to PageOut
Topic Tackler Demo
NetTutor Demo

Online Instructor Center
Instructor's Manual
PowerPoint® files
Solutions Manual
Downloadable Images From the Text
Alternate Problems and Solutions
SPATS Problems and Solutions
Links to Professional Resources

Online Student Center
Sample Study Guide and Working Papers
Learning Objectives
Chapter Overviews
Glossary of Key Terms
Chapter 4 FIFO supplement
PowerPoint® files
Internet Exercises
Online Quizzes
Links to URLs referenced in the text

Online Tutorial
SPATS Exercises
Link to ALEKS Math Skills Assessor
Practice Midterm and Final Exams
Link to NetTutor Live Online Tutoring
Downloadable Images From the Text

Other updates will be added throughout the term.

Introduction to Managerial Accounting

Jeannie M. Folk
College of DuPage

Ray H. Garrison
Professor Emeritus, Brigham Young University

Eric W. Noreen
University of Washington and INSEAD

McGraw-Hill
Irwin

Boston   Burr Ridge, IL   Dubuque, IA   Madison, WI   New York   San Francisco   St. Louis
Bangkok   Bogotá   Caracas   Kuala Lumpur   Lisbon   London   Madrid   Mexico City
Milan   Montreal   New Delhi   Santiago   Seoul   Singapore   Sydney   Taipei   Toronto

McGraw-Hill Higher Education ⚛

*A Division of The **McGraw-Hill** Companies*

INTRODUCTION TO MANAGERIAL ACCOUNTING

Published by McGraw-Hill/Irwin, an imprint of The McGraw-Hill Companies, Inc., 1221 Avenue of the Americas, New York, NY, 10020. Copyright © 2002 by The McGraw-Hill Companies, Inc. All rights reserved. No part of this publication may be reproduced or distributed in any form or by any means, or stored in a database or retrieval system, without the prior written consent of The McGraw-Hill Companies, Inc., including, but not limited to, in any network or other electronic storage or transmission, or broadcast for distance learning.

Some ancillaries, including electronic and print components, may not be available to customers outside the United States.

This book is printed on acid-free paper.

domestic   1 2 3 4 5 6 7 8 9 0 VNH/VNH 0 9 8 7 6 5 4 3 2 1
international   1 2 3 4 5 6 7 8 9 0 VNH/VNH 0 9 8 7 6 5 4 3 2 1

ISBN 0-07-242224-6

Vice president and editor-in-chief: *Robin J. Zwettler*
Senior sponsoring editor: *Stewart Mattson*
Senior development editors: *Tracey Douglas* and *Kristin Leahy*
Marketing manager: *Ryan Blankenship*
Senior project manager: *Pat Frederickson*
Lead production supervisor: *Heather Burbridge*
Lead designer: *Laurie J. Entringer*
Photo research coordinator: *Judy Kausal*
Photo researcher: *Sarah Evertson*
Senior supplement producer: *Carol Loreth*
Media producer: *Ed Przyzycki*
Cover images: © PhotoDisc
Compositor: *GAC Indianapolis*
Typeface: *10.5/12 Times Roman*
Printer: *Von Hoffmann Press, Inc.*

Library of Congress Cataloging-in-Publication Data

Folk, Jeannie M.
    Introduction to managerial accounting / Jeannie M. Folk, Ray H. Garrison, Eric W. Noreen.
      p. cm.
    Includes index.
    ISBN 0-07-242224-6 (alk. paper)
    1. Managerial accounting. I. Garrison, Ray H. II. Noreen, Eric W. III. Title.
  HF5657.4.F65 2002
  658.15'11--dc21   2001030306

INTERNATIONAL EDITION ISBN 0-07-112335-0
Copyright © 2002. Exclusive rights by The McGraw-Hill Companies, Inc. for manufacture and export.
This book cannot be re-exported from the country to which it is sold by McGraw-Hill.
The International Edition is not available in North America.

www.mhhe.com

Dedication

To my grandmother, Mary, and my children, Andy, Jessica, and Kevin.

Jeannie M. Folk

To our families and to our many colleagues who use this book.

Ray H. Garrison and Eric W. Noreen

About the Authors

Jeannie M. Folk is a professor of accounting at College of DuPage, one of the nation's largest community colleges. Professor Folk teaches financial and managerial accounting and auditing at College of DuPage and mentors accounting students working in cooperative education positions. In addition, Professor Folk is active in the area of on-line, distance education. She has developed and taught several on-line accounting courses.

Professor Folk serves on the Scholarship Committee of TACTYC (Teachers of Accounting at Two-Year Colleges) and the Illinois CPA Society's Outstanding Educator Award Task Force. She is also a member of the American Accounting Association and the American Institute of Certified Public Accountants. She was honored with the Illinois CPA Society Outstanding Educator Award and was a recipient of the Women in Management, Inc., Charlotte Danstrom Woman of Achievement Award.

Before entering academe, she was a general practice auditor with Coopers & Lybrand (now PricewaterhouseCoopers). She received her BBA from Loyola University Chicago and MAS in Accountancy from Northern Illinois University. She is the author of a wide variety of instructional materials for both financial and managerial accounting courses.

Professor Folk enjoys travel, camping, hiking, and community activities with her three children.

Ray H. Garrison is *emeritus* professor of accounting at Brigham Young University, Provo, Utah. He received his BS and MS degrees from Brigham Young University and his DBA degree from Indiana University.

As a certified public accountant, Professor Garrison has been involved in management consulting work with both national and regional accounting firms. He has published articles in *The Accounting Review, Management Accounting,* and other professional journals. Innovation in the classroom has earned Professor Garrison the Karl G. Maeser Distinguished Teaching Award from Brigham Young University.

Eric W. Noreen is a globe-trotting academic who has held appointments at institutions in the United States, Europe, and Asia. He is currently a professor of accounting at the University of Washington and Visiting Professor of Management Information & Control at INSEAD, an international graduate school of business located in France.

He received his BA degree from the University of Washington and MBA and PhD degrees from Stanford University. A Certified Management Accountant, he was awarded a Certificate of Distinguished Performance by the Institute of Certified Management Accountants.

Professor Noreen has served as associate editor of *The Accounting Review* and the *Journal of Accounting and Economics.* He has numerous articles in academic journals including: the *Journal of Accounting Research; The Accounting Review;* the *Journal of Accounting and Economics; Accounting Horizons; Accounting, Organizations and Society; Contemporary Accounting Research;* the *Journal of Management Accounting Research;* and the *Review of Accounting Studies.*

Professor Noreen teaches management accounting at the undergraduate and masters levels and has won a number of awards from students for his teaching.

Preface

The decision to publish *Introduction to Managerial Accounting* resulted from discussions with selected groups of faculty members, business leaders, and students. Our goal was to create an introductory textbook that meets the current needs and desires of each of these groups. Faculty members expressed a need for an introductory managerial accounting textbook that would support their efforts to prepare students for successful careers in today's economy. Business leaders stated that greater emphasis is being placed on the skills that candidates must demonstrate during the interview process. The definition of a "traditional" accounting student is changing, as students struggle to balance their desire for quality education with their professional and personal lives. These students value their time and resources.

What Do Faculty Members Want?

Faculty members describe the introductory managerial accounting textbook that would meet their needs by citing three important characteristics. The textbook must be manageable, that is, consist of material that can be covered in one semester. In addition to being understandable, the textbook must be accurate, relevant, and up-to-date, and have high-quality end-of-chapter materials. The textbook must also have a strong pedagogical framework that facilitates both learning and the development of skills that employers require of new hires.

What Do Business Leaders Want?

Business leaders assume that the students who make it into the interview process have the required technical expertise. The accounting candidates who receive job offers clearly demonstrate that they also have the skills that are essential for success in the business world. The sought-after skills include: an aptitude for both oral and written communication, a talent for analyzing information and making effective decisions, a willingness to work effectively with team members, and a high level of comfort with technology (including familiarity with spreadsheets and the use of the Internet to gather information for decision making). Faculty members referred to these same skills and stressed the need for textbook support for the development of these proficiencies in their students.

These skills are consistent with the SCANS competencies. The Secretary of Labor appointed a commission, the Secretary's Commission on Achieving Necessary Skills (SCANS), to identify the skills people need to succeed in the workplace. SCANS' fundamental purpose is to encourage a high-performance economy characterized by high-skill, high-wage employment. The commission's message to educators is: Help your students connect what they learn in class to the world outside. To help educators prepare their students for the workplace, SCANS identified five workplace competencies that should be taught: (1) resource skills (the ability to allocate time, money, materials, space, and staff);

(2) interpersonal skills (the ability to work on teams, teach others, serve customers, lead, negotiate, and work well with people from culturally diverse backgrounds); (3) information ability (the ability to acquire and evaluate data, organize and maintain files, interpret and communicate, and use computers to process information); (4) systems understanding (the ability to operate within various social, organizational, and technological systems and to monitor and correct performance to design or improve systems); and (5) technological ability (the ability to select equipment and tools, apply technology to specific tasks, and maintain and troubleshoot equipment). The pedagogical tools in this text and package are designed to facilitate these SCANS competencies.

What Do Students Want?

Like instructors, students desire a clear and understandable introductory managerial accounting textbook that is engaging and interesting to read. They need interesting examples to help them understand and appreciate how managerial accounting concepts are applied in the real world. They want to be able to practice and apply their grasp of key concepts as they work through manageable end-of-chapter exercises and problems. Finally, students who view managerial accounting as an essential and practical component of their education (rather than just one of those required courses) expressed a desire for meaningful supplemental materials. They must balance other commitments with the additional time required to use such materials. As such, they stressed the need for these materials to focus on the hard-to-master concepts, be directly related to and use terminology consistent with that used in the textbook, and be interactive.

How Did We Respond to the Demand for an Accurate, Up-to-Date, and Manageable Text?

By focusing on the **core concepts** that faculty cover in one semester, we have been able to create a 14-chapter managerial accounting text. Based on feedback, 14 chapters appeared to be the number of chapters most faculty cover in a semester. Faculty advised which **topics** to include in an introductory course and which would be best covered in an advanced course. In addition to the standard managerial accounting topics that you expect to see, this text does introduce newer topics such as activity-based costing, theory of constraints, just-in-time, and others. Our primary concern when discussing these newer topics is to present the material in an understandable manner for the student. The emphasis has been on a clear **writing style,** use of appropriate **examples,** and solid end-of-chapter materials for **reinforcement.**

We realize that many instructors choose to cover the statement of cash flows using a worksheet approach, while others prefer to introduce the statement using T-accounts. In response, both approaches have been included. The worksheet approach is used in the body of the chapter while the appendix uses a T-account format. The **two approaches** complement one another. We believe that many students will benefit by the dual coverage whether or not their instructors choose to cover both approaches in class.

We feel that the **skills** outlined earlier are so important that throughout the text we have end-of-chapter material that help build these skills. Within each chapter, we have included relevant real world examples to help students see how these concepts are applied in business.

The Prologue provides an introduction to the revolutionary **changes** that today's managers are facing. Companies have gone through several waves of improvement programs, starting with just-in-time and continuing with total quality management, process reengineering, theory of constraints, and benchmarking. These changes are having a profound effect on the practice of management accounting.

The chapter **organization** is designed to expose students to fundamental managerial accounting concepts such as job-order costing and process costing before introducing decision-making tools such as CVP, activity-based costing, standard costs, and budgeting.

Pedagogy

Chapter One

An Introduction to Managerial Accounting and Cost Concepts

A Look Back

We addressed some of the challenges faced by managers during the 1980s and 1990s in the Prologue, and described the significant improvement programs that were adopted by many companies during that period. You were introduced to Good Vibrations, an international retailer of music CDs, and learned about their organizational structure. After describing the role of the controller, we stressed the importance of professional ethics and codes of conduct, and provided information about the Certified Management Accountant designation.

A Look at This Chapter

After describing the three major activities of managers in the context of Good Vibrations, Inc., this chapter compares and contrasts financial and managerial accounting. We define many of the terms that are used to classify costs in business. Because these terms will be used throughout the text, you should ensure that you are familiar with each of them.

A Look Ahead

Chapters 2, 3, and 4 describe managerial costing systems that are used to compute product costs. Chapter 2 describes job-order costing. Chapter 3 describes activity-based costing, an elaboration of job-order costing. Chapter 4 covers process costing.

Chapter Outline

The Work of Management and the Need for Managerial Accounting Information
- Planning
- Directing and Motivating
- Controlling
- The End Results of Managers' Activities
- The Planning and Control Cycle

Comparison of Financial and Managerial Accounting
- Emphasis on the Future
- Relevance and Flexibility of Data
- Less Emphasis on Precision
- Segments of an Organization
- Generally Accepted Accounting Principles (GAAP)
- Managerial Accounting—Not Mandatory

General Cost Classifications
- Manufacturing Costs
- Nonmanufacturing Costs

Product Costs versus Period Costs
- Product Costs
- Period Costs

Cost Classifications on Financial Statements
- The Balance Sheet
- The Income Statement
- Schedule of Cost of Goods Manufactured

Product Costs—A Closer Look
- Inventoriable Costs
- An Example of Cost Flows

Cost Classifications for Predicting Cost Behavior
- Variable Cost
- Fixed Cost

Cost Classifications for Assigning Costs to Cost Objects
- Direct Cost
- Indirect Cost

Cost Classifications for Decision Making
- Differential Cost and Revenue
- Opportunity Cost
- Sunk Cost

Appendix 1A: Cost of Quality
- Quality of Conformance
- Distribution of Quality Cost
- Quality Cost Report

Each chapter begins with a two-page chapter opening designed to help orient the student and prepare for the material that is covered in the chapter.

The **A Look Back, A Look at This Chapter,** and **A Look Ahead** features launch the chapter and establish bridges between chapters, assisting the student in linking concepts across the topics and in understanding how the chapters fit together.

The **Chapter Outline** provides students with an outline of the topics that will be covered in the chapter.

Decision Feature **Managing the Marines**

Many businesses are challenged by rapidly changing conditions and increasingly complex situations. Few would look to the military, especially the Marines, for ideas on how to succeed in today's business environment. Marines are soldiers, who blindly follow the orders given them, aren't they? This may be true in boot camp, but is no longer the case outside of that arena. In order to survive in today's world, the Marine Corps has reexamined its organizational structure. Innovative solutions enable the Corps to react promptly and creatively to the same types of threats that are facing today's business managers.

Their success in dealing with immediate challenges is attributed to four principles.

Fast decisions are essential.
- Even though there is a downside to making a decision with incomplete and hastily analyzed information, the alternative of not reacting to an immediate threat presents an unacceptable risk. Breaking the problem down into pieces facilitates the process.

All members of the organization are empowered to make decisions.
- The organization chart of the Marine Corps is much more of a pyramid than that illustrated in Exhibit 3 of the Prologue. After studying the effectiveness of the many layers of management, the Marines concluded that the pyramidal structure works best. However, they also recognized that decisions made by high-level officers couldn't always be communicated on timely basis to Marines engaged in combat. Accordingly, men and women fighting on the front lines are allowed to change or make decisions and take the steps necessary to implement the decisions.

People learn by making mistakes.
- When you make a mistake and have to live with the consequences, you learn from that experience. The Marines tolerate mistakes for the same reason. In fact, a Marine who doesn't make mistakes occasionally is viewed as someone who doesn't take enough risk.

Seek the advice of people outside of the organization.
- To keep pace with the changing world, the Marine Corps taps into the creativity and expertise of others. A psychologist who has extensively studied the decision-making process was brought in to assist in the redesign of the training that is provided to Marines who will be required to make decisions in combat.

In many ways, the work of management, whether in business or in the Marines Corps, is the same.

Source: David H. Freedman, "A Few Good Principles—What the Marines Can Teach Silicon Valley,"

Learning Objectives
After studying Chapter 1, you should be able to:

LO1 Identify and give examples of each of the three basic manufacturing cost categories.

LO2 Distinguish between product costs and period costs and give examples of each.

LO3 Prepare an income statement including calculation of the cost of goods sold.

LO4 Prepare a schedule of cost of goods manufactured.

LO5 Define and give examples of variable costs and fixed costs.

LO6 Define and give examples of direct and indirect costs.

LO7 Define and give examples of cost classifications used in making decisions: differential costs, opportunity costs, and sunk costs.

LO8 (Appendix 1A) Identify the four types of quality costs and explain how they interact.

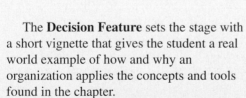

The **Decision Feature** sets the stage with a short vignette that gives the student a real world example of how and why an organization applies the concepts and tools found in the chapter.

The **Learning Objectives** are listed at the beginning of each chapter and are tied directly to the summaries at the end of the chapter. These objectives help students preview and review what they are expected to know and understand after reading the chapter.

The **In Business Today** feature provides examples of how companies throughout the world apply or are affected by a managerial accounting issue, concept, or tool.

in business today **A Return on Investment of 100%**

During negotiations to build a replacement for the old Fenway Park in Boston, the Red Sox offered the city approximately $2 million per year over 30 years in exchange for an investment of $150 million by the city for land acquisition and cleanup. In May 2000, after denying his lack of support for the project, Boston Mayor Thomas M. Menino stated that his goal is a 100% rate of return on any investment that is made by the city. Some doubt that the Red Sox would be able to pay players' salaries if the team were required to meet the mayor's goal. The mayor has countered with a list of suggestions for raising private funds (such as selling shares to the public, as the Celtics did in 1986). Private funds would reduce the investment that would need to be made by the city and, as a result, reduce the future payments made to the city by the Red Sox. Negotiations continue.

Source: Meg Vaillancourt, "Boston Mayor Wants High Return on Investment in New Ballpark," *Knight-Ridder/Tribune Business News*, May 11, 2000, pITEM00133018. Reprinted with permission of Knight Ridder/Tribune Information Services.

Managerial Accounting in Action

The Wrap Up

Hampton Freeze, Inc.

After completing the master budget, Larry Giano took the documents to Tom Wills, chief executive officer of Hampton Freeze, for his review.

Larry: Here's the budget. Overall, the net income is excellent, and the net cash flow for the entire year is positive.
Tom: Yes, but I see on this cash budget that we have the same problem with negative cash flows in the first and second quarters that we had last year.
Larry: That's true. I don't see any way around that problem. However, there is no doubt in my mind that if you take this budget to the bank today, they'll approve an open line of credit that will allow you to borrow enough to make it through the first two quarters without any problem.
Tom: Are you sure? They didn't seem very happy to see me last year when I came in for an emergency loan.
Larry: Did you repay the loan on time?
Tom: Sure.
Larry: I don't see any problem. You won't be asking for an emergency loan this time. The bank will have plenty of warning. And with this budget, you have a solid plan that shows when and how you are going to pay off the loan. Trust me, they'll go for it.
Tom: Fantastic! It would sure make life a lot easier this year.

The **Managerial Accounting in Action** feature is used to introduce core concepts and stimulate interest. They incorporate real products and services to which students can relate.

The **Decision Maker** feature fosters critical thinking and decision-making skills by providing real world business scenarios that require the resolution of a business issue. The suggested solution is located at the end of each chapter.

decision maker **Hospital Administrator**

You are the administrator of a community hospital. The hospital's board of directors has questioned the pricing of certain services and noted that the fees charged for these services seem to be considerably lower than those charged by nearby hospitals. After interviewing one of the hospital's costs analysts, you learn that a hospital-wide rate has been used to assign a single pool of overhead costs to services. After reading about activity-based costing, you make a list of other cost pools that might be more appropriate and plan to ask the cost analyst to identify the cost drivers that might relate to those cost pools. What cost pools would you include on the list?

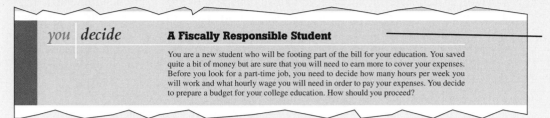

The **You Decide** feature challenges students to apply the tools of analysis and make decisions. The suggested solution is found at the end of the chapter.

The **Review Problem** found at the end of each chapter helps students reinforce the material learned in the chapter. The review problem is followed by a solution.

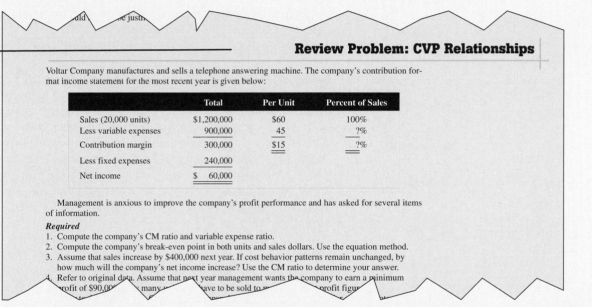

Review Problem: CVP Relationships

Voltar Company manufactures and sells a telephone answering machine. The company's contribution format income statement for the most recent year is given below:

	Total	Per Unit	Percent of Sales
Sales (20,000 units)	$1,200,000	$60	100%
Less variable expenses	900,000	45	?%
Contribution margin	300,000	$15	?%
Less fixed expenses	240,000		
Net income	$ 60,000		

Management is anxious to improve the company's profit performance and has asked for several items of information.

Required
1. Compute the company's CM ratio and variable expense ratio.
2. Compute the company's break-even point in both units and sales dollars. Use the equation method.
3. Assume that sales increase by $400,000 next year. If cost behavior patterns remain unchanged, by how much will the company's net income increase? Use the CM ratio to determine your answer.
4. Refer to original data. Assume that next year management wants the company to earn a minimum profit of $90,000 ... many ... ave to be sold to ... profit figu ...

The **Summary** describes the chapter in terms of the learning objectives and assists the reader in identifying key concepts and analyses.

The **Glossary** describes key terms used in the chapter. It provides a page reference to the first use in that chapter.

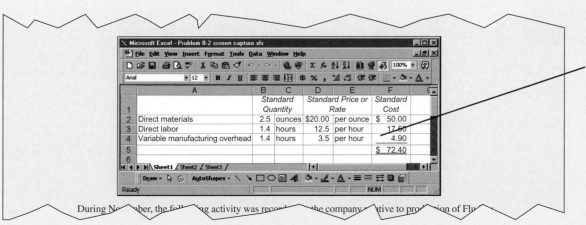

Exhibits in selected chapters are presented in **Excel Spreadsheet** screen captures. Such spreadsheets are routinely used in business to prepare analyses and reports.

During No ... ber, the f ... ng activity was reco ... the company ... tive to pro ... ion of Fl ...

End-of-Chapter Material

This author team has always been known for their quality and quantity of assignment material. *Introduction to Managerial Accounting* has a wide variety of end-of-chapter materials to assist students.

The **Questions** are short questions that students can use to ensure that they have mastered concepts. Faculty can also use the questions to ensure that the students are grasping the concepts.

Each **Brief Exercise** covers a single learning objective. These simple exercises serve as building blocks to prepare the student for the longer exercises and problems. Faculty can use the brief exercises as quick in-class exercises.

The **Exercises** cover multiple learning objectives.

The **Problems** challenge students to apply themselves. Alternate problems for each chapter may be found on the text's website at www.mhhe.com/folk1e.

The **Building Your Skills** section contains problem materials that help students develop communication, teamwork, Internet, and analytical skills.

- **Analytical Thinking** problems challenge students to think critically and apply their analytical skills to find the solutions.
- **Communicating in Practice** problems stress oral and written communication skills. Students are provided with opportunities to either interview accountants and managers to gain insights into decisions made in business or analyze solutions, and then are asked to present their findings and conclusions in writing.
- **Ethics Challenges** provide the opportunity for role-playing in business situations with ethical consequences. The goal of these exercises is to reinforce the need for ethical behavior. Guidance answers are provided for instructors.
- **Taking It to the Net** calls for students to access websites and obtain and use relevant information. In addition to highlighting the possibilities of the Internet as a source of information, these questions help students to become more comfortable with using the Internet. The Taking It to the Net exercises are posted at the website www.mhhe.com/folk1e. We have placed these exercises on the Internet so that they can be periodically updated throughout the life of this edition.
- **Teamwork in Action** requires teams to prepare, analyze, and use information to solve problems and then present their ideas to the class.

Topic Tackler

Topic Tackler is an exciting, interactive CD created by Jeannie Folk to help students with the concepts they typically find the most difficult to learn. These concepts are highlighted in the text with the topic tackler icon, which tells the student that they can refer to the CD for additional instruction. The material on the CD includes a video segment, a PowerPoint® slide show, a practice session, and a self-test for each of the 28 difficult-to-master concepts. It also contains a student tutorial.

The following are examples of the difficult-to-master topics that are included in Topic Tackler:

- Application of Overhead
- Computing Activity Rates and Product Costs
- Calculation of Equivalent Units
- Process-Costing Cost Reconciliation
- Contribution Format Income Statement
- Budgeting Process
- Flexible Budgets
- Variance Analysis (Direct Materials, Direct Labor, and Overhead)
- Adding or Dropping Product Lines or Segments
- Make or Buy Decisions
- Net Present Value Method for Capital Budgeting
- Classifying Cash Flows

Instructor Supplements

 ***Instructor CD-ROM* ISBN 0-07-246632-4**
An all-in-one resource that allows instructors to create a customized multimedia presentation that incorporates the Test Bank, PowerPoint® Slides, Instructor's Resource Guide, Solutions Manual, Links to PageOut, and Spreadsheet Application Template Software.

***Instructor's Resource Guide* ISBN 0-07-246621-9**
Extensive chapter-by-chapter lecture notes to help with classroom presentation. Useful suggestions for presenting key concepts and ideas are included. This supplement contains the teaching transparency masters.

***Solutions Manual* ISBN 0-07-246830-0**
The manual contains solutions for all assignment materials, including a general discussion of how to use the group exercises. The print supplement is packaged with a CD-ROM.

***Solutions Acetates* ISBN 0-07-246625-1**
Overhead transparencies are available for the Solutions Manual.

***Ready Shows* ISBN 0-07-246832-7 Available on Web and instructor CD-ROM only.**
A multimedia lecture slide package using PowerPoint® Slides, version 7, to illustrate key objectives and topics. A viewer is included so that screens can be shown with or without Microsoft® PowerPoint® software.

***Diploma for Windows* ISBN 0-07-246624-3**
A computerized version of the Test Bank, delivered in the Brownstone Diploma shell. It can be used to create different versions of the same test, change the answer order, edit and add questions, and conduct on-line testing.

***Test Bank* ISBN 0-07-246623-5**
A wide variety of test materials organized by chapter, including true/false, multiple-choice, and problems.

 ***Instructor Spreadsheet Application Template Software (SPATS)* ISBN 0-07-246831-9 Available on Web and instructor CD-ROM only.**
Prepared by Jack Terry of ComSource Associates Inc., these Excel templates offer solutions to the Student SPATS version. SPATS is available on the Web.

***Check Figures* ISBN 0-07-246834-3 Available on Web only.**
The list of check figures gives key answers for selected assignment materials.

***Video Library* ISBN 0-07-237617-1**
These short, action-oriented videos, developed by Dallas County Community College, provide the impetus for lively classroom discussion. The focus is on the preparation, analysis, and use of accounting information for business decision-making. (To acquire the complete telecourse, Accounting in Action, call Dallas TeleLearning at 972-669-6666, or FAX 972-669-6668 or visit their website at www.lecroy.dcccd.edu.)

Student Supplements

***Topic Tackler CD-ROM* ISBN 0-07-246617-0**
Free with the text, the Topic Tackler CD-ROM helps students master difficult concepts in managerial accounting through a creative, interactive learning process. Designed for study outside the classroom, the Topic Tackler is a complete tutorial focusing on challenging topics in managerial accounting. This multimedia CD delves into chapter concepts with graphical slides and diagrams, web links, video clips, and animations, all centered around engaging exercises designed to put students in control of their learning of managerial accounting topics.

***Workbook/Study Guide* ISBN 0-07-246636-7**
This study aid provides suggestions for studying chapter material, summarizes essential points in each chapter, and tests students' knowledge using self-test questions and exercises.

***Ready Notes* ISBN 0-07-246642-1**
This booklet provides the PowerPoint® exhibits in a workbook format for efficient note taking.

***Student Lecture Aid* ISBN 0-07-246643-X**
Similar to Ready Notes, this booklet offers a print version of all of the Teaching Transparencies. Students can annotate the material during the lecture and take notes in the spaces provided.

***Working Papers* ISBN 0-07-246640-5**
This booklet study aid contains partially completed forms for use in completing homework problems. Not only will students save time by using the working papers, they will be guided in how to organize their answers and solutions.

 ***Spreadsheet Application Template Software (SPATS)* ISBN 0-07-246842-4 Available on Web only.**
Excel templates, prepared by Jack Terry of ComSource Associates Inc., can be used to solve selected problems and cases in the text. These selected problems and cases are identified in the margin of the text with an appropriate icon. SPATS is available on the Web.

Mansuetti & Weidkamp: Ramblewood Manufacturing, Inc. Windows-Based Practice Set
Student ISBN 0-07-234815-1
Instructor's Manual ISBN 0-07-234642-6
Ramblewood Manufacturing, Inc. by Leland Mansuetti and Keith Weidkamp of Sierra College is a computerized practice set. It presents a simulation of business transactions for a corporation that manufactures metal fencing. The practice set is intended for use after coverage of job-order cost accounting using a JIT inventory system. Estimated completion time is 10–14 hours.

The Interactive Managerial Accounting Lab
ISBN 0-07-236138-7
This software provides exercises related to managerial accounting. It is presented in the same style as the Interactive Financial Accounting Lab. (Developed by Diane Pattison of the University of San Diego and Patrick McKenzie and Rick Birney of Arizona State University.)

Online Learning Center www.mhhe.com/folk1e

The comprehensive Online Learning Center (OLC) is organized by chapter and provides students with a wealth of useful resources.

A password-protected **Instructor Center** contains the instructor materials and other useful resources such as links to Spreadsheet Application Software, professional resources, web-based projects, and sample syllabi.

The **Student Center** contains a variety of relevant materials designed to support and enhance student learning, such as self-study quizzes (with a feedback mechanism) and Spreadsheet Application templates. In addition, a supplement to Chapter Four, "Process Costing Using the FIFO Method," is included here. Selected supplemental end-of-chapter materials, such as the Alternate Problems and the Taking It to the Net exercises, are also housed in The Student Center.

 *NetTutor* allows tutors and students to communicate with each other in a variety of ways: through a Live Tutor Center, a Q&A Center, an Archive Center, and a Management Center. Students are issued 10 hours of free NetTutor time when they purchase a new copy of the text. Additional time may be purchased in 5-hour increments. Live tutor availability will vary throughout the course of the term, with a peak availability of around 60 hours a week.

- The Live Tutor Center enables a tutor to hold an interactive on-line tutorial for several students.

- The Q&A Center allows students to submit questions and retrieve answers within 24 hours.

- The Archive Center allows students to browse previously asked questions for their answers. They can also search for questions pertinent to a particular topic. If they encounter an answer they do not understand, they can ask a follow-up question.

- The Management Center makes it easy to create, update, and delete groups and members, as well as to customize the site to suit the needs of the group. The OLC website also serves as a doorway to other technology solutions.

PageOut, an exclusive McGraw-Hill product, provides simple steps to enable instructors to create a professional course website. A team of product specialists is available to help. The instructor can supplement the website by using the interactive course syllabus functions. Pageout's online grade book automatically stores quiz and test grades and allows scores to be posted to the whole class or individually. The discussion board offers the instructor and students a forum to pose questions, exchange ideas, and talk about topics relating to the course.

 PowerWeb extends the learning experience beyond the core textbook by offering all of the latest news and developments pertinent to the course, via the Internet. It offers current articles related to managerial accounting, weekly updates with assessment tools, informative and timely world news culled by an expert, refereed web links, and more. In addition, PowerWeb provides a trove of helpful learning aids, including self-grading quizzes and interactive glossaries and exercises. Students may also access study tips, conduct online research, and learn about different career paths. Visit the PowerWeb site at www.dushkin.com/powerweb.

The Online Learning Center offers different delivery platforms:

WebCT is one of the most popular and easy-to-use platforms available. McGraw-Hill will prepay the WebCT site license for students and there are also two service agreements available with WebCT.

EColleges.com is one of the most robust and stable online course authoring and management platforms in on-line education. It provides course-hosting development services for faculty and around-the-clock service.

Blackboard.com is one of the fastest and easiest ways to manage on-line courses. The courses are hosted on Blackboard's servers.

TopClass provides on-line discussion and message boards. On-line testing scores can be recorded and automatically placed in an instructor's grade book.

As a full service publisher of quality educational products, McGraw-Hill does much more than just sell textbooks to your students. We create and publish an extensive array of print, video, and digital supplements to support instruction on your campus. Orders of new (versus used) textbooks help us to defray the cost of developing such supplements, which is substantial. Please consult your local McGraw-Hill representative to learn about the availability of the supplements that accompany this text.

Acknowledgments

We appreciate the encouragement and support that we have received from instructors throughout the world. Each person who has offered comments and suggestions has our thanks.

We would like to thank the following instructors for their recommendations:

Reviewers

Betty Jo Browning, Bradley University
Alan Czyzewski, Indiana State University
Deborah Davis, Hampton University
James Emig, Villanova University
Harriet Farney, University of Hartford
Jackson Gillespie, University of Delaware
Joe Goetz, Louisiana State University
Art Goldman, University of Kentucky

David Jacobson, Salem State College
Holly Johnston, Boston University
Lisa Martin, Western Michigan University
Michael O'Neill, Seattle Central Community College
Leonardo Rodriguez, Florida International University
Eldon Schafer, University of Arizona
Soliman Soliman, Tulane University

Consultants

Wagdy Abdallah, Seton Hall University
Sheila Ammons, Austin Community College
Mohamed Bayou, University of Michigan—Dearborn
Suzanne Breitenbach, Keller Graduate School of Business
Thomas Buttros, Indiana University at Kokomo
Larry Carney, Fontbonne College
Robert Close, Consumnes River College
Gail Cook, University of Wisconsin—Parkside
Jeremy Cripps, Heidelberg College
Patricia Doherty, Boston University
Pete Dorff, Kent State University
Alan Doyle, Pima College
Sheila Handy, Lafayette College
Thomas Hoar, Houston Community College
Bonnie Holloway, Lake-Sumter Community College
Susan Hughes, Butler University
Phillip Jones, University of Richmond
Carol Keller, Coastal Carolina University
Janice Klimek, Missouri Western State College
Terry Lindenberg, Rock Valley College
Lawrence Logan, University of Massachusetts—Dartmouth
Rex Mahlman, Northwestern Oklahoma State University
Carol Mannino, Milwaukee School of Engineering

Duncan McDougall, Plymouth State College
Noel McKeon, Florida Community College
David Morris, North Georgia College and State University
Doug Moses, Naval Postgraduate School
Kevin Nathan, Oakland University
Kathy Otero, University of Texas at El Paso
Michael Pearson, Kent State University
Vaughan Radcliffe, Case Western Reserve University
David Remmele, University of Wisconsin—Whitewater
John Roberts, St. John's River Community College
Don Schwartz, National University
Mayda Shorney, St. Gregory's University
Donald Simons, Frostburg State University
Parvez Sopariwala, Grand Valley State University
Mel Stinnett, Oklahoma Christian University
Ephraim Sudit, Rutgers University—Newark
Kimberly Temme, Maryville University
Nicole Turner, Florida Community College—Jacksonville
Kiran Verma, University of Massachusetts—Boston
Lee Warren, Boston College
Ronald Wood, Pittsburg State University
Martha Woodman, University of Vermont

Survey Respondents

L. M. Abney, LaSalle University
Robert Appleton, University of North Carolina—Wilmington
Leonard Bacon, California State University, Bakersfield

Larry Bitner, Hood College
Jay Blazer, Milwaukee Area Technical College
Nancy Bledsoe, Millsaps College
William Blouch, Loyola College

Eugene Blue, Governor State University

Casey Bradley, Troy State University

Marley Brown, Mt. Hood Community College

Myra Bruegger, Southeastern Community College

Francis Bush, Virginia Military Institute

Rebecca Butler, Gateway Community College

June Calahan, Redlands Community College

Elizabeth Cannata, Stonehill College

John Chandler, University of Illinois—Champaign

Lawrence Chin, Golden Gate University

Carolyn Clark, St. Joseph's University

Joanne Collins, California State University—Los Angeles

Judith Cook, Grossmont College

Charles Croxford, Merced College

Richard Cummings, Benedictine College

Jill Cunningham, Santa Fe Community College

G. DiLorenzo, Gloucester County College

Michael Farina, Cerritos College

M. A. Fekrat, Georgetown University

W. L. Ferrara, Stetson University

James Franklin, Troy State University Montgomery

David Gibson, Hampden-Sydney College

John Gill, Jackson State University

James Gravel, Husson College

Linda Hadley, University of Dayton

Anita Hape, Farrant County Jr. College

Dan Hary, Southwestern Oklahoma State University

Susan Hass, Simmons College

Robert Hayes, Tennessee State University

James Hendricks, Northern Illinois University

Nancy Thorley Hill, DePaul University

Kathy Ho, Niagra University

Ronald Huntsman, Texas Lutheran University

Wayne Ingalls, University of Maine College

Martha Janis, University of Wisconsin—Waukesha

Sanford Kahn, University of Cincinnati

Greg Kordecki, Clayton College and State University

Michael Kulper, Santa Barbara City College

Christopher Kwak, Ohlone College

Robert Larson, Penn State University

Barry Lewis, Southwest Missouri State University

Joan Litton, Ferrum College

G. D. Lorenzo, Gloucester Community College

Bob Mahan, Milligan College

Leland Mansuetti, Sierra College

Laura Morgan, University of New Hampshire

Anthony Moses, Saint Anselm College

Daniel Mugavero, Lake Superior State University

Presha Neidermeyer, Union College

Eustace Phillip, Emmanuel College

Anthony Piltz, Rocky Mountain College

H. M. Pomroy, Elizabethtown College

Alan Porter, Eastern New Mexico University

Barbara Prince, Cambridge Community College

Ahmad Rahman, La Roch College

Joan Reicosky, University of Minnesota—Morris

Gary Ross, College of the Southwest

Martha Sampsell, Elmhurst College

Roger Scherser, Edison Community College

Deborah Shafer, Temple College

Ola Smith, Michigan State University

John Snyder, Florida Technical

Alice Steljes, Illinois Valley Community College

Joseph Ugras, LaSalle University

Edward Walker, University of Texas—Pan American

Frank Walker, Lee College

Robert Weprin, Lourdes College

Brent Wickham, Owens Community College

Geri Wink, University of Texas at Tyler

James Wolfson, Wilson College

The authors would like to thank the following students who helped them immensely in many ways: Andy Folk, Jessica Folk, Suzanne Gelderman, Steve Groszik, Crystal Hoyer, Brenda Iino, Annika Noreen, Olga Ugarova, and Lisa Waiblinger.

The authors would like to thank the team at McGraw-Hill/Irwin: Stewart Mattson, senior sponsoring editor; Tracey Douglas and Kristin Leahy, senior developmental editors; Erin Cibula, editorial coordinator; Jackie Scruggs, senior software coordinator; Ed Przyzycki, media technology producer; Ryan Blankenship, marketing manager; Laurie Entringer, lead designer; Carol Loreth, senior supplements producer; Pat Frederickson, senior project manager; Michael McCormick, senior production supervisor; Judy Kausal, photo research coordinator, and Sarah Evertson, photo researcher. Special thanks go to Barbara Schnathorst and Beth Woods, our accuracy checkers, and Diane Colwyn, our permissions researcher.

We also thank the Institute of Certified Management Accountants for permission to use questions and/or unofficial answers from past Certificate in Management Accountant (CMA) examinations. Likewise we thank the American Institute of Certified Public Accountants, the Society of Management Accountants of Canada, and the Chartered Institute of Management Accountants (United Kingdom) for permission to use (or to adapt) selected problems from their examinations. These problems bear the notations CMA, CPA, SMA, and CIMA, respectively.

Brief | Table of Contents

Table of Contents

Prologue

Managerial Accounting and the Business Environment

Prologue Outline

Just-in-Time (JIT)
- The JIT Approach
- Zero Defects and JIT
- Benefits of a JIT System

Total Quality Management (TQM)
- The Plan-Do-Check-Act Cycle
- An Example of TQM in Practice

Process Reengineering
- The Problem of Employee Morale

The Theory of Constraints (TOC)
- An Example of TOC
- TOC and Continuous Improvement

International Competition

Organizational Structure
- Decentralization
- Line and Staff Relationships
- The Controller

Professional Ethics
- Code of Conduct for Management Accountants
- Company Codes of Conduct
- Codes of Conduct on the International Level

The Certified Management Accountant (CMA)

A Look at the Prologue

Just as you are amazed as you listen to your grandparents and parents talk about the "good old days," today's managers are amazed to discover that their world is constantly changing and becoming even more complex. Before we get down to the basics, this Prologue will expose you to a few of the revolutionary concepts that today's managers are facing. These managers would not be able to make effective decisions in today's rapidly changing environment if they did not have a solid base to build on.

A Look Ahead

Chapter 1 describes the work performed by managers, stresses the need for managerial accounting information, contrasts managerial and financial accounting, and defines many of the cost terms that will be used throughout the textbook. You will begin to build your base there.

The last two decades have been a period of tremendous turmoil and change in the business environment. Competition in many industries has become worldwide in scope, and the pace of innovation in products and services has accelerated. This has been good news for consumers, since intensified competition has generally led to lower prices, higher quality, and more choices. However, the last two decades have been a period of wrenching change for many businesses and their employees. Many managers have learned that cherished ways of doing business do not work anymore and that major changes must be made in the way organizations are managed and work gets done. These changes are so great that some observers view them as a second industrial revolution. And to add even more dynamism, the Internet has been changing the fundamental ways of doing business in more and more industries since the mid 1990s.

These changes are having a profound effect on the practice of management accounting—as we will see throughout the rest of the text. First, however, it is necessary to have an appreciation of the ways in which organizations are transforming themselves to become more competitive. Since the early 1980s, many companies have gone through several waves of improvement programs, starting with just-in-time (JIT) and passing on to total quality management (TQM), process reengineering, and various other management programs—including in some companies the theory of constraints (TOC). When properly implemented, these improvement programs can enhance quality, reduce cost, increase output, eliminate delays in responding to customers, and ultimately increase profits. They have not, however, always been wisely implemented, and considerable controversy exists concerning the ultimate value of each of these programs. Nevertheless, the current business environment cannot be properly understood without an appreciation of what each of these approaches attempts to accomplish. Each is worthy of extended study, but we will discuss them only in the broadest terms. The details are best handled in operations management courses.

Just-in-Time (JIT)

Traditionally, managers in manufacturing companies have sought to minimize the unit costs of products on the theory that in the long run only the lowest cost producer will survive and prosper. This strategy led managers to maximize production to spread the fixed costs of investments in equipment and other assets over as many units as possible. In addition, managers have traditionally felt that an important part of their job was to keep everyone busy—idleness wastes money. These traditional views, often aided and abetted by traditional management accounting practices, resulted in a number of practices that have come under severe criticism in recent years. The critics point to excessive inventories as the most visible symptom of outdated management practices. Why do excessive inventories result from the desire to maximize production and to keep everyone busy and why are they a problem?

In a traditional manufacturing company, work is *pushed* through the system. Enough materials are released to workstations to keep everyone busy, and when a workstation completes its tasks, the partially completed goods are "pushed" forward to the next workstation regardless of whether that workstation is ready to receive them. The result is that partially completed goods stack up, waiting for the next workstation to become available. They may not be completed for days, weeks, or even months. Additionally, when the units are finally completed, customers may or may not want them. If finished goods are produced faster than the market will absorb, the result is bloated finished goods inventories.

In addition, companies maintained large amounts of inventories as a form of insurance so that operations could proceed smoothly even if unanticipated disruptions occurred. Suppliers might be late with deliveries, so companies maintained inventories of key supplies. A workstation might be unable to operate due to a breakdown or other reason, so companies maintained inventories of partially completed goods. And customers might suddenly place big unexpected orders, so companies maintained large inventories of finished goods.

While these inventories provide some insurance against unforeseen events, they have a cost. According to experts, in addition to tying up money, maintaining inventories encourages inefficient and sloppy work, results in too many defects, and dramatically increases the amount of time required to complete a product. For example, when partially completed products are stored for long periods of time before being processed by the next workstation, defects introduced by the preceding workstation go unnoticed. If a machine is out of calibration or incorrect procedures are being followed, many defective units will be produced before the problem is discovered. And when the defects are finally discovered, it may be very difficult to track down the source of the problem. In addition, units may be obsolete or out of fashion by the time they are finally completed.

Large inventories of partially completed goods create many other operating problems that are best discussed in more advanced courses. These problems are not obvious—if they were, companies would have long ago reduced their inventories. Managers at Toyota are credited with the insight that large inventories often create many more problems than they solve, and Toyota pioneered the *JIT approach.*

The JIT Approach

In contrast to the traditional approach, companies that use the **just-in-time (JIT)** approach purchase materials and produce units only as needed to meet actual customer demand. The theory is that producing things doesn't do the company any good unless someone buys them and that excess inventories create a multitude of operating problems. In a JIT system, inventories are reduced to an absolute minimum. Under ideal conditions, a company operating a just-in-time system would purchase only enough materials each day to meet that day's needs. Moreover, the company would have no goods still in process at the end of the day, and all goods completed during the day would have been shipped immediately to customers. As this sequence suggests, "just-in-time" means that raw materials are received just in time to go into production, manufactured parts are completed just in time to be assembled into products, and products are completed just in time to be shipped to customers.

Although few companies have been able to reach this ideal, many companies have been able to reduce inventories to only a fraction of their previous levels. The results have been a substantial reduction in ordering and warehousing costs and much more effective operations.

The change from a traditional to a JIT approach is more profound than it may appear to be. Among other things, producing only in response to a customer order means that workers will be idle whenever demand falls below the company's production capacity. This can be an extremely difficult cultural change for an organization to make. It challenges the core beliefs of many managers and raises anxieties in workers who have become accustomed to being kept busy all of the time. It also requires fundamental changes in managerial accounting practices, as we will see in later chapters.

Zero Defects and JIT

Defective units create big problems in a JIT environment. If a completed order contains a defective unit, the company must ship the order with less than the promised quantity or it must restart the whole production process to make just one unit. At minimum, this creates a delay in shipping the order and may generate a ripple effect that delays other orders. For this and other reasons, defects cannot be tolerated in a JIT system. Companies that are deeply involved in JIT tend to become zealously committed to a goal of *zero defects.* Even though it may be next to impossible to attain the zero defect goal, companies have found that they can come very close. For example, Motorola, Allied Signal, and many other companies now measure defects in terms of the number of defects per *million* units of product.

In a traditional company, parts and materials are inspected for defects when they are received from suppliers, and quality inspectors inspect units as they progress along the production line. In a JIT system, the company's suppliers are responsible for the quality of incoming parts and materials. And instead of using quality inspectors, the company's production workers are directly responsible for spotting defective units. A worker who discovers a defect is supposed to punch an alarm button that stops the production flow line and sets off flashing lights. Supervisors and other workers go immediately to the workstation to determine the cause of the defect and correct it before any further defective units are produced. This procedure ensures that problems are quickly identified and corrected, but it does require that defects are rare—otherwise there would be constant disruptions to the production process.

in business today Adopters of the JIT Approach

Many companies—large and small—have employed JIT with great success. Among the major companies using JIT are Bose, Goodyear, Westinghouse, General Motors, Hughes Aircraft, Ford Motor Company, Black and Decker, Chrysler, Borg-Warner, John Deere, Xerox, Tektronix, and Intel.

Benefits of a JIT System

The main benefits of JIT are:

1. Funds that have been tied up in inventories can be used elsewhere.
2. Areas previously used to store inventories are made available for other, more productive uses.
3. The time required to fill an order is reduced, resulting in quicker response to customers and consequentially greater potential sales.
4. Defect rates are reduced, resulting in less waste and greater customer satisfaction.

As a result of benefits such as those cited above, more companies are embracing JIT each year. Most companies find, however, that simply reducing inventories is not enough. To remain competitive in an ever-changing and ever-more competitive business environment, companies must strive for *continuous improvement*.

Total Quality Management (TQM)

The most popular approach to continuous improvement is known as *total quality management*. There are two major characteristics of **total quality management (TQM)**: (1) a focus on serving customers and (2) systematic problem solving using teams made up of front-line workers. A variety of specific tools is available to aid teams in their problem solving. One of these tools, **benchmarking**, involves studying organizations that are among the best in the world at performing a particular task. For example, when Xerox wanted to improve its procedures for filling customer orders, it studied how the mail-order company L. L. Bean processes its customer orders.

The Plan-Do-Check-Act Cycle

Perhaps the most important and pervasive TQM problem-solving tool is the *plan-do-check-act (PDCA) cycle*, which is also referred to as the Deming Wheel.[1] The **plan-do-check-act cycle** is a systematic, fact-based approach to continuous improvement. The

---

[1] Dr. W. Edwards Deming, a pioneer in TQM, introduced many of the elements of TQM to Japanese industry after World War II. TQM was further refined and developed at Japanese companies such as Toyota.

Exhibit P–1
The Plan-Do-Check-Act Cycle

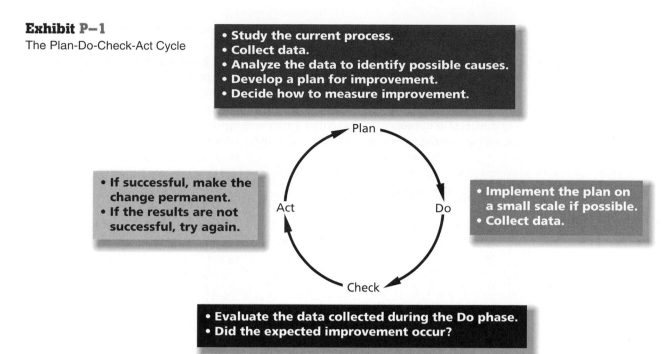

- Study the current process.
- Collect data.
- Analyze the data to identify possible causes.
- Develop a plan for improvement.
- Decide how to measure improvement.

- If successful, make the change permanent.
- If the results are not successful, try again.

- Implement the plan on a small scale if possible.
- Collect data.

- Evaluate the data collected during the Do phase.
- Did the expected improvement occur?

Plan

Act

Do

Check

basic elements of the PDCA cycle are illustrated in Exhibit P–1. The PDCA cycle applies the scientific method to problem solving. In the Plan phase, the problem-solving team analyzes data to identify possible causes for the problem and then proposes a solution. In the Do phase, an experiment is conducted. In the Check phase, the results of the experiment are analyzed. And in the Act phase, if the results of the experiment are favorable, the plan is implemented. If the results of the experiment are not favorable, the team goes back to the original data and starts all over again.

An Example of TQM in Practice

Sterling Chemicals, Inc., a producer of basic industrial chemicals, provides a good example of the use of TQM.[2] Among many other problems, the company had been plagued by pump failures. In one year, a particular type of pump had failed 22 times at an average cost of about $10,000 per failure. The company first tried to solve the problem using a traditional, non-TQM approach. A committee of "experts"—in this case engineers and manufacturing supervisors—was appointed to solve the problem. A manager at Sterling Chemicals describes the results:

> This team immediately concluded that each of the 22 pump failures . . . was due to a special or one-of-a-kind cause. There was some finger pointing by team members trying to assign blame. Maintenance engineers claimed that production personnel didn't know how to operate the pumps, and production supervisors blamed maintenance people for poor repair work.

One year later, a TQM team was formed to tackle the same pump failure problem. The team consisted primarily of hourly workers with hands-on experience working with the pumps. The team brainstormed and came up with a list of 57 theories that could potentially explain the high pump-failure rate. Each of these theories was tested against the data and all but two were rejected. The team made recommendations to address both of these

---

[2]The information about Sterling Chemicals in this section was taken from Karen Hopper Wruck and Michael C. Jensen, "Science, Specific Knowledge, and Total Quality Management," *Journal of Accounting and Economics* 18 (1994), pp. 247–287. The quotations are from pages 260 and 261 of this article and are used with permission.

theories, and once the recommendations were implemented, there were no more pump failures.

Notice how the plan-do-check-act cycle was used to solve this pump-failure problem. Instead of bickering over who was responsible for the problem, the team began by collecting data. They then hypothesized a number of possible causes for the problem, and these hypotheses were checked against the data. Perhaps the most important feature of TQM is that "it improves productivity by encouraging the use of science in decision-making and discouraging counterproductive defensive behavior."[3]

in business today TQM Is Widely Used

Thousands of organizations have been involved in TQM and similar programs. Some of the more well-known companies are American Express, AT&T, Cadillac Motor Car, Corning, Dun & Bradstreet, Ericsson of Sweden, Federal Express, GTE Directories, Bank One, Florida Power and Light, General Electric, Hospital Corporation of America, IBM, Johnson & Johnson, KLM Royal Dutch Airlines, LTV, 3M, Milliken & Company, Motorola, Northern Telecom of Canada, Phillips of the Netherlands, Ritz Carlton Hotel, Texas Instruments, Westinghouse Electric, and Xerox. As this list illustrates, TQM is international in scope and is not confined to manufacturing. Indeed, a survey by the American Hospital Association of 3,300 hospitals found that 69 percent have launched quality-improvement programs. For example, Intermountain Healthcare's LDS Hospital in Salt Lake City is using total quality management techniques to reduce infection rates among surgery patients and the toxic side effects of chemotherapy.

Source: Ron Wilson, "Excising Waste: Health-Care Providers Try Industrial Tactics in U.S. to Cut Costs," *The Wall Street Journal Europe*, November 10, 1993, pp. 1, 8.

In sum, TQM provides tools and techniques for continuous improvement based on facts and analysis and, if properly implemented, it avoids counterproductive organizational infighting.

Process Reengineering

Process reengineering is a more radical approach to improvement than TQM. Instead of tweaking the existing system by making a series of small incremental improvements, **process reengineering** diagrams a *business process* in detail, questions it, and then completely redesigns it in order to eliminate unnecessary steps, reduce opportunities for errors, and reduce costs. A **business process** is any series of steps that are followed in order to carry out some task in a business. For example, the steps followed to make a large pineapple and Canadian bacon pizza at Godfather's Pizza are a business process. The steps followed by your bank when you deposit a check are a business process. While process reengineering is similar in some respects to TQM, its proponents view it as a more sweeping approach to change. One difference is that while TQM emphasizes a team approach involving people who work directly in the processes, process reengineering is more likely to be imposed from above and to use outside consultants.

Process reengineering focuses on *simplification* and *elimination of wasted effort*. A central idea of process reengineering is that *all activities that do not add value to a product or service should be eliminated*. Activities that do not add value to a product or service that customers are willing to pay for are known as **non-value-added activities**. For example, moving large batches of partially completed goods from one workstation to

---

[3]Ibid., p. 247.

another is a non-value-added activity that can be eliminated by redesigning the factory layout to bring the workstations closer together.[4]

Process Reengineering in Practice

in business | today

Process reengineering has been used by many companies to deal with a wide variety of problems. For example, the EMI Records Group was having difficulty filling orders for its most popular CDs. Retailers and recording stars were rebelling—it took the company as much as 20 days to deliver a big order for a hit CD, and then nearly 20 percent of the order would be missing. Small, incremental improvements would not have been adequate, so the company reengineered its entire distribution process with dramatic effects on on-time delivery and order fill rates.

Source: Glenn Rifkin, "EMI: Technology Brings the Music Giant a Whole New Spin," *Forbes ASAP*, February 27, 1995, pp. 32–38.

Another example is provided by Reynolds & Reynolds Co. of Dayton, Ohio, which produces business forms. Filling an order for a customer used to take 90 separate steps. By reengineering, the number of steps was slashed to 20 and the time required to fill an order was cut from three weeks to one week.

Source: William M. Bulkeley, "Pushing the Pace: The Latest Big Thing at Many Companies Is Speed, Speed, Speed," *The Wall Street Journal*, December 23, 1994, pp. A1, A7.

Massachusetts General Hospital is even using process reengineering to standardize and improve surgical procedures.

Source: George Anders, "Required Surgery: Health Plans Force Even Elite Hospitals to Cut Costs Sharply," *The Wall Street Journal*, March 8, 1994, pp. A1, A6.

The Problem of Employee Morale

Employee resistance is a recurrent problem in process reengineering. The cause of much of this resistance is the fear that employees may lose their jobs. Employees reason that if process reengineering succeeds in eliminating non-value-added activities, there will be less work to do and management may be tempted to reduce the payroll. Process reengineering, if carried out insensitively and without regard to such fears, can undermine morale and will ultimately fail to improve the bottom line (i.e., profits). As with other improvement projects, employees must be convinced that the end result of the improvement will be more secure, rather than less secure, jobs. Real improvement can have this effect if management uses the improvement to generate more business rather than to cut the workforce. If by improving processes the company is able to produce a better product at lower cost, the company will have the competitive strength to prosper. And a prosperous company is a much more secure employer than a company that is in trouble.

The Theory of Constraints (TOC)

A **constraint** is anything that prevents you from getting more of what you want. Every individual and every organization faces at least one constraint. You may not have enough time to study thoroughly for every subject and to go out with your friends on the weekend, so time is your constraint. United Airlines has only a limited number of loading gates available at its busy O'Hare hub, so its constraint is loading gates. Vail Associates has only a limited amount of land to develop as home sites and commercial lots at its ski areas, so its constraint is land.

---

[4]Activity-based costing and activity-based management, both of which are discussed in a later chapter, can be helpful in identifying areas in the company that could benefit from process reengineering.

The theory of constraints (TOC) focuses on effectively managing the constraint as the key to success. For example, United Airlines should concentrate on quickly turning around its aircraft on the ground so they do not tie up precious gates. Delays on the ground decrease the number of flights that can be flown out of O'Hare and therefore result in lost business for United.

An Example of TOC

ProSport Equipment, Inc., manufactures aluminum tennis rackets on the production flow line sketched in Exhibit P–2. The capacity of each workstation is stated in terms of the maximum number of rackets that can be processed in a week. For example, the aluminum extruding workstation can extrude enough aluminum each week to build as many as 2,500 tennis rackets. Referring to Exhibit P–2, what is the maximum rate of output of tennis rackets that can be sustained in a week? The rate of output of the entire system is limited by the rate of output of the slowest workstation, which is frame assembly with a rate of output of only 1,800 rackets per week. Even though the other workstations can process

Exhibit P–2

A Flowchart of an Aluminum Tennis Racket Production Line

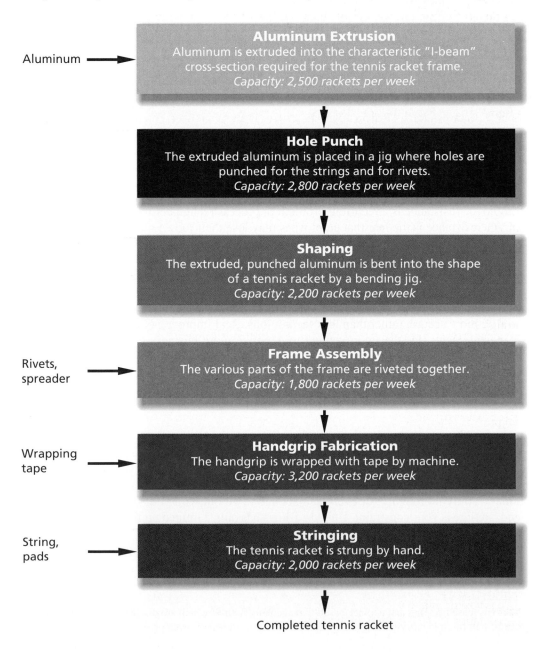

Aluminum →

Aluminum Extrusion
Aluminum is extruded into the characteristic "I-beam" cross-section required for the tennis racket frame.
Capacity: 2,500 rackets per week

Hole Punch
The extruded aluminum is placed in a jig where holes are punched for the strings and for rivets.
Capacity: 2,800 rackets per week

Shaping
The extruded, punched aluminum is bent into the shape of a tennis racket by a bending jig.
Capacity: 2,200 rackets per week

Rivets, spreader →

Frame Assembly
The various parts of the frame are riveted together.
Capacity: 1,800 rackets per week

Wrapping tape →

Handgrip Fabrication
The handgrip is wrapped with tape by machine.
Capacity: 3,200 rackets per week

String, pads →

Stringing
The tennis racket is strung by hand.
Capacity: 2,000 rackets per week

Completed tennis racket

more than 1,800 rackets per week, the entire production line can process only 1,800 rackets per week since each racket must go through frame assembly whose capacity is only 1,800 rackets. The frame assembly workstation is the *bottleneck*. In addition, if demand exceeds 1,800 rackets per week, the frame assembly workstation is the constraint.

Several important observations can be made using this simple example. First, if managers try to keep each workstation busy all of the time, the result will be frustration and an ever-increasing pile of uncompleted units waiting to be processed through the frame assembly workstation. Shaping can process 2,200 units per week whereas frame assembly can process only 1,800 units per week. If both workstations are kept busy all of the time processing units, the inevitable result will be 400 units being added each week to the pile of uncompleted units waiting to be processed through the frame assembly workstation.

Second, if demand exceeds 1,800 units per week, the only way the company can satisfy demand (and thereby increase profits) is to increase the capacity of the constraint, which is frame assembly. There are several ways the capacity of the constraint can be increased. These will be discussed in detail in a later chapter, but one way to increase capacity is to focus TQM and process reengineering efforts on the constraint.

Consider what would happen if process reengineering were used to improve one of the workstations that is not a constraint. Suppose, for example, that the handgrip fabrication process is reengineered so that it requires only half as much time to wrap a handgrip. Will this increase profits? The answer is "Probably not." Handgrip fabrication already has plenty of excess capacity; it is capable of processing 3,200 rackets per week, which is far more than the bottleneck can handle. Speeding up this process will simply create more excess capacity. Unless resources can now be shifted from handgrip fabrication to the constraint area (frame assembly) or unless spending can be cut in the handgrip fabrication work center, there will be no increase in profits. In contrast, if the processing time were cut in half in frame assembly, which is the constraint, the company could produce and sell more tennis rackets, and this should have a direct and immediate positive impact on profits.

TOC and Continuous Improvement

In TOC, an analogy is often drawn between a business process—such as the tennis racket production line—and a chain. What is the most effective way to increase the strength of a chain? Should you concentrate your efforts on strengthening the strongest link, the largest link, all the links, or the weakest link? Clearly, focusing effort on the weakest link will bring the biggest benefit.

Continuing with this analogy, the procedure to follow in strengthening the chain is straightforward. First, identify the weakest link, which is the constraint. Second, don't place a greater strain on the system than the weakest link can handle. Third, concentrate improvement efforts on strengthening the weakest link. Fourth, if the improvement efforts are successful, eventually the weakest link will improve to the point where it is no longer the weakest link. At this point, the new weakest link (i.e., the new constraint) must be identified, and improvement efforts must be shifted over to that link. This simple sequential process provides a powerful strategy for continuous improvement. The TOC approach is a perfect complement to TQM and process reengineering—it focuses improvement efforts where they are likely to be most effective.

International Competition

Over the last several decades, reductions in tariffs, quotas, and other barriers to free trade; improvements in global transportation systems; and increasing sophistication in international markets have led to worldwide competition in many industries. These factors work together to reduce the costs of conducting international trade and make it possible for foreign companies to compete on a more equal footing with local firms. These changes have been most dramatic within the European Union (EU) and the North American Free Trade Association (NAFTA) free trade zones.

Very few firms can afford to be complacent. A company that is currently very successful in its local market may suddenly find itself facing competition from halfway around the globe. It is likely that this threat will become even more potent as business migrates more and more to the Internet. As a matter of survival, even firms that are presently doing very well in their home markets must become world-class competitors. On the bright side, the freer international movement of goods and services presents tremendous export opportunities for those companies that can transform themselves into world-class competitors. And from the standpoint of consumers, heightened competition promises an even greater variety of goods, at higher quality and lower prices.

What are the implications for managerial accounting of increased global competition? It would be very difficult for a firm to become world-class if it plans, directs, and controls its operations and makes decisions using a second-class management accounting system. An excellent management accounting system will not by itself guarantee success, but a poor management accounting system can stymie the best efforts of people in an organization to make the firm truly competitive.

Throughout this text we will highlight the differences between obsolete management accounting systems that get in the way of success and well-designed management accounting systems that can enhance a firm's performance. It is noteworthy that elements of well-designed management accounting systems have originated in many countries. More and more, managerial accounting has become a discipline that is worldwide in scope.

Organizational Structure

Since organizations are made up of people, management must accomplish its objectives by working through people. Presidents of companies with more than a few employees cannot possibly execute all of their company's strategies alone; they must rely on other people. This is done by creating an organizational structure that permits *decentralization* of management responsibilities.

Decentralization

Decentralization is the delegation of decision-making authority throughout an organization by providing managers at various operating levels with the authority to make decisions relating to their area of responsibility. Some organizations are more decentralized than others. For example, consider Good Vibrations, Inc., an international retailer of music CDs with shops in major cities scattered around the Pacific Rim. Because of Good Vibrations, Inc.'s geographic dispersion and the peculiarities of local markets, the company is highly decentralized.

Good Vibrations, Inc.'s president (also called chief executive officer, or CEO) sets the broad strategy for the company and makes major strategic decisions such as opening stores in new markets, but much of the remaining decision-making authority is delegated to managers on various levels throughout the organization. Each of the company's numerous retail stores has a store manager as well as a separate manager for each section such as international rock and classical/jazz. In addition, the company has support departments such as a central Purchasing Department and a Personnel Department. The organizational structure of the company is depicted in Exhibit P–3.

The arrangement of boxes shown in Exhibit P–3 is called an **organization chart**. The purpose of an organization chart is to show how responsibility has been divided among managers and to show formal lines of reporting and communication, or *chain of command*. Each box depicts an area of management responsibility, and the lines between the boxes show the lines of formal authority between managers. The chart tells us, for example, that the store managers are responsible to the operations vice president. In turn, the latter is responsible to the company president, who in turn is responsible to the board of directors. Following the lines of authority and communication on the organization chart, we can see that the manager of the Hong Kong store would ordinarily report to the operations vice president rather than directly to the president of the company.

Exhibit P–3
Organization Chart, Good Vibrations, Inc.

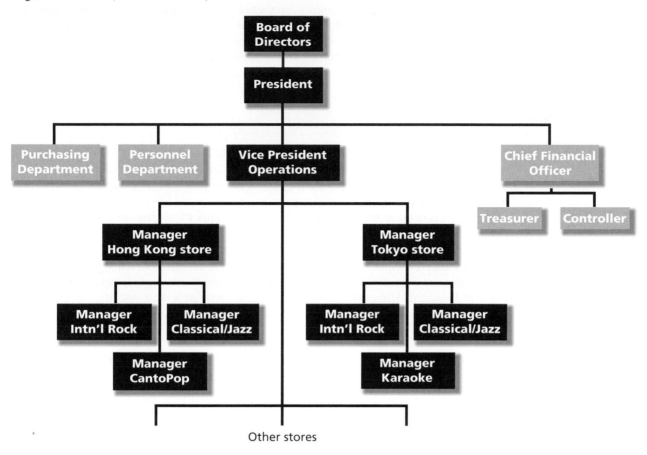

Informal relationships and channels of communication often develop outside the formal reporting relationships on the organization chart as a result of personal contacts between managers. The informal structure does not appear on the organization chart, but it is often vital to effective operations.

Line and Staff Relationships

An organization chart also depicts *line* and *staff* positions in an organization. A person in a **line** position is *directly* involved in achieving the basic objectives of the organization. A person in a **staff** position, by contrast, is only *indirectly* involved in achieving those basic objectives. Staff positions *support* or provide assistance to line positions or other parts of the organization, but they do not have direct authority over line positions. Refer again to the organization chart in Exhibit P–3. Since the basic objective of Good Vibrations, Inc. is to sell recorded music at a profit, those managers whose areas of responsibility are directly related to the sales effort occupy line positions. These positions, which are shown in a darker color in the exhibit, include the managers of the various music departments in each store, the store managers, the operations vice president, and members of top management.

By contrast, the manager of the central Purchasing Department occupies a staff position, since the only function of the Purchasing Department is to support and serve the line departments by doing their purchasing for them.

The Controller

In the United States the manager in charge of the accounting department is often known as the *controller*. The **controller** is the member of the top management team who is given the responsibility of providing relevant and timely data to managers and of preparing financial statements for external users. Accountants inside a company often refer to themselves as part of the finance team or group.

The controller's office combines a number of important functions including, quite often, management of the company's computer services. Because the controller becomes familiar with all parts of a company's operations by working with managers throughout the company, it is not unusual for the controller's office to be a stepping-stone to the top position in a company.

Professional Ethics

Many concerns have been raised regarding ethical behavior in business and in public life. Allegations and scandals of unethical conduct have been directed toward managers in virtually all segments of society, including government, business, charitable organizations, and even religion. Although these allegations and scandals have received a lot of attention, it is important to remember that hundreds of millions of transactions are conducted every day that remain untainted. Nevertheless, it is important to have an appreciation of what is and is not acceptable behavior in business and why. Fortunately, the Institute of Management Accountants (IMA) of the United States has developed a very useful ethical code called the *Standards of Ethical Conduct for Practitioners of Management Accounting and Financial Management*. Even though the standards were specifically developed for management accountants, they have much broader application.

Code of Conduct for Management Accountants

The IMA's Standards of Ethical Conduct for Practitioners of Management Accounting and Financial Management is presented in full in Exhibit P–4. The standards contain two parts. The first part provides general guidelines for ethical behavior. In a nutshell, the management accountant has four broad ethical responsibilities: (1) maintaining a high level of professional competence; (2) treating sensitive matters with confidentiality; (3) maintaining personal integrity; and (4) being objective in all disclosures. The second part of the standards gives specific guidance concerning what should be done if an individual finds evidence of ethical misconduct within an organization. We recommend that you stop at this point and read the standards in Exhibit P–4.

The ethical standards provide sound, practical advice for management accountants and managers. Most of the rules in the ethical standards are motivated by a very practical consideration—if these rules were not generally followed in business, then the economy would come to a screeching halt. Consider the following specific examples of the consequences of not abiding by the standards:

- Suppose employees could not be trusted with confidential information. Then top managers would be reluctant to distribute confidential information within the company. As a result, decisions would be based on incomplete information and operations would deteriorate.
- Suppose employees accepted bribes from suppliers. Then contracts would tend to go to suppliers who pay the highest bribes rather than to the most competent suppliers. Would you like to fly in an aircraft whose wings were made by the subcontractor who was willing to pay the highest bribe to a purchasing agent? What would happen to the airline industry if its safety record deteriorated due to shoddy workmanship on contracted parts and assemblies?
- Suppose the presidents of companies routinely lied in their annual reports to shareholders and grossly distorted financial statements. If the basic integrity of a company's financial statements could not be relied on, investors and creditors would have little basis for making informed decisions. Suspecting the worst, rational investors would pay less for securities issued by companies. As a consequence, fewer funds would be available for productive investments and many firms might be

Exhibit P-4
Standards of Ethical Conduct for
Practitioners of Management
Accounting and Financial
Management

Practitioners of management accounting and financial management have an obligation to the public, their profession, the organization they serve, and themselves, to maintain the highest standards of ethical conduct. In recognition of this obligation, the Institute of Management Accountants has promulgated the following standards of ethical conduct for practitioners of management accounting and financial management. Adherence to these standards, both domestically and internationally, is integral to achieving the Objectives of Management Accounting. Practitioners of management accounting and financial management shall not commit acts contrary to these standards nor shall they condone the commission of such acts by others within their organizations.

Competence. Practitioners of management accounting and financial management have a responsibility to:

- Maintain an appropriate level of professional competence by ongoing development of their knowledge and skills.
- Perform their professional duties in accordance with relevant laws, regulations, and technical standards.
- Prepare complete and clear reports and recommendations after appropriate analysis of relevant and reliable information.

Confidentiality. Practitioners of management accounting and financial management have a responsibility to:

- Refrain from disclosing confidential information acquired in the course of their work except when authorized, unless legally obligated to do so.
- Inform subordinates as appropriate regarding the confidentiality of information acquired in the course of their work and monitor their activities to assure the maintenance of that confidentiality.
- Refrain from using or appearing to use confidential information acquired in the course of their work for unethical or illegal advantage either personally or through third parties.

Integrity. Practitioners of management accounting and financial management have a responsibility to:

- Avoid actual or apparent conflicts of interest and advise all appropriate parties of any potential conflict.
- Refrain from engaging in any activity that would prejudice their ability to carry out their duties ethically.
- Refuse any gift, favor, or hospitality that would influence or would appear to influence their actions.
- Refrain from either actively or passively subverting the attainment of the organization's legitimate and ethical objectives.
- Recognize and communicate professional limitations or other constraints that would preclude responsible judgment or successful performance of an activity.
- Communicate unfavorable as well as favorable information and professional judgments or opinions.
- Refrain from engaging in or supporting any activity that would discredit the profession.

Objectivity. Practitioners of management accounting and financial management have a responsibility to:

- Communicate information fairly and objectively.
- Disclose fully all relevant information that could reasonably be expected to influence an intended user's understanding of the reports, comments, and recommendations presented.

continued

unable to raise any funds at all. Ultimately, this would lead to slower economic growth, fewer goods and services, and higher prices.

As these examples suggest, if ethical standards were not generally adhered to, there would be undesirable consequences for everyone. Essentially, abandoning ethical standards would lead to a lower standard of living with lower-quality goods and services, less to choose from, and higher prices. In short, following ethical rules such as those in the

Exhibit P–4
(concluded)

Resolution of Ethical Conflict. In applying the standards of ethical conduct, practitioners of management accounting and financial management may encounter problems in identifying unethical behavior or in resolving an ethical conflict. When faced with significant ethical issues, practitioners of management accounting and financial management should follow the established policies of the organization bearing on the resolution of such conflict. If these policies do not resolve the ethical conflict, such practitioner should consider the following courses of action:

- Discuss such problems with the immediate superior except when it appears that the superior is involved, in which case the problem should be presented initially to the next higher managerial level. If a satisfactory resolution cannot be achieved when the problem is initially presented, submit the issues to the next higher managerial level.
- If the immediate superior is the chief executive officer, or equivalent, the acceptable reviewing authority may be a group such as the audit committee, executive committee, board of directors, board of trustees, or owners. Contact with levels above the immediate superior should be initiated only with the superior's knowledge, assuming the superior is not involved. Except where legally prescribed, communication of such problems to authorities or individuals not employed or engaged by the organization is not considered appropriate.
- Clarify relevant ethical issues by confidential discussion with an objective advisor (e.g., IMA Ethics Counseling Service) to obtain a better understanding of possible courses of action.
- Consult your own attorney as to legal obligations and rights concerning the ethical conflict.
- If the ethical conflict still exists after exhausting all levels of internal review, there may be no other recourse on significant matters than to resign from the organization and to submit an informative memorandum to an appropriate representative of the organization. After resignation, depending on the nature of the ethical conflict, it may also be appropriate to notify other parties.

*Institute of Management Accountants, formerly National Association of Accountants, *Statements on Management Accounting: Objectives of Management Accounting,* Statement No. 1B, New York, NY, June 17, 1982, as revised in 1997.

Standards of Ethical Conduct for Practitioners of Management Accounting and Financial Management is not just a matter of being "nice"; it is absolutely essential for the smooth functioning of an advanced market economy.

in business today **An Ethical Environment**

Robert Gebring of Olin Corporation, a producer of metals, ammunition, and chemicals, summarizes one of the company's key themes as, "Ethics is in everything we do." His title, Vice President, Auditing, Business Ethics and Integrity, signifies the importance of ethical behavior at this company. Olin emphasizes a commitment to "doing the right thing" rather than mindless compliance with rules. The company's chief executive officer, Don Griffin, quit his first job at Olin because he perceived that management displayed an uncaring attitude toward customers. He adds that, "If we fail to do the right thing, the company suffers, along with its employees." Olin's approach to ethics is multifaceted. Although certainly not limited to the following, "it includes:

- Special brochures and training on effective communication and respect—because communication lapses and lack of mutual respect appear to be a root cause of many employee concerns.
- An intranet site that provides ready access to company policies and standards and to lively interactive resources such as video messages and news items."

Source: Michael Rion and Robert K. Gebring, "Doing the Right Things," *Internal Auditor*, December 1999, pp. 33–35. Reprinted with permission from the December 1999 issue of *Internal Auditor*, published by the Institute of Internal Auditors, Inc.

Company Codes of Conduct

"Those who engage in unethical behavior often justify their actions with one or more of the following reasons: (1) the organization expects unethical behavior, (2) everyone else is unethical, and/or (3) behaving unethically is the only way to get ahead."[5]

To counter the first justification for unethical behavior, many companies have adopted formal ethics codes of conduct. These codes are generally broad-based statements of a company's responsibilities to its employees, its customers, its suppliers, and the communities in which the company operates. Codes rarely spell out specific do's and don'ts or suggest proper behavior in specific situations. Instead, they give broad guidelines.

Unfortunately, the single-minded emphasis placed on short-term profits in some companies may make it seem like the only way to get ahead is to act unethically. When top managers say, in effect, that they will only be satisfied with bottom-line results and will accept no excuses, they are asking for trouble.

Undue Pressure Can Lead to Unethical Behavior   *in business* today

Top managers at Sears, Roebuck & Company created a situation in its automotive service business that led to unethical actions by its front-line employees.

> Consumers and attorneys general in more than 40 states had accused the company of misleading customers and selling them unnecessary parts and services, from brake jobs to front-end alignments. It would be a mistake, however, to see this situation . . . in terms of any one individual's moral failings. Nor did management set out to defraud Sears customers . . .
>
> In the face of declining revenues, shrinking market share, and an increasingly competitive market, . . . Sears management attempted to spur performance of its auto centers . . . The company increased minimum work quotas and introduced productivity incentives for mechanics. The automotive service advisers were given product-specific sales quotas—sell so many springs, shock absorbers, alignments, or brake jobs per shift—and paid a commission based on sales. According to advisers, failure to meet quotas could lead to a transfer or a reduction in work hours. Some employees spoke of the "pressure, pressure, pressure" to bring in sales.

This pressure-cooker atmosphere created conditions under which employees felt that the only way to satisfy top management was by selling customers products and services they didn't really need.

Shortly after the allegations against Sears became public, CEO Edward Brennan acknowledged management's responsibility for putting in place compensation and goal-setting systems that "created an environment in which mistakes did occur."

Source: Reprinted by permission of Harvard Business Review. Excerpt from Lynn Sharp Paine, "Managing for Organizational Integrity," *Harvard Business Review*, March–April 1994. Copyright © 1994 by the President and Fellows of Harvard College. All rights reserved.

Codes of Conduct on the International Level

The *Guideline on Ethics for Professional Accountants*, issued in July 1990 by the International Federation of Accountants (IFAC), governs the activities of *all* professional accountants throughout the world, regardless of whether they are practicing as independent CPAs, employed in government service, or employed as internal accountants.[6] In addition to outlining ethical requirements in matters dealing with competence, objectivity, independence, and confidentiality, the IFAC's code also outlines the accountant's ethical responsibilities in matters relating to taxes, fees and commissions, advertising and solicitation, the handling of

---

[5]Michael K. McCuddy, Karl E. Reichardt, and David Schroeder, "Ethical Pressures: Fact or Fiction?" *Management Accounting*, April 1993, pp. 57–61.

[6]A copy of this code can be obtained on the International Federation of Accountants' website at www.ifac.org.

monies, and cross-border activities. Where cross-border activities are involved, the IFAC ethical requirements must be followed if these requirements are stricter than the ethical requirements of the country in which the work is being performed.[7]

In addition to professional and company codes of ethical conduct, accountants and managers in the United States are subject to the legal requirements of *The Foreign Corrupt Practices Act of 1977*. The Act requires that companies devise and maintain a system of internal controls sufficient to ensure that all transactions are properly executed and recorded. The Act specifically prohibits giving bribes, even if giving bribes is common practice in the country in which the company is doing business.

The Certified Management Accountant (CMA)

A management accountant who possesses the necessary qualifications and who passes a rigorous professional exam earns the right to be known as a *Certified Management Accountant (CMA)*. In addition to the prestige that accompanies a professional designation, CMAs are often given greater responsibilities and higher compensation than those who do not have such a designation. Information about becoming a CMA and the CMA program can be accessed on the Institute of Management Accountants' (IMA) website at www.imanet.org or by calling 1-800-638-4427.

To become a Certified Management Accountant, the following four steps must be completed:

1. File an Application for Admission and register for the CMA examination.
2. Pass all four parts of the CMA examination within a three-year period.
3. Satisfy the experience requirement of two continuous years of professional experience in management and/or financial accounting prior to or within seven years of passing the CMA examination.
4. Comply with the Standards of Ethical Conduct for Practitioners of Management Accounting and Financial Management.

in business today **Certified Management Accountant**

Students often ask Joseph Martin, Assistant Controller of IBM, why they should become Certified Management Accountants. Martin stresses that the Certified Management Accountant designation demonstrates two important leadership qualities. First, that the candidate has mastered the body of knowledge necessary for decision-making in today's global economy. Second, that the candidate is making the commitment to stay current (through continuing education courses) as the fast-paced economy continues to evolve. Martin attributes his career advancement, in part, to his CMA designation.

Source: Joseph J. Martin, "Why Should I Pursue the CMA & CFM," reprinted with permission from *Management Accounting imastudents.org Supplement*, August 1997, pp. 18–20.

---

[7]*Guideline on Ethics for Professional Accountants* (New York: International Federation of Accountants, July 1990), p. 23.

Summary

The business environment in recent years has been characterized by increasing competition and a relentless drive for continuous improvement. Several approaches have been developed to assist organizations in meeting these challenges—including just-in-time (JIT), total quality management (TQM), process reengineering, and the theory of constraints (TOC).

JIT emphasizes the importance of reducing inventories to the barest minimum possible. This reduces working capital requirements, frees up space, reduces throughput time, reduces defects, and eliminates waste.

TQM involves focusing on the customer, and it employs systematic problem solving using teams made up of front-line workers. Specific TQM tools include benchmarking and the plan-do-check-act (PDCA) cycle. By emphasizing teamwork, a focus on the customer, and facts, TQM can avoid the organizational infighting that might otherwise block improvement.

Process reengineering involves completely redesigning a business process in order to eliminate non-value-added activities and to reduce opportunities for errors. Process reengineering relies more on outside specialists than TQM and is more likely to be imposed by top management.

The theory of constraints emphasizes the importance of managing the organization's constraints. Since the constraint is whatever is holding back the organization, improvement efforts usually must be focused on the constraint in order to be really effective.

Most organizations are decentralized to some degree. The organization chart depicts who works for whom in the organization and which units perform staff functions rather than line functions. Accountants perform a staff function—they support and provide assistance to others inside the organization.

Ethical standards serve a very important practical function in an advanced market economy. Without widespread adherence to ethical standards, the economy would slow down dramatically. Ethics is the lubrication that keeps a market economy functioning smoothly. The Standards of Ethical Conduct for Practitioners of Management Accounting and Financial Management provide sound, practical guidelines for resolving ethics problems that might arise in an organization.

Glossary

At the end of each chapter, a list of key terms for review is given, along with the definition of each term. (These terms are printed in boldface where they are defined in the chapter.) Carefully study each term to be sure you understand its meaning, since these terms are used repeatedly in the chapters that follow. The list for the Prologue follows.

Benchmarking A study of organizations that are among the best in the world at performing a particular task. (p. 4)

Business process A series of steps that are followed in order to carry out some task in a business. (p. 6)

Controller The member of the top management team who is responsible for providing relevant and timely data to managers and for preparing financial statements for external users. (p. 11)

Constraint Anything that prevents an organization or individual from getting more of what it wants. (p. 7)

Decentralization The delegation of decision-making authority throughout an organization by providing managers at various operating levels with the authority to make key decisions relating to their area of responsibility. (p. 10)

Just-in-time (JIT) A production and inventory control system in which materials are purchased and units are produced only as needed to meet actual customer demand. (p. 3)

Line A position in an organization that is directly related to the achievement of the organization's basic objectives. (p. 11)

Non-value-added activity An activity that consumes resources or takes time but that does not add value for which customers are willing to pay. (p. 6)

Organization chart A visual diagram of a firm's organizational structure that depicts formal lines of reporting, communication, and responsibility between managers. (p. 10)

Plan-do-check-act (PDCA) cycle A systematic approach to continuous improvement that applies the scientific method to problem solving. (p. 4)

Process reengineering An approach to improvement that involves completely redesigning business processes in order to eliminate unnecessary steps, reduce errors, and reduce costs. (p. 6)

Staff A position in an organization that is only indirectly related to the achievement of the organization's basic objectives. Such positions are supportive in nature in that they provide service or assistance to line positions or to other staff positions. (p. 11)

Theory of constraints (TOC) A management approach that emphasizes the importance of managing constraints. (p. 8)

Total quality management (TQM) An approach to continuous improvement that focuses on customers and using teams of front-line workers to systematically identify and solve problems. (p. 4)

Chapter One

An Introduction to Managerial Accounting and Cost Concepts

A Look Back

We addressed some of the challenges faced by managers during the 1980s and 1990s in the Prologue, and described the significant improvement programs that were adopted by many companies during that period. You were introduced to Good Vibrations, an international retailer of music CDs, and learned about their organizational structure. After describing the role of the controller, we stressed the importance of professional ethics and codes of conduct, and provided information about the Certified Management Accountant designation.

A Look at This Chapter

After describing the three major activities of managers in the context of Good Vibrations, Inc., this chapter compares and contrasts financial and managerial accounting. We define many of the terms that are used to classify costs in business. Because these terms will be used throughout the text, you should ensure that you are familiar with each of them.

A Look Ahead

Chapters 2, 3, and 4 describe managerial costing systems that are used to compute product costs. Chapter 2 describes job-order costing. Chapter 3 describes activity-based costing, an elaboration of job-order costing. Chapter 4 covers process costing.

Chapter Outline

The Work of Management and the Need for Managerial Accounting Information
- Planning
- Directing and Motivating
- Controlling
- The End Results of Managers' Activities
- The Planning and Control Cycle

Comparison of Financial and Managerial Accounting
- Emphasis on the Future
- Relevance and Flexibility of Data
- Less Emphasis on Precision
- Segments of an Organization
- Generally Accepted Accounting Principles (GAAP)
- Managerial Accounting—Not Mandatory

General Cost Classifications
- Manufacturing Costs
- Nonmanufacturing Costs

Product Costs versus Period Costs
- Product Costs
- Period Costs

Cost Classifications on Financial Statements
- The Balance Sheet
- The Income Statement
- Schedule of Cost of Goods Manufactured

Product Costs—A Closer Look
- Inventoriable Costs
- An Example of Cost Flows

Cost Classifications for Predicting Cost Behavior
- Variable Cost
- Fixed Cost

Cost Classifications for Assigning Costs to Cost Objects
- Direct Cost
- Indirect Cost

Cost Classifications for Decision Making
- Differential Cost and Revenue
- Opportunity Cost
- Sunk Cost

Appendix 1A: Cost of Quality
- Quality of Conformance
- Distribution of Quality Costs
- Quality Cost Report

Decision Feature **Managing the Marines**

Many businesses are challenged by rapidly changing conditions and increasingly complex situations. Few would look to the Marines for ideas on how to succeed in today's business environment. Don't Marines blindly follow orders? Maybe in boot camp. In order to survive in today's world, the Marine Corps has reexamined its organizational structure. Innovative solutions enable the Corps to react promptly and creatively to the same types of threats that are facing today's business managers.

Their success in dealing with immediate challenges is attributed to four principles.

Fast decisions are essential.
- Even though there is a downside to making a decision with incomplete and hastily analyzed information, the alternative of not reacting to an immediate threat presents an unacceptable risk. Breaking the problem down into pieces facilitates the process.

All members of the organization are empowered to make decisions.
- The organization chart of the Marine Corps is much more of a pyramid than that illustrated in Exhibit 3 of the Prologue. After studying the effectiveness of the many layers of management, the Marines concluded that the pyramidal structure works best. However, they also recognized that decisions made by high-level officers couldn't always be communicated on timely basis to Marines engaged in combat. Accordingly, men and women fighting on the front lines are allowed to change or make decisions and take the steps necessary to implement the decisions.

People learn by making mistakes.
- When you make a mistake and have to live with the consequences, you learn from that experience. The Marines tolerate mistakes for the same reason. In fact, a Marine who doesn't make mistakes occasionally is viewed as someone who doesn't take enough risk.

Seek the advice of people outside of the organization.
- To keep pace with the changing world, the Marine Corps taps into the creativity and expertise of others. A psychologist who has extensively studied the decision-making process was brought in to assist in the redesign of the training that is provided to Marines who will be required to make decisions in combat.

In many ways, the work of management, in business or in the Marines Corps, is the same.

Source: David H. Freedman, "A Few Good Principles—What the Marines Can Teach Silicon Valley," *Forbes ASAP*, May 29, 2000, pp. 201–209.

Learning Objectives
After studying Chapter 1, you should be able to:

LO1 Identify and give examples of each of the three basic manufacturing cost categories.

LO2 Distinguish between product costs and period costs and give examples of each.

LO3 Prepare an income statement including calculation of the cost of goods sold.

LO4 Prepare a schedule of cost of goods manufactured.

LO5 Define and give examples of variable costs and fixed costs.

LO6 Define and give examples of direct and indirect costs.

LO7 Define and give examples of cost classifications used in making decisions: differential costs, opportunity costs, and sunk costs.

LO8 (Appendix 1A) Identify the four types of quality costs and explain how they interact.

Managerial accounting is concerned with providing information to managers—that is, people *inside* an organization who direct and control its operations. In contrast, **financial accounting** is concerned with providing information to stockholders, creditors, and others who are *outside* an organization. Managerial accounting provides the essential data with which organizations are actually run. Financial accounting provides the scorecard by which a company's past performance is judged.

The Work of Management and the Need for Managerial Accounting Information

Every organization—large and small—has managers. Someone must be responsible for making plans, organizing resources, directing personnel, and controlling operations. This is true of the Bank of America, the Peace Corps, the University of Illinois, the Catholic Church, and the Coca-Cola Corporation, as well as the local 7-Eleven convenience store. We will use a particular organization—Good Vibrations, Inc.—to illustrate the work of management. What we have to say about the management of Good Vibrations, Inc., however, is very general and can be applied to virtually any organization.

Good Vibrations runs a chain of retail outlets that sell a full range of music CDs. The chain's stores are concentrated in Pacific Rim cities such as Sydney, Singapore, Hong Kong, Beijing, Tokyo, and Vancouver, British Columbia. The company has found that the best way to generate sales, and profits, is to create an exciting shopping environment. Consequently, the company puts a great deal of effort into planning the layout and decor of its stores—which are often quite large and extend over several floors in key downtown locations. Management knows that different types of clientele are attracted to different kinds of music. The international rock section is generally decorated with bold, brightly colored graphics, and the aisles are purposely narrow to create a crowded feeling much like one would experience at a popular nightclub on Friday night. In contrast, the classical music section is wood-paneled and fully sound insulated, with the rich, spacious feeling of a country club meeting room.

Managers at Good Vibrations, like managers everywhere, carry out three major activities—*planning, directing and motivating,* and *controlling.* **Planning** involves selecting a course of action and specifying how the action will be implemented. **Directing and motivating** involves mobilizing people to carry out plans and run routine operations. **Controlling** involves ensuring that the plan is actually carried out and is appropriately modified as circumstances change. Management accounting information plays a vital role in these basic management activities—but most particularly in the planning and control functions.

in business today **Furthering the Organization's Objectives in More Ways than One**

The electronic brokerage unit of Charles Schwab & Co. has established a free online learning center for existing and potential customers. The interactive learning center is expected to reduce the number of customer requests for information. However, Janet Lecuyer, Schwab's Vice President of Electronic Learning, noted that the resulting decrease in costs was not the primary reason for this course of action. Education lessens fears and may nudge customers toward investment decisions. Schwab may see an increase in revenues and a decrease in costs as a result of this course of action.

Source: Monica Sambataro, "Just-in-Time Learning," *Computerworld*, April 3, 2000, p. 50.

Planning

The first step in planning is to identify alternatives and then to select from among the alternatives the one that does the best job of furthering the organization's objectives. The basic objective of Good Vibrations is to earn profits for the owners of the company by providing superior service at competitive prices in as many markets as possible. To further this objective, every year top management carefully considers a number of alternatives for expanding into new geographic markets. This year management is considering opening new stores in Shanghai, Los Angeles, and Auckland.

When making this and other choices, management must balance the opportunities against the demands made on the company's resources. Management knows from bitter experience that opening a store in a major new market is a big step that cannot be taken lightly. It requires enormous amounts of time and energy from the company's most experienced, talented, and busy professionals. When the company attempted to open stores in both Beijing and Vancouver in the same year, resources were stretched too thinly. The result was that neither store opened on schedule, and operations in the rest of the company suffered. Therefore, entering new markets is planned very, very carefully.

Among other data, top management looks at the sales volumes, profit margins, and costs of the company's established stores in similar markets. These data, supplied by the management accountant, are combined with projected sales volume data at the proposed new locations to estimate the profits that would be generated by the new stores. In general, virtually all important alternatives considered by management in the planning process have some effect on revenues or costs, and management accounting data are essential in estimating those effects.

After considering all of the alternatives, Good Vibrations, Inc.'s top management decided to open a store in the burgeoning Shanghai market in the third quarter of the year, but to defer opening any other new stores to another year. As soon as this decision was made, detailed plans were drawn up for all parts of the company that would be involved in the Shanghai opening. For example, the Personnel Department's travel budget was increased, since it would be providing extensive on-the-site training to the new personnel hired in Shanghai.

As in the Personnel Department example, the plans of management are often expressed formally in **budgets,** and the term *budgeting* is applied to generally describe this part of the planning process. Budgets are usually prepared under the direction of the controller, who is the manager in charge of the Accounting Department. Typically, budgets are prepared annually and represent management's plans in specific, quantitative terms. In addition to a travel budget, the Personnel Department will be given goals in terms of new hires, courses taught, and detailed breakdowns of expected expenses. Similarly, the manager of each store will be given a target for sales volume, profit, expenses, pilferage losses, and employee training. These data will be collected, analyzed, and summarized for management use in the form of budgets prepared by management accountants.

Directing and Motivating

In addition to planning for the future, managers must oversee day-to-day activities and keep the organization functioning smoothly. This requires the ability to motivate and effectively direct people. Managers assign tasks to employees, arbitrate disputes, answer questions, solve on-the-spot problems, and make many small decisions that affect customers and employees. In effect, directing is that part of managers' work that deals with the routine and the here and now. Managerial accounting data, such as daily sales reports, are often used in this type of day-to-day decision making.

Controlling

In carrying out the **control** function, managers seek to ensure that the plan is being followed. **Feedback,** which signals whether operations are on track, is the key to effective

in business today **Planning without Direction**

Joe works for a large technology company. Unfortunately, the company's sales, profits, and stock price leave much to be desired. Simon, one of the company's vice presidents, had convinced the company's chairman that a new corporate culture would do the trick. Joe accepted a job to lead the cultural change project even though all that he could ascertain was that the project was big. He was enticed by the offer of money and his curiosity.

During his first day on the job, Joe attended a project team meeting. None of the ideas put on the table by the team came close to what was envisioned by the vice president. After the meeting, the team members informed him that this was their fourth attempt at trying to figure out what Simon was thinking. Joe was able to get the team to develop an outline for the project that simply made sense without worrying about whether or not it was what Simon had in mind.

Source: Joe Kay, "My Year at a Big High Tech Company," *Forbes ASAP,* May 29, 2000, pp. 195–198. *(As noted in the article, because Joe does not want to lose his job, his name as well as the name of the company and certain details have been changed.)*

control. In sophisticated organizations this feedback is provided by detailed reports of various types. One of these reports, which compares budgeted to actual results, is called a **performance report.** Performance reports suggest where operations are not proceeding as planned and where some parts of the organization may require additional attention. For example, before the opening of the new Shanghai store in the third quarter of the year, the store's manager will be given sales volume, profit, and expense targets for the fourth quarter of the year. As the fourth quarter progresses, periodic reports will be made in which the actual sales volume, profit, and expenses are compared to the targets. If the actual results fall below the targets, top management is alerted that the Shanghai store requires more attention. Experienced personnel can be flown in to help the new manager, or top management may come to the conclusion that plans will have to be revised. As we shall see in following chapters, providing this kind of feedback to managers is one of the central purposes of managerial accounting.

The End Results of Managers' Activities

As a customer enters one of the Good Vibrations stores, the results of management's planning, directing and motivating, and control activities will be evident in the many details that make the difference between a pleasant and an irritating shopping experience. The store will be clean, fashionably decorated, and logically laid out. Featured artists' videos will be displayed on TV monitors throughout the store, and the background rock music will be loud enough to send older patrons scurrying for the classical music section. Popular CDs will be in stock, and the latest hits will be available for private listening on earphones. Specific titles will be easy to find. Regional music, such as CantoPop in Hong Kong, will be prominently featured. Checkout clerks will be alert, friendly, and efficient. In short, what the customer experiences doesn't simply happen; it is the result of the efforts of managers who must visualize and fit together the processes that are needed to get the job done.

The Planning and Control Cycle

The work of management can be summarized in a model such as the one shown in Exhibit 1–1. The model, which depicts the **planning and control cycle,** illustrates the smooth flow of management activities from planning through directing and motivating, controlling, and then back to planning again. All of these activities involve decision making, so it is depicted as the hub around which the other activities revolve.

Exhibit 1–1
The Planning and Control Cycle

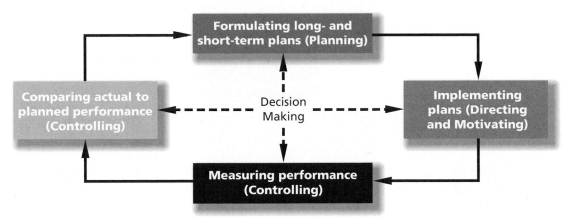

Comparison of Financial and Managerial Accounting

Financial accounting reports are prepared for the use of external parties such as share-holders and creditors, whereas managerial accounting reports are prepared for managers inside the organization. This contrast in basic orientation results in a number of major differences between financial and managerial accounting, even though both financial and managerial accounting rely on the same underlying financial data. These differences are summarized in Exhibit 1–2.

As shown in Exhibit 1–2, in addition to the difference in who the reports are prepared for, financial and managerial accounting also differ in their emphasis between the past and the future, in the type of data provided to users, and in several other ways. These differences are discussed in the following paragraphs.

Emphasis on the Future

Since *planning* is such an important part of the manager's job, managerial accounting has a strong future orientation. In contrast, financial accounting primarily provides summaries of past financial transactions. These summaries may be useful in planning, but only to a point. The difficulty with summaries of the past is that the future is not simply a reflection of what has happened in the past. Changes are constantly taking place in economic conditions, customer needs and desires, competitive conditions, and so on. All of these changes demand that the manager's planning be based in large part on estimates of what will happen rather than on summaries of what has already happened.

Relevance and Flexibility of Data

Financial accounting data are expected to be objective and verifiable. However, for internal uses, the manager wants information that is relevant even if it is not completely objective or verifiable. By relevant, we mean *appropriate for the problem at hand.* For example, it is difficult to verify estimated sales volumes for a proposed new store at Good Vibrations, Inc., but this is exactly the type of information that is most useful to managers in their decision making. The managerial accounting information system should be flexible enough to provide whatever data are relevant for a particular decision.

Less Emphasis on Precision

Timeliness is often more important than precision to managers. If a decision must be made, a manager would much rather have a good estimate now than wait a week for a

Exhibit 1–2
Comparison of Financial and Managerial Accounting

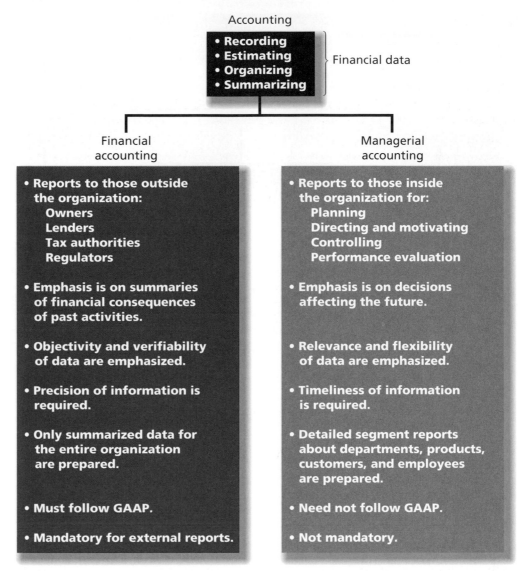

more precise answer. A decision involving tens of millions of dollars does not have to be based on estimates that are precise down to the penny, or even to the dollar. Estimates that are accurate to the nearest million dollars may be precise enough to make a good decision. Since precision is costly in terms of both time and resources, managerial accounting places less emphasis on precision than does financial accounting. In addition, managerial accounting places considerable weight on nonmonetary data. For example, information about customer satisfaction is tremendously important even though it would be difficult to express such data in a monetary form.

Segments of an Organization

Financial accounting is primarily concerned with reporting for the company as a whole. By contrast, managerial accounting focuses much more on the parts, or **segments,** of a company. These segments may be product lines, sales territories, divisions, departments, or any other categorization of the company's activities that management finds useful. Financial accounting does require some breakdowns of revenues and costs by major segments in external reports, but this is a secondary emphasis. In managerial accounting, segment reporting is the primary emphasis.

Recordkeeping for the Future

in business | *today*

Taking into account the ongoing nature of litigation, executives in the tobacco industry might consider company records to be a liability. However, properly maintained corporate records have significant future benefit and, as such, should be considered an essential asset. Reviews of recordkeeping policies should be performed periodically to ensure that important information, needed for reference in the future, is documented and can be retrieved. Most of the problems uncovered in such reviews tend to relate to how the records are organized rather than how much information is being documented. There is little value in information that cannot be retrieved when it is needed for decision making.

Source: J. Edwin Dietal, "Improving Corporate Performance," reprinted with permission from the *Information Management Journal*, April 2000, pp. 18–26 © 2000 ARMA International.

Generally Accepted Accounting Principles (GAAP)

Financial accounting statements prepared for external users must be prepared in accordance with generally accepted accounting principles (GAAP). External users must have some assurance that the reports have been prepared in accordance with a common set of ground rules. These common ground rules enhance comparability and help reduce fraud and misrepresentation, but they do not necessarily lead to the type of reports that would be most useful in internal decision making. For example, GAAP requires that land be stated at its historical cost on financial reports. However, if management is considering moving a store to a new location and then selling the land the store currently sits on, management would like to know the current market value of the land—a vital piece of information that is ignored under GAAP.

Managerial accounting is not bound by generally accepted accounting principles. Managers set their own ground rules concerning the content and form of internal reports. The only constraint is that the expected benefits from using the information should outweigh the costs of collecting, analyzing, and summarizing the data. Nevertheless, as we shall see in subsequent chapters, it is undeniably true that financial reporting requirements have heavily influenced management accounting practice.

Managerial Accounting—Not Mandatory

Financial accounting is mandatory; that is, it must be done. Various outside parties such as the Securities and Exchange Commission (SEC) and the tax authorities require periodic financial statements. Managerial accounting, on the other hand, is not mandatory. A company is completely free to do as much or as little as it wishes. There are no regulatory bodies or other outside agencies that specify what is to be done, or, for that matter, whether anything is to be done at all. Since managerial accounting is completely optional, the important question is always, "Is the information useful?" rather than, "Is the information required?"

As explained above, the work of management focuses on (1) planning, which includes setting objectives and outlining how to attain these objectives; and (2) control, which includes the steps to take to ensure that objectives are realized. To carry out these planning and control responsibilities, managers need *information* about the organization. From an accounting point of view, this information often relates to the *costs* of the organization.

In managerial accounting, the term *cost* is used in many different ways. The reason is that there are many types of costs, and these costs are classified differently according to the immediate needs of management. For example, managers may want cost data to prepare external financial reports, to prepare planning budgets, or to make decisions. Each different use of cost data demands a different classification and definition of costs. For example, the preparation of external financial reports requires the use of historical cost data, whereas decision making may require current cost data.

General Cost Classifications

Concept 1–1

Costs are associated with all types of organizations—business, nonbusiness, manufacturing, retail, and service. Generally, the kinds of costs that are incurred and the way in which these costs are classified depends on the type of organization involved. Managerial accounting is as applicable to one type of organization as to another. For this reason, we will consider in our discussion the cost characteristics of a variety of organizations—manufacturing, merchandising, and service.

Our initial focus in this chapter is on manufacturing companies, since their basic activities include most of the activities found in other types of business organizations. Manufacturing companies such as Texas Instruments, Ford, and Kodak are involved in acquiring raw materials, producing finished goods, marketing, distributing, billing, and almost every other business activity. Therefore, an understanding of costs in a manufacturing company can be very helpful in understanding costs in other types of organizations.

In this chapter, we develop cost concepts that apply to diverse organizations. For example, these cost concepts apply to fast-food outlets such as Kentucky Fried Chicken, Pizza Hut, and Taco Bell; movie studios such as Disney, Paramount, and United Artists; consulting firms such as Accenture and McKinsey; and your local hospital. The exact terms used in these industries may not be the same as those used in manufacturing, but the same basic concepts apply. With some slight modifications, these basic concepts also apply to merchandising companies such as Wal-Mart, The Gap, 7-Eleven, Nordstrom, and Tower Records that resell finished goods acquired from manufacturers and other sources. With that in mind, let us begin our discussion of manufacturing costs.

Manufacturing Costs

Most manufacturing companies divide manufacturing costs into three broad categories: direct materials, direct labor, and manufacturing overhead. A discussion of each of these categories follows.

Direct Materials The materials that go into the final product are called **raw materials.** This term is somewhat misleading, since it seems to imply unprocessed natural resources like wood pulp or iron ore. Actually, raw materials refer to any materials that are used in the final product; and the finished product of one company can become the raw materials of another company. For example, the plastics produced by Du Pont are a raw material used by Compaq Computer in its personal computers.

Direct materials are those materials that become an integral part of the finished product and that can be physically and conveniently traced to it. This would include, for example, the seats Boeing purchases from subcontractors to install in its commercial aircraft. Also included is the tiny electric motor Panasonic uses in its CD players to make the CD spin.

Sometimes it isn't worth the effort to trace the costs of relatively insignificant materials to the end products. Such minor items would include the solder used to make electrical connections in a Sony TV or the glue used to assemble an Ethan Allen chair. Materials such as solder and glue are called **indirect materials** and are included as part of manufacturing overhead, which is discussed later in this section.

Direct Labor The term **direct labor** is reserved for those labor costs that can be easily (i.e., physically and conveniently) traced to individual units of product. Direct labor is sometimes called *touch labor,* since direct labor workers typically touch the product while it is being made. The labor costs of assembly-line workers, for example, would be direct labor costs, as would the labor costs of carpenters, bricklayers, and machine operators.

Labor costs that cannot be physically traced to the creation of products, or that can be traced only at great cost and inconvenience, are termed **indirect labor** and treated as part of manufacturing overhead, along with indirect materials. Indirect labor includes the labor costs of janitors, supervisors, materials handlers, and night security guards. Although the efforts of these workers are essential to production, it would be either impractical or impossible to accurately trace their costs to specific units of product. Hence, such labor costs are treated as indirect labor.

In some industries, major shifts are taking place in the structure of labor costs. Sophisticated automated equipment, run and maintained by skilled indirect workers, is increasingly replacing direct labor. In a few companies, direct labor has become such a minor element of cost that it has disappeared altogether as a separate cost category. More is said in later chapters about this trend and about the impact it is having on cost systems. However, the vast majority of manufacturing and service companies throughout the world continue to recognize direct labor as a separate cost category.

Manufacturing Overhead **Manufacturing overhead,** the third element of manufacturing cost, includes all costs of manufacturing except direct materials and direct labor. Manufacturing overhead includes items such as indirect materials; indirect labor; maintenance and repairs on production equipment; and heat and light, property taxes, depreciation, and insurance on manufacturing facilities. A company also incurs costs for heat and light, property taxes, insurance, depreciation, and so forth, associated with its selling and administrative functions, but these costs are not included as part of manufacturing overhead. Only those costs associated with *operating the factory* are included in the manufacturing overhead category.

Various names are used for manufacturing overhead, such as *indirect manufacturing cost, factory overhead,* and *factory burden.* All of these terms are synonymous with *manufacturing overhead.*

Manufacturing overhead combined with direct labor is called **conversion cost.** This term stems from the fact that direct labor costs and overhead costs are incurred to convert raw materials into finished products. Direct labor combined with direct materials is called **prime cost.**

Nonmanufacturing Costs

Generally, nonmanufacturing costs are subclassified into two categories:

1. Marketing or selling costs.
2. Administrative costs.

Marketing or selling costs include all costs necessary to secure customer orders and get the finished product or service into the hands of the customer. These costs are often called *order-getting and order-filling costs.* Examples of marketing costs include advertising, shipping, sales travel, sales commissions, sales salaries, and costs of finished goods warehouses.

Administrative costs include all executive, organizational, and clerical costs associated with the *general management* of an organization rather than with manufacturing, marketing, or selling. Examples of administrative costs include executive compensation, general accounting, secretarial, public relations, and similar costs involved in the overall, general administration of the organization *as a whole.*

Product Costs versus Period Costs

> **Learning Objective 2**
> Distinguish between product costs and period costs and give examples of each.

In addition to the distinction between manufacturing and nonmanufacturing costs, there are other ways to look at costs. For instance, they can also be classified as either *product costs* or *period costs.* To understand the difference between product costs and period costs, we must first refresh our understanding of the matching principle from financial accounting.

Generally, costs are recognized as expenses on the income statement in the period that benefits from the cost. For example, if a company pays for liability insurance in advance for two years, the entire amount is not considered an expense of the year in which the payment is made. Instead, one-half of the cost would be recognized as an expense each year. The reason is that both years—not just the first year—benefit from the insurance payment. The unexpensed portion of the insurance payment is carried on the balance sheet as an asset called *prepaid insurance.* You should be familiar with this type of *accrual* from your financial accounting coursework.

The *matching principle* is based on the accrual concept and states that *costs incurred to generate a particular revenue should be recognized as expenses in the same period that the revenue is recognized.* This means that if a cost is incurred to acquire or make something that will eventually be sold, then the cost should be recognized as an expense only when the sale takes place—that is, when the benefit occurs. Such costs are called *product costs.*

Product Costs

For financial accounting purposes, **product costs** include all the costs that are involved in acquiring or making a product. In the case of manufactured goods, these costs consist of direct materials, direct labor, and manufacturing overhead. Product costs are viewed as "attaching" to units of product as the goods are purchased or manufactured, and they remain attached as the goods go into inventory awaiting sale. So initially, product costs are assigned to an inventory account on the balance sheet. When the goods are sold, the costs are released from inventory as expenses (typically called *cost of goods sold*) and matched against sales revenue. Since product costs are initially assigned to inventories, they are also known as **inventoriable costs.**

We want to emphasize that product costs are not necessarily treated as expenses in the period in which they are incurred. Rather, as explained above, they are treated as expenses in the period in which the related products *are sold.* This means that a product cost such as direct materials or direct labor might be incurred during one period but not treated as an expense until a following period when the completed product is sold.

Period Costs

Period costs are all the costs that are not included in product costs. These costs are expensed on the income statement in the period in which they are incurred, using the usual rules of accrual accounting you have already learned in financial accounting. Period costs are not included as part of the cost of either purchased or manufactured goods. Sales commissions and office rent are good examples of the kind of costs we are talking about. Neither commissions nor office rent are included as part of the cost of purchased or manufactured goods. Rather, both items are treated as expenses on the income statement in the period in which they are incurred. Thus, they are said to be period costs.

As suggested above, *all selling and administrative expenses are considered to be period costs.* Therefore, advertising, executive salaries, sales commissions, public relations, and other nonmanufacturing costs discussed earlier would all be period costs. They will appear on the income statement as expenses in the period in which they are incurred.

Exhibit 1–3 contains a summary of the cost terms that we have introduced so far.

Cost Classifications on Financial Statements

In your prior accounting training, you learned that firms prepare periodic financial reports for creditors, stockholders, and others to show the financial condition of the firm and the firm's earnings performance over some specified interval. The reports you studied were probably those of merchandising companies, such as retail stores, which simply purchase goods from suppliers for resale to customers.

The financial statements prepared by a *manufacturing* company are more complex than the statements prepared by a merchandising company. Manufacturing companies are more complex organizations than merchandising companies because the manufacturing company must produce its goods as well as market them. The production process gives rise to many costs that do not exist in a merchandising company, and somehow these costs must be accounted for on the manufacturing company's financial statements. In this section, we focus our attention on how this accounting is carried out in the balance sheet and income statement.

Exhibit 1–3
Summary of Cost Terms

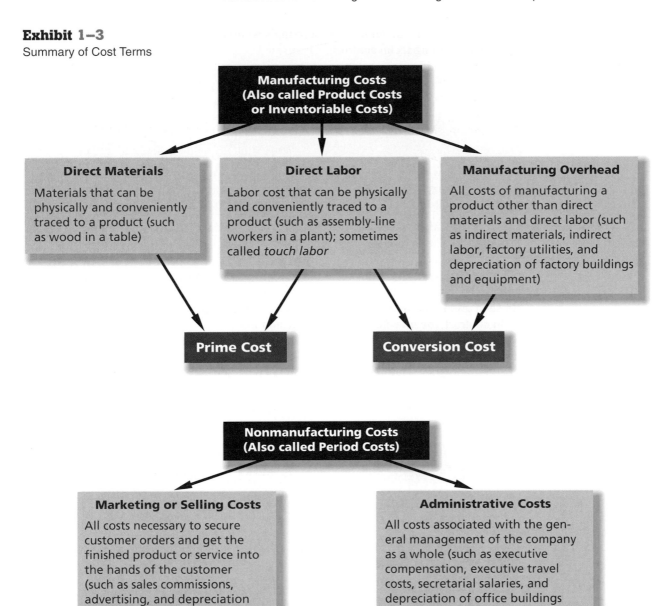

The Balance Sheet

The balance sheet, or statement of financial position, of a manufacturing company is similar to that of a merchandising company. However, the inventory accounts differ between the two types of companies. A merchandising company has only one class of inventory—goods purchased from suppliers that are awaiting resale to customers. In contrast, manufacturing companies have three classes of inventories—*raw materials*, *work in process*, and *finished goods*. Raw materials, as we've noted, are the materials that are used to make a product. **Work in process** consists of units of product that are only partially complete and will require further work before they are ready for sale to a customer. **Finished goods** consist of units of product that have been completed but have not yet been sold to customers. The overall inventory figure is usually broken down into these three classes of inventories in a footnote to the financial statements.

We will use two companies—Graham Manufacturing and Reston Bookstore—to illustrate the concepts discussed in this section. Graham Manufacturing is located in Portsmouth, New Hampshire, and makes precision brass fittings for yachts. Reston Bookstore is a small bookstore in Reston, Virginia, specializing in books about the Civil War.

The footnotes to Graham Manufacturing's Annual Report reveal the following information concerning its inventories:

GRAHAM MANUFACTURING CORPORATION		
Inventory Accounts		
	Beginning Balance	Ending Balance
Raw materials	$ 60,000	$ 50,000
Work in process	90,000	60,000
Finished goods	125,000	175,000
Total inventory accounts	$275,000	$285,000

Graham Manufacturing's raw materials inventory consists largely of brass rods and brass blocks. The work in process inventory consists of partially completed brass fittings. The finished goods inventory consists of brass fittings that are ready to be sold to customers.

In contrast, the inventory account at Reston Bookstore consists entirely of the costs of books the company has purchased from publishers for resale to the public. In merchandising companies like Reston, these inventories may be called *merchandise inventory.* The beginning and ending balances in this account appear as follows:

RESTON BOOKSTORE		
Inventory Accounts		
	Beginning Balance	Ending Balance
Merchandise inventory	$100,000	$150,000

The Income Statement

Concept 1–2

Learning Objective 3
Prepare an income statement including calculation of the cost of goods sold.

Exhibit 1–4 compares the income statements of Reston Bookstore and Graham Manufacturing. For purposes of illustration, these statements contain more detail about cost of goods sold than you will generally find in published financial statements.

At first glance, the income statements of merchandising and manufacturing firms like Reston Bookstore and Graham Manufacturing are very similar. The only apparent difference is in the labels of some of the entries in the computation of the cost of goods sold. In the exhibit, the computation of cost of goods sold relies on the following basic equation for inventory accounts:

BASIC EQUATION FOR INVENTORY ACCOUNTS

$$\begin{array}{c} \text{Beginning} \\ \text{balance} \end{array} + \begin{array}{c} \text{Additions} \\ \text{to inventory} \end{array} = \begin{array}{c} \text{Ending} \\ \text{balance} \end{array} + \begin{array}{c} \text{Withdrawals} \\ \text{from inventory} \end{array}$$

The logic underlying this equation, which applies to any inventory account, is illustrated in Exhibit 1–5. During a period, additions to the inventory account come through purchases or other means. The sum of the additions to the account and the beginning balance represents the total amount of inventory that is available for use during the period. At the end of the period, all of the inventory that was available either must be in ending inventory or must have been withdrawn from the inventory account.

These concepts are applied to determine the cost of goods sold for a merchandising company like Reston Bookstore as follows:

Exhibit 1–4

Comparative Income Statements: Merchandising and Manufacturing Companies

MERCHANDISING COMPANY
Reston Bookstore

Sales		$1,000,000
Cost of goods sold:		
Beginning merchandise inventory	$100,000	
Add: Purchases	650,000	
Goods available for sale	750,000	
Deduct: Ending merchandise inventory	150,000	600,000
Gross margin		400,000
Less operating expenses:		
Selling expense	100,000	
Administrative expense	200,000	300,000
Net income		$ 100,000

The cost of merchandise inventory purchased from outside suppliers during the period. →

MANUFACTURING COMPANY
Graham Manufacturing

Sales		$1,500,000
Cost of goods sold:		
Beginning finished goods inventory	$125,000	
Add: Cost of goods manufactured	850,000	
Goods available for sale	975,000	
Deduct: Ending finished goods inventory	175,000	800,000
Gross margin		700,000
Less operating expenses:		
Selling expense	250,000	
Administrative expense	300,000	550,000
Net income		$ 150,000

The manufacturing costs associated with the goods that were finished during the period. (See Exhibits 1–6 and 1–7 for details.) →

COST OF GOODS SOLD IN A MERCHANDISING COMPANY

$$\text{Beginning merchandise inventory} + \text{Purchases} = \text{Ending merchandise inventory} + \text{Cost of goods sold}$$

or

$$\text{Cost of goods sold} = \text{Beginning merchandise inventory} + \text{Purchases} - \text{Ending merchandise inventory}$$

The cost of goods sold for a manufacturing company like Graham Manufacturing is determined as follows:

COST OF GOODS SOLD IN A MANUFACTURING COMPANY

$$\text{Beginning finished goods inventory} + \text{Cost of goods manufactured} = \text{Ending finished goods inventory} + \text{Cost of goods sold}$$

or

$$\text{Cost of goods sold} = \text{Beginning finished goods inventory} + \text{Cost of goods manufactured} - \text{Ending finished goods inventory}$$

Exhibit 1–5

Inventory Flows

Exhibit 1–6

Schedule of Cost of Goods Manufactured

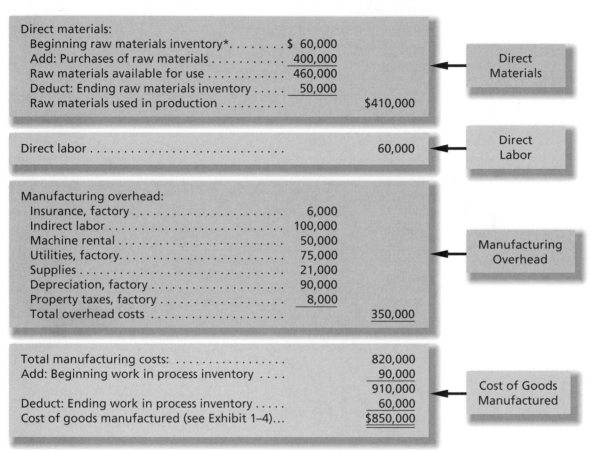

*We assume in this example that the Raw Materials inventory account contains only direct materials and that indirect materials are carried in a separate Supplies account. Using a Supplies account for indirect materials is a common practice among companies. In Chapter 2, we discuss the procedure to be followed if *both* direct and indirect materials are carried in a single account.

To determine the cost of goods sold in a merchandising company like Reston Bookstore, we only need to know the beginning and ending balances in the Merchandise Inventory account and the purchases. Total purchases can be easily determined in a merchandising company by simply adding together all purchases from suppliers.

To determine the cost of goods sold in a manufacturing company like Graham Manufacturing, we need to know the *cost of goods manufactured* and the beginning and ending balances in the Finished Goods inventory account. The **cost of goods manufactured** consists of the manufacturing costs associated with goods that were *finished* during the period. The cost of goods manufactured figure for Graham Manufacturing is derived in Exhibit 1–6, which contains a *schedule of cost of goods manufactured.*

Learning Objective 4

Prepare a schedule of cost of goods manufactured.

Schedule of Cost of Goods Manufactured

At first glance, the **schedule of cost of goods manufactured** in Exhibit 1–6 appears complex and perhaps even intimidating. However, it is all quite logical. Notice that the sched-

Exhibit 1–7

An Alternative Approach to Computation of Cost of Goods Sold

Computation of Raw Materials Used in Production

Beginning raw materials inventory	$ 60,000
+ Purchases of raw materials	400,000
− Ending raw materials inventory	50,000
= Raw materials used in production	$410,000

Computation of Total Manufacturing Cost

Raw materials used in production	$410,000
+ Direct labor	60,000
+ Total manufacturing overhead costs	350,000
= Total manufacturing cost	$820,000

Computation of Cost of Goods Manufactured

Beginning work in process inventory	$ 90,000
+ Total manufacturing cost	820,000
− Ending work in process inventory	60,000
= Cost of goods manufactured	$850,000

Computation of Cost of Goods Sold

Beginning finished goods inventory	$125,000
+ Cost of goods manufactured	850,000
− Ending finished goods inventory	175,000
= Cost of goods sold	$800,000

ule of cost of goods manufactured contains the three elements of product costs that we discussed earlier—direct materials, direct labor, and manufacturing overhead. The total of these three cost elements is *not* the cost of goods manufactured, however. The reason is that some of the materials, labor, and overhead costs incurred during the period relate to goods that are not yet completed. The costs that relate to goods that are not yet completed are shown in the work in process inventory figures at the bottom of the schedule. Note that the beginning work in process inventory must be added to the manufacturing costs of the period, and the ending work in process inventory must be deducted, to arrive at the cost of goods manufactured.

The logic underlying the schedule of cost of goods manufactured and the computation of cost of goods sold is laid out in a different format in Exhibit 1–7. To compute the cost of goods sold, go to the top of the exhibit and work your way down using the following steps:

1. Compute the raw materials used in production in the top section of the exhibit.
2. Insert the total raw materials used in production ($410,000) into the second section of the exhibit and compute the total manufacturing cost.
3. Insert the total manufacturing cost ($820,000) into the third section of the exhibit and compute the cost of goods manufactured.
4. Insert the cost of goods manufactured ($850,000) into the bottom section of the exhibit and compute the cost of goods sold.

Product Costs—A Closer Look

Earlier in the chapter, we defined product costs as consisting of those costs that are involved in either the purchase or the manufacture of goods. For manufactured goods, we stated that these costs consist of direct materials, direct labor, and manufacturing overhead. To understand product costs more fully, it will be helpful at this point to look briefly

Exhibit 1–8
Cost Flows and Classifications in a Manufacturing Company

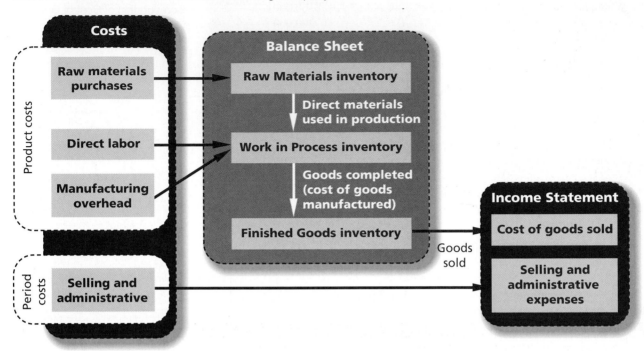

at the flow of costs in a manufacturing company. By doing so, we will be able to see how product costs move through the various accounts and affect the balance sheet and the income statement in the course of producing and selling products.

Exhibit 1–8 illustrates the flow of costs in a manufacturing company. Raw materials purchases are recorded in the Raw Materials inventory account. When raw materials are used in production, their costs are transferred to the Work in Process inventory account as direct materials. Notice that direct labor cost and manufacturing overhead cost are added directly to Work in Process. Work in Process can be viewed most simply as an assembly line where workers are stationed and where products slowly take shape as they move from one end of the assembly line to the other. The direct materials, direct labor, and manufacturing overhead costs added to Work in Process in Exhibit 1–8 are the costs needed to complete these products as they move along this assembly line.

Notice from the exhibit that as goods are completed, their cost is transferred from Work in Process to Finished Goods. Here the goods await sale to a customer. As goods are sold, their cost is then transferred from Finished Goods to Cost of Goods Sold. At this point the various material, labor, and overhead costs that are required to make the product are finally treated as expenses.

Inventoriable Costs

As stated earlier, product costs are often called inventoriable costs. The reason is that these costs go directly into inventory accounts as they are incurred (first into Work in Process and then into Finished Goods), rather than going into expense accounts. Thus, they are termed *inventoriable costs. This is a key concept since such costs can end up on the balance sheet as assets if goods are only partially completed or are unsold at the end of a period.* To illustrate this point, refer again to Exhibit 1–8. At the end of the period, the materials, labor, and overhead costs that are associated with the units in the Work in Process and Finished Goods inventory accounts will appear on the balance sheet as part of the company's assets. As explained earlier, these costs will not become expenses until later when the goods are completed and sold.

Selling and administrative expenses are not involved in the manufacture of a product. For this reason, they are not treated as product costs but rather as period costs that go directly into expense accounts as they are incurred as shown in Exhibit 1–8.

Benetton and the Value Chain

in business | today

United Colors of Benetton, an Italian apparel company headquartered in Ponzano, is unusual in that it is involved in all activities in the "value chain" from clothing design through manufacturing, distribution, and ultimate sale to customers in Benetton retail outlets. Most companies are involved in only one or two of these activities. Looking at this company allows us to see how costs are distributed across the entire value chain. A recent income statement from the company contained the following data:

	Billions of Italian Lire	Percent of Net Sales
Net sales	2,768	100.0%
Cost of sales	1,721	62.2
Selling and general and administrative expenses:		
Payroll and related cost	166	6.0
Distribution and transport	57	2.1
Sales commissions	115	4.2
Advertising and promotion	120	4.3
Depreciation and amortization	42	1.5
Other expenses	275	9.9
Total selling and general and administrative expenses	775	28.0%

Even though this company spends large sums on advertising and runs its own shops, the cost of sales is still quite high in relation to the net sales—62% of net sales. And despite the company's lavish advertising campaigns, advertising and promotion costs amounted to only a little over 4% of net sales. (Note: One U.S. dollar was worth about 1,600 Italian lire at the time of this financial report.)

An Example of Cost Flows

To provide a numerical example of cost flows in a manufacturing company, assume that a company's annual insurance cost is $2,000. Three-fourths of this amount ($1,500) applies to factory operations, and one-fourth ($500) applies to selling and administrative activities. Therefore, $1,500 of the $2,000 insurance cost would be a product (inventoriable) cost and would be added to the cost of the goods produced during the year. This concept is illustrated in Exhibit 1–9, where $1,500 of insurance cost is added into Work in Process. As shown in the exhibit, this portion of the year's insurance cost will not become an expense until the goods that are produced during the year are sold—which may not happen until the following year or even later. Until the goods are sold, the $1,500 will remain as part of inventory (either as part of Work in Process or as part of Finished Goods), along with the other costs of producing the goods.

By contrast, the $500 of insurance cost that applies to the company's selling and administrative activities will go into an expense account immediately as a charge against the period's revenue.

Thus far, we have been mainly concerned with classifications of manufacturing costs for the purpose of determining inventory valuations on the balance sheet and cost of

Exhibit 1–9
An Example of Cost Flows in a Manufacturing Company

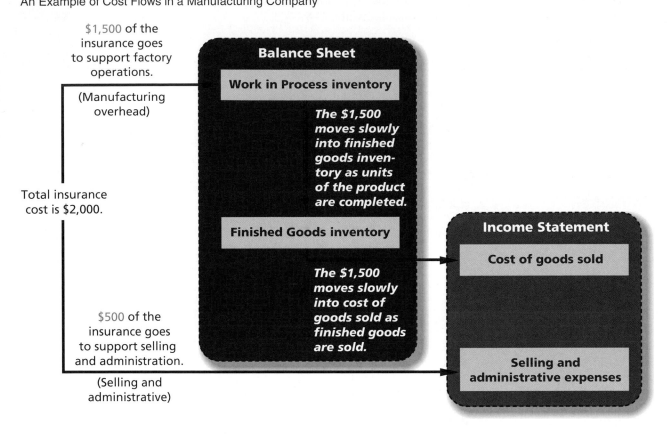

goods sold on the income statement of external financial reports. There are, however, many other purposes for which costs are used, and each purpose requires a different classification of costs. We will consider several different purposes for cost classifications in the remaining sections of this chapter. These purposes and the corresponding cost classifications are summarized in Exhibit 1–10. To maintain focus, we suggest that you refer back to this exhibit frequently as you progress through the rest of this chapter.

in business today **Product or Period Cost?—Not Just an Academic Distinction**

Whether a cost is considered a product or period cost can have an important impact on a company's financial statements and can create conflicts inside an organization. Consider the following excerpts from a conversation recorded on the Institute of Management Accountants' Ethics Hot Line:

Caller: My problem basically is that my boss, the division general manager, wants me to put costs into inventory that I know should be expensed.
Counselor: Have you expressed your doubts to your boss?
Caller: Yes, but he is basically a salesman and claims he knows nothing about GAAP. He just wants the "numbers" to back up the good news he keeps telling corporate [headquarters], which is what corporate demands. Also, he asks if I am ready to make the entries that I think are improper. It seems he wants to make it look like my idea all along. Our company had legal problems a few years ago with some government contracts, and it was the lower level people who were "hung out to dry" rather than the higher-ups who were really at fault.
Counselor: What does he say when you tell him these matters need resolution?

Caller: He just says we need a meeting, but the meetings never solve anything.

Counselor: Does your company have an ethics hot line?

Caller: Yes, but my boss would view use of the hot line as snitching or even whistle-blowing.

Counselor: If you might face reprisals for using the hot line, perhaps you should evaluate whether or not you really want to work for a company whose ethical climate is one you are uncomfortable in.

Caller: I have already asked . . . for a transfer back to the corporate office.

Source: Curtis C. Verschoor, "Using a Hot Line Isn't Whistle-Blowing," *Strategic Finance*, April 1999, pp. 27–28. Used with permission from *Strategic Finance* and the Institute of Management Accountants.

Purpose of Cost Classification	Cost Classifications

Preparing external financial statements	• Product costs (inventoriable)
	   • Direct materials
	   • Direct labor
	   • Manufacturing overhead
	 • Period costs (expensed)
	   • Nonmanufacturing costs
	     • Marketing or selling costs
	     • Administrative costs

Predicting cost behavior in response to changes in activity	• Variable cost (proportional to activity) • Fixed cost (constant in total)
Assigning costs to cost objects such as departments or products	• Direct cost (can be easily traced) • Indirect cost (cannot be easily traced; must be allocated)
Making decisions	• Differential cost (differs between alternatives) • Sunk cost (past cost not affected by a decision) • Opportunity cost (forgone benefit)
Cost of quality (Appendix 1A)	• Prevention costs • Appraisal costs • Internal failure costs • External failure costs

Exhibit 1–10
Summary of Cost Classifications

Cost Classifications for Predicting Cost Behavior

Quite frequently, it is necessary to predict how a certain cost will behave in response to a change in activity. For example, a manager at AT&T may want to estimate the impact a 5% increase in long-distance calls would have on the company's total electric bill or on the total wages the company pays its long-distance operators. **Cost behavior** is the way a cost will react or respond to changes in the level of business activity. As the activity level rises and falls, a particular cost may rise and fall as well—or it may remain constant. For planning purposes, a manager must be able to anticipate which of these will happen; and

Learning Objective 5
Define and give examples of variable costs and fixed costs.

if a cost can be expected to change, the manager must know by how much it will change. To help make such distinctions, costs are often categorized as variable or fixed.

Variable Cost

A **variable cost** is a cost that varies, in total, in direct proportion to changes in the level of activity. The activity can be expressed in many ways, such as units produced, units sold, miles driven, beds occupied, lines of print, hours worked, and so forth. Direct materials is a good example of a variable cost. The cost of direct materials used during a period will vary, in total, in direct proportion to the number of units that are produced. As an example, consider the Saturn Division of GM. Each auto requires one battery. As the output of autos increases and decreases, the number of batteries used will increase and decrease proportionately. If auto production goes up 10%, then the number of batteries used will also go up 10%. The concept of a variable cost is shown in graphic form in Exhibit 1–11.

It is important to note that when we speak of a cost as being variable, we mean the *total* cost rises and falls as the activity level rises and falls. This idea is presented below, assuming that a Saturn's battery costs $24:

Number of Autos Produced		Cost per Battery	Total Variable Cost— Batteries
1	. . . .	$24	$ 24
500	. . . .	24	12,000
1,000	. . . .	24	24,000

One interesting aspect of variable cost behavior is that a variable cost is constant if expressed on a *per unit* basis. Observe from the tabulation above that the per unit cost of batteries remains constant at $24 even though the total amount of cost involved increases and decreases with activity.

There are many examples of costs that are variable with respect to the products and services provided by a company. In a manufacturing company, variable costs include items such as direct materials and some elements of manufacturing overhead such as lubricants, shipping costs, and sales commissions. For the present we will also assume that direct labor is a variable cost, although as we shall see in a later chapter, direct labor may

Exhibit 1–11
Variable and Fixed Cost Behavior

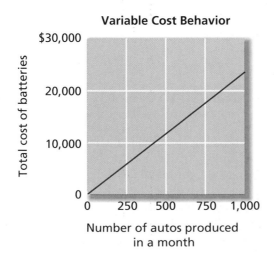

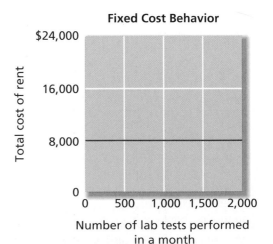

act more like a fixed cost in many situations. In a merchandising company, variable costs include items such as cost of goods sold, commissions to salespersons, and billing costs. In a hospital, the variable costs of providing health care services to patients would include the costs of the supplies, drugs, meals, and perhaps nursing services.

The activity causing changes in a variable cost need not be how much output is produced or sold. For example, the wages paid to employees at a Blockbuster Video outlet will depend on the number of hours the store is open and not strictly on the number of videos rented. In this case, we would say that wage costs are variable with respect to the hours of operation. Nevertheless, when we say that a cost is variable, we ordinarily mean it is variable with respect to the volume of revenue-generating output—in other words, how many units are produced and sold, how many videos are rented, how many patients are treated, and so on.

Fixed Cost

A **fixed cost** is a cost that remains constant, in total, regardless of changes in the level of activity. Unlike variable costs, fixed costs are not affected by changes in activity. Consequently, as the activity level rises and falls, the fixed costs remain constant in total amount unless influenced by some outside force, such as a price change. Rent is a good example of a fixed cost. Suppose the Mayo Clinic rents a machine for $8,000 per month that tests blood samples for the presence of leukemia cells. The $8,000 monthly rental cost will be sustained regardless of the number of tests that may be performed during the month. The concept of a fixed cost is shown in graphic form in Exhibit 1–11.

Very few costs are completely fixed. Most will change if there is a large enough change in activity. For example, suppose that the capacity of the leukemia diagnostic machine at the Mayo Clinic is 2,000 tests per month. If the clinic wishes to perform more than 2,000 tests in a month, it would be necessary to rent an additional machine, which would cause a jump in the fixed costs. When we say a cost is fixed, we mean it is fixed within some *relevant range*. The **relevant range** is the range of activity within which the assumptions about variable and fixed costs are valid. For example, the assumption that the rent for diagnostic machines is $8,000 per month is valid within the relevant range of 0 to 2,000 tests per month.

Fixed costs can create confusion if they are expressed on a per-unit basis. This is because the average fixed cost per unit increases and decreases *inversely* with changes in activity. In the Mayo Clinic, for example, the average cost per test will fall as the number of tests performed increases. This is because the $8,000 rental cost will be spread over more tests. Conversely, as the number of tests performed in the clinic declines, the average cost per test will rise as the $8,000 rental cost is spread over fewer tests. This concept is illustrated in the table below:

Monthly Rental Cost	Number of Tests Performed	Average Cost per Test
$8,000	10	$800
8,000	500	16
8,000	2,000	4

Note that if the Mayo Clinic performs only 10 tests each month, the rental cost of the equipment will average $800 per test. But if 2,000 tests are performed each month, the average cost will drop to only $4 per test. More will be said later about the problems created for both the accountant and the manager by this variation in unit costs.

Examples of fixed costs include straight-line depreciation, insurance, property taxes, rent, supervisory salaries, administrative salaries, and advertising.

A summary of both variable and fixed cost behavior is presented in Exhibit 1–12.

Exhibit 1–12
Summary of Variable and Fixed
Cost Behavior

Cost	Behavior of the Cost (within the relevant range)	
	In Total	**Per Unit**
Variable cost	Total variable cost increases and decreases in proportion to changes in the activity level.	Variable cost remains constant per unit.
Fixed cost	Total fixed cost is not affected by changes in the activity level within the relevant range.	Fixed cost per unit decreases as the activity level rises and increases as the activity level falls.

decision | maker   Financial Analyst

You are a financial analyst for several clients who are interested in making investments in stable companies. You become aware of a privately owned airline that has been in business for 20 years and needs to raise $75 million in new capital. When you call one of your clients, she replies that she avoids investing in airlines because of the high proportion of fixed costs in this industry. How would you reply to this statement?

Cost Classifications for Assigning Costs to Cost Objects

Learning Objective 6
Define and give examples of direct and indirect costs.

Costs are assigned to objects for a variety of purposes including pricing, profitability studies, and control of spending. A **cost object** is anything for which cost data are desired—including products, product lines, customers, jobs, and organizational subunits. For purposes of assigning costs to cost objects, costs are classified as either *direct* or *indirect.*

Direct Cost

A **direct cost** is a cost that can be easily and conveniently traced to the particular cost object under consideration. The concept of direct cost extends beyond just direct materials and direct labor. For example, if Reebok is assigning costs to its various regional and national sales offices, then the salary of the sales manager in its Tokyo office would be a direct cost of that office.

Indirect Cost

An **indirect cost** is a cost that cannot be easily and conveniently traced to the particular cost object under consideration. For example, a Campbell Soup factory may produce dozens of varieties of canned soups. The factory manager's salary would be an indirect cost of a particular variety such as chicken noodle soup. The reason is that the factory manager's salary is not caused by any one variety of soup but rather is incurred as a consequence of running the entire factory. *To be traced to a cost object such as a particular product, the cost must be caused by the cost object.* The factory manager's salary is called a *common cost* of producing the various products of the factory. A **common cost** is a cost that is incurred to support a number of costing objects but that cannot be traced to them individually. A common cost is a particular type of indirect cost.

A particular cost may be direct or indirect, depending on the cost object. While the Campbell Soup factory manager's salary is an *indirect* cost of manufacturing chicken noodle soup, it is a *direct* cost of the manufacturing division. In the first case, the cost object is the chicken noodle soup product. In the second case, the cost object is the entire manufacturing division.

Cost Classifications for Decision Making

Costs are an important feature of many business decisions. In making decisions, it is essential to have a firm grasp of the concepts *differential cost, opportunity cost,* and *sunk cost.*

Learning Objective 7
Define and give examples of cost classifications used in making decisions: differential costs, opportunity costs, and sunk costs.

Differential Cost and Revenue

Decisions involve choosing between alternatives. In business decisions, each alternative will have certain costs and benefits that must be compared to the costs and benefits of the other available alternatives. A difference in costs between any two alternatives is known as a **differential cost.** A difference in revenues between any two alternatives is known as **differential revenue.**

A differential cost is also known as an **incremental cost,** although technically an incremental cost should refer only to an increase in cost from one alternative to another; decreases in cost should be referred to as *decremental costs.* Differential cost is a broader term, encompassing both cost increases (incremental costs) and cost decreases (decremental costs) between alternatives.

The accountant's differential cost concept can be compared to the economist's marginal cost concept. In speaking of changes in cost and revenue, the economist employs the terms *marginal cost* and *marginal revenue.* The revenue that can be obtained from selling one more unit of product is called marginal revenue, and the cost involved in producing one more unit of product is called marginal cost. The economist's marginal concept is basically the same as the accountant's differential concept applied to a single unit of output.

Differential costs can be either fixed or variable. To illustrate, assume that Nature Way Cosmetics, Inc., is thinking about changing its marketing method from distribution through retailers to distribution by door-to-door direct sale. Present costs and revenues are compared to projected costs and revenues in the following table:

	Retailer Distribution (present)	Direct Sale Distribution (proposed)	Differential Costs and Revenues
Revenues (V)	$700,000	$800,000	$100,000
Cost of goods sold (V)	350,000	400,000	50,000
Advertising (F)	80,000	45,000	(35,000)
Commissions (V)	–0–	40,000	40,000
Warehouse depreciation (F)	50,000	80,000	30,000
Other expenses (F)	60,000	60,000	–0–
Total	540,000	625,000	85,000
Net income	$160,000	$175,000	$ 15,000

V = Variable; F = Fixed.

According to the above analysis, the differential revenue is $100,000 and the differential costs total $85,000, leaving a positive differential net income of $15,000 under the proposed marketing plan.

The decision of whether Nature Way Cosmetics should stay with the present retail distribution or switch to door-to-door direct selling could be made on the basis of the net incomes of the two alternatives. As we see in the above analysis, the net income under the present distribution method is $160,000, whereas the net income under door-to-door direct selling is estimated to be $175,000. Therefore, the door-to-door direct distribution method is preferred, since it would result in $15,000 higher net income. Note that we would have arrived at exactly the same conclusion by simply focusing on the differential revenues, differential costs, and differential net income, which also show a $15,000 advantage for the direct selling method.

In general, only the differences between alternatives are relevant in decisions. Those items that are the same under all alternatives are not affected by the decision and can be ignored. For example, in the Nature Way Cosmetics example above, the "Other expenses" category, which is $60,000 under both alternatives, can be ignored, since it is not affected by the decision. If it were removed from the calculations, the door-to-door direct selling method would still be preferred by $15,000. This is an extremely important principle in management accounting that we will return to in later chapters.

Opportunity Cost

Opportunity cost is the potential benefit that is given up when one alternative is selected over another. To illustrate this important concept, consider the following examples:

EXAMPLE 1
Vicki has a part-time job that pays her $200 per week while attending college. She would like to spend a week at the beach during spring break, and her employer has agreed to give her the time off, but without pay. The $200 in lost wages would be an opportunity cost of taking the week off to be at the beach.

EXAMPLE 2
Suppose that Neiman Marcus is considering investing a large sum of money in land that may be a site for a future store. Rather than invest the funds in land, the company could invest the funds in high-grade securities. If the land is acquired, the opportunity cost will be the investment income that could have been realized if the securities had been purchased instead.

EXAMPLE 3
Steve is employed with a company that pays him a salary of $30,000 per year. He is thinking about leaving the company and returning to school. Since returning to school would require that he give up his $30,000 salary, the forgone salary would be an opportunity cost of seeking further education.

Opportunity cost is not usually recorded in the accounts of an organization, but it is a cost that must be explicitly considered in every decision a manager makes. Virtually every alternative has some opportunity cost attached to it. In example 3 above, for instance, if Steve decides to stay at his job, there still is an opportunity cost involved: it is the greater income that could be realized in future years as a result of returning to school.

Your Decision to Attend Class

you | *decide*

When you make the decision to attend class, what are the opportunity costs that are inherent in that decision?

Sunk Cost

A **sunk cost** is a cost *that has already been incurred* and that cannot be changed by any decision made now or in the future. Since sunk costs cannot be changed by any decision, they are not differential costs. Therefore, they can and should be ignored when making a decision.

To illustrate a sunk cost, assume that a company paid $50,000 several years ago for a special-purpose machine. The machine was used to make a product that is now obsolete and is no longer being sold. Even though in hindsight the purchase of the machine may have been unwise, no amount of regret can undo that decision. And it would be folly to continue making the obsolete product in a misguided attempt to "recover" the original cost of the machine. In short, the $50,000 originally paid for the machine has already been incurred and cannot be a differential cost in any future decision. For this reason, such costs are said to be sunk and should be ignored in decisions.

Summary

LO1   Identify and give examples of each of the three basic manufacturing cost categories.
Manufacturing costs consist of two categories of costs that can be conveniently and directly traced to units of product—direct materials and direct labor—and one category that cannot be conveniently traced to units of product—manufacturing overhead.

LO2   Distinguish between product costs and period costs and give examples of each.
For purposes of valuing inventories and determining expenses for the balance sheet and income statement, costs are classified as either product costs or period costs. Product costs are assigned to inventories and are considered assets until the products are sold. A product cost becomes an expense—cost of goods sold—only when the product is sold. In contrast, period costs are taken directly to the income statement as expenses in the period in which they are incurred.

In a merchandising company, product cost is whatever the company paid for its merchandise. For external financial reports in a manufacturing company, product costs consist of all manufacturing costs. In both kinds of companies, selling and administrative costs are considered to be period costs and are expensed as incurred.

LO3   Prepare an income statement including calculation of the cost of goods sold.
See Exhibit 1–4 for examples of income statements for both a merchandising and a manufacturing company. In general, net income is computed by deducting the cost of goods sold and operating expenses from sales. Cost of goods sold is calculated by adding purchases to the beginning merchandise or finished goods inventory and then deducting the ending merchandise or finished goods inventory.

LO4   Prepare a schedule of cost of goods manufactured.
See Exhibit 1–6 for an example of a schedule of cost of goods manufactured. In general, the cost of goods manufactured is the sum of direct materials, direct labor, and manufacturing overhead incurred during the period.

LO5   Define and give examples of variable costs and fixed costs.
For purposes of predicting cost behavior—how costs will react to changes in activity—costs are commonly categorized as variable or fixed. Variable costs, in total, are strictly proportional to activity. Thus, the variable cost per unit is constant. Fixed costs, in total, remain at the same level for changes in activity within the relevant range. Thus, the average fixed cost per unit decreases as the number of units increases.

LO6   Define and give examples of direct and indirect costs.

A direct cost is a cost that can be easily and conveniently traced to a costing object. Direct materials is a direct cost of making a product. An indirect cost is a cost that cannot be easily and conveniently traced to a cost object. The salary of the administrator of a hospital is an indirect cost of serving a particular patient.

LO7   Define and give examples of cost classifications used in making decisions: differential costs, opportunity costs, and sunk costs.

The concepts of differential costs and revenue, opportunity cost, and sunk cost are vitally important for purposes of making decisions. Differential costs and revenues are the cost and revenue items that differ between alternatives. Opportunity cost is the benefit that is forgone when one alternative is selected over another. Sunk cost is a cost that occurred in the past and cannot be altered. Differential costs and opportunity costs should be carefully considered in decisions. Sunk costs are always irrelevant in decisions and should be ignored.

The various cost classifications discussed in this chapter are different ways of looking at costs. A particular cost, such as the cost of cheese in a taco served at Taco Bell, can be a manufacturing cost, a product cost, a variable cost, a direct cost, and a differential cost—all at the same time. Taco Bell can be considered to be a manufacturer of fast food. The cost of the cheese in a taco would be considered a manufacturing cost and, as such, it would be a product cost as well. In addition, the cost of cheese would be considered variable with respect to the number of tacos served and would be a direct cost of serving tacos. Finally, the cost of the cheese in a taco would be considered a differential cost of the taco.

Guidance Answers to Decision Maker and You Decide

FINANCIAL ANALYST (p. 40)

Fixed and *variable* are terms used to describe cost behavior or how a given cost will react or respond to changes in the level of business activity. A fixed cost is a cost that remains constant, in total, regardless of changes in the level of activity. However, on a per unit basis, a fixed cost varies inversely with changes in activity. The cost structures of a number of industries lean toward fixed costs because of the nature of their operations. Obviously, the cost of airplanes would be fixed, and within some relevant range, such costs would not change if the number of passengers flown changed. This would also be true in other industries, such as trucking and rail transportation. You might suggest that it would be worthwhile to research the prospects for growth in this industry and for this company. If a downturn in business is not anticipated, a cost structure weighted toward fixed costs should not be used as the primary reason for turning down the investment opportunity. On the other hand, if a period of decline is anticipated, your client's initial impression might be on target.

YOUR DECISION TO ATTEND CLASS (p. 43)

Every alternative has some opportunity cost attached to it. If you brainstormed a bit, you probably came up with a few opportunity costs that accompany your choice to attend class. If you had trouble answering the question, think about what you could be doing instead of attending class.

- You could have been working at a part-time job; you could quantify that cost by multiplying your pay rate by the time you spend in class.
- You could have spent the time studying for another class; the opportunity cost could be measured by the improvement in the grade that would result from spending more time on that class.
- You could have slept in or taken a nap; depending on your level of sleep deprivation, this opportunity cost might be priceless.

Review Problem 1: Cost Terms

Many new cost terms have been introduced in this chapter. It will take you some time to learn what each term means and how to properly classify costs in an organization. Consider the following example: Porter Company manufactures furniture, including tables. Selected costs are given below:
1. The tables are made of wood that costs $100 per table.
2. The tables are assembled by workers, at a wage cost of $40 per table.
3. Workers assembling the tables are supervised by a factory supervisor who is paid $25,000 per year.
4. Electrical costs are $2 per machine-hour. Four machine-hours are required to produce a table.
5. The depreciation cost of the machines used to make the tables totals $10,000 per year.
6. The salary of the president of Porter Company is $100,000 per year.

7. Porter Company spends $250,000 per year to advertise its products.
8. Salespersons are paid a commission of $30 for each table sold.
9. Instead of producing the tables, Porter Company could rent its factory space out at a rental income of $50,000 per year.

Required:

Classify these costs according to various cost terms used in the chapter. *Carefully study the classification of each cost.* If you don't understand why a particular cost is classified the way it is, reread the section of the chapter discussing the particular cost term. The terms *variable cost* and *fixed cost* refer to how costs behave with respect to the number of tables produced in a year.

SOLUTION TO REVIEW PROBLEM 1

	Variable Cost	Fixed Cost	Period (selling and adminis- trative) Cost	Product Cost — Direct Materials	Product Cost — Direct Labor	Product Cost — Manufacturing Overhead	To Units of Product — Direct	To Units of Product — Indirect	Sunk Cost	Opportunity Cost
1. Wood used in a table ($100 per table)	X			X			X			
2. Labor cost to assemble a table ($40 per table)	X				X		X			
3. Salary of the factory supervisor ($25,000 per year)		X				X		X		
4. Cost of electricity to produce tables ($2 per machine- hour)	X					X		X		
5. Depreciation of machines used to produce tables ($10,000 per year)		X				X		X	X*	
6. Salary of the company president ($100,000 per year)		X	X							
7. Advertising expense ($250,000 per year)		X	X							
8. Commissions paid to salespersons ($30 per table sold)	X		X							
9. Rental income forgone on factory space ($50,000 per year)										X†

*This is a sunk cost, since the outlay for the equipment was made in a previous period.

†This is an opportunity cost, since it represents the potential benefit that is lost or sacrificed as a result of using the factory space to produce tables. Opportunity cost is a special category of cost that is not ordinarily recorded in an organization's accounting books. To avoid possible confusion with other costs, we will not attempt to classify this cost in any other way except as an opportunity cost.

Review Problem 2: Schedule of Cost of Goods Manufactured and Income Statement

The following information has been taken from the accounting records of Klear-Seal Company for last year:

Selling expenses	$ 140,000
Raw materials inventory, January 1	90,000
Raw materials inventory, December 31	60,000
Utilities, factory	36,000
Direct labor cost	150,000
Depreciation, factory	162,000
Purchases of raw materials	750,000
Sales	2,500,000
Insurance, factory	40,000
Supplies, factory	15,000
Administrative expenses	270,000
Indirect labor	300,000
Maintenance, factory	87,000
Work in process inventory, January 1	180,000
Work in process inventory, December 31	100,000
Finished goods inventory, January 1	260,000
Finished goods inventory, December 31	210,000

Management wants these data organized in a better format so that financial statements can be prepared for the year.

Required:
1. Prepare a schedule of cost of goods manufactured as in Exhibit 1–6.
2. Compute the cost of goods sold.
3. Using data as needed from (1) and (2) above, prepare an income statement.

SOLUTION TO REVIEW PROBLEM 2
1.

KLEAR-SEAL COMPANY
Schedule of Cost of Goods Manufactured
For the Year Ended December 31

Direct materials:		
Raw materials inventory, January 1	$ 90,000	
Add: Purchases of raw materials	750,000	
Raw materials available for use	840,000	
Deduct: Raw materials inventory, December 31	60,000	
Raw materials used in production		$ 780,000
Direct labor		150,000
Manufacturing overhead:		
Utilities, factory	36,000	
Depreciation, factory	162,000	
Insurance, factory	40,000	
Supplies, factory	15,000	
Indirect labor	300,000	
Maintenance, factory	87,000	
Total overhead costs		640,000
Total manufacturing costs		1,570,000
Add: Work in process inventory, January 1		180,000
		1,750,000
Deduct: Work in process inventory, December 31		100,000
Cost of goods manufactured		$1,650,000

2. The cost of goods sold would be computed as follows:

Finished goods inventory, January 1	$ 260,000
Add: Cost of goods manufactured	1,650,000
Goods available for sale	1,910,000
Deduct: Finished goods inventory, December 31	210,000
Cost of goods sold	$1,700,000

3.

KLEAR-SEAL COMPANY
Income Statement
For the Year Ended December 31

Sales		$2,500,000
Less cost of goods sold (above)		1,700,000
Gross margin		800,000
Less selling and administrative expenses:		
Selling expenses	$140,000	
Administrative expenses	270,000	
Total expenses		410,000
Net income		$ 390,000

Glossary

Administrative costs   All executive, organizational, and clerical costs associated with the general management of an organization rather than with manufacturing, marketing, or selling. (p. 27)

Budget   A detailed plan for the future, usually expressed in formal quantitative terms. (p. 21)

Common costs   A cost that is incurred to support a number of costing objects but cannot be traced to them individually. For example, the wage cost of the pilot of a 747 airliner is a common cost of all of the passengers on the aircraft. Without the pilot, there would be no flight and no passengers. But no part of the pilot's wage is caused by any one passenger taking the flight. (p. 40)

Control   The process of instituting procedures and then obtaining feedback to ensure that all parts of the organization are functioning effectively and moving toward overall company goals. (p. 21)

Controlling   Ensuring that the plan is actually carried out and is appropriately modified as circumstances change. (p. 20)

Conversion cost   Direct labor cost plus manufacturing overhead cost. (p. 27)

Cost behavior   The way in which a cost reacts or responds to changes in the level of business activity. (p. 37)

Cost object   Anything for which cost data are desired. Examples of possible cost objects are products, product lines, customers, jobs, and organizational subunits such as departments or divisions of a company. (p. 40)

Cost of goods manufactured   The manufacturing costs associated with the goods that were finished during the period. (p. 32)

Differential cost   A difference in cost between any two alternatives. Also see *Incremental cost*. (p. 41)

Differential revenue   The difference in revenue between any two alternatives. (p. 41)

Direct cost   A cost that can be easily and conveniently traced to a particular cost object. (p. 40)

Direct labor   Those factory labor costs that can be easily traced to individual units of product. Also called *touch labor*. (p. 26)

Direct materials   Those materials that become an integral part of a finished product and can be conveniently traced to it. (p. 26)

Directing and motivating   Mobilizing people to carry out plans and run routine operations. (p. 20)

Feedback   Accounting and other reports that help managers monitor performance and focus on problems and/or opportunities that might otherwise go unnoticed. (p. 21)

Financial accounting   The phase of accounting concerned with providing information to stockholders, creditors, and others outside the organization. (p. 20)

Finished goods   Units of product that have been completed but have not yet been sold to customers. (p. 29)

Fixed cost   A cost that remains constant, in total, regardless of changes in the level of activity within the relevant range. If a fixed cost is expressed on a per unit basis, it varies inversely with the level of activity. (p. 39)

Incremental cost   An increase in cost between two alternatives. Also see *Differential cost*. (p. 41)

Indirect cost   A cost that cannot be easily and conveniently traced to a particular cost object. (p. 40)

Indirect labor   The labor costs of janitors, supervisors, materials handlers, and other factory workers that cannot be conveniently traced directly to particular products. (p. 26)

Indirect materials   Small items of material such as glue and nails. These items may become an integral part of a finished product but are traceable to the product only at great cost or inconvenience. (p. 26)

Inventoriable costs   Synonym for *product costs*. (p. 28)

Managerial accounting   The phase of accounting concerned with providing information to managers for use in planning and controlling operations and in decision making. (p. 20)

Manufacturing overhead   All costs associated with manufacturing except direct materials and direct labor. (p. 27)

Marketing or selling costs   All costs necessary to secure customer orders and get the finished product or service into the hands of the customer. (p. 27)

Opportunity cost   The potential benefit that is given up when one alternative is selected over another. (p. 42)

Performance report   A detailed report comparing budgeted data to actual data. (p. 22)

Period costs   Those costs that are taken directly to the income statement as expenses in the period in which they are incurred or accrued; such costs consist of selling (marketing) and administrative expenses. (p. 28)

Planning   Selecting a course of action and specifying how the action will be implemented. (p. 20)

Planning and control cycle   The flow of management activities through planning, directing and motivating, and controlling, and then back to planning again. (p. 22)

Prime cost   Direct materials cost plus direct labor cost. (p. 27)

Product costs   All costs that are involved in the purchase or manufacture of goods. In the case of manufactured goods, these costs consist of direct materials, direct labor, and manufacturing overhead. Also see *Inventoriable costs*. (p. 28)

Raw materials   Materials that are used to make a product. (p. 26)

Relevant range   The range of activity within which assumptions about variable and fixed cost behavior are valid. (p. 39)

Schedule of cost of goods manufactured   A schedule showing the direct materials, direct labor, and manufacturing overhead costs incurred for a period and assigned to Work in Process and completed goods. (p. 32)

Segment   Any part of an organization that can be evaluated independently of other parts and about which the manager seeks financial data. Examples include a product line, a sales territory, a division, or a department. (p. 24)

Sunk cost   Any cost that has already been incurred and that cannot be changed by any decision made now or in the future. (p. 43)

Variable cost   A cost that varies, in total, in direct proportion to changes in the level of activity. (p. 38)

Work in process   Units of product that are only partially complete and will require further work before they are ready for sale to a customer. (p. 29)

Appendix 1A | Cost of Quality

A company may have a product that has a high quality design and that uses high quality components, but if the product is defective the company will have high warranty costs and dissatisfied customers. People who are dissatisfied with a product won't buy it again. They are also likely to tell others about their bad experiences. One study found that "[c]ustomers who have bad experiences tell approximately 11 people about it."[1] This is the worst possible sort of advertising. To prevent such problems, companies have been expending a great deal of effort to reduce defects. The objective is to have high *quality of conformance*.

Learning Objective 8
Identify the four types of quality costs and explain how they interact.

Quality of Conformance

A product that meets or exceeds its design specifications and is free of defects is said to have high **quality of conformance.** Note that if an economy car is free of defects, it can have a quality of conformance that is just as high as a defect-free luxury car. The purchasers of economy cars cannot expect their cars to be as opulently equipped as luxury cars, but they can and do expect them to be free of defects.

Preventing, detecting, and correcting defects cause costs that are called *quality costs* or the *cost of quality*. The use of the term *quality cost* is confusing to some people. It does not refer to costs such as using a higher-grade leather to make a wallet or using 14K gold instead of gold-plating in jewelry. Instead, the term **quality cost** refers to all of the costs that are incurred to prevent defects or that result from the occurrence of defects.

Quality costs can be broken down into four broad groups. Two of these groups—known as *prevention costs* and *appraisal costs*—are incurred to keep defective products from falling into the hands of customers. The other two groups of costs—known as *internal failure costs* and *external failure costs*—are incurred because defects happen despite efforts to prevent them.

Prevention Costs Generally, the most effective way to manage quality costs is to avoid having defects in the first place. It is much less costly to prevent a problem from ever happening than it is to find and correct the problem after it has occurred. **Prevention costs** support activities whose purpose is to reduce the number of defects. Companies employ many techniques to prevent defects including statistical process control, quality engineering, training, and a variety of tools from Total Quality Management.

Appraisal Costs Any defective parts and products should be caught as early as possible in the production process. **Appraisal costs,** which are sometimes called *inspection costs*, are incurred to identify defective products *before* the products are shipped to customers. Unfortunately, performing appraisal activities doesn't keep defects from happening again, and most managers now realize that maintaining an army of inspectors is a costly (and ineffective) approach to quality control.

---

[1]Christopher W. L. Hart, James L. Heskett, and W. Earl Sasser, Jr., "The Profitable Art of Service Recovery," *Harvard Business Review,* July–August 1990, p. 153.

Professor John K. Shank of Dartmouth College has aptly stated, "The old-style approach was to say, 'We've got great quality. We have 40 quality control inspectors in the factory.' Then somebody realized that if you need 40 inspectors, it must be a lousy factory. So now the trick is to run a factory without any quality control inspectors; each employee is his or her own quality control person."[2]

Increasingly, companies are asking employees to be responsible for their own quality control. Taking this approach, along with designing products easy to manufacture properly, allows manufacturers to build quality into products rather than rely on inspection to get the defects out.

Internal Failure Costs   Failure costs are incurred when a product fails to conform to its design specifications. Failure costs can be either internal or external. **Internal failure costs** result from identification of defects before they are shipped to customers. These costs include scrap, rejected products, reworking of defective units, and downtime caused by quality problems. In some companies, as little as 10% of the company's products make it through the production process without rework of some kind. Of course, the more effective a company's appraisal activities, the greater the chance of catching defects internally and the greater the level of internal failure costs (as compared to external failure costs).

External Failure Costs   **External failure costs** result when a defective product is delivered to a customer. These costs include warranty repairs and replacements, product recalls, legal liability, and lost sales arising from a reputation for poor quality. Such costs can devastate profits.

In the past, some managers have taken the attitude, "Let's go ahead and ship everything to customers, and we'll take care of any problems under the warranty." This attitude generally results in high external failure costs, customer ill will, and declining market share and profits.

Distribution of Quality Costs

Quality costs often exceed 10% of total sales, whereas experts say that these costs should be more in the 2% to 4% range. How does a company reduce its total quality cost? The answer lies in how the quality costs are distributed.

[2]Robert W. Casey, "The Changing World of the CEO," *PPM World* 24, no. 2 (1990), p. 31.

When the defect rate is high, total quality cost is high and most of this cost consists of costs of internal and external failure. However, as a company spends more and more on prevention and appraisal, the percentage of defective units drops. This results in lower costs of internal and external failure. Ordinarily, total quality cost drops rapidly as the defect rate improves. Thus, a company can reduce its total quality cost by focusing its efforts on prevention and appraisal. The cost savings from reduced defects usually swamp the costs of the additional prevention and appraisal efforts. As a company's quality program becomes more refined and as its failure costs begin to fall, prevention activities usually become more effective than appraisal activities. Appraisal can only find defects, whereas prevention can eliminate them.

Quality Cost Report

As an aid to management, prevention and appraisal costs and the costs of internal and external failure can be summarized on a **quality cost report.** This report shows the type of quality costs being incurred and their significance and trends. The report helps managers understand the importance of quality costs, spot problem areas, and assess the way in which the quality costs are distributed. For further details, see Appendix B in Ray Garrison and Eric Noreen, *Managerial Accounting*, ninth edition, Irwin/McGraw-Hill, 2000.

Summary of Appendix 1A

LO8 (Appendix 1A) Identify the four types of quality costs and explain how they interact.
Defects cause costs, which can be classified into prevention costs, appraisal costs, internal failure costs, and external failure costs. Prevention costs are incurred to keep defects from happening. Appraisal costs are incurred to ensure that defective products are not shipped to customers. Internal failure costs result from detecting defective products before they are shipped to customers. External failure costs result from delivering defective products to customers; they include the cost of repairs, servicing, and lost future business. Most experts agree that management effort should be focused on preventing defects. Small investments in prevention can lead to dramatic reductions in appraisal costs and costs of internal and external failure.

Glossary for Appendix 1A

Appraisal costs Costs that are incurred to identify defective products before they are shipped to customers. (p. 49)
External failure costs Costs that are incurred when a defective product is delivered to a customer. (p. 50)
Internal failure costs Costs that are incurred as a result of identifying defective products before they are shipped to customers. (p. 50)
Prevention costs Costs that are incurred to keep defects from happening. (p. 49)
Quality cost Costs that are incurred to prevent defective products from falling into the hands of customers or that are incurred as a result of defective units. (p. 49)
Quality cost report A report that details prevention costs, appraisal costs, and the costs of internal and external failures. (p. 51)
Quality of conformance The degree to which a product or service meets or exceeds its design specifications and is free of defects or other problems that mar its appearance or degrade its performance. (p. 49)

Questions

1–1　What is the basic difference in orientation between financial and managerial accounting?
1–2　What are the three major activities of a manager?
1–3　Describe the four steps in the planning and control cycle.
1–4　Distinguish between line and staff positions in an organization.
1–5　What are the major differences between financial and managerial accounting?

1–6 What are the three major elements of product costs in a manufacturing company?

1–7 Distinguish between the following: (a) direct materials, (b) indirect materials, (c) direct labor, (d) indirect labor, and (e) manufacturing overhead.

1–8 Explain the difference between a product cost and a period cost.

1–9 Describe how the income statement of a manufacturing company differs from the income statement of a merchandising company.

1–10 Of what value is the schedule of cost of goods manufactured? How does it tie into the income statement?

1–11 Describe how the inventory accounts of a manufacturing company differ from the inventory account of a merchandising company.

1–12 Why are product costs sometimes called inventoriable costs? Describe the flow of such costs in a manufacturing company from the point of incurrence until they finally become expenses on the income statement.

1–13 Is it possible for costs such as salaries or depreciation to end up as assets on the balance sheet? Explain.

1–14 What is meant by the term *cost behavior*?

1–15 "A variable cost is a cost that varies per unit of product, whereas a fixed cost is constant per unit of product." Do you agree? Explain.

1–16 How do fixed costs create difficulties in costing units of product?

1–17 Why is manufacturing overhead considered an indirect cost of a unit of product?

1–18 Define the following terms: differential cost, opportunity cost, and sunk cost.

1–19 Only variable costs can be differential costs. Do you agree? Explain.

1–20 (Appendix 1A) Costs associated with the quality of conformance can be broken down into four broad groups. What are these four groups and how do they differ?

1–21 (Appendix 1A) In their efforts to reduce the total cost of quality, should companies generally focus on decreasing prevention costs and appraisal costs?

1–22 (Appendix 1A) What is probably the most effective way to reduce a company's total quality costs?

Brief Exercises

BRIEF EXERCISE 1–1   Classifying Manufacturing Costs (LO1)
The PC Works assembles custom computers from components supplied by various manufacturers. The company is very small and its assembly shop and retail sales store are housed in a single facility in a Redmond, Washington, industrial park. Listed below are some of the costs that are incurred at the company.

Required:
For each cost, indicate whether it would most likely be classified as direct labor, direct materials, manufacturing overhead, marketing and selling, or an administrative cost.
1. The cost of a hard drive installed in a computer.
2. The cost of advertising in the *Puget Sound Computer User* newspaper.
3. The wages of employees who assemble computers from components.
4. Sales commissions paid to the company's salespeople.
5. The wages of the assembly shop's supervisor.
6. The wages of the company's accountant.
7. Depreciation on equipment used to test assembled computers before release to customers.
8. Rent on the facility in the industrial park.

BRIEF EXERCISE 1–2   Identifying Product and Period Costs (LO2)
A product cost is also known as an inventoriable cost. Classify the following costs as either product (inventoriable) costs or period (noninventoriable) costs in a manufacturing company:
1. Depreciation on salespersons' cars.
2. Rent on equipment used in the factory.
3. Lubricants used for maintenance of machines.
4. Salaries of finished goods warehouse personnel.
5. Soap and paper towels used by factory workers at the end of a shift.
6. Factory supervisors' salaries.
7. Heat, water, and power consumed in the factory.
8. Materials used in boxing units of finished product for shipment overseas. (Units are not normally boxed.)
9. Advertising outlays.
10. Workers' compensation insurance on factory employees.

11. Depreciation on chairs and tables in the factory lunchroom.
12. The salary of the switchboard operator for the company.
13. Depreciation on a Lear Jet used by the company's executives.
14. Rent on rooms at a Florida resort for the annual sales conference.
15. Attractively designed box for packaging breakfast cereal.

BRIEF EXERCISE 1–3   Constructing an Income Statement (LO3)

Last month CyberGames, a computer game retailer, had total sales of $1,450,000, selling expenses of $210,000, and administrative expenses of $180,000. The company had beginning merchandise inventory of $240,000, purchased additional merchandise inventory for $950,000, and had ending merchandise inventory of $170,000.

Required:
Prepare an income statement for the company for the month in good form.

BRIEF EXERCISE 1–4   Prepare a Schedule of Cost of Goods Manufactured (LO4)

Lompac Products manufactures a variety of products in its factory. Data for the most recent month's operations appear below:

Beginning raw materials inventory	$ 60,000
Purchases of raw materials	690,000
Ending raw materials inventory	45,000
Direct labor	135,000
Manufacturing overhead	370,000
Beginning work in process inventory	120,000
Ending work in process inventory	130,000

Required:
Prepare in good form a schedule of cost of goods manufactured for the company for the month.

BRIEF EXERCISE 1–5   Identifying Variable and Fixed Costs (LO5)

Below are a number of costs that are incurred in a variety of organizations.

Required:
Classify each cost as being variable or fixed with respect to the number of units of product or services sold by the organization.

	Cost Behavior	
Cost Item	**Variable**	**Fixed**

Place an *X* in the appropriate column for each cost to indicate whether the cost involved would be variable or fixed with respect to the number of units of products or services sold by the organization.

1. X-ray film used in the radiology lab at Virginia Mason Hospital in Seattle.
2. The costs of advertising a Madonna rock concert in New York City.
3. Depreciation on the Planet Hollywood restaurant building in Hong Kong.
4. The electrical costs of running a roller coaster at Magic Mountain.
5. Property taxes on your local cinema.
6. Commissions paid to salespersons at Nordstrom.
7. Property insurance on a Coca-Cola bottling plant.
8. The costs of synthetic materials used to make Nike running shoes.
9. The costs of shipping Panasonic televisions to retail stores.
10. The cost of leasing an ultra-scan diagnostic machine at the American Hospital in Paris.

BRIEF EXERCISE 1–6   Identifying Direct and Indirect Costs (LO6)

Northwest Hospital is a full-service hospital that provides everything from major surgery and emergency room care to outpatient clinics.

Required:

For each cost incurred at Northwest Hospital, indicate whether it would most likely be a direct cost or an indirect cost of the specified costing object by placing an *X* in the appropriate column.

	Cost	Costing object	Direct Cost	Indirect Cost
Ex.	Catered food served to patients	A particular patient	X	
1.	The wages of pediatric nurses	The pediatric department		
2.	Prescription drugs	A particular patient		
3.	Heating the hospital	The pediatric department		
4.	The salary of the head of pediatrics	The pediatric department		
5.	The salary of the head of pediatrics	A particular pediatric patient		
6.	Hospital chaplain's salary	A particular patient		
7.	Lab tests by outside contractor	A particular patient		
8.	Lab tests by outside contractor	A particular department		

BRIEF EXERCISE 1–7   Differential, Opportunity, and Sunk Costs (LO7)

Northwest Hospital is a full-service hospital that provides everything from major surgery and emergency room care to outpatient clinics. The hospital's Radiology Department is considering replacing an old inefficient X-ray machine with a state-of-the-art digital X-ray machine. The new machine would provide higher quality X-rays in less time and at a lower cost per X-ray. The new machine would require less power consumption and would use a color laser printer to produce easily readable X-ray images. Instead of investing the funds in the new X-ray machine, the Laboratory Department is lobbying the hospital's management to buy a new DNA analyzer.

Required:

For each of the items below, indicate by placing an *X* in the appropriate column whether it should be considered a differential cost, an opportunity cost, or a sunk cost in the decision to replace the old X-ray machine with a new machine. If none of the categories applies for a particular item, leave all columns blank.

	Item	Differential Cost	Opportunity Cost	Sunk Cost
Ex.	Cost of X-ray film used in the old machine	X		
1.	Cost of the old X-ray machine			
2.	The salary of the head of the Radiology Department			
3.	The salary of the head of the Pediatrics Department			
4.	Cost of the new color laser printer			
5.	Rent on the space occupied by Radiology			
6.	The cost of maintaining the old machine			
7.	Benefits from a new DNA analyzer			
8.	Cost of electricity to run the X-ray machines			

BRIEF EXERCISE 1–8   Categorization of Quality Costs (LO8)

Listed below are a number of terms relating to quality management:

Appraisal costs	Prevention costs
Quality cost report	External failure costs
Quality of conformance	Quality costs
Internal failure costs	

Required:
Choose the term or terms that most appropriately complete the following statements. The terms can be used more than once. (A fill-in blank can hold more than one word.)
1. A product that has a high rate of defects is said to have a low _____ .
2. All of the costs associated with preventing and dealing with defects once they occur are known as _____ .
3. A company incurs _____ and _____ in an effort to keep defects from occurring.
4. A company incurs _____ and _____ because defects have occurred.
5. Of the four groups of costs associated with quality of conformance, _____ are generally the most damaging to a company.
6. Inspection, testing, and other costs incurred to keep defective products from being shipped to customers are known as _____ .
7. The costs relating to defects, rejected products, and downtime caused by quality problems are known as _____ .
8. When a product that is defective in some way is delivered to a customer, _____ are incurred.
9. Over time a company's total quality costs should decrease if it redistributes its quality costs by placing its greatest emphasis on _____ and _____ .
10. One way to ensure that management is aware of the costs associated with quality is to summarize such costs on a _____ .

Exercises

EXERCISE 1–1   Cost Identification (LO1, LO2, LO5, LO7)
Wollogong Group Ltd. of New South Wales, Australia, acquired its factory building about 10 years ago. For several years the company has rented out a small annex attached to the rear of the building. The company has received a rental income of $30,000 per year on this space. The renter's lease will expire soon, and rather than renew the lease, the company has decided to use the space itself to manufacture a new product.

Direct materials cost for the new product will total $80 per unit. To have a place to store finished units of product, the company will rent a small warehouse nearby. The rental cost will be $500 per month. In addition, the company must rent equipment for use in producing the new product; the rental cost will be $4,000 per month. Workers will be hired to manufacture the new product, with direct labor cost amounting to $60 per unit. The space in the annex will continue to be depreciated on a straight-line basis, as in prior years. This depreciation is $8,000 per year.

Advertising costs for the new product will total $50,000 per year. A supervisor will be hired to oversee production; her salary will be $1,500 per month. Electricity for operating machines will be $1.20 per unit. Costs of shipping the new product to customers will be $9 per unit.

To provide funds to purchase materials, meet payrolls, and so forth, the company will have to liquidate some temporary investments. These investments are presently yielding a return of about $3,000 per year.

Required:
Prepare an answer sheet with the following column headings:

Name of the Cost	Variable Cost	Fixed Cost	Product Cost			Period (selling and administrative) Cost	Opportunity Cost	Sunk Cost
			Direct Materials	Direct Labor	Manufacturing Overhead			

List the different costs associated with the new product decision down the extreme left column (under Name of the Cost). Then place an X under each heading that helps to describe the type of cost involved. There may be X's under several column headings for a single cost. (For example, a cost may be a fixed cost, a period cost, and a sunk cost; you would place an X under each of these column headings opposite the cost.)

EXERCISE 1–2   Definitions of Cost Terms (LO2, LO5, LO7)
Following are a number of cost terms introduced in the chapter:

Variable cost	Product cost
Fixed cost	Sunk cost
Prime cost	Conversion cost
Opportunity cost	Period cost

Choose the term or terms above that most appropriately describe the cost identified in each of the following situations. A cost term can be used more than once.

1. Lake Company produces a tote bag that is very popular with college students. The cloth going into the manufacture of the tote bag would be called direct materials and classified as a _____ cost. In terms of cost behavior, the cloth could also be described as a _____ cost.
2. The direct labor cost required to produce the tote bags, combined with the manufacturing overhead cost involved, would be known as _____ cost.
3. The company could have taken the funds that it has invested in production equipment and invested them in interest-bearing securities instead. The interest forgone on the securities would be called _____ cost.
4. Taken together, the direct materials cost and the direct labor cost required to produce tote bags would be called _____ cost.
5. The company used to produce a smaller tote bag that was not very popular. Some three hundred of these smaller bags are stored in one of the company's warehouses. The amount invested in these bags would be called a _____ cost.
6. The tote bags are sold through agents who are paid a commission on each bag sold. These commissions would be classified by Lake Company as a _____ cost. In terms of cost behavior, commissions would be classified as a _____ cost.
7. Depreciation on the equipment used to produce tote bags would be classified by Lake Company as a _____ cost. However, depreciation on any equipment used by the company in selling and administrative activities would be classified as a _____ cost. In terms of cost behavior, depreciation would probably be classified as a _____ cost.
8. A _____ cost is also known as an inventoriable cost, since such costs go into the Work in Process inventory account and then into the Finished Goods inventory account before appearing on the income statement as part of cost of goods sold.
9. The salary of Lake Company's president would be classified as a _____ cost, since the salary will appear on the income statement as an expense in the time period in which it is incurred.
10. Costs can often be classified in several ways. For example, Lake Company pays $5,000 rent each month on its factory building. The rent would be part of manufacturing overhead. In terms of cost behavior, it would be classified as a _____ cost. The rent can also be classified as a _____ cost and as part of _____ cost.

EXERCISE 1–3 Cost Flows (LO3)

The Devon Motor Company produces automobiles. During April, the company purchased 8,000 batteries at a cost of $10 per battery. Devon withdrew 7,600 batteries from the storeroom during the month. Of these, 100 were used to replace batteries in autos being used by the company's traveling sales staff. The remaining 7,500 batteries withdrawn from the storeroom were placed in autos being produced by the company. Of the autos in production during April, 90% were completed and transferred from work in process to finished goods. Of the cars completed during the month, 30% were unsold at April 30.

There were no inventories of any type on April 1.

Required:
1. Determine the cost of batteries that would appear in each of the following accounts at April 30:
    a. Raw Materials.
    b. Work in Process.
    c. Finished Goods.
    d. Cost of Goods Sold.
    e. Selling Expense.
2. Specify whether each of the above accounts would appear on the balance sheet or on the income statement at April 30.

EXERCISE 1–4 Classification of Variable, Fixed, Period, and Product Costs (LO2, LO5)

Below are listed various costs that are found in organizations.
1. Hamburger buns in a McDonald's outlet.
2. Advertising by a dental office.
3. Apples processed and canned by Del Monte Corporation.
4. Shipping canned apples from a Del Monte plant to customers.
5. Insurance on a Bausch & Lomb factory producing contact lenses.
6. Insurance on IBM's corporate headquarters.
7. Salary of a supervisor overseeing production of circuit boards at Hewlett-Packard.
8. Commissions paid to Encyclopedia Britannica salespersons.
9. Depreciation of factory lunchroom facilities at a General Electric plant.
10. Steering wheels installed in BMWs.

Required:

Classify each cost as being either variable or fixed with respect to the number of units sold. Also classify each cost as either a selling and administrative cost or a product cost. Prepare your answer sheet as shown below.

Cost Item	Cost Behavior		Selling and Administrative Cost	Product Cost
	Variable	**Fixed**		

Place an *X* in the appropriate columns to show the proper classification of each cost.

EXERCISE 1–5   Determining Cost of Goods Sold (LO3, LO4)

The following cost and inventory data are taken from the accounting records of Mason Company for the year just completed:

Costs incurred:

Direct labor cost	$ 70,000
Purchases of raw materials	118,000
Indirect labor	30,000
Maintenance, factory equipment	6,000
Advertising expense	90,000
Insurance, factory equipment	800
Sales salaries	50,000
Rent, factory facilities	20,000
Supplies	4,200
Depreciation, office equipment	3,000
Depreciation, factory equipment	19,000

	Beginning of the Year	End of the Year
Inventories:		
Raw materials	$ 7,000	$15,000
Work in process	10,000	5,000
Finished goods	20,000	35,000

Required:

1. Prepare a schedule of cost of goods manufactured in good form.
2. Prepare the cost of goods sold section of Mason Company's income statement for the year.

EXERCISE 1–6   Classification of Variable, Fixed, Direct, and Indirect Costs (LO5, LO6)

Various costs associated with the operation of a factory are given below:

1. Electricity used in operating machines.
2. Rent on a factory building.
3. Cloth used in drapery production.
4. Production superintendent's salary.
5. Wages of laborers assembling a product.
6. Depreciation of air purification equipment used in furniture production.
7. Janitorial salaries.
8. Peaches used in canning fruit.
9. Lubricants needed for machines.
10. Sugar used in soft-drink production.
11. Property taxes on the factory.
12. Wages of workers painting a product.
13. Depreciation on cafeteria equipment.
14. Insurance on a building used in producing TV sets.
15. Picture tubes used in TV sets.

Required:

Classify each cost as being either variable or fixed with respect to the number of units produced and sold. Also indicate whether each cost would typically be treated as a direct cost or an indirect cost with respect to units of product. Prepare your answer sheet as shown below:

Cost Item	Cost Behavior		To Units of Product	
	Variable	**Fixed**	**Direct**	**Indirect**
Example: Factory insurance		X		X

EXERCISE 1–7   Classification of Quality Costs (LO8)

Listed below are a number of costs that are incurred in connection with a company's quality control system.

a. Product testing.
b. Product recalls.
c. Rework labor and overhead.
d. Downtime caused by defects.
e. Cost of field servicing.
f. Inspection of finished goods.
g. Warranty repairs.
h. Statistical process control.
i. Net cost of scrap.
j. Depreciation of test equipment.
k. Returns and allowances arising from poor quality.
l. Disposal of defective products.
m. Warranty replacements.

Required:

1. Classify each of the costs above into one of the following categories: prevention cost, appraisal cost, internal failure cost, or external failure cost.
2. Which of the costs in (1) above are incurred in an effort to keep poor quality of conformance from occurring? Which of the costs in (1) above are incurred because poor quality of conformance has occurred?

Problems

CHECK FIGURE
Clay and glaze: variable, direct materials

PROBLEM 1–1   Cost Identification (LO1, LO2, LO5, LO7)

Staci Valek began dabbling in pottery several years ago as a hobby. Her work is quite creative, and it has been so popular with friends and others that she has decided to quit her job with an aerospace firm and manufacture pottery full time. The salary from Staci's aerospace job is $2,500 per month.

Staci will rent a small building near her home to use as a place for manufacturing the pottery. The rent will be $500 per month. She estimates that the cost of clay and glaze will be $2 for each finished piece of pottery. She will hire workers to produce the pottery at a labor rate of $8 per pot. To sell her pots, Staci feels that she must advertise heavily in the local area. An advertising agency states that it will handle all advertising for a fee of $600 per month. Staci's brother will sell the pots; he will be paid a commission of $4 for each pot sold. Equipment needed to manufacture the pots will be rented at a cost of $300 per month.

Staci has already paid the legal and filing fees associated with incorporating her business in the state. These fees amounted to $500. A small room has been located in a tourist area that Staci will use as a sales office. The rent will be $250 per month. A phone installed in the room for taking orders will cost $40 per month. In addition, a recording device will be attached to the phone for taking after-hours messages.

Staci has some money in savings that is earning interest of $1,200 per year. These savings will be withdrawn and used to get the business going. For the time being, Staci does not intend to draw any salary from the new company.

Required:

1. Prepare an answer sheet with the following column headings:

Name of the Cost	Variable Cost	Fixed Cost	Product Cost			Period (selling and administrative) Cost	Opportunity Cost	Sunk Cost
			Direct Materials	**Direct Labor**	**Manufacturing Overhead**			

List the different costs associated with the new company down the extreme left column (under Name of the Cost). Then place an X under each heading that helps to describe the type of cost involved.

There may be X's under several column headings for a single cost. (That is, a cost may be a fixed cost, a period cost, and a sunk cost; you would place an X under each of these column headings opposite the cost.)

Under the Variable Cost column, list only those costs that would be variable with respect to the number of units of pottery that are produced and sold.

2. All of the costs you have listed above, except one, would be differential costs between the alternatives of Staci producing pottery or staying with the aerospace firm. Which cost is *not* differential? Explain.

PROBLEM 1–2 Classification of Salary Cost (LO2)

You have just been hired by Ogden Company to fill a new position that was created in response to rapid growth in sales. It is your responsibility to coordinate shipments of finished goods from the factory to distribution warehouses located in various parts of the United States so that goods will be available as orders are received from customers.

The company is unsure how to classify your annual salary in its cost records. The company's cost analyst says that your salary should be classified as a manufacturing (product) cost; the controller says that it should be classified as a selling expense; and the president says that it doesn't matter which way your salary cost is classified.

Required:
1. Which viewpoint is correct? Why?
2. From the point of view of the reported net income for the year, is the president correct in his statement that it doesn't matter which way your salary cost is classified? Explain.

PROBLEM 1–3 Cost Classification (LO2, LO5, LO6)

Listed below are a number of costs typically found in organizations.

CHECK FIGURE
Boxes for packaging:
variable, direct

1. Property taxes, factory.
2. Boxes used for packaging detergent.
3. Salespersons' commissions.
4. Supervisor's salary, factory.
5. Depreciation, executive automobiles.
6. Wages of workers assembling computers.
7. Packing supplies for out-of-state shipments.
8. Insurance, finished goods warehouses.
9. Lubricants for machines.
10. Advertising costs.
11. "Chips" used in producing calculators.
12. Shipping costs on merchandise sold.
13. Magazine subscriptions, factory lunchroom.
14. Thread in a garment factory.
15. Billing costs.
16. Executive life insurance.
17. Ink used in textbook production.
18. Fringe benefits, assembly-line workers.
19. Yarn used in sweater production.
20. Wages of receptionist, executive offices.

Required:
Prepare an answer sheet with column headings as shown below. For each cost item, indicate whether it would be variable or fixed with respect to the number of units produced and sold; and then whether it would be a selling cost, an administrative cost, or a manufacturing cost. If it is a manufacturing cost, indicate whether it would typically be treated as a direct cost or an indirect cost with respect to units of product. Three sample answers are provided for illustration.

Cost Item	Variable or Fixed	Selling Cost	Administrative Cost	Manufacturing (product) Cost	
				Direct	Indirect
Direct labor	V			X	
Executive salaries	F		X		
Factory rent	F				X

PROBLEM 1–4 Cost Identification and Cost Concepts (LO2, LO5, LO6)

The Dorilane Company specializes in producing a set of wood patio furniture consisting of a table and four chairs. The set enjoys great popularity, and the company has ample orders to keep production going at its full capacity of 2,000 sets per year. Annual cost data at full capacity follow:

Factory labor, direct	$118,000
Advertising	50,000
Factory supervision	40,000
Property taxes, factory building	3,500
Sales commissions	80,000
Insurance, factory	2,500
Depreciation, office equipment	4,000
Lease cost, factory equipment	12,000
Indirect materials, factory	6,000
Depreciation, factory building	10,000
General office supplies (billing)	3,000
General office salaries	60,000
Direct materials used (wood, bolts, etc.)	94,000
Utilities, factory	20,000

Required:

1. Prepare an answer sheet with the column headings shown below. Enter each cost item on your answer sheet, placing the dollar amount under the appropriate headings. As examples, this has been done already for the first two items in the list above. Note that each cost item is classified in two ways: first, as variable or fixed, with respect to the number of units produced and sold; and second, as a selling and administrative cost or a product cost. (If the item is a product cost, it should also be classified as being either direct or indirect as shown.)

	Cost Behavior		Selling or Administrative Cost	Product Cost	
Cost Item	Variable	Fixed		Direct	Indirect*
Factory labor, direct	$118,000			$118,000	
Advertising		$50,000	$50,000		

*To units of product.

2. Total the dollar amounts in each of the columns in (1) above. Compute the average product cost per patio set.

3. Assume that production drops to only 1,000 sets annually. Would you expect the average product cost per patio set to increase, decrease, or remain unchanged? Explain. No computations are necessary.

4. Refer to the original data. The president's brother-in-law has considered making himself a patio set and has priced the necessary materials at a building supply store. The brother-in-law has asked the president if he could purchase a patio set from the Dorilane Company "at cost," and the president agreed to let him do so.

   a. Would you expect any disagreement between the two men over the price the brother-in-law should pay? Explain. What price does the president probably have in mind? The brother-in-law?

   b. Since the company is operating at full capacity, what cost term used in the chapter might be justification for the president to charge the full, regular price to the brother-in-law and still be selling "at cost"?

PROBLEM 1–5   Supplying Missing Data (LO3, LO4)

Supply the missing data in the following cases. Each case is independent of the others.

CHECK FIGURE
Case 1: Goods available for
sale = $19,000

	Case			
	1	2	3	4
Direct materials	$ 4,500	$ 6,000	$ 5,000	$ 3,000
Direct labor	?	3,000	7,000	4,000
Manufacturing overhead	5,000	4,000	?	9,000
Total manufacturing costs	18,500	?	20,000	?
Beginning work in process inventory	2,500	?	3,000	?
Ending work in process inventory ...	?	1,000	4,000	3,000
Cost of goods manufactured	18,000	14,000	?	?
Sales	30,000	21,000	36,000	40,000
Beginning finished goods inventory	1,000	2,500	?	2,000
Cost of goods manufactured	?	?	?	17,500
Goods available for sale	?	?	?	?
Ending finished goods inventory	?	1,500	4,000	3,500
Cost of goods sold	17,000	?	18,500	?
Gross margin	13,000	?	17,500	?
Operating expenses	?	3,500	?	?
Net income	$ 4,000	?	$ 5,000	$ 9,000

PROBLEM 1–6   Preparing Financial Statements for a Manufacturer (LO3, LO4)

Swift Company was organized on March 1 of the current year. After five months of start-up losses, management had expected to earn a profit during August, the most recent month. Management was disappointed, however, when the income statement for August also showed a loss. August's income statement follows:

CHECK FIGURE
(1) COGM: $310,000

SWIFT COMPANY
Income Statement
For the Month Ended August 31

Sales		$450,000
Less operating expenses:		
Indirect labor cost	$ 12,000	
Utilities	15,000	
Direct labor cost	70,000	
Depreciation, factory equipment	21,000	
Raw materials purchased	165,000	
Depreciation, sales equipment	18,000	
Insurance	4,000	
Rent on facilities	50,000	
Selling and administrative salaries	32,000	
Advertising	75,000	462,000
Net loss		$(12,000)

After seeing the $12,000 loss for August, Swift's president stated, "I was sure we'd be profitable within six months, but our six months are up and this loss for August is even worse than July's. I think it's time to start looking for someone to buy out the company's assets—if we don't, within a few months there won't be any assets to sell. By the way, I don't see any reason to look for a new controller. We'll just limp along with Sam for the time being."

The company's controller resigned a month ago. Sam, a new assistant in the controller's office, prepared the income statement above. Sam has had little experience in manufacturing operations. Additional information about the company follows:

a. Some 60% of the utilities cost and 75% of the insurance apply to factory operations. The remaining amounts apply to selling and administrative activities.

b. Inventory balances at the beginning and end of August were:

	August 1	August 31
Raw materials	$ 8,000	$13,000
Work in process	16,000	21,000
Finished goods	40,000	60,000

c. Only 80% of the rent on facilities applies to factory operations; the remainder applies to selling and administrative activities.

The president has asked you to check over the income statement and make a recommendation as to whether the company should look for a buyer for its assets.

Required:
1. As one step in gathering data for a recommendation to the president, prepare a schedule of cost of goods manufactured in good form for August.
2. As a second step, prepare a new income statement for August.
3. Based on your statements prepared in (1) and (2) above, would you recommend that the company look for a buyer?

PROBLEM 1–7   Financial Statements; Cost Behavior (LO3, LO4, LO5)
Various cost and sales data for Meriwell Company for the just completed year follow:

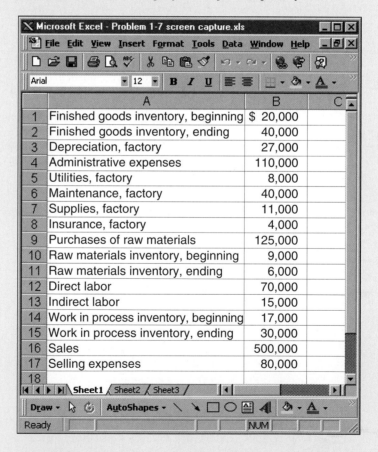

	A	B
1	Finished goods inventory, beginning	$ 20,000
2	Finished goods inventory, ending	40,000
3	Depreciation, factory	27,000
4	Administrative expenses	110,000
5	Utilities, factory	8,000
6	Maintenance, factory	40,000
7	Supplies, factory	11,000
8	Insurance, factory	4,000
9	Purchases of raw materials	125,000
10	Raw materials inventory, beginning	9,000
11	Raw materials inventory, ending	6,000
12	Direct labor	70,000
13	Indirect labor	15,000
14	Work in process inventory, beginning	17,000
15	Work in process inventory, ending	30,000
16	Sales	500,000
17	Selling expenses	80,000
18		

Required:
1. Prepare a schedule of cost of goods manufactured.
2. Prepare an income statement.

3. Assume that the company produced the equivalent of 10,000 units of product during the year just completed. What was the average cost per unit for direct materials? What was the average cost per unit for factory depreciation?

4. Assume that the company expects to produce 15,000 units of product during the coming year. What average cost per unit and what total cost would you expect the company to incur for direct materials at this level of activity? For factory depreciation? (In preparing your answer, assume that direct materials is a variable cost and that depreciation is a fixed cost; also assume that depreciation is computed on a straight-line basis.)

5. As the manager responsible for production costs, explain to the president any difference in the average cost per unit between (3) and (4) above.

PROBLEM 1–8   Financial Statements; Cost Behavior (LO3, LO4, LO5)

Selected account balances for the year ended December 31 are provided below for Superior Company:

CHECK FIGURE
(1) COGM: $690,000

Selling and administrative salaries	$110,000
Insurance, factory	8,000
Utilities, factory	45,000
Purchases of raw materials	290,000
Indirect labor	60,000
Direct labor	?
Advertising expense	80,000
Cleaning supplies, factory	7,000
Sales commissions	50,000
Rent, factory building	120,000
Maintenance, factory	30,000

Inventory balances at the beginning and end of the year were as follows:

	Beginning of the Year	End of the Year
Raw materials	$40,000	$10,000
Work in process	?	35,000
Finished goods	50,000	?

The total manufacturing costs for the year were $683,000; the goods available for sale totaled $740,000; and the cost of goods sold totaled $660,000.

Required:

1. Prepare a schedule of cost of goods manufactured in good form and the cost of goods sold section of the company's income statement for the year.

2. Assume that the dollar amounts given above are for the equivalent of 40,000 units produced during the year. Compute the average cost per unit for direct materials used and the average cost per unit for rent on the factory building.

3. Assume that in the following year the company expects to produce 50,000 units. What average cost per unit and total cost would you expect to be incurred for direct materials? For rent on the factory building? (In preparing your answer, you may assume that direct materials is a variable cost and that rent is a fixed cost.)

4. As the manager in charge of production costs, explain to the president the reason for any difference in average cost per unit between (2) and (3) above.

Building Your Skills

CHECK FIGURE
(1) COGM: $870,000

S

ANALYTICAL THINKING   (LO3, LO4)

Visic Company, a manufacturing firm, produces a single product. The following information has been taken from the company's production, sales, and cost records for the just completed year.

Production in units	29,000
Sales in units	?
Ending finished goods inventory in units	?
Sales in dollars	$1,300,000
Costs:	
Advertising	105,000
Entertainment and travel	40,000
Direct labor	90,000
Indirect labor	85,000
Raw materials purchased	480,000
Building rent (production uses 80% of the space; administrative and sales offices use the rest)	40,000
Utilities, factory	108,000
Royalty paid for use of production patent, $1.50 per unit produced	?
Maintenance, factory	9,000
Rent for special production equipment, $7,000 per year plus $0.30 per unit produced	?
Selling and administrative salaries	210,000
Other factory overhead costs	6,800
Other selling and administrative expenses	17,000

	Beginning of the Year	End of the Year
Inventories:		
Raw materials	$20,000	$30,000
Work in process	50,000	40,000
Finished goods	–0–	?

The finished goods inventory is being carried at the average unit production cost for the year. The selling price of the product is $50 per unit.

Required:
1. Prepare a schedule of goods manufactured for the year.
2. Compute the following:
   a. The number of units in the finished goods inventory at the end of the year.
   b. The cost of the units in the finished goods inventory at the end of the year.
3. Prepare an income statement for the year.

COMMUNICATING IN PRACTICE   (LO2, LO3, LO4)

CHECK FIGURE
(2) COGM: $780,000

"I was sure that when our battery hit the market it would be an instant success," said Roger Strong, founder and president of Solar Technology, Inc. "But just look at the gusher of red ink for the first quarter. It's obvious that we're better scientists than we are businesspeople." The data to which Roger was referring follow:

SOLAR TECHNOLOGY, INC.
Income Statement
For the Quarter Ended March 31

Sales (32,000 batteries)		$960,000
Less operating expenses:		
Selling and administrative salaries	$110,000	
Advertising	90,000	
Maintenance, production	43,000	
Indirect labor cost	120,000	
Cleaning supplies, production	7,000	
Purchases of raw materials	360,000	
Rental cost, facilities	75,000	
Insurance, production	8,000	
Depreciation, office equipment	27,000	
Utilities	80,000	
Depreciation, production equipment	100,000	
Direct labor cost	70,000	
Travel, salespersons	40,000	
Total operating expenses		1,130,000
Net loss		$ (170,000)

"At this rate we'll be out of business within a year," said Cindy Zhang, the company's accountant. "But I've double-checked these figures, so I know they're right."

Solar Technology was organized at the beginning of the current year to produce and market a revolutionary new solar battery. The company's accounting system was set up by Margie Wallace, an experienced accountant who recently left the company to do independent consulting work. The statement above was prepared by Zhang, her assistant.

"We may not last a year if the insurance company doesn't pay the $226,000 it owes us for the 8,000 batteries lost in the warehouse fire last week," said Roger. "The insurance adjuster says our claim is inflated, but he's just trying to pressure us into a lower figure. We have the data to back up our claim, and it will stand up in any court."

On April 3, just after the end of the first quarter, the company's finished goods storage area was swept by fire and all 8,000 unsold batteries were destroyed. (These batteries were part of the 40,000 units completed during the first quarter.) The company's insurance policy states that the company will be reimbursed for the "cost" of any finished batteries destroyed or stolen. Zhang has determined this cost as follows:

$$\frac{\text{Total costs for the quarter, \$1,130,000}}{\text{Batteries produced during the quarter, 40,000}} = \$28.25 \text{ per battery}$$

$$8,000 \text{ batteries} \times \$28.25 \text{ per battery} = \$226,000$$

The following additional information is available on the company's activities during the quarter ended March 31:

a. Inventories at the beginning and end of the quarter were as follows:

	Beginning of the Quarter	End of the Quarter
Raw materials	–0–	$10,000
Work in process	–0–	50,000
Finished goods	–0–	?

b. Eighty percent of the rental cost for facilities and 90% of the utilities cost relate to manufacturing operations. The remaining amounts relate to selling and administrative activities.

Required:
1. Write a brief memorandum to the president that identifies what conceptual errors, if any, were made in preparing the income statement above.
2. Prepare a schedule of cost of goods manufactured for the first quarter.
3. Prepare a corrected income statement for the first quarter. Your statement should show in detail how the cost of goods sold is computed.
4. Do you agree that the insurance company owes Solar Technology, Inc., $226,000? Explain your answer in another brief memorandum to the president.

ETHICS CHALLENGE   (LO2)
M. K. Gallant is president of Kranbrack Corporation, a company whose stock is traded on a national exchange. In a meeting with investment analysts at the beginning of the year, Gallant had predicted that the company's earnings would grow by 20% this year. Unfortunately, sales have been less than expected for the year, and Gallant concluded within two weeks of the end of the fiscal year that it would be impossible to ultimately report an increase in earnings as large as predicted unless some drastic action was taken. Accordingly, Gallant has ordered that wherever possible, expenditures should be postponed to the new year—including canceling or postponing orders with suppliers, delaying planned maintenance and training, and cutting back on end-of-year advertising and travel. Additionally, Gallant ordered the company's controller to carefully scrutinize all costs that are currently classified as period costs and reclassify as many as possible as product costs. The company is expected to have substantial inventories of work in process and finished goods at the end of the year.

Required:
1. Why would reclassifying period costs as product costs increase this period's reported earnings?
2. Do you believe Gallant's actions are ethical? Why or why not?

TAKING IT TO THE NET
As you know, the World Wide Web is a medium that is constantly evolving. Sites come and go and change without notice. To enable periodic update of site addresses, this problem has been posted to the textbook website (www.mhhe.com/folk1e). After accessing the site, enter the Student Center and select this chapter. Select and complete the Taking It to the Net problem.

TEAMWORK IN ACTION   (LO5)
Steel production involves a large amount of fixed costs. Since competition is defined primarily in terms of price, American steel manufacturers (and many of their manufacturing and service industry counterparts) try to gain a competitive advantage by using economies of scale and investment in technology to increase productivity and drive unit costs lower. Their substantial fixed costs are the result of their size.

Required:
1. The team should discuss and then write up descriptions of the definitions of fixed costs and variable costs.
2. Each member of the team should select one of the following types of businesses and perform the following: (a) give examples of fixed costs and variable costs that would be incurred by that type of business, (b) choose a relevant measure of production or service activity for that type of business, and (c) explain the relationship between the production (or service) output and each of the following: total fixed costs, fixed cost per unit, total variable costs, and variable cost per unit.
   a. Steel company
   b. Hospital
   c. University
   d. Auto manufacturer
   Each team member should present his or her notes to the other teammates, who should confirm or correct the presentation. Then, work together as a team to complete steps 3 through 6 below.

3. Using the examples of fixed and variable costs for steel companies from (a) above, explain the relationship between production output at a steel company and each of the following: total fixed costs, fixed cost per unit, total variable costs, variable cost per unit, total costs, and average unit cost.
4. With an X axis (horizontal axis) of tons produced and a Y axis (vertical axis) of total costs, graph total fixed costs, total variable costs, and total costs against tons produced.
5. With an X axis of tons produced and a Y axis of unit costs, graph fixed cost per unit, variable cost per unit, and total (or average) cost per unit against tons produced.
6. Explain how costs (total and per unit) behave with changes in demand once capacity has been set.

Chapter Two

Systems Design: Job-Order Costing

Chapter Outline

Decision Feature **Managing a Successful Furniture Company**

Bush Industries, Inc., was included on *Forbes'* 1997 and 1996 lists of the 200 Best Small Companies in America. Founded by Paul Bush in 1959 in Little Valley, New York, as a manufacturer of bathroom accessories, the company is now the 8th largest and the fastest-growing furniture manufacturer in the United States. The company's focus shifted to furniture in the mid 1970s when it first produced a pedestal TV table with a wood finish. The company's product line has expanded to include ready-to-assemble home-entertainment, bedroom, home office, and business furniture. Potential customers can view the company's online furniture showroom via a link from its home page at www.bushfurniture.com.

The company went public in the mid-1980s, but Bush and his children still control its voting shares. Now headquartered in Jamestown, New York, the company employs 3,500. Its manufacturing and distribution centers, totaling almost 4 million square feet, are located in New York, North Carolina, Pennsylvania, Florida, California, and Mexico. Bush's furniture is shipped to retailers, mass merchandisers, and dealers throughout the United States and in over 40 countries throughout the world.

The popularity of the company's products can be attributed to price and quality. Noting that sales doubled between 1990 and 1995, the company's vice president of corporate development emphasized the importance of its approach to customer service. Bush's 20 customer service representatives field calls from customers 24 hours a day, 7 days a week. Bush, the company's CEO and chairman, credits the company's ability to manage its unparalleled growth to its employees and their work environment, which is based on teamwork and empowerment.

Bush Industries earned $5.7 million on sales of $441.7 million in 1999 and had $55 million of inventory on hand at the end of the year. Obviously, the accuracy of information relating to the costs of the company's various products is critical to the company's continued success. Product costs impact a wide assortment of management decisions—from pricing and profitability to adding and dropping product lines.

Sources: Bush Industries, Inc., website, June 2000; "Ranking the 200 Best Small Companies in America," *Forbes*, 11/3/97, p. 276; "Ranking the Best Small Companies in America," *Forbes*, 11/4/96, p. 288; Tom Hartley, "Sales Growing Piece-by-Piece at Jamestown Furniture Maker," *Business First of Buffalo – Western New York*, 9/23/96, p. 1; Stephanie Burdo, "Bush Industries: Doin' It Right," *Business First of Buffalo – Western New York*, 12/12/94, p. 12.

2

Learning Objectives

After studying Chapter 2, you should be able to:

LO1 Distinguish between process costing and job-order costing and identify companies that would use each costing method.

LO2 Identify the documents used in a job-order costing system.

LO3 Compute predetermined overhead rates and explain why estimated overhead costs (rather than actual overhead costs) are used in the costing process.

LO4 Prepare journal entries to record costs in a job-order costing system.

LO5 Apply overhead cost to Work in Process using a predetermined overhead rate.

LO6 Prepare T-accounts to show the flow of costs in a job-order costing system and prepare schedules of cost of goods manufactured and cost of goods sold.

LO7 Compute under- or overapplied overhead cost and prepare the journal entry to close the balance in Manufacturing Overhead to the appropriate accounts.

As discussed in the previous chapter, product costing is the process of assigning costs to the products and services provided by a company. An understanding of this costing process is vital to managers, since the way in which a product or service is costed can have a substantial impact on reported net income, as well as on key management decisions.

We should keep in mind that the essential purpose of any managerial costing system should be to provide cost data to help managers plan, control, direct, and make decisions. Nevertheless, external financial reporting and tax reporting requirements often heavily influence how costs are accumulated and summarized on managerial reports. This is true of product costing.

In this chapter, we use an *absorption costing* approach to determine product costs. This was also the method that was used in the previous chapter. In **absorption costing,** *all* manufacturing costs, fixed and variable, are assigned to units of product—units are said to *fully absorb manufacturing costs.* The absorption costing approach is also known as the **full cost** approach. In a later chapter, we look at product costing from a different point of view called *variable costing,* which is often advocated as an alternative to absorption costing.

In one form or another, most countries—including the United States—require absorption costing for both external financial reporting and for tax reporting. In addition, the vast majority of companies throughout the world also use absorption costing for managerial accounting purposes. Since absorption costing is the most common approach to product costing, we discuss it first and then deal with alternatives in subsequent chapters.

Process and Job-Order Costing

> **Learning Objective 1**
>
> Distinguish between process costing and job-order costing and identify companies that would use each costing method.

In computing the cost of a product or a service, managers are faced with a difficult problem. Many costs (such as rent) do not change much from month to month, whereas production may change frequently, with production going up in one month and then down in another. In addition to variations in the level of production, several different products or services may be produced in a given period in the same facility. Under these conditions, how is it possible to accurately determine the cost of a product or service? In practice, assigning costs to products and services involves an averaging of some type across time periods and across products. The way in which this averaging is carried out will depend heavily on the type of production process involved. Two costing systems are commonly used in manufacturing and in many service companies; these two systems are known as *process costing* and *job-order costing.*

Process Costing

A **process costing system** is used in situations where the company produces many units of a single product (such as frozen orange juice concentrate) for long periods at a time. Examples include producing paper at Weyerhaeuser, refining aluminum ingots at Reynolds Aluminum, mixing and bottling beverages at Coca-Cola, and making wieners at Oscar Meyer. All of these industries are characterized by an essentially homogeneous product that flows evenly through the production process on a continuous basis.

The basic approach in process costing is to accumulate costs in a particular operation or department for an entire period (month, quarter, year) and then to divide this total by the number of units produced during the period. The basic formula for process costing is:

$$\frac{\text{Unit cost}}{\text{(per gallon, pound, bottle)}} = \frac{\text{Total manufacturing cost}}{\text{Total units produced (gallons, pounds, bottles)}}$$

Since one unit of product (gallon, pound, bottle) is indistinguishable from any other unit of product, each unit is assigned the same average cost as any other unit produced during the period. This costing technique results in a broad, average unit cost figure that applies to homogeneous units flowing in a continuous stream out of the production process.

Job-Order Costing

A **job-order costing system** is used in situations where many *different* products are produced each period. For example, a Levi Strauss clothing factory would typically make many different types of jeans for both men and women during a month. A particular order might consist of 1,000 stonewashed men's blue denim jeans, style number A312, with a 32-inch waist and a 30-inch inseam. This order of 1,000 jeans is called a *batch* or a *job*. In a job-order costing system, costs are traced and allocated to jobs and then the costs of the job are divided by the number of units in the job to arrive at an average cost per unit.

Other examples of situations where job-order costing would be used include large-scale construction projects managed by Bechtel International, commercial aircraft produced by Boeing, greeting cards designed and printed at Hallmark, and airline meals prepared by LSG Sky Chefs. All of these examples are characterized by diverse outputs. Each Bechtel project is unique and different from every other—the company may be simultaneously constructing a dam in Zaire and a bridge in Indonesia. Likewise, each airline orders a different type of meal from LSG Sky Chefs' catering service.

Job-order costing is also used extensively in service industries. Hospitals, law firms, movie studios, accounting firms, advertising agencies, and repair shops, for example, all use a variation of job-order costing to accumulate costs for accounting and billing purposes. Although the detailed example of job-order costing provided in the following section deals with a manufacturing firm, the same basic concepts and procedures are used by many service organizations.

The record-keeping and cost assignment problems are more complex when a company sells many different products and services than when it has only a single product. Since the products are different, the costs are typically different. Consequently, cost records must be maintained for each distinct product or job. For example, an attorney in a large criminal law practice would ordinarily keep separate records of the costs of advising and defending each of her clients. And the Levi Strauss factory mentioned above would keep separate track of the costs of filling orders for particular styles, sizes, and colors of jeans. Thus, a job-order costing system requires more effort than a process-costing system.

In this chapter, we focus on the design of a job-order costing system. In the following chapter, we focus on process costing and also look more closely at the similarities and differences between the two costing methods.

Popularity of Costing Methods   *in business today*

Job-order costing appears to be the dominant product costing system in the United States. Of the manufacturing firms surveyed throughout the United States, 51.1% used job-order costing, 14.2% used process costing, and 10.6% used operation or hybrid costing. The other companies surveyed responded that they used standard costing (discussed in Chapter 8).

Source: Eun-Sup Shim and Joseph M. Larkin, "A Survey of Current Managerial Accounting Practices: Where Do We Stand?" Reprinted with permission from The Ohio Society of CPAs, *Ohio CPA Journal*, February 1994, p. 21 (4 pages).

Job-Order Costing—An Overview

To introduce job-order costing, we will follow a specific job as it progresses through the manufacturing process. This job consists of two experimental couplings that Yost Precision Machining has agreed to produce for Loops Unlimited, a manufacturer of roller coasters. The couplings connect the cars on the roller coaster and are a critical component in the performance and safety of the ride. Before we begin our discussion, recall from the

> **Learning Objective 2**
> Identify the documents used in a job-order costing system.

previous chapter that companies generally classify manufacturing costs into three broad categories: (1) direct materials, (2) direct labor, and (3) manufacturing overhead. As we study the operation of a job-order costing system, we will see how each of these three types of costs is recorded and accumulated.

Yost Precision Machining is a small company in Michigan that specializes in fabricating precision metal parts that are used in a variety of applications ranging from deep-sea exploration vehicles to the inertial triggers in automobile air bags. The company's top managers gather every morning at 8:00 A.M. in the company's conference room for the daily planning meeting. Attending the meeting this morning are: Jean Yost, the company's president; David Cheung, the marketing manager; Debbie Turner, the production manager; and Marcus White, the company controller. The president opened the meeting:

Jean: The production schedule indicates we'll be starting job 2B47 today. Isn't that the special order for experimental couplings, David?
David: That's right, Jean. That's the order from Loops Unlimited for two couplings for their new roller coaster ride for Magic Mountain.
Debbie: Why only two couplings? Don't they need a coupling for every car?
David: That's right. But this is a completely new roller coaster. The cars will go faster and will be subjected to more twists, turns, drops, and loops than on any other existing roller coaster. To hold up under these stresses, Loops Unlimited's engineers had to completely redesign the cars and couplings. They want to thoroughly test the design before proceeding to large-scale production. So they want us to make just two of these new couplings for testing purposes. If the design works, then we'll have the inside track on the order to supply couplings for the whole ride.
Jean: We agreed to take on this initial order at our cost just to get our foot in the door. Marcus, will there be any problem documenting our cost so we can get paid?
Marcus: No problem. The contract with Loops stipulates that they will pay us an amount equal to our cost of goods sold. With our job-order costing system, I can tell you that number on the day the job is completed.
Jean: Good. Is there anything else we should discuss about this job at this time? No? Well then let's move on to the next item of business.

Measuring Direct Materials Cost

Yost Precision Machining will require four G7 Connectors and two M46 Housings to make the two experimental couplings for Loops Unlimited. If this were a standard product, there would be a *bill of materials* for the product. A **bill of materials** is a document that lists the type and quantity of each item of materials needed to complete a unit of product. In this case, there is no established bill of materials, so Yost's production staff determined the materials requirements from the blueprints submitted by the customer. Each coupling requires two connectors and one housing, so to make two couplings, four connectors and two housings are required.

When an agreement has been reached with the customer concerning the quantities, prices, and shipment date for the order, a *production order* is issued. The Production Department then prepares a *materials requisition form* similar to the form in Exhibit 2–1. The **materials requisition form** is a detailed source document that (1) specifies the type and quantity of materials to be drawn from the storeroom, and (2) identifies the job to which the costs of the materials are to be charged. The form is used to control the flow of materials into production and also for making entries in the accounting records.

The Yost Precision Machining materials requisition form in Exhibit 2–1 shows that the company's Milling Department has requisitioned two M46 Housings and four G7 Connectors for job 2B47. This completed form is presented to the storeroom clerk who then issues the necessary raw materials. The storeroom clerk is not allowed to release materials without such a form bearing an authorized signature.

Exhibit 2–1
Materials Requisition Form

Materials Requisition Number _14873_   Date _March 2_
Job Number to Be Charged _2B47_
Department _Milling_

Description	Quantity	Unit Cost	Total Cost
M46 Housing	2	$124	$248
G7 Connector	4	103	412
			$660

Authorized
Signature _Bill White_

Job Cost Sheet

After being notified that the production order has been issued, the Accounting Department prepares a *job cost sheet* similar to the one presented in Exhibit 2–2. A **job cost sheet** is a form prepared for each separate job that records the materials, labor, and overhead costs charged to the job.

After direct materials are issued, the Accounting Department records their costs directly on the job cost sheet. Note from Exhibit 2–2, for example, that the $660 cost for direct materials shown earlier on the materials requisition form has been charged to job 2B47 on its job cost sheet. The requisition number 14873 is also recorded on the job cost sheet to make it easier to identify the source document for the direct materials charge.

In addition to serving as a means for charging costs to jobs, the job cost sheet also serves as a key part of a firm's accounting records. The job cost sheets form a subsidiary ledger to the Work in Process account. They are detailed records for the jobs in process that add up to the balance in Work in Process.

Concept 2–1

Measuring Direct Labor Cost

Direct labor cost is handled in much the same way as direct materials cost. Direct labor consists of labor charges that are easily traced to a particular job. Labor charges that cannot be easily traced directly to any job are treated as part of manufacturing overhead. As discussed in the previous chapter, this latter category of labor costs is called *indirect labor* and includes tasks such as maintenance, supervision, and cleanup.

Relationship of Direct Labor to Product Cost   *in business today*

How much direct labor is in the products you buy? Sometimes not very much. During a visit to the Massachusetts Institute of Technology, Chinese Prime Minister Zhu Rongji claimed that, of the $120 retail cost of a pair of athletic shoes made in China, only $2 goes to the Chinese workers who assemble them. The National Labor Committee based in New York estimates that the labor cost to assemble a $90 pair of Nike sneakers is only $1.20.

Source: Robert A. Senser, letter to the editor, *Business Week*, May 24, 1999, pp. 11–12.

Workers use *time tickets* to record the time they spend on each job and task. A completed **time ticket** is an hour-by-hour summary of the employee's activities throughout the day. An example of an employee time ticket is shown in Exhibit 2–3. When working on a specific job, the employee enters the job number on the time ticket and notes the amount of time spent on that job. When not assigned to a particular job, the employee

Exhibit 2–2
Job Cost Sheet

JOB COST SHEET

Job Number __2B47__   Date Initiated __March 2__
                             Date Completed _____

Department __Milling__   Units Completed _____
Item __Special order coupling__
For Stock _____

Direct Materials		Direct Labor			Manufacturing Overhead		
Req. No.	Amount	Ticket	Hours	Amount	Hours	Rate	Amount
14873	$660	843	5	$45			

Cost Summary		Units Shipped		
		Date	Number	Balance
Direct Materials	$			
Direct Labor	$			
Manufacturing Overhead	$			
Total Cost	$			
Unit Cost	$			

Exhibit 2–3
Employee Time Ticket

Time Ticket No. 843   Date __March 3__
Employee __Mary Holden__   Station __4__

Started	Ended	Time Completed	Rate	Amount	Job Number
7:00	12:00	5.0	$9	$45	2B47
12:30	2:30	2.0	9	18	2B50
2:30	3:30	1.0	9	9	Maintenance
Totals		8.0		$72	

Supervisor __R.W. Pace__

records the nature of the indirect labor task (such as cleanup and maintenance) and the amount of time spent on the task.

At the end of the day, the time tickets are gathered and the Accounting Department enters the direct labor-hours and costs on individual job cost sheets. (See Exhibit 2–2 for an example of how direct labor costs are entered on the job cost sheet.) The daily time tickets are source documents that are used as the basis for labor cost entries into the accounting records.

in business today More Productive Use of Time

Is it always worth the trouble to fill out labor time tickets? In a word, no. United Electric Controls, Inc., located in Waterton, Massachusetts, makes temperature and pressure sensors and controls. In the late 1980s the manufacturing vice president decided he wanted the workers to spend their time focusing on getting products out the door rather than on filling out labor time tickets. The company converted everyone into salaried workers and stopped producing labor reports.

Source: Richard L. Jenson, James W. Brackner, and Clifford Skousen. Reprinted with permission from *Management Accounting in Support of Manufacturing Excellence*, 1996, The IMA Foundation for Applied Research, Inc., Montvale, New Jersey, p. 12.

The system we have just described is a manual method for recording and posting labor costs. Many companies now rely on computerized systems and no longer record labor time by hand on sheets of paper. One computerized approach uses bar codes to enter the basic data into a computer. Each employee and each job has a unique bar code. When an employee begins work on a job, he or she scans three bar codes using a handheld device much like the bar code readers at grocery store check-out stands. The first bar code indicates that a job is being started; the second is the unique bar code on his or her identity badge; and the third is the unique bar code of the job itself. This information is fed automatically via an electronic network to a computer that notes the time and then records all of the data. When the employee completes the task, he or she scans a bar code indicating the task is complete, the bar code on his or her identity badge, and the bar code attached to the job. This information is relayed to the computer that again notes the time, and a time ticket is automatically prepared. Since all of the source data are already in computer files, the labor costs can be automatically posted to job cost sheets (or their electronic equivalents). Computers, coupled with technology such as bar codes, can eliminate much of the drudgery involved in routine bookkeeping activities while at the same time increasing timeliness and accuracy.

Concept 2–2

Tracking Time in Strawberry Fields

Advanced technology for recording data is even found in strawberry fields where the pay of workers is traditionally based on the amount of berries they pick. The Bob Jones Ranch in Oxnard, California, is using dime-sized metal buttons to record how many boxes of fruit each worker picks. The buttons, which are stuffed with microelectronics, are carried by the field workers. The buttons can be read in the field with a wand-like probe that immediately downloads data to a laptop computer. The information picked up by the probe includes the name of the worker; the type and quality of the crop; and the time, date, and location of the field being picked. Not only does the system supply the data needed to pay over 700 field workers but it also provides farm managers with information about which fields are most productive. Previously, two people were required every night to process the time tickets for the field workers.

Source: Mark Boslet, "Metal Buttons Carried by Crop Pickers Serve as Mini Databases for Farmers," *The Wall Street Journal,* May 31, 1994, p. A11A.

Application of Manufacturing Overhead

Manufacturing overhead must be included with direct materials and direct labor on the job cost sheet since manufacturing overhead is also a product cost. However, assigning manufacturing overhead to units of product can be a difficult task. There are three reasons for this.

1. Manufacturing overhead is an *indirect cost.* This means that it is either impossible or difficult to trace these costs to a particular product or job.
2. Manufacturing overhead consists of many different items ranging from the grease used in machines to the annual salary of the production manager.

> **Learning Objective 3**
> Compute predetermined overhead rates and explain why estimated overhead costs (rather than actual overhead costs) are used in the costing process.

3. Even though output may fluctuate due to seasonal or other factors, manufacturing overhead costs tend to remain relatively constant due to the presence of fixed costs.

Given these problems, about the only way to assign overhead costs to products is to use an allocation process. This allocation of overhead costs is accomplished by selecting an *allocation base* that is common to all of the company's products and services. An **allocation base** is a measure such as direct labor-hours (DLH) or machine-hours (MH) that is used to assign overhead costs to products and services.

The most widely used allocation bases are direct labor-hours and direct labor cost, with machine-hours and even units of product (where a company has only a single product) also used to some extent.

The allocation base is used to compute the **predetermined overhead rate** in the following formula:

$$\text{Predetermined overhead rate} = \frac{\text{Estimated total manufacturing overhead cost}}{\text{Estimated total units in the allocation base}}$$

Note that the predetermined overhead rate is based on *estimates* rather than actual results.[1] This is because the *predetermined* overhead rate is computed *before* the period begins and is used to *apply* overhead cost to jobs throughout the period. The process of assigning overhead cost to jobs is called **overhead application.** The formula for determining the amount of overhead cost to apply to a particular job is:

$$\frac{\text{Overhead applied to}}{\text{a particular job}} = \frac{\text{Predetermined}}{\text{overhead rate}} \times \frac{\text{Amount of the allocation}}{\text{base incurred by the job}}$$

For example, if the predetermined overhead rate is $8 per direct labor-hour, then $8 of overhead cost is *applied* to a job for each direct labor-hour incurred by the job. When the allocation base is direct labor-hours, the formula becomes:

$$\frac{\text{Overhead applied to}}{\text{a particular job}} = \frac{\text{Predetermined}}{\text{overhead rate}} \times \frac{\text{Actual direct labor-hours}}{\text{charged to the job}}$$

Using the Predetermined Overhead Rate To illustrate the steps involved in computing and using a predetermined overhead rate, let's return to Yost Precision Machining. The company has estimated its total manufacturing overhead costs to be $320,000 for the year and its total direct labor-hours to be 40,000. Its predetermined overhead rate for the year would be $8 per direct labor-hour, as shown below:

$$\text{Predetermined overhead rate} = \frac{\text{Estimated total manufacturing overhead cost}}{\text{Estimated total units in the allocation base}}$$

$$\frac{\$320,000}{40,000 \text{ direct labor-hours}} = \$8 \text{ per direct labor-hour}$$

The job cost sheet in Exhibit 2–4 indicates that 27 direct labor-hours (i.e., DLHs) were charged to job 2B47. Therefore, a total of $216 of overhead cost would be applied to the job:

$$\frac{\text{Overhead applied to}}{\text{job 2B47}} = \frac{\text{Predetermined}}{\text{overhead rate}} \times \frac{\text{Actual direct labor-hours}}{\text{charged to job 2B47}}$$

$8 per direct labor-hour × 27 direct labor-hours = $216 of overhead applied to job 2B47

This amount of overhead has been entered on the job cost sheet in Exhibit 2–4. Note that this is *not* the actual amount of overhead caused by the job. There is no attempt to trace actual overhead costs to jobs—if that could be done, the costs would be direct costs, not overhead. The overhead assigned to the job is simply a share of the total overhead that was estimated at the beginning of the year. When a company applies overhead cost to jobs

---

[1]Some experts argue that the predetermined overhead rate should be based on activity at capacity rather than on estimated activity. See Appendix 3A of Ray Garrison and Eric Noreen, *Managerial Accounting,* 9th edition, for details.

Exhibit 2–4
A Completed Job Cost Sheet

JOB COST SHEET

Job Number __2B47__   Date Initiated __March 2__

                             Date Completed __March 8__

Department __Milling__

Item __Special order coupling__   Units Completed __2__

For Stock _____

Direct Materials		Direct Labor			Manufacturing Overhead		
Req. No.	Amount	Ticket	Hours	Amount	Hours	Rate	Amount
14873	$ 660	843	5	$ 45	27	$8/DLH	$216
14875	506	846	8	60			
14912	238	850	4	21			
	$1,404	851	10	54			
			27	$180			

Cost Summary		Units Shipped		
Direct Materials	$1,404	Date	Number	Balance
Direct Labor	$ 180	March 8	—	2
Manufacturing Overhead	$ 216			
Total Cost	$1,800			
Unit Cost	$ 900*			

*$1,800 ÷ 2 units = $900 per unit.

as we have done—that is, by multiplying actual activity times the predetermined overhead rate—it is called a **normal cost system.**

The overhead may be applied as direct labor-hours are charged to jobs, or all of the overhead can be applied at once when the job is completed. The choice is up to the company. If a job is not completed at year-end, however, overhead should be applied to value the work in process inventory.

The Need for a Predetermined Rate   Instead of using a predetermined rate, a company could wait until the end of the accounting period to compute an actual overhead rate based on the *actual* total manufacturing costs and the *actual* total units in the allocation base for the period. However, managers cite several reasons for using predetermined overhead rates instead of actual overhead rates:

1. Managers would like to know the accounting system's valuation of completed jobs *before* the end of the accounting period. Suppose, for example, that Yost Precision Machining waits until the end of the year to compute its overhead rate. Then there would be no way for managers to know the cost of goods sold for job 2B47 until the close of the year, even though the job was completed and shipped to the customer in March. The seriousness of this problem can be reduced to some extent by computing the actual overhead more frequently, but that immediately leads to another problem as discussed below.
2. If actual overhead rates are computed frequently, seasonal factors in overhead costs or in the allocation base can produce fluctuations in the overhead rates. Managers generally feel that such fluctuations in overhead rates serve no useful purpose and are misleading.
3. The use of a predetermined overhead rate simplifies record keeping. To determine the overhead cost to apply to a job, the accounting staff at Yost Precision Machining

simply multiplies the direct labor-hours recorded for the job by the predetermined overhead rate of $8 per direct labor-hour.

For these reasons, most companies use predetermined overhead rates rather than actual overhead rates in their cost accounting systems.

Choice of an Allocation Base for Overhead Cost

Ideally, the allocation base should be a *cost driver* of the overhead cost. A **cost driver** is a factor, such as machine-hours, beds occupied, computer time, or flight-hours, that causes overhead costs. If a base is used to compute overhead rates that does not "drive" overhead costs, then the result will be inaccurate overhead rates and distorted product costs. For example, if direct labor-hours are used to allocate overhead, but in reality overhead has little to do with direct labor-hours, then products with high direct labor-hour requirements will shoulder an unrealistic burden of overhead and will be overcosted.

Most companies use direct labor-hours or direct labor cost as the allocation base for manufacturing overhead. However, as discussed in earlier chapters, major shifts are taking place in the structure of costs in many industries. In the past, direct labor accounted for up to 60% of the cost of many products, with overhead cost making up only a portion of the remainder. This situation has been changing—for two reasons. First, sophisticated automated equipment has taken over functions that used to be performed by direct labor workers. Since the costs of acquiring and maintaining such equipment are classified as overhead, this increases overhead while decreasing direct labor. Second, products are themselves becoming more sophisticated and complex and change more frequently. This increases the need for highly skilled indirect workers such as engineers. As a result of these two trends, direct labor is becoming less of a factor and overhead is becoming more of a factor in the cost of products in many industries.

In companies where direct labor and overhead costs have been moving in opposite directions, it would be difficult to argue that direct labor "drives" overhead costs. Accordingly, in recent years, managers in some companies have used *activity-based costing* principles to redesign their cost accounting systems. Activity-based costing is a costing technique that is designed to more accurately reflect the demands that products, customers, and other cost objects make on overhead resources. The activity-based approach is discussed in more detail in Chapter 3.

We hasten to add that although direct labor may not be an appropriate allocation base in some industries, in others it continues to be a significant driver of manufacturing overhead. The key point is that the allocation base used by the company should really drive, or cause, overhead costs, and direct labor is not always an appropriate allocation base.

in business today The Potential for Inaccurate Product Costs

There was a time when direct labor was the predominant product cost, and the allocation of overhead was not as critical as it is today. However, as discussed in the chapter, a significant shift in the cost structure has taken place in manufacturing plants. Factory automation is now common. Forty-three percent of the surveyed manufacturing firms indicated that their factories were either moderately or mostly automated. At the other end of the spectrum, only 5% of the firms reported a total lack of automation. Further, 91% of the firms manufacture more than one product. Not surprisingly, direct labor accounted for only 15% of product costs of the firms surveyed; direct materials and overhead accounted for 47% and 33%, respectively.*

Even so, a survey of managerial accounting practices indicated that 62% to 74% of manufacturing companies in the United States use direct labor as the primary or secondary allocation base for overhead.†

Companies that use a direct labor overhead allocation base should consider whether it does indeed drive overhead. If there is not a strong correlation between the two costs, product costs may be misleading and may adversely impact a variety of decisions that rely on such data.

*Eun-Sup Shim and Joseph M. Larkin, "A Survey of Current Managerial Accounting Practices: Where Do We Stand?" Reprinted with permission from The Ohio Society of CPAs, *Ohio CPA Journal*, February 1994, p. 21 (4 pages).
†Jeffrey R. Cohen and Laurence Paquette, "Management Accounting Practices: Perceptions of Controllers," *Journal of Cost Management* 5, no. 3 (Fall 1991), p. 75 and James R. Emore and Joseph A. Ness, "The Slow Pace of Meaningful Change in Cost Systems," *Journal of Cost Management* 4, no. 4 (Winter 1991).

Computation of Unit Costs

With the application of Yost Precision Machining's $216 manufacturing overhead to the job cost sheet in Exhibit 2–4, the job cost sheet is almost complete. There are two final steps. First, the totals for direct materials, direct labor, and manufacturing overhead are transferred to the Cost Summary section of the job cost sheet and added together to obtain the total cost for the job. Then the total cost ($1,800) is divided by the number of units (2) to obtain the unit cost ($900). As indicated earlier, *this unit cost is an average cost and should not be interpreted as the cost that would actually be incurred if another unit were produced.* Much of the actual overhead would not change at all if another unit were produced, so the incremental cost of an additional unit is something less than the average unit cost of $900.

The completed job cost sheet is now ready to be transferred to the Finished Goods inventory account, where it will serve as the basis for valuing unsold units in ending inventory and determining cost of goods sold.

Treasurer, Class Reunion Committee

It is hard to believe that 10 years has passed so quickly since your graduation from high school. Take a minute to reflect on what has happened in that time frame. After high school, you attended the local community college, transferred to the state university, and graduated on time. You're juggling a successful career, classes in an evening MBA program, and a new family. And now, after reminiscing with one of your high school classmates, you've somehow agreed to handle the financial arrangements for your 10-year reunion. What were you thinking? Well, at least you can fall back on those accounting skills.

You call the restaurant where the reunion will be held and jot down the most important information. The meal cost (including beverages) will be $30 per person plus a 15% gratuity. An additional $200 will be charged for a banquet room with a dance floor. (You do not remember dancing in high school.) A band has been hired for $500. One of the members of the reunion committee informs you that there is just enough money left in the class bank account to cover the printing and mailing costs. He mentions that at least one-half of the class of 400 will attend the reunion and wonders if he should add the 15% gratuity to the $30 per person meal cost when he drafts the invitation, which will indicate that a check must be returned with the reply card.

How should you respond? How much will you need to charge to cover the various costs? After making your decision, label your answer with the managerial accounting terms covered in this chapter. Finally, identify any issues that should be investigated further.

Summary of Document Flows

The sequence of events discussed above is summarized in Exhibit 2–5. A careful study of the flow of documents in this exhibit will provide a good overview of the overall operation of a job-order costing system.

Managerial Accounting in Action

The Wrap-Up

YOST ☆
PRECISION MACHINING

In the 8:00 A.M. daily planning meeting on March 9, Jean Yost, the president of Yost Precision Machining, once again drew attention to job 2B47, the experimental couplings:

Jean: I see job 2B47 is completed. Let's get those couplings shipped immediately to Loops Unlimited so they can get their testing program under way. Marcus, how much are we going to bill Loops for those two units?

Marcus: Just a second, let me check the job cost sheet for that job. Here it is. We agreed to sell the experimental units at cost, so we will be charging Loops Unlimited just $900 a unit.

Jean: Fine. Let's hope the couplings work out and we make some money on the big order later.

Job-Order Costing—The Flow of Costs

Learning Objective 4
Prepare journal entries to record costs in a job-order costing system.

We are now ready to take a more detailed look at the flow of costs through the company's formal accounting system. To illustrate, we shall consider a single month's activity for Rand Company, a producer of gold and silver commemorative medallions. Rand Company has two jobs in process during April, the first month of its fiscal year. Job A, a special minting of 1,000 gold medallions commemorating the invention of motion pictures, was started during March. By the end of March, $30,000 in manufacturing costs had been recorded for the job. Job B, an order for 10,000 silver medallions commemorating the fall of the Berlin Wall, was started in April.

The Purchase and Issue of Materials

On April 1, Rand Company had $7,000 in raw materials on hand. During the month, the company purchased an additional $60,000 in raw materials. The purchase is recorded in journal entry (1) below:

(1)

Raw Materials	60,000	
Accounts Payable		60,000

As explained in the previous chapter, Raw Materials is an asset account. Thus, when raw materials are purchased, they are initially recorded as an asset—not as an expense.

Issue of Direct and Indirect Materials   During April, $52,000 in raw materials were requisitioned from the storeroom for use in production. Entry (2) records the issue of the materials to the production departments.

(2)

Work in Process	50,000	
Manufacturing Overhead	2,000	
Raw Materials		52,000

The materials charged to Work in Process represent direct materials for specific jobs. As these materials are entered into the Work in Process account, they are also recorded on the appropriate job cost sheets. This point is illustrated in Exhibit 2–6, where $28,000 of the $50,000 in direct materials is charged to job A's cost sheet and the remaining $22,000

Exhibit 2-5
The Flow of Documents in a Job-Order Costing System

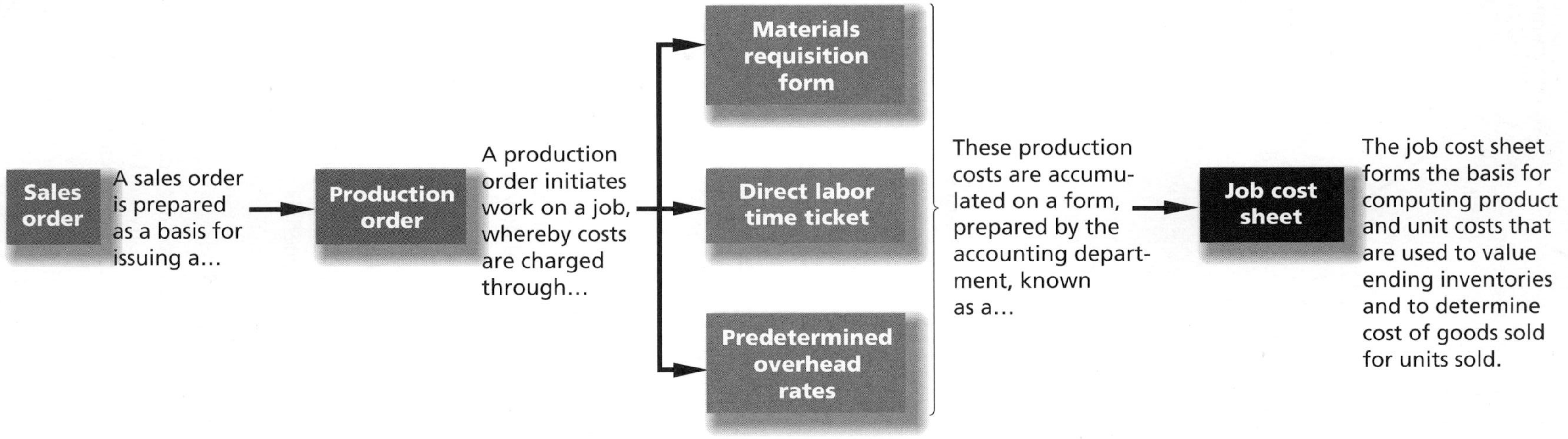

Sales order

A sales order is prepared as a basis for issuing a...

Production order

A production order initiates work on a job, whereby costs are charged through...

Materials requisition form

Direct labor time ticket

Predetermined overhead rates

These production costs are accumulated on a form, prepared by the accounting department, known as a...

Job cost sheet

The job cost sheet forms the basis for computing product and unit costs that are used to value ending inventories and to determine cost of goods sold for units sold.

Exhibit 2–6
Raw Materials Cost Flows

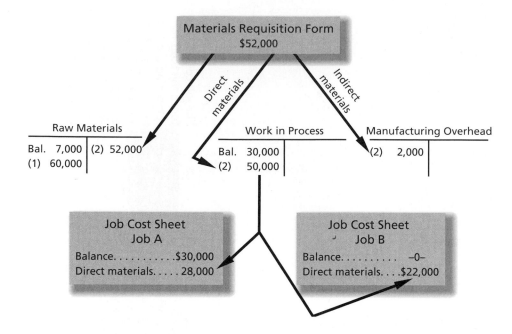

is charged to job B's cost sheet. (In this example, all data are presented in summary form and the job cost sheet is abbreviated.)

The $2,000 charged to Manufacturing Overhead in entry (2) represents indirect materials used in production during April. Observe that the Manufacturing Overhead account is separate from the Work in Process account. The purpose of the Manufacturing Overhead account is to accumulate all manufacturing overhead costs as they are incurred during a period.

Before leaving Exhibit 2–6 we need to point out one additional thing. Notice from the exhibit that the job cost sheet for job A contains a beginning balance of $30,000. We stated earlier that this balance represents the cost of work done during March that has been carried forward to April. Also note that the Work in Process account contains the same $30,000 balance. *The reason the $30,000 appears in both places is that the Work in Process account is a control account and the job cost sheets form a subsidiary ledger. Thus, the Work in Process account contains a summarized total of all costs appearing on the individual job cost sheets for all jobs in process at any given point in time.* (Since Rand Company had only job A in process at the beginning of April, job A's $30,000 balance on that date is equal to the balance in the Work in Process account.)

Issue of Direct Materials Only   Sometimes the materials drawn from the Raw Materials inventory account are all direct materials. In this case, the entry to record the issue of the materials into production would be as follows:

Work in Process	XXX	
Raw Materials		XXX

Labor Cost

As work is performed each day in various departments of Rand Company, employee time tickets are filled out by workers, collected, and forwarded to the Accounting Department. In the Accounting Department, the tickets are costed according to the various employee wage rates, and the resulting costs are classified as either direct or indirect labor. This costing and classification for April resulted in the following summary entry:

(3)

Work in Process	60,000	
Manufacturing Overhead	15,000	
Salaries and Wages Payable		75,000

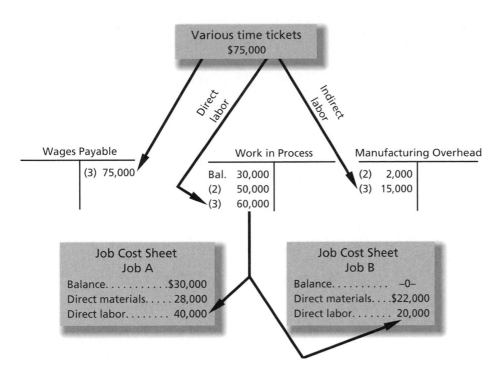

Exhibit 2–7
Labor Cost Flows

Only direct labor is added to the Work in Process account. For Rand Company, this amounted to $60,000 for April.

At the same time that direct labor costs are added to Work in Process, they are also added to the individual job cost sheets, as shown in Exhibit 2–7. During April, $40,000 of direct labor cost was charged to job A and the remaining $20,000 was charged to job B.

The labor costs charged to Manufacturing Overhead represent the indirect labor costs of the period, such as supervision, janitorial work, and maintenance.

Manufacturing Overhead Costs

Recall that all costs of operating the factory other than direct materials and direct labor are classified as manufacturing overhead costs. These costs are entered directly into the Manufacturing Overhead account as they are incurred. To illustrate, assume that Rand Company incurred the following general factory costs during April:

Utilities (heat, water, and power)	$21,000
Rent on factory equipment	16,000
Miscellaneous factory costs	3,000
Total	$40,000

The following entry records the incurrence of these costs:

(4)

Manufacturing Overhead	40,000	
Accounts Payable		40,000

In addition, let us assume that during April, Rand Company recognized $13,000 in accrued property taxes and that $7,000 in prepaid insurance expired on factory buildings and equipment. The following entry records these items:

(5)

Manufacturing Overhead	20,000	
Property Taxes Payable		13,000
Prepaid Insurance		7,000

Finally, let us assume that the company recognized $18,000 in depreciation on factory equipment during April. The following entry records the accrual of this depreciation:

(6)

Manufacturing Overhead	18,000	
Accumulated Depreciation		18,000

In short, *all* manufacturing overhead costs are recorded directly into the Manufacturing Overhead account as they are incurred day by day throughout a period. It is important to understand that Manufacturing Overhead is a control account for many—perhaps thousands—of subsidiary accounts such as Indirect Materials, Indirect Labor, Factory Utilities, and so forth. As the Manufacturing Overhead account is debited for costs during a period, the various subsidiary accounts are also debited. In the example above and also in the assignment material for this chapter, we omit the entries to the subsidiary accounts for the sake of brevity.

The Application of Manufacturing Overhead

Learning Objective 5

Apply overhead cost to Work in Process using a predetermined overhead rate.

Since actual manufacturing costs are charged to the Manufacturing Overhead control account rather than to Work in Process, how are manufacturing overhead costs assigned to Work in Process? The answer is, by means of the predetermined overhead rate. Recall from our discussion earlier in the chapter that a predetermined overhead rate is established at the beginning of each year. The rate is calculated by dividing the estimated total manufacturing overhead cost for the year by the estimated total units in the allocation base (measured in machine-hours, direct labor-hours, or some other base). The predetermined overhead rate is then used to apply overhead costs to jobs. For example, if direct labor-hours is the allocation base, overhead cost is applied to each job by multiplying the number of direct labor-hours charged to the job by the predetermined overhead rate.

To illustrate, assume that Rand Company has used machine-hours to compute its predetermined overhead rate and that this rate is $6 per machine-hour. Also assume that during April, 10,000 machine-hours were worked on job A and 5,000 machine-hours were worked on job B (a total of 15,000 machine-hours). Thus, $90,000 in overhead cost (15,000 machine-hours × $6 per machine-hour = $90,000) would be applied to Work in Process. The following entry records the application of Manufacturing Overhead to Work in Process:

(7)

Work in Process	90,000	
Manufacturing Overhead		90,000

The flow of costs through the Manufacturing Overhead account is shown in Exhibit 2–8.

The "actual overhead costs" in the Manufacturing Overhead account in Exhibit 2–8 are the costs that were added to the account in entries (2)–(6). Observe that the incurrence of these actual overhead costs [entries (2)–(6)] and the application of overhead to Work in Process [entry (7)] represent two separate and entirely distinct processes.

The Concept of a Clearing Account   The Manufacturing Overhead account operates as a clearing account. As we have noted, actual factory overhead costs are debited to the accounts as they are incurred day by day throughout the year. At certain intervals during the year, usually when a job is completed, overhead cost is released from the Manufacturing Overhead account and is applied to the Work in Process account by means of the predetermined overhead rate. This sequence of events is illustrated below:

Manufacturing Overhead
(a clearing account)

Actual overhead costs are charged to the account as these costs are incurred day by day throughout the period.	Overhead is applied to Work in Process using the predetermined overhead rate.

Exhibit 2–8
The Flow of Costs in Overhead Application

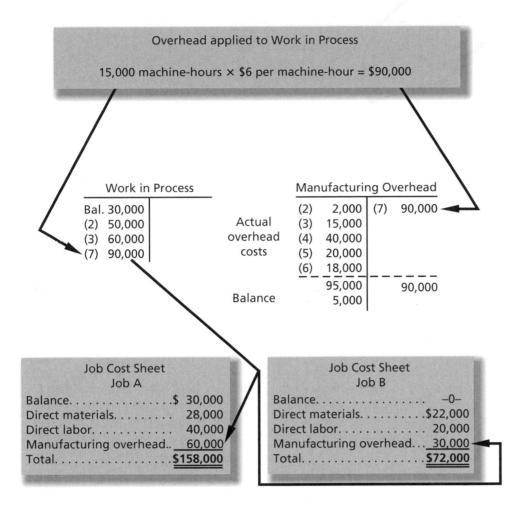

As we emphasized earlier, the predetermined overhead rate is based entirely on estimates of what overhead costs are *expected* to be, and it is established before the year begins. As a result, the overhead cost applied during a year will almost certainly turn out to be more or less than the overhead cost that is actually incurred. For example, notice from Exhibit 2–8 that Rand Company's actual overhead costs for the period are $5,000 greater than the overhead cost that has been applied to Work in Process, resulting in a $5,000 debit balance in the Manufacturing Overhead account. We will reserve discussion of what to do with this $5,000 balance until the next section, Problems of Overhead Application.

For the moment, we can conclude by noting from Exhibit 2–8 that the cost of a completed job consists of the actual materials cost of the job, the actual labor cost of the job, and the overhead cost *applied* to the job. Pay particular attention to the following subtle but important point: *Actual overhead costs are not charged to jobs; actual overhead costs do not appear on the job cost sheet nor do they appear in the Work in Process account. Only the applied overhead cost, based on the predetermined overhead rate, appears on the job cost sheet and in the Work in Process account.* Study this point carefully.

Nonmanufacturing Costs

In addition to manufacturing costs, companies also incur marketing and selling costs. As explained in the previous chapter, these costs should be treated as period expenses and charged directly to the income statement. *Nonmanufacturing costs should not go into the Manufacturing Overhead account.* To illustrate the correct treatment of nonmanufacturing costs, assume that Rand Company incurred the following selling and administrative costs during April:

Top-management salaries	$21,000
Other office salaries	9,000
Total salaries	$30,000

The following entry records these salaries:

(8)

Salaries Expense	30,000	
Salaries and Wages Payable		30,000

Assume that depreciation on office equipment during April was $7,000. The entry would be:

(9)

Depreciation Expense	7,000	
Accumulated Depreciation		7,000

Pay particular attention to the difference between this entry and entry (6) where we recorded depreciation on factory equipment. In journal entry (6), depreciation on factory equipment was debited to Manufacturing Overhead and is therefore a product cost. In journal entry (9) above, depreciation on office equipment was debited to Depreciation Expense. Depreciation on office equipment is considered to be a period expense rather than a product cost.

Finally, assume that advertising was $42,000 and that other selling and administrative expenses in April totaled $8,000. The following entry records these items:

(10)

Advertising Expense	42,000	
Other Selling and Administrative Expense	8,000	
Accounts Payable		50,000

Since the amounts in entries (8) through (10) all go directly into expense accounts, they will have no effect on the costing of Rand Company's production for April. The same will be true of any other selling and administrative expenses incurred during April, including sales commissions, depreciation on sales equipment, rent on office facilities, insurance on office facilities, and related costs.

Cost of Goods Manufactured

When a job has been completed, the finished output is transferred from the production departments to the finished goods warehouse. By this time, the accounting department will have charged the job with direct materials and direct labor cost, and manufacturing overhead will have been applied using the predetermined rate. A transfer of these costs must be made within the costing system that *parallels* the physical transfer of the goods to the finished goods warehouse. The costs of the completed job are transferred out of the Work in Process account and into the Finished Goods account. The sum of all amounts transferred between these two accounts represents the cost of goods manufactured for the period. (This point was illustrated earlier in Exhibit 1–8 in Chapter 1.)

In the case of Rand Company, let us assume that job A was completed during April. The following entry transfers the cost of job A from Work in Process to Finished Goods:

(11)

Finished Goods	158,000	
Work in Process		158,000

The $158,000 represents the completed cost of job A, as shown on the job cost sheet in Exhibit 2–8. Since job A was the only job completed during April, the $158,000 also represents the cost of goods manufactured for the month.

Job B was not completed by month-end, so its cost will remain in the Work in Process account and carry over to the next month. If a balance sheet is prepared at the end of April, the cost accumulated thus far on job B will appear as "Work in process inventory" in the assets section.

Cost of Goods Sold

As units in finished goods are shipped to fill customers' orders, the unit cost appearing on the job cost sheets is used as a basis for transferring the cost of the items sold from the Finished Goods account into the Cost of Goods Sold account. If a complete job is shipped, as in the case where a job has been done to a customer's specifications, then it is a simple matter to transfer the entire cost appearing on the job cost sheet into the Cost of Goods Sold account. In most cases, however, only a portion of the units involved in a particular job will be immediately sold. In these situations, the unit cost must be used to determine how much product cost should be removed from Finished Goods and charged to Cost of Goods Sold.

For Rand Company, we will assume 750 of the 1,000 gold medallions in job A were shipped to customers by the end of the month for total sales revenue of $225,000. Since 1,000 units were produced and the total cost of the job from the job cost sheet was $158,000, the unit product cost was $158. The following journal entries would record the sale (all sales are on account):

(12)

| Accounts Receivable | 225,000 | |
| Sales | | 225,000 |

(13)

| Cost of Goods Sold | 118,500 | |
| Finished Goods | | 118,500 |

($158 per unit × 750 units = $118,500)

With entry (13), the flow of costs through our job-order costing system is completed.

Summary of Cost Flows

To pull the entire Rand Company example together, journal entries (1) through (13) are summarized in Exhibit 2–9. The flow of costs through the accounts is presented in T-account form in Exhibit 2–10.

Exhibit 2–11 presents a schedule of cost of goods manufactured and a schedule of cost of goods sold for Rand Company. Note particularly from Exhibit 2–11 that the manufacturing overhead cost on the schedule of cost of goods manufactured is the overhead applied to jobs during the month—not the actual manufacturing overhead costs incurred. The reason for this can be traced back to journal entry (7) and the T-account for Work in Process that appears in Exhibit 2–10. Under a normal costing system as illustrated in this chapter, applied—not actual—overhead costs are applied to jobs and thus to Work in Process inventory. Note also the cost of goods manufactured for the month ($158,000) agrees with the amount transferred from Work in Process to Finished Goods for the month as recorded earlier in entry (11). Also note that this $158,000 figure is used in computing the cost of goods sold for the month.

An income statement for April is presented in Exhibit 2–12. Observe that the cost of goods sold figure on this statement ($123,500) is carried down from Exhibit 2–11.

> **Learning Objective 6**
> Prepare T-accounts to show the flow of costs in a job-order costing system and prepare schedules of cost of goods manufactured and cost of goods sold.

Exhibit 2–9
Summary of Rand Company
Journal Entries

(1)		
Raw Materials	60,000	
Accounts Payable		60,000
(2)		
Work in Process	50,000	
Manufacturing Overhead	2,000	
Raw Materials		52,000
(3)		
Work in Process	60,000	
Manufacturing Overhead	15,000	
Salaries and Wages Payable		75,000
(4)		
Manufacturing Overhead	40,000	
Accounts Payable		40,000
(5)		
Manufacturing Overhead	20,000	
Property Taxes Payable		13,000
Prepaid Insurance		7,000
(6)		
Manufacturing Overhead	18,000	
Accumulated Depreciation		18,000
(7)		
Work in Process	90,000	
Manufacturing Overhead		90,000
(8)		
Salaries Expense	30,000	
Salaries and Wages Payable		30,000
(9)		
Depreciation Expense	7,000	
Accumulated Depreciation		7,000
(10)		
Advertising Expense	42,000	
Other Selling and Administrative Expense	8,000	
Accounts Payable		50,000
(11)		
Finished Goods	158,000	
Work in Process		158,000
(12)		
Accounts Receivable	225,000	
Sales		225,000
(13)		
Cost of Goods Sold	118,500	
Finished Goods		118,500

Exhibit 2–10

Summary of Cost Flows—Rand Company

Accounts Receivable		
(12)	XX* 225,000	

Prepaid Insurance		
	XX	(5) 7,000

Raw Materials		
Bal.	7,000	(2) 52,000
(1)	60,000	
Bal.	15,000	

Work in Process		
Bal.	30,000	(11) 158,000
(2)	50,000	
(3)	60,000	
(7)	90,000	
Bal.	72,000	

Finished Goods		
Bal.	10,000	(13) 118,500
(11)	158,000	
Bal.	49,500	

Accumulated Depreciation		
		XX
	(6)	18,000
	(9)	7,000

Manufacturing Overhead		
(2)	2,000	(7) 90,000
(3)	15,000	
(4)	40,000	
(5)	20,000	
(6)	18,000	
Bal.	5,000	

Accounts Payable		
		XX
(1)	60,000	
(4)	40,000	
(10)	50,000	

Salaries and Wages Payable		
		XX
(3)	75,000	
(8)	30,000	

Property Taxes Payable		
		XX
(5)	13,000	

Capital Stock		
		XX

Retained Earnings		
		XX

Sales		
	(12)	225,000

Cost of Goods Sold		
(13)	118,500	

Salaries Expense		
(8)	30,000	

Depreciation Expense		
(9)	7,000	

Advertising Expense		
(10)	42,000	

Other Selling and Administrative Expense		
(10)	8,000	

Explanation of entries:

(1) Raw materials purchased.
(2) Direct and indirect materials issued into production.
(3) Direct and indirect factory labor cost incurred.
(4) Utilities and other factory costs incurred.
(5) Property taxes and insurance incurred on the factory.
(6) Depreciation recorded on factory assets.
(7) Overhead cost applied to Work in Process.

(8) Administrative salaries expense incurred.
(9) Depreciation recorded on office equipment.
(10) Advertising and other expense incurred.
(11) Cost of goods manufactured transferred into finished goods.
(12) Sale of job A recorded.
(13) Cost of goods sold recorded for job A.

*XX = Normal balance in the account (for example, Accounts Receivable normally carries a debit balance).

Exhibit 2–11
Schedules of Cost of Goods
Manufactured and Cost of
Goods Sold

Cost of Goods Manufactured

Direct materials:		
Raw materials inventory, beginning	$ 7,000	
Add: Purchases of raw materials	60,000	
Total raw materials available	67,000	
Deduct: Raw materials inventory, ending	15,000	
Raw materials used in production	52,000	
Less indirect materials included in manufacturing overhead	2,000	$ 50,000
Direct labor		60,000
Manufacturing overhead applied to work in process		90,000
Total manufacturing costs		200,000
Add: Beginning work in process inventory		30,000
		230,000
Deduct: Ending work in process inventory		72,000
Cost of goods manufactured		$158,000

Cost of Goods Sold

Finished goods inventory, beginning		$ 10,000
Add: Cost of goods manufactured		158,000
Goods available for sale		168,000
Deduct: Finished goods inventory, ending		49,500
Unadjusted cost of goods sold		118,500
Add: Underapplied overhead		5,000
Adjusted cost of goods sold		$123,500

*Note that the underapplied overhead is added to cost of goods sold. If overhead were overapplied, it would be deducted from cost of goods sold.

Exhibit 2–12
Income Statement

RAND COMPANY
Income Statement
For the Month Ending April 30

Sales		$225,000
Less cost of goods sold ($118,500 + $5,000)		123,500
Gross margin		101,500
Less selling and administrative expenses:		
Salaries expense	$30,000	
Depreciation expense	7,000	
Advertising expense	42,000	
Other expense	8,000	87,000
Net income		$ 14,500

Problems of Overhead Application

We need to consider two complications relating to overhead application. These are (1) the computation of underapplied and overapplied overhead and (2) the disposition of any balance remaining in the Manufacturing Overhead account at the end of a period.

Underapplied and Overapplied Overhead

Since the predetermined overhead rate is established before a period begins and is based entirely on estimated data, there generally will be a difference between the amount of overhead cost applied to Work in Process and the amount of overhead cost actually incurred during a period. In the case of Rand Company, for example, the predetermined overhead rate of $6 per hour resulted in $90,000 of overhead cost being applied to Work in Process, whereas actual overhead costs for April proved to be $95,000 (see Exhibit 2–8). The difference between the overhead cost applied to Work in Process and the actual overhead costs of a period is termed either **underapplied** or **overapplied overhead.** For Rand Company, overhead was underapplied because the applied cost ($90,000) was $5,000 less than the actual cost ($95,000). If the tables had been reversed and the company had applied $95,000 in overhead cost to Work in Process while incurring actual overhead costs of only $90,000, then the overhead would have been overapplied.

What is the cause of underapplied or overapplied overhead? The causes can be complex, and a full explanation will have to wait for later chapters. Nevertheless, the basic problem is that the method of applying overhead to jobs using a predetermined overhead rate assumes that actual overhead costs will be proportional to the actual amount of the allocation base incurred during the period. If, for example, the predetermined overhead rate is $6 per machine-hour, then it is assumed that actual overhead costs incurred will be $6 for every machine-hour that is actually worked. There are at least two reasons why this may not be true. First, much of the overhead often consists of fixed costs that do not grow as the number of machine-hours incurred increases. Second, spending on overhead items may or may not be under control. If individuals who are responsible for overhead costs do a good job, those costs should be less than were expected at the beginning of the period. If they do a poor job, those costs will be more than expected. As we indicated above, however, a fuller explanation of the causes of underapplied and overapplied overhead will have to wait for later chapters.

To illustrate what can happen, suppose that two companies—Turbo Crafters and Black & Howell—have prepared the following estimated data for the coming year:

	Company	
	Turbo Crafters	**Black & Howell**
Predetermined overhead rate based on ...	Machine-hours	Direct materials cost
Estimated manufacturing overhead	$300,000 (a)	$120,000 (a)
Estimated machine-hours	75,000 (b)	—
Estimated direct materials cost	—	$ 80,000 (b)
Predetermined overhead rate, (a) ÷ (b) ...	$4 per machine-hour	150% of direct materials cost

Now assume that because of unexpected changes in overhead spending and changes in demand for the companies' products, the *actual* overhead cost and the *actual* activity recorded during the year in each company are as follows:

	Company	
	Turbo Crafters	**Black & Howell**
Actual manufacturing overhead costs	$290,000	$130,000
Actual machine-hours	68,000	—
Actual direct materials costs	—	$ 90,000

Exhibit 2–13
Summary of Overhead Concepts

At the beginning of the period:

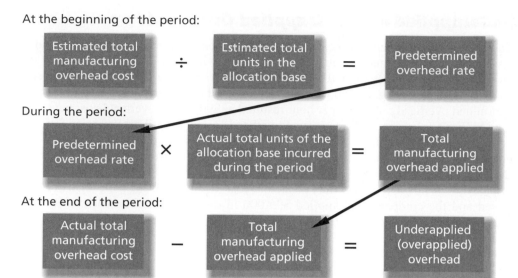

For each company, note that the actual data for both cost and activity differ from the estimates used in computing the predetermined overhead rate. This results in underapplied and overapplied overhead as follows:

	Company	
	Turbo Crafters	Black & Howell
Actual manufacturing overhead costs	$290,000	$130,000
Manufacturing overhead cost applied to		
Work in process during the year:		
68,000 *actual* machine-hours ×		
$4 per machine-hour	272,000	
$90,000 *actual* direct materials cost × 150% ...		135,000
Underapplied (overapplied) overhead	$ 18,000	$ (5,000)

For Turbo Crafters, notice that the amount of overhead cost that has been applied to Work in Process ($272,000) is less than the actual overhead cost for the year ($290,000). Therefore, overhead is underapplied. Also notice that the original estimate of overhead in Turbo Crafters ($300,000) is not directly involved in this computation. Its impact is felt only through the $4 predetermined overhead rate that is used.

For Black & Howell, the amount of overhead cost that has been applied to Work in Process ($135,000) is greater than the actual overhead cost for the year ($130,000), and so overhead is overapplied.

A summary of the concepts discussed above is presented in Exhibit 2–13.

Disposition of Under- or Overapplied Overhead Balances

What disposition of any under- or overapplied balance remaining in the Manufacturing Overhead account should managers make at the end of a period? The simplest method is to close out the balance to Cost of Goods Sold. More complicated methods are sometimes used, but they are beyond the scope of this book. To illustrate the simplest method, recall that Rand Company had underapplied overhead of $5,000. The entry to close this underapplied overhead to Cost of Goods Sold would be:

(14)

Cost of Goods Sold	5,000	
Manufacturing Overhead		5,000

Note that since the Manufacturing Overhead account has a debit balance, Manufacturing Overhead must be credited to close out the account. This has the effect of increasing Cost of Goods Sold for April to $123,500:

Unadjusted cost of goods sold [from entry (13)]	$118,500
Add underapplied overhead [entry (14) above]	5,000
Adjusted cost of goods sold	$123,500

After this adjustment has been made, Rand Company's income statement for April will appear as was shown earlier in Exhibit 2–12.

Remaining Balance in the Overhead Account

you decide

The simplest method for disposing of any balance remaining in the Overhead account is to close it out to Cost of Goods Sold. If there is a debit balance (that is, overhead has been underapplied), the entry to dispose of the balance would include a debit to Cost of Goods Sold. That debit would increase the balance in the Cost of Goods Sold account. On the other hand, if there is a credit balance, the entry to dispose of the balance would include a credit to Cost of Goods Sold. That credit would decrease the balance in the Cost of Goods Sold account. If you were the company's controller, would you want a debit balance, a credit balance, or no balance in the Overhead account at the end of the period?

A General Model of Product Cost Flows

The flow of costs in a product costing system is presented in the form of a T-account model in Exhibit 2–14. This model applies as much to a process costing system as it does to a job-order costing system. Examination of this model can be very helpful in gaining a perspective as to how costs enter a system, flow through it, and finally end up as Cost of Goods Sold on the income statement.

Multiple Predetermined Overhead Rates

Our discussion in this chapter has assumed that there is a single predetermined overhead rate for an entire factory called a **plantwide overhead rate.** This is, in fact, a common practice—particularly in smaller companies. But in larger companies, *multiple predetermined overhead rates* are often used. In a **multiple predetermined overhead rate** system each production department will usually have a different overhead rate. Such a system, while more complex, is considered to be more accurate, since it can reflect differences across departments in how overhead costs are incurred. For example, overhead might be allocated based on direct labor-hours in departments that are relatively labor intensive and based on machine-hours in departments that are relatively machine intensive. When multiple predetermined overhead rates are used, overhead is applied in each department according to its own overhead rate as a job proceeds through the department.

Enhancing the Accuracy of Product Costs

in business today

Only 34% of surveyed manufacturing firms reported that they used a single, plantwide overhead rate. The use of multiple overhead rates to obtain more accurate product costs was reported by 44% of the firms. The remaining 22% use activity-based costing (discussed in Chapter 3)—an even more complex approach to the allocation of overhead costs to products.

Source: Eun-Sup Shim and Joseph M. Larkin, "A Survey of Current Managerial Accounting Practices: Where Do We Stand?" Reprinted with permission from The Ohio Society of CPAs, *Ohio CPA Journal*, February 1994, p. 21 (4 pages).

Exhibit 2–14
A General Model of Cost Flows

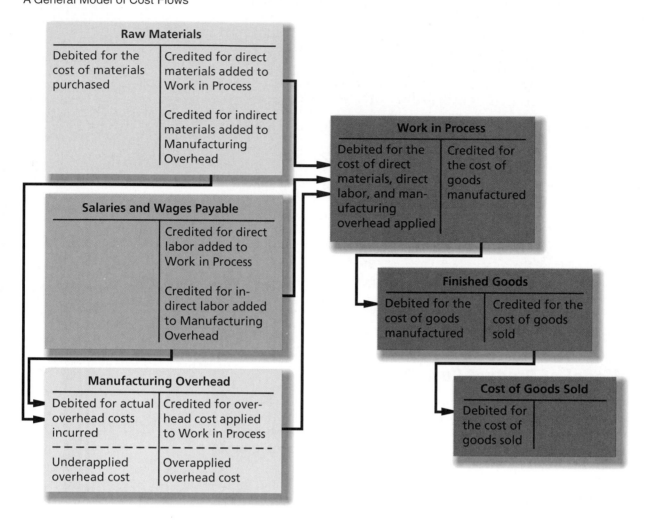

Job-Order Costing in Service Companies

We stated earlier in the chapter that job-order costing is also used in service organizations such as law firms, movie studios, hospitals, and repair shops, as well as in manufacturing companies. In a law firm, for example, each client represents a "job," and the costs of that job are accumulated day by day on a job cost sheet as the client's case is handled by the firm. Legal forms and similar inputs represent the direct materials for the job; the time expended by attorneys represents the direct labor; and the costs of secretaries, clerks, rent, depreciation, and so forth, represent the overhead.

In a movie studio such as Columbia Pictures, each film produced by the studio is a "job," and costs for direct materials (costumes, props, film, etc.) and direct labor (actors, directors, and extras) are accounted for and charged to each film's job cost sheet. A share of the studio's overhead costs, such as utilities, depreciation of equipment, salaries of maintenance workers, and so forth, is also charged to each film. However, there is considerable controversy about the methods used by some studios to distribute overhead costs among movies, and these controversies sometimes result in lawsuits.

In sum, job-order costing is a versatile and widely used costing method that may be encountered in virtually any organization with diverse products or services.

A Fair Share of Profits

"Net profit participation" contracts in which writers, actors, and directors share in the net profits of movies are common in Hollywood. For example, Winston Groom, the author of the novel *Forrest Gump,* has a contract with Paramount Pictures Corp. that calls for him to receive 3% of the net profits on the movie. However, Paramount claims that *Forrest Gump* has yet to show any profits even though it has the third-highest gross receipts of any film in history. How can this be?

Movie studios assess a variety of overhead charges including a charge of about 15% on production costs for production overhead, a charge of about 30% of gross rentals for distribution overhead, and a charge for marketing overhead that amounts to about 10% of advertising costs. After all of these overhead charges and other hotly contested accounting practices, it is a rare film that shows a profit. Fewer than 5% of released films show a profit for net profit participation purposes. Examples of "money-losing" films include *Rain Man, Batman,* and *Who Framed Roger Rabbit?* as well as *Forrest Gump.* Disgruntled writers and actors are increasingly suing studios, claiming unreasonable accounting practices that are designed to cheat them of their share of profits.

Source: Ross Engel and Bruce Ikawa, "Where's the Profit?" Reprinted with permission from *Management Accounting,* January 1997, pp. 40–47.

Summary

LO1 Distinguish between process costing and job-order costing and identify companies that would use each costing method.

Job-order costing and process costing are widely used to track costs. Job-order costing is used in situations where the organization offers many different products or services, such as in furniture manufacturing, hospitals, and legal firms. Process costing is used where units of product are homogeneous, such as in flour milling or cement production.

LO2 Identify the documents used in a job-order costing system.

In a job-order costing system, each job has its own job cost sheet. Materials requisition forms and labor time tickets are used to record direct materials and direct labor costs. These costs, together with manufacturing overhead, are accumulated on the job cost sheet for a job.

LO3 Compute predetermined overhead rates and explain why estimated overhead costs (rather than actual overhead costs) are used in the costing process.

Manufacturing overhead costs are assigned to jobs using a predetermined overhead rate. The rate is determined at the beginning of the period so that jobs can be costed throughout the period rather than waiting until the end of the period. The predetermined overhead rate is determined by dividing the estimated total manufacturing cost for the period by the estimated total allocation base for the period.

LO4 Prepare journal entries to record costs in a job-order costing system.

Direct materials costs are debited to Work in Process when they are released for use in production. Direct labor costs are debited to Work in Process as incurred. Actual manufacturing overhead costs are debited to the Manufacturing Overhead control account as incurred. Manufacturing overhead costs are applied to Work in Process using the predetermined overhead rate. The journal entry that accomplishes this is a debit to Work in Process and a credit to the Manufacturing Overhead control account.

LO5 Apply overhead cost to Work in Process using a predetermined overhead rate.

Overhead is applied to jobs by multiplying the predetermined overhead rate by the actual amount of the allocation base used by the job.

LO6 Prepare T-accounts to show the flow of costs in a job-order costing system and prepare schedules of cost of goods manufactured and cost of goods sold.

See Exhibit 2–14 for a summary of the cost flows through the T-accounts.

LO7 **Compute under- or overapplied overhead cost and prepare the journal entry to close the balance in Manufacturing Overhead to the appropriate accounts.**

The difference between the actual overhead cost incurred during a period and the amount of overhead cost applied to production is referred to as under- or overapplied overhead. Under- or overapplied overhead is closed out to Cost of Goods Sold. When overhead is underapplied, the balance in the Manufacturing Overhead control account is debited to Cost of Goods Sold. This has the effect of increasing the Cost of Goods Sold and occurs because costs assigned to products have been understated. When overhead is overapplied, the balance in the Manufacturing Overhead control account is credited to Cost of Goods Sold. This has the effect of decreasing the Cost of Goods Sold and occurs because costs assigned to products have been overstated.

Guidance Answers to Decision Maker and You Decide

TREASURER, CLASS REUNION COMMITTEE (p. 79)
You should charge $38.00 per person to cover the costs calculated as follows:

Meal cost	$30.00	Direct material cost
Gratuity ($30 × 0.15)	4.50	Direct labor cost
Room charge ($200 ÷ 200 expected attendees)	1.00	Overhead cost
Band cost ($500 ÷ 200 expected attendees)	2.50	Overhead cost
Total cost	$38.00	

The number of expected attendees (or estimated units in the allocation base) was used to allocate the band cost. Attendees who plan to leave immediately after dinner might object to this allocation. However, this personal choice probably should not override the decision to base the allocation on this very simple base.

If exactly 200 classmates attend the reunion, the $7,600 of receipts (200 @ $38) will exactly cover the expenditures of $7,600 [meal cost of $6,000 (or 200 @ $30) plus gratuity cost of $900 (or $6,000 × 0.15) plus the $200 room charge plus the $500 band cost]. Unfortunately, if less than 200 attend, the Reunion Committee will come up short in an amount equal to the difference between the 200 estimated attendees and the actual number of attendees times $3.50 (the total per person overhead charge). As such, you should talk to the members of the Reunion Committee to ensure that (1) the estimate is as reasonable as possible, and (2) there is a plan to deal with the shortage. On the other hand, if more than 200 attend, the Reunion Committee will collect more money than it needs to disburse. The amount would be equal to the difference between the actual number of attendees and the 200 estimated attendees times $3.50. Again, a plan should be in place to deal with this situation. (Perhaps the funds could be used to cover the mailing costs for the next reunion.)

REMAINING BALANCE IN THE OVERHEAD ACCOUNT (p. 93)
A quick response on your part might have been that you would prefer a credit balance in the Overhead account. The entry to dispose of the balance would decrease the balance in the Cost of Goods Sold account and would cause the company's gross margin and net income to be higher than might have otherwise been expected. However, the impact on decision-making during the period should be carefully considered.

Ideally, a controller would want the balance in the Overhead account to be zero. If there is no remaining balance in the Overhead account at the end of the period, that means that the actual overhead costs for the period (which are debited to the Overhead account) exactly equaled the overhead costs that were applied (or allocated to the products made by being added to the Work in Process account) during the period. As a result, the products made during the period would have had the "correct" amount of overhead assigned as they moved from the factory floor to the finished goods area to the customer. Typically, this would not be the case because the predetermined overhead rate (used to apply or allocate overhead to the products made) is developed using two estimates (the total amount of overhead expected and the total units in the allocation base expected during the period). It would be difficult, if not impossible, to accurately predict one or both estimates.

If there is a remaining balance in the Overhead account, then the products manufactured during the period either received too little overhead (if there is a debit or underapplied balance) or too much overhead (if there is a credit or overapplied balance). As such, units carried along with them inaccurate product costs as the costs flowed through system. Decisions that relied on those inaccurate product costs may have been faulty.

Review Problem: Job-Order Costing

Hogle Company is a manufacturing firm that uses job-order costing. On January 1, the beginning of its fiscal year, the company's inventory balances were as follows:

Raw materials	$20,000
Work in process	15,000
Finished goods	30,000

The company applies overhead cost to jobs on the basis of machine-hours worked. For the current year, the company estimated that it would work 75,000 machine-hours and incur $450,000 in manufacturing overhead cost. The following transactions were recorded for the year:

a. Raw materials were purchased on account, $410,000.
b. Raw materials were requisitioned for use in production, $380,000 ($360,000 direct materials and $20,000 indirect materials).
c. The following costs were incurred for employee services: direct labor, $75,000; indirect labor, $110,000; sales commissions, $90,000; and administrative salaries, $200,000.
d. Sales travel costs were incurred, $17,000.
e. Utility costs were incurred in the factory, $43,000.
f. Advertising costs were incurred, $180,000.
g. Depreciation was recorded for the year, $350,000 (80% relates to factory operations, and 20% relates to selling and administrative activities).
h. Insurance expired during the year, $10,000 (70% relates to factory operations, and the remaining 30% relates to selling and administrative activities).
i. Manufacturing overhead was applied to production. Due to greater than expected demand for its products, the company worked 80,000 machine-hours during the year.
j. Goods costing $900,000 to manufacture according to their job cost sheets were completed during the year.
k. Goods were sold on account to customers during the year at a total selling price of $1,500,000. The goods cost $870,000 to manufacture according to their job cost sheets.

Required:
1. Prepare journal entries to record the preceding transactions.
2. Post the entries in (1) above to T-accounts (don't forget to enter the opening balances in the inventory accounts).
3. Is Manufacturing Overhead underapplied or overapplied for the year? Prepare a journal entry to close any balance in the Manufacturing Overhead account to Cost of Goods Sold. Do not allocate the balance between ending inventories and Cost of Goods Sold.
4. Prepare an income statement for the year.

SOLUTION TO REVIEW PROBLEM

1. *a.* Raw Materials	410,000	
Accounts Payable		410,000
b. Work in Process	360,000	
Manufacturing Overhead	20,000	
Raw Materials		380,000
c. Work in Process	75,000	
Manufacturing Overhead	110,000	
Sales Commissions Expense	90,000	
Administrative Salaries Expense	200,000	
Salaries and Wages Payable		475,000
d. Sales Travel Expense	17,000	
Accounts Payable		17,000
e. Manufacturing Overhead	43,000	
Accounts Payable		43,000
f. Advertising Expense	180,000	
Accounts Payable		180,000
g. Manufacturing Overhead	280,000	
Depreciation Expense	70,000	
Accumulated Depreciation		350,000

h. Manufacturing Overhead 7,000
　　Insurance Expense 3,000
　　　　Prepaid Insurance   10,000

i. The predetermined overhead rate for the year would be computed as follows:

$$\frac{\text{Estimated manufacturing overhead, \$450,000}}{\text{Estimated machine-hours, 75,000}} = \$6 \text{ per machine-hour}$$

Based on the 80,000 machine-hours actually worked during the year, the company would have applied $480,000 in overhead cost to production: 80,000 machine-hours × $6 per machine-hour = $480,000. The following entry records this application of overhead cost:

　　Work in Process 480,000
　　　　Manufacturing Overhead   480,000
j. Finished Goods 900,000
　　　　Work in Process   900,000
k. Accounts Receivable 1,500,000
　　　　Sales   1,500,000
　　Cost of Goods Sold 870,000
　　　　Finished Goods   870,000

2.

Accounts Receivable				Manufacturing Overhead					Sales		
(k)	1,500,000			(b)	20,000	(i)	480,000			(k)	1,500,000
				(c)	110,000						
				(e)	43,000						

Prepaid Insurance

		(h)	10,000

Manufacturing Overhead (continued):
(g)	280,000		
(h)	7,000		
	460,000		480,000
Bal.		20,000	

Cost of Goods Sold

(k)	870,000		

Raw Materials

Bal.	20,000	(b)	380,000
(a)	410,000		
Bal.	50,000		

Commissions Expense

(c)	90,000		

Accumulated Depreciation

		(g)	350,000

Administrative Salary Expense

(c)	200,000		

Work in Process

Bal.	15,000	(j)	900,000
(b)	360,000		
(c)	75,000		
(i)	480,000		
Bal.	30,000		

Accounts Payable

		(a)	410,000
		(d)	17,000
		(e)	43,000
		(f)	180,000

Sales Travel Expense

(d)	17,000		

Finished Goods

Bal.	30,000	(k)	870,000
(j)	900,000		
Bal.	60,000		

Salaries and Wages Payable

		(c)	475,000

Advertising Expense

(f)	180,000		

Depreciation Expense

(g)	70,000		

Insurance Expense

(h)	3,000		

3. Manufacturing overhead is overapplied for the year. The entry to close it out to Cost of Goods Sold is as follows:

Manufacturing Overhead	20,000	
Cost of Goods Sold		20,000

4.

HOGLE COMPANY Income Statement For the Year Ended December 31		
Sales		$1,500,000
Less cost of goods sold ($870,000 − $20,000)		850,000
Gross margin		650,000
Less selling and administrative expenses:		
Commissions expense	$ 90,000	
Administrative salaries expense	200,000	
Sales travel expense	17,000	
Advertising expense	180,000	
Depreciation expense	70,000	
Insurance expense	3,000	560,000
Net income		$ 90,000

Glossary

Absorption costing   A costing method that includes all manufacturing costs—direct materials, direct labor, and both variable and fixed overhead—as part of the cost of a finished unit of product. This term is synonymous with *full cost.* (p. 70)

Allocation base   A measure of activity such as direct labor-hours or machine-hours that is used to assign costs to cost objects. (p. 76)

Bill of materials   A document that shows the type and quantity of each major item of materials required to make a product. (p. 72)

Cost driver   A factor, such as machine-hours, beds occupied, computer time, or flight-hours, that causes overhead costs. (p. 78)

Full cost   See *Absorption costing.* (p. 70)

Job cost sheet   A form prepared for each job that records the materials, labor, and overhead costs charged to the job. (p. 73)

Job-order costing system   A costing system used in situations where many different products, jobs, or services are produced each period. (p. 71)

Materials requisition form   A detailed source document that specifies the type and quantity of materials that are to be drawn from the storeroom and identifies the job to which the costs of materials are to be charged. (p. 72)

Multiple predetermined overhead rates   A costing system in which there are multiple overhead cost pools with a different predetermined rate for each cost pool, rather than a single predetermined overhead rate for the entire company. Frequently, each production department is treated as a separate overhead cost pool. (p. 93)

Normal cost system   A costing system in which overhead costs are applied to jobs by multiplying a predetermined overhead rate by the actual amount of the allocation base incurred by the job. (p. 77)

Overapplied overhead   A credit balance in the Manufacturing Overhead account that arises when the amount of overhead cost applied to Work in Process is greater than the amount of overhead cost actually incurred during a period. (p. 91)

Overhead application   The process of charging manufacturing overhead cost to job cost sheets and to the Work in Process account. (p. 76)

Plantwide overhead rate   A single predetermined overhead rate that is used throughout a plant. (p. 93)

Predetermined overhead rate   A rate used to charge overhead cost to jobs in production; the rate is established in advance for each period by use of estimates of total manufacturing overhead cost and of the total allocation base for the period. (p. 76)

Process costing system   A costing system used in those manufacturing situations where a single, homogeneous product (such as cement or flour) is produced for long periods of time. (p. 70)

Time ticket   A detailed source document that is used to record an employee's hour-by-hour activities during a day. (p. 73)

Underapplied overhead   A debit balance in the Manufacturing Overhead account that arises when the amount of overhead cost actually incurred is greater than the amount of overhead cost applied to Work in Process during a period. (p. 91)

Questions

2–1   Why aren't actual overhead costs traced to jobs just as direct materials and direct labor costs are traced to jobs?

2–2   When would job-order costing be used in preference to process costing?

2–3   What is the purpose of the job cost sheet in a job-order costing system?

2–4   What is a predetermined overhead rate, and how is it computed?

2–5   Explain how a sales order, a production order, a materials requisition form, and a labor time ticket are involved in producing and costing products.

2–6   Explain why some production costs must be assigned to products through an allocation process. Name several such costs. Would such costs be classified as *direct* or as *indirect* costs?

2–7   Why do firms use predetermined overhead rates rather than actual manufacturing overhead costs in applying overhead to jobs?

2–8   What factors should be considered in selecting a base to be used in computing the predetermined overhead rate?

2–9   If a company fully allocates all of its overhead costs to jobs, does this guarantee that a profit will be earned for the period?

2–10   What account is credited when overhead cost is applied to Work in Process? Would you expect the amount applied for a period to equal the actual overhead costs of the period? Why or why not?

2–11   What is underapplied overhead? Overapplied overhead? What disposition is made of these amounts at the end of the period?

2–12   Give two reasons why overhead might be underapplied in a given year.

2–13   What adjustment is made for underapplied overhead on the schedule of cost of goods sold? What adjustment is made for overapplied overhead?

2–14   Sigma Company applies overhead cost to jobs on the basis of direct labor cost. Job A, which was started and completed during the current period, shows charges of $5,000 for direct materials, $8,000 for direct labor, and $6,000 for overhead on its job cost sheet. Job B, which is still in process at year-end, shows charges of $2,500 for direct materials and $4,000 for direct labor. Should any overhead cost be added to job B at year-end? Explain.

2–15   A company assigns overhead cost to completed jobs on the basis of 125% of direct labor cost. The job cost sheet for job 313 shows that $10,000 in direct materials has been used on the job and that $12,000 in direct labor cost has been incurred. If 1,000 units were produced in job 313, what is the cost per unit?

2–16   What is a plantwide overhead rate? Why are multiple overhead rates, rather than a plantwide rate, used in some companies?

2–17   What happens to overhead rates based on direct labor when automated equipment replaces direct labor?

Brief Exercises

BRIEF EXERCISE 2–1   Process versus Job-Order Costing (LO1)
Which method of determining product costs, job-order costing or process costing, would be more appropriate in each of the following situations?
a. An Elmer's glue factory.
b. A textbook publisher such as McGraw-Hill.
c. An Exxon oil refinery.
d. A facility that makes Minute Maid frozen orange juice.
e. A Scott paper mill.
f. A custom home builder.

g. A shop that customizes vans.
h. A manufacturer of specialty chemicals.
i. An auto repair shop.
j. A Firestone tire manufacturing plant.
k. An advertising agency.
l. A law office.

BRIEF EXERCISE 2–2 Job-Order Costing Documents (LO2)

Cycle Gear Corporation has incurred the following costs on job number W456, an order for 20 special sprockets to be delivered at the end of next month.

Direct materials:

On April 10, requisition number 15673 was issued for 20 titanium blanks to be used in the special order. The blanks cost $15.00 each.

On April 11, requisition number 15678 was issued for 480 hardened nibs also to be used in the special order. The nibs cost $1.25 each.

Direct labor:

On April 12, Jamie Unser worked from 11:00 AM until 2:45 PM on Job W456. He is paid $9.60 per hour.

On April 18, Melissa Chan worked from 8:15 AM until 11:30 AM on Job W456. She is paid $12.20 per hour.

Required:
1. On what documents would these costs be recorded?
2. How much cost should have been recorded on each of the documents for Job W456?

BRIEF EXERCISE 2–3 Compute the Predetermined Overhead Rate (LO3)

Harris Fabrics computes its predetermined overhead rate annually on the basis of direct labor hours. At the beginning of the year it estimated that its total manufacturing overhead would be $134,000 and the total direct labor would be 20,000 hours. Its actual total manufacturing overhead for the year was $123,900 and its actual total direct labor was 21,000 hours.

Required:
Compute the company's predetermined overhead rate for the year.

BRIEF EXERCISE 2–4 Prepare Journal Entries (LO4)

Larned Corporation recorded the following transactions for the just completed month.
a. $80,000 in raw materials were purchased on account.
b. $71,000 in raw materials were requisitioned for use in production. Of this amount, $62,000 was for direct materials and the remainder was for indirect materials.
c. Total labor wages of $112,000 were incurred. Of this amount, $101,000 was for direct labor and the remainder was for indirect labor.
d. Additional manufacturing overhead costs of $175,000 were incurred.

Required:
Record the above transactions in journal entries.

BRIEF EXERCISE 2–5 Apply Overhead (LO5)

Luthan Company uses a predetermined overhead rate of $23.40 per direct labor-hour. This predetermined rate was based on 11,000 estimated direct labor-hours and $257,400 of estimated total manufacturing overhead.

The company incurred actual total manufacturing overhead costs of $249,000 and 10,800 total direct labor-hours during the period.

Required:
Determine the amount of manufacturing overhead that would have been applied to units of product during the period.

BRIEF EXERCISE 2–6 Prepare T-Accounts (LO6, LO7)

Jurvin Enterprises recorded the following transactions for the just completed month. The company had no beginning inventories.
a. $94,000 in raw materials were purchased for cash.

b. $89,000 in raw materials were requisitioned for use in production. Of this amount, $78,000 was for direct materials and the remainder was for indirect materials.

c. Total labor wages of $132,000 were incurred and paid. Of this amount, $112,000 was for direct labor and the remainder was for indirect labor.

d. Additional manufacturing overhead costs of $143,000 were incurred and paid.

e. Manufacturing overhead costs of $152,000 were applied to jobs using the company's predetermined overhead rate.

f. All of the jobs in progress at the end of the month were completed and shipped to customers.

g. The underapplied or overapplied overhead for the period was closed out to Cost of Goods Sold.

Required:

1. Post the above transactions to T-accounts.
2. Determine the cost of goods sold for the period.

BRIEF EXERCISE 2–7   Under- and Overapplied Overhead (LO7)

Osborn Manufacturing uses a predetermined overhead rate of $18.20 per direct labor-hour. This predetermined rate was based on 12,000 estimated direct labor-hours and $218,400 of estimated total manufacturing overhead.

The company incurred actual total manufacturing overhead costs of $215,000 and 11,500 total direct labor-hours during the period.

Required:

1. Determine the amount of underapplied or overapplied manufacturing overhead for the period.
2. Assuming that the entire amount of the underapplied or overapplied overhead is closed out to Cost of Goods Sold, what would be the effect of the underapplied or overapplied overhead on the company's gross margin for the period?

Exercises

EXERCISE 2–1   Applying Overhead in a Service Firm (LO2, LO3, LO5)

Leeds Architectural Consultants began operations on January 2. The following activity was recorded in the company's Work in Process account for the first month of operations:

Work in Process

Costs of subcontracted work	230,000	To completed projects	390,000
Direct staff costs	75,000		
Studio overhead	120,000		

Leeds Architectural Consultants is a service firm, so the names of the accounts it uses are different from the names used in manufacturing firms. Costs of Subcontracted Work is basically the same thing as Direct Materials; Direct Staff Costs is the same as Direct Labor; Studio Overhead is the same as Manufacturing Overhead; and Completed Projects is the same as Finished Goods. Apart from the difference in terms, the accounting methods used by the company are identical to the methods used by manufacturing companies.

Leeds Architectural Consultants uses a job-order costing system and applies studio overhead to Work in Process on the basis of direct staff costs. At the end of January, only one job was still in process. This job (Lexington Gardens Project) had been charged with $6,500 in direct staff costs.

Required:

1. Compute the predetermined overhead rate that was in use during January.
2. Complete the following job cost sheet for the partially completed Lexington Gardens Project.

Job Cost Sheet—Lexington Gardens Project
As of January 31

Costs of subcontracted work	$?
Direct staff costs	?
Studio overhead	?
Total cost to January 31	$?

EXERCISE 2–2   Varying Predetermined Overhead Rates (LO3, LO5)
Kingsport Containers, Ltd., of the Bahamas experiences wide variation in demand for the 200-liter steel drums it fabricates. The leakproof, rustproof steel drums have a variety of uses from storing liquids and bulk materials to serving as makeshift musical instruments. The drums are made to order and are painted according to the customer's specifications—often in bright patterns and designs. The company is well known for the artwork that appears on its drums. Unit costs are computed on a quarterly basis by dividing each quarter's manufacturing costs (materials, labor, and overhead) by the quarter's production in units. The company's estimated costs, by quarter, for the coming year follow:

	Quarter			
	First	**Second**	**Third**	**Fourth**
Direct materials	$240,000	$120,000	$ 60,000	$180,000
Direct labor	128,000	64,000	32,000	96,000
Manufacturing overhead	300,000	220,000	180,000	260,000
Total manufacturing costs	$668,000	$404,000	$272,000	$536,000
Number of units to be produced	80,000	40,000	20,000	60,000
Estimated cost per unit	$8.35	$10.10	$13.60	$8.93

Management finds the variation in unit costs to be confusing and difficult to work with. It has been suggested that the problem lies with manufacturing overhead, since it is the largest element of cost. Accordingly, you have been asked to find a more appropriate way of assigning manufacturing overhead cost to units of product. After some analysis, you have determined that the company's overhead costs are mostly fixed and therefore show little sensitivity to changes in the level of production.

Required:
1. The company uses a job-order costing system. How would you recommend that manufacturing overhead cost be assigned to production? Be specific, and show computations.
2. Recompute the company's unit costs in accordance with your recommendations in (1) above.

EXERCISE 2–3   Journal Entries and T-Accounts (LO4, LO5, LO6)
The Polaris Company uses a job-order costing system. The following data relate to October, the first month of the company's fiscal year.
a. Raw materials purchased on account, $210,000.
b. Raw materials issued to production, $190,000 ($178,000 direct materials and $12,000 indirect materials).
c. Direct labor cost incurred, $90,000; indirect labor cost incurred, $110,000.
d. Depreciation recorded on factory equipment, $40,000.
e. Other manufacturing overhead costs incurred during October, $70,000 (credit Accounts Payable).
f. The company applies manufacturing overhead cost to production on the basis of $8 per machine-hour. There were 30,000 machine-hours recorded for October.
g. Production orders costing $520,000 according to their job cost sheets were completed during October and transferred to Finished Goods.
h. Production orders that had cost $480,000 to complete according to their job cost sheets were shipped to customers during the month. These goods were sold at 25% above cost. The goods were sold on account.

Required:
1. Prepare journal entries to record the information given above.
2. Prepare T-accounts for Manufacturing Overhead and Work in Process. Post the relevant information above to each account. Compute the ending balance in each account, assuming that Work in Process has a beginning balance of $42,000.

EXERCISE 2–4   Applying Overhead; Cost of Goods Manufactured (LO5, LO7)
The following cost data relate to the manufacturing activities of Chang Company during the just completed year:

Manufacturing overhead costs incurred:

Indirect materials	$ 15,000
Indirect labor	130,000
Property taxes, factory	8,000
Utilities, factory	70,000
Depreciation, factory	240,000
Insurance, factory	10,000
Total actual costs incurred	$473,000

Other costs incurred:

Purchases of raw materials (both direct and indirect)	$400,000
Direct labor cost	60,000

Inventories:

Raw materials, beginning	20,000
Raw materials, ending	30,000
Work in process, beginning	40,000
Work in process, ending	70,000

The company uses a predetermined overhead rate to apply overhead cost to production. The rate for the year was $25 per machine-hour. A total of 19,400 machine-hours was recorded for the year.

Required:
1. Compute the amount of under- or overapplied overhead cost for the year.
2. Prepare a schedule of cost of goods manufactured for the year.

EXERCISE 2–5   Applying Overhead with Differing Bases (LO3, LO5, LO7)
Estimated cost and operating data for three companies for the upcoming year follow:

	Company		
	X	**Y**	**Z**
Direct labor-hours	80,000	45,000	60,000
Machine-hours	30,000	70,000	21,000
Direct materials cost	$400,000	$290,000	$300,000
Manufacturing overhead cost	536,000	315,000	480,000

Predetermined overhead rates are computed using the following bases in the three companies:

Company	Overhead Rate Based on—
X	Direct labor-hours
Y	Machine-hours
Z	Direct materials cost

Required:
1. Compute the predetermined overhead rate to be used in each company during the upcoming year.
2. Assume that Company X works on three jobs during the upcoming year. Direct labor-hours recorded by job are: job 418, 12,000 hours; job 419, 36,000 hours; job 420, 30,000 hours. How much overhead cost will the company apply to Work in Process for the year? If actual overhead costs total $530,000 for the year, will overhead be under- or overapplied? By how much?

EXERCISE 2–6   Journal Entries; Applying Overhead (LO4, LO7)
The following information is taken from the accounts of Latta Company. The entries in the T-accounts are summaries of the transactions that affected those accounts during the year.

Manufacturing Overhead			
(a)	460,000	(b)	390,000
Bal.	70,000		

Work in Process			
Bal.	5,000	(c)	710,000
	270,000		
	85,000		
(b)	390,000		
Bal.	40,000		

Finished Goods			
Bal.	50,000	(d)	640,000
(c)	710,000		
Bal.	120,000		

Cost of Goods Sold			
(d)	640,000		

The overhead that had been applied to Work in Process during the year is distributed among the ending balances in the accounts as follows:

Work in Process, ending	$ 19,500
Finished Goods, ending	58,500
Cost of Goods Sold	312,000
Overhead applied	$390,000

For example, of the $40,000 ending balance in Work in Process, $19,500 was overhead that had been applied during the year.

Required:
1. Identify reasons for entries (a) through (d).
2. Assume that the company closes any balance in the Manufacturing Overhead account directly to Cost of Goods Sold. Prepare the necessary journal entry.

EXERCISE 2–7   Applying Overhead; Journal Entries; T-Accounts (LO3, LO4, LO5, LO6)
Dillon Products manufactures various machined parts to customer specifications. The company uses a job-order costing system and applies overhead cost to jobs on the basis of machine-hours. At the beginning of the year, it was estimated that the company would work 240,000 machine-hours and incur $4,800,000 in manufacturing overhead costs.

The company spent the entire month of January working on a large order for 16,000 custom-made machined parts. The company had no work in process at the beginning of January. Cost data relating to January follow:
a. Raw materials purchased on account, $325,000.
b. Raw materials requisitioned for production, $290,000 (80% direct materials and 20% indirect materials).
c. Labor cost incurred in the factory, $180,000 (one-third direct labor and two-thirds indirect labor).
d. Depreciation recorded on factory equipment, $75,000.
e. Other manufacturing overhead costs incurred, $62,000 (credit Accounts Payable).
f. Manufacturing overhead cost was applied to production on the basis of 15,000 machine-hours actually worked during the month.
g. The completed job was moved into the finished goods warehouse on January 31 to await delivery to the customer. (In computing the dollar amount for this entry, remember that the cost of a completed job consists of direct materials, direct labor, and *applied* overhead.)

Required:
1. Prepare journal entries to record items (a) through (f) above [ignore item (g) for the moment].
2. Prepare T-accounts for Manufacturing Overhead and Work in Process. Post the relevant items from your journal entries to these T-accounts.
3. Prepare a journal entry for item (g) above.
4. Compute the unit cost that will appear on the job cost sheet.

Problems

CHECK FIGURE
(2) Overhead applied to job
203: $870

PROBLEM 2–1   Departmental Overhead Rates (LO2, LO3, LO5)
White Company has two departments, Cutting and Finishing. The company uses a job-order cost system and computes a predetermined overhead rate in each department. The Cutting Department bases its rate on machine-hours, and the Finishing Department bases its rate on direct labor cost. At the beginning of the year, the company made the following estimates:

	Department	
	Cutting	**Finishing**
Direct labor-hours	6,000	30,000
Machine-hours	48,000	5,000
Manufacturing overhead cost	$360,000	$486,000
Direct labor cost	50,000	270,000

Required:
1. Compute the predetermined overhead rate to be used in each department.
2. Assume that the overhead rates that you computed in (1) above are in effect. The job cost sheet for job 203, which was started and completed during the year, showed the following:

	Department	
	Cutting	**Finishing**
Direct labor-hours	6	20
Machine-hours	80	4
Materials requisitioned	$500	$310
Direct labor cost	70	150

Compute the total overhead cost applied to job 203.
3. Would you expect substantially different amounts of overhead cost to be assigned to some jobs if the company used a plantwide overhead rate based on direct labor cost, rather than using departmental rates? Explain. No computations are necessary.

CHECK FIGURE
(3) Underapplied by $4,000

PROBLEM 2–2   Applying Overhead; T-Accounts; Journal Entries (LO3, LO4, LO5, LO6, LO7)
Harwood Company is a manufacturing firm that operates a job-order costing system. Overhead costs are applied to jobs on the basis of machine-hours. At the beginning of the year, management estimated that the company would incur $192,000 in manufacturing overhead costs and work 80,000 machine-hours.

Required:
1. Compute the company's predetermined overhead rate.
2. Assume that during the year the company works only 75,000 machine-hours and incurs the following costs in the Manufacturing Overhead and Work in Process accounts:

Manufacturing Overhead				Work in Process		
(Maintenance)	21,000		?	(Direct materials)	710,000	
(Indirect materials)	8,000			(Direct labor)	90,000	
(Indirect labor)	60,000			(Overhead)	?	
(Utilities)	32,000					
(Insurance)	7,000					
(Depreciation)	56,000					

Copy the data in the T-accounts above onto your answer sheet. Compute the amount of overhead cost that would be applied to Work in Process for the year and make the entry in your T-accounts.

3. Compute the amount of under- or overapplied overhead for the year and show the balance in your Manufacturing Overhead T-account. Prepare a general journal entry to close out the balance in this account to Cost of Goods Sold.
4. Explain why the manufacturing overhead was under- or overapplied for the year.

PROBLEM 2–3 Applying Overhead in a Service Firm; Journal Entries (LO4, LO5, LO7)

CHECK FIGURE
(3) Balance in WIP: $16,700

Vista Landscaping uses a job-order costing system to track the costs of its landscaping projects. The company provides garden design services as well as actually carrying out the landscaping for the client. The table below provides data concerning the three landscaping projects that were in progress during April. There was no work in process at the beginning of April.

	Project		
	Harris	**Chan**	**James**
Designer-hours	120	100	90
Direct materials cost	$4,500	$3,700	$1,400
Direct labor cost	9,600	8,000	7,200

Actual overhead costs were $30,000 for April. Overhead costs are applied to projects on the basis of designer-hours since most of the overhead is related to the costs of the garden design studio. The predetermined overhead rate is $90 per designer-hour. The Harris and Chan projects were completed in April; the James project was not completed by the end of the month.

Required:
1. Compute the amount of overhead cost that would have been charged to each project during April.
2. Prepare a journal entry showing the completion of the Harris and Chan projects and the transfer of costs to the Completed Projects (i.e., Finished Goods) account.
3. What is the balance in the Work in Process account at the end of the month?
4. What is the balance in the Overhead account at the end of the month? What is this balance called?

PROBLEM 2–4 Comprehensive Problem (LO3, LO4, LO5, LO6, LO7)

CHECK FIGURE
(3) Overapplied by
Rmb7,000
(4) NI: Rmb247,000

Gold Nest Company of Guandong, China, is a family-owned enterprise that makes birdcages for the South China market. A popular pastime among older Chinese men is to take their pet birds on daily excursions to teahouses and public parks where they meet with other bird owners to talk and play mahjong. A great deal of attention is lavished on these birds, and the birdcages are often elaborately constructed from exotic woods and contain porcelain feeding bowls and silver roosts. Gold Nest Company makes a broad range of birdcages that it sells through an extensive network of street vendors who receive commissions on their sales. The Chinese currency is the renminbi, which is denoted by Rmb. All of the company's transactions with customers, employees, and suppliers are conducted in cash; there is no credit.

The company uses a job-order costing system in which overhead is applied to jobs on the basis of direct labor cost. At the beginning of the year, it was estimated that the total direct labor cost for the year would be Rmb200,000 and the total manufacturing overhead cost would be Rmb330,000. At the beginning of the year, the inventory balances were as follows:

Raw materials	Rmb25,000
Work in process	10,000
Finished goods	40,000

During the year, the following transactions were completed:

a. Raw materials purchased for cash, Rmb275,000.

b. Raw materials requisitioned for use in production, Rmb280,000 (materials costing Rmb220,000 were charged directly to jobs; the remaining materials were indirect).

c. Costs for employee services were incurred as follows:

Direct labor	Rmb180,000
Indirect labor	72,000
Sales commissions	63,000
Administrative salaries	90,000

d. Rent for the year was Rmb18,000 (Rmb13,000 of this amount related to factory operations, and the remainder related to selling and administrative activities).

e. Utility costs incurred in the factory, Rmb57,000.

f. Advertising costs incurred, Rmb140,000.

g. Depreciation recorded on equipment, Rmb100,000. (Rmb88,000 of this amount was on equipment used in factory operations; the remaining Rmb12,000 was on equipment used in selling and administrative activities.)

h. Manufacturing overhead cost was applied to jobs, Rmb ____?____ .

i. Goods that cost Rmb675,000 to manufacture according to their job cost sheets were completed during the year.

j. Sales for the year totaled Rmb1,250,000. The total cost to manufacture these goods according to their job cost sheets was Rmb700,000.

Required:

1. Prepare journal entries to record the transactions for the year.

2. Prepare T-accounts for inventories, Manufacturing Overhead, and Cost of Goods Sold. Post relevant data from your journal entries to these T-accounts (don't forget to enter the beginning balances in your inventory accounts). Compute an ending balance in each account.

3. Is Manufacturing Overhead underapplied or overapplied for the year? Prepare a journal entry to close any balance in the Manufacturing Overhead account to Cost of Goods Sold.

4. Prepare an income statement for the year. (Do not prepare a schedule of cost of goods manufactured; all of the information needed for the income statement is available in the journal entries and T-accounts you have prepared.)

CHECK FIGURE
(3) Indirect labor: $30,000
(7) Overapplied: $10,000

PROBLEM 2–5   T-Account Analysis of Cost Flows (LO3, LO6, LO7)

Selected ledger accounts of Moore Company are given below for the just completed year:

Raw Materials

Bal. 1/1	15,000	Credits	?
Debits	120,000		
Bal. 12/31	25,000		

Manufacturing Overhead

Debits	230,000	Credits	?

Work in Process

Bal. 1/1	20,000	Credits	470,000
Direct materials	90,000		
Direct labor	150,000		
Overhead	240,000		
Bal. 12/31	?		

Factory Wages Payable

Debits	185,000	Bal. 1/1	9,000
		Credits	180,000
		Bal. 12/31	4,000

Finished Goods

Bal. 1/1	40,000	Credits	?
Debits	?		
Bal. 12/31	60,000		

Cost of Goods Sold

Debits	?	

Required:

1. What was the cost of raw materials put into production during the year?

2. How much of the materials in (1) above consisted of indirect materials?
3. How much of the factory labor cost for the year consisted of indirect labor?
4. What was the cost of goods manufactured for the year?
5. What was the cost of goods sold for the year (before considering under- or overapplied overhead)?
6. If overhead is applied to production on the basis of direct labor cost, what rate was in effect during the year?
7. Was manufacturing overhead under- or overapplied? By how much?
8. Compute the ending balance in the Work in Process inventory account. Assume that this balance consists entirely of goods started during the year. If $8,000 of this balance is direct labor cost, how much of it is direct materials cost? Manufacturing overhead cost?

PROBLEM 2–6   Overhead Analysis; Schedule of Cost of Goods Manufactured (LO3, LO5, LO7)
Gitano Products operates a job-order cost system and applies overhead cost to jobs on the basis of direct materials *used in production* (*not* on the basis of raw materials purchased). In computing a predetermined overhead rate at the beginning of the year, the company's estimates were: manufacturing overhead cost, $800,000; and direct materials to be used in production, $500,000. The company's inventory accounts at the beginning and end of the year were:

CHECK FIGURE
(2) COGM: $1,340,000

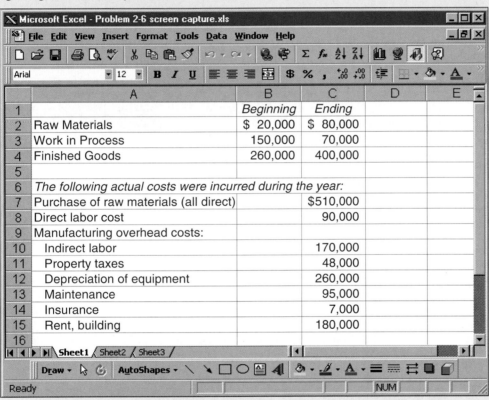

	Beginning	Ending
Raw Materials	$ 20,000	$ 80,000
Work in Process	150,000	70,000
Finished Goods	260,000	400,000

The following actual costs were incurred during the year:

Purchase of raw materials (all direct)	$510,000
Direct labor cost	90,000
Manufacturing overhead costs:	
Indirect labor	170,000
Property taxes	48,000
Depreciation of equipment	260,000
Maintenance	95,000
Insurance	7,000
Rent, building	180,000

Required:
1. a. Compute the predetermined overhead rate for the year.
   b. Compute the amount of under- or overapplied overhead for the year.
2. Prepare a schedule of cost of goods manufactured for the year.
3. Compute the Cost of Goods Sold for the year. (Do not include any under- or overapplied overhead in your Cost of Goods Sold figure.)
4. Job 215 was started and completed during the year. What price would have been charged to the customer if the job required $8,500 in direct materials and $2,700 in direct labor cost and the company priced its jobs at 25% above cost to manufacture?
5. Direct materials made up $24,000 of the $70,000 ending Work in Process inventory balance. Supply the information missing below:

Direct materials	$24,000
Direct labor	?
Manufacturing overhead	?
Work in process inventory	$70,000

PROBLEM 2–7   Multiple Departments; Applying Overhead (LO3, LO5, LO7)
High Desert Potteryworks makes a variety of pottery products that it sells to retailers such as Home Depot. The company uses a job-order costing system in which predetermined overhead rates are used to apply manufacturing overhead cost to jobs. The predetermined overhead rate in the Molding Department is based on machine-hours, and the rate in the Painting Department is based on direct labor cost. At the beginning of the year, the company's management made the following estimates:

	Department	
	Molding	Painting
Direct labor-hours	12,000	60,000
Machine-hours	70,000	8,000
Direct materials cost	$510,000	$650,000
Direct labor cost	130,000	420,000
Manufacturing overhead cost	602,000	735,000

Job 205 was started on August 1 and completed on August 10. The company's cost records show the following information concerning the job:

	Department	
	Molding	Painting
Direct labor-hours	30	85
Machine-hours	110	20
Materials placed into production	$470	$332
Direct labor cost	290	680

Required:
1. Compute the predetermined overhead rate used during the year in the Molding Department. Compute the rate used in the Painting Department.
2. Compute the total overhead cost applied to job 205.
3. What would be the total cost recorded for job 205? If the job contained 50 units, what would be the cost per unit?
4. At the end of the year, the records of High Desert Potteryworks revealed the following *actual* cost and operating data for all jobs worked on during the year:

	Department	
	Molding	Painting
Direct labor-hours	10,000	62,000
Machine-hours	65,000	9,000
Direct materials cost	$430,000	$680,000
Direct labor cost	108,000	436,000
Manufacturing overhead cost	570,000	750,000

What was the amount of under- or overapplied overhead in each department at the end of the year?

PROBLEM 2–8   T-Accounts; Applying Overhead (LO5, LO6, LO7)
Hudson Company's trial balance as of January 1, the beginning of the fiscal year, is given below:

Cash	$ 7,000	
Accounts Receivable	18,000	
Raw Materials	9,000	
Work in Process	20,000	
Finished Goods	32,000	
Prepaid Insurance	4,000	
Plant and Equipment	210,000	
Accumulated Depreciation		$ 53,000
Accounts Payable		38,000
Capital Stock		160,000
Retained Earnings		49,000
Total	$300,000	$300,000

Hudson Company is a manufacturing firm and employs a job-order costing system. During the year, the following transactions took place:

a. Raw materials purchased on account, $40,000.
b. Raw materials were requisitioned for use in production, $38,000 (85% direct and 15% indirect).
c. Factory utility costs incurred, $19,100.
d. Depreciation was recorded on plant and equipment, $36,000. Three-fourths of the depreciation related to factory equipment, and the remainder related to selling and administrative equipment.
e. Advertising expense incurred, $48,000.
f. Costs for salaries and wages were incurred as follows:

Direct labor	$45,000
Indirect labor	10,000
Administrative salaries	30,000

g. Prepaid insurance expired during the year, $3,000 (80% related to factory operations, and 20% related to selling and administrative activities).
h. Miscellaneous selling and administrative expenses incurred, $9,500.
i. Manufacturing overhead was applied to production. The company applies overhead on the basis of $8 per machine-hour; 7,500 machine-hours were recorded for the year.
j. Goods that cost $140,000 to manufacture according to their job cost sheets were transferred to the finished goods warehouse.
k. Sales for the year totaled $250,000 and were all on account. The total cost to manufacture these goods according to their job cost sheets was $130,000.
l. Collections from customers during the year totaled $245,000.
m. Payments to suppliers on account during the year, $150,000; payments to employees for salaries and wages, $84,000.

Required:
1. Prepare a T-account for each account in the company's trial balance and enter the opening balances shown above.
2. Record the transactions above directly into the T-accounts. Prepare new T-accounts as needed. Key your entries to the letters (a) through (m) above. Find the ending balance in each account.
3. Is manufacturing overhead underapplied or overapplied for the year? Make an entry in the T-accounts to close any balance in the Manufacturing Overhead account to Cost of Goods Sold.
4. Prepare an income statement for the year. (Do not prepare a schedule of cost of goods manufactured; all of the information needed for the income statement is available in the T-accounts.)

PROBLEM 2–9   Journal Entries; T-Accounts; Cost Flows (LO4, LO5, LO6, LO7)
Almeda Products, Inc., uses a job-order cost system. The company's inventory balances on April 1, the start of its fiscal year, were as follows:

CHECK FIGURE
(3) Underapplied by $4,000
(4) NI: $57,000

Raw materials	$32,000
Work in process	20,000
Finished goods	48,000

During the year, the following transactions were completed:

a. Raw materials were purchased on account, $170,000.

b. Raw materials were issued from the storeroom for use in production, $180,000 (80% direct and 20% indirect).

c. Employee salaries and wages were accrued as follows: direct labor, $200,000; indirect labor, $82,000; and selling and administrative salaries, $90,000.

d. Utility costs were incurred in the factory, $65,000.

e. Advertising costs were incurred, $100,000.

f. Prepaid insurance expired during the year, $20,000 (90% related to factory operations, and 10% related to selling and administrative activities).

g. Depreciation was recorded, $180,000 (85% related to factory assets, and 15% related to selling and administrative assets).

h. Manufacturing overhead was applied to jobs at the rate of 175% of direct labor cost.

i. Goods that cost $700,000 to manufacture according to their job cost sheets were transferred to the finished goods warehouse.

j. Sales for the year totaled $1,000,000 and were all on account. The total cost to manufacture these goods according to their job cost sheets was $720,000.

Required:

1. Prepare journal entries to record the transactions for the year.

2. Prepare T-accounts for Raw Materials, Work in Process, Finished Goods, Manufacturing Overhead, and Cost of Goods Sold. Post the appropriate parts of your journal entries to these T-accounts. Compute the ending balance in each account. (Don't forget to enter the beginning balances in the inventory accounts.)

3. Is Manufacturing Overhead underapplied or overapplied for the year? Prepare a journal entry to close this balance to Cost of Goods Sold.

4. Prepare an income statement for the year. (Do not prepare a schedule of cost of goods manufactured; all of the information needed for the income statement is available in the journal entries and T-accounts you have prepared.)

CHECK FIGURE
(3) Overapplied by $9,400
(4) NI: $78,400

PROBLEM 2–10 Cost Flows; T-Accounts; Income Statement (LO3, LO5, LO6, LO7)
Supreme Videos, Inc., produces short musical videos for sale to retail outlets. The company's balance sheet accounts as of January 1, the beginning of the fiscal year, are given below.

SUPREME VIDEOS, INC.
Balance Sheet
January 1

Assets

Current assets:		
Cash		$ 63,000
Accounts receivable		102,000
Inventories:		
Raw materials (film, costumes)	$ 30,000	
Videos in process	45,000	
Finished videos awaiting sale	81,000	156,000
Prepaid insurance		9,000
Total current assets		330,000
Studio and equipment	730,000	
Less accumulated depreciation	210,000	520,000
Total assets		$850,000

Liabilities and Stockholders' Equity

Accounts payable		$160,000
Capital stock	$420,000	
Retained earnings	270,000	690,000
Total liabilities and stockholders' equity		$850,000

Since the videos differ in length and in complexity of production, the company uses a job-order costing system to determine the cost of each video produced. Studio (manufacturing) overhead is charged to videos on the basis of camera-hours of activity. At the beginning of the year, the company estimated that it would work 7,000 camera-hours and incur $280,000 in studio overhead cost. The following transactions were recorded for the year:

a. Film, costumes, and similar raw materials purchased on account, $185,000.
b. Film, costumes, and other raw materials issued to production, $200,000 (85% of this material was considered direct to the videos in production, and the other 15% was considered indirect).
c. Utility costs incurred in the production studio, $72,000.
d. Depreciation recorded on the studio, cameras, and other equipment, $84,000. Three-fourths of this depreciation related to actual production of the videos, and the remainder related to equipment used in marketing and administration.
e. Advertising expense incurred, $130,000.
f. Costs for salaries and wages were incurred as follows:

Direct labor (actors and directors)	$ 82,000
Indirect labor (carpenters to build sets, costume designers, and so forth)	110,000
Administrative salaries	95,000

g. Prepaid insurance expired during the year, $7,000 (80% related to production of videos, and 20% related to marketing and administrative activities).
h. Miscellaneous marketing and administrative expenses incurred, $8,600.
i. Studio (manufacturing) overhead was applied to videos in production. The company recorded 7,250 camera-hours of activity during the year.
j. Videos that cost $550,000 to produce according to their job cost sheets were transferred to the finished videos warehouse to await sale and shipment.
k. Sales for the year totaled $925,000 and were all on account. The total cost to produce these videos according to their job cost sheets was $600,000.
l. Collections from customers during the year totaled $850,000.
m. Payments to suppliers on account during the year, $500,000; payments to employees for salaries and wages, $285,000.

Required:

1. Prepare a T-account for each account on the company's balance sheet and enter the opening balances.
2. Record the transactions directly into the T-accounts. Prepare new T-accounts as needed. Key your entries to the letters (a) through (m) above. Find the ending balance in each account.
3. Is the Studio (manufacturing) Overhead account underapplied or overapplied for the year? Make an entry in the T-accounts to close any balance in the Studio Overhead account to Cost of Goods Sold.
4. Prepare an income statement for the year. (Do not prepare a schedule of cost of goods manufactured; all of the information needed for the income statement is available in the T-accounts.)

Building Your Skills

ANALYTICAL THINKING (LO3, LO5)

Kelvin Aerospace, Inc., manufactures parts such as rudder hinges for the aerospace industry. The company uses a job-order costing system with a plantwide predetermined overhead rate based on direct labor-hours. On December 16, 1999, the company's controller made a preliminary estimate of the predetermined overhead rate for the year 2000. The new rate was based on the estimated total manufacturing overhead cost of $3,402,000 and the estimated 63,000 total direct labor-hours for 2000:

$$\text{Predetermined overhead rate} = \frac{\$3,402,000}{63,000 \text{ direct labor-hours}}$$
$$= \$54 \text{ per direct labor-hour}$$

This new predetermined overhead rate was communicated to top managers in a meeting on December 19. The rate did not cause any comment because it was within a few pennies of the overhead rate that had been used during 1999. One of the subjects discussed at the meeting was a proposal by the production manager to purchase an automated milling machine built by Sunghi Industries. The president of Kelvin Aerospace, Harry Arcany, agreed to meet with the sales representative from Sunghi Industries to discuss the proposal.

On the day following the meeting, Mr. Arcany met with Jasmine Chang, Sunghi Industries' sales representative. The following discussion took place:

Arcany: Wally, our production manager, asked me to meet with you since he is interested in installing an automated milling machine. Frankly, I'm skeptical. You're going to have to show me this isn't just another expensive toy for Wally's people to play with.

Chang: This is a great machine with direct bottom-line benefits. The automated milling machine has three major advantages. First, it is much faster than the manual methods you are using. It can process about twice as many parts per hour as your present milling machines. Second, it is much more flexible. There are some up-front programming costs, but once those have been incurred, almost no setup is required to run a standard operation. You just punch in the code for the standard operation, load the machine's hopper with raw material, and the machine does the rest.

Arcany: What about cost? Having twice the capacity in the milling machine area won't do us much good. That center is idle much of the time anyway.

Chang: I was getting there. The third advantage of the automated milling machine is lower cost. Wally and I looked over your present operations, and we estimated that the automated equipment would eliminate the need for about 6,000 direct labor-hours a year. What is your direct labor cost per hour?

Arcany: The wage rate in the milling area averages about $32 per hour. Fringe benefits raise that figure to about $41 per hour.

Chang: Don't forget your overhead.

Arcany: Next year the overhead rate will be $54 per hour.

Chang: So including fringe benefits and overhead, the cost per direct labor-hour is about $95.

Arcany: That's right.

Chang: Since you can save 6,000 direct labor-hours per year, the cost savings would amount to about $570,000 a year. And our 60-month lease plan would require payments of only $348,000 per year.

Arcany: That sounds like a no-brainer. When could you install the equipment?

Shortly after this meeting, Mr. Arcany informed the company's controller of the decision to lease the new equipment, which would be installed over the Christmas vacation period. The controller realized that this decision would require a recomputation of the predetermined overhead rate for the year 2000 since the decision would affect both the manufacturing overhead and the direct labor-hours for the year. After talking with both the production manager and the sales representative from Sunghi Industries, the controller discovered that in addition to the annual lease cost of $348,000, the new machine would also require a skilled technician/programmer who would have to be hired at a cost of $50,000 per year to maintain and program the equipment. Both of these costs would be included in factory overhead. There would be no other changes in total manufacturing overhead cost, which is almost entirely fixed. The controller assumed that the new machine would result in a reduction of 6,000 direct labor-hours for the year from the levels that had initially been planned.

When the revised predetermined overhead rate for the year 2000 was circulated among the company's top managers, there was considerable dismay.

Required:
1. Recompute the predetermined rate assuming that the new machine will be installed. Explain why the new predetermined overhead rate is higher (or lower) than the rate that was originally estimated for the year 2000.
2. What effect (if any) would this new rate have on the cost of jobs that do not use the new automated milling machine?
3. Why would managers be concerned about the new overhead rate?
4. After seeing the new predetermined overhead rate, the production manager admitted that he probably wouldn't be able to eliminate all of the 6,000 direct labor-hours. He had been hoping to accomplish the reduction by not replacing workers who retire or quit, but that had not been possible. As a result, the real labor savings would be only about 2,000 hours—one worker. In the light of this additional information, evaluate the original decision to acquire the automated milling machine from Sunghi Industries.

COMMUNICATING IN PRACTICE   (LO1, LO3, LO5)
Look in the yellow pages or contact your local chamber of commerce or local chapter of the Institute of Certified Management Accountants to find the names of manufacturing companies in your area. Call or make an appointment to meet with the controller or chief financial officer of one of these companies.

Required:
Ask the following questions and write a brief memorandum to your instructor that addresses what you found out.

1. What are the company's main products?
2. Does the company use job-order costing, process costing, or some other method of determining product costs?
3. How is overhead assigned to products? What is the overhead rate? What is the basis of allocation? Is more than one overhead rate used?
4. Has the company recently changed its cost system or is it considering changing its cost system? If so, why? What changes were made or what changes are being considered?

ETHICS CHALLENGE   (LO3, LO5)

Terri Ronsin had recently been transferred to the Home Security Systems Division of National Home Products. Shortly after taking over her new position as divisional controller, she was asked to develop the division's predetermined overhead rate for the upcoming year. The accuracy of the rate is of some importance, since it is used throughout the year and any overapplied or underapplied overhead is closed out to Cost of Goods Sold only at the end of the year. National Home Products uses direct labor-hours in all of its divisions as the allocation base for manufacturing overhead.

To compute the predetermined overhead rate, Terri divided her estimate of the total manufacturing overhead for the coming year by the production manager's estimate of the total direct labor-hours for the coming year. She took her computations to the division's general manager for approval but was quite surprised when he suggested a modification in the base. Her conversation with the general manager of the Home Security Systems Division, Harry Irving, went like this:

Ronsin: Here are my calculations for next year's predetermined overhead rate. If you approve, we can enter the rate into the computer on January 1 and be up and running in the job-order costing system right away this year.

Irving: Thanks for coming up with the calculations so quickly, and they look just fine. There is, however, one slight modification I would like to see. Your estimate of the total direct labor-hours for the year is 440,000 hours. How about cutting that to about 420,000 hours?

Ronsin: I don't know if I can do that. The production manager says she will need about 440,000 direct labor-hours to meet the sales projections for the year. Besides, there are going to be over 430,000 direct labor-hours during the current year and sales are projected to be higher next year.

Irving: Teri, I know all of that. I would still like to reduce the direct labor-hours in the base to something like 420,000 hours. You probably don't know that I had an agreement with your predecessor as divisional controller to shave 5% or so off the estimated direct labor-hours every year. That way, we kept a reserve that usually resulted in a big boost to net income at the end of the fiscal year in December. We called it our Christmas bonus. Corporate headquarters always seemed as pleased as punch that we could pull off such a miracle at the end of the year. This system has worked well for many years, and I don't want to change it now.

Required:
1. Explain how shaving 5% off the estimated direct labor-hours in the base for the predetermined overhead rate usually results in a big boost in net income at the end of the fiscal year.
2. Should Terri Ronsin go along with the general manager's request to reduce the direct labor-hours in the predetermined overhead rate computation to 420,000 direct labor-hours?

TAKING IT TO THE NET

As you know, the World Wide Web is a medium that is constantly evolving. Sites come and go, and change without notice. To enable periodic update of site addresses, this problem has been posted to the textbook website (www.mhhe.com/folk1e). After accessing the site, enter the Student Center and select this chapter. Select and complete the Taking It to the Net problem.

TEAMWORK IN ACTION   (LO3, LO4, LO5, LO6, LO7)

CHECK FIGURE
(3) WIP inventory: $14,300

In an attempt to conceal a theft of funds, Snake N. Grass, controller of Bucolic Products, Inc., placed a bomb in the company's record vault. The ensuing explosion left only fragments of the company's factory ledger, as shown below:

Raw Materials		Manufacturing Overhead	
Bal. 6/1 8,000		Actual costs for June 79,000	
		Overapplied overhead 6,100	

Work in Process		
Bal. 6/1	7,200	

Accounts Payable		
		Bal. 6/30 16,000

Finished Goods		
Bal. 6/30	21,000	

Cost of Goods Sold		

To bring Mr. Grass to justice, the company must reconstruct its activities for June. Your team has been assigned to perform the task of reconstruction. After interviewing selected employees and sifting through charred fragments, you have determined the following additional information:

a. According to the company's treasurer, the accounts payable are for purchases of raw materials only. The company's balance sheet, dated May 31, shows that Accounts Payable had a $20,000 balance at the beginning of June. The company's bank has provided photocopies of all checks that cleared the bank during June. These photocopies show that payments to suppliers during June totaled $119,000. (All materials used during the month were direct materials.)

b. The production superintendent states that manufacturing overhead cost is applied to jobs on the basis of direct labor-hours. However, he does not remember the rate currently being used by the company.

c. Cost sheets kept in the production superintendent's office show that only one job was in process on June 30, at the time of the explosion. The job had been charged with $6,600 in materials, and 500 direct labor-hours at $8 per hour had been worked on the job.

d. A log is kept in the finished goods warehouse showing all goods transferred in from the factory. This log shows that the cost of goods transferred into the finished goods warehouse from the factory during June totaled $280,000.

e. The company's May 31 balance sheet indicates that the finished goods inventory totaled $36,000 at the beginning of June.

f. A charred piece of the payroll ledger, found after sifting through piles of smoking debris, indicates that 11,500 direct labor-hours were recorded for June. The company's Personnel Department has verified that, as a result of a union contract, all factory employees earn the same $8 per hour rate.

g. The production superintendent states that there was no under- or overapplied overhead in the Manufacturing Overhead account at May 31.

Required:

1. Each member of the team should determine what types of transactions would be posted to one of the following sets of accounts:

   a. Raw materials and accounts payable.

   b. Work in process and manufacturing overhead.

   c. Finished goods and cost of goods sold.

   Each team member should present a summary of the types of transactions that would be posted to the accounts to the other team members, who should confirm or correct the summary. Then, the team should work together to complete steps 2 through 7.

2. Determine the transaction that should be reflected in the manufacturing overhead account and then determine the company's predetermined overhead rate.

3. Determine the June 30 balance in the company's work in process account.

4. Determine the transactions that should be reflected in the work in process account. (You will need to back into the amount of direct materials that must have been used during the month to complete the T-account analysis.)

5. Determine the transactions that should be reflected in the finished goods account. (You will need to back into the cost of the finished goods that were sold during the month to complete the T-account analysis.)

6. Determine the transactions that should be reflected in the cost of goods sold account.

7. Determine the transactions that should be reflected in the accounts payable account.

8. Determine the transactions that should be reflected in the raw materials account.

   (Hint: A good method for determining the transactions that were recorded in a given account is to update the related fragmented T-account by posting whatever entries can be developed from the information provided above.)

Chapter Three

Systems Design: Activity-Based Costing

Chapter Outline

Decision Feature Peddling to Oblivion

Claudia Post started Diamond Courier of Philadelphia in 1990 shortly after having been fired as a salesperson for another courier service. Her downtown bicycle messenger service grew quickly—reaching $1 million in sales within 17 months. Seeing opportunities to sell other services, she added truck deliveries, airfreight services, a parts distribution service, and a legal service that served subpoenas and prepared court filings. Within three years of beginning operations, Diamond Courier had $3.1 million in annual sales and employed about 40 bike messengers and 25 back-office staffers in addition to providing work for about 50 independent drivers. There was only one problem—the company was losing money.

Post had to sell her jewelry to meet the payroll and pay bills. With the help of an adviser, Post took a serious look at the profitability of each of the company's lines of business. Post had assumed that if she charged a competitive rate, kept clients happy, and increased sales, she would make money. However, an activity-based costing analysis of her overhead costs indicated that the average cost of a bike delivery—including overhead—was $9.24 but she was charging only $4.69. "The bicycle division, which she thought of as Diamond's core business, generated just 10% of total revenues and barely covered its own direct-labor and insurance costs. Worse, the division created more logistical and customer-service nightmares than any other single business, thereby generating a disproportionate share of overhead costs." Since smaller, focused competitors were charging as little as $3 per delivery, there was little alternative except to drop the bicycle messenger business and concentrate on the other, more profitable, lines of business. A similar analysis also led to closing the airfreight and parts distribution businesses.

Post turned the company around by making these changes; the company reported a profit in 1995. Although up-to-date financial information is not readily available for this privately owned entity, the company did report that it surpassed the one million-delivery mark in its 10th year of operations. Post keeps her customers informed and advertises the company's services on its website at www.diamondcourier.com. The company recently moved into a larger facility in Philadelphia and expanded its services. In addition to delivering letters, documents, and packages the same day by vehicle in the Northeast and by air throughout the United States, the company now provides warehousing and distribution services. A growing enterprise, such as Diamond Courier, can continue to use activity-based costing to provide the costing information required to make decisions that impact the profitability of the business.

Source: Susan Greco, "Are We Making Money Yet?" *INC.*, July 1996, pp. 52–61.

Learning Objectives

After studying Chapter 3, you should be able to:

LO1 Understand the basic approach in activity-based costing and how it differs from conventional costing.

LO2 Compute activity rates for an activity-based costing system.

LO3 Compute product costs using activity-based costing.

LO4 Contrast the product costs computed under activity-based costing and conventional costing methods.

LO5 Record the flow of costs in an activity-based costing system.

As discussed in earlier chapters, direct materials and direct labor costs can be directly traced to products. Overhead costs, on the other hand, cannot be easily traced to products and some other means must be found for assigning them to products for financial reporting and other purposes. In the previous chapter, overhead costs were assigned to products using a plantwide predetermined overhead rate. This method is simpler than the other methods of assigning overhead costs to products that will be described in this chapter, but this simplicity has a cost. A plantwide predetermined overhead rate spreads overhead costs uniformly over products in proportion to whatever allocation base is used—most commonly, direct labor-hours. This procedure results in high overhead costs for products with a high direct labor-hour content and low overhead costs for products with a low direct labor-hour content. However, the real causes of overhead may have little to do with direct labor-hours and as a consequence, product costs may be distorted. Activity-based costing attempts to correct these distortions by more accurately assigning overhead costs to products.

Assigning Overhead Costs to Products

Learning Objective 1
Understand the basic approach in activity-based costing and how it differs from conventional costing.

Companies use three common approaches to assign overhead costs to products. The simplest method is to use a plantwide overhead rate. A slightly more refined approach is to use departmental overhead rates. The most complex method is activity-based costing, which is the most accurate of the three approaches to overhead cost assignment.

Plantwide Overhead Rate

Our discussion in the two preceding chapters assumed that a single overhead rate, called a *plantwide overhead rate*, was being used throughout an entire factory. This simple approach to overhead assignment can result in distorted unit product costs, as we shall see below.

Direct Labor as a Base   When cost systems were developed in the 1800s, direct labor was a larger component of product costs than it is today. Data relating to direct labor were readily available and convenient to use, and managers believed there was a high positive correlation between direct labor and overhead costs. (A positive correlation between two things means that they tend to move together in the same direction.) Consequently, direct labor was considered to be a useful allocation base for overhead.

Changing Environment   However, a plantwide overhead rate based on direct labor may no longer be satisfactory. First, in many companies direct labor may no longer be highly correlated with overhead costs. Second, because of the large variety of activities encompassed in overhead, no single allocation basis may be able to adequately reflect the demands that products place on overhead resources.

On an economywide basis, direct labor and overhead costs have been moving in opposite directions for a long time. As a percentage of total cost, direct labor has been declining, whereas overhead has been increasing.[1] Many tasks that used to be done by hand are now done with largely automated equipment—a component of overhead. Furthermore, product diversity has increased. Companies are creating new products and services

---

[1]Germain Böer provides some data concerning these trends in "Five Modern Management Accounting Myths," *Management Accounting*, January 1994, pp. 22–27. Since 1849, on average, material cost as a percentage of manufacturing cost has been fairly constant at 55% of sales. Labor cost has always been relatively less important and has declined steadily from 23% in 1849 to about 10% in 1987. Overhead has grown from about 18% of sales to about 33% of sales over the last 50 years.

at an ever-accelerating rate that differ in volume, batch size, and complexity. Managing and sustaining this product diversity requires many more overhead resources such as production schedulers and product design engineers, and many of these overhead resources have no obvious connection with direct labor.

Nevertheless, direct labor remains a viable base for applying overhead to products in many companies—particularly for external reports. In some companies there is still a high positive correlation between overhead costs and direct labor. And most companies throughout the world continue to base overhead allocations on direct labor or machine-hours. However, in those instances in which plantwide overhead costs are not highly correlated with plantwide direct labor, some other means of assigning costs must be found or product costs will be distorted.

Departmental Overhead Rates

Rather than use a plantwide overhead rate, many companies use departmental overhead rates. The allocation bases depend on the nature of the work performed in each department. For example, overhead costs in a machining department may be allocated on the basis of the machine-hours in that department. In contrast, the overhead costs in an assembly department may be allocated on the basis of direct labor-hours in that department.

Unfortunately, even departmental overhead rates will not correctly assign overhead costs in situations where a company has a range of products and complex overhead costs.[2] The reason is that the departmental approach usually relies on volume as the factor in allocating overhead cost to products. For example, if the machining department's overhead is applied to products on the basis of machine-hours, it is assumed that the department's overhead costs are caused by, and are directly proportional to, machine-hours. However, the department's overhead costs are probably more complex than this and are caused by a variety of factors, including the range of products processed in the department, the number of batch setups that are required, the complexity of the products, and so on. A more sophisticated method like *activity-based costing* is required to adequately account for these diverse factors.

How Internal Auditors Can Help

in business today

Internal auditors often identify operational problems when they are checking to see if a company's policies and procedures are being followed. The following conditions may suggest to an internal auditor that a company may need to replace its conventional approach to assigning overhead with an activity-based costing technique:

- Overhead has become the largest component of product costs.
- Significant increases are noted in the company's plantwide overhead rate.
- The sales of some products far outpace the sales of other products in the same product line.

Source: S. J. Lambert III, Kung H. Chen, and Joyce C. Lambert, "Overhead Cost Pools," *Internal Auditor*, October 1996, pp. 62–67. Reprinted with permission from the Institute of Internal Auditors, Inc.

Activity-Based Costing (ABC)

Activity-based costing (ABC) is a technique that attempts to assign overhead costs more accurately to products than the simpler methods discussed thus far. The basic idea underlying the activity-based costing approach is illustrated in Exhibit 3–1. A customer order triggers a number of activities. For example, if Nordstrom orders a line of women's skirts

Concept 3–1

[2]Robin Cooper and Robert S. Kaplan, "How Cost Accounting Distorts Product Costs," *Management Accounting*, April 1988, pp. 20–27.

Exhibit 3–1
The Activity-Based Costing
Model

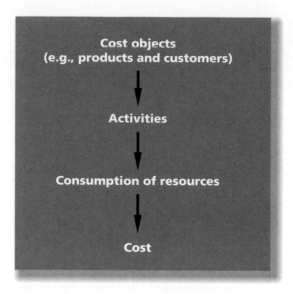

from Calvin Klein, a production order is generated, materials are ordered, patterns are created, textiles are cut to pattern and then sewn, and the finished products are packed for shipping. These activities consume resources. For example, ordering the appropriate materials consumes clerical time—a resource the company must pay for. In activity-based costing, an attempt is made to trace these costs directly to the products that cause them.

Rather than a single allocation base such as direct labor-hours or machine-hours, in activity-based costing a company uses a number of allocation bases for assigning costs to products. Each allocation base in an activity-based costing system represents a major *activity* that causes overhead costs. An **activity** in activity-based costing is an event that causes the consumption of overhead resources. Examples of activities in various organizations include the following:

- Setting up machines.
- Admitting patients to a hospital.
- Scheduling production.
- Performing blood tests at a clinic.
- Billing customers.
- Maintaining equipment.

- Ordering materials or supplies.
- Stocking shelves at a store.
- Meeting with clients at a law firm.
- Preparing shipments.
- Inspecting materials for defects.
- Opening an account at a bank.

Activity-based costing centers on these activities. Each major activity has its own overhead cost pool (also known as an *activity cost pool*), its own *activity measure*, and its own predetermined overhead rate (also known as an *activity rate*). An **activity cost pool** is a "cost bucket" in which costs related to a particular activity are accumulated. The **activity measure** expresses how much of the activity is carried out and it is used as the allocation basis for applying overhead costs to products and services. For example, *the number of patients admitted* is a natural choice of an activity measure for the activity *admitting patients to the hospital*. An **activity rate** is a predetermined overhead rate in an activity-based costing system. Each activity has its own activity rate that is used to apply overhead costs.

For example, the activity *setting up machines to process a batch* would have its own activity cost pool. Products are ordinarily processed in batches. And since each product has its own machine settings, machines must be set up when changing over from a batch of one product to another. If the total cost in this activity cost pool is $150,000 and the total expected activity is 1,000 machine setups, the predetermined overhead rate (i.e., activity rate) for this activity would be $150 per machine setup ($150,000 ÷ 1,000 machine setups = $150 per machine setup). Each product that requires a machine setup would be charged $150. Note that this charge does not depend on how many units are produced after the machine is set up. A small job requiring a machine setup would be charged $150— just the same as a large job.

Taking each activity in isolation, this system works exactly like the job-order costing system described in the last chapter. A predetermined overhead rate is computed for each activity and then applied to jobs and products based on the amount of activity required by the job or product.

Designing an Activity-Based Costing System

The most important decisions in designing an activity-based costing system concern what activities will be included in the system and how the activities will be measured. In most companies, hundreds or even thousands of different activities cause overhead costs. These activities range from taking a telephone order to training new employees. Setting up and maintaining a complex costing system that includes all of these activities would be prohibitively expensive. The challenge in designing an activity-based costing system is to identify a reasonably small number of activities that explain the bulk of the variation in overhead costs. This is usually done by interviewing a broad range of managers in the organization to find out what activities they think are important and that consume most of the resources they manage. This often results in a long list of potential activities that could be included in the activity-based costing system. This list is refined and pruned in consultation with top managers. Related activities are frequently combined to reduce the amount of detail and record-keeping cost. For example, several actions may be involved in handling and moving raw materials, but these may be combined into a single activity titled *material handling*. The end result of this stage of the design process is an *activity dictionary* that defines each of the activities that will be included in the activity-based costing system and how the activities will be measured.

Some of the activities commonly found in activity-based costing systems in manufacturing companies are listed in Exhibit 3–2. In the exhibit, activities have been grouped into a four-level hierarchy: *unit-level activities, batch-level activities, product-level activities,* and *facility-level activities.* This cost hierarchy is useful in understanding the impact of activity-based costing. It also serves as a guide in simplifying an activity-based costing system. In general, activities and costs should be combined in the activity-based costing system only if they fall within the same level in the cost hierarchy.

Hierarchy of Activities

Unit-level activities are performed each time a unit is produced. The costs of unit-level activities should be proportional to the number of units produced. For example, providing

Level	Activities	Activity Measures
Unit-level	Processing units on machines	Machine-hours
	Processing units by hand	Direct labor-hours
	Consuming factory supplies	Units produced
Batch-level	Processing purchase orders	Purchase orders processed
	Processing production orders	Production orders processed
	Setting up equipment	Number of setups; setup hours
	Handling material	Pounds of material handled; number of times material moved
Product-level	Testing new products	Hours of testing time
	Administering parts inventories	Number of part types
	Designing products	Hours of design time
Facility-level	General factory administration	Direct labor-hours*
	Plant building and grounds	Direct labor-hours*

*Facility-level costs cannot be traced on a cause-and-effect basis to individual products. Nevertheless, these costs are usually allocated to products using some arbitrary basis such as direct labor-hours—particularly for purposes of external reporting.

Exhibit 3–2
Examples of Activities and Activity Measures in Manufacturing Companies

power to run processing equipment would be a unit-level activity since power tends to be consumed in proportion to the number of units produced.

Batch-level activities consist of tasks that are performed each time a batch is processed, such as processing purchase orders, setting up equipment, packing shipments to customers, and handling material. Costs at the batch level depend on *the number of batches processed* rather than on the number of units produced. For example, the cost of processing a purchase order is the same regardless of whether one unit or 5,000 units of an item are ordered. Thus, the total cost of a batch-level activity such as purchasing is a function of the *number* of orders placed.

Product-level activities (sometimes called *product-sustaining activities*) relate to specific products and typically must be carried out regardless of how many batches or units of the product are manufactured. Product-level activities include maintaining inventories of parts for a product, issuing engineering change notices to modify a product to meet a customer's specifications, and developing special test routines when a product is first placed into production.

in business today ABC and the Virtual Bakery

Super Bakery, Inc., founded by former Pittsburgh Steelers' running back Franco Harris, is a "virtual corporation" that supplies donuts and other baked goods to schools, hospitals, and other institutions. "In a virtual corporation, only the core, strategic functions of the business are performed inside the company. The remaining support activities are outsourced to a network of external companies that specialize in each function." A network of independent brokers sells Super Bakery's products and the company contracts out baking, warehousing, and shipping. What does Super Bakery itself do? The company's master baker develops products and the company formulates and produces its own dry mixes from ingredients it has purchased. The contracted bakeries simply add water to the mix and follow the baking instructions. Super Bakery maintains four regional sales managers, and a small office staff processes orders and handles bookkeeping and accounting.

As much as possible, actual costs are traced to individual customer accounts. The remaining costs of the company are assigned to customer accounts using the following activity cost pools and activity measures:

Activity Description	Activity Measure
Advertising, trade shows, and bonds	Projected number of cases sold
Order department	Number of orders
Sales management	Time spent in each sales territory
Research and development (R&D)	Hours of R&D for each product line

Since the independent sales brokers are paid a flat 5% commission on sales, they have little incentive to make sure that the sales are actually profitable to Super Bakery. It is in the interests of the brokers to deeply discount prices if that is necessary to make a sale. Consequently, Super Bakery's regional sales managers must approve all price discounts and they use the ABC data to evaluate the profitability of the deals proposed by the brokers.

Source: Tim R. V. Davis and Bruce L. Darling, "ABC in a Virtual Corporation," *Management Accounting*, October 1996, pp. 18–26. Reprinted with permission.

Facility-level activities (also called *organization-sustaining activities*) are activities that are carried out regardless of which products are produced, how many batches are run, or how many units are made. Facility-level costs include items such as factory management salaries, insurance, property taxes, and building depreciation. The costs of facility-level activities are often combined into a single cost pool and allocated to products using an arbitrary basis such as direct labor-hours. As we will see later in the book, allocating

Exhibit 3–3
Graphic Example of Activity-Based Costing

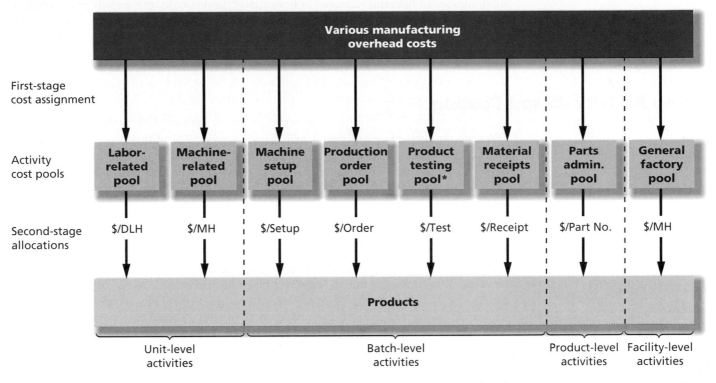

* Standard tests are performed on a few randomly selected units in each batch.

such costs to products will result in misleading data that can lead to bad decisions. However, facility-level costs must be allocated to products for external financial reports.

An Example of an Activity-Based Costing System Design

The complexity of an activity-based costing system will differ from company to company. For some companies, the structure of the activity-based costing system will be simple with only one or two activity cost pools at the unit, batch, and product levels. For other companies, the structure will be much more complex.

Exhibit 3–3 provides a graphic example of a relatively simple activity-based costing system. The purpose of this exhibit is to tie together the concepts discussed on preceding pages and also to present a bird's-eye view of an activity-based costing system.

The unallocated manufacturing overhead costs are at the top of Exhibit 3–3. These costs are ultimately allocated to products via the two-stage procedure illustrated in the exhibit. In the first stage, overhead costs are assigned to the activity cost pools. In the second stage, the costs that have been accumulated in the activity cost pools are allocated to products using activity rates and activity measures. For example, in the first stage cost assignment, various manufacturing overhead costs are assigned to the material receipts activity cost pool. These costs could include wages of workers who receive materials, wages of the clerks who handle shipping documents, and other costs that are incurred as a consequence of receiving materials. We will not go into the details of how these first-stage cost assignments are made. In all of the examples and assignments in this book, the first-stage cost assignments have already been completed. Once the amount of cost in the material receipts activity cost pool is known, procedures from Chapter 2 can be followed. The activity rate for material receipts is computed by dividing the total cost in the material receipts activity cost pool by the anticipated number of times material will be received in the up-coming year. For example, the total cost in the activity cost pool might be $50,000 and the total number of material receipts might be 2,500. In that case, the activity rate would be $20 per material receipt. If a job requires three shipments of incoming materials, it would be charged $60 for material receipts. This is really no different from the way overhead was applied to jobs in Chapter 2 except that the number of material receipts is the allocation basis rather than direct labor-hours.

Using Activity-Based Costing

Different products place different demands on resources. This difference in demand on resources is not recognized by traditional costing systems, which assume that overhead resources are consumed in direct proportion to direct labor-hours. The following example illustrates the distortions in product costs that can result from using a traditional costing system.

Managerial Accounting in Action

The Issue

Comtek Sound, Inc., makes two products, a radio with a built-in tape player (called a *tape unit*) and a radio with a built-in compact disc player (called a *CD unit*). Both of these products are sold to automobile manufacturers for installation in new vehicles. The president of the company, Sarah Kastler, recently returned from a management conference at which activity-based costing was discussed. Following the conference, she called a meeting of the top managers in the company to discuss what she had learned. Attending the meeting were the production manager, Frank Hines; the marketing manager, Nicole Sermone; and the accounting manager, Tom Frazier.

Sarah: I learned some things at the conference I just attended that may help resolve some long-standing puzzles here at Comtek Sound.
Frank: Did anyone at the conference explain why my equipment always breaks down at the worst possible moment?
Sarah: Sorry, Frank, I guess it must be bad karma or something.
Nicole: Did they tell you why we've been losing all those bids lately on our bread-and-butter tape units and winning every bid on our specialty CD units?
Sarah: Nicole, you probably weren't expecting this answer, but yes, there may be a simple explanation. We may have been shooting ourselves in the foot.
Nicole: How so? I don't know about anyone else, but we have been hustling like crazy to get more business for the company.
Frank: Wait a minute, Nicole, my production people have been turning in tremendous improvements in defect rates, on-time delivery, you name it.
Sarah: Whoa, everybody. Calm down. I don't think anyone is to blame for us losing so many bids on our high-volume bread-and-butter product. Nicole, when you talk with our customers, what reasons do they give for taking their tape unit business to our competitors? Is it a problem with quality or on-time delivery?
Nicole: No, our customers readily admit that we're among the best in the business.
Sarah: Then what's the problem?
Nicole: Price. The competition is undercutting our price on the tape units and then bidding high on the CD units. As a result, they're stealing our high-volume tape business and leaving us with just the low-volume CD business.
Sarah: Why is our price so high for the tape units that the competition is able to undercut us?
Nicole: Our price isn't too high. Theirs is too low. Our competitors must be pricing below their costs on the tape units.
Sarah: Why do you think that?
Nicole: Well, if we charged the prices for our tape units that our competitors are quoting, we'd be pricing below *our* cost, and I know we're just as efficient as any competitor.

Frank: Nicole, why would our competitors price below their cost?

Nicole: They're out to grab market share.

Frank: Does that make any sense? What good does more market share do them if they're pricing below their cost?

Sarah: I think Frank has a point. Tom, you're the expert with the numbers. Can you suggest another explanation?

Tom: I was hoping you'd ask that. Those product cost figures my department reports to you are primarily intended to be used to value inventories and determine cost of goods sold for our external financial statements. I am awfully uncomfortable about using them for bidding. In fact, I have mentioned this several times, but no one was interested.

Sarah: Now I'm interested. Tom, are you telling us that the product cost figures we have been using for bidding may be wrong? Are you suggesting that we really don't know what the manufacturing cost is for either the tape units or the CD units?

Tom: Yes, that could be the problem. Our cost system isn't designed to recognize that our two products place different demands on our resources. The tape units are simple to manufacture, and the CD units are more complex. For example, both products take the same amount of labor time for assembly, but the more complex CD units take a disproportionate amount of machine and testing time. We need a cost system that recognizes this difference in demand on resources.

Sarah: That's exactly the point made at the conference. The conference speakers suggested we recost our products using something called activity-based costing. Tom, can we do this?

Tom: You bet! But we need to do it as a team. Can each person in the room appoint one of their top people to work with me?

Sarah: Let's do it! I'd like the special ABC team to report back to this group as soon as possible. If there's a problem with our costs, we need to know it before the competition plows us under.

Comtek Sound, Inc.'s Basic Data

Tom Frazier and the ABC team immediately began gathering basic information relating to the company's two products. As a basis for its study, the team decided to use the cost and other data planned for the current year. A summary of some of this information follows. For the current year, the company's budget provides for selling 50,000 CD units and 200,000 tape units. Both products require two direct labor-hours to complete. Therefore, the company plans to work 500,000 direct labor-hours (DLHs) during the current year, computed as follows:

	Hours
CD units: 50,000 units × 2 DLHs per unit	100,000
Tape units: 200,000 units × 2 DLHs per unit	400,000
Total direct labor-hours	500,000

Costs for materials and labor for one unit of each product are given below:

	CD Units	Tape Units
Direct materials	$90	$50
Direct labor (at $10 per DLH)	20	20

The company's estimated manufacturing overhead costs for the current year total $10,000,000. The ABC team discovered that although the same amount of direct labor time is required for each product, the more complex CD units require more machine time, more machine setups, and more testing than the tape units. Also, the team found that it is necessary to manufacture the CD units in smaller lots, so they require a relatively large number of production orders as compared to the tape units.

The company has always used direct labor-hours as the base for assigning overhead costs to its products.

With this data in hand, the ABC team was prepared to begin the design of the new activity-based costing system. But first, they wanted to compute the cost of each product using the company's existing cost system.

Direct Labor-Hours as a Base

Under the company's existing costing system, the company's predetermined overhead rate would be $20 per direct labor-hour. The rate is computed as follows:

$$\text{Predetermined overhead rate} = \frac{\text{Estimated total manufacturing overhead}}{\text{Estimated total direct labor-hours (DLHs)}}$$

$$= \frac{\$10,000,000}{500,000 \text{ DLHs}} = \$20 \text{ per DLH}$$

Using this rate, the ABC team then computed the unit product costs as given below:

	CD Units	Tape Units
Direct materials (above)	$90	$50
Direct labor (above)	20	20
Manufacturing overhead (2 DLHs × $20 per DLH)	40	40
Unit product cost	$150	$110

Tom Frazier explained to the ABC team that the problem with this costing approach is that it relies entirely on labor time in assigning overhead cost to products and does not consider the impact of other factors—such as setups and testing—on the overhead costs of the company. Since these other factors are being ignored and the two products require equal amounts of labor time, they are assigned equal amounts of overhead cost.

Tom explained that while this method of computing costs is fast and simple, it is accurate only in those situations where other factors affecting overhead costs are not significant. Tom stated that he believed these other factors are significant in the case of Comtek Sound, Inc., and he was anxious for the team to analyze the various activities of the company to see what impact they have on costs.

Computing Activity Rates

The ABC team then analyzed Comtek Sound, Inc.'s operations and identified eight major activities to be included in the new activity-based costing system. (These eight activities are identical to those illustrated earlier in Exhibit 3–3.) Cost and other data relating to the activities are presented in Exhibit 3–4.

As shown in the Basic Data at the top of Exhibit 3–4, the ABC team estimated the amount of overhead cost for each activity cost pool, along with the expected amount of activity for the current year. The machine setups activity cost pool, for example, has been assigned $1,600,000 in overhead cost. The company expects to complete 4,000 setups during the year, of which 3,000 will be for CD units and 1,000 will be for tape units. Data for other activities are also shown in the exhibit.

The ABC team then computed an activity rate for each activity. (See the middle panel in Exhibit 3–4.) The rate for machine setups, for example, was computed by dividing the total estimated overhead cost in the activity cost pool, $1,600,000, by the expected

Exhibit 3–4
Comtek Sound's Activity-Based Costing System

Basic Data

Activities and Activity Measures	Estimated Overhead Cost	Total	CD Units	Tape Units
		Expected Activity		
Labor related (direct labor-hours)	$ 800,000	500,000	100,000	400,000
Machine related (machine-hours)	2,100,000	1,000,000	300,000	700,000
Machine setups (setups)	1,600,000	4,000	3,000	1,000
Production orders (orders)	450,000	1,200	400	800
Product testing (tests)	1,700,000	20,000	16,000	4,000
Material receipts (receipts)	1,000,000	5,000	1,800	3,200
Parts administration (part types)	350,000	700	400	300
General factory (machine-hours)	2,000,000	1,000,000	300,000	700,000
	$10,000,000			

Computation of Activity Rates

Activities	(a) Estimated Overhead Cost	(b) Total Expected Activity	(a) ÷ (b) Activity Rate
Labor related	$ 800,000	500,000 DLHs	$ 1.60 per DLH
Machine related	2,100,000	1,000,000 MHs	2.10 per MH
Machine setups	1,600,000	4,000 setups	400.00 per setup
Production orders	450,000	1,200 orders	375.00 per order
Product testing	1,700,000	20,000 tests	85.00 per test
Material receipts	1,000,000	5,000 receipts	200.00 per receipt
Parts administration	350,000	700 part types	500.00 per part type
General factory	2,000,000	1,000,000 MHs	2.00 per MH

Computation of the Overhead Cost per Unit of Product

Activities and Activity Rates	CD Units Expected Activity	CD Units Amount	Tape Units Expected Activity	Tape Units Amount
Labor related, at $1.60 per DLH	100,000	$ 160,000	400,000	$ 640,000
Machine related, at $2.10 per MH	300,000	630,000	700,000	1,470,000
Machine setups, at $400 per setup	3,000	1,200,000	1,000	400,000
Production orders, at $375 per order	400	150,000	800	300,000
Product testing, at $85 per test	16,000	1,360,000	4,000	340,000
Materials receipts, at $200 per receipt	1,800	360,000	3,200	640,000
Parts administration, at $500 per part type	400	200,000	300	150,000
General factory, at $2.00 per MH	300,000	600,000	700,000	1,400,000
Total overhead costs assigned (a)		$4,660,000		$5,340,000
Number of units produced (b)		50,000		200,000
Overhead cost per unit (a) ÷ (b)		$93.20		$26.70

amount of activity, 4,000 setups. The result was the activity rate of $400 per setup. This process was repeated for each of the other activities in the activity-based costing system.

in business | *today* **Shifting the Focus of a Bank**

The Co-Operative Bank of the United Kingdom uses activity-based costing to analyze the profitability of its personal banking products such as financial advice, checking accounts, credit cards, mortgages, and personal loans. Overhead costs are assigned to the banking products using the following activity cost pools and activity measures:

Activity Description	Activity Measure
Provide ATM service	ATM transactions
Clear debit items	Number of debits processed
Branch operations for debit items	Number of branch counter debits
Issue personal checkbook	Number of checkbooks issued
Clear credit items	Number of credits processed
Branch operations for credit items	Number of branch counter credits
Lending control and security	Number of interventions
Customer inquiries	Number of telephone minutes
Marketing and sales activities	Number of accounts opened
Computer processing	Number of computer transactions
Statementing and postage	Number of statements issued
Advise on investments and insurance	Hours of advice given
Process VISA transactions	Number of VISA transactions
Issue VISA statements	Number of VISA statements issued
Open/maintain Handyloans	Number of Handyloan accounts
Open and close accounts	Number of accounts opened/closed
Administer mortgages	Number of mortgages

The bank excludes organization-sustaining costs such as accounting, finance, strategy, planning, human resource management, and information technology from this ABC analysis. These organization-sustaining costs, which are not traceable to any particular banking products, are about 15% of the bank's operating expenses.

The ABC analysis indicated that several banking products were failing to generate adequate profits. In particular, the provision of financial advice and the sale of associated investment products appeared to be generating only small profits. This product had always been considered a highly profitable business and had been targeted as a growth area for the bank. In contrast, the credit card business was highly profitable according to the ABC analysis. As a consequence, the bank decided to focus its limited marketing resources on personal account and credit card business.

Source: Srikant Datar and Robert S. Kaplan, *The Co-Operative Bank*, Harvard Business School, Case 9-193-196, Copyright © 1995 (revised April 1996) by the President and Fellows of Harvard College. Harvard Business School Exhibit 6. Reprinted by permission of Harvard Business School.

Computing Product Costs

Learning Objective 3
Compute product costs using activity-based costing.

Once the activity rates were determined, it was then an easy matter to compute the overhead cost that would be allocated to each product. (See the bottom panel of Exhibit 3–4.) For example, the amount of machine setup cost allocated to CD units was determined by multiplying the activity rate of $400 per setup by the 3,000 expected setups for CD units during the year. This yielded a total of $1,200,000 in machine setup costs to be assigned to the CD units.

Note from the exhibit that the use of an activity approach has resulted in $93.20 in overhead cost being assigned to each CD unit and $26.70 to each tape unit. The ABC team then used these amounts to determine unit product costs under activity-based costing, as presented in the table below. For comparison, the table also shows the unit costs derived earlier when direct labor was used as the base for assigning overhead costs to the products.

	Activity-Based Costing		Direct-Labor Based Costing	
	CD Units	Tape Units	CD Units	Tape Units
Direct materials	$ 90.00	$50.00	$ 90.00	$ 50.00
Direct labor	20.00	20.00	20.00	20.00
Manufacturing overhead ..	93.20	26.70	40.00	40.00
Unit product cost	$203.20	$96.70	$150.00	$110.00

The ABC team members were shocked by their findings, which Tom Frazier summarized as follows in the team's report:

> In the past, the company has been charging $40.00 in overhead cost to a unit of either product, whereas it should have been charging $93.20 in overhead cost to each CD unit and only $26.70 to each tape unit. Thus, as a result of using direct labor as the base for overhead costing, unit product costs had been badly distorted. The company may even have been suffering a loss on the CD units without knowing it because the cost of these units has been so vastly understated. Through activity-based costing, we have been able to better identify the overhead costs of each product and thus derive more accurate cost data.

The pattern of cost distortion shown by the ABC team's findings is quite common. Such distortion can happen in any company that relies on direct labor-hours or machine-hours in assigning overhead cost to products and ignores other significant factors affecting overhead cost incurrence.

The ABC team presented the results of its work in a meeting attended by all of the top managers of Comtek Sound including the president, Sarah Kastler; the production manager, Frank Hines; the marketing manager, Nicole Sermone; and the accounting manager, Tom Frazier. After the formal presentation by the ABC team, the following discussion took place:

Sarah: I would like to personally thank the ABC team for all the work they have done. I am now beginning to wonder about some of the decisions we have made in the past using our old cost accounting system.

Tom: I hope I don't have to remind anyone that I have been warning people about this problem for quite some time.

Sarah: No, you don't have to remind us, Tom. I guess we just didn't understand the problem before.

Nicole: It's obvious from this activity-based costing information that we had everything backwards. We thought the competition was pricing below cost on the tape units, but in fact *we* were overcharging for these units because our costs were overstated. And we thought the competition was overpricing CD units, but in fact *our* prices were way too low because our costs for these units were understated. I'll bet the competition has really been laughing behind our backs!

Sarah: You can bet they won't be laughing when they see our next bids.

Shifting of Overhead Cost

When a company implements activity-based costing, overhead cost often shifts from high-volume products to low-volume products, with a higher unit product cost resulting for the

Managerial Accounting in Action

Wrap-Up

comtek
SOUND, INC.

Learning Objective 4
Contrast the product costs computed under activity-based costing and conventional costing methods.

low-volume products. We saw this happen in the example above, where overhead cost was shifted to the CD units—the low-volume product—and their unit product cost increased from $150.00 to $203.20 per unit. This results from the existence of batch-level and product-level costs. When these costs are spread across lower volumes, higher average costs result. For example, consider the cost of issuing production orders, which is a batch activity. As shown in Exhibit 3–4, the average cost to Comtek Sound to issue a single production order is $375. This cost is assigned to a production order regardless of how many units are to be processed under that product order. The key here is to realize that fewer CD units (the low-volume product) are processed per production order than tape units:

	CD Units	Tape Units
Number of units produced per year (a)	50,000	200,000
Number of production orders issued per year (b)	400	800
Number of units processed per production order (a) ÷ (b) ...	125	250

If the $375 cost to issue a production order is spread over the number of units processed per order, we get the following average cost per unit:

	CD Units	Tape Units
Cost to issue a production order (a)	$375	$375
Number of units processed per production order (above) (b)	125	250
Production order cost per unit (a) ÷ (b)	$3.00	$1.50

Thus, the production order cost for a CD unit (the low-volume product) is $3, which is *double* the $1.50 cost for a tape unit.

Product-level costs—such as parts administration—have a similar impact. In a conventional costing system, these costs are spread more or less uniformly across all units that are produced. In an activity-based costing system, these costs are assigned more appropriately to products. Since product-level costs are fixed with respect to the number of units that are processed, the average cost per unit of something like parts administration will be higher for low-volume products than for high-volume products.

Targeting Process Improvements

Activity-based costing can also be used to identify activities that would benefit from process improvements. Indeed, this is the most widely cited benefit of activity-based costing by managers.[3] When used in this way, activity-based costing is often called *activity-based management*. Basically, **activity-based management** involves focusing on activities to eliminate waste, decrease processing time, and reduce defects. Activity-based management is used in organizations as diverse as manufacturing companies, hospitals, and the U.S. Marine Corps.[4] When "40 percent of the cost of running a hospital involves storing, collecting and moving information," there is obviously a great deal of room for eliminating waste.[5]

The first step in any improvement program is to decide what to improve. The Theory of Constraints approach discussed in the Prologue is a powerful tool for targeting the area

---

[3]Dan Swenson, "The Benefits of Activity-Based Cost Management to the Manufacturing Industry," *Journal of Management Accounting Research* 7, (Fall 1995), pp. 167–180.

[4]Julian Freeman, "Marines Embrace Continuous Improvement: Highlight of CAM-I's Meeting," *Management Accounting*, February 1997, p. 64.

[5]Kambiz Foroohar, "Rx: software," *Forbes*, April 7, 1997, p. 114.

in an organization whose improvement will yield the greatest benefit. Activity-based management provides another approach. The activity rates computed in activity-based costing can provide valuable clues concerning where there is waste and scope for improvement in an organization. For example, looking at the activity rates in Exhibit 3–4, Comtek's managers may wonder why it costs $375 on average to process a purchase order. That may seem like an awful lot of money for an activity that adds no value to the product. As a consequence, the purchase order processing activity may be targeted for process improvement using TQM or process reengineering as discussed in the Prologue. *Benchmarking* is often advocated as a way to leverage the information in activity rates.

Benchmarking is a systematic approach to identifying the activities with the greatest room for improvement. It is based on comparing the performance in an organization with the performance of other, similar organizations known for their outstanding performance. If a particular part of the organization performs far below the world-class standard, managers will be likely to target that area for an improvement program.

Benchmarking the Back Office   *in business* | *today*

The Marketing Resources Group of Qwest, the telephone company, performed an activity-based costing analysis of the activities carried out in its accounting department. Managers computed the activity rates for the activities and then compared these rates to the costs of carrying out the same activities in other companies. Two benchmarks were used: (1) a sample of Fortune 100 companies, which are the largest 100 companies in the United States and (2) "world class" companies that had been identified by a consultant as having the best accounting practices in the world. These comparisons appear below:

Activity	Activity Measure	Qwest Activity Rate	Fortune 100 Benchmark	World Class Benchmark
Processing accounts receivable	Number of invoices processed	$3.80 per invoice	$15.00 per invoice	$4.60 per invoice
Processing accounts payable	Number of invoices processed	$8.90 per invoice	$7.00 per invoice	$1.80 per invoice
Processing payroll checks	Number of checks processed	$7.30 per check	$5.00 per check	$1.72 per check
Managing customer credit	Number of customer accounts	$12.00 per account	$16.00 per account	$5.60 per account

It is clear from this analysis that Qwest does a good job of processing accounts receivables. Its average cost per invoice is $3.80, whereas the cost in other companies that are considered world class is even higher—$4.60 per invoice. On the other hand, the cost of processing payroll checks is significantly higher at Qwest than at benchmark companies. The cost per payroll check at Qwest is $7.30 versus $5.00 at Fortune 100 companies and $1.72 at world-class companies. This suggests that it may be possible to wring waste out of this activity. As a consequence, the payroll processing activity may be targeted for a TQM effort or for process reengineering.

Source: Steve Coburn, Hugh Grove, and Cynthia Fukami, "Benchmarking with ABCM," *Management Accounting*, January 1995, pp. 56–60. Reprinted with permission.

Evaluation of Activity-Based Costing

Activity-based costing improves the accuracy of product costs, helps managers to understand the nature of overhead costs, and helps managers target areas for improvement through benchmarking and other techniques. These benefits are discussed in this section.

The Benefits of Activity-Based Costing

Activity-based costing improves the accuracy of product costs in three ways. First, activity-based costing usually increases the number of cost pools used to accumulate overhead costs. Rather than accumulating all overhead costs in a single, plantwide pool, or accumulating them in departmental pools, the company accumulates costs for each major activity. Second, the activity cost pools are more homogeneous than departmental cost pools. In principle, all of the costs in an activity cost pool pertain to a single activity. In contrast, departmental cost pools contain the costs of many different activities carried out in the department. Third, activity-based costing changes the bases used to assign overhead costs to products. Rather than assign costs on the basis of direct labor or some other measure of volume, managers assign costs on the basis of the activities that cause overhead costs.

In a traditional costing system, overhead is typically applied to products on the basis of direct labor-hours. As a consequence, it may appear that overhead costs are caused by direct labor-hours. In activity-based costing, managers see that batch setups, engineering change orders, and other activities cause overhead costs rather than just direct labor. Better understanding can lead to better decisions and better control over overhead costs.

Finally, activity-based costing can be used as part of a program to improve the overall operations in an organization. It can provide valuable clues concerning the activities that could benefit most from TQM, process reengineering, and other improvement initiatives.

Limitations of Activity-Based Costing

Any discussion of activity-based costing is incomplete without some cautionary warnings. First, the cost of implementing and maintaining an activity-based costing system may outweigh the benefits. Second, it would be naïve to assume that product costs provided even by an activity-based costing are always relevant when making decisions. These limitations are discussed below.

The Cost of Implementing Activity-Based Costing   Implementing ABC is a major project that involves a great deal of effort. First, the cost system must be designed—preferably by a cross-functional team. This requires taking valued employees away from other tasks for a major project. In addition, the data used in the activity-based costing system must be collected and verified. In some cases, this requires collecting data that has never been collected before. In short, implementing and maintaining an activity-based costing system can present a formidable challenge, and management may decide that the costs are too great to justify the expected benefits. Nevertheless, it should be kept in mind that the costs of collecting and processing data have dropped dramatically over the last several decades due to bar coding and other technologies, and these costs can be expected to continue to fall.

When are the benefits of activity-based costing most likely to be worth the cost? Companies that have some of the following characteristics are most likely to benefit from activity-based costing:

1. Products differ substantially in volume, lot size, and in the activities they require.
2. Conditions have changed substantially since the existing cost system was established.
3. Overhead costs are high and increasing and no one seems to understand why.
4. Management does not trust the existing cost system and ignores cost data from the system when making decisions.

Limitations of the ABC Model   The activity-based costing model relies on a number of critical assumptions.[6] Perhaps the most important of these assumptions is that the

---

[6]Eric Noreen, "Conditions under Which Activity-Based Cost Systems Provide Relevant Costs," *Journal of Management Accounting Research*, Fall 1991, pp. 159–168.

cost in each activity cost pool is strictly proportional to its activity measure. What little evidence we have on this issue suggests that overhead costs are less than proportional to activity.[7] As a practical matter, this means that product costs will be overstated for the purposes of making decisions. The product costs generated by activity-based costing are almost certainly more accurate than those generated by a conventional costing system, but the product costs should nevertheless be viewed with caution. Managers should be particularly alert to product costs that contain allocations of facility-level costs. As we shall see later in the book, such product costs can easily lead managers astray in decisions.

Modifying the ABC Model   The discussion in this chapter has assumed that the primary purpose of the activity-based costing system is to provide more accurate product costs for external reports. If the product costs are to be used by managers for internal decisions, some modifications should be made. For example, for decision-making purposes, the distinction between manufacturing costs on the one hand and selling and general administrative expenses on the other hand is unimportant. Managers need to know what costs a product causes, and it doesn't matter whether the costs are manufacturing costs or selling and general administrative expenses. Consequently, for decision-making purposes, some selling and general administrative expenses should be assigned to products as well as manufacturing costs. Moreover, as mentioned above, facility-level costs should be removed from product costs when making decisions. Nevertheless, the techniques covered in this chapter provide a good basis for understanding the mechanics of activity-based costing. For a more complete coverage of the use of activity-based costing in decisions, see more advanced texts.[8]

Activity-Based Costing and Service Industries

Although initially developed as a tool for manufacturing companies, activity-based costing is also being used in service industries. Successful implementation of an activity-based costing system depends on identifying the key activities that generate costs and tracking how many of those activities are performed for each service the organization provides. Activity-based costing has been implemented in a wide variety of service industries including railroads, hospitals, banks, and data services companies.

ABC for Cities

in business | *today*

To keep taxes in check, city governments often decide to charge user fees for certain services (such as the issuance of permits) or to contract for certain services (such as garbage collection) rather than providing those services directly with city employees. These decisions should at least in part be based on the cost of providing such services.

The City of Indianapolis now uses activity-based costing to determine how much it costs to provide a given service. Previously, the city had used direct labor to allocate overhead costs to its services.

Source: Wayne K. Simpson and Michael J. Williams, "Activity-Based: Costing, Management and Budgeting," *Government Accountants Journal*, Spring 1996, pp. 26–28. Copyright 1996. Reprinted with the permission of the Association of Government Accountants.

---

[7]Eric Noreen and Naomi Soderstrom, "The Accuracy of Proportional Cost Models: Evidence from Hospital Service Departments," *Review of Accounting Studies* 2, 1997 and Eric Noreen and Naomi Soderstrom, "Are Overhead Costs Proportional to Activity? Evidence from Hospital Service Departments," *Journal of Accounting and Economics*, January 1994, pp. 253–278.

[8]See, for example, Chapter 8 in Ray Garrison and Eric Noreen, *Managerial Accounting*, ninth edition, Irwin/McGraw-Hill, © 2000.

decision *maker* **Hospital Administrator**

You are the administrator of a community hospital. The hospital's board of directors has questioned the pricing of certain services and noted that the fees charged for these services seem to be lower than those charged by nearby hospitals. After interviewing one of the hospital's costs analysts, you learn that a hospital-wide rate has been used to assign a single pool of overhead costs to services. After reading about activity-based costing, you make a list of other cost pools that might be more appropriate and plan to ask the cost analyst to identify the cost drivers that might relate to those cost pools. What cost pools would you include on the list?

Cost Flows in an Activity-Based Costing System

Learning Objective 5
Record the flow of costs in an activity-based costing system.

In Chapter 2, we discussed the flow of costs in a job-order costing system. The flow of costs through Raw Materials, Work in Process, and other accounts is the same under activity-based costing. The only difference in activity-based costing is that more than one predetermined overhead rate is used to apply overhead costs to products. Our purpose in this section is to provide a detailed example of cost flows in an activity-based costing system.

An Example of Cost Flows

The company in the following example has five activity cost pools and therefore must compute five predetermined overhead rates (i.e., activity rates). Except for that detail, the journal entries, T-accounts, and general cost flows are the same as described in Chapter 2.

Basic Data Sarvik Company uses activity-based costing for its external financial reports. The company has five activity cost pools, which are listed below along with relevant data for the coming year.

Activity Cost Pool	Activity Measure	Estimated Overhead Cost	Expected Activity
Machine related ..	Machine-hours	$175,000	5,000 MHs
Purchase orders ..	Number of orders	63,000	700 orders
Machine setups ...	Number of setups	92,000	460 setups
Product testing ...	Number of tests	160,000	200 tests
General factory ...	Direct labor-hours	300,000	25,000 DLHs

At the beginning of the year, the company had inventory balances as follows:

Raw materials	$3,000
Work in process	4,000
Finished goods	–0–

Selected transactions recorded by the company during the year are given below:

  a. Raw materials were purchased on account, $915,000.
  b. Raw materials were requisitioned for use in production, $900,000 ($810,000 direct and $90,000 indirect).
  c. Labor costs were incurred in the factory, $370,000 ($95,000 direct labor and $275,000 indirect labor).
  d. Depreciation was recorded on factory assets, $180,000.
  e. Miscellaneous manufacturing overhead costs were incurred, $230,000.

f. Manufacturing overhead cost was applied to production. Actual activity during the year was as follows:

Activity Cost Pool	Actual Activity
Machine related	4,600 MHs
Purchase orders	800 orders
Machine setups	500 setups
Product testing	190 tests
General factory	23,000 DLHs

g. Goods costing $1,650,000 to manufacture were completed during the year.

Tracking the Flow of Costs   The predetermined overhead rates (i.e., activity rates) for the activity cost pools would be computed as follows:

Activity Cost Pools	(a) Estimated Overhead Cost	(b) Total Expected Activity	(a) ÷ (b) Activity Rate
Machine related	$175,000	5,000 machine-hours	$35 per machine-hour
Purchase orders	63,000	700 orders	$90 per order
Machine setups	92,000	460 setups	$200 per setup
Product testing	160,000	200 tests	$800 per test
General factory	300,000	25,000 direct labor-hours	$12 per direct labor-hour

The following journal entries would be used to record transactions (a) through (g) above:

a.	Raw Materials	915,000	
	Accounts Payable		915,000
b.	Work in Process	810,000	
	Manufacturing Overhead	90,000	
	Raw Materials		900,000
c.	Work in Process	95,000	
	Manufacturing Overhead	275,000	
	Salaries and Wages Payable		370,000
d.	Manufacturing Overhead	180,000	
	Accumulated Depreciation		180,000
e.	Manufacturing Overhead	230,000	
	Accounts Payable		230,000

Recall from Chapter 2 the formula for computing applied overhead cost, which is:

Predetermined overhead rate × Actual activity = Applied overhead cost

In activity-based costing, this formula is applied for each activity cost pool using its own predetermined overhead rate (i.e., activity rate). The computations are as follows:

Activities	(1) Activity Rate	(2) Actual Activity	(1) × (2) Applied Overhead Cost
Machine related	$ 35 per MH	4,600 MHs	$161,000
Purchase orders	90 per order	800 orders	72,000
Machine setups	200 per setup	500 setups	100,000
Product testing	800 per test	190 tests	152,000
General factory	12 per DLH	23,000 DLHs	276,000
Total			$761,000

By totaling these five applied overhead cost figures, we find that the company applied $761,000 in overhead cost to products during the year. The following entry would be used to record this application of overhead cost:

f.	Work in Process	761,000	
	Manufacturing Overhead		761,000

Finally, the following journal entry would be used to record the completion of work in process as described in transaction (g) above:

g.	Finished Goods	1,650,000	
	Work in Process		1,650,000

The T-accounts corresponding to the above journal entries appear below:

Raw Materials			
Bal.	3,000	(b)	900,000
(a)	915,000		
Bal.	18,000		

Work in Process			
Bal.	4,000	(g)	1,650,000
(b)	810,000		
(c)	95,000		
(f)	761,000		
Bal.	20,000		

Finished Goods			
Bal.	–0–		
(g)	1,650,000		

Accumulated Depreciation			
		(d)	180,000

Accounts Payable			
		(a)	915,000
		(e)	230,000

Salaries and Wages Payable			
		(c)	370,000

Manufacturing Overhead			
(b)	90,000	(f)	761,000
(c)	275,000		
(d)	180,000		
(e)	230,000		
	775,000		761,000
Bal.	14,000		

The overhead is underapplied by $14,000. This can be determined directly, as shown below, or by reference to the balance in the Manufacturing Overhead T-account above.

Actual manufacturing overhead incurred	$775,000
Manufacturing overhead applied	761,000
Overhead underapplied	$ 14,000

you *decide*   ## Entrepreneur

You are the owner of a small manufacturing firm. You are considering whether you should continue to use direct labor as the base for assigning overhead or implement activity-based costing. How would you go about making this decision?

Summary

LO1   Understand the basic approach in activity-based costing and how it differs from conventional costing.

Activity-based costing was developed as a way of more accurately assigning overhead to products. Activity-based costing differs from conventional costing as described in Chapter 2 in two major ways. First, in activity-based costing, each major activity that consumes overhead resources has its own cost pool and its own activity rate, whereas in Chapter 2 there was only a single overhead cost pool and a single predetermined overhead rate. Second, the allocation bases (or activity measures) in activity-based costing are diverse. They may include machine setups, purchase orders, engineering change orders, and so on, in addition to direct labor-hours or machine-hours. Nevertheless, within each activity cost pool, the mechanics of computing overhead rates and of applying overhead to products are the same as described in Chapter 2. However, the increase in the number of cost pools and the use of better measures of activity generally result in more accurate product costs.

LO2   Compute activity rates for an activity-based costing system.

Each activity in an activity-based costing system has its own cost pool and its own measure of activity. The activity rate for a particular activity is computed by dividing the total cost in the activity's cost pool by the total amount of activity.

LO3   Compute product costs using activity-based costing.

Product costs in activity-based costing, as in conventional costing systems, consist of direct materials, direct labor, and overhead. In both systems, overhead is applied to products using predetermined overhead rates. In the case of an activity-based costing system, each activity has its own predetermined overhead rate (i.e., activity rate). The activities required by a product are multiplied by their respective activity rates to determine the amount of overhead that is applied to the product.

LO4   Contrast the product costs computed under activity-based costing and conventional costing methods.

Under conventional costing methods, overhead costs are allocated to products on the basis of some measure of volume such as direct labor-hours or machine-hours. This results in most of the overhead cost being allocated to high-volume products. In contrast, under activity-based costing, some overhead costs are allocated on the basis of batch-level or product-level activities. This change in allocation bases results in shifting overhead costs from the high-volume products to low-volume products. Accordingly, product costs for high-volume products are commonly lower under activity-based costing than under conventional costing methods, and product costs for low-volume products are higher.

LO5   Record the flow of costs in an activity-based costing system.

The journal entries and general flow of costs in an activity-based costing system are the same as they are in a conventional costing system. The only difference is the use of more than one predetermined overhead rate (i.e., activity rate) to apply overhead to products.

Guidance Answers to Decision Maker and You Decide

HOSPITAL ADMINISTRATOR (p. 136)

Cost pools that could be segregated in a small community hospital might include, but probably would not be limited to, the following: various patient departments (such as pediatrics and maternity), the emergency room, operating rooms, the radiology (X-ray) department, physical therapy, the pharmacy, the cafeteria, the gift shop, and the admitting, housekeeping, laundry, maintenance, accounting, and personnel departments. [Source: John B. MacArthur and Harriet A. Stranahan, "Cost Driver Analysis in Hospitals: A Simultaneous Equations Approach," *Journal of Management Accounting Research* 10, 1998, pp. 279–312.]

ENTREPRENEUR (p. 138)

Your decision should weigh both the costs and the benefits of adopting activity-based costing. The primary benefit of activity-based costing is an improvement in the accuracy of product costs. The conventional approach applies (or assigns) overhead to products on the basis of direct labor-hours. If there is a correlation between direct labor and overhead (that is, when direct labor increases, overhead increases and vice versa), this approach may be sufficient. However, if this correlation does not exist, activity-based costing may result in more accurate product costs because more of the overhead would be assigned to products on the basis of the activities that cause the overhead costs. The primary cost of an activity-based costing system includes the cost of implementing and maintaining the system. A team must be formed to handle the implementation and data must be collected and analyzed during implementation and then on an ongoing basis.

You might also consider the following characteristics, which are common to a company that is likely to benefit from activity-based costing:

- The company produces a variety of products that differ in terms of the manufacturing process (for example, certain products may require different machine setups, etc.).
- Conditions have changed (for example, the factory has been enlarged).
- Overhead costs have increased in relation to direct material and direct labor costs.
- Managers ignore cost data from the company's accounting system when making decisions because they do not believe that the cost data reflect the true costs of the company's products.

Review Problem: Activity-Based Costing

Aerodec, Inc., manufactures and sells two types of wooden deck chairs: Deluxe and Tourist. Annual sales in units, direct labor-hours (DLHs) per unit, and total direct labor-hours per year are provided below:

	Total Hours
Deluxe deck chair: 2,000 units × 5 DLHs per unit	10,000
Tourist deck chair: 10,000 units × 4 DLHs per unit	40,000
Total direct labor-hours	50,000

Costs for materials and labor for one unit of each product are given below:

	Deluxe	Tourist
Direct materials	$25	$17
Direct labor (at $12 per DLH)	60	48

Manufacturing overhead costs total $800,000 each year. The breakdown of these costs among the company's six activity cost pools is given below. The activity measures are shown in parentheses.

Activities and Activity Measures	Estimated Overhead Cost	Expected Activity		
		Total	Deluxe	Tourist
Labor related (direct labor-hours)	$ 80,000	50,000	10,000	40,000
Machine setups (number of setups)	150,000	5,000	3,000	2,000
Parts administration (number of parts)	160,000	80	50	30
Production orders (number of orders)	70,000	400	100	300
Material receipts (number of receipts)	90,000	750	150	600
General factory (machine-hours)	250,000	40,000	12,000	28,000
	$800,000			

Required:
1. Classify each of Aerodec's activities as either a unit-level, batch-level, product-level, or facility-level activity.
2. Assume that the company applies overhead cost to products on the basis of direct labor-hours.
   a. Compute the predetermined overhead rate that would be used.
   b. Determine the unit product cost of each product, using the predetermined overhead rate computed in (2)(a) above.
3. Assume that the company uses activity-based costing to compute overhead rates.
   a. Compute the activity rate (i.e., predetermined overhead rate) for each of the six activity centers listed above.
   b. Using the rates developed in (3)(a) above, determine the amount of overhead cost that would be assigned to a unit of each product.
   c. Determine the unit product cost of each product and compare this cost to the cost computed in (2)(b) above.

SOLUTION TO REVIEW PROBLEM

1.

Activity Cost Pool	Type of Activity
Labor related	Unit level
Machine setups	Batch level
Parts administration	Product level
Production orders	Batch level
Material receipts	Batch level
General factory	Facility level

2. a.

$$\text{Predetermined overhead rate} = \frac{\text{Estimated total manufacturing overhead}}{\text{Estimated total direct labor-hours (DLHs)}} = \frac{\$800,000}{50,000 \text{ DLHs}} = \$16 \text{ per DLH}$$

b.

	Deluxe	Tourist
Direct materials	$ 25	$ 17
Direct labor	60	48
Manufacturing overhead applied:		
Deluxe: 5 DLHs × $16 per DLH	80	
Tourist: 4 DLHs × $16 per DLH		64
Unit product cost	$165	$129

3. a.

Activities	(a) Estimated Overhead Cost	(b) Total Expected Activity	(a) ÷ (b) Activity Rate
Labor related	$ 80,000	50,000 DLHs	$1.60 per DLH
Machine setups	150,000	5,000 setups	$30.00 per setup
Parts administration	160,000	80 parts	$2,000.00 per part
Production orders	70,000	400 orders	$175.00 per order
Material receipts	90,000	750 receipts	$120.00 per receipt
General factory	250,000	40,000 MHs	$6.25 per MH

b.

Activities and Activity Rates	Deluxe Expected Activity	Amount	Tourist Expected Activity	Amount
Labor related, at $1.60 per DLH	10,000	$ 16,000	40,000	$ 64,000
Machine setups, at $30 per setup	3,000	90,000	2,000	60,000
Parts administration, at $2,000 per part	50	100,000	30	60,000
Production orders, at $175 per order	100	17,500	300	52,500
Material receipts, at $120 per receipt	150	18,000	600	72,000
General factory, at $6.25 per MH	12,000	75,000	28,000	175,000
Total overhead cost assigned (a)		$316,500		$483,500
Number of units produced (b)		2,000		10,000
Overhead cost per unit, (a) ÷ (b)		$158.25		$48.35

c.

	Deluxe	Tourist
Direct materials	$ 25.00	$ 17.00
Direct labor	60.00	48.00
Manufacturing overhead (see above)	158.25	48.35
Unit product cost	$243.25	$113.35

Under activity-based costing, the unit product cost of the Deluxe deck chair is much greater than the cost computed in (2)(b) above, and the unit product cost of the Tourist deck chair is much less. Using volume (direct labor-hours) in (2)(b) as a basis for applying overhead cost to products has resulted in too little overhead cost being applied to the Deluxe deck chair (the low-volume product) and too much overhead cost being applied to the Tourist deck chair (the high-volume product).

Glossary

Activity An event that causes the consumption of overhead resources in an organization. (p. 122)
Activity-based costing (ABC) A two-stage costing method in which overhead costs are assigned to products on the basis of the activities they require. (p. 121)
Activity-based management A management approach that focuses on managing activities as a way of eliminating waste and reducing delays and defects. (p. 132)
Activity cost pool A "bucket" in which costs are accumulated that relate to a single activity in the activity-based costing system. (p. 122)
Activity measure An allocation base in an activity-based costing system; ideally, a measure of whatever causes the costs in an activity cost pool. (p. 122)
Activity rate A predetermined overhead rate in activity-based costing. Each activity cost pool has its own activity rate which is used to apply overhead to products and services. (p. 122)
Batch-level activities Activities that are performed each time a batch of goods is handled or processed, regardless of how many units are in a batch. The amount of resources consumed depends on the number of batches run rather than on the number of units in the batch. (p. 124)
Benchmarking A systematic approach to identifying the activities with the greatest room for improvement. It is based on comparing the performance in an organization with the performance of other, similar organizations known for their outstanding performance. (p. 133)
Facility-level activities Activities that relate to overall production and therefore can't be traced to specific products. Costs associated with these activities pertain to a plant's general manufacturing process. (p. 124)
Product-level activities Activities that relate to specific products that must be carried out regardless of how many units are produced and sold or batches run. (p. 124)
Unit-level activities Activities that arise as a result of the total volume of goods and services that are produced, and that are performed each time a unit is produced. (p. 123)

Questions

3–1   What are the three common approaches for assigning overhead costs to products?
3–2   Why is activity-based costing growing in popularity?
3–3   Why do departmental overhead rates sometimes result in inaccurate product costs?
3–4   What are the four hierarchical levels of activity discussed in the chapter?
3–5   Why is activity-based costing described as a "two-stage" costing method?
3–6   Why do overhead costs often shift from high-volume products to low-volume products when a company switches from a conventional costing method to activity-based costing?
3–7   What are the three major ways in which activity-based costing improves the accuracy of product costs?
3–8   What are the major limitations of activity-based costing?

Brief Exercises

BRIEF EXERCISE 3–1   ABC Cost Hierarchy (LO1)
The following activities occur at Greenwich Corporation, a company that manufactures a variety of products.
a. Receive raw materials from suppliers.

b. Manage parts inventories.
c. Do rough milling work on products.
d. Interview and process new employees in the personnel department.
e. Design new products.
f. Perform periodic preventative maintenance on general-use equipment.
g. Use the general factory building.
h. Issue purchase orders for a job.

Required:
Classify each of the activities above as either a unit-level, batch-level, product-level, or facility-level activity.

BRIEF EXERCISE 3–2   Compute Activity Rates (LO2)
Kramer Corporation is a diversified manufacturer of consumer goods. The company's activity-based costing system has the following seven activity cost pools:

Activity Cost Pool	Estimated Overhead Cost	Expected Activity
Labor related	$ 48,000	20,000 direct labor-hours
Machine related	67,500	45,000 machine-hours
Machine setups	84,000	600 setups
Production orders	112,000	400 orders
Product testing	58,500	900 tests
Packaging	90,000	6,000 packages
General factory	672,000	20,000 direct labor-hours

Required:
1. Compute the activity rate for each activity cost pool.
2. Compute the company's predetermined overhead rate, assuming that the company uses a single plantwide predetermined overhead rate based on direct labor-hours.

BRIEF EXERCISE 3–3   Compute ABC Product Costs (LO3)
Klumper Corporation is a diversified manufacturer of industrial goods. The company's activity-based costing system has the following six activity cost pools and activity rates:

Activity Cost Pool	Activity Rates
Labor related	$ 6.00 per direct labor-hour
Machine related	4.00 per machine-hour
Machine setups	50.00 per setup
Production orders	90.00 per order
Shipments	14.00 per shipment
General factory	9.00 per direct labor-hour

Cost and activity data have been supplied for the following products:

	K425	M67
Direct materials cost per unit	$13.00	$56.00
Direct labor cost per unit	$5.60	$3.50
Number of units produced per year	200	2,000

	Total Expected Activity	
	K425	M67
Direct labor-hours	80	500
Machine-hours	100	1,500
Machine setups	1	4
Production orders	1	4
Shipments	1	10

Required:
Compute the unit product cost of each of the products listed above.

BRIEF EXERCISE 3–4   Contrast ABC and Conventional Product Costs (LO4)
Midwest Industrial Products Corporation makes two products, Product H and Product L. Product H is expected to sell 50,000 units next year and Product L is expected to sell 10,000 units. A unit of either product requires 0.2 direct labor-hours.

The company's total manufacturing overhead for the year is expected to be $1,920,000.

Required:
1. The company currently applies manufacturing overhead to products using direct labor-hours as the allocation base. If this method is followed, how much overhead cost would be applied to each product? Compute both the overhead cost per unit and the total amount of overhead cost that would be applied to each product. (In other words, how much overhead cost is applied to a unit of Product H? Product L? How much overhead cost is applied in total to all the units of Product H? Product L?)
2. Management is considering an activity-based costing system and would like to know what impact this change might have on product costs. For purposes of discussion, it has been suggested that all of the manufacturing overhead be treated as a product-level cost. The total manufacturing overhead would be divided in half between the two products, with $960,000 assigned to Product H and $960,000 assigned to Product L.

   If this suggestion is followed, how much overhead cost per unit would be applied to each product?
3. Explain the impact on unit product costs of the switch in costing systems.

BRIEF EXERCISE 3–5   Cost Flows in an ABC System (LO5)
Larker Corporation implemented activity-based costing several years ago and uses it for its external financial reports. The company has four activity cost pools, which are listed below.

Activity Cost Pool	Activity Rate
Machine related	$24 per MH
Purchase orders	$85 per order
Machine setups	$175 per setup
General factory	$16 per DLH

At the beginning of the year, the company had inventory balances as follows:

Raw materials	$18,000
Work in process	24,000
Finished goods	46,000

Selected transactions recorded by the company during the year are given below:
a. Raw materials were purchased on account, $854,000.
b. Raw materials were requisitioned for use in production, $848,000 ($780,000 direct and $68,000 indirect).
c. Labor costs were incurred in the factory, $385,000 ($330,000 direct labor and $55,000 indirect labor).
d. Depreciation was recorded on factory assets, $225,000.
e. Miscellaneous manufacturing overhead costs were incurred, $194,000.
f. Manufacturing overhead cost was applied to production. Actual activity during the year was as follows:

Activity Cost Pool	Actual Activity
Machine related	3,800 MHs
Purchase orders	700 orders
Machine setups	400 setups
General factory	22,000 DLHs

g. Completed products were transferred to the company's finished goods warehouse. According to the company's costing system, these products cost $1,690,000.

Required:

1. Prepare journal entries to record transactions (a) through (g) above.
2. Post the entries in (1) above to T-accounts.
3. Compute the underapplied or overapplied overhead cost in the Manufacturing Overhead account.

Exercises

EXERCISE 3–1   ABC Cost Hierarchy (LO1)

The following activities are carried out in Greenberry Company, a manufacturer of consumer goods.

a. Direct labor workers assemble a product.
b. Engineers design a new product.
c. A machine is set up to process a batch.
d. Numerically controlled machines cut and shape materials.
e. The personnel department trains new employees concerning company policies.
f. Raw materials are moved from the receiving dock to the production line.
g. A random sample of 10 units is inspected for defects in each batch.

Required:

1. Classify each activity as a unit-level, batch-level, product-level, or facility-level cost.
2. Provide at least one example of an allocation base (i.e., activity measure) that could be used to allocate the cost of each activity listed above.

EXERCISE 3–2   Contrast ABC and Conventional Product Costs (LO2, LO3, LO4)

Harrison Company makes two products and uses a conventional costing system in which a single plantwide predetermined overhead rate is computed based on direct labor-hours. Data for the two products for the upcoming year follow:

	Rascon	Parcel
Direct materials cost per unit	$13.00	$22.00
Direct labor cost per unit	$6.00	$3.00
Direct labor-hours per unit	0.40	0.20
Number of units produced	20,000	80,000

These products are customized to some degree for specific customers.

Required:

1. The company's manufacturing overhead costs for the year are expected to be $576,000. Using the company's conventional costing system, compute the unit product costs for the two products.
2. Management is considering an activity-based costing system in which half of the overhead would continue to be allocated on the basis of direct labor-hours and half would be allocated on the basis of engineering design time. This time is expected to be distributed as follows during the upcoming year:

	Rascon	Parcel	Total
Engineering design time (in hours)	3,000	3,000	6,000

Compute the unit product costs for the two products using the proposed ABC system.

3. Explain why the product costs differ between the two systems.

EXERCISE 3–3   Cost Flows in Activity-Based Costing (LO2, LO5)

Sylvan Company uses activity-based costing to determine product costs for external financial reports. Some of the entries have been completed to the Manufacturing Overhead account for the current year, as shown by entry (a) below:

Manufacturing Overhead

(a) 1,302,000	

Required:
1. What does the entry (a) above represent?
2. At the beginning of the year, the company made the following estimates of cost and activity for its five activity cost pools:

Activity Cost Pool	Activity Measure	Estimated Overhead Cost	Expected Activity
Labor related	Direct labor-hours	$280,000	40,000 DLHs
Purchase orders	Number of orders	90,000	1,500 orders
Parts management	Number of part types	120,000	400 part types
Board etching	Number of boards	360,000	2,000 boards
General factory	Machine-hours	400,000	80,000 MHs

Compute the activity rate (i.e., predetermined overhead rate) for each of the activity cost pools.
3. During the year, actual activity was recorded as follows:

Activity Cost Pool	Actual Activity
Labor related	41,000 DLHs
Purchase orders	1,300 orders
Parts management	420 part types
Board etching	2,150 boards
General factory	82,000 MHs

Determine the amount of manufacturing overhead cost applied to production for the year.
4. Determine the amount of underapplied or overapplied overhead cost for the year.

EXERCISE 3–4   Assigning Overhead to Products in ABC (LO3)

Refer to the data in Exercise 3-3 for Sylvan Company. The activities during the year were distributed across the company's four products as follows:

Activity Cost Pool	Actual Activity	Product A	Product B	Product C	Product D
Labor related	41,000 DLHs	8,000	12,000	15,000	6,000
Purchase orders . .	1,300 orders	100	300	400	500
Parts management	420 part types	20	90	200	110
Board etching	2,150 boards	–0–	1,500	650	–0–
General factory . . .	82,000 MHs	16,000	24,000	30,000	12,000

Required:
Compute the amount of overhead cost applied to each product during the year.

EXERCISE 3–5   Computing ABC Product Costs (LO2, LO3)

Fogerty Company makes two products, titanium Hubs and Sprockets. Data regarding the two products follow:

	Direct Labor-Hours per Unit	Annual Production
Hubs	0.80	10,000 units
Sprockets	0.40	40,000 units

Additional information about the company follows:
a. Hubs require $32 in direct materials per unit, and Sprockets require $18.

b. The direct labor wage rate is $15 per hour.
c. Hubs are more complex to manufacture than Sprockets and they require special equipment.
d. The ABC system has the following activity cost pools:

Activity Cost Pool	Activity Measure	Estimated Overhead Cost	Activity		
			Total	Hubs	Sprockets
Machine setups	Number of setups	$ 72,000	400	100	300
Special processing ...	Machine-hours	200,000	5,000	5,000	—
General factory	Direct labor-hours	816,000	24,000	8,000	16,000
		$1,088,000			

Required:
1. Compute the activity rate (i.e., predetermined overhead rate) for each activity cost pool.
2. Determine the unit product cost of each product.

Problems

PROBLEM 3–1   ABC Cost Hierarchy (LO1)
Juneau Company manufactures a variety of products in a single facility. Consultants hired by the company to do an activity-based costing analysis have identified the following activities carried out in the company on a routine basis:
a. Machines are set up between batches of different products.
b. The company's grounds crew maintains planted areas surrounding the factory.
c. A percentage of all completed goods are inspected on a random basis.
d. Milling machines are used to make components for products.
e. Employees are trained in general procedures.
f. Purchase orders are issued for materials required in production.
g. The maintenance crew does routine periodic maintenance on general-purpose equipment.
h. The plant controller prepares periodic accounting reports.
i. Material is received on the receiving dock and moved to the production area.
j. The engineering department makes modifications in the designs of products.
k. The human resources department screens and hires new employees.
l. Production orders are issued for jobs.

Required:
1. Classify each of the above activities as a unit-level, batch-level, product-level, or facility-level activity.
2. For each of the above activities, suggest an activity measure that could be used to allocate its costs to products.

PROBLEM 3–2   Contrasting ABC and Conventional Product Costs (LO2, LO3, LO4)
Siegel Corporation manufactures a product that is available in both a deluxe and a regular model. The company has made the regular model for years; the deluxe model was introduced several years ago to tap a new segment of the market. Since introduction of the deluxe model, the company's profits have steadily declined, and management has become concerned about the accuracy of its costing system. Sales of the deluxe model have been increasing rapidly.

Overhead is applied to products on the basis of direct labor-hours. At the beginning of the current year, management estimated that $2,000,000 in overhead costs would be incurred and the company would produce and sell 5,000 units of the deluxe model and 40,000 units of the regular model. The deluxe model requires 1.6 hours of direct labor time per unit, and the regular model requires 0.8 hours. Materials and labor costs per unit are given below:

	Deluxe	Regular
Direct materials cost per unit	$150	$112
Direct labor cost per unit	16	8

CHECK FIGURE
(3b) Regular: $152 per unit

Required:

1. Compute the predetermined overhead rate using direct labor-hours as the basis for allocating overhead costs to products. Compute the unit product cost for one unit of each model.
2. An intern suggested that the company use activity-based costing to cost its products. A team was formed to investigate this idea and it came back with the recommendation that four activity cost pools be used. These cost pools and their associated activities are listed below:

Activity Cost Pool and Activity Measure	Estimated Overhead Cost	Activity		
		Total	Deluxe	Regular
Purchase orders (number of orders)	$ 84,000	1,200	400	800
Rework requests (number of requests) ...	216,000	900	300	600
Product testing (number of tests)	450,000	15,000	4,000	11,000
Machine-related (machine-hours)	1,250,000	50,000	20,000	30,000
	$2,000,000			

Compute the activity rate (i.e., predetermined overhead rate) for each of the activity cost pools.
3. Assume that actual activity is as expected for the year. Using activity-based costing, do the following:
   a. Determine the total amount of overhead that would be applied to each model for the year.
   b. Compute the unit product cost for one unit of each model.
4. Can you identify a possible explanation for the company's declining profits? If so, what is it?

CHECK FIGURE
(2d) Total overhead
overapplied: $15,000

PROBLEM 3–3   Cost Flows and Unit Product Costs in Activity-Based Costing (LO2, LO3, LO5)

Hunter Corporation uses activity-based costing to determine product costs for external financial reports. At the beginning of the year, management made the following estimates of cost and activity in the company's five activity cost pools:

Activity Cost Pool	Activity Measure	Estimated Overhead Cost	Expected Activity
Labor related	Direct labor-hours	$270,000	30,000 DLHs
Production orders	Number of orders	60,000	750 orders
Material receipts	Number of receipts	180,000	1,200 receipts
Relay assembly	Number of relays	320,000	8,000 relays
General factory	Machine-hours	840,000	60,000 MHs

Required:

1. Compute the activity rate (i.e., predetermined overhead rate) for each of the activity cost pools.
2. During the year, actual overhead cost and activity were recorded as follows:

Activity Cost Pool	Actual Overhead Cost	Actual Activity
Labor related	$ 279,000	32,000 DLHs
Production orders	58,000	700 orders
Material receipts	190,000	1,300 receipts
Relay assembly	320,000	7,900 relays
General factory	847,000	61,000 MHs
Total overhead cost	$1,694,000	

   a. Prepare a journal entry to record the incurrence of actual manufacturing overhead cost for the year (credit Accounts Payable). Post the entry to the company's Manufacturing Overhead T-account.
   b. Determine the amount of overhead cost applied to production during the year.
   c. Prepare a journal entry to record the application of manufacturing overhead cost to work in process for the year. Post the entry to the company's Manufacturing Overhead T-account.

d. Determine the amount of underapplied or overapplied manufacturing overhead for the year.

3. The actual activity for the year was distributed among the company's four products as follows:

Activity Cost Pool	Actual Activity	Product A	Product B	Product C	Product D
Labor related	32,000 DLHs	8,000	11,000	4,000	9,000
Production orders	700 orders	160	200	130	210
Materials receipts	1,300 receipts	100	460	240	500
Relay assembly	7,900 relays	2,700	–0–	5,200	–0–
General factory	61,000 MHs	13,000	18,000	14,000	16,000

a. Determine the total amount of overhead cost applied to each product.
b. Does the total amount of overhead cost applied to the products above "tie in" to the T-accounts in any way? Explain.

PROBLEM 3–4   Contrast Activity-Based Costing and Conventional Product Costs (LO2, LO3, LO4)

CHECK FIGURE
(2b) X200 unit product cost: $213

Ellix Company manufactures two models of ultra-high fidelity speakers, the X200 model and the X99 model. Data regarding the two products follow:

	Direct Labor-Hours per Unit	Annual Production	Total Direct Labor-Hours
Model X200	1.8	5,000 units	9,000
Model X99	0.9	30,000 units	27,000
			36,000

Additional information about the company follows:
a. Model X200 requires $72 in direct materials per unit, and model X99 requires $50.
b. The direct labor wage rate is $10 per hour.
c. The company has always used direct labor-hours as the base for applying manufacturing overhead cost to products.
d. Model X200 is more complex to manufacture than model X99 and requires the use of special equipment. Consequently, the company is considering the use of activity-based costing to apply manufacturing overhead cost to products for external financial reports. Three activity cost pools have been identified as follows:

Activity Cost Pool	Activity Measure	Estimated Overhead Cost
Machine setups	Number of setups	$ 360,000
Special processing	Machine-hours	180,000
General factory	Direct labor-hours	1,260,000
		$1,800,000

	Expected Activity		
Activity Measure	Model X200	Model X99	Total
Number of setups	50	100	150
Machine-hours	12,000	–0–	12,000
Direct labor-hours	9,000	27,000	36,000

Required:

1. Assume that the company continues to use direct labor-hours as the base for applying overhead cost to products.
   a. Compute the predetermined overhead rate.
   b. Compute the unit product cost of each model.
2. Assume that the company decides to use activity-based costing to apply manufacturing overhead cost to products.
   a. Compute the predetermined overhead rate for each activity cost pool and determine the amount of overhead cost that would be applied to each model using the activity-based costing system.
   b. Compute the unit product cost of each model.
3. Explain why manufacturing overhead cost shifts from Model X99 to Model X200 under activity-based costing.

CHECK FIGURE
(2d) Total overhead
underapplied: $17,000

PROBLEM 3–5   Activity-Based Costing Cost Flows (LO2, LO3, LO5)

Munoz Corporation uses activity-based costing to determine product costs for external financial reports. At the beginning of the year, management made the following estimates of cost and activity in the company's five activity cost pools:

Activity Cost Pool	Activity Measure	Estimated Overhead Cost	Expected Activity
Labor related	Direct labor-hours	$210,000	35,000 DLHs
Purchase orders	Number of orders	72,000	900 orders
Product testing	Number of tests	168,000	1,400 tests
Template etching	Number of templates	315,000	10,500 templates
General factory	Machine-hours	840,000	70,000 MHs

Required:

1. Compute the activity rate (i.e., predetermined overhead rate) for each of the activity cost pools.
2. During the year, actual overhead cost and activity were recorded as follows:

Activity Cost Pool	Actual Overhead Cost	Actual Activity
Labor related	$ 205,000	32,000 DLHs
Purchase orders	74,000	950 orders
Product testing	160,000	1,300 tests
Template etching	338,000	11,500 relays
General factory	825,000	68,000 MHs
Total overhead cost	$1,602,000	

   a. Prepare a journal entry to record the incurrence of actual manufacturing overhead cost for the year (credit Accounts Payable). Post the entry to the company's Manufacturing Overhead T-account.
   b. Determine the amount of overhead cost applied to production during the year.
   c. Prepare a journal entry to record the application of manufacturing overhead cost to work in process for the year. Post the entry to the company's Manufacturing Overhead T-account.
   d. Determine the amount of underapplied or overapplied manufacturing overhead for the year.
3. The actual activity for the year was distributed among the company's four products as follows:

Activity Cost Pool	Actual Activity	Product A	Product B	Product C	Product D
Labor related	32,000 DLHs	6,000	7,500	10,000	8,500
Purchase orders	950 orders	150	300	100	400
Product testing	1,300 tests	400	175	225	500
Template etching	11,500 templates	–0–	4,500	–0–	7,000
General factory	68,000 MHs	10,000	20,000	17,000	21,000

   a. Determine the total amount of overhead cost applied to each product.
   b. Does the total amount of overhead cost applied to the products above "tie in" to the T-accounts in any way? Explain.

PROBLEM 3–6   Activity-Based Costing Cost Flows and Income Statement (LO2, LO5)

Aucton Corporation is a manufacturing company that uses activity-based costing for its external financial reports. The company's activity cost pools and associated data for the coming year appear below:

CHECK FIGURE
(4) Total overhead
overapplied: $8,000

Activity Cost Pool	Activity Measure	Estimated Overhead Cost	Expected Activity
Machining	Machine-hours	$180,000	1,000 MHs
Purchase orders	Number of orders	90,000	600 orders
Parts management	Number of part types	60,000	300 part types
Testing	Number of tests	150,000	250 tests
General factory	Direct labor-hours	280,000	20,000 DLHs

At the beginning of the year, the company had inventory balances as follows:

Raw materials	$ 7,000
Work in process	6,000
Finished goods	10,000

The following transactions were recorded for the year:
a. Raw materials were purchased on account, $595,000.
b. Raw materials were withdrawn from the storeroom for use in production, $600,000 ($560,000 direct and $40,000 indirect).
c. The following costs were incurred for employee services: direct labor, $90,000; indirect labor, $300,000; sales commissions, $85,000; and administrative salaries, $245,000.
d. Sales travel costs were incurred, $38,000.
e. Various factory overhead costs were incurred, $237,000.
f. Advertising costs were incurred, $190,000.
g. Depreciation was recorded for the year, $270,000 ($210,000 related to factory operations and $60,000 related to selling and administrative activities).
h. Manufacturing overhead was applied to products. Actual activity for the year was as follows:

Activity Cost Pool	Actual Activity
Machining	1,050 MHs
Purchase orders	580 orders
Parts management	330 part types
Testing	265 tests
General factory	21,000 DLHs

i. Goods were completed and transferred to the finished goods warehouse. According to the company's activity-based costing system, these finished goods cost $1,450,000 to manufacture.
j. Goods were sold on account to customers during the year for a total of $2,100,000. According to the company's activity-based costing system, the goods cost $1,400,000 to manufacture.

Required:
1. Compute the predetermined overhead rate (i.e., activity rate) for each activity cost pool.
2. Prepare journal entries to record transactions (a) through (j) above.
3. Post the entries in (2) above to T-accounts.
4. Compute the underapplied or overapplied manufacturing overhead cost. Prepare a journal entry to close any balance in the Manufacturing Overhead account to Cost of Goods Sold. Post the entry to the appropriate T-accounts.
5. Prepare an income statement for the year.

PROBLEM 3–7   Contrasting ABC and Conventional Product Costs (LO2, LO3, LO4)

For many years, Zapro Company manufactured a single product called a mono-relay. Then three years ago, the company automated a portion of its plant and at the same time introduced a second product called a bi-relay that has become increasingly popular. The bi-relay is a more complex product, requiring one hour of direct labor time per unit to manufacture and extensive machining in the automated portion of the plant. The mono-relay requires only 0.75 hour of direct labor time per unit and only a small amount of machining. Manufacturing overhead costs are currently assigned to products on the basis of direct labor-hours.

CHECK FIGURE
(3a) Mono-relay overhead
cost: $10.80

Despite the growing popularity of the company's new bi-relay, profits have been declining steadily. Management is beginning to believe that there may be a problem with the company's costing system. Material and labor costs per unit are as follows:

	Mono-Relay	Bi-Relay
Direct materials	$35	$48
Direct labor (0.75 hour and 1.0 hour @ $12 per hour)	9	12

Management estimates that the company will incur $1,000,000 in manufacturing overhead costs during the current year and 40,000 units of the mono-relay and 10,000 units of the bi-relay will be produced and sold.

Required:
1. Compute the predetermined manufacturing overhead rate assuming that the company continues to apply manufacturing overhead cost on the basis of direct labor-hours. Using this rate and other data from the problem, determine the unit product cost of each product.
2. Management is considering using activity-based costing to apply manufacturing overhead cost to products for external financial reports. The activity-based costing system would have the following four activity cost pools:

Activity Cost Pool	Activity Measure	Estimated Overhead Cost
Maintaining parts inventory	Number of part types	$ 180,000
Processing purchase orders	Number of purchase orders	90,000
Quality control	Number of tests run	230,000
Machine related	Machine-hours	500,000
		$1,000,000

	Expected Activity		
Activity Measure	Mono-Relay	Bi-Relay	Total
Number of part types	75	150	225
Number of purchase orders	800	200	1,000
Number of tests run	2,500	3,250	5,750
Machine-hours	4,000	6,000	10,000

Determine the activity rate (i.e., predetermined overhead rate) for each of the four activity cost pools.
3. Using the activity rates you computed in (2) above, do the following:
   a. Compute the total amount of manufacturing overhead cost that would be applied to each product using the activity-based costing system. After these totals have been computed, determine the amount of manufacturing overhead cost per unit of each product.
   b. Compute the unit product cost of each product.
4. From the data you have developed in (1) through (3) above, identify factors that may account for the company's declining profits.

CHECK FIGURE
(3b) $11.95 per diner

PROBLEM 3–8 Compute and Use Activity Rates to Determine the Costs of Serving Customers
(LO2, LO3, LO4)
Jordan's Lakeside is a popular restaurant located on Lake Washington in Seattle. The owner of the restaurant has been trying to better understand costs at the restaurant and has hired a student intern to conduct an activity-based costing study. The intern, in consultation with the owner, identified the following major activities:

Activity Cost Pool	Activity Measure
Serving a party of diners	Number of parties served
Serving a diner	Number of diners served
Serving drinks	Number of drinks ordered

A group of diners who ask to sit at the same table are counted as a party. Some costs, such as the costs of cleaning linen, are the same whether one person is at a table or the table is full. Other costs, such as washing dishes, depend on the number of diners served.

Data concerning these activities are displayed below.

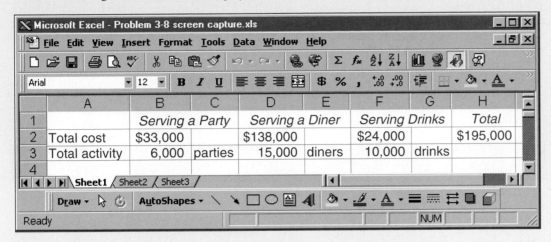

	Serving a Party		Serving a Diner		Serving Drinks		Total
Total cost	$33,000		$138,000		$24,000		$195,000
Total activity	6,000	parties	15,000	diners	10,000	drinks	

Prior to the activity-based costing study, the owner knew very little about the costs of the restaurant. She knew that the total cost for the month was $195,000 and that 15,000 diners had been served. Therefore, the average cost per diner was $13 ($195,000 ÷ 15,000 diners = $13 per diner).

Required:

1. Compute the activity rates for each of the three activities.
2. According to the activity-based costing system, what is the total cost of serving each of the following parties of diners?
    a. A party of four diners who order three drinks in total.
    b. A party of two diners who do not order any drinks.
    c. A lone diner who orders two drinks.
3. Convert the total costs you computed in (1) above to costs per diner. In other words, what is the average cost per diner for serving each of the following parties of diners?
    a. A party of four diners who order three drinks in total.
    b. A party of two diners who do not order any drinks.
    c. A lone diner who orders two drinks.
4. Why do the costs per diner for the three different parties differ from each other and from the overall average cost of $13 per diner?

Building Your Skills

ANALYTICAL THINKING*   (LO2, LO3, LO4)

"A dollar of gross margin per briefcase? That's ridiculous!" roared Art Dejans, president of CarryAll, Inc. "Why do we go on producing those standard briefcases when we're able to make over $15 per unit on our specialty items? Maybe it's time to get out of the standard line and focus the whole plant on specialty work."

Mr. Dejans is referring to a summary of unit costs and revenues that he had just received from the company's Accounting Department:

CHECK FIGURE
(2) Standard model
unit product cost:
$29.98 per unit

	Standard Briefcases	Specialty Briefcases
Selling price per unit	$36	$40
Unit product cost	35	25
Gross margin per unit	$ 1	$15

*Adapted from a case written by Harold P. Roth and Imogene Posey, "Management Accounting Case Study: CarryAll Company," *Management Accounting Campus Report,* Institute of Management Accountants (Fall 1991), p. 9. Used by permission.

CarryAll produces briefcases from leather, fabric, and synthetic materials in a single plant. The basic product is a standard briefcase that is made from leather lined with fabric. The standard briefcase is a high-quality item and has sold well for many years.

Last year, the company decided to expand its product line and produce specialty briefcases for special orders. These briefcases differ from the standard in that they vary in size, they contain the finest synthetic materials, and they are imprinted with the buyer's name. To reduce labor costs on the specialty briefcases, most of the cutting and stitching is done by automated machines. These machines are used to a much lesser degree in the production of standard briefcases.

"I agree that the specialty business is looking better and better," replied Sally Henrie, the company's marketing manager. "And there seems to be plenty of specialty work out there, particularly since the competition hasn't been able to touch our price. Did you know that Armor Company, our biggest competitor, charges over $50 a unit for its specialty items? Now that's what I call gouging the customer!"

A breakdown of the manufacturing cost for each of CarryAll's product lines is given below:

	Standard Briefcases		Specialty Briefcases	
Units produced each month ..		10,000		2,500
Direct materials:				
Leather	1.0 sq. yd.	$15.00	0.5 sq. yd.	$ 7.50
Fabric	1.0 sq. yd.	5.00	1.0 sq. yd.	5.00
Synthetic		—		5.00
Total materials		20.00		17.50
Direct labor	0.5 hr. @ $12	6.00	0.25 hr. @ $12	3.00
Manufacturing overhead	0.5 hr. @ $18	9.00	0.25 hr. @ $18	4.50
Unit product cost		$35.00		$25.00

Manufacturing overhead is applied to products on the basis of direct labor-hours. The rate of $18 per direct labor-hour is determined by dividing the total manufacturing overhead cost for a month by the direct labor-hours:

$$\frac{\text{Manufacturing overhead cost, \$101,250}}{\text{Direct labor-hours, 5,625}} = \$18 \text{ per DLH}$$

The following additional information is available about the company and its products:

a. Standard briefcases are produced in batches of 200 units, and specialty briefcases are produced in batches of 25 units. Thus, the company does 50 setups for the standard items each month and 100 setups for the specialty items. A setup for the standard items requires one hour of time, whereas a setup for the specialty items requires two hours of time.

b. All briefcases are inspected to ensure that quality standards are met. A total of 300 hours of inspection time is spent on the standard briefcases and 500 hours of inspection time is spent on the specialty briefcases each month.

c. A standard briefcase requires 0.5 hour of machine time, and a specialty briefcase requires 2 hours of machine time.

d. The company is considering the use of activity-based costing as an alternative to its traditional costing system for computing unit product costs. Since these unit product costs will be used for external financial reporting, all manufacturing overhead costs are to be allocated to products and nonmanufacturing costs are to be excluded from product costs. The activity-based costing system has already been designed and costs allocated to the activity cost pools. The activity cost pools and activity measures are detailed below:

Activity Cost Pool	Activity Measure	Estimated Overhead Cost
Purchasing	Number of orders	$ 12,000
Material handling	Number of receipts	15,000
Production orders and setup	Setup hours	20,250
Inspection	Inspection-hours	16,000
Frame assembly	Assembly-hours	8,000
Machine related	Machine-hours	30,000
		$101,250

Activity Measure	Expected Activity		
	Standard Briefcase	Specialty Briefcase	Total
Number of orders:			
Leather	34	6	40
Fabric	48	12	60
Synthetic material	—	100	100
Number of receipts:			
Leather	52	8	60
Fabric	64	16	80
Synthetic material	—	160	160
Setup hours	?	?	?
Inspection-hours	?	?	?
Assembly-hours	800	800	1,600
Machine-hours	?	?	?

Required:

1. Using activity-based costing and the simplified approach described at the end of the chapter, determine the amount of manufacturing overhead cost that would be applied to each standard briefcase and each specialty briefcase.
2. Using the data computed in (1) above and other data from the case as needed, determine the unit product cost of each product line from the perspective of the activity-based costing system.
3. Within the limitations of the data that have been provided, evaluate the president's concern about the profitability of the two product lines. Would you recommend that the company shift its resources entirely to production of specialty briefcases? Explain.
4. Sally Henrie stated that "the competition hasn't been able to touch our price" on specialty business. Why do you suppose the competition hasn't been able to touch CarryAll's price?

COMMUNICATING IN PRACTICE   (LO1, LO4)

You often provide advice to Maria Graham, a client who is interested in diversifying her company. Maria is considering the purchase of a small manufacturing concern that assembles and packages its many products by hand. She plans to automate the factory and her projections indicate that the company will once again be profitable within two to three years. During her review of the company's records, she discovered that the company currently uses direct labor-hours to allocate overhead to its products. Because of its simplicity, Maria hopes that this approach can continue to be used.

Required:

Write a memorandum to Maria that addresses whether or not direct labor should continue to be used as an allocation base for overhead.

ETHICS CHALLENGE   (LO1)

You and your friends go to a restaurant as a group. At the end of the meal, the issue arises of how the bill for the group should be shared. One alternative is to figure out the cost of what each individual consumed and divide up the bill accordingly. Another alternative is to split the bill equally among the individuals.

Required:

Which system for dividing the bill is more equitable? Which system is easier to use? How does this issue relate to the material covered in this chapter?

TAKING IT TO THE NET

As you know, the World Wide Web is a medium that is constantly evolving. Sites come and go and change without notice. To enable periodic update of site addresses, this problem has been posted to the textbook website (www.mhhe.com/folk1e). After accessing the site, enter the Student Center and select this chapter. Select and complete the Taking It to the Net problem.

TEAMWORK IN ACTION   (LO1)

This activity requires teamwork to reinforce the understanding of the hierarchy of activities commonly found in activity-based costing systems in manufacturing companies.

Required:

1. The team should discuss and then write up a brief description of how the activity-based costing allocates overhead to products. All team members should agree with and understand the description.

2. Without referring to the related section in the text, each member of the team should choose one of the following levels of activities, define the level of activity chosen and provide one or more examples of the tasks that are performed at that level of activity in a manufacturing firm:

   a. Unit-level activities.
   b. Batch-level activities.
   c. Product-level activities
   d. Facility-level activities.

3. Each team member should present his or her answers from part 2 to the other teammates who should confirm or correct those answers.

Chapter Four

Systems Design: Process Costing

Decision Feature **Sweet Dreams**

John Asher, the grandson of the founder of Asher's Chocolates, had second thoughts while driving up the Jersey Turnpike in 1966 to sell the company. Turning around, he convinced his brother Bob that they should try to rescue the troubled company. The brothers made substantial investments to modernize the company's production facilities and to increase operating efficiency. When they turned the business over to their sons in 1997, the company had sales of $21 million and was successful. John's son David is now the president and CEO; David's cousin Jeff is the vice president of sales and marketing. The younger generation continues to focus on operating efficiencies. Both David and Jeff dream of turning the business over to a fifth generation of candy makers.

In 1892, at age 24, Chester Asher opened a candy shop in Philadelphia with $200. He moved to a building in the city's Germantown community four years later. Over the years, the company acquired four additional buildings in the area. After 100 years in the candy-making business, the company acquired a $1.2 million chocolate shell-molding line from Denmark in 1992. Then, in 1998, Asher's Chocolates built a $9 million factory on 31 acres in Souderton, a suburb of Philadelphia.

At 125,000 square feet, the new, linear-design factory is only slightly larger than the combined total of the five-century-old buildings that housed the company's operations in Germantown. However, with receiving at one end and shipping at the other, and $1 million of new equipment, the increase in operating efficiencies has already surpassed expectations. In addition, because the company is now able to receive chocolate from its suppliers in liquid form, material costs will be lower and raw material handling will be much easier.

The cousins foresee a need to expand in the next three to five years. This need for additional space was considered when the facility was designed. One wall can be knocked down to double the size of the facility.

Sources: Asher's Chocolates website www.ashers.com, July 2000; Susan Tiffany, "Trouble-Free Partnership Conceives and Builds Dream Factory for Asher's Chocolates," *Candy Industry Magazine*/Stagnito Communications, Inc., April 1999, p. 52 (3 pages); Susan Tiffany, "New Factory Stretches Opportunities for Asher's Chocolates," *Candy Industry Magazine*/Stagnito Communications, Inc., August 1998, p. 22 (5 pages); "Four Generations Guide Asher's Chocolates," *Candy Industry Magazine*/Stagnito Communications, Inc., August 1994, p. 90.

Learning Objectives

After studying Chapter 4, you should be able to:

LO1 Prepare journal entries to record the flow of materials, labor, and overhead through a process costing system.

LO2 Compute the equivalent units of production using the weighted-average method.

LO3 Prepare a quantity schedule using the weighted-average method.

LO4 Compute the costs per equivalent unit using the weighted-average method.

LO5 Prepare a cost reconciliation using the weighted-average method.

As explained in Chapter 2, two basic costing systems are in use: job-order costing and process costing. A job-order costing system is used in situations where many different jobs or products are worked on each period. Examples of industries that would typically use job-order costing include furniture manufacture, special-order printing, shipbuilding, and many types of service organizations.

By contrast, **process costing** is most commonly used in industries that produce essentially homogenous (i.e., uniform) products on a continuous basis, such as bricks, corn flakes, or paper. Process costing is particularly used in companies that convert basic raw materials into homogenous products, such as Reynolds Aluminum (aluminum ingots), Scott Paper (toilet paper), General Mills (flour), Exxon (gasoline and lubricating oils), Coppertone (sunscreens), and Kellogg (breakfast cereals). In addition, process costing is often used in companies with assembly operations, such as Panasonic (video monitors), Compaq (personal computers), General Electric (refrigerators), Toyota (automobiles), Amana (washing machines), and Sony (CD players). A form of process costing may also be used in utilities that produce gas, water, and electricity. As suggested by the length of this list, process costing is in very wide use.

Our purpose in this chapter is to extend the discussion of product costing to include a process costing system.

Comparison of Job-Order and Process Costing

In some ways process costing is very similar to job-order costing, and in some ways it is very different. In this section, we focus on these similarities and differences in order to provide a foundation for the detailed discussion of process costing that follows.

Similarities between Job-Order and Process Costing

Much of what was learned in Chapter 2 about costing and about cost flows applies equally well to process costing in this chapter. That is, we are not throwing out all that we have learned about costing and starting from "scratch" with a whole new system. The similarities that exist between job-order and process costing can be summarized as follows:

1. The same basic purposes exist in both systems, which are to assign material, labor, and overhead cost to products and to provide a mechanism for computing unit costs.
2. Both systems maintain and use the same basic manufacturing accounts, including Manufacturing Overhead, Raw Materials, Work in Process, and Finished Goods.
3. The flow of costs through the manufacturing accounts is basically the same in both systems.

As can be seen from this comparison, much of the knowledge that we have already acquired about costing is applicable to a process costing system. Our task now is simply to refine and extend this knowledge to process costing.

Differences between Job-Order and Process Costing

The differences between job-order and process costing arise from two factors. The first is that the flow of units in a process costing system is more or less continuous, and the second is that these units are indistinguishable from one another. Under process costing, it makes no sense to try to identify materials, labor, and overhead costs with a particular order from a customer (as we did with job-order costing), since each order is just one of many that are filled from a continuous flow of virtually identical units from the production line. Under process costing, we accumulate costs *by department,* rather than by order, and assign these costs uniformly to all units that pass through the department during a period.

Job-Order Costing	Process Costing
1. Many different jobs are worked on during each period, with each job having different production requirements.	1. A single product is produced either on a continuous basis or for long periods of time. All units of product are identical.
2. Costs are accumulated by individual job.	2. Costs are accumulated by department.
3. The *job cost sheet* is the key document controlling the accumulation of costs by a job.	3. The *department production report* is the key document showing the accumulation and disposition of costs by a department.
4. Unit costs are computed *by job* on the job cost sheet.	4. Unit costs are computed *by department* on the department production report.

Exhibit 4–1
Differences between Job-Order and Process Costing

A further difference between the two costing systems is that the job cost sheet has no use in process costing, since the focal point of that method is on departments. Instead of using job cost sheets, a **production report** is prepared for each department in which work is done on products. The production report serves several functions. It provides a summary of the number of units moving through a department during a period, and it also provides a computation of unit costs. In addition, it shows what costs were charged to the department and what disposition was made of these costs. The department production report is the key document in a process costing system.

The major differences between job-order and process costing are summarized in Exhibit 4–1.

A Hybrid Approach

in business today

Managers of successful pharmacies understand product costs. Some pharmacies use a hybrid approach to costing drugs. For example, a hospital pharmacy may use process costing to develop the cost of formulating the base solution for parenterals (that is, drugs delivered by injection or through the blood stream), and then use job-order costing to accumulate the additional costs incurred to create specific parenteral solutions. These additional costs include the ingredients added to the base solution and the time spent by the pharmacist to prepare the specific prescribed drug solution.

Source: "Pharmaceutical Care: Cost Estimation and Cost Management," *Drug Store News*, February 16, 1998, p. CP21 (5 pages).

A Perspective of Process Cost Flows

Before presenting a detailed example of process costing, it will be helpful to see how manufacturing costs flow through a process costing system.

Processing Departments

A **processing department** is any location in an organization where work is performed on a product and where materials, labor, or overhead costs are added to the product. For example, a potato chip factory operated by Nalley's might have three processing departments—one for preparing potatoes, one for cooking, and one for inspecting and packaging. A brick factory might have two processing departments—one for mixing and molding clay into brick form and one for firing the molded brick. A company can have as many or as few processing departments as are needed to complete a product or service.

Exhibit 4–2
Sequential Processing Departments

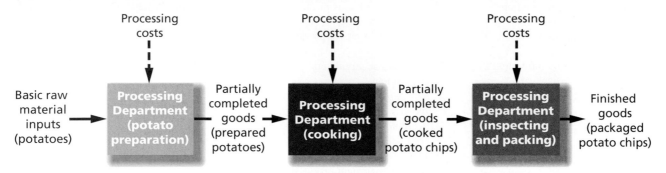

Some products and services may go through several processing departments, while others may go through only one or two. Regardless of the number of departments involved, all processing departments have two essential features. First, the activity performed in the processing department must be performed uniformly on all of the units passing through it. Second, the output of the processing department must be homogeneous.

The processing departments involved in making a product such as bricks or potato chips would probably be organized in a *sequential* pattern. By sequential processing, we mean that units flow in sequence from one department to another as in Exhibit 4–2.

in business today **Transforming the Process**

Honeytop Foods has transformed the preparation of naan, a flavored flatbread served with a variety of ethnic meals. With the exception of one step, the 60-minute process is now automated. High-speed machinery is used to measure and mix the ingredients, roll, shape, and flame-bake the dough, and package the bread before it is refrigerated or frozen. Humans are still needed to perform the final shaping step, the outcome of which is a teardrop shape.

Source: "Naan Bread Revolution," *Food Manufacture*, February 2000, pp. 38–39.

The Flow of Materials, Labor, and Overhead Costs

Cost accumulation is simpler in a process costing system than in a job-order costing system. In a process costing system, instead of having to trace costs to hundreds of different jobs, costs are traced to only a few processing departments.

A T-account model of materials, labor, and overhead cost flows in a process costing system is given in Exhibit 4–3. Several key points should be noted from this exhibit. First, note that a separate Work in Process account is maintained for *each processing department*. In contrast, in a job-order costing system there may be only a single Work in Process account for the entire company. Second, note that the completed production of the first processing department (Department A in the exhibit) is transferred into the Work in Process account of the second processing department (Department B), where it undergoes further work. After this further work, the completed units are then transferred into Finished Goods. (In Exhibit 4–3, we show only two processing departments, but there can be many such departments in a company.)

Finally, note that materials, labor, and overhead costs can be added in *any* processing department—not just the first. Costs in Department B's Work in Process account would consist of the materials, labor, and overhead costs incurred in Department B plus the costs attached to partially completed units transferred in from Department A (called **transferred-in costs**).

Exhibit 4–3
T-Account Model of Process Costing Flows

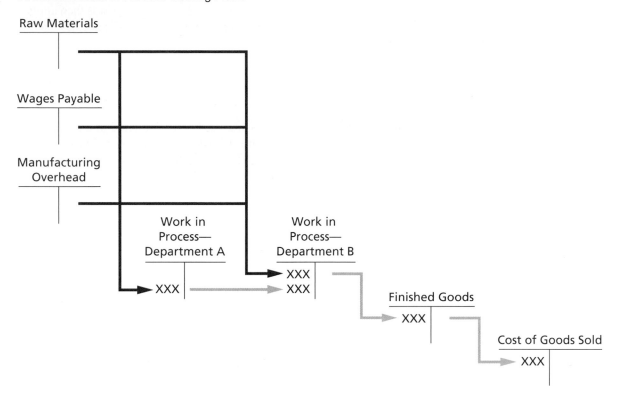

Materials, Labor, and Overhead Cost Entries

To complete our discussion of cost flows in a process costing system, in the following paragraphs we show journal entries relating to materials, labor, and overhead costs.

Materials Costs   As in job-order costing, materials are drawn from the storeroom using a materials requisition form. As stated earlier, materials can be added in any processing department, although it is not unusual for materials to be added only in the first processing department, with subsequent departments adding only labor and overhead costs as the partially completed units move along toward completion.

    Assuming that the first processing department in a company is Department A, the journal entry for placing materials into production is:

Work in Process—Department A	XXX	
Raw Materials		XXX

If other materials are subsequently added in Department B, the entry is the following:

Work in Process—Department B	XXX	
Raw Materials		XXX

Labor Costs   In process costing, labor costs do not have to be traced to specific jobs since it is only necessary to keep track of how much labor cost is incurred in each department. The following journal entry will record the labor costs for a period in Department A:

Work in Process—Department A	XXX	
Salaries and Wages Payable		XXX

Learning Objective 1
Prepare journal entries to record the flow of materials, labor, and overhead through a process costing system.

Overhead Costs   In process costing, as in job-order costing, predetermined overhead rates are usually used to charge overhead costs to products. Each department has its own separate rate, which is computed as discussed in Chapter 2. Overhead cost is then applied to units of product as the units move through the department using a journal entry such as the following for Department A:

Work in Process—Department A	XXX	
Manufacturing Overhead		XXX

Completing the Cost Flows   Once processing has been completed in a department, the units are transferred to the next department for further processing, as illustrated earlier in the T-accounts in Exhibit 4–3. The following journal entry is used to transfer the costs of partially completed units from Department A to Department B:

Work in Process—Department B	XXX	
Work in Process—Department A		XXX

After processing has been completed in Department B, the costs of the completed units are then transferred to the Finished Goods inventory account:

Finished Goods	XXX	
Work in Process—Department B		XXX

Finally, when a customer's order is filled and units are sold, the cost of the units is transferred to Cost of Goods Sold:

Cost of Goods Sold	XXX	
Finished Goods		XXX

To summarize, cost flows between accounts are basically the same in a process costing system as they are in a job-order costing system. The only noticeable difference at this point is that in a process costing system there is a separate Work in Process account for each department.

Managerial Accounting in Action

The Issue

Samantha Trivers, president of Double Diamond Skis, was worried about the future of her company. After a rocky start, the company had come out with a completely redesigned ski called The Ultimate, made of exotic materials and featuring flashy graphics. Exhibit 4–4 illustrates how this ski is manufactured. The ski was a runaway best seller—particularly among younger skiers—and had provided the company with much-needed cash for two years. However, last year a dismal snowfall in the Rocky Mountains had depressed sales, and Double Diamond was once again short of cash. Samantha was worried that another bad ski season would force Double Diamond into bankruptcy.

Just before starting production of next year's model of The Ultimate, Samantha called Jerry Madison, the company controller, into her office to discuss the reports she would need in the coming year.

Samantha: Jerry, I am going to need more frequent cost information this year. I really have to stay on top of things.
Jerry: What do you have in mind?
Samantha: I'd like reports at least once a month that detail our production costs for each department and for each pair of skis.
Jerry: That shouldn't be much of a problem. We already compile almost all of the necessary data for the annual report. The only complication is our work in process inventories. They haven't been a problem in our annual reports, since our fiscal year ends

Wood, aluminum, plastic sheets

Exhibit 4–4
The Production Process at
Double Diamond Skis*

Shaping and Milling Department

Computer-assisted milling machines shape the wood core and aluminum sheets that serve as the backbone of the ski.

Graphics Application Department

Graphics are applied to the back of the clear plastic top sheets using a heat-transfer process.

Molding Department

The wooden core and various layers are stacked in a mold, polyurethane foam is injected into the mold, and then the mold is placed in a press that fuses the parts together.

Grinding and Sanding Department

The semi-finished skis are tuned by stone grinding and belt sanding. The ski edges are beveled and polished.

Finishing and Pairing Department

A skilled technician selects skis to form a pair and adjusts the skis' camber.

Finished goods

Source: *Adapted from Bill Gout, Jesse James Doquilo, and Studio M D, "Capped Crusaders," *Skiing,* October 1993, pp. 138–144.

at a time when we have finished producing skis for the last model year and haven't yet started producing for the new model year. Consequently, there aren't any work in process inventories to value for the annual report. But that won't be true for monthly reports.
Samantha: I'm not sure why that is a problem, Jerry. But I'm confident you can figure out how to solve it.
Jerry: You can count on me.

Equivalent Units of Production

Jerry Madison, the controller of Double Diamond Skis, was concerned with the following problem: After materials, labor, and overhead costs have been accumulated in a department, the department's output must be determined so that unit costs can be computed. The difficulty is that a department usually has some partially completed units in its ending inventory. It does not seem reasonable to count these partially completed units as equivalent to fully completed units when counting the department's output. Therefore, Jerry will mathematically convert those partially completed units into an *equivalent* number of fully completed units. In process costing, this is done using the following formula:

Concept 4–1

Equivalent units = Number of partially completed units × Percentage completion

As the formula states, **equivalent units** is defined to be the product of the number of partially completed units and the percentage completion of those units. The equivalent units is the number of complete units that could have been obtained from the materials and effort that went into the partially complete units.

For example, suppose the Molding Department at Double Diamond has 500 units in its ending work in process inventory that are 60% complete. These 500 partially complete units are equivalent to 300 fully complete units (500 × 60% =300). Therefore, the ending work in process inventory would be said to contain 300 equivalent units. These equivalent units would be added to any fully completed units to determine the period's output for the department—called the *equivalent units of production.*

The equivalent units of production can be computed using either the *weighted-average method* or the *FIFO method.* The weighted-average method is a little simpler, and for that reason, it is the method used in this chapter. If you are interested in the details of the FIFO method, a supplement to this chapter on the FIFO method can be downloaded at www.mhhe.com/folk1e. In broad terms, in the **FIFO method** the equivalent units and unit costs relate only to work done during the current period. In contrast, the **weighted-average method** blends together units and costs from the current period with units and costs from the prior period. In the weighted-average method, the **equivalent units of production** for a department are the number of units transferred to the next department (or to finished goods) plus the equivalent units in the department's ending work in process inventory.

---

in business today **Equivalent Container Units**

A record 3.5 million TEUs (total equivalent units) moved through the Port of Long Beach, the busiest container port in the United States. A TEU is a 20-foot container unit equivalent, which is used as the industry standard.

Source: "Long Beach Port Moves Record Volume," *Orange County Business Journal/Los Angeles Business Journal,* February 9, 1998, p. 18.

Weighted-Average Method

Learning Objective 2

Compute the equivalent units of production using the weighted-average method.

Under the weighted-average method, a department's equivalent units are computed as follows:

Weighted-Average Method
(a separate calculation is made for each cost category in
each processing department)

Equivalent units of production = Units transferred to the next department or to
finished goods
+ Equivalent units in ending work in process
inventory

We do not have to make an equivalent units calculation for units transferred to the next department. We can assume that they would not have been transferred unless they were 100% complete with respect to the work performed in the transferring department.

Consider the Shaping and Milling Department at Double Diamond. This department uses computerized milling machines to precisely shape the wooden core and metal sheets that will be used to form the backbone of the ski. (See Exhibit 4–4 for an overview of the production process at Double Diamond.) The following activity took place in the department in May, several months into the production of the new model of The Ultimate ski:

Shaping and Milling Department

	Units	Percent Completed	
		Materials	Conversion
Work in process, May 1	200	50%	30%
Units started into production during May . . .	5,000		
Units completed during May and transferred to the next department	4,800	100%*	100%*
Work in process, May 31	400	40%	25%

*It is always assumed that units transferred out of a department are 100% complete with respect to the processing done in that department.

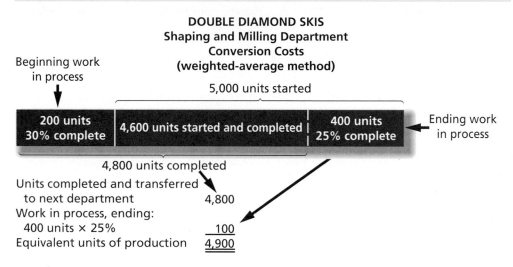

Shaping and Milling Department

	Materials	Conversion
Units transferred to the next department	4,800	4,800
Work in process, May 31:		
400 units × 40%	160	
400 units × 25%		100
Equivalent units of production	4,960	4,900

Exhibit 4–5
Equivalent Units of Production:
Weighted-Average Method

Exhibit 4–6
Visual Perspective of Equivalent
Units of Production

Note the use of the term *conversion* in the table on the previous page. **Conversion cost,** as defined in Chapter 1, is direct labor cost plus manufacturing overhead cost. In process costing, conversion cost is often—but not always—treated as a single element of product cost.

Also note that the May 1 beginning work in process was 50% complete with respect to materials costs and 30% complete with respect to conversion costs. This means that 50% of the materials costs required to complete the units had already been incurred. Likewise, 30% of the conversion costs required to complete the units had already been incurred.

Since Double Diamond's work in process inventories are at different stages of completion in terms of the amounts of materials cost and conversion cost that have been added in the department, two equivalent unit figures must be computed. The equivalent units computations are given in Exhibit 4–5.

Note from the computation in Exhibit 4–5 that units in the beginning work in process inventory are ignored. The weighted-average method is concerned only with the fact that there are 4,900 equivalent units for conversion cost in ending inventories and in units transferred to the next department—the method is not concerned with the additional fact that some of this work was accomplished in prior periods. This is a key point in the weighted-average method that is easy to overlook.

The weighted-average method blends together the work that was accomplished in prior periods with the work that was accomplished in the current period. In the FIFO method, the units and costs of prior periods are cleanly separated from the units and costs of the current period. Some managers believe the FIFO method is more accurate for this reason. However, the FIFO method is more complex than the weighted-average method.

Computation of equivalent units of production is illustrated in Exhibit 4–6. Study this exhibit carefully before going on.

Writer of Term Papers

you decide

Assume that all of your professors have assigned short papers this term. In fact, you have to turn in four separate five-page papers early next month. During the month, you purchased all of the paper that you will need, began and finished two papers, and wrote the first two and one-half pages of the other two papers. You turned in the papers that you had finished to your instructors on the last day of the month.

If instead you had focused all your efforts into starting *and* completing papers this month, how many papers would you have written this month? After answering that question, reconfigure your answer as a computation of equivalent units of production by (1) preparing a quantity schedule and (2) computing the number of equivalent units for labor.

Production Report—Weighted-Average Method

The production report developed in this section contains the information requested by the president of Double Diamond Skis. The purpose of the production report is to summarize for management all of the activity that takes place in a department's Work in Process account for a period. This activity includes the units and costs that flow through the Work in Process account. As illustrated in Exhibit 4–7, a separate production report is prepared for each department.

Remember the summer of 1999? Rawlings, the ball manufacturer, was forced to open its Turrialba facility in Costa Rica to a delegation from Major League Baseball to dispel rumors that Rawlings balls were behind the record numbers of home runs.

The delegation found that the production process is unchanged from earlier years. The red pills (rubber-coated corks purchased from a company in Mississippi) are wound three times with wool yarn and then once with cotton string. The balls are weighed, measured, and inspected after each wind. The covers, cut from sheets of rawhide, are hand-stitched and then machine-rolled. After a trip through a drying room to remove the moisture that kept the leather soft during the sewing process, the balls are stamped with logos. After they are weighed, measured, and inspected once again, the balls are wrapped in tissue and packed in boxes. Balls that don't meet Major League specifications (5–5 ¼ ounces and 9–9 ¼ inches in circumference) are sold commercially.

A trip to Mississippi is next on the agenda.

Source: "Behind-the-Seams Look Rawlings Throws Open Baseball Plant Door," *USA TODAY*, May 24, 2000, pp. 1C–2C. Copyright 2000, *USA TODAY*. Reprinted with permission.

Assume that you are a cost analyst in the Rawlings plant in Costa Rica that supplies baseballs to Major League Baseball. Your assignment is to identify the production departments in that facility. How many production reports will be needed to summarize the activity in each department?

Earlier, when we outlined the differences between job-order costing and process costing, we stated that the production report takes the place of a job cost sheet in a process costing system. The production report is a key management document. The production report has three separate (though highly interrelated) parts:

Exhibit 4–7
The Position of the Production Report in the Flow of Costs

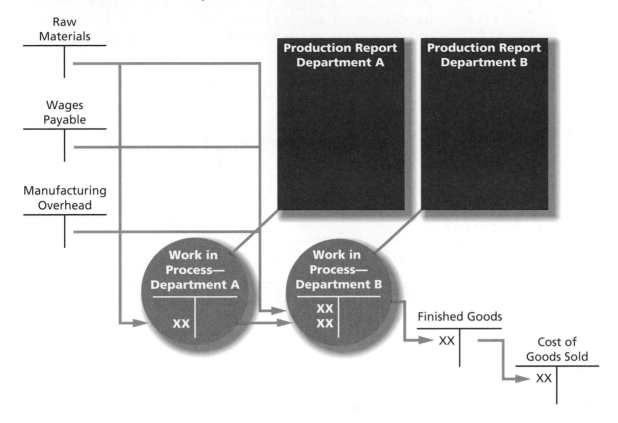

1. A quantity schedule, which shows the flow of units through the department and a computation of equivalent units.
2. A computation of costs per equivalent unit.
3. A reconciliation of all cost flows into and out of the department during the period.

We will use the data that follows for the May operations of the Shaping and Milling Department of Double Diamond Skis to illustrate the production report. Keep in mind that this report is only one of the five reports that would be prepared for the company since the company has five processing departments.

Shaping and Milling Department		
Work in process, beginning:		
Units in process		200
Stage of completion with respect to materials		50%
Stage of completion with respect to conversion		30%
Costs in the beginning inventory:		
Materials cost	$	3,000
Conversion cost		1,000
Total cost in process	$	4,000
Units started into production during May		5,000
Units completed and transferred out		4,800
Costs added to production during May:		
Materials cost	$	74,000
Conversion cost		70,000
Total cost added in the department	$	144,000

Work in process, ending:	
Units in process	400
Stage of completion with respect to materials	40%
Stage of completion with respect to conversion	25%

In this section, we show how a production report is prepared when the weighted-average method is used to compute equivalent units and unit costs.

Step 1: Prepare a Quantity Schedule and Compute the Equivalent Units

Learning Objective 3
Prepare a quantity schedule using the weighted-average method.

The first part of a production report consists of a **quantity schedule,** which shows the flow of units through the department and a computation of equivalent units.

**Shaping and Milling Department
Quantity Schedule and
Computation of Equivalent Units**

	Quantity Schedule		
Units to be accounted for:			
Work in process, May 1 (50% materials; 30% conversion added last month)	200		
Started into production	5,000		
Total units	5,200		
		Equivalent Units	
		Materials	**Conversion**
Units accounted for as follows:			
Transferred to the next department . . .	4,800	4,800	4,800
Work in process, May 31 (40% materials; 25% conversion added this month)	400	160*	100†
Total units and equivalent units of production	5,200	4,960	4,900

*40% × 400 units = 160 equivalent units.
†25% × 400 units = 100 equivalent units.

The quantity schedule shows how many units moved through the department during the period as well as the stage of completion of any in-process units. In addition to providing this information, the quantity schedule serves as an essential guide in preparing and tying together the remaining parts of a production report.

Step 2: Compute Costs per Equivalent Unit

Learning Objective 4
Compute the costs per equivalent unit using the weighted-average method.

As stated earlier, the weighted-average method blends together the work that was accomplished in the prior period with the work that was accomplished in the current period. That is why it is called the weighted-average method; it averages together units and costs from both the prior and current periods by adding the cost in the beginning work in process inventory to the current period costs. These computations are shown below for the Shaping and Milling Department for May:

Shaping and Milling Department

	Total Cost	Materials	Conversion	Whole Unit
Cost to be accounted for:				
Work in process, May 1	$ 4,000	$ 3,000	$ 1,000	
Cost added in the Shaping and Milling Department ...	144,000	74,000	70,000	
Total cost (a)	$148,000	$77,000	$71,000	
Equivalent units of production (Step 1 above) (b)		4,960	4,900	
Cost per EU, (a) ÷ (b)		$15.524 +	$14.490 =	$30.014

The cost per equivalent unit (EU) that we have computed for the Shaping and Milling Department will be used to apply cost to units that are transferred to the next department, graphics application, and will also be used to compute the cost in the ending work in process inventory. For example, each unit transferred out of the Shaping and Milling Department to the Graphics Application Department will carry with it a cost of $30.014. Since the costs are passed on from department to department, the unit cost of the last department, Finishing and Pairing, will represent the final unit cost of a completed unit of product.

Step 3: Prepare a Cost Reconciliation

The purpose of a **cost reconciliation** is to show how the costs that have been charged to a department during a period are accounted for. Typically, the costs charged to a department will consist of the following:

1. Cost in the beginning work in process inventory.
2. Materials, labor, and overhead costs added during the period.
3. Cost (if any) transferred in from the preceding department.

In a production report, these costs are generally titled "Cost to be accounted for." They are accounted for in a production report by computing the following amounts:

1. Cost transferred out to the next department (or to Finished Goods).
2. Cost remaining in the ending work in process inventory.

In short, when a cost reconciliation is prepared, the "Cost to be accounted for" from step 2 is reconciled with the sum of the cost transferred out during the period plus the cost in the ending work in process inventory. This concept is shown graphically in Exhibit 4–8. Study this exhibit carefully before going on to the cost reconciliation below for the Shaping and Milling Department.

Example of a Cost Reconciliation To prepare a cost reconciliation, follow the quantity schedule line for line and show the cost associated with each group of units. This is done in Exhibit 4–9, where we present a completed production report for the Shaping and Milling Department.

The quantity schedule in the exhibit shows that 200 units were in process on May 1 and that an additional 5,000 units were started into production during the month. Looking at the "Cost to be accounted for" in the middle part of the exhibit, notice that the units in process on May 1 had $4,000 in cost attached to them and that the Shaping and Milling Department added another $144,000 in cost to production during the month. Thus, the department has $148,000 ($4,000 + $144,000) in cost to be accounted for.

This cost is accounted for in two ways. As shown on the quantity schedule, 4,800 units were transferred to the Graphics Application Department, the next department in the production process. Another 400 units were still in process in the Shaping and Milling Department at the end of the month. Thus, part of the $148,000 "Cost to be accounted

Concept 4–2

Exhibit 4-8
Graphic Illustration of the Cost Reconciliation Part of a Production Report

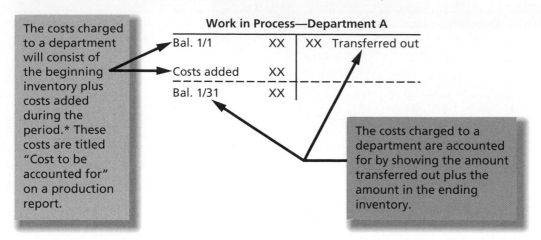

The costs charged to a department will consist of the beginning inventory plus costs added during the period.* These costs are titled "Cost to be accounted for" on a production report.

Work in Process—Department A

Bal. 1/1	XX	XX	Transferred out
Costs added	XX		
Bal. 1/31	XX		

The costs charged to a department are accounted for by showing the amount transferred out plus the amount in the ending inventory.

* Departments that follow Department A (Department B and so forth) will need to show the amount of cost transferred in from the preceding department

for" goes with the 4,800 units to the Graphics Application Department, and part of it remains with the 400 units in the ending work in process inventory in the Shaping and Milling Department.

Each of the 4,800 units transferred to the Graphics Application Department is assigned $30.014 in cost, for a total $144,067. The 400 units still in process at the end of the month are assigned costs according to their stage of completion. To determine the stage of completion, we refer to the equivalent units computation and bring the equivalent units figures down to the cost reconciliation part of the report. We then assign costs to these units, using the cost per equivalent unit figures already computed.

After cost has been assigned to the ending work in process inventory, the total cost that we have accounted for ($148,000) agrees with the amount that we had to account for ($148,000). Thus, the cost reconciliation is complete.

Managerial Accounting in Action

The Wrap-Up

Jerry: Here's an example of the kind of report I can put together for you every month. This particular report is for the Shaping and Milling Department. It follows a fairly standard format for industries like ours and is called a production report. I hope this is what you have in mind.

Samantha: The quantity schedule makes sense to me. I can see we had a total of 5,200 units to account for in the department, and 4,800 of those were transferred to the next department while 400 were still in process at the end of the month. What are these "equivalent units"?

Jerry: That's the problem I mentioned earlier. The 400 units that are still in process are far from complete. When we compute the unit costs, it wouldn't make sense to count them as whole units.

Samantha: I suppose not. I see what you are driving at. Since those 400 units are only 25% complete with respect to our conversion costs, they should only be counted as 100 units when we compute the unit costs for conversion.

Jerry: That's right. Is the rest of the report clear?

Samantha: Yes, it does seem pretty clear, although I want to work the numbers through on my own to make sure I thoroughly understand the report.

Jerry: Does this report give you the information you wanted?

Samantha: Yes, it does. I can tell how many units are in process, how complete they are, what happened to them, and their costs. While I know the unit costs are averages and are heavily influenced by our volume, they still can give me some idea of how well we are doing on the cost side. Thanks, Jerry.

Exhibit 4-9
Production Report—Weighted-Average Method

DOUBLE DIAMOND SKIS
Shaping and Milling Department Production Report
(weighted-average method)

Quantity Schedule and Equivalent Units

	Quantity Schedule
Units to be accounted for:	
Work in process, May 1 (50% materials; 30% conversion added last month)	200
Started into production	5,000
Total units	5,200

		Equivalent Units (EU)	
		Materials	Conversion
Units accounted for as follows:			
Transferred to the next department	4,800	4,800	4,800
Work in process, May 31 (40% materials; 25% conversion added this month)	400	160*	100†
Total units and equivalent units of production	5,200	4,960	4,900

Costs per Equivalent Unit

	Total Cost	Materials	Conversion	Whole Unit
Cost to be accounted for:				
Work in process, May 1	$ 4,000	$ 3,000	$ 1,000	
Cost added in the Shaping and Milling Department	144,000	74,000	70,000	
Total cost (a)	$148,000	$77,000	$71,000	
Equivalent units of production (above) (b)		4,960	4,900	
Cost per EU, (a) ÷ (b)		$15.524 +	$14.490 =	$30.014

Cost Reconciliation

	Total Cost	Equivalent Units (above)	
		Materials	Conversion
Cost accounted for as follows:			
Transferred to next department:			
4,800 units × $30.014 per unit	$144,067	4,800	4,800
Work in process, May 31:			
Materials, at $15.524 per EU	2,484	160	
Conversion, at $14.490 per EU	1,449		100
Total work in process, May 31	3,933		
Total cost	$148,000		

*40% × 400 units = 160 equivalent units.
†25% × 400 units = 100 equivalent units.
EU = Equivalent unit.

A Comment about Rounding Errors

If you use a calculator or computer spreadsheet and do not round off the costs per equivalent unit, there shouldn't be any discrepancy between the "Cost to be accounted for" and the "Cost accounted for" in the cost reconciliation. However, if you round off the costs per equivalent unit, the two figures will not always exactly agree. For the report in Exhibit 4–9, the two figures do agree, but this will not always happen. In all of the homework assignments and other materials, we follow two rules: (1) all the costs per equivalent unit are rounded off to three decimal places as in Exhibit 4–9, and (2) any adjustment needed to reconcile the "Cost accounted for" with the "Cost to be accounted for" is made to the cost "transferred" amount rather than to the ending inventory.

Summary

LO1 Prepare journal entries to record the flow of materials, labor, and overhead through a process costing system.

The journal entries to record the flow of costs in process costing are basically the same as in job-order costing. Direct materials costs are debited to Work in Process when they are released for use in production. Direct labor costs are debited to Work in Process as incurred. Manufacturing overhead costs are applied to Work in Process using predetermined overhead rates. Costs are accumulated by department in process costing and by job in job-order costing. In addition, each department will have its own predetermined overhead rate in process costing.

LO2 Compute the equivalent units of production using the weighted-average method.

To compute unit costs for a department, the department's output in terms of equivalent units must be determined. In the weighted-average method, the equivalent units for a period are the sum of the units transferred out of the department during the period and the equivalent units in ending work in process inventory at the end of the period.

LO3 Prepare a quantity schedule using the weighted-average method.

The activity in a department is summarized on a production report which has three separate (though highly interrelated) parts. The first part is a quantity schedule, which includes a computation of equivalent units and shows the flow of units through the department during the period. The quantity schedule shows the units to be accounted for—the units in beginning Work in Process inventory and the units started into production. These units are accounted for by detailing the units transferred to the next department and the units still in process in the department at the end of the period. This part of the report also shows the equivalent units of production for the units still in process.

LO4 Compute the costs per equivalent unit using the weighted-average method.

The cost per equivalent unit is computed by dividing the total cost for a particular cost category such as conversion costs by the equivalent units of production for that cost category.

LO5 Prepare a cost reconciliation using the weighted-average method.

In the cost reconciliation report, the costs of beginning Work in Process inventory and the costs added during the period are reconciled with the costs of the units transferred out of the department and the costs of ending Work in Process inventory.

Guidance Answers to You Decide and Decision Maker

WRITER OF TERM PAPERS (p. 167)

You wrote a total of 15 pages (5 + 5 + 2.5 + 2.5) this month. If you had placed all of your efforts into starting *and* completing papers, you could have written three complete five-page papers.

	Quantity Schedule
Units (papers) to be accounted for:	
Work in process, beginning of month	
Started into production	4
Total units	4

	Equivalent Units
	Labor
Units accounted for as follows:	
Transferred (handed in) to instructors	2	2
Work in process, end of month (all materials and 50% of labor and overhead added this month)	2	1*
Total units and equivalent units of production	4	3

*2 units (papers) × 50% (or 2.5 pages out of 5) = 1

COST ANALYST (p. 168)

The Rawlings baseball production facility in Costa Rica might include the following production departments: winding, cutting, stitching, rolling, drying, stamping, inspecting, and packaging. Each department would have its own production report.

Review Problem: Process Cost Flows and Reports

Luxguard Home Paint Company produces exterior latex paint, which it sells in one-gallon containers. The company has two processing departments—Base Fab and Finishing. White paint, which is used as a base for all the company's paints, is mixed from raw ingredients in the Base Fab Department. Pigments are added to the basic white paint, the pigmented paint is squirted under pressure into one-gallon containers, and the containers are labeled and packed for shipping in the Finishing Department. Information relating to the company's operations for April follows:

a. Raw materials were issued for use in production: Base Fab Department, $851,000; and Finishing Department, $629,000.
b. Direct labor costs were incurred: Base Fab Department, $330,000; and Finishing Department, $270,000.
c. Manufacturing overhead cost was applied: Base Fab Department, $665,000; and Finishing Department, $405,000.
d. The cost of basic white paint transferred from the Base Fab Department to the Finishing Department was $1,850,000.
e. Paint that had been prepared for shipping was transferred from the Finishing Department to Finished Goods. Its cost according to the company's cost system was $3,200,000.

Required:

1. Prepare journal entries to record items (a) through (e) above.
2. Post the journal entries from (1) above to T-accounts. The balance in the Base Fab Department's Work in Process account on April 1 was $150,000; the balance in the Finishing Department's Work in Process account was $70,000. After posting entries to the T-accounts, find the ending balance in each department's Work in Process account.
3. Prepare a production report for the Base Fab Department for April. The following additional information is available regarding production in the Base Fab Department during April:

Production data:

Units (gallons) in process, April 1: 100% complete as to materials,
60% complete as to labor and overhead 30,000

Units (gallons) started into production during April 420,000

Units (gallons) completed and transferred to the Finishing Department 370,000

Units (gallons) in process, April 30: 50% complete as to materials,
25% complete as to labor and overhead 80,000

Cost data:

Work in process inventory, April 1:

Materials	$	92,000
Labor		21,000
Overhead		37,000
Total cost	$	150,000

Cost added during April:

Materials	$	851,000
Labor		330,000
Overhead		665,000
Total cost	$	1,846,000

SOLUTION TO REVIEW PROBLEM

1. a.	Work in Process—Base Fab Department	851,000	
	Work in Process—Finishing Department	629,000	
	Raw Materials		1,480,000
b.	Work in Process—Base Fab Department	330,000	
	Work in Process—Finishing Department	270,000	
	Salaries and Wages Payable		600,000
c.	Work in Process—Base Fab Department	665,000	
	Work in Process—Finishing Department	405,000	
	Manufacturing Overhead		1,070,000
d.	Work in Process—Finishing Department	1,850,000	
	Work in Process—Base Fab Department		1,850,000
e.	Finished Goods	3,200,000	
	Work in Process—Finishing Department		3,200,000

2.

Raw Materials				Salaries and Wages Payable			
Bal.	XXX	(a)	1,480,000			(b)	600,000

Work in Process— Base Fab Department				Manufacturing Overhead			
Bal.	150,000	(d)	1,850,000	(Various actual		(c)	1,070,000
(a)	851,000			costs)			
(b)	330,000						
(c)	665,000						
Bal.	146,000						

Work in Process— Finishing Department				Finished Goods			
Bal.	70,000	(e)	3,200,000	Bal.	XXX		
(a)	629,000			(e)	3,200,000		
(b)	270,000						
(c)	405,000						
(d)	1,850,000						
Bal.	24,000						

LUXGUARD HOME PAINT COMPANY
Production Report—Base Fab Department
For the Month Ended April 30

Quantity Schedule and Equivalent Units

	Quantity Schedule
Units (gallons) to be accounted for:	
Work in process, April 1 (all materials, 60% labor and overhead added last month)	30,000
Started into production	420,000
Total units	450,000

		Equivalent Units (EU)		
		Materials	Labor	Overhead
Units (gallons) accounted for as follows:				
Transferred to Finishing Department	370,000	370,000	370,000	370,000
Work in process, April 30 (50% materials, 25% labor and overhead added this month)	80,000	40,000*	20,000*	20,000*
Total units and equivalent units of production	450,000	410,000	390,000	390,000

Costs per Equivalent Unit

	Total Cost	Materials	Labor	Overhead	Whole Unit
Cost to be accounted for:					
Work in process, April 1	$ 150,000	$ 92,000	$ 21,000	$ 37,000	
Cost added by the Base Fab Department	1,846,000	851,000	330,000	665,000	
Total cost (a)	$1,996,000	$943,000	$351,000	$702,000	
Equivalent units of production (b)		410,000	390,000	390,000	
Cost per EU, (a) ÷ (b)		$2.30 +	$0.90 +	$1.80 =	$5.00

Cost Reconciliation

	Total Cost	Equivalent Units (above)		
		Materials	Labor	Overhead
Cost accounted for as follows:				
Transferred to Finishing Department: 370,000 units × $5.00 each	$1,850,000	370,000	370,000	370,000
Work in process, April 30:				
Materials, at $2.30 per EU	92,000	40,000		
Labor, at $0.90 per EU	18,000		20,000	
Overhead, at $1.80 per EU	36,000			20,000
Total work in process	146,000			
Total cost	$1,996,000			

*Materials: 80,000 units × 50% =40,000 equivalent units; labor and overhead: 80,000 units × 25% =20,000 equivalent units.
EU = Equivalent unit.

Glossary

Conversion cost Direct labor cost plus manufacturing overhead cost. (p. 167)

Cost reconciliation The part of a department's production report that shows the cost to be accounted for during a period and how those costs are accounted for. (p. 171)

Equivalent units The product of the number of partially completed units and their percentage of completion with respect to a particular cost. Equivalent units are the number of complete whole units one could obtain from the materials and effort contained in partially completed units. (p. 165)

Equivalent units of production (weighted-average method) The units transferred to the next department (or to finished goods) during the period plus the equivalent units in the department's ending work in process inventory. (p. 166)

FIFO method A method of accounting for cost flows in a process costing system in which equivalent units and unit costs relate only to work done during the current period. (p. 166)

Process costing A costing method used in situations where essentially homogeneous products are produced on a continuous basis. (p. 160)

Processing department Any location in an organization where work is performed on a product and where materials, labor, or overhead costs are added to the product. (p. 161)

Production report A report that summarizes all activity in a department's Work in Process account during a period and that contains three parts: a quantity schedule and a computation of equivalent units, a computation of total and unit costs, and a cost reconciliation. (p. 161)

Quantity schedule The part of a production report that shows the flow of units through a department during a period and a computation of equivalent units. (p. 170)

Transferred-in cost The cost attached to products that have been received from a prior processing department. (p. 162)

Weighted-average method A method of process costing that blends together units and costs from both the current and prior periods. (p. 166)

Questions

4–1 Under what conditions would it be appropriate to use a process costing system?

4–2 In what ways are job-order and process costing similar?

4–3 Costs are accumulated by job in a job-order costing system; how are costs accumulated in a process costing system?

4–4 Why is cost accumulation easier under a process costing system than it is under a job-order costing system?

4–5 How many Work in Process accounts are maintained in a company using process costing?

4–6 Assume that a company has two processing departments, Mixing and Firing. Prepare a journal entry to show a transfer of partially completed units from the Mixing Department to the Firing Department.

4–7 Assume again that a company has two processing departments, Mixing and Firing. Explain what costs might be added to the Firing Department's Work in Process account during a period.

4–8 What is meant by the term *equivalent units of production* when the weighted-average method is used?

4–9 What is a quantity schedule, and what purpose does it serve?

4–10 Under process costing, it is often suggested that a product is like a rolling snowball as it moves from department to department. Why is this an apt comparison?

4–11 Watkins Trophies, Inc., produces thousands of medallions made of bronze, silver, and gold. The medallions are identical except for the materials used in their manufacture. What costing system would you advise the company to use?

Brief Exercises

BRIEF EXERCISE 4–1 Process Costing Journal Entries (LO1)

Quality Brick Company produces bricks in two processing departments—molding and firing. Information relating to the company's operations in March follows:

a. Raw materials were issued for use in production: Molding Department, $23,000; and Firing Department, $8,000.

b. Direct labor costs were incurred: Molding Department, $12,000; and Firing Department, $7,000.

c. Manufacturing overhead was applied: Molding Department, $25,000; and Firing Department, $37,000.

d. Unfired, molded bricks were transferred from the Molding Department to the Firing Department. According to the company's process costing system, the cost of the unfired, molded bricks was $57,000.

e. Finished bricks were transferred from the Firing Department to the finished goods warehouse. According to the company's process costing system, the cost of the finished bricks was $103,000.

f. Finished bricks were sold to customers. According to the company's process costing system, the cost of the finished bricks sold was $101,000.

Required:
Prepare journal entries to record items (a) through (f) above.

BRIEF EXERCISE 4–2   Computation of Equivalent Units—Weighted-Average Method (LO2)
Clonex Labs, Inc., uses a process costing system. The following data are available for one department for October:

	Units	Percent Completed	
		Materials	Conversion
Work in process, October 1	30,000	65%	30%
Work in process, October 31	15,000	80%	40%

The department started 175,000 units into production during the month and transferred 190,000 completed units to the next department.

Required:
Compute the equivalent units of production for October assuming that the company uses the weighted-average method of accounting for units and costs.

BRIEF EXERCISE 4–3   Preparation of Quantity Schedule—Weighted-Average Method (LO3)
Hielta Oy, a Finnish company, processes wood pulp for various manufacturers of paper products. Data relating to tons of pulp processed during June are provided below:

	Tons of Pulp	Percent Completed	
		Materials	Labor and Overhead
Work in process, June 1	20,000	90%	80%
Work in process, June 30	30,000	60%	40%
Started into processing during June	190,000	—	—

Required:
1. Compute the number of tons of pulp completed and transferred out during June.
2. Prepare a quantity schedule for June assuming that the company uses the weighted-average method.

BRIEF EXERCISE 4–4   Cost per Equivalent Unit—Weighted-Average Method (LO4)
Superior Micro Products uses the weighted-average method in its process costing system. Data for the Assembly Department for May appear below:

	Materials	Labor	Overhead
Work in process, May 1	$18,000	$5,500	$27,500
Cost added during May	$238,900	$80,300	$401,500
Equivalent units of production	35,000	33,000	33,000

Required:
1. Compute the cost per equivalent unit for materials, for labor, and for overhead.
2. Compute the total cost per equivalent whole unit.

BRIEF EXERCISE 4–5   Cost Reconciliation—Weighted-Average Method (LO5)
Superior Micro Products uses the weighted-average method in its process costing system. During January, the Delta Assembly Department completed its processing of 25,000 units and transferred them to the next department. The cost of beginning inventory and the costs added during January amounted to $599,780 in total. The ending inventory in January consisted of 3,000 units, which were 80% complete with respect to materials and 60% complete with respect to labor and overhead. The costs per equivalent unit for the month were as follows:

	Materials	Labor	Overhead
Cost per equivalent unit	$12.50	$3.20	$6.40

Required:
1. Compute the total cost per equivalent unit for the month.
2. Compute the equivalent units of material, of labor, and of overhead in the ending inventory for the month.
3. Prepare the cost reconciliation portion of the department's production report for January.

Exercises

EXERCISE 4–1   Process Costing Journal Entries (LO1)
Chocolaterie de Geneve, SA, is located in a French-speaking canton in Switzerland. The company makes chocolate truffles that are sold in popular embossed tins. The company has two processing departments— Cooking and Molding. In the Cooking Department, the raw ingredients for the truffles are mixed and then cooked in special candy-making vats. In the Molding Department, the melted chocolate and other ingredients from the Cooking Department are carefully poured into molds and decorative flourishes are applied by hand. After cooling, the truffles are packed for sale. The company uses a process costing system. The T-accounts below show the flow of costs through the two departments in April (all amounts are in Swiss francs):

Work in Process—Cooking

Bal. 4/1	8,000	Transferred out	160,000
Direct materials	42,000		
Direct labor	50,000		
Overhead	75,000		

Work in Process—Molding

Bal. 4/1	4,000	Transferred out	240,000
Transferred in	160,000		
Direct labor	36,000		
Overhead	45,000		

Required:
Prepare journal entries showing the flow of costs through the two processing departments during April.

EXERCISE 4–2   Quantity Schedule and Equivalent Units—Weighted-Average Method (LO2, LO3)
The Alaskan Fisheries, Inc., processes salmon for various distributors. Two departments are involved— Department 1 and Department 2. Data relating to pounds of salmon processed in Department 1 during July are presented below:

	Pounds of Salmon	Percent Completed*
Work in process, July 1	20,000	30%
Started into processing during July	380,000	—
Work in process, July 31	25,000	60%

*Labor and overhead only.

All materials are added at the beginning of processing in Department 1. Labor and overhead (conversion) costs are incurred uniformly throughout processing.

Required:
Prepare a quantity schedule and a computation of equivalent units for July for Department 1 assuming that the company uses the weighted-average method of accounting for units.

EXERCISE 4–3   Equivalent Units and Cost per Equivalent Unit—Weighted-Average Method
(LO2, LO4)
Helox, Inc., manufactures a product that passes through two production processes. A quantity schedule for a recent month for the first process follows:

	Quantity Schedule	Equivalent Units	
		Materials	Conversion
Units to be accounted for:			
Work in process, May 1 (all materials, 40% conversion cost added last month) ...	5,000		
Started into production	180,000		
Total units	185,000		
Units accounted for as follows:			
Transferred to the next process	175,000	?	?
Work in process, May 31 (all materials, 30% conversion cost added this month) ...	10,000	?	?
Total units	185,000	?	?

Costs in the beginning work in process inventory of the first processing department were: materials, $1,200; and conversion cost, $3,800. Costs added during the month were: materials, $54,000; and conversion cost, $352,000.

Required:
1. Assume that the company uses the weighted-average method of accounting for units and costs. Determine the equivalent units for the month for the first process.
2. Compute the costs per equivalent unit for the month for the first process.

EXERCISE 4–4   Cost Reconciliation—Weighted-Average Method (LO5)
(This exercise should be assigned only if Exercise 4–3 is also assigned.) Refer to the data for Helox, Inc., in Exercise 4–3 and to the equivalent units and costs per equivalent unit you have computed there.

Required:
Complete the following cost reconciliation for the first process:

Cost Reconciliation

	Total Cost	Equivalent Units	
		Materials	Conversion
Cost accounted for as follows:			
Transferred to the next process: (? units × $?)	$?		
Work in process, May 31:			
Materials, at _____ per EU	?	?	
Conversion, at _____ per EU	?		?
Total work in process	?		
Total cost	$?		

EXERCISE 4–5   Quantity Schedule, Equivalent Units, and Cost per Equivalent Unit—Weighted-Average Method (LO2, LO3, LO4)

Pureform, Inc., manufactures a product that passes through two departments. Data for a recent month for the first department follow:

	Units	Materials	Labor	Overhead
Work in process, beginning	5,000	$ 4,500	$ 1,250	$ 1,875
Units started in process	45,000			
Units transferred out	42,000			
Work in process, ending	8,000			
Cost added during the month	—	52,800	21,500	32,250

The beginning work in process inventory was 80% complete as to materials and 60% complete as to processing. The ending work in process inventory was 75% complete as to materials and 50% complete as to processing.

Required:

1. Assume that the company uses the weighted-average method of accounting for units and costs. Prepare a quantity schedule and a computation of equivalent units for the month.
2. Determine the costs per equivalent unit for the month.

Problems

CHECK FIGURE
(2) 6/30 WIP: $4,510

PROBLEM 4–1   Equivalent Units; Cost Reconciliation—Weighted-Average Method (LO2, LO5)

Martin Company manufactures a single product. The company uses the weighted-average method in its process costing system. Activity for June has just been completed. An incomplete production report for the first processing department follows:

Quantity Schedule and Equivalent Units

	Quantity Schedule
Units to be accounted for:	
Work in process, June 1 (all materials, 75% labor and overhead added last month)	8,000
Started into production	45,000
Total units	53,000

	Quantity Schedule	Equivalent Units (EU)		
		Materials	Labor	Overhead
Units accounted for as follows:				
Transferred to the next department	48,000	?	?	?
Work in process, June 30 (all materials, 40% labor and overhead added this month)	5,000	?	?	?
Total units......................	53,000	?	?	?

Costs per Equivalent Unit

	Total Cost	Materials	Labor	Overhead	Whole Unit
Cost to be accounted for:					
Work in process, June 1	$ 7,130	$ 5,150	$ 660	$ 1,320	
Cost added by the department	58,820	29,300	9,840	19,680	
Total cost (a)	$65,950	$34,450	$10,500	$21,000	
Equivalent units (b)		53,000	50,000	50,000	
Cost per EU, (a) ÷ (b)		$0.65 +	$0.21 +	$0.42 =	$1.28

Cost Reconciliation

	Total Cost
Cost accounted for as follows:	
?	?

Required:

1. Prepare a schedule showing how the equivalent units were computed for the first processing department.
2. Complete the "Cost Reconciliation" part of the production report for the first processing department.

PROBLEM 4–2   Interpreting a Production Report—Weighted-Average Method (LO2, LO3, LO4)
Cooperative San José of southern Sonora state in Mexico makes a unique syrup using cane sugar and local herbs. The syrup is sold in small bottles and is prized as a flavoring for drinks and for use in desserts. The bottles are sold for $12 each. (The Mexican currency is the peso and is denoted by $.) The first stage in the production process is carried out in the Mixing Department, which removes foreign matter from the raw materials and mixes them in the proper proportions in large vats. The company uses the weighted-average method in its process costing system.

A hastily prepared report for the Mixing Department for April appears below:

CHECK FIGURE
(1) Materials: 220,000 equivalent units
(2) Conversion: $1.30 per unit
(3) 160,000 units

Quantity Schedule

Units to be accounted for:	
Work in process, April 1 (90% materials, 80% conversion cost added last month)	30,000
Started into production	200,000
Total units	230,000
Units accounted for as follows:	
Transferred to the next department	190,000
Work in process, April 30 (75% materials, 60% conversion cost added this month)	40,000
Total units .:..............................	230,000

Total Cost

Cost to be accounted for:	
Work in process, April 1	$ 98,000
Cost added during the month	827,000
Total cost	$925,000

Cost Reconciliation

Cost accounted for as follows:	
Transferred to the next department	$805,600
Work in process, April 30	119,400
Total cost	$925,000

Cooperative San José has just been acquired by another company, and the management of the acquiring company wants some additional information about Cooperative San José's operations.

Required:

1. What were the equivalent units for the month?
2. What were the costs per equivalent unit for the month? The beginning inventory consisted of the following costs: materials, $67,800; and conversion cost, $30,200. The costs added during the month consisted of: materials, $579,000; and conversion cost, $248,000.
3. How many of the units transferred to the next department were started and completed during the month?
4. The manager of the Mixing Department, anxious to make a good impression on the new owners, stated, "Materials prices jumped from about $2.50 per unit in March to $3 per unit in April, but due to good cost control I was able to hold our materials cost to less than $3 per unit for the month." Should this manager be rewarded for good cost control? Explain.

CHECK FIGURE
6/30 WIP: $87,500

PROBLEM 4–3   Production Report—Weighted-Average Method (LO2, LO3, LO4, LO5)

Sunspot Beverages, Ltd., of Fiji makes blended tropical fruit drinks in two stages. Fruit juices are extracted from fresh fruits and then blended in the Blending Department. The blended juices are then bottled and packed for shipping in the Bottling Department. The following information pertains to the operations of the Blending Department for June. (The currency in Fiji is the Fijian dollar.)

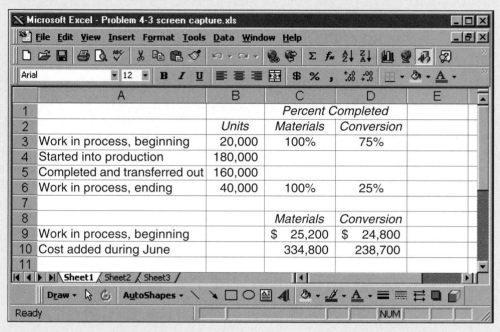

Required:

Prepare a production report for the Blending Department for June assuming that the company uses the weighted-average method.

CHECK FIGURE
(2) Materials: $1.50 per unit
(3) 5/31 WIP: $16,500

PROBLEM 4–4   Step-by-Step Production Report—Weighted-Average Method (LO2, LO3, LO4, LO5)

Builder Products, Inc., manufactures a caulking compound that goes through three processing stages prior to completion. Information on work in the first department, Cooking, is given below for May:

Production data:	
Units in process, May 1: 100% complete as to materials and 80% complete as to labor and overhead	10,000
Units started into production during May	100,000
Units completed and transferred out	95,000
Units in process, May 31: 60% complete as to materials and 20% complete as to labor and overhead	?

Cost data:
Work in process inventory, May 1:
Materials cost .... $ 1,500
Labor cost 1,800
Overhead cost 5,400
Cost added during May:
Materials cost 154,500
Labor cost 22,700
Overhead cost 68,100

Materials are added at several stages during the cooking process, whereas labor and overhead costs are incurred uniformly. The company uses the weighted-average method.

Required:
Prepare a production report for the Cooking Department for May. Use the following three steps in preparing your report:
1. Prepare a quantity schedule and a computation of equivalent units.
2. Compute the costs per equivalent unit for the month.
3. Using the data from (1) and (2) above, prepare a cost reconciliation.

PROBLEM 4–5   Preparation of Production Report from Analysis of Work in Process—Weighted-Average Method (LO2, LO3, LO4, LO5)
Weston Products manufactures an industrial cleaning compound that goes through three processing departments—Grinding, Mixing, and Cooking. All raw materials are introduced at the start of work in the Grinding Department, with conversion costs being incurred evenly throughout the grinding process. The Work in Process T-account for the Grinding Department for a recent month is given below:

CHECK FIGURE
(1) Materials: $0.80 per unit;
5/31 WIP: $25,000

Work in Process—Grinding Department

Inventory, May 1 (18,000 lbs., 1/3 processed)	21,800	Completed and transferred to mixing (? lbs.)	?
May costs added:			
Raw materials (167,000 lbs.)	133,400		
Labor and overhead	226,800		
Inventory, May 31 (15,000 lbs., 2/3 processed)	?		

The May 1 work in process inventory consists of $14,600 in materials cost and $7,200 in labor and overhead cost. The company uses the weighted-average method to account for units and costs.

Required:
1. Prepare a production report for the Grinding Department for the month.
2. What criticism can be made of the unit costs that you have computed on your production report?

PROBLEM 4–6   Costing Inventories; Journal Entries; Cost of Goods Sold—Weighted-Average Method (LO1, LO2, LO4, LO5)
You are employed by Spirit Company, a manufacturer of digital watches. The company's chief financial officer is trying to verify the accuracy of the ending work in process and finished goods inventories prior to closing the books for the year. You have been asked to assist in this verification. The year-end balances shown on Spirit Company's books are as follows:

CHECK FIGURE
(1) Labor: $2.20 per unit
(2) 12/31 WIP: $903,000
(4) COGS: $3,339,000

	Units	Costs
Work in process, December 31 (50% complete as to labor and overhead)	300,000	$660,960
Finished goods, December 31	200,000	1,009,800

Materials are added to production at the beginning of the manufacturing process, and overhead is applied to each product at the rate of 60% of direct labor cost. There was no finished goods inventory at the beginning of the year. A review of Spirit Company's inventory and cost records has disclosed the following data, all of which are accurate:

	Units	Costs Materials	Costs Labor
Work in process, January 1 (80% complete as to labor and overhead)	200,000	$ 200,000	$ 315,000
Units started into production	1,000,000		
Cost added during the year:			
Materials cost		1,300,000	
Labor cost			1,995,000
Units completed during the year	900,000		

The company uses the weighted-average cost method.

Required:
1. Determine the equivalent units and costs per equivalent unit for materials, labor, and overhead for the year.
2. Determine the amount of cost that should be assigned to the ending work in process and finished goods inventories.
3. Prepare the necessary correcting journal entry to adjust the work in process and finished goods inventories to the correct balances as of December 31.
4. Determine the cost of goods sold for the year assuming there is no under- or overapplied overhead.

(CPA, adapted)

PROBLEM 4–7   Comprehensive Process Costing Problem—Weighted-Average Method
(LO1, LO2, LO3, LO4, LO5)
Lubricants, Inc., produces a special kind of grease that is widely used by race car drivers. The grease is produced in two processes: refining and blending.

Raw oil products are introduced at various points in the Refining Department; labor and overhead costs are incurred evenly throughout the refining operation. The refined output is then transferred to the Blending Department.

The following incomplete Work in Process account is available for the Refining Department for March:

Work in Process—Refining Department

March 1 inventory (20,000 gal.; 100% complete as to materials; 90% complete as to labor and overhead)	38,000	Completed and transferred to blending (? gal.)	?
March costs added:			
Raw oil materials (390,000 gal.)	495,000		
Direct labor	72,000		
Overhead	181,000		
March 31 inventory (40,000 gal.; 75% complete as to materials; 25% complete as to labor and overhead)	?		

The March 1 work in process inventory in the Refining Department consists of the following cost elements: raw materials, $25,000; direct labor, $4,000; and overhead, $9,000.

Costs incurred during March in the Blending Department were: materials used, $115,000; direct labor, $18,000; and overhead cost applied to production, $42,000. The company accounts for units and costs by the weighted-average method.

Required:
1. Prepare journal entries to record the costs incurred in both the Refining Department and Blending Department during March. Key your entries to the items (a) through (g) below.

a. Raw materials were issued for use in production.

b. Direct labor costs were incurred.

c. Manufacturing overhead costs for the entire factory were incurred, $225,000. (Credit Accounts Payable.)

d. Manufacturing overhead cost was applied to production using a predetermined overhead rate.

e. Units that were complete as to processing in the Refining Department were transferred to the Blending Department, $740,000.

f. Units that were complete as to processing in the Blending Department were transferred to Finished Goods, $950,000.

g. Completed units were sold on account, $1,500,000. The Cost of Goods Sold was $900,000.

2. Post the journal entries from (1) above to T-accounts. The following account balances existed at the beginning of March. (The beginning balance in the Refining Department's Work in Process account is given above.)

Raw Materials	$618,000
Work in Process—Blending Department	65,000
Finished Goods	20,000

After posting the entries to the T-accounts, find the ending balance in the inventory accounts and the manufacturing overhead account.

3. Prepare a production report for the Refining Department for March.

PROBLEM 4–8 Comprehensive Process Costing Problem—Weighted-Average Method
(LO1, LO2, LO3, LO4, LO5)

CHECK FIGURE
(2) 5/31 Cooking
Dept. WIP:
$66,000

Hilox, Inc., produces an antacid product that goes through two departments—Cooking and Bottling. The company has recently hired a new assistant accountant, who has prepared the following summary of production and costs for the Cooking Department for May using the weighted-average method.

Cooking Department costs:	
Work in process inventory, May 1: 70,000 quarts, 60% complete as to materials and 30% complete as to labor and overhead	$ 61,000*
Materials added during May	570,000
Labor added during May	100,000
Overhead applied during May	235,000
Total departmental costs	$966,000
Cooking Department costs assigned to:	
Quarts completed and transferred to the Bottling Department: 400,000 quarts at __?__ per quart	$?
Work in process inventory, May 31: 50,000 quarts, 70% complete as to materials and 40% complete as to labor and overhead	?
Total departmental costs assigned	$?

*Consists of materials, $39,000; labor, $5,000; and overhead, $17,000.

The new assistant accountant has determined the cost per quart transferred to be $2.415, as follows:

$$\frac{\text{Total departmental costs, } \$966,000}{\text{Quarts completed and transferred, } 400,000} = \$2.415 \text{ per quart}$$

However, the assistant accountant is unsure how to use this unit cost figure in assigning cost to the ending work in process inventory. In addition, the company's general ledger shows only $900,000 in cost transferred from the Cooking Department to the Bottling Department, which does not agree with the $966,000 figure above.

The general ledger also shows the following costs incurred in the Bottling Department during May: materials used, $130,000; direct labor cost incurred, $80,000; and overhead cost applied to products, $158,000.

Required:
1. Prepare journal entries as follows to record activity in the company during May. Key your entries to the letters (a) through (g) below.
   a. Raw materials were issued to the two departments for use in production.
   b. Direct labor costs were incurred in the two departments.
   c. Manufacturing overhead costs were incurred, $400,000. (Credit Accounts Payable.) The company maintains a single Manufacturing Overhead account for the entire plant.
   d. Manufacturing overhead cost was applied to production in each department using predetermined overhead rates.
   e. Units completed as to processing in the Cooking Department were transferred to the Bottling Department, $900,000.
   f. Units completed as to processing in the Bottling Department were transferred to Finished Goods, $1,300,000.
   g. Units were sold on account, $2,000,000. The Cost of Goods Sold was $1,250,000.
2. Post the journal entries from (1) above to T-accounts. Balances in selected accounts on May 1 are given below:

Raw Materials	$710,000
Work in Process—Bottling Department	85,000
Finished Goods	45,000

After posting the entries to the T-accounts, find the ending balance in the inventory accounts and the Manufacturing Overhead account.
3. Prepare a production report for the Cooking Department for May.

Building Your Skills

ANALYTICAL THINKING   (LO2, LO3, LO4, LO5)
"I think we goofed when we hired that new assistant controller," said Ruth Scarpino, president of Provost Industries. "Just look at this production report that he prepared for last month for the Finishing Department. I can't make heads or tails out of it."

Finishing Department costs:	
Work in process inventory, April 1, 450 units; 100% complete as to materials; 60% complete as to conversion costs	$ 8,208*
Costs transferred in during the month from the preceding department, 1,950 units	17,940
Materials cost added during the month (materials are added when processing is 50% complete in the Finishing Department)	6,210
Conversion costs incurred during the month	13,920
Total departmental costs	$46,278
Finishing Department costs assigned to:	
Units completed and transferred to finished goods, 1,800 units at $25.71 per unit	$46,278
Work in process inventory, April 30, 600 units; 0% complete as to materials; 35% complete as to processing	–0–
Total departmental costs assigned	$46,278

*Consists of: cost transferred in, $4,068; materials cost, $1,980; and conversion cost, $2,160.

"He's struggling to learn our system," replied Frank Harrop, the operations manager. "The problem is that he's been away from process costing for a long time, and it's coming back slowly."

"It's not just the format of his report that I'm concerned about. Look at that $25.71 unit cost that he's come up with for April. Doesn't that seem high to you?" said Ms. Scarpino.

"Yes, it does seem high; but on the other hand, I know we had an increase in materials prices during April, and that may be the explanation," replied Mr. Harrop. "I'll get someone else to redo this report and then we may be able to see what's going on."

Provost Industries manufactures a ceramic product that goes through two processing departments—Molding and Finishing. The company uses the weighted-average method to account for units and costs.

Required:
1. Prepare a revised production report for the Finishing Department.
2. Explain to the president why the unit cost on the new assistant controller's report is so high.

COMMUNICATING IN PRACTICE   (LO5)
Assume that you are the cost analyst who prepared the Production Report that appears in Exhibit 4–9. You receive a call from Minesh Patel, a new hire in the company's accounting staff who is not sure what needs to be done with the cost reconciliation portion of the report. He wants to know what journal entries should be prepared and what balances need to be checked in the company's accounts.

Required:
Write a memorandum to Mr. Patel that explains the steps that should be taken. Refer to specific amounts on the Cost Reconciliation portion of the Production Report to ensure that he properly completes the steps.

ETHICS CHALLENGE   (LO2, LO4, LO5)
Gary Stevens and Mary James are production managers in the Consumer Electronics Division of General Electronics Company, which has several dozen plants scattered in locations throughout the world. Mary manages the plant located in Des Moines, Iowa, while Gary manages the plant in El Segundo, California. Production managers are paid a salary and get an additional bonus equal to 5% of their base salary if the entire division meets or exceeds its target profits for the year. The bonus is determined in March after the company's annual report has been prepared and issued to stockholders.

Shortly after the beginning of the new year, Mary received a phone call from Gary that went like this:

Gary: How's it going, Mary?
Mary: Fine, Gary. How's it going with you?
Gary: Great! I just got the preliminary profit figures for the division for last year and we are within $200,000 of making the year's target profits. All we have to do is to pull a few strings, and we'll be over the top!
Mary: What do you mean?
Gary: Well, one thing that would be easy to change is your estimate of the percentage completion of your ending work in process inventories.
Mary: I don't know if I can do that, Gary. Those percentage completion figures are supplied by Tom Winthrop, my lead supervisor, who I have always trusted to provide us with good estimates. Besides, I have already sent the percentage completion figures to the corporate headquarters.
Gary: You can always tell them there was a mistake. Think about it, Mary. All of us managers are doing as much as we can to pull this bonus out of the hat. You may not want the bonus check, but the rest of us sure could use it.

The final processing department in Mary's production facility began the year with no work in process inventories. During the year, 210,000 units were transferred in from the prior processing department and 200,000 units were completed and sold. Costs transferred in from the prior department totaled $39,375,000. No materials are added in the final processing department. A total of $20,807,500 of conversion cost was incurred in the final processing department during the year.

Required:
1. Tom Winthrop estimated that the units in ending inventory in the final processing department were 30% complete with respect to the conversion costs of the final processing department. If this estimate of the percentage completion is used, what would be the Cost of Goods Sold for the year?
2. Does Gary Stevens want the estimated percentage completion to be increased or decreased? Explain why.
3. What percentage completion would result in increasing reported net income by $200,000 over the net income that would be reported if the 30% figure were used?
4. Do you think Mary James should go along with the request to alter estimates of the percentage completion?

TAKING IT TO THE NET

As you know, the World Wide Web is a medium that is constantly evolving. Sites come and go and change without notice. To enable periodic update of site addresses, this problem has been posted to the textbook website (www.mhhe.com/folk1e). After accessing the site, enter the Student Center and select this chapter. Select and complete the Taking It to the Net problem.

TEAMWORK IN ACTION   (LO2, LO3, LO4, LO5)

The production report includes a quantity schedule, the computation of equivalent costs and costs per equivalent units, and a cost reconciliation.

Required:

1. *Learning teams* of three (or more) members should be formed. Each team member must select one of the following sections of the production report (as illustrated in Exhibit 4–9) as an area of expertise (each team must have at least one expert in each section).
    a. Quantity Schedule and Equivalent Units.
    b. Costs per Equivalent Unit.
    c. Cost Reconciliation.
2. *Expert teams* should be formed from the individuals who have selected the same area of expertise. Expert teams should discuss and write up a brief summary that each expert will present to his/her learning team that addresses the following:
    a. The purpose of the section of the production report.
    b. The manner in which the amounts appearing in this section of the report are determined.
3. Each expert should return to his/her learning team. In rotation, each member should present his/her expert team's report to the learning team.

Chapter Five

Cost Behavior: Analysis and Use

Decision Feature A Costly Mistake

After spending countless hours tracking down the hardware and fixtures he needed to restore his Queen Anne Victorian house, Stephen Gordon recognized an opportunity. In 1980, he opened Restoration Hardware, Inc., a specialty store carrying antique hardware and fixtures.

The company, based in Corte Madera, California, now sells fine furniture, lighting, hardware, home accessories, garden products, and gifts. The company's products, described by some as nostalgic, old-fashioned, and obscure, appeal to wealthy baby boomers. Customers can shop at one of the 90 Restoration Hardware stores, by catalog, or online at the company's website www.restorationhardware.com.

1998 was a year of phenomenal growth and change for Restoration Hardware. Twenty-four new stores were opened, increasing the total number in the chain to 65. The company's newly launched catalog business was an instant success. Net sales approached $200 million, an increase of almost 114% from the prior year. Gordon, chairman and CEO, took the company public.

The success enjoyed by the company in 1998 did not recur in 1999. Gordon's biggest mistake was a failure to consider cost behavior when making decisions to promote the company's products. The most popular furniture items in the store were discounted during the first quarter to encourage customer interest. The company spent $1 million to advertise this big sale, which was far more "successful" than Gordon had imagined. Sales for the first quarter increased by 84% to $60 million. However, much of the increase arose from sales of discounted goods. As a result, margins (that is, differences between sale prices and the cost of the goods that were sold) were lower than usual. Further, because the items placed on sale were larger and heavier than average, the costs to move them from the distribution centers to the stores were considerably higher. The company ended up reporting a loss of $2.7 million for the quarter.

Sources: Restoration Hardware website July 2000; Stephen Gordon, "My Biggest Mistake," *Inc.*, September 1999, p. 103; and Heather Chaplin, "Past? Perfect," *American Demographics*, May 1999, pp. 68–69.

Learning Objectives

After studying Chapter 5, you should be able to:

LO1 Understand how fixed and variable costs behave and how to use them to predict costs.

LO2 Analyze a mixed cost using the high-low method.

LO3 Analyze a mixed cost using the scattergraph method.

LO4 Prepare an income statement using the contribution format.

In our discussion of cost terms and concepts in Chapter 1, we stated that one way in which costs can be classified is by behavior. We defined cost behavior as the way a cost reacts or changes as changes take place in the level of business activity. An understanding of cost behavior is the key to many decisions in an organization. Managers who understand how costs behave are better able to predict what costs will be under various operating circumstances. Attempts at decision-making without a thorough understanding of the costs involved—and how these costs may change with the activity level—can lead to disaster. For example, a decision to cut back a particular product line might result in far less cost savings than managers had assumed if they confuse variable and fixed costs—leading to a decline in profits. To avoid such problems, a manager must be able to accurately predict what costs will be at various activity levels. In this chapter, we shall find that the key to effective cost prediction lies in understanding variable and fixed costs.

We briefly review in this chapter the definitions of variable costs and fixed costs and then discuss the behavior of these costs in greater depth than we were able to do in Chapter 1. After this review and discussion, we turn our attention to the analysis of mixed costs. We conclude the chapter by introducing a new income statement format—called the contribution format—in which costs are organized by behavior rather than by the traditional functions of production, sales, and administration.

Types of Cost Behavior Patterns

Concept 5–1

In Chapter 1 we mentioned only variable and fixed costs. In this chapter we will discuss a third behavior pattern, generally known as a *mixed* or *semivariable* cost. All three cost behavior patterns—variable, fixed, and mixed—are found in most organizations. The relative proportion of each type of cost present in a firm is known as the firm's **cost structure**. For example, a firm might have many fixed costs but few variable or mixed costs. Alternatively, it might have many variable costs but few fixed or mixed costs. A firm's cost structure can have a significant impact on decisions. In this chapter we will concentrate on gaining a fuller understanding of the behavior of each type of cost. In the next chapter we will discuss more fully how cost structure impacts decisions.

in business today **Selling Online**

By making investments in technology, many firms have created cost structures radically different from those of traditional companies. John Labbett, the CFO of Onsale, an Internet auctioneer of discontinued computers, was previously employed at House of Fabrics, a traditional retailer. The two companies have roughly the same total revenues of about $250 million. However, House of Fabrics, with 5,500 employees, has a revenue per employee of about $90,000. At Onsale, with only 200 employees, the figure is $1.18 million per employee. Moreover, Internet companies are often able to grow at very little cost. If demand grows, an Internet company just adds another computer server. If demand grows at a traditional retailer, the company may have to invest in a new building and additional inventory and may have to hire additional employees.

Source: George Donnelly, "New@ttitude," *CFO*, June 1999, pp. 42–54.

Learning Objective 1
Understand how fixed and variable costs behave and how to use them to predict costs.

Variable Costs

We explained in Chapter 1 that a variable cost is a cost whose total dollar amount varies in direct proportion to changes in the activity level. If the activity level doubles, the total dollar amount of the variable cost also doubles. If the activity level increases by only 10%, then the total dollar amount of the variable cost increases by 10% as well.

We also found in Chapter 1 that a variable cost remains constant if expressed on a *per unit* basis. To provide an example, consider Nooksack Expeditions, a small company that provides daylong whitewater rafting excursions on rivers in the North Cascade Mountains. The company provides all of the necessary equipment and experienced guides, and it serves gourmet meals to its guests. The meals are purchased from an exclusive caterer for $30 a person for a daylong excursion. If we look at the cost of the meals on a *per person* basis, the cost remains constant at $30. This $30 cost per person will not change, regardless of how many people participate in a daylong excursion. The behavior of this variable cost, on both a per unit and a total basis, is tabulated below:

Number of Guests	Cost of Meals per Guest	Total Cost of Meals
250	$30	$ 7,500
500	30	15,000
750	30	22,500
1,000	30	30,000

The idea that a variable cost is constant per unit but varies in total with the activity level is crucial to an understanding of cost behavior patterns. We shall rely on this concept again and again in this chapter and in chapters ahead.

Exhibit 5–1 provides a graphic illustration of variable cost behavior. Note that the graph of the total cost of the meals slants upward to the right. This is because the total cost of the meals is directly proportional to the number of guests. In contrast, the graph of the per unit cost of meals is flat. This is because the cost of the meals per guest is constant at $30 per guest.

The Activity Base   For a cost to be variable, it must be variable *with respect to something*. That "something" is its *activity base*. An **activity base** is a measure of whatever causes the incurrence of variable cost. An activity base is also sometimes referred to as a *cost driver.* Some of the most common activity bases are direct labor-hours, machine-hours, units produced, and units sold. Other activity bases (cost drivers) might include the number

Exhibit 5–1
Variable Cost Behavior

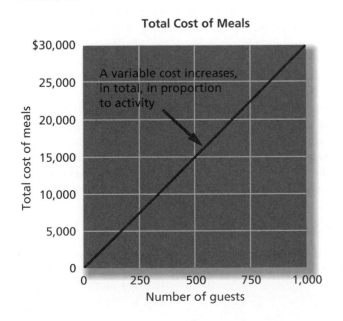

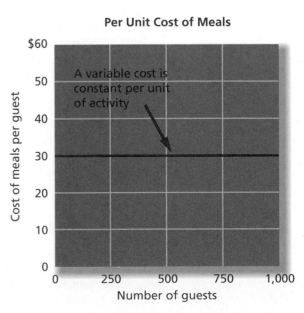

of miles driven by salespersons, the number of pounds of laundry cleaned by a hotel, the number of letters typed by a secretary, and the number of beds occupied in a hospital.

To plan and control variable costs, a manager must be well acquainted with the various activity bases within the firm. People sometimes get the notion that if a cost doesn't vary with production or with sales, then it is not really a variable cost. This is not correct. As suggested by the range of bases listed above, costs are caused by many different activities within an organization. Whether a cost is considered to be variable depends on whether it is caused by the activity under consideration. For example, if a manager is analyzing the cost of service calls under a product warranty, the relevant activity measure will be the number of service calls made. Those costs that vary in total with the number of service calls made are the variable costs of making service calls.

Nevertheless, unless stated otherwise, you can assume that the activity base under consideration is the total volume of goods and services provided by the organization. So, for example, if we ask whether direct materials at Ford is a variable cost, the answer is yes, since the cost of direct materials is variable with respect to Ford's total volume of output. We will specify the activity base only when it is something other than total output.

decision | *maker*   **Budget Analyst**

You are the budget analyst for a firm that provides janitorial services to other companies. You have been asked to estimate the costs that will be incurred on the janitorial jobs that will be performed next year. What types of costs would you expect? How would you characterize these costs in terms of behavior? What activity would you need to measure in order to estimate the costs?

Extent of Variable Costs   The number and type of variable costs present in an organization will depend in large part on the organization's structure and purpose. A public utility like Florida Power and Light, with large investments in equipment, will tend to have few variable costs. Most of the costs are associated with its plant, and these costs tend to be insensitive to changes in levels of service provided. A manufacturing company like Black and Decker, by contrast, will often have many variable costs; these costs will be associated with both the manufacture and distribution of its products to customers.

A merchandising company like Wal-Mart or J. K. Gill will usually have a high proportion of variable costs in its cost structure. In most merchandising companies, the cost of merchandise purchased for resale, a variable cost, constitutes a very large component of total cost. Service companies, by contrast, have diverse cost structures. Some service companies, such as the Skippers restaurant chain, have fairly large variable costs because of the costs of their raw materials. On the other hand, service companies involved in consulting, auditing, engineering, dental, medical, and architectural activities have very large fixed costs in the form of expensive facilities and highly trained salaried employees.

Some of the more frequently encountered variable costs are listed in Exhibit 5–2. This exhibit is not a complete listing of all costs that can be considered variable. Moreover, some of the costs listed in the exhibit may behave more like fixed than variable costs in some firms. We will see some examples of this later in the chapter. Nevertheless, Exhibit 5–2 provides a useful listing of many of the costs that normally would be considered variable with respect to the volume of output.

True Variable versus Step-Variable Costs

Not all variable costs have exactly the same behavior pattern. Some variable costs behave in a *true variable* or *proportionately variable* pattern. Other variable costs behave in a *step-variable* pattern.

Exhibit 5-2
Examples of Variable Costs

Type of Organization	Costs that Are Normally Variable with Respect to Volume of Output
Merchandising company	Cost of goods (merchandise) sold

Manufacturing company	Manufacturing costs:
	    Direct materials
	    Direct labor*
	Variable portion of manufacturing overhead:
	    Indirect materials
	    Lubricants
	    Supplies

Both merchandising and manufacturing companies	Selling, general, and administrative costs:
	    Commissions
	    Clerical costs, such as invoicing
	    Shipping costs

Service organizations	Supplies, travel, clerical

*Direct labor may or may not be variable in practice. See the discussion later in this chapter.

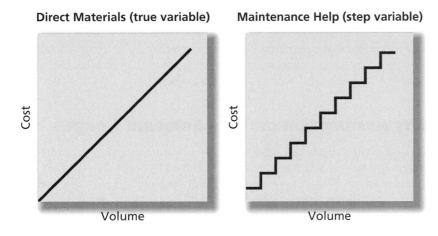

Direct Materials (true variable)   **Maintenance Help (step variable)**

Exhibit 5-3
True Variable versus Step-Variable Costs

True Variable Costs   Direct materials is a true or proportionately variable cost because the amount used during a period will vary in direct proportion to the level of production activity. Moreover, any amounts purchased but not used can be stored and carried forward to the next period as inventory.

Step-Variable Costs   The wages of maintenance workers are often considered to be a variable cost, but this labor cost doesn't behave in quite the same way as the cost of direct materials. Unlike direct materials, the time of maintenance workers is obtainable only in large chunks. Moreover, any maintenance time not utilized cannot be stored as inventory and carried forward to the next period. If the time is not used effectively, it is gone forever. Furthermore, a maintenance crew can work at a fairly leisurely pace if pressures are light but intensify its efforts if pressures build up. For this reason, somewhat small changes in the level of production may have no effect on the number of maintenance people employed.

A cost that is obtainable only in large chunks (such as the labor cost of maintenance workers) and that increases or decreases only in response to fairly wide changes in the activity level is known as a **step-variable cost.** The behavior of a step-variable cost, contrasted with the behavior of a true variable cost, is illustrated in Exhibit 5–3.

Notice that the need for maintenance help changes only with fairly wide changes in volume and that when additional maintenance time is obtained, it comes in large, indivisible

Exhibit 5–4

Curvilinear Costs and the
Relevant Range

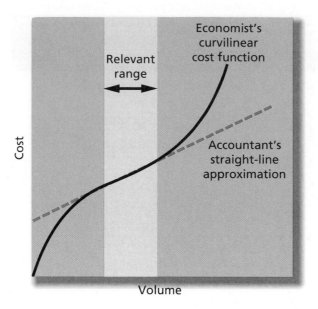

chunks. The strategy of management in dealing with step-variable costs must be to obtain the fullest use of services possible for each separate step. Great care must be taken in working with these kinds of costs to prevent "fat" from building up in an organization. There may be a tendency to employ additional help more quickly than needed, and there is a natural reluctance to lay people off when volume declines.

The Linearity Assumption and the Relevant Range

In dealing with variable costs, we have assumed a strictly linear relationship between cost and volume, except in the case of step-variable costs. Economists correctly point out that many costs that the accountant classifies as variable actually behave in a *curvilinear* fashion. The behavior of a **curvilinear cost** is shown in Exhibit 5–4.

Although many costs are not strictly linear when plotted as a function of volume, a curvilinear cost can be satisfactorily approximated with a straight line within a narrow band of activity known as the *relevant range*. The **relevant range** is that range of activity within which the assumptions made about cost behavior by the manager are valid. For example, note that the dashed line in Exhibit 5–4 can be used as an approximation to the curvilinear cost with very little loss of accuracy within the shaded relevant range. However, outside of the relevant range this particular straight line is a poor approximation to the curvilinear cost relationship. Managers should always keep in mind that a particular assumption made about cost behavior may be very inappropriate if activity falls outside of the relevant range.

Fixed Costs

In our discussion of cost behavior patterns in Chapter 1, we stated that fixed costs remain constant in total dollar amount within the relevant range of activity. To continue the Nooksack Expeditions example, assume the company decides to rent a building for $500 per month to store its equipment. The *total* amount of rent paid is the same regardless of the number of guests the company takes on its expeditions during any given month. This cost behavior pattern is shown graphically in Exhibit 5–5.

Since fixed costs remain constant in total, the amount of fixed cost computed on a *per unit* basis becomes progressively smaller as the level of activity increases. If Nooksack Expeditions has only 250 guests in a month, the $500 fixed rental cost would amount to

Exhibit 5–5
Fixed Cost Behavior

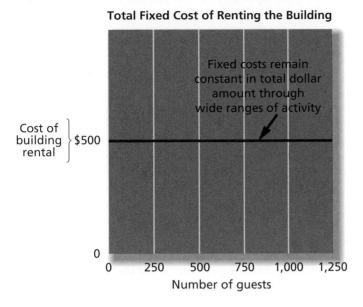

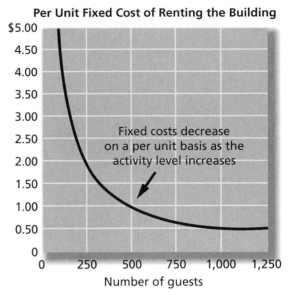

$2 per guest. If there are 1,000 guests, the fixed rental cost would amount to only 50 cents per guest. This aspect of the behavior of fixed costs is also displayed in Exhibit 5–5. Note that as the number of guests increases, the average unit cost drops, but it drops at a decreasing rate. The first guests have the biggest impact on unit costs.

As we noted in Chapter 1, this aspect of fixed costs can be confusing, although it is necessary in some contexts to express fixed costs on an average per unit basis. We found in Chapter 2, for example, that a broad unit cost figure containing both variable and fixed cost elements is used to determine unit product costs for *external* financial statements. For *internal* uses, however, fixed costs should not be expressed on a per unit basis because of the potential confusion. Experience has shown that for internal uses, fixed costs are most easily (and most safely) dealt with on a total basis rather than on a per unit basis.

Less Legroom

in business today

Airlines have long recognized that once a flight is scheduled, the variable cost of filling a seat with a passenger is very small. The costs of the cockpit flight crew, fuel, gate rentals, maintenance, aircraft depreciation, and so on, are all basically fixed with respect to the number of passengers who actually take a particular flight. The cost of the cabin flight crew is a step-variable cost—the number of flight attendants assigned to a flight will vary with the number of passengers on the flight. The only true variable costs are the costs of meals and a small increase in fuel consumption. Therefore, adding one passenger to a flight brings in additional revenue but has very little effect on total cost. Consequently, airlines have been stuffing more and more seats into their aircraft. Boeing 747s were configured originally with 9 seats across a row, but now they frequently have 10. One major airline has raised the number of seats in its fleet of DC-10 planes from 232 to nearly 300.

Source: Michael J. McCarthy, "Airline Squeeze Play: More Seats, Less Legroom," *The Wall Street Journal,* April 18, 1994, pp. B1 and B6.

Types of Fixed Costs

Fixed costs are sometimes referred to as capacity costs, since they result from outlays made for buildings, equipment, skilled professional employees, and other items needed to provide the basic capacity for sustained operations. For planning purposes, fixed costs can be viewed as being either *committed* or *discretionary*.

Committed Fixed Costs   **Committed fixed costs** relate to the investment in facilities, equipment, and the basic organizational structure of a firm. Examples of such costs include depreciation of buildings and equipment, taxes on real estate, insurance, and salaries of top management and operating personnel.

Committed fixed costs are long term in nature and can't be reduced to zero even for short periods of time without seriously impairing the profitability or long-run goals of the organization. Even if operations are interrupted or cut back, the committed fixed costs will still continue largely unchanged. During a recession, for example, a firm won't usually discharge key executives or sell off key facilities. The basic organizational structure and facilities ordinarily are kept intact. The costs of restoring them later are likely to be far greater than any short-run savings that might be realized.

Since it is difficult to change a committed fixed cost once the commitment has been made, management should approach these decisions with particular care. Decisions to acquire major equipment or to take on other committed fixed costs involve a long planning horizon. Management should make such commitments only after careful analysis of the available alternatives. Once a decision is made to build a certain size facility, a firm becomes locked into that decision for many years to come. Decisions relating to committed fixed costs will be examined in Chapter 12.

in business today **Sharing Office Space**

Even committed fixed costs may be more flexible than they would appear at first glance. Doctors in private practice have been under enormous pressure in recent years to cut costs. Dr. Edward Betz of Encino, California, has reduced the committed fixed costs of maintaining his office by letting a urologist use the office on Wednesday afternoons and Friday mornings for $1,500 a month. Dr. Betz uses this time to work on paperwork at home and he makes up for the lost time in the office by treating some patients on Saturdays.

Source: Gloria Lau and Tim W. Ferguson, "Doc's Just an Employee Now," *Forbes*, May 18, 1998, pp. 162–172.

Discretionary Fixed Costs   **Discretionary fixed costs** (often referred to as *managed fixed costs*) usually arise from *annual* decisions by management to spend in certain fixed cost areas. Examples of discretionary fixed costs include advertising, research, public relations, management development programs, and internships for students.

Basically, two key differences exist between discretionary fixed costs and committed fixed costs. First, the planning horizon for a discretionary fixed cost is fairly short term—usually a single year. By contrast, as we indicated earlier, committed fixed costs have a planning horizon that encompasses many years. Second, discretionary fixed costs can be cut for short periods of time with minimal damage to the long-run goals of the organization. For example, spending on management development programs can be cut back because of poor economic conditions. Although some unfavorable consequences may result from the cutback, it is doubtful that these consequences would be as great as those that would result if the company decided to economize during the year by laying off key personnel.

Whether a particular cost is regarded as committed or discretionary may depend on management's strategy. For example, during recessions when the level of home building is down, many construction companies lay off most of their workers and virtually disband operations. Other construction companies retain large numbers of employees on the payroll, even though the workers have little or no work to do. While these latter companies may be faced with short-term cash flow problems, it will be easier for them to respond quickly when economic conditions improve. And the higher morale and loyalty of their employees may give these companies a significant competitive advantage.

The most important characteristic of discretionary fixed costs is that management is not locked into a decision regarding such costs. They can be adjusted from year to year or even perhaps during the course of a year if circumstances demand such a modification.

The Trend Toward Fixed Costs   The trend in many industries is toward greater fixed costs relative to variable costs. Chores that used to be performed by hand have been taken over by machines. For example, grocery clerks at Safeway and Kroger used to key in prices by hand on cash registers. Now, most stores are equipped with barcode readers that enter price and other product information automatically. In general, competition has created pressure to give customers more value for their money—a demand that often can only be satisfied by automating business processes. For example, an H & R Block employee used to fill out tax returns for customers by hand and the advice given to a customer largely depended on the knowledge of that particular employee. Now, sophisticated computer software is used to complete tax returns, and the software provides the customer with tax planning and other advice tailored to the customer's needs based on the accumulated knowledge of many experts.

As machines take over more and more of the tasks that were performed by humans, the overall demand for human workers has not diminished. The demand for "knowledge" workers—those who work primarily with their minds rather than their muscles—has grown tremendously. And knowledge workers tend to be salaried, highly trained, and difficult to replace. As a consequence, the costs of compensating knowledge workers are often relatively fixed and are committed rather than discretionary costs.

Is Labor a Variable or a Fixed Cost?   As the preceding discussion suggests, wages and salaries may be fixed or variable. The behavior of wage and salary costs will differ from one country to another, depending on labor regulations, labor contracts, and custom. In some countries, such as France, Germany, China, and Japan, management has little flexibility in adjusting the labor force to changes in business activity. In countries such as the United States and the United Kingdom, management typically has much greater latitude. However, even in these less restrictive environments, managers may choose to treat employee compensation as a fixed cost for several reasons.

First, many companies have become much more reluctant to adjust the work force in response to short-term fluctuations in sales. Most companies realize that their employees are a very valuable asset. More and more, highly skilled and trained employees are required to run a successful business, and these workers are not easy to replace. Trained workers who are laid off may never return, and layoffs undermine the morale of those workers who remain.

In addition, managers do not want to be caught with a bloated payroll in an economic downturn. Therefore, there is an increased reluctance to add workers when sales activity picks up. Many companies are turning to temporary and part-time workers to take up the slack when their permanent, full-time employees are unable to handle all of the demand for the company's products and services. In such companies, labor costs are a mixture of fixed and variable costs.

Many major companies have undergone waves of downsizing in recent years in which large numbers of employees—particularly middle managers—have lost their jobs. It may seem that this downsizing proves that even management salaries should be regarded as variable costs, but this would not be a valid conclusion. Downsizing has been the result of attempts to reengineer business processes and cut costs rather than a response to a decline in sales activity. This underscores an important, but subtle, point. Fixed costs can change—they just don't change in response to small changes in activity.

In sum, we cannot provide a clear-cut answer to the question "Is labor a variable or fixed cost?" It depends on how much flexibility management has and management's strategy. Nevertheless, we will assume in this text that, unless otherwise stated, direct labor is a variable cost. This assumption is more likely to be valid for companies in the United States than in countries where employment laws permit much less flexibility.

in business today **Labor Laws and Cost Behavior**

The labor laws in the country in which the company operates often affect whether employee staff costs are fixed or variable. In Europe, banks have historically had very large numbers of branches, some of which serve very small villages. These branches are expensive to staff and maintain, and banks have argued that they are a drain on profits. In Denmark and the United Kingdom, the number of branches were cut by 34% and 22%, respectively, over a span of 10 years. In both cases, this led to a 15% reduction in staff employees. In contrast, countries with more restrictive labor laws that make it difficult to lay off workers have been unable to reduce staff or the number of branches significantly. For example, in Germany the number of branches was reduced by only 2% and the number of staff by only two-tenths of a percent during the same period.

Source: Charles Fleming, "Kinder Cuts: Continental Banks Seek to Expand Their Way Out of Retail Trouble," *The Wall Street Journal Europe,* March 11, 1997, pp. 1 and 8.

Fixed Costs and the Relevant Range

The concept of the relevant range, which was introduced in the discussion of variable costs, is also important in understanding fixed costs—particularly discretionary fixed costs. The levels of discretionary fixed costs are typically decided at the beginning of the year and depend on the support needs of planned programs such as advertising and training. The scope of these programs will depend, in turn, on the overall anticipated level of activity for the year. At very high levels of activity, programs are usually broadened or expanded. For example, if the company hopes to increase sales by 25%, it would probably plan for much larger advertising costs than if no sales increase were planned. So the *planned* level of activity might affect total discretionary fixed costs. However, once the total discretionary fixed costs have been budgeted, they are unaffected by the *actual* level of activity. For example, once the advertising budget has been decided on and has been spent, it will not be affected by how many units are actually sold. Therefore, the cost is fixed with respect to the *actual* number of units sold.

Discretionary fixed costs are easier to adjust than committed fixed costs. They also tend to be less "lumpy." Committed fixed costs consist of costs such as buildings, equipment, and the salaries of key personnel. It is difficult to buy half a piece of equipment or to hire a quarter of a product-line manager, so the step pattern depicted in Exhibit 5–6 is typical for such costs. The relevant range of activity for a fixed cost is the range of activity over which the graph of the cost is flat as in Exhibit 5–6. As a company expands its level of activity, it may outgrow its present facilities, or the key management team may need to be expanded. The result, of course, will be increased committed fixed costs as larger facilities are built and as new management positions are created.

One reaction to the step pattern depicted in Exhibit 5–6 is to say that discretionary and committed fixed costs are really just step-variable costs. To some extent this is true, since almost *all* costs can be adjusted in the long run. There are two major differences, however, between the step-variable costs depicted earlier in Exhibit 5–3 and the fixed costs depicted in Exhibit 5–6.

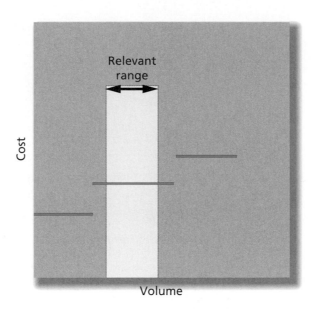

Exhibit 5–6
Fixed Costs and the Relevant Range

The first difference is that the step-variable costs can often be adjusted quickly as conditions change, whereas once fixed costs have been set, they often can't be changed easily. A step-variable cost such as maintenance labor, for example, can be adjusted upward or downward by hiring and laying off maintenance workers. By contrast, once a company has signed a lease for a building, it is locked into that level of lease cost for the life of the contract.

The second difference is that the *width of the steps* depicted for step-variable costs is much narrower than the width of the steps depicted for the fixed costs in Exhibit 5–6. The width of the steps relates to volume or level of activity. For step-variable costs, the width of a step might be 40 hours of activity or less if one is dealing, for example, with maintenance labor cost. For fixed costs, however, the width of a step might be *thousands* or even *tens of thousands* of hours of activity. In essence, the width of the steps for step-variable costs is generally so narrow that these costs can be treated essentially as variable costs for most purposes. The width of the steps for fixed costs, on the other hand, is so wide that these costs must generally be treated as being entirely fixed within the relevant range.

Mixed Costs

A **mixed cost** is one that contains both variable and fixed cost elements. Mixed costs are also known as semivariable costs. To continue the Nooksack Expeditions example, the company must pay a license fee of $25,000 per year plus $3 per rafting party to the state's Department of Natural Resources. If the company runs 1,000 rafting parties this year, then the total fees paid to the state would be $28,000, made up of $25,000 in fixed cost plus $3,000 in variable cost. The behavior of this mixed cost is shown graphically in Exhibit 5–7.

Even if Nooksack fails to attract any customers, the company will still have to pay the license fee of $25,000. This is why the cost line in Exhibit 5–7 intersects the vertical cost axis at the $25,000 point. For each rafting party the company organizes, the total cost of the state fees will increase by $3. Therefore, the total cost line slopes upward as the variable cost element is added to the fixed cost element.

Since the mixed cost in Exhibit 5–7 is represented by a straight line, the following equation for a straight line can be used to express the relationship between mixed cost and the level of activity:

Exhibit 5–7
Mixed Cost Behavior

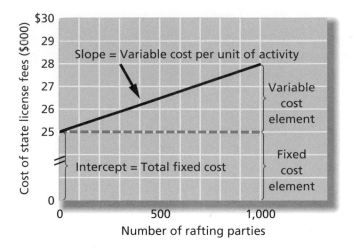

$$Y = a + bX$$

In this equation,

    Y = The total mixed cost
    a = The total fixed cost (the vertical intercept of the line)
    b = The variable cost per unit of activity (the slope of the line)
    X = The level of activity

In the case of the state fees paid by Nooksack Expeditions, the equation is written as follows:

$$Y = \$25{,}000 + \$3.00X$$

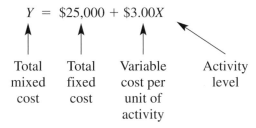

| Total mixed cost | Total fixed cost | Variable cost per unit of activity | Activity level |

This equation makes it very easy to calculate what the total mixed cost would be for any level of activity within the relevant range. For example, suppose that the company expects to organize 800 rafting parties in the next year. Then the total state fees would be $27,400 calculated as follows:

$$Y = \$25{,}000 + (\$3.00 \text{ per rafting party} \times 800 \text{ rafting parties})$$

$$= \$27{,}400$$

The Analysis of Mixed Costs

In practice, mixed costs are very common. For example, the cost of providing X-ray services to patients at the Harvard Medical School Hospital is a mixed cost. There are substantial fixed costs for equipment depreciation and for salaries for radiologists and technicians, but there are also variable costs for X-ray film, power, and supplies. At Southwest Airlines, maintenance costs are mixed costs. The company must incur fixed costs for renting maintenance facilities and for keeping skilled mechanics on the payroll, but the costs of replacement parts, lubricating oils, tires, and so forth, are variable with respect to how often and how far the company's aircraft are flown.

    The fixed portion of a mixed cost represents the basic, minimum cost of just having a service *ready and available* for use. The variable portion represents the cost incurred for *actual consumption* of the service. The variable element varies in proportion to the amount of service that is consumed.

How does management go about actually estimating the fixed and variable components of a mixed cost? The most common methods used in practice and in this text are *account analysis* and the *engineering approach.*

In **account analysis,** each account under consideration is classified as either variable or fixed based on the analyst's prior knowledge of how the cost in the account behaves. For example, direct materials would be classified as variable and a building lease cost would be classified as fixed because of the nature of those costs. The total fixed cost of an organization is the sum of the costs for the accounts that have been classified as fixed. The variable cost per unit is estimated by dividing the sum of the costs for the accounts that have been classified as variable by the total activity.

The **engineering approach** to cost analysis involves a detailed analysis of what cost behavior should be, based on an industrial engineer's evaluation of the production methods to be used, the materials specifications, labor requirements, equipment usage, efficiency of production, power consumption, and so on. For example, Pizza Hut might use the engineering approach to estimate the cost of serving a particular take-out pizza. The cost of the pizza would be estimated by carefully costing the specific ingredients used to make the pizza, the power consumed to cook the pizza, and the cost of the container the pizza is delivered in. The engineering approach must be used in those situations where no past experience is available concerning activity and costs. In addition, it is sometimes used together with other methods to improve the accuracy of cost analysis.

Account analysis works best when analyzing costs at a fairly aggregated level, such as the cost of serving patients in the emergency room (ER) of Cook County General Hospital. The costs of drugs, supplies, forms, wages, equipment, and so on, can be roughly classified as variable or fixed and a mixed cost formula for the overall cost of the emergency room can be estimated fairly quickly. However, this method glosses over the fact that some of the accounts may have elements of both fixed and variable costs. For example, the cost of electricity for the ER is a mixed cost. Most of the electricity is used for heating and lighting and is a fixed cost. However, the consumption of electricity increases with activity in the ER since diagnostic equipment, operating theater lights, defibrillators, and so on, all consume electricity. The most effective way to estimate the fixed and variable elements of such a mixed cost may be to analyze past records of cost and activity data. These records should reveal whether electrical costs vary significantly with the number of patients and if so, by how much. The remainder of this section will be concerned with how to conduct such an analysis of past cost and activity data.

Dr. Derek Chalmers, the chief executive officer of Brentline Hospital, motioned Kinh Nguyen, the chief financial officer of the hospital, into his office.

Derek: Kinh, come on in.
Kinh: What can I do for you?
Derek: Well for one, could you get the government to rescind the bookcase full of regulations against the wall over there?
Kinh: Sorry, that's a bit beyond my authority.
Derek: Just wishing, Kinh. Actually, I wanted to talk to you about our maintenance expenses. I don't usually pay attention to such things, but these expenses seem to be bouncing around a lot. Over the last half year or so they have been as low as $7,400 and as high as $9,800 per month.
Kinh: Actually, that's a pretty normal variation in those expenses.
Derek: Well, we budgeted a constant $8,400 a month. Can't we do a better job of predicting what these costs are going to be? And how do we know when we've spent too much in a month? Shouldn't there be some explanation for these variations?

Managerial Accounting in Action

The Issue

Kinh: Now that you mention it, we are in the process right now of tightening up our budgeting process. Our first step is to break all of our costs down into fixed and variable components.

Derek: How will that help?

Kinh: Well, that will permit us to predict what the level of costs will be. Some costs are fixed and shouldn't change much. Other costs go up and down as our activity goes up and down. The trick is to figure out what is driving the variable component of the costs.

Derek: What about the maintenance costs?

Kinh: My guess is that the variations in maintenance costs are being driven by our overall level of activity. When we treat more patients, our equipment is used more intensively, which leads to more maintenance expense.

Derek: How would you measure the level of overall activity? Would you use patient-days?

Kinh: I think so. Each day a patient is in the hospital counts as one patient-day. The greater the number of patient-days in a month, the busier we are. Besides, our budgeting is all based on projected patient-days.

Derek: Okay, so suppose you are able to break the maintenance costs down into fixed and variable components. What will that do for us?

Kinh: Basically, I will be able to predict what maintenance costs should be as a function of the number of patient-days.

Derek: I can see where that would be useful. We could use it to predict costs for budgeting purposes.

Kinh: We could also use it as a benchmark. Based on the actual number of patient-days for a period, I can predict what the maintenance costs should have been. We can compare this to the actual spending on maintenance.

Derek: Sounds good to me. Let me know when you get the results.

We will examine three methods that Kinh Nguyen might use to break down mixed costs into their fixed and variable elements—the *high-low method,* the *scattergraph method,* and the *least-squares regression method.* All three methods are based on analyzing cost and activity records from a number of prior periods. In the case of Brentline Hospital, we will use the following records of maintenance costs and patient-days for the first seven months of the year to estimate the fixed and variable elements of maintenance costs:

Month	Activity Level: Patient-Days	Maintenance Cost Incurred
January	5,600	$7,900
February	7,100	8,500
March	5,000	7,400
April	6,500	8,200
May	7,300	9,100
June	8,000	9,800
July	6,200	7,800

The High-Low Method

To analyze mixed costs with the **high-low method,** you begin by identifying the period with the lowest level of activity and the period with the highest level of activity. The difference in cost observed at the two extremes is divided by the change in activity between the extremes to estimate the variable cost per unit of activity.

Since total maintenance cost at Brentline Hospital appears to generally increase as the activity level increases, it is likely that some variable cost element is present. Using the high-low method, we first identify the periods with the highest and lowest *activity*—in this case, June and March. We then use the activity and cost data from these two periods to estimate the variable cost component as follows:

	Patient-Days	Maintenance Cost Incurred
High activity level (June)	8,000	$9,800
Low activity level (March)	5,000	7,400
Change	3,000	$2,400

$$\text{Variable cost} = \frac{\text{Change in cost}}{\text{Change in activity}} = \frac{\$2,400}{3,000 \text{ patient days}} = \$0.80 \text{ per patient-day}$$

Having determined that the variable rate for maintenance cost is 80 cents per patient-day, we can now determine the amount of fixed cost. This is done by taking total cost at *either* the high or the low activity level and deducting the variable cost element. In the computation below, total cost at the high activity level is used in computing the fixed cost element:

$$\text{Fixed cost element} = \text{Total cost} - \text{Variable cost element}$$
$$= \$9,800 - (\$0.80 \text{ per patient-day} \times 8,000 \text{ patient-days})$$
$$= \$3,400$$

Both the variable and fixed cost elements have now been isolated. The cost of maintenance can be expressed as $3,400 per month plus 80 cents per patient-day.

The cost of maintenance can also be expressed in terms of the equation for a straight line as follows:

$$Y = \$3,400 + \$0.80X$$

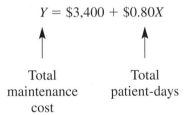

Total maintenance cost   Total patient-days

The data used in this illustration are shown graphically in Exhibit 5–8. Three things should be noted in relation to this exhibit:

1. The total maintenance cost, *Y,* is plotted on the vertical axis. Cost is known as the **dependent variable,** since the amount of cost incurred during a period depends on the level of activity for the period. (That is, as the level of activity increases, total cost will also increase.)
2. The activity, *X* (patient-days in this case), is plotted on the horizontal axis. Activity is known as the **independent variable,** since it causes variations in the cost.
3. A straight line has been drawn through the points corresponding to the low and high levels of activity. In essence, that is what the high-low method does—it draws a straight line through those two points.[1]

---

[1]The formula for the variable cost, $\dfrac{\text{Change in cost (i.e., change in } Y)}{\text{Change in activity (i.e., change in } X)}$, is basically the same as the formula for the slope of the line, $\dfrac{\text{Rise (i.e., change in } Y)}{\text{Run (i.e., change in } X)}$, that you are familiar with from high school algebra. This is because the slope of the line *is* the variable cost per unit. The higher the variable cost per unit, the steeper the line.

Sometimes the high and low levels of activity don't coincide with the high and low amounts of cost. For example, the period that has the highest level of activity may not have the highest amount of cost. Nevertheless, the highest and lowest levels of *activity* are always used to analyze a mixed cost under the high-low method. The reason is that the activity presumably causes costs, so the analyst would like to use data that reflects the greatest possible variation in activity.

The high-low method is very simple to apply, but it suffers from a major (and sometimes critical) defect—it utilizes only two data points. Generally, two points are not enough to produce accurate results in cost analysis work. Additionally, periods in which the activity level is unusually low or unusually high will tend to produce inaccurate results. A cost formula that is estimated solely using data from these unusual periods may seriously misrepresent the true cost relationship that holds during normal periods. Such a distortion is evident in Exhibit 5–8. The straight line should probably be shifted down somewhat so that it is closer to more of the data points. For these reasons, other methods of cost analysis that utilize a greater number of points will generally be more accurate than the high-low method. If a manager chooses to use the high-low method, he or she should do so with a full awareness of the method's limitations.

The Scattergraph Method

Learning Objective 3
Analyze a mixed cost using the scattergraph method.

A more accurate way of analyzing mixed costs is to use the **scattergraph method,** which takes into account all of the cost data. A graph like the one that we used in Exhibit 5–8 is constructed in which cost is shown on the vertical axis and the level of activity is shown on the horizontal axis. Costs observed at various levels of activity are then plotted on the graph, and a line is fitted to the plotted points. However, rather than just fitting the line to the high and low points, all points are considered when the line is drawn. This is done through simple visual inspection of the data, with the analyst taking care that the placement of the line is representative of all points, not just the high and low ones. Typically, the line is placed so that approximately equal numbers of points fall above and below it. A graph of this type is known as a *scattergraph,* and the line fitted to the plotted points is known as a **regression line.**

The scattergraph approach using the Brentline Hospital maintenance data is illustrated in Exhibit 5–9. Note that the regression line has been placed in such a way that approximately equal numbers of points fall above and below it. Also note that the line has been drawn so that it goes through one of the points. This is not absolutely necessary, but it makes subsequent calculations a little easier.

Since the regression line strikes the vertical cost axis at $3,300, that amount represents the fixed cost element. The variable cost element can be computed by subtracting the fixed cost of $3,300 from the total cost for any point lying on the regression line. Since the point representing 7,300 patient-days lies on the regression line, we can use it. The variable cost (to the nearest tenth of a cent) would be 79.5 cents per patient-day, computed as follows:

Total cost for 7,300 patient-days (a point falling on the regression line)	$9,100
Less fixed cost element	3,300
Variable cost element	$5,800

$5,800 ÷ 7,300 patient-days = $0.795 per patient-day

Thus, the cost formula using the regression line in Exhibit 5–9 would be $3,300 per month plus 79.5 cents per patient-day. In terms of the linear equation $Y = a + bX,$ the cost formula can be written as:

$$Y = \$3,300 + \$0.795X$$

where activity (X) is expressed in patient-days.

Exhibit 5–8
High-Low Method of Cost Analysis

Activity Level	Patient-Days	Maintenance Cost
High	8,000	$9,800
Low	5,000	$7,400

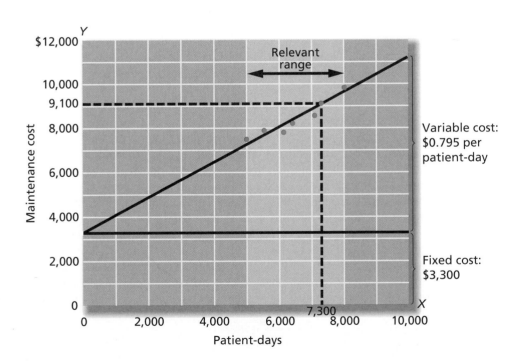

Exhibit 5–9
Scattergraph Method of Cost Analysis

In this example, there is not a great deal of difference between the cost formula derived using the high-low method and the cost formula derived using the scattergraph method. However, sometimes there *will* be a big difference. In those situations, more reliance should ordinarily be placed on the results of the scattergraph approach.

Also note that all of the points in Exhibit 5–9 lie reasonably close to the straight line. In other words, the estimates of the fixed and variable costs are reasonably accurate within this range of activity, so the relevant range extends at least from 5,000 to 8,000 patient-days. It may also be accurate below 5,000 patient-days and above 8,000 patient-days—we can't tell for sure without looking at more data.

A scattergraph can be an extremely useful tool in the hands of an experienced analyst. Quirks in cost behavior due to strikes, bad weather, breakdowns, and so on, become immediately apparent to the trained observer, who can make appropriate adjustments to the data when fitting the regression line. Some cost analysts would argue that a scattergraph should be the beginning point in all cost analyses, due to the benefits to be gained from having the data visually available in graph form.

However, the scattergraph method has two major drawbacks. First, it is subjective. No two analysts who look at the same scattergraph are likely to draw exactly the same regression line. Second, the estimates are not as precise as they are with other methods. Some managers are uncomfortable with these elements of subjectivity and imprecision and desire a method that will yield a precise answer that will be the same no matter who does the analysis. Fortunately, modern computer software makes it very easy to use sophisticated statistical methods, such as *least-squares regression,* that are capable of providing much more information than just the estimates of variable and fixed costs. The details of these statistical methods are beyond the scope of this text, but the basic approach is discussed below. Nevertheless, even if the least-squares regression approach is used, it is always a good idea to plot the data in a scattergraph. By simply looking at the scattergraph, you can quickly verify whether it makes sense to fit a straight line to the data using least-squares regression or some other method.

The Least-Squares Regression Method

The **least-squares regression method** is a more objective and precise approach to estimating the regression line than the scattergraph method. Rather than fitting a regression line through the scattergraph data by visual inspection, the least-squares regression method uses mathematical formulas to fit the regression line. Also, unlike the high-low method, the least-squares regression method takes all of the data into account when estimating the cost formula.

The basic idea underlying the least-squares regression method is illustrated in Exhibit 5–10 using hypothetical data points. Notice from the exhibit that the deviations from the plotted points to the regression line are measured vertically on the graph. These vertical deviations are called the regression errors and are the key to understanding what least-squares regression does. There is nothing mysterious about the least-squares regression method. It simply computes the regression line that minimizes the sum of these squared errors. The formulas that accomplish this are fairly complex and involve numerous calculations, but the principle is simple.

Fortunately, computers are adept at carrying out the computations required by the least-squares regression formulas. The data—the observed values of X and Y—are entered into the computer, and software does the rest. In the case of the Brentline Hospital maintenance cost data, we used a statistical software package on a personal computer to calculate the following least-squares regression estimates of the total fixed cost (a) and the variable cost per unit of activity (b):

$$a = \$3,431$$

$$b = \$0.759$$

Therefore, using the least-squares regression method, the fixed element of the maintenance cost is \$3,431 per month and the variable portion is 75.9 cents per patient-day.

In terms of the linear equation $Y = a + bX,$ the cost formula can be written as

$$Y = \$3,431 + \$0.759X$$

where activity (X) is expressed in patient-days.

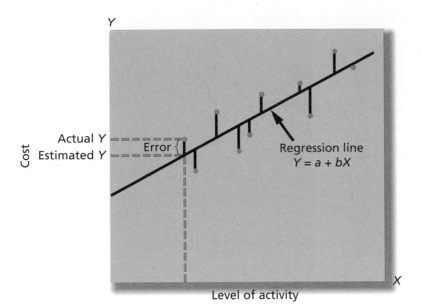

Exhibit 5–10
The Concept of Least-Squares
Regression

After completing the analysis of maintenance costs, Kinh Nguyen met with Dr. Derek Chalmers to discuss the results.

Kinh: We used least-squares regression analysis to estimate the fixed and variable components of maintenance costs. According to the results, the fixed cost per month is $3,431 and the variable cost per patient-day is 75.9 cents.

Derek: Okay, so if we plan for 7,800 patient-days next month, what is your estimate of the maintenance costs?

Kinh: That will take just a few seconds to figure out. [Kinh wrote the following calculations on a pad of paper.]

Fixed costs	$3,431
Variable costs:	
7,800 patient-days × $0.759 per patient-day	5,920
Total expected maintenance costs	$9,351

Derek: Nine thousand three hundred and fifty *one* dollars; isn't that a bit *too* precise?

Kinh: Sure. I don't really believe the maintenance costs will be exactly this figure. However, based on the information we have, this is the best estimate we can come up with.

Derek: Don't let me give you a hard time. Even though it is an estimate, it will be a lot better than just guessing like we have done in the past. Thanks. I hope to see more of this kind of analysis.

*Managerial
Accounting in
Action*

The Wrap-Up

Managing Power Consumption

in business | *today*

The Tata Iron Steel Company Ltd. is one of the largest companies in India. The company is faced with frequent power shortages and must carefully manage its power consumption—allocating scarce power to the most profitable uses. Estimating the power requirements of each processing station in the steel mill was the first step in building a model to better manage power consumption. Management used simple least-squares regression to estimate the fixed and variable components of the power load. Total power consumption was the dependent variable and tons of steel processed was the independent variable. The fixed component estimated from the least-squares regression was the fixed power consumption (in KWHs) per month and the variable component was the power consumption (again in KWHs) per ton of steel processed.

Source: "How Tata Steel Optimized Its Results," *The Management Accountant* (India), May 1996, pp. 372–376.

The Contribution Format

> **Learning Objective 4**
> Prepare an income statement using the contribution format.

Once the manager has separated costs into fixed and variable elements, what is done with the data? We have already answered this question somewhat by showing how a cost formula can be used to predict costs. To answer this question more fully will require most of the remainder of this text, since much of what the manager does rests in some way on an understanding of cost behavior. One immediate and very significant application of the ideas we have developed, however, is found in a new income statement format known as the **contribution approach.** The unique thing about the contribution approach is that it provides the manager with an income statement geared directly to cost behavior.

Why a New Income Statement Format?

An income statement prepared using the *traditional approach,* as illustrated in Chapter 1, is not organized in terms of cost behavior. Rather, it is organized in a "functional" format—emphasizing the functions of production, administration, and sales in the classification and presentation of cost data. No attempt is made to distinguish between the behavior of costs included under each functional heading. Under the heading "Administrative expense," for example, one can expect to find both variable and fixed costs lumped together.

Although an income statement prepared in the functional format may be useful for external reporting purposes, it has serious limitations when used for internal purposes. Internally, the manager needs cost data organized in a format that will facilitate planning, control, and decision-making. As we shall see in chapters ahead, these tasks are much easier when cost data are available in a fixed and variable format. The contribution approach to the income statement has been developed in response to this need.

Concept 5–2

The Contribution Approach

Exhibit 5–11 illustrates the contribution approach to the income statement with a simple example, along with the traditional approach discussed in Chapter 1.

Notice that the contribution approach separates costs into fixed and variable categories, first deducting variable expenses from sales to obtain what is known as the *contribution margin.* The **contribution margin** is the amount remaining from sales revenues after variable expenses have been deducted. This amount *contributes* toward covering fixed expenses and then toward profits for the period.

The contribution approach to the income statement is used as an internal planning and decision-making tool. Its emphasis on costs by behavior facilitates cost-volume-profit analysis, such as we shall be doing in the next chapter. The approach is also very useful

Exhibit 5–11
Comparison of the Contribution Income Statement with the Traditional Income Statement

Traditional Approach (costs organized by function)			Contribution Approach (costs organized by behavior)		
Sales		$12,000	Sales		$12,000
Less cost of goods sold		6,000*	Less variable expenses:		
Gross margin		6,000	Variable production	$2,000	
Less operating expenses:			Variable selling	600	
Selling	$3,100*		Variable administrative	400	3,000
Administrative	1,900*	5,000	Contribution margin		9,000
Net income		$ 1,000			
			Less fixed expenses:		
			Fixed production	4,000	
			Fixed selling	2,500	
			Fixed administrative	1,500	8,000
			Net income		$ 1,000

*Contains both variable and fixed expenses. This is the income statement for a manufacturing company; thus, when the income statement is placed in the contribution format, the "cost of goods sold" figure is divided between variable production costs and fixed production costs. If this were the income statement for a *merchandising* company (which simply purchases completed goods from a supplier), then the cost of goods sold would *all* be variable.

in appraising management performance, in segmented reporting of profit data, and in budgeting. Moreover, the contribution approach helps managers organize data pertinent to all kinds of special decisions such as product-line analysis, pricing, use of scarce resources, and make or buy analysis. All of these topics are covered in later chapters.

Entrepreneur

you decide

You are the owner of a small manufacturing firm. You are in the process of applying for a loan. The loan officer would like to compare your company to others in the industry and has requested a copy of your company's income statement. Should you submit an income statement prepared using the traditional approach or the contribution approach?

Summary

LO1 Understand how fixed and variable costs behave and how to use them to predict costs.
A variable cost is proportional to the level of activity within the relevant range. The cost per unit of activity for a variable cost is constant as the level of activity changes.

A fixed cost is constant in total for changes of activity within the relevant range. The cost per unit of activity decreases as the level of activity increases since a constant amount is divided by a larger number.

To predict costs at a new level of activity, multiply the variable cost per unit by the new level of activity and then add to the result the constant fixed cost.

LO2 Analyze a mixed cost using the high-low method.
To use the high-low method, first identify the periods in which the highest and the lowest levels of activity have occurred. Second, estimate the variable cost element by dividing the change in total cost by the change in activity for these two periods. Third, estimate the fixed cost element by subtracting the total variable cost from the total cost at either the highest or the lowest level of activity.

The high-low method relies on only two, often unusual, data points rather than all of the available data and therefore may provide misleading estimates of variable and fixed costs.

LO3 Analyze a mixed cost using the scattergraph method.

The scattergraph method begins with plotting the available cost and activity data. Activity is plotted on the horizontal, X, axis and cost is plotted on the vertical, Y, axis. The analyst then draws a straight line that is representative of the relation between cost and activity revealed by the pattern of points on the plot.

The scattergraph method is criticized because it is subjective and is relatively imprecise. However, a scattergraph is an excellent means of gaining insight into the behavior of the cost under investigation.

LO4 Prepare an income statement using the contribution format.

Managers use costs organized by behavior in many decisions. To help managers make such decisions, the income statement can be prepared in a contribution format. The traditional income statement format emphasizes the purposes for which costs were incurred (i.e., to manufacture the product, to sell the product, or to administer the organization). In contrast, the contribution format classifies costs on the income statement by cost behavior (i.e., variable versus fixed).

Guidance Answers to Decision Maker and You Decide

BUDGET ANALYST (p. 196)

A janitorial service company is likely to incur most of the following types of costs:

Cost	Type	Activity Base (if variable)
Cleaning supplies	Variable	Square footage of client's spaces
Depreciation (vacuum cleaners, etc.)	Fixed	Not applicable
Reimbursement of employee mileage	Variable	Distance (miles) to client
Salary of supervisor(s)	Fixed	Not applicable
Wages of janitorial employees	Variable	Square footage of client's spaces

ENTREPRENEUR (p. 213)

In order to make useful comparisons to financial information published by other companies, the loan officer would expect an income statement prepared using the approach used for external reporting purposes. As such, you should provide an income statement prepared using the traditional approach. The information that can be obtained from an income statement prepared using the contribution approach would normally only be used internally for planning and decision-making. Such income statements are not normally distributed outside of the company.

Review Problem 1: Cost Behavior

Neptune Rentals offers a boat rental service. Consider the following costs of the company over the relevant range of 5,000 to 8,000 hours of operating time for its boats:

	Hours of Operating Time			
	5,000	6,000	7,000	8,000
Total costs:				
Variable costs	$ 20,000	$?	$?	$?
Fixed costs	168,000	?	?	?
Total costs	$188,000	$?	$?	$?
Cost per hour:				
Variable cost	$?	$?	$?	$?
Fixed cost	?	?	?	?
Total cost per hour	$?	$?	$?	$?

Required:
Compute the missing amounts, assuming that cost behavior patterns remain unchanged within the relevant range of 5,000 to 8,000 hours.

SOLUTION TO REVIEW PROBLEM 1
The variable cost per hour can be computed as follows:

$$\$20,000 \div 5,000 \text{ hours} = \$4 \text{ per hour}$$

Therefore, in accordance with the behavior of variable and fixed costs, the missing amounts are as follows:

| | Hours of Operating Time | | | |
	5,000	6,000	7,000	8,000
Total costs:				
Variable costs	$ 20,000	$ 24,000	$ 28,000	$ 32,000
Fixed costs	168,000	168,000	168,000	168,000
Total costs	$188,000	$192,000	$196,000	$200,000
Cost per hour:				
Variable cost	$ 4.00	$ 4.00	$ 4.00	$ 4.00
Fixed cost	33.60	28.00	24.00	21.00
Total cost per hour	$37.60	$32.00	$28.00	$25.00

Observe that the total variable costs increase in proportion to the number of hours of operating time, but that these costs remain constant at $4 if expressed on a per hour basis.

In contrast, the total fixed costs do not change with changes in the level of activity. They remain constant at $168,000 within the relevant range. With increases in activity, however, the fixed costs decrease on a per hour basis, dropping from $33.60 per hour when the boats are operated 5,000 hours a period to only $21.00 per hour when the boats are operated 8,000 hours a period. *Because of this troublesome aspect of fixed costs, they are most easily (and most safely) dealt with on a total basis, rather than on a unit basis, in cost analysis work.*

Review Problem 2: High-Low Method

The administrator of Azalea Hills Hospital would like a cost formula linking the costs involved in admitting patients to the number of patients admitted during a month. The admitting department's costs and the number of patients admitted during the immediately preceding eight months are given in the following table:

Month	Number of Patients Admitted	Admitting Department Costs
May	1,800	$14,700
June	1,900	15,200
July	1,700	13,700
August	1,600	14,000
September	1,500	14,300
October	1,300	13,100
November	1,100	12,800
December	1,500	14,600

Required:
1. Use the high-low method to establish the fixed and variable components of admitting costs.
2. Express the fixed and variable components of admitting costs as a cost formula in the linear equation form $Y = a + bX$.

SOLUTION TO REVIEW PROBLEM 2
1. The first step in the high-low method is to identify the periods of the lowest and highest activity. Those periods are November (1,100 patients admitted) and June (1,900 patients admitted).
   The second step is to compute the variable cost per unit using those two points:

Month	Number of Patients Admitted	Admitting Department Costs
High activity level (June)	1,900	$15,200
Low activity level (November)	1,100	12,800
Change	800	$ 2,400

$$\text{Variable cost} = \frac{\text{Change in cost}}{\text{Change in activity}} = \frac{\$2,400}{800 \text{ patients admitted}} = \$3 \text{ per patient admitted}$$

The third step is to compute the fixed cost element by deducting the variable cost element from the total cost at either the high or low activity. In the computation below, the high point of activity is used:

$$\begin{aligned}
\text{Fixed cost element} &= \text{Total cost} - \text{Variable cost element} \\
&= \$15,200 - (\$3 \text{ per patient admitted} \times 1,900 \text{ patients admitted}) \\
&= \$9,500
\end{aligned}$$

2. The cost formula expressed in the linear equation form is $Y = \$9,500 + \$3X$.

Glossary

Account analysis   A method for analyzing cost behavior in which each account is classified as either variable or fixed based on the analyst's prior knowledge of how the cost in the account behaves. (p. 205)

Activity base   A measure of whatever causes the incurrence of a variable cost. For example, the total cost of X-ray film in a hospital will increase as the number of X-rays taken increases. Therefore, the number of X-rays is an activity base for explaining the total cost of X-ray film. (p. 195)

Committed fixed costs   Those fixed costs that are difficult to adjust and that relate to the investment in facilities, equipment, and the basic organizational structure of a firm. (p. 200)

Contribution approach   An income statement format that is geared to cost behavior in that costs are separated into variable and fixed categories rather than being separated according to the functions of production, sales, and administration. (p. 212)

Contribution margin   The amount remaining from sales revenues after all variable expenses have been deducted. (p. 212)

Cost structure   The relative proportion of fixed, variable, and mixed costs found within an organization. (p. 194)

Curvilinear costs   A relation between cost and activity that is a curve rather than a straight line. (p. 198)

Dependent variable   A variable that reacts or responds to some causal factor; total cost is the dependent variable, as represented by the letter Y, in the equation $Y = a + bX$. (p. 207)

Discretionary fixed costs   Those fixed costs that arise from annual decisions by management to spend in certain fixed cost areas, such as advertising and research. (p. 200)

Engineering approach   A detailed analysis of cost behavior based on an industrial engineer's evaluation of the inputs that are required to carry out a particular activity and of the prices of those inputs. (p. 205)

High-low method   A method of separating a mixed cost into its fixed and variable elements by analyzing the change in cost between the high and low levels of activity. (p. 206)

Independent variable   A variable that acts as a causal factor; activity is the independent variable, as represented by the letter X, in the equation $Y = a + bX$. (p. 207)

Least-squares regression method   A method of separating a mixed cost into its fixed and variable elements by fitting a regression line that minimizes the sum of the squared errors. (p. 210)

Mixed cost   A cost that contains both variable and fixed cost elements. (p. 203)

Regression line   A line fitted to an array of plotted points. The slope of the line, denoted by the letter b in the linear equation $Y = a + bX$, represents the variable cost per unit of activity. The point where the line intersects the cost axis, denoted by the letter a in the above equation, represents the total fixed cost. (p. 208)

Relevant range   The range of activity within which assumptions about variable and fixed cost behavior are valid. (p. 198)

Scattergraph method   A method of separating a mixed cost into its fixed and variable elements. Under this method, a regression line is fitted to an array of plotted points by drawing a line with a straight-edge. (p. 208)

Step-variable cost   A cost (such as the cost of a maintenance worker) that is obtainable only in large chunks and that increases and decreases only in response to fairly wide changes in activity. (p. 197)

Questions

5–1   Distinguish between (a) a variable cost, (b) a fixed cost, and (c) a mixed cost.
5–2   What effect does an increase in volume have on—
a.   Unit fixed costs?
b.   Unit variable costs?
c.   Total fixed costs?
d.   Total variable costs?
5–3   Define the following terms: (a) cost behavior, and (b) relevant range.

5–4 What is meant by an *activity base* when dealing with variable costs? Give several examples of activity bases.

5–5 Distinguish between (a) a variable cost, (b) a mixed cost, and (c) a step-variable cost. Chart the three costs on a graph, with activity plotted horizontally and cost plotted vertically.

5–6 Managers often assume a strictly linear relationship between cost and volume. How can this practice be defended in light of the fact that many costs are curvilinear?

5–7 Distinguish between discretionary fixed costs and committed fixed costs.

5–8 Classify the following fixed costs as normally being either committed or discretionary:
   a. Depreciation on buildings.
   b. Advertising.
   c. Research.
   d. Long-term equipment leases.
   e. Pension payments to the firm's retirees.
   f. Management development and training.

5–9 Does the concept of the relevant range apply to fixed costs? Explain.

5–10 What is the major disadvantage of the high-low method?

5–11 What methods are available for separating a mixed cost into its fixed and variable elements using past records of cost and activity data? Which method is considered to be most accurate? Why?

5–12 What is meant by a regression line? Give the general formula for a regression line. Which term represents the variable cost? The fixed cost?

5–13 Once a regression line has been drawn, how does one determine the fixed cost element? The variable cost element?

5–14 What is meant by the term *least-squares regression?*

5–15 What is the difference between the contribution approach to the income statement and the traditional approach to the income statement?

5–16 What is the contribution margin?

Brief Exercises

BRIEF EXERCISE 5–1   Fixed and Variable Cost Behavior (LO1)

Espresso Express operates a number of espresso coffee stands in busy suburban malls. The fixed weekly expense of a coffee stand is $1,200 and the variable cost per cup of coffee served is $0.22.

Required:
1. Fill in the following table with your estimates of total costs and cost per cup of coffee at the indicated levels of activity for a coffee stand. Round off the cost of a cup of coffee to the nearest tenth of a cent.

	Cups of Coffee Served in a Week		
	2,000	**2,100**	**2,200**
Fixed cost	?	?	?
Variable cost	?	?	?
Total cost	?	?	?
Cost per cup of coffee served	?	?	?

2. Does the cost per cup of coffee served increase, decrease, or remain the same as the number of cups of coffee served in a week increases? Explain.

BRIEF EXERCISE 5–2   High-Low Method (LO2)

The Cheyenne Hotel in Big Sky, Montana, has accumulated records of the total electrical costs of the hotel and the number of occupancy-days over the last year. An occupancy-day represents a room rented out for one day. The hotel's business is highly seasonal, with peaks occurring during the ski season and in the summer.

Month	Occupancy-Days	Electrical Costs
January	1,736	$4,127
February	1,904	4,207
March	2,356	5,083
April	960	2,857
May	360	1,871
		continued

Month	Occupancy-Days	Electrical Costs
June	744	$2,696
July	2,108	4,670
August	2,406	5,148
September	840	2,691
October	124	1,588
November	720	2,454
December	1,364	3,529

Required:

1. Using the high-low method, estimate the fixed cost of electricity per month and the variable cost of electricity per occupancy-day. Round off the fixed cost to the nearest whole dollar and the variable cost to the nearest whole cent.
2. What other factors other than occupancy-days are likely to affect the variation in electrical costs from month to month?

BRIEF EXERCISE 5–3   Scattergraph Analysis (LO3)

Oki Products, Ltd., has observed the following processing costs at various levels of activity over the last 15 months:

Month	Units Produced	Processing Cost
1	4,500	$38,000
2	11,000	52,000
3	12,000	56,000
4	5,500	40,000
5	9,000	47,000
6	10,500	52,000
7	7,500	44,000
8	5,000	41,000
9	11,500	52,000
10	6,000	43,000
11	8,500	48,000
12	10,000	50,000
13	6,500	44,000
14	9,500	48,000
15	8,000	46,000

Required:

1. Prepare a scattergraph by plotting the above data on a graph. Plot cost on the vertical axis and activity on the horizontal axis. Fit a line to your plotted points by visual inspection.
2. What is the approximate monthly fixed cost? The approximate variable cost per unit processed? Show your computations.

BRIEF EXERCISE 5–4   Contribution Format Income Statement (LO4)

The Alpine House, Inc., is a large retailer of winter sports equipment. An income statement for the company's Ski Department for a recent quarter is presented below:

THE ALPINE HOUSE, INC.
Income Statement—Ski Department
For the Quarter Ended March 31

Sales		$150,000
Less cost of goods sold		90,000
Gross margin		60,000
Less operating expenses:		
Selling expenses	$30,000	
Administrative expenses	10,000	40,000
Net income		$ 20,000

Skis sell, on the average, for $750 per pair. Variable selling expenses are $50 per pair of skis sold. The remaining selling expenses are fixed. The administrative expenses are 20% variable and 80% fixed. The company does not manufacture its own skis; it purchases them from a supplier for $450 per pair.

Required:
1. Prepare an income statement for the quarter using the contribution approach.
2. For every pair of skis sold during the quarter, what was the contribution toward covering fixed expenses and toward earning profits?

Exercises

EXERCISE 5–1   High-Low Method; Predicting Cost (LO1, LO2)

The Lakeshore Hotel's guest-days of occupancy and custodial supplies expense over the last seven months were:

Month	Guest-Days of Occupancy	Custodial Supplies Expense
March	4,000	$ 7,500
April	6,500	8,250
May	8,000	10,500
June	10,500	12,000
July	12,000	13,500
August	9,000	10,750
September	7,500	9,750

Guest-days is a measure of the overall activity at the hotel. For example, a guest who stays at the hotel for three days is counted as three guest-days.

Required:
1. Using the high-low method, estimate a cost formula for custodial supplies expense.
2. Using the cost formula you derived above, what amount of custodial supplies expense would you expect to be incurred at an occupancy level of 11,000 guest-days?

EXERCISE 5–2   High-Low Analysis and Scattergraph Analysis (LO2, LO3)

Refer to the data in Exercise 5–1.

Required:
1. Prepare a scattergraph using the data from Exercise 5–1. Plot cost on the vertical axis and activity on the horizontal axis. Fit a regression line to your plotted points by visual inspection.
2. What is the approximate monthly fixed cost? The approximate variable cost per guest-day?
3. Scrutinize the points on your graph and explain why the high-low method would or would not yield an accurate cost formula in this situation.

EXERCISE 5–3   High-Low Analysis and Scattergraph Analysis (LO2, LO3)

The following data relating to units shipped and total shipping expense have been assembled by Archer Company, a manufacturer of large, custom-built air-conditioning units for commercial buildings:

Month	Units Shipped	Total Shipping Expense
January	3	$1,800
February	6	2,300
March	4	1,700
April	5	2,000
May	7	2,300
June	8	2,700
July	2	1,200

Required:
1. Using the high-low method, estimate a cost formula for shipping expense.
2. For the scattergraph method, do the following:

a. Prepare a scattergraph, using the data given above. Plot cost on the vertical axis and activity on the horizontal axis. Fit a regression line to your plotted points by visual inspection.

b. Using your scattergraph, estimate the approximate variable cost per unit shipped and the approximate fixed cost per month.

3. What factors, other than the number of units shipped, are likely to affect the company's total shipping expense? Explain.

EXERCISE 5–4   High-Low Method; Predicting Cost (LO1, LO2)

Hoi Chong Transport, Ltd., operates a fleet of delivery trucks in Singapore. The company has determined that if a truck is driven 105,000 kilometers during a year, the average operating cost is 11.4 cents per kilometer. If a truck is driven only 70,000 kilometers during a year, the average operating cost increases to 13.4 cents per kilometer. (The Singapore dollar is the currency used in Singapore.)

Required:

1. Using the high-low method, estimate the variable and fixed cost elements of the annual cost of truck operation.
2. Express the variable and fixed costs in the form $Y = a + bX$.
3. If a truck were driven 80,000 kilometers during a year, what total cost would you expect to be incurred?

EXERCISE 5–5   Cost Behavior and Contribution Format Income Statement (LO1, LO4)

Harris Company manufactures and sells a single product. A partially completed schedule of the company's total and per unit costs over the relevant range of 30,000 to 50,000 units produced and sold annually is given below:

	Units Produced and Sold		
	30,000	40,000	50,000
Total costs:			
Variable costs	$180,000	?	?
Fixed costs	300,000	?	?
Total costs	$480,000	?	?
Cost per unit:			
Variable cost	?	?	?
Fixed cost	?	?	?
Total cost per unit	?	?	?

Required:

1. Complete the schedule of the company's total and unit costs above.
2. Assume that the company produces and sells 45,000 units during a year at a selling price of $16 per unit. Prepare an income statement in the contribution format for the year.

Problems

PROBLEM 5–1   High-Low Method and Predicting Cost (LO1, LO2)

St. Mark's Hospital contains 450 beds. The average occupancy rate is 80% per month. In other words, on average, 80% of the hospital's beds are occupied by patients. At this level of occupancy, the hospital's operating costs are $32 per occupied bed per day, assuming a 30-day month. This $32 figure contains both variable and fixed cost elements.

During June, the hospital's occupancy rate was only 60%. A total of $326,700 in operating cost was incurred during the month.

Required:

1. Using the high-low method, estimate:
   a. The variable cost per occupied bed on a daily basis.
   b. The total fixed operating costs per month.
2. Assume an occupancy rate of 70% per month. What amount of total operating cost would you expect the hospital to incur?

CHECK FIGURE
(1) Net income is $8,000

PROBLEM 5–2   Contribution Format Income Statement (LO4)

Marwick's Pianos, Inc., purchases pianos from a large manufacturer and sells them at the retail level. The pianos cost, on the average, $2,450 each from the manufacturer. Marwick's Pianos, Inc., sells the pianos to its customers at an average price of $3,125 each. The selling and administrative costs that the company incurs in a typical month are presented below:

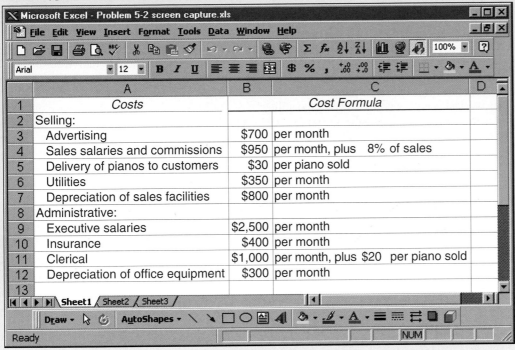

During August, Marwick's Pianos, Inc., sold and delivered 40 pianos.

Required:

1. Prepare an income statement for Marwick's Pianos, Inc., for August. Use the traditional format, with costs organized by function.
2. Redo (1) above, this time using the contribution format, with costs organized by behavior. Show costs and revenues on both total and a per unit basis down through contribution margin.
3. Refer to the income statement you prepared in (2) above. Why might it be misleading to show the fixed costs on a per unit basis?

PROBLEM 5–3   Scattergraph Analysis (LO3)

Molina Company is a value-added computer resaler that specializes in providing services to small companies. The company owns and maintains several autos for use by the sales staff. All expenses of operating these autos have been entered into an Automobile Expense account on the company's books. Along with this record of expenses, the company has also kept a careful record of the number of miles the autos have been driven each month.

The company's records of miles driven and total auto expenses over the past 10 months are given below:

Month	Total Mileage (000)	Total Cost
January	4	$3,000
February	8	3,700
March	7	3,300
April	12	4,000
May	6	3,300
June	11	3,900
July	14	4,200
August	10	3,600
September	13	4,100
October	15	4,400

Molina Company's president wants to know the cost of operating the fleet of cars in terms of the fixed monthly cost and the variable cost per mile driven.

Required:

1. Prepare a scattergraph using the data given above. Place cost on the vertical axis and activity (miles driven) on the horizontal axis. Fit a regression line to the plotted points by simple visual inspection.
2. By analyzing your scattergraph, estimate fixed cost per month and the variable cost per mile driven.

CHECK FIGURE
(1) $1,000 per month plus
$20 per scan

PROBLEM 5–4   High-Low and Scattergraph Analysis (LO2, LO3)

Pleasant View Hospital of British Columbia has just hired a new chief administrator who is anxious to employ sound management and planning techniques in the business affairs of the hospital. Accordingly, she has directed her assistant to summarize the cost structure existing in the various departments so that data will be available for planning purposes.

The assistant is unsure how to classify the utilities costs in the Radiology Department since these costs do not exhibit either strictly variable or fixed cost behavior. Utilities costs are very high in the department due to a CAT scanner that draws a large amount of power and is kept running at all times. The scanner can't be turned off due to the long warm-up period required for its use. When the scanner is used to scan a patient, it consumes an additional burst of power. The assistant has accumulated the following data on utilities costs and use of the scanner since the first of the year.

Month	Number of Scans	Utilities Cost
January	60	$2,200
February	70	2,600
March	90	2,900
April	120	3,300
May	100	3,000
June	130	3,600
July	150	4,000
August	140	3,600
September	110	3,100
October	80	2,500

The chief administrator has informed her assistant that the utilities cost is probably a mixed cost that will have to be broken down into its variable and fixed cost elements by use of a scattergraph. The assistant feels, however, that if an analysis of this type is necessary, then the high-low method should be used, since it is easier and quicker. The controller has suggested that there may be a better approach.

Required:

1. Using the high-low method, estimate a cost formula for utilities. Express the formula in the form $Y = a + bX$. (The variable rate should be stated in terms of cost per scan.)
2. Prepare a scattergraph by plotting the above data on a graph. (The number of scans should be placed on the horizontal axis, and utilities cost should be placed on the vertical axis.) Fit a regression line to the plotted points by visual inspection and estimate a cost formula for utilities.

CHECK FIGURE
(2) Shipping: A$18,000
per month plus A$4 per
unit

PROBLEM 5–5   Cost Behavior; High-Low Analysis; Contribution Format Income Statement (LO1, LO2, LO4)

Morrisey & Brown, Ltd., of Sydney is a merchandising firm that is the sole distributor of a product that is increasing in popularity among Australian consumers. The company's income statements for the three most recent months follow:

MORRISEY & BROWN, LTD.
Income Statements
For the Three Months Ending September 30

	July	August	September
Sales in units	4,000	4,500	5,000
Sales revenue	A$400,000	A$450,000	A$500,000
Less cost of goods sold	240,000	270,000	300,000
Gross margin	160,000	180,000	200,000

continued

Less operating expenses:			
Advertising expense	21,000	21,000	21,000
Shipping expense	34,000	36,000	38,000
Salaries and commissions	78,000	84,000	90,000
Insurance expense	6,000	6,000	6,000
Depreciation expense	15,000	15,000	15,000
Total operating expenses	154,000	162,000	170,000
Net income	A$ 6,000	A$ 18,000	A$ 30,000

(Note: Morrisey & Brown, Ltd.'s Australian-formatted income statement has been recast in the format common in the United States. The Australian dollar is denoted by A$.)

Required:
1. Identify each of the company's expenses (including cost of goods sold) as being either variable, fixed, or mixed.
2. By use of the high-low method, separate each mixed expense into variable and fixed elements. State the cost formula for each mixed expense.
3. Redo the company's income statement at the 5,000-unit level of activity using the contribution format.

PROBLEM 5–6   Identifying Cost Behavior Patterns (LO1)

A number of graphs displaying cost behavior patterns that might be found in a company's cost structure are shown below. The vertical axis on each graph represents total cost and the horizontal axis represents the level of activity (volume).

Required:
1. For each of the following situations, identify the graph below or from the next page that illustrates the cost pattern involved. Any graph may be used more than once.
   a. Cost of raw materials used.
   b. Electricity bill—a flat fixed charge, plus a variable cost after a certain number of kilowatt-hours are used.
   c. City water bill, which is computed as follows:

First 1,000,000 gallons or less	$1,000 flat fee
Next 10,000 gallons	0.003 per gallon used
Next 10,000 gallons	0.006 per gallon used
Next 10,000 gallons	0.009 per gallon used
Etc.	Etc.

   d. Depreciation of equipment, where the amount is computed by the straight-line method. When the depreciation rate was established, it was anticipated that the obsolescence factor would be greater than the wear and tear factor.
   e. Rent on a factory building donated by the city, where the agreement calls for a fixed fee payment unless 200,000 labor-hours or more are worked, in which case no rent need be paid.
   f. Salaries of maintenance workers, where one maintenance worker is needed for every 1,000 hours of machine-hours or less (that is, 0 to 1,000 hours requires one maintenance worker, 1,001 to 2,000 hours requires two maintenance workers, etc.)
   g. Cost of raw materials, where the cost starts at $7.50 per unit and then decreases by 5 cents per unit for each of the first 100 units purchased, after which it remains constant at $2.50 per unit.
   h. Rent on a factory building donated by the county, where the agreement calls for rent of $100,000 less $1 for each direct labor-hour worked in excess of 200,000 hours, but a minimum rental payment of $20,000 must be paid.
   i. Use of a machine under a lease, where a minimum charge of $1,000 is paid for up to 400 hours of machine time. After 400 hours of machine time, an additional charge of $2 per hour is paid up to a maximum charge of $2,000 per period.

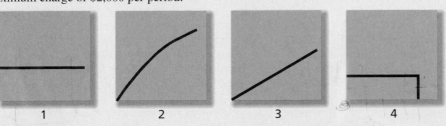

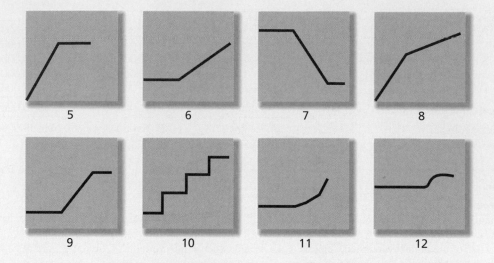

2. How would a knowledge of cost behavior patterns such as those above be of help to a manager in analyzing the cost structure of his or her firm?

(CPA, adapted)

CHECK FIGURE
(2) ¥1,500,000 per year
plus ¥35 per DLH

PROBLEM 5–7   High-Low Analysis and Cost Behavior (LO1, LO2)

Sawaya Co., Ltd., of Japan is a manufacturing company whose total factory overhead costs fluctuate considerably from year to year according to increases and decreases in the number of direct labor-hours worked in the factory. Total factory overhead costs (in Japanese yen, denoted ¥) at high and low levels of activity for recent years are given below:

	Level of Activity	
	Low	High
Direct labor-hours	50,000	75,000
Total factory overhead costs	¥14,250,000	¥17,625,000

The factory overhead costs above consist of indirect materials, rent, and maintenance. The company has analyzed these costs at the 50,000-hour level of activity as follows:

Indirect materials (V)	¥ 5,000,000
Rent (F)	6,000,000
Maintenance (M)	3,250,000
Total factory overhead costs	¥14,250,000

V = variable; F = fixed; M = mixed.

To have data available for planning, the company wants to break down the maintenance cost into its variable and fixed cost elements.

Required:

1. Estimate how much of the ¥17,625,000 factory overhead cost at the high level of activity consists of maintenance cost. (Hint: To do this, it may be helpful to first determine how much of the ¥17,625,000 consists of indirect materials and rent. Think about the behavior of variable and fixed costs!)
2. By means of the high-low method of cost analysis, estimate a cost formula for maintenance.
3. What total factory overhead costs would you expect the company to incur at an operating level of 70,000 direct labor-hours?

PROBLEM 5–8   High-Low Analysis and Predicting Cost (LO1, LO2)

Nova Company's total overhead costs at various levels of activity are presented below:

Month	Machine-Hours	Total Overhead Costs
April	70,000	$198,000
May	60,000	174,000
June	80,000	222,000
July	90,000	246,000

Assume that the total overhead costs above consist of utilities, supervisory salaries, and maintenance. The breakdown of these costs at the 60,000 machine-hour level of activity is:

Utilities (V)	$ 48,000
Supervisory salaries (F)	21,000
Maintenance (M)	105,000
Total overhead costs	$174,000

V = variable; F = fixed; M = mixed.

Nova Company's management wants to break down the maintenance cost into its basic variable and fixed cost elements.

Required:
1. As shown above, overhead costs in July amounted to $246,000. Determine how much of this consisted of maintenance cost. (Hint: To do this, it may be helpful to first determine how much of the $246,000 consisted of utilities and supervisory salaries. Think about the behavior of variable and fixed costs!)
2. By means of the high-low method, estimate a cost formula for maintenance.
3. Express the company's *total* overhead costs in the linear equation form $Y = a + bX$.
4. What *total* overhead costs would you expect to be incurred at an operating activity level of 75,000 machine-hours?

PROBLEM 5–9   High-Low Analysis; Cost of Goods Manufactured (LO1, LO2)

Amfac Company manufactures a single product. The company keeps careful records of manufacturing activities from which the following information has been extracted:

	Level of Activity	
	March-Low	June-High
Number of units produced	6,000	9,000
Cost of goods manufactured	$168,000	$257,000
Work in process inventory, beginning	9,000	32,000
Work in process inventory, ending	15,000	21,000
Direct materials cost per unit	6	6
Direct labor cost per unit	10	10
Manufacturing overhead cost, total	?	?

The company's manufacturing overhead cost consists of both variable and fixed cost elements. To have data available for planning, management wants to determine how much of the overhead cost is variable with units produced and how much of it is fixed per month.

Required:
1. For both March and June, determine the amount of manufacturing overhead cost added to production. The company had no under- or overapplied overhead in either month. (Hint: A useful way to proceed might be to construct a schedule of cost of goods manufactured.)
2. By means of the high-low method of cost analysis, estimate a cost formula for manufacturing overhead. Express the variable portion of the formula in terms of a variable rate per unit of product.
3. If 7,000 units are produced during a month, what would be the cost of goods manufactured? (Assume that work in process inventories do not change and that there is no under- or overapplied overhead cost for the month.)

Building Your Skills

ANALYTICAL THINKING (LO2, LO3)

The Ramon Company manufactures a wide range of products at several plant locations. The Franklin plant, which manufactures electrical components, has been experiencing difficulties with fluctuating monthly overhead costs. The fluctuations have made it difficult to estimate the level of overhead that will be incurred for any one month.

Management wants to be able to estimate overhead costs accurately in order to better plan its operational and financial needs. A trade association publication to which Ramon Company subscribes indicates that for companies manufacturing electrical components, overhead tends to vary with direct labor-hours.

One member of the accounting staff has proposed the cost behavior pattern of the overhead costs be determined. Then overhead costs could be predicted from the budgeted direct labor-hours.

Another member of the accounting staff has suggested that a good starting place for determining the cost behavior pattern of overhead costs would be an analysis of historical data. The historical cost behavior pattern would provide a basis for estimating future overhead costs. Ramon Company has decided to employ the high-low method and the scattergraph method. Data on direct labor-hours and the respective overhead costs incurred have been collected for the past two years. The raw data are as follows:

| | Prior Year | | Current Year | |
Month	Direct Labor-Hours	Overhead Costs	Direct Labor-Hours	Overhead Costs
January	20,000	$84,000	21,000	$86,000
February	25,000	99,000	24,000	93,000
March	22,000	89,500	23,000	93,000
April	23,000	90,000	22,000	87,000
May	20,000	81,500	20,000	80,000
June	19,000	75,500	18,000	76,500
July	14,000	70,500	12,000	67,500
August	10,000	64,500	13,000	71,000
September	12,000	69,000	15,000	73,500
October	17,000	75,000	17,000	72,500
November	16,000	71,500	15,000	71,000
December	19,000	78,000	18,000	75,000

All equipment in the Franklin plant is leased under an arrangement calling for a flat fee up to 19,500 direct labor-hours of activity in the plant, after which lease charges are assessed on an hourly basis. Lease expense is a major item of overhead cost.

Required:

1. Using the high-low method, estimate the cost formula for overhead in the Franklin plant.
2. Prepare a scattergraph, including on it all data for the two-year period. Fit a regression line or lines to the plotted points by visual inspection. In this part it is not necessary to compute the fixed and variable cost elements.
3. Assume that the Franklin plant works 22,500 direct labor-hours during a month. Compute the expected overhead cost for the month using the cost formulas developed above with:
   a. The high-low method.
   b. The scattergraph method [read the expected costs directly off the graph prepared in (2) above].
4. Of the two proposed methods, which one should the Ramon Company use to estimate monthly overhead costs in the Franklin plant? Explain fully, indicating the reasons why the other method is less desirable.
5. Would a relevant range concept probably be more or less important in the Franklin plant than in most companies?

(CMA, adapted)

COMMUNICATING IN PRACTICE (LO1, LO4)

Maria Chavez owns a catering company that serves food and beverages at parties and business functions. Chavez's business is seasonal, with a heavy schedule during the summer months and holidays and a lighter schedule at other times.

One of the major events requested by Chavez's customers is a cocktail party. She offers a standard cocktail party and has estimated the total cost per guest as follows:

Food and beverages	$15.00
Labor (0.5 hours @ $10.00 per hour)	5.00
Overhead (0.5 hours @ $13.98 per hour)	6.99
Total cost per guest	$26.99

The standard cocktail party lasts three hours, and she hires one worker for every six guests, which works out to one-half hour of direct labor per guest. The servers work only as needed and are paid only for the hours they actually work.

When bidding on cocktail parties, Chavez adds a 15% markup to yield a price of $31 per guest. Chavez is confident about her estimates of the costs of food and beverages and labor, but is not as comfortable with the estimate of overhead cost. The overhead cost per guest was determined by dividing total overhead expenses for the last 12 months by total labor hours for the same period. Her overhead includes such costs as annual rent for office space, administrative costs (including those relating to hiring and paying workers), etc.

Chavez has received a request to bid on a large fund-raising cocktail party to be given next month by an important local charity. (The party would last three hours.) She would really like to win this contract—the guest list for this charity event includes many prominent individuals she would like to land as future clients. Other caterers have also been invited to bid on the event, and she believes that one, if not more, of those companies will bid less than $31 per guest. She is not willing to lose money on the event and needs your input before making any decisions.

Required:

Write a memorandum to Ms. Chavez that addresses the validity of her concern about her estimate of overhead costs and whether or not she should base her bid on the estimated cost of $26.99 per guest. (Hint: Start by discussing the need to consider cost behavior when estimating costs. You can safely assume that she will not incur any additional fixed costs if she wins the bid on this cocktail party.)

TAKING IT TO THE NET

As you know, the World Wide Web is a medium that is constantly evolving. Sites come and go, and change without notice. To enable periodic update of site addresses, this problem has been posted to the textbook website (www.mhhe.com/folk1e). After accessing the site, enter the Student Center and select this chapter. Select and complete the Taking It to the Net problem.

TEAMWORK IN ACTION (LO 1)

Assume that your team is going to form a company that will manufacture chocolate chip cookies. The team is responsible for preparing a list of all product components and costs necessary to manufacture this product.

Required:

1. The team should discuss and then write up a brief description of the definitions of variable, fixed, and mixed costs. All team members should agree with and understand the definitions.
2. After preparing a list of all product components and costs necessary to manufacture your cookies, identify each of the product costs as direct materials, direct labor, or factory overhead. Then, identify each of those costs as variable, fixed, or mixed.
3. Prepare to report this information in class. (Each teammate can assume responsibility for a different part of the presentation.)

Chapter Six

Cost-Volume-Profit Relationships

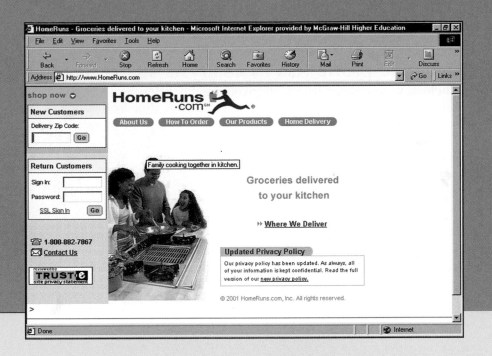

Decision Feature Buying Your Groceries Online

Online grocers such as Peapod.com, Webvan, Streamline.com, HomeRuns.com, Netgrocer.com, and HomeGrocer.com have interesting cost structures. Large investments in fixed costs are necessary to create appealing web pages and for bricks and mortar infrastructure such as warehouses and delivery vans. Variable costs come in at least two varieties. One kind of variable cost is related to the number of deliveries made. These variable costs include fuel, maintenance, and depreciation on vehicles. The other kind of variable cost is related to the amount of groceries ordered by a customer.

The cost structure in this industry combined with the low gross margins prevalent in the grocery business has made it very difficult for online grocers to break even. In addition, until recently online grocers were charging very little or nothing for delivery in an effort to attract and maintain loyal customers. This competitive practice has put additional pressure on contribution margins and caused the break-even points of these companies to be even higher than they would otherwise be. Even so, analysts project an increase in online grocery sales from just over $500 million in 1999 to almost $17 billion in 2004.

HomeRuns.com, which was launched in Massachusetts in 1996 by Hannaford Bros. Co., a national food retailer, now serves 40,000 customers in the Boston area. Through mid-1999, HomeRuns.com did not charge a delivery fee if a customer's order exceeded $60 and added a flat $10 delivery charge to orders under $60. At that time, HomeRuns needed 8,000 orders per week to break even; it was filling less than a third of that amount in a decent week. In mid-2000, the company announced that it was implementing a minimum order requirement of $50 and a flat delivery charge of $2.50 per order. The elimination of smaller orders combined with the delivery charge should increase the average contribution margin on an order and reduce the company's break-even point. Whether HomeRuns can surpass its break-even point and become profitable remains to be seen.

Sources: HomeRuns.com website March 2001; Bruce Mohl, "Online Grocer Peapod to Sharply Raise Delivery Prices in Massachusetts," *The Boston Globe*, February 27, 2001; Bruce Mohl, "Burlington, Mass. Online Grocer Charges for Delivery," *The Boston Globe*, August 30, 2000; "Boston-Area Online Grocer Announces Leadership Change," *The Boston Globe*, March 10, 2000; Timothy J. Mullaney and David Leonhardt, "A Hard Sell Online? Guess Again," *Business Week*, July 12, 1999, pp. 142–143.

Learning Objectives

After studying Chapter 6, you should be able to:

LO1 Explain how changes in activity affect contribution margin and net income.

LO2 Compute the contribution margin ratio (CM ratio) and use it to compute changes in contribution margin and net income.

LO3 Show the effects on contribution margin of changes in variable costs, fixed costs, selling price, and volume.

LO4 Compute the break-even point by both the equation method and the contribution margin method.

LO5 Prepare a cost-volume-profit (CVP) graph and explain the significance of each of its components.

LO6 Use the CVP formulas to determine the activity level needed to achieve a desired target profit.

LO7 Compute the margin of safety and explain its significance.

LO8 Compute the degree of operating leverage at a particular level of sales and explain how the degree of operating leverage can be used to predict changes in net income.

LO9 Compute the break-even point for a multiple product company and explain the effects of shifts in the sales mix on contribution margin and the break-even point.

Cost-volume-profit (CVP) analysis is one of the most powerful tools that managers have at their command. It helps them understand the interrelationship between cost, volume, and profit in an organization by focusing on interactions between the following five elements:

1. Prices of products.
2. Volume or level of activity.
3. Per unit variable costs.
4. Total fixed costs.
5. Mix of products sold.

Because CVP analysis helps managers understand the interrelationship between cost, volume, and profit, it is a vital tool in many business decisions. These decisions include, for example, what products to manufacture or sell, what pricing policy to follow, what marketing strategy to employ, and what type of production facilities to acquire. To help understand the role of CVP analysis in business decisions, consider the case of Acoustic Concepts, Inc., a company founded by Prem Narayan.

Managerial Accounting in Action

The Issue

Accoustic Concepts, Inc.

Prem, who was a graduate student in engineering at the time, started Acoustic Concepts to market a radically new speaker he had designed for automobile sound systems. The speaker, called the Sonic Blaster, uses an advanced microprocessor chip to boost amplification to awesome levels. Prem contracted with a Taiwanese electronics manufacturer to produce the speaker. With seed money provided by his family, Prem placed an order with the manufacturer and ran advertisements in auto magazines.

The Sonic Blaster was an almost immediate success, and sales grew to the point that Prem moved the company's headquarters out of his apartment and into rented quarters in a neighboring industrial park. He also hired a receptionist, an accountant, a sales manager, and a small sales staff to sell the speakers to retail stores. The accountant, Bob Luchinni, had worked for several small companies where he had acted as a business advisor as well as accountant and bookkeeper. The following discussion occurred soon after Bob was hired:

Prem: Bob, I've got a lot of questions about the company's finances that I hope you can help answer.
Bob: We're in great shape. The loan from your family will be paid off within a few months.
Prem: I know, but I am worried about the risks I've assumed by expanding operations. What would happen if a competitor entered the market and our sales slipped? How far could sales drop without putting us into the red? Another question I've been trying to resolve is how much our sales would have to increase in order to justify the big marketing campaign the sales staff is pushing for.
Bob: Marketing always wants more money for advertising.
Prem: And they are always pushing me to drop the selling price on the speaker. I agree with them that a lower price will boost our volume, but I'm not sure the increased volume will offset the loss in revenue from the lower price.
Bob: It sounds like these questions all are related in some way to the relationships between our selling prices, our costs, and our volume. We shouldn't have a problem coming up with some answers. I'll need a day or two, though, to gather some data.
Prem: Why don't we set up a meeting for three days from now? That would be Thursday.
Bob: That'll be fine. I'll have some preliminary answers for you as well as a model you can use for answering similar questions in the future.
Prem: Good. I'll be looking forward to seeing what you come up with.

The Basics of Cost-Volume-Profit (CVP) Analysis

Bob Luchinni's preparation for the Thursday meeting begins where our study of cost behavior in the preceding chapter left off—with the contribution income statement. The contribution income statement emphasizes the behavior of costs and therefore is extremely helpful to a manager in judging the impact on profits of changes in selling price, cost, or volume. Bob will base his analysis on the following contribution income statement he prepared last month:

ACOUSTIC CONCEPTS, INC. Contribution Income Statement For the Month of June		
	Total	**Per Unit**
Sales (400 speakers)	$100,000	$250
Less variable expenses	60,000	150
Contribution margin	40,000	$100
Less fixed expenses	35,000	
Net income	$ 5,000	

Notice that sales, variable expenses, and contribution margin are expressed on a per unit basis as well as in total. This is a good idea on income statements prepared for management's own use, since it facilitates profitability analysis.

Contribution Margin

As explained in the previous chapter, contribution margin is the amount remaining from sales revenue after variable expenses have been deducted. Thus, it is the amount available to cover fixed expenses and then to provide profits for the period. Notice the sequence here—contribution margin is used *first* to cover the fixed expenses, and then whatever remains goes toward profits. If the contribution margin is not sufficient to cover the fixed expenses, then a loss occurs for the period. To illustrate with an extreme example, assume that by the middle of a particular month Acoustic Concepts has been able to sell only one speaker. At that point, the company's income statement will appear as follows:

Learning Objective 1
Explain how changes in activity affect contribution margin and net income.

	Total	**Per Unit**
Sales (1 speaker)	$ 250	$250
Less variable expenses	150	150
Contribution margin	100	$100
Less fixed expenses	35,000	
Net loss	$(34,900)	

For each additional speaker that the company is able to sell during the month, $100 more in contribution margin will become available to help cover the fixed expenses. If a second speaker is sold, for example, then the total contribution margin will increase by $100 (to a total of $200) and the company's loss will decrease by $100, to $34,800:

	Total	Per Unit
Sales (2 speakers)	$ 500	$250
Less variable expenses	300	150
Contribution margin	200	$100
Less fixed expenses	35,000	
Net loss	$(34,800)	

If enough speakers can be sold to generate $35,000 in contribution margin, then all of the fixed costs will be covered and the company will have managed to at least *break even* for the month—that is, to show neither profit nor loss but just cover all of its costs. To reach the break-even point, the company will have to sell 350 speakers in a month, since each speaker sold yields $100 in contribution margin:

	Total	Per Unit
Sales (350 speakers)	$87,500	$250
Less variable expenses	52,500	150
Contribution margin	35,000	$100
Less fixed expenses	35,000	
Net income	$ –0–	

Computation of the break-even point is discussed in detail later in the chapter; for the moment, note that the **break-even point** can be defined as the level of sales at which profit is zero.

Once the break-even point has been reached, net income will increase by the unit contribution margin for each additional unit sold. For example, if 351 speakers are sold in a month, then we can expect that the net income for the month will be $100, since the company will have sold 1 speaker more than the number needed to break even:

	Total	Per Unit
Sales (351 speakers)	$87,750	$250
Less variable expenses	52,650	150
Contribution margin	35,100	$100
Less fixed expenses	35,000	
Net income	$ 100	

If 352 speakers are sold (2 speakers above the break-even point), then we can expect that the net income for the month will be $200, and so forth. To know what the profits will be at various levels of activity, therefore, it is not necessary to prepare a whole series of income statements. The manager can simply take the number of units to be sold over the break-even point and multiply that number by the unit contribution margin. The result represents the anticipated profits for the period. Or, to estimate the effect of a planned increase in sales on profits, the manager can simply multiply the increase in units sold by the unit contribution margin. The result will be the expected increase in profits. To illustrate, if Acoustic Concepts is currently selling 400 speakers per month and plans to increase sales to 425 speakers per month, the anticipated impact on profits can be computed as follows:

Increased number of speakers to be sold	25
Contribution margin per speaker	$\times$ \$100
Increase in net income	\$2,500

These calculations can be verified as follows:

	Sales Volume			
	400 Speakers	**425 Speakers**	**Difference 25 Speakers**	**Per Unit**
Sales	\$100,000	\$106,250	\$6,250	\$250
Less variable expenses ..	60,000	63,750	3,750	150
Contribution margin	40,000	42,500	2,500	\$100
Less fixed expenses	35,000	35,000	–0–	
Net income	\$ 5,000	\$ 7,500	\$2,500	

To summarize the series of examples given above, if there were no sales, the company's loss would equal its fixed expenses. Each unit that is sold reduces the loss by the amount of the unit contribution margin. Once the break-even point has been reached, each additional unit sold increases the company's profit by the amount of the unit contribution margin.

Contribution Margin Ratio (CM Ratio)

In addition to being expressed on a per unit basis, sales revenues, variable expenses, and contribution margin for Acoustic Concepts can also be expressed as a percentage of sales:

	Total	**Per Unit**	**Percent of Sales**
Sales (400 speakers)	\$100,000	\$250	100%
Less variable expenses	60,000	150	60
Contribution margin	40,000	\$100	40%
Less fixed expenses	35,000		
Net income	\$ 5,000		

> **Learning Objective 2**
> Compute the contribution margin ratio (CM ratio) and use it to compute changes in contribution margin and net income.

The contribution margin as a percentage of total sales is referred to as the **contribution margin ratio (CM ratio).** This ratio is computed as follows:

$$\text{CM ratio} = \frac{\text{Contribution margin}}{\text{Sales}}$$

For Acoustic Concepts, the computations are as follows:

$$\frac{\text{Total contribution margin, \$40,000}}{\text{Total sales, \$100,000}} = 40\%$$

In a company such as Acoustic Concepts that has only one product, the CM ratio can also be computed as follows:

$$\frac{\text{Per unit contribution margin, \$100}}{\text{Per unit sales, \$250}} = 40\%$$

The CM ratio is extremely useful since it shows how the contribution margin will be affected by a change in total sales. To illustrate, notice that Acoustic Concepts has a CM ratio of 40%. This means that for each dollar increase in sales, total contribution margin will increase by 40 cents ($1 sales × CM ratio of 40%). Net income will also increase by 40 cents, assuming that there are no changes in fixed costs.

As this illustration suggests, *the impact on net income of any given dollar change in total sales can be computed in seconds by simply applying the CM ratio to the dollar change.* If Acoustic Concepts plans a $30,000 increase in sales during the coming month, for example, management can expect contribution margin to increase by $12,000 ($30,000 increased sales × CM ratio of 40%). As we noted above, net income will also increase by $12,000 if fixed costs do not change.

This is verified by the following table:

	Sales Volume			Percent of Sales
	Percent	Expected	Increase	
Sales	$100,000	$130,000	$30,000	100%
Less variable expenses	60,000	78,000*	18,000	60
Contribution margin	40,000	52,000	12,000	40%
Less fixed expenses	35,000	35,000	–0–	
Net income	$ 5,000	$ 17,000	$12,000	

*$130,000 expected sales ÷ $250 per unit = 520 units. 520 units × $150 per unit = $78,000.

Some managers prefer to work with the CM ratio rather than the unit contribution margin figure. The CM ratio is particularly valuable in those situations where the manager must make trade-offs between more dollar sales of one product versus more dollar sales of another. Generally speaking, when trying to increase sales, products that yield the greatest amount of contribution margin per dollar of sales should be emphasized.

Some Applications of CVP Concepts

Learning Objective 3
Show the effects on contribution margin of changes in variable costs, fixed costs, selling price, and volume.

Bob Luchinni, the accountant at Acoustic Concepts, wanted to demonstrate to the company's president Prem Narayan how the concepts developed on the preceding pages of this text can be used in planning and decision making. Bob gathered the following basic data:

	Per Unit	Percent of Sales
Sales price	$250	100%
Less variable expenses	150	60
Contribution margin	$100	40%

Concept 6–1

Recall that fixed expenses are $35,000 per month. Bob Luchinni will use these data to show the effects of changes in variable costs, fixed costs, sales price, and sales volume on the company's profitability.

Change in Fixed Cost and Sales Volume   Acoustic Concepts is currently selling 400 speakers per month (monthly sales of $100,000). The sales manager feels that a $10,000 increase in the monthly advertising budget would increase monthly sales to 520 units, thus increasing sales revenue by $30,000. Should the advertising budget be increased?

The following table shows the effect of the proposed change in monthly advertising budget:

	Current Sales	Sales with Additional Advertising Budget	Difference	Percent of Sales
Sales	$100,000	$130,000	$30,000	100%
Less variable expenses ..	60,000	78,000*	18,000	60
Contribution margin	40,000	52,000	12,000	40%
Less fixed expenses	35,000	45,000†	10,000	
Net income	$ 5,000	$ 7,000	$ 2,000	

*520 units $\times$ $150 per unit = $78,000.
†$35,000 plus additional $10,000 monthly advertising budget = $45,000.

Assuming no other factors need to be considered, the increase in the advertising budget should be approved since it would lead to an increase in net income of $2,000. There are two shorter ways to present this solution. The first alternative solution follows:

ALTERNATIVE SOLUTION 1

Expected total contribution margin:	
$130,000 $\times$ 40% CM ratio	$52,000
Present total contribution margin:	
$100,000 $\times$ 40% CM ratio	40,000
Incremental contribution margin	12,000
Change in fixed costs:	
Less incremental advertising expense	10,000
Increased net income	$ 2,000

Since in this case only the fixed costs and the sales volume change, the solution can be presented in an even shorter format, as follows:

ALTERNATIVE SOLUTION 2

Incremental contribution margin:	
$30,000 $\times$ 40% CM ratio	$12,000
Less incremental advertising expense	10,000
Increased net income	$ 2,000

Notice that this approach does not depend on a knowledge of previous sales. Also notice that it is unnecessary under either shorter approach to prepare an income statement. Both of the solutions above involve an **incremental analysis** in that they consider only those items of revenue, cost, and volume that will change if the new program is implemented. Although in each case a new income statement could have been prepared, most managers would prefer the incremental approach. It is simpler and more direct and focuses attention on the specific items involved in the decision.

Change in Variable Costs and Sales Volume   Refer to the original data. Recall that Acoustic Concepts is currently selling 400 speakers per month. Management is contemplating the use of higher-quality components, which would increase variable costs (and thereby reduce the contribution margin) by $10 per speaker. However, the sales manager predicts that the higher overall quality would increase sales to 480 speakers per month. Should the higher-quality components be used?

The $10 increase in variable costs will cause the unit contribution margin to decrease from $100 to $90.

SOLUTION

Expected total contribution margin with higher-quality components:	
480 speakers × $90 per speaker	$43,200
Present total contribution margin:	
400 speakers × $100 per speaker	40,000
Increase in total contribution margin	$ 3,200

Yes, based on the information above, the higher-quality components should be used. Since fixed costs will not change, net income should increase by the $3,200 increase in contribution margin shown above.

Change in Fixed Cost, Sales Price, and Sales Volume   Refer to the original data and recall again that the company is currently selling 400 speakers per month. To increase sales, the sales manager would like to cut the selling price by $20 per speaker and increase the advertising budget by $15,000 per month. The sales manager argues that if these two steps are taken, unit sales will increase by 50% to 600 speakers per month. Should the changes be made?

A decrease of $20 per speaker in the selling price will cause the unit contribution margin to decrease from $100 to $80.

SOLUTION

Expected total contribution margin with lower selling price:	
600 speakers × $80 per speaker	$48,000
Present total contribution margin:	
400 speakers × $100 per speaker	40,000
Incremental contribution margin	8,000
Change in fixed costs:	
Less incremental advertising expense	15,000
Reduction in net income	$(7,000)

No, based on the information above, the changes should not be made. The same solution can be obtained by preparing comparative income statements as follows:

	Present 400 Speakers per Month		Expected 600 Speakers per Month		
	Total	Per Unit	Total	Per Unit	Difference
Sales	$100,000	$250	$138,000	$230	$38,000
Less variable expenses . .	60,000	150	90,000	150	30,000
Contribution margin . . .	40,000	$100	48,000	$ 80	8,000
Less fixed expenses	35,000		50,000*		15,000
Net income (loss)	$ 5,000		$ (2,000)		$(7,000)

*35,000 + Additional monthly advertising budget of $15,000 = $50,000.

Notice that the effect on net income is the same as that obtained by the incremental analysis above.

Change in Variable Cost, Fixed Cost, and Sales Volume   Refer to the original data. As before, the company is currently selling 400 speakers per month. The sales manager would like to place the sales staff on a commission basis of $15 per speaker sold, rather than on flat salaries that now total $6,000 per month. The sales manager is confident that the change will increase monthly sales by 15% to 460 speakers per month. Should the change be made?

SOLUTION

Changing the sales staff from a salaried basis to a commission basis will affect both fixed and variable costs. Fixed costs will decrease by $6,000, from $35,000 to $29,000. Variable costs will increase by $15, from $150 to $165, and the unit contribution margin will decrease from $100 to $85.

Expected total contribution margin with sales staff on commissions:	
460 speakers × $85 per speaker	$39,100
Present total contribution margin:	
400 speakers × $100 per speaker	40,000
Decrease in total contribution margin	(900)
Change in fixed costs:	
Add salaries avoided if a commission is paid	6,000
Increase in net income	$ 5,100

Yes, based on the information above, the changes should be made. Again, the same answer can be obtained by preparing comparative income statements:

	Present 400 Speakers per Month		Expected 460 Speakers per Month		Difference: Increase or (Decrease) in Net Income
	Total	**Per Unit**	**Total**	**Per Unit**	
Sales	$100,000	$250	$115,000	$250	$15,000
Less variable expenses . .	60,000	150	75,900	165	(15,900)
Contribution margin . . .	40,000	$100	39,100	$ 85	(900)
Less fixed expenses	35,000		29,000		6,000
Net income	$ 5,000		$ 10,100		$ 5,100

Change in Regular Sales Price   Refer to the original data where Acoustic Concepts is currently selling 400 speakers per month. The company has an opportunity to make a bulk sale of 150 speakers to a wholesaler if an acceptable price can be worked out. This sale would not disturb the company's regular sales. What price per speaker should be quoted to the wholesaler if Acoustic Concepts wants to increase its monthly profits by $3,000?

SOLUTION

Variable cost per speaker	$150
Desired profit per speaker:	
$3,000 ÷ 150 speakers	20
Quoted price per speaker	$170

Notice that no element of fixed cost is included in the computation. This is because fixed costs are not affected by the bulk sale, so all of the additional revenue in excess of variable costs increases the profits of the company.

Importance of the Contribution Margin

As stated in the introduction to the chapter, CVP analysis seeks the most profitable combination of variable costs, fixed costs, selling price, and sales volume. The above examples show that the effect on the contribution margin is a major consideration in deciding on the most profitable combination of these factors. We have seen that profits can sometimes be improved by reducing the contribution margin if fixed costs can be reduced by a greater amount. More commonly, however, we have seen that the way to improve profits is to increase the total contribution margin figure. Sometimes this can be done by reducing the selling price and thereby increasing volume; sometimes it can be done by increasing the fixed costs (such as advertising) and thereby increasing volume; and sometimes it can be done by trading off variable and fixed costs with appropriate changes in volume. Many other combinations of factors are possible.

The size of the unit contribution margin figure (and the size of the CM ratio) will have a heavy influence on what steps a company is willing to take to improve profits. For example, the greater the unit contribution margin for a product, the greater is the amount that a company will be willing to spend in order to increase unit sales of the product by a given percentage. This explains in part why companies with high unit contribution margins (such as auto manufacturers) advertise so heavily, while companies with low unit contribution margins (such as dishware manufacturers) tend to spend much less for advertising.

In short, the effect on the contribution margin holds the key to many decisions.

Break-Even Analysis

Concept 6–2

> **Learning Objective 4**
> Compute the break-even point by both the equation method and the contribution margin method.

CVP analysis is sometimes referred to simply as break-even analysis. This is unfortunate because break-even analysis is only one element of CVP analysis—although an important element. Break-even analysis is designed to answer questions such as those asked by Prem Narayan, the president of Acoustic Concepts, concerning how far sales could drop before the company begins to lose money.

Break-Even Computations

Earlier in the chapter we defined the break-even point to be the level of sales at which the company's profit is zero. The break-even point can be computed using either the *equation method* or the *contribution margin method*—the two methods are equivalent.

The Equation Method The **equation method** centers on the contribution approach to the income statement illustrated earlier in the chapter. The format of this income statement can be expressed in equation form as follows:

$$\text{Profits} = \text{Sales} - (\text{Variable expenses} + \text{Fixed expenses})$$

Rearranging this equation slightly yields the following equation, which is widely used in CVP analysis:

$$\text{Sales} = \text{Variable expenses} + \text{Fixed expenses} + \text{Profits}$$

At the break-even point, profits are zero. Therefore, the break-even point can be computed by finding that point where sales just equal the total of the variable expenses plus the fixed expenses. For Acoustic Concepts, the break-even point in unit sales, Q, can be computed as follows:

Sales = Variable expenses + Fixed expenses + Profits

$$\$250Q = \$150Q + \$35,000 + \$0$$
$$\$100Q = \$35,000$$
$$Q = \$35,000 \div \$100 \text{ per speaker}$$
$$Q = 350 \text{ speakers}$$

where:

Q = Number (quantity) of speakers sold
$\$250$ = Unit sales price
$\$150$ = Unit variable expenses
$\$35,000$ = Total fixed expenses

The break-even point in sales dollars can be computed by multiplying the break-even level of unit sales by the selling price per unit:

350 speakers $\times$ $250 per speaker = $87,500

The break-even in total sales dollars, X, can also be directly computed as follows:

Sales = Variable expenses + Fixed expenses + Profits

$$X = 0.60X + \$35,000 + \$0$$
$$0.40X = \$35,000$$
$$X = \$35,000 \div 0.40$$
$$X = \$87,500$$

where:

X = Total sales dollars
0.60 = Variable expenses as a percentage of sales
$\$35,000$ = Total fixed expenses

Firms often have data available only in percentage form, and the approach we have just illustrated must then be used to find the break-even point. Notice that use of percentages in the equation yields a break-even point in sales dollars rather than in units sold. The break-even point in units sold is the following:

$87,500 $\div$ $250 per speaker = 350 speakers

Recruit

you decide

Assume that you are being recruited by the ConneXus Corp. and have an interview scheduled later this week. You are interested in working for this company for a variety of reasons. In preparation for the interview, you did some research at your local library and gathered the following information about the company. ConneXus is a company set up by two young engineers, George Searle and Humphrey Chen, to allow consumers to order music CDs on their mobile phones. Suppose you hear on the radio a cut from a CD that you would like to own. Pick up your mobile phone, punch "*CD," and enter the radio station's frequency and the time you heard the song, and the CD will be on its way to you.

ConneXus charges about $17 for a CD, including shipping. The company pays its supplier about $13, leaving a contribution margin of $4 per CD. Because of the fixed costs of running the service, Searle expects the company to lose $1.5 million on sales of $1.5 million in its first year of operations. That assumes the company sells in excess of 88,000 CDs.

What are your initial impressions of this company based on the information you gathered? What other information would you want to obtain during the job interview?

Adapted from: Peter Kafka, "Play It Again," *Forbes*, July 26, 1999, p. 94.

The Contribution Margin Method   The **contribution margin method** is actually just a shortcut version of the equation method already described. The approach centers on the idea discussed earlier that each unit sold provides a certain amount of contribution margin that goes toward covering fixed costs. To find how many units must be sold to break even, divide the total fixed costs by the unit contribution margin:

$$\text{Break-even point in units sold} = \frac{\text{Fixed expenses}}{\text{Unit contribution margin}}$$

Each speaker generates a contribution margin of $100 ($250 selling price, less $150 variable expenses). Since the total fixed expenses are $35,000, the break-even point is as follows:

$$\frac{\text{Fixed expenses}}{\text{Unit contribution margin}} = \frac{\$35,000}{\$100 \text{ per speaker}} = 350 \text{ speakers}$$

A variation of this method uses the CM ratio instead of the unit contribution margin. The result is the break-even in total sales dollars rather than in total units sold.

$$\text{Break-even point in total sales dollars} = \frac{\text{Fixed expenses}}{\text{CM ratio}}$$

In the Acoustic Concepts example, the calculations are as follows:

$$\frac{\text{Fixed expenses}}{\text{CM ratio}} = \frac{\$35,000}{40\%} = \$87,500$$

This approach, based on the CM ratio, is particularly useful in those situations where a company has multiple product lines and wishes to compute a single break-even point for the company as a whole. More is said on this point in a later section titled The Concept of Sales Mix.

in business today **Operating on a Shoestring**

Hesh Kestin failed in his attempt at publishing an English-language newspaper in Israel in the 1980s. His conclusion: "Never start a business with too many people or too much furniture." Kestin's newest venture is *The American*, a Sunday-only newspaper for overseas Americans. His idea is to publish *The American* on the one day of the week that the well-established *International Herald Tribune* (circulation, 190,000 copies) does not publish. But following what he learned from his first failed venture, he is doing it on a shoestring.

In contrast to the Paris-based *International Herald Tribune* with its eight-story office tower and staff of 250, Kestin has set up business in a small clapboard building on Long Island. Working at desks purchased from a thrift shop, Kestin's staff of 12 assemble the tabloid from stories pulled off wire services. The result of this frugality is that *The American*'s break-even point is only 14,000 copies. Sales topped 20,000 copies just two months after the paper's first issue.

Source: Jerry Useem, "American Hopes to Conquer the World—from Long Island," *Inc,* December 1996, p. 23.

CVP Relationships in Graphic Form

The relationships among revenue, cost, profit, and volume can be expressed graphically by preparing a **cost-volume-profit (CVP) graph.** A CVP graph highlights CVP relationships over wide ranges of activity and can give managers a perspective that can be obtained in no other way. To help explain his analysis to Prem Narayan, Bob Luchinni decided to prepare a CVP graph for Acoustic Concepts.

Learning Objective 5
Prepare a cost-volume-profit (CVP) graph and explain the significance of each of its components.

Preparing the CVP Graph   Preparing a CVP graph (sometimes called a *break-even chart*) involves three steps. These steps are keyed to the graph in Exhibit 6–1:

1. Draw a line parallel to the volume axis to represent total fixed expenses. For Acoustic Concepts, total fixed expenses are $35,000.
2. Choose some volume of sales and plot the point representing total expenses (fixed and variable) at the activity level you have selected. In Exhibit 6–1, Bob Luchinni chose a volume of 600 speakers. Total expenses at that activity level would be as follows:

Fixed expenses	$ 35,000
Variable expenses (600 speakers × $150 per speaker)	90,000
Total expenses	$125,000

After the point has been plotted, draw a line through it back to the point where the fixed expenses line intersects the dollars axis.
3. Again choose some volume of sales and plot the point representing total sales dollars at the activity level you have selected. In Exhibit 6–1, Bob Luchinni again chose a volume of 600 speakers. Sales at that activity level total $150,000 (600 speakers × $250 per speaker). Draw a line through this point back to the origin.

The interpretation of the completed CVP graph is given in Exhibit 6–2. The anticipated profit or loss at any given level of sales is measured by the vertical distance between the total revenue line (sales) and the total expenses line (variable expenses plus fixed expenses).

The break-even point is where the total revenue and total expenses lines cross. The break-even point of 350 speakers in Exhibit 6–2 agrees with the break-even point obtained for Acoustic Concepts in earlier computations.

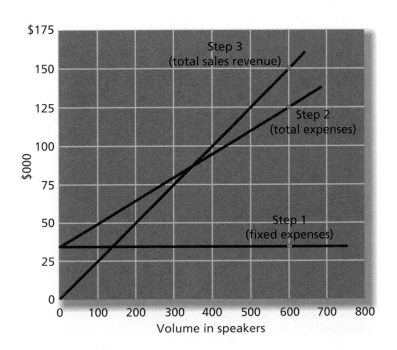

Exhibit 6–1
Preparing the CVP Graph

Exhibit 6–2
The Completed CVP Graph

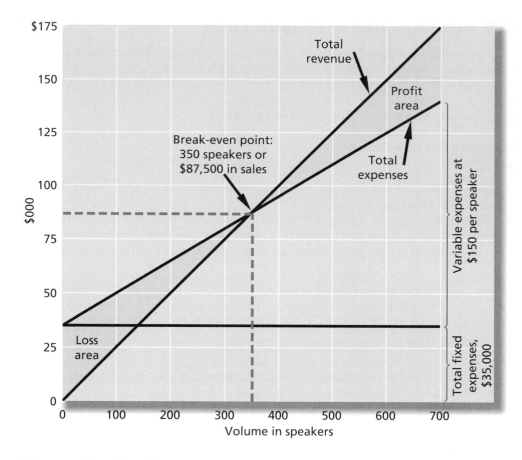

Target Profit Analysis

CVP formulas can be used to determine the sales volume needed to achieve a target profit. Suppose that Prem Narayan of Acoustic Concepts would like to earn a target profit of $40,000 per month. How many speakers would have to be sold?

The CVP Equation   One approach is to use the equation method. Instead of solving for the unit sales where profits are zero, you instead solve for the unit sales where profits are $40,000.

$$\text{Sales} = \text{Variable expenses} + \text{Fixed expenses} + \text{Profits}$$
$$\$250Q = \$150Q + \$35,000 + \$40,000$$
$$\$100Q = \$75,000$$
$$Q = \$75,000 \div \$100 \text{ per speaker}$$
$$Q = 750 \text{ speakers}$$

where:

Q = Number of speakers sold
$\$250$ = Unit sales price
$\$150$ = Unit variable expenses
$\$35,000$ = Total fixed expenses
$\$40,000$ = Target profit

Thus, the target profit can be achieved by selling 750 speakers per month, which represents $187,500 in total sales ($250 per speaker × 750 speakers).

The Contribution Margin Approach   A second approach involves expanding the contribution margin formula to include the target profit:

$$\text{Units sold to attain the target profit} = \frac{\text{Fixed expenses} + \text{Target profit}}{\text{Unit contribution margin}}$$

$$\frac{\$35,000 + \$40,000}{\$100 \text{ per speaker}} = 750 \text{ speakers}$$

This approach gives the same answer as the equation method since it is simply a shortcut version of the equation method.

The Margin of Safety

The **margin of safety** is the excess of budgeted (or actual) sales over the break-even volume of sales. It states the amount by which sales can drop before losses begin to be incurred. The formula for its calculation is:

Learning Objective 7
Compute the margin of safety and explain its significance.

$$\text{Margin of safety} = \text{Total budgeted (or actual) sales} - \text{Break-even sales}$$

The margin of safety can also be expressed in percentage form. This percentage is obtained by dividing the margin of safety in dollar terms by total sales:

$$\text{Margin of safety percentage} = \frac{\text{Margin of safety in dollars}}{\text{Total budgeted (or actual) sales}}$$

The calculations for the margin of safety for Acoustic Concepts are as follows:

Sales (at the current volume of 400 speakers) (a)	$100,000
Break-even sales (at 350 speakers)	87,500
Margin of safety (in dollars) (b)	$ 12,500
Margin of safety as a percentage of sales, (b) ÷ (a)	12.5%

This margin of safety means that at the current level of sales and with the company's current prices and cost structure, a reduction in sales of $12,500, or 12.5%, would result in just breaking even.

In a single-product firm like Acoustic Concepts, the margin of safety can also be expressed in terms of the number of units sold by dividing the margin of safety in dollars by the selling price per unit. In this case, the margin of safety is 50 speakers ($12,500 ÷ $250 per speaker = 50 speakers).

Loan Officer

decision *maker*

Pak Melwani and Kumar Hathiramani, former silk merchants from Bombay, opened a soup store in Manhattan after watching a Seinfeld episode featuring the "soup Nazi." The episode parodied a real-life soup vendor, Ali Yeganeh, whose loyal customers put up with hour-long lines and "snarling customer service." Melwani and Hathiramani approached Yeganeh about turning his soup kitchen into a chain, but they were gruffly rebuffed. Instead of giving up, the two hired a French chef with a repertoire of 500 soups and opened a store called Soup Nutsy. For $6 per serving, Soup Nutsy offers 12 homemade soups each day, such as sherry crab bisque and Thai coconut shrimp. Melwani and Hathiramani report that in their first year of operation, they netted $210,000 on sales of $700,000. They report that it costs about $2 per serving to make the soup.

Assume that Melwani and Hathiramani have approached your bank for a loan. As the loan officer, you should consider a variety of factors, including the company's margin of safety. Assuming that other information about the company is favorable, would you consider Soup Nutsy's margin of safety to be comfortable enough to extend the loan?

Adapted from: Silva Sansoni, "The Starbucks of Soup?" *Forbes*, July 7, 1997, pp. 90–91.

It is Thursday morning, and Prem Narayan and Bob Luchinni are discussing the results of Bob's analysis.

Prem: Bob, everything you have shown me is pretty clear. I can see what impact some of the sales manager's suggestions would have on our profits. Some of those suggestions are quite good and some are not so good. I also understand that our break-even is 350 speakers, so we have to make sure we don't slip below that level of sales. What really bothers me is that we are only selling 400 speakers a month now. What did you call the 50-speaker cushion?

Bob: That's the margin of safety.

Prem: Such a small cushion makes me very nervous. What can we do to increase the margin of safety?

Bob: We have to increase total sales or decrease the break-even point or both.

Prem: And to decrease the break-even point, we have to either decrease our fixed expenses or increase our unit contribution margin?

Bob: Exactly.

Prem: And to increase our unit contribution margin, we have to either increase our selling price or decrease the variable cost per unit?

Bob: Correct.

Prem: So what do you suggest?

Bob: Well, the analysis doesn't tell us which of these to do, but it does indicate we have a potential problem here.

Prem: If you don't have any immediate suggestions, I would like to call a general meeting next week to discuss ways we can work on increasing the margin of safety. I think everyone will be concerned about how vulnerable we are to even small downturns in sales.

Bob: I agree. This is something everyone will want to work on.

CVP Considerations in Choosing a Cost Structure

We stated in the preceding chapter that *cost structure* refers to the relative proportion of fixed and variable costs in an organization. We also stated that an organization often has some latitude in trading off between fixed and variable costs. Such a trade-off is possible, for example, by automating facilities rather than using direct labor workers.

In this section, we discuss various considerations involved in choosing a cost structure. We look first at the matter of cost structure and profit stability, and then we discuss an important concept known as *operating leverage*. Finally, we conclude the section by comparing capital-intensive (automated) and labor-intensive companies in terms of the potential risks and rewards that are inherent in the cost structures these companies have chosen.

Cost Structure and Profit Stability

When a manager has some latitude in trading off between fixed and variable costs, which cost structure is better—high variable costs and low fixed costs, or the opposite? No categorical answer to this question is possible; there may be advantages either way, depending on the specific circumstances. To show what we mean by this statement, refer to the income statements given below for two blueberry farms. Bogside Farm depends on migrant workers to pick its berries by hand, whereas Sterling Farm has invested in expensive berry-picking machines. Consequently, Bogside Farm has higher variable costs, but Sterling Farm has higher fixed costs:

	Bogside Farm		Sterling Farm	
	Amount	Percent	Amount	Percent
Sales	$100,000	100%	$100,000	100%
Less variable expenses ...	60,000	60	30,000	30
Contribution margin	40,000	40%	70,000	70%
Less fixed expenses	30,000		60,000	
Net income	$ 10,000		$ 10,000	

The question as to which farm has the better cost structure depends on many factors, including the long-run trend in sales, year-to-year fluctuations in the level of sales, and the attitude of the owners toward risk. If sales are expected to be above $100,000 in the future, then Sterling Farm probably has the better cost structure. The reason is that its CM ratio is higher, and its profits will therefore increase more rapidly as sales increase. To illustrate, assume that each farm experiences a 10% increase in sales without any increase in fixed costs. The new income statements would be as follows:

	Bogside Farm		Sterling Farm	
	Amount	Percent	Amount	Percent
Sales	$110,000	100%	$110,000	100%
Less variable expenses ...	66,000	60	33,000	30
Contribution margin	44,000	40%	77,000	70%
Less fixed expenses	30,000		60,000	
Net income	$ 14,000		$ 17,000	

Sterling Farm has experienced a greater increase in net income due to its higher CM ratio even though the increase in sales was the same for both farms.

What if sales drop below $100,000 from time to time? What are the break-even points of the two farms? What are their margins of safety? The computations needed to answer these questions are carried out below using the contribution margin method:

	Bogside Farm	Sterling Farm
Fixed expenses	$ 30,000	$ 60,000
Contribution margin ratio	÷ 40%	÷ 70%
Break-even in total sales dollars	$ 75,000	$ 85,714
Total current sales (a)	$100,000	$100,000
Break-even sales	75,000	85,714
Margin of safety in sales dollars (b)	$ 25,000	$ 14,286
Margin of safety as a percentage of sales, (b) ÷ (a)	25.0%	14.3%

This analysis makes it clear that Bogside Farm is less vulnerable to downturns than Sterling Farm. We can identify two reasons why it is less vulnerable. First, due to its lower fixed expenses, Bogside Farm has a lower break-even point and a higher margin of safety, as shown by the computations above. Therefore, it will not incur losses as quickly as Sterling Farm in periods of sharply declining sales. Second, due to its lower CM ratio,

Bogside Farm will not lose contribution margin as rapidly as Sterling Farm when sales fall off. Thus, Bogside Farm's income will be less volatile. We saw earlier that this is a drawback when sales increase, but it provides more protection when sales drop.

To summarize, without knowing the future, it is not obvious which cost structure is better. Both have advantages and disadvantages. Sterling Farm, with its higher fixed costs and lower variable costs, will experience wider swings in net income as changes take place in sales, with greater profits in good years and greater losses in bad years. Bogside Farm, with its lower fixed costs and higher variable costs, will enjoy greater stability in net income and will be more protected from losses during bad years, but at the cost of lower net income in good years.

Operating Leverage

A lever is a tool for multiplying force. Using a lever, a massive object can be moved with only a modest amount of force. In business, *operating leverage* serves a similar purpose. **Operating leverage** is a measure of how sensitive net income is to percentage changes in sales. Operating leverage acts as a multiplier. If operating leverage is high, a small percentage increase in sales can produce a much larger percentage increase in net income.

Operating leverage can be illustrated by returning to the data given above for the two blueberry farms. We previously showed that a 10% increase in sales (from $100,000 to $110,000 in each farm) results in a 70% increase in the net income of Sterling Farm (from $10,000 to $17,000) and only a 40% increase in the net income of Bogside Farm (from $10,000 to $14,000). Thus, for a 10% increase in sales, Sterling Farm experiences a much greater percentage increase in profits than does Bogside Farm. Therefore, Sterling Farm has greater operating leverage than Bogside Farm.

The **degree of operating leverage** at a given level of sales is computed by the following formula:

$$\text{Degree of operating leverage} = \frac{\text{Contribution margin}}{\text{Net income}}$$

The degree of operating leverage is a measure, at a given level of sales, of how a percentage change in sales volume will affect profits. To illustrate, the degree of operating leverage for the two farms at a $100,000 sales level would be computed as follows:

$$\text{Bogside Farm: } \frac{\$40,000}{\$10,000} = 4$$

$$\text{Sterling Farm: } \frac{\$70,000}{\$10,000} = 7$$

Since the degree of operating leverage for Bogside Farm is 4, the farm's net income grows four times as fast as its sales. Similarly, Sterling Farm's net income grows seven times as fast as its sales. Thus, if sales increase by 10%, then we can expect the net income of Bogside Farm to increase by four times this amount, or by 40%, and the net income of Sterling Farm to increase by seven times this amount, or by 70%.

	(1) Percent Increase in Sales	(2) Degree of Operating Leverage	(3) Percent Increase in Net Income (1) × (2)
Bogside Farm	10%	4	40%
Sterling Farm	10%	7	70%

What is responsible for the higher operating leverage at Sterling Farm? The only difference between the two farms is their cost structure. If two companies have the same total revenue and same total expense but different cost structures, then the company with the higher proportion of fixed costs in its cost structure will have higher operating leverage. Referring back to the original example on pages 244–245, when both farms have sales of $100,000 and total expenses of $90,000, one-third of Bogside Farm's costs are fixed but two-thirds of Sterling Farm's costs are fixed. As a consequence, Sterling's degree of operating leverage is higher than Bogside's.

The degree of operating leverage is greatest at sales levels near the break-even point and decreases as sales and profits rise. This can be seen from the tabulation below, which shows the degree of operating leverage for Bogside Farm at various sales levels. (Data used earlier for Bogside Farm are shown in color.)

Sales	$75,000	$80,000	$100,000	$150,000	$225,000
Less variable expenses	45,000	48,000	60,000	90,000	135,000
Contribution margin (a)	30,000	32,000	40,000	60,000	90,000
Less fixed expenses	30,000	30,000	30,000	30,000	30,000
Net income (b)	$ -0-	$ 2,000	$ 10,000	$ 30,000	$ 60,000
Degree of operating leverage, (a) ÷ (b)	∞	16	4	2	1.5

Thus, a 10% increase in sales would increase profits by only 15% (10% × 1.5) if the company were operating at a $225,000 sales level, as compared to the 40% increase we computed earlier at the $100,000 sales level. The degree of operating leverage will continue to decrease the farther the company moves from its break-even point. At the break-even point, the degree of operating leverage will be infinitely large ($30,000 contribution margin ÷ $0 net income = ∞).

A manager can use the degree of operating leverage to quickly estimate what impact various percentage changes in sales will have on profits, without the necessity of preparing detailed income statements. As shown by our examples, the effects of operating leverage can be dramatic. If a company is near its break-even point, then even small percentage increases in sales can yield large percentage increases in profits. *This explains why management will often work very hard for only a small increase in sales volume.* If the degree of operating leverage is 5, then a 6% increase in sales would translate into a 30% increase in profits.

Fan Appreciation

in business today

Operating leverage can be a good thing when business is booming but can turn the situation ugly when sales slacken. Jerry Colangelo, the managing partner of the Arizona Diamondbacks professional baseball team, spent over $100 million to sign six free agents—doubling the team's payroll cost—on top of the costs of operating and servicing the debt on the team's new stadium. With annual expenses of about $100 million, the team needs to average 40,000 fans per game to just break even.

Faced with a financially risky situation, Colangelo decided to raise ticket prices by 12%. And he did it during Fan Appreciation Weekend! Attendance for the season dropped by 15%, turning what should have been a $20 million profit into a loss of over $10 million for the year. Note that a drop of attendance of 15% did not cut profit by just 15%—that's the magic of operating leverage at work.

Source: Mary Summers, "Bottom of the Ninth, Two Out," *Forbes*, November 1, 1999, pp. 69–70.

Structuring Sales Commissions

Companies generally compensate salespeople by paying them either a commission based on sales or a salary plus a sales commission. Commissions based on sales dollars can lead to lower profits in a company. To illustrate, consider Pipeline Unlimited, a producer of surfing equipment. Salespeople for the company sell the company's product to retail sporting goods stores throughout North America and the Pacific Basin. Data for two of the company's surfboards, the XR7 and Turbo models, appear below:

	Model	
	XR7	Turbo
Selling price	$100	$150
Less variable expenses	75	132
Contribution margin	$ 25	$ 18

Which model will salespeople push hardest if they are paid a commission of 10% of sales revenue? The answer is the Turbo, since it has the higher selling price. On the other hand, from the standpoint of the company, profits will be greater if salespeople steer customers toward the XR7 model since it has the higher contribution margin.

To eliminate such conflicts, some companies base salepersons' commissions on contribution margin rather than on sales. The reasoning goes like this: Since contribution margin represents the amount of sales revenue available to cover fixed expenses and profits, a firm's well-being will be maximized when contribution margin is maximized. By tying salespersons' commissions to contribution margin, the salespersons are automatically encouraged to concentrate on the element that is of most importance to the firm. There is no need to worry about what mix of products the salespersons sell because they will *automatically* sell the mix of products that will maximize the contribution margin. In effect, by maximizing their own well-being, they automatically maximize the well-being of the firm—assuming there is no change in fixed expenses.

in business today Compensation Plan Backfires

The method of compensating salespersons must be chosen with a great deal of care. Digital Equipment Corporation's founder believed that salespersons should never sell customers something they don't need, and accordingly Digital paid them salaries rather than sales commissions. This approach worked fine for many years because "Digital's products were the hottest alternative to expensive mainframe computers, and because they were cheaper, they almost sold themselves. But when competition arrived, the Digital sales staff was hopelessly outclassed." When commissions were introduced in an attempt to stem the tide, the new system backfired. "Some salesmen sold product at little, or no profit to pump up volume—and their compensation."

Source: John R. Wilke, "At Digital Equipment, a Resignation Reveals Key Problem: Selling," *The Wall Street Journal,* April 26, 1994, pp. A1, A11.

The Concept of Sales Mix

The preceding sections have given us some insights into the principles involved in CVP analysis, as well as some selected examples of how these principles are used by the manager. Before concluding our discussion, it will be helpful to consider one additional application of the ideas that we have developed—the use of CVP concepts in analyzing sales mix.

The Definition of Sales Mix

The term **sales mix** means the relative proportions in which a company's products are sold. Managers try to achieve the combination, or mix, that will yield the greatest amount of profits. Most companies have many products, and often these products are not equally profitable. Where this is true, profits will depend to some extent on the company's sales mix. Profits will be greater if high-margin rather than low-margin items make up a relatively large proportion of total sales.

Changes in the sales mix can cause interesting (and sometimes confusing) variations in a company's profits. A shift in the sales mix from high-margin items to low-margin items can cause total profits to decrease even though total sales may increase. Conversely, a shift in the sales mix from low-margin items to high-margin items can cause the reverse effect—total profits may increase even though total sales decrease. It is one thing to achieve a particular sales volume; it is quite a different thing to sell the most profitable mix of products.

Sales Mix and Break-Even Analysis

If a company sells more than one product, break-even analysis is somewhat more complex than discussed earlier in the chapter. The reason is that different products will have different selling prices, different costs, and different contribution margins. Consequently, the break-even point will depend on the mix in which the various products are sold. To illustrate, consider Sound Unlimited, a small company that imports CD-ROMs from France for use in personal computers. At present, the company distributes the following to retail computer stores: the Le Louvre CD, a multimedia free-form tour of the famous art museum in Paris; and the Le Vin CD, which features the wines and wine-growing regions of France. Both multimedia products have sound, photos, video clips, and sophisticated software. The company's September sales, expenses, and break-even point are shown in Exhibit 6–3.

As shown in the exhibit, the break-even point is $60,000 in sales. This is computed by dividing the fixed costs by the company's *overall* CM ratio of 45%. The sales mix is currently 20% for the Le Louvre CD and 80% for the Le Vin CD. If this sales mix is constant, then at the break-even total sales of $60,000, the sales of the Le Louvre CD would be $12,000 (20% of $60,000) and the sales of the Le Vin CD would be $48,000 (80% of $60,000). As shown in Exhibit 6–3, at these levels of sales the company would indeed break even. But $60,000 in sales represents the break-even point for the company only so long as the sales mix does not change. *If the sales mix changes, then the break-even point will also change.* This is illustrated by the results for October in which the sales mix shifted away from the more profitable Le Vin CD (which has a 50% CM ratio) toward the less profitable Le Louvre CD (which has only a 25% CM ratio). These results appear in Exhibit 6–4.

Although sales have remained unchanged at $100,000, the sales mix is exactly the reverse of what it was in Exhibit 6–3, with the bulk of the sales now coming from the less profitable Le Louvre CD. Notice that this shift in the sales mix has caused both the overall CM ratio and total profits to drop sharply from the prior month—the overall CM ratio has dropped from 45% in September to only 30% in October, and net income has dropped from $18,000 to only $3,000. In addition, with the drop in the overall CM ratio, the company's break-even point is no longer $60,000 in sales. Since the company is now realizing less average contribution margin per dollar of sales, it takes more sales to cover the

Exhibit 6–3
Multiple-Product Break-Even Analysis

SOUND UNLIMITED
Contribution Income Statement
For the Month of September

	Le Louvre CD		Le Vin CD		Total	
	Amount	Percent	Amount	Percent	Amount	Percent
Sales	$20,000	100%	$80,000	100%	$100,000	100%
Less variable expenses	15,000	75	40,000	50	55,000	55
Contribution margin	$ 5,000	25%	$40,000	50%	45,000	45%
Less fixed expenses					27,000	
Net income					$ 18,000	

Computation of the break-even point:

$$\frac{\text{Fixed expenses, \$27,000}}{\text{Overall CM ratio, 45\%}} = \$60,000$$

Verification of the breakeven:

	Le Louvre CD	Le Vin CD	Total
Current dollar sales	$20,000	$80,000	$100,000
Percentage of total dollar sales	20%	80%	100%
Sales at break-even	$12,000	$48,000	$60,000

	Le Louvre CD		Le Vin CD		Total	
	Amount	Percent	Amount	Percent	Amount	Percent
Sales	$12,000	100%	$48,000	100%	$60,000	100%
Less variable expenses	9,000	75	24,000	50	33,000	55
Contribution margin	$ 3,000	25%	$24,000	50%	27,000	45%
Less fixed expenses					27,000	
Net income					$ –0–	

Exhibit 6–4
Multiple-Product Break-Even Analysis: A Shift in Sales Mix (see Exhibit 6–3)

SOUND UNLIMITED
Contribution Income Statement
For the Month of October

	Le Louvre CD		Le Vin CD		Total	
	Amount	Percent	Amount	Percent	Amount	Percent
Sales	$80,000	100%	$20,000	100%	$100,000	100%
Less variable expenses	60,000	75	10,000	50	70,000	70
Contribution margin	$20,000	25%	$10,000	50%	30,000	30%
Less fixed expenses					27,000	
Net income					$ 3,000	

Computation of the break-even point:

$$\frac{\text{Fixed expenses, \$27,000}}{\text{Overall CM ratio, 30\%}} = \$90,000$$

same amount of fixed costs. Thus, the break-even point has increased from $60,000 to $90,000 in sales per year.

In preparing a break-even analysis, some assumption must be made concerning the sales mix. Usually the assumption is that it will not change. However, if the manager knows that shifts in various factors (consumer tastes, market share, and so forth) are causing shifts in the sales mix, then these factors must be explicitly considered in any CVP computations. Otherwise, the manager may make decisions on the basis of outmoded or faulty data.

Benefiting from a Shift in Sales Mix

in business today

Roger Maxwell grew up near a public golf course where he learned the game and worked as a caddie. After attending Oklahoma State on a golf scholarship, he became a golf pro and eventually rose to become vice president at Marriott, responsible for Marriott's golf courses in the United States. Sensing an opportunity to serve a niche market, Maxwell invested his life savings in opening his own golfing superstore, In Celebration of Golf (ICOG), in Scottsdale, Arizona. Maxwell says, "I'd rather sacrifice profit up front for sizzle . . . [P]eople are bored by malls. They're looking for something different." Maxwell has designed his store to be a museum-like mecca for golfing fanatics. For example, maintenance work is done in a replica of a turn-of-the-century club maker's shop.

Maxwell's approach seems to be working. In the second year of operation, Maxwell projected a profit of $81,000 on sales of $2.4 million as follows:

	Projected	Percent of Sales
Sales	$2,400,000	100 %
Cost of sales	1,496,000	62⅓
Other variable expenses	296,000	12⅓
Contribution margin	608,000	25⅓%
Fixed expenses	527,000	
Net income	$ 81,000	

Happily for Maxwell, sales for the year were even better than expected—reaching $3.0 million. In the absence of any other changes, the net income should have been approximately $233,000, computed as follows:

	Projected	Percent of Sales
Sales	$3,000,000	100 %
Cost of sales	1,870,000	62⅓
Other variable expenses	370,000	12⅓
Contribution margin	760,000	25⅓%
Fixed expenses	527,000	
Net income	$ 233,000	

However, net income for the year was actually $289,000—apparently because of a favorable shift in the sales mix toward higher margin items. A 25% increase in sales over the projections at the beginning of the year resulted in a 356% increase in net income. That's leverage!

Source: Edward O. Welles, "Going for the Green," *Inc,* July 1996, pp. 68–75.

Assumptions of CVP Analysis

A number of assumptions typically underlie CVP analysis:

1. Selling price is constant throughout the entire relevant range. The price of a product or service will not change as volume changes.
2. Costs are linear throughout the entire relevant range, and they can be accurately divided into variable and fixed elements. The variable element is constant per unit, and the fixed element is constant in total over the entire relevant range.
3. In multiproduct companies, the sales mix is constant.
4. In manufacturing companies, inventories do not change. The number of units produced equals the number of units sold.

While some of these assumptions may be technically violated, the violations are usually not serious enough to call into question the basic validity of CVP analysis. For example, in most multiproduct companies, the sales mix is constant enough so that the results of CVP analysis are reasonably valid.

Perhaps the greatest danger lies in relying on simple CVP analysis when a manager is contemplating a large change in volume that lies outside of the relevant range. For example, a manager might contemplate increasing the level of sales far beyond what the company has ever experienced before. However, even in these situations a manager can adjust the model as we have done in this chapter to take into account anticipated changes in selling prices, fixed costs, and the sales mix that would otherwise violate the assumptions. For example, in a decision that would affect fixed costs, the change in fixed costs can be explicitly taken into account as illustrated earlier in the chapter in the Acoustic Concepts example on page 235.

Variable Costing

The last assumption, that inventories do not change, is important when a company uses absorption costing to compute its unit product costs. Under absorption costing, fixed manufacturing overhead costs are absorbed by the products made during a period. If some of these products are not sold (i.e., inventories increase), then the fixed manufacturing overhead costs absorbed by these products will appear as a part of ending inventories on the balance sheet rather than as an expense as shown on the contribution format income statement illustrated in this chapter.

Variable costing is an alternative approach to computing unit product costs. In contrast to absorption costing, under **variable costing** only the *variable* manufacturing costs are assigned to products. Fixed manufacturing costs under variable costing are considered to be period costs and go directly to the income statement as expenses of the current period. Consequently, under variable costing none of the fixed manufacturing overhead costs are on the balance sheet in the form of ending inventories.

Variable costing has a number of advantages over absorption costing including simplicity, compatibility with CVP analysis, and freedom from distortions caused by changes in ending inventories. For further discussion of variable costing, see Chapter 7 of Garrison & Noreen, *Managerial Accounting*, 9th edition, Irwin/McGraw-Hill.

Summary

LO1 Explain how changes in activity affect contribution margin and net income.

The unit contribution margin, which is the difference between a unit's selling price and its variable cost, indicates how net income will change as the result of selling one more or one fewer unit. For example, if a product's unit contribution margin is $10, then selling one more unit will add $10 to the company's profit.

LO2 Compute the contribution margin ratio (CM ratio) and use it to compute changes in contribution margin and net income.

The contribution margin ratio is computed by dividing the unit contribution margin by the unit selling price, or by dividing the total contribution margin by the total sales.

The contribution margin shows by how much a dollar increase in sales will affect the total contribution margin and net income. For example, if a product has a 40% contribution margin ratio, then a $100 increase in sales should result in a $40 increase in contribution margin and in net income.

LO3 Show the effects on contribution margin of changes in variable costs, fixed costs, selling price, and volume.

Contribution margin concepts can be used to estimate the effects of changes in various parameters such as variable costs, fixed costs, selling prices, and volume on the total contribution margin and net income.

LO4 Compute the break-even point by both the equation method and the contribution margin method.

The break-even point is the level of sales at which profits are zero. It can be computed using several methods. The break-even in units can be determined by dividing total fixed expenses by the unit contribution margin. The break-even in sales dollars can be determined by dividing total fixed expenses by the contribution margin ratio.

LO5 Prepare a cost-volume-profit (CVP) graph and explain the significance of each of its components.

A cost-volume-profit graph displays sales revenues and expenses as a function of unit sales. Revenue is depicted as a straight line slanting upward to the right from the origin. Total expenses consist of both a fixed element and a variable element. The fixed element is flat on the graph. The variable element slants upward to the right. The break-even point is the point at which the total sales revenue and total expenses lines intersect on the graph.

LO6 Use the CVP formulas to determine the activity level needed to achieve a desired target profit.

The sales, in units, required to attain a desired target profit can be determined by summing the total fixed expenses and the desired target profit and then dividing the result by the unit contribution margin.

LO7 Compute the margin of safety and explain its significance.

The margin of safety is the difference between the total budgeted (or actual) sales of a period and the break-even sales. It expresses how much cushion there is in the current level of sales above the break-even point.

LO8 Compute the degree of operating leverage at a particular level of sales and explain how the degree of operating leverage can be used to predict changes in net income.

The degree of operating leverage is computed by dividing the total contribution margin by net income. The degree of operating leverage can be used to determine impact a given percentage change in sales would have on net income. For example, if a company's degree of operating leverage is 2.5, then a 10% increase in sales from current levels of sales should result in a 25% increase in net income.

LO9 Compute the break-even point for a multiple product company and explain the effects of shifts in the sales mix on contribution margin and the break-even point.

The break-even for a multiproduct company can be computed by dividing the company's total fixed expenses by the overall contribution margin ratio.

This method for computing the break-even assumes that the sales mix is constant. If the sales mix shifts toward products with a lower contribution margin ratio, then more total sales are required to attain any given level of profits.

Guidance Answers to You Decide and Decision Maker

RECRUIT (p. 239)

You can get a feel for the challenges that this company will face by determining its break-even point. Start by estimating the company's variable expense ratio:

Variable cost per unit ÷ Selling price per unit = Variable expense ratio

$$\$13 \div \$17 = 76.5\%$$

Then, estimate the company's variable expenses:

Sales × Variable expense ratio = Estimated amount of variable expenses

$$\$1,500,000 \times 0.765 = \$1,147,500$$

Next, put the contribution format income statement into an equation format to estimate the company's current level of fixed expenses:

Sales = Variable expenses + Fixed expenses + Net income (loss)

$$\$1,500,000 = \$1,147,500 + X + (\$1,500,000)$$

$$X = \$1,500,000 - \$1,147,500 + \$1,500,000$$

$$X = \$1,852,500$$

Finally, use the equation approach to estimate the company's break-even point:

Sales = Variable expenses + Fixed expenses + Profits

$$\$17Q = \$13Q + \$1,852,500 + \$0$$

$$\$4Q = \$1,852,500$$

$$Q = 463,125$$

Assuming that its cost structure stays the same, ConneXus needs to increase its sales by 527%—from 88,000 to 463,125 CDs—just to break even. After it reaches that break-even point, net income will increase by $4 (the contribution margin) for each additional CD that it sells. Joining the company would be a risky proposition; you should be prepared with some probing questions when you arrive for your interview. (For example, what steps does the company plan to take to increase sales? How might the company reduce its fixed and/or variable expenses so as to lower its break-even point?)

LOAN OFFICER (p. 243)

To determine the company's margin of safety, you need to determine its break-even point. Start by estimating the company's variable expense ratio:

Variable cost per unit ÷ Selling price per unit = Variable expense ratio

$$\$2 \div \$6 = 33.3\% \text{ or } \frac{1}{3}$$

Then, estimate the company's variable expenses:

Sales × Variable expense ratio = Estimated amount of variable expenses

$$\$700,000 \times \frac{1}{3} = \$233,333$$

Next, put the contribution format income statement into an equation format to estimate the company's current level of fixed expenses:

Sales = Variable expenses + Fixed expenses + Net income

$$\$700,000 = \$233,333 + X + \$210,000$$

$$X = \$700,000 - \$233,333 - \$210,000$$

$$X = \$256,667$$

Use the equation approach to estimate the company's break-even point:

Sales = Variable expenses + Fixed expenses + Profits

$$X = \frac{1}{3}X + \$256,667 + \$0$$

$$\frac{2}{3}X = \$256,667$$

$$X = \$385,000$$

Finally, compute the company's margin of safety:

$$\text{Margin of safety} = (\text{Sales} - \text{Break-even sales}) \div \text{Sales}$$
$$= (\$700,000 - \$385,000) \div \$700,000$$
$$= 45\%$$

The margin of safety appears to be adequate, so if the other information about the company is favorable, a loan would seem to be justified.

Review Problem: CVP Relationships

Voltar Company manufactures and sells a telephone answering machine. The company's contribution format income statement for the most recent year is given below:

	Total	Per Unit	Percent of Sales
Sales (20,000 units)	$1,200,000	$60	100%
Less variable expenses	900,000	45	?%
Contribution margin	300,000	$15	?%
Less fixed expenses	240,000		
Net income	$ 60,000		

Management is anxious to improve the company's profit performance and has asked for several items of information.

Required:
1. Compute the company's CM ratio and variable expense ratio.
2. Compute the company's break-even point in both units and sales dollars. Use the equation method.
3. Assume that sales increase by $400,000 next year. If cost behavior patterns remain unchanged, by how much will the company's net income increase? Use the CM ratio to determine your answer.
4. Refer to original data. Assume that next year management wants the company to earn a minimum profit of $90,000. How many units will have to be sold to meet this target profit figure?
5. Refer to the original data. Compute the company's margin of safety in both dollar and percentage form.
6. a. Compute the company's degree of operating leverage at the present level of sales.
   b. Assume that through a more intense effort by the sales staff the company's sales increase by 8% next year. By what percentage would you expect net income to increase? Use the operating leverage concept to obtain your answer.
   c. Verify your answer to (b) by preparing a new income statement showing an 8% increase in sales.
7. In an effort to increase sales and profits, management is considering the use of a higher-quality speaker. The higher-quality speaker would increase variable costs by $3 per unit, but management could eliminate one quality inspector who is paid a salary of $30,000 per year. The sales manager estimates that the higher-quality speaker would increase annual sales by at least 20%.
   a. Assuming that changes are made as described above, prepare a projected income statement for next year. Show data on a total, per unit, and percentage basis.
   b. Compute the company's new break-even point in both units and dollars of sales. Use the contribution margin method.
   c. Would you recommend that the changes be made?

SOLUTION TO REVIEW PROBLEM
1. CM ratio:

$$\frac{\text{Contribution margin, }\$15}{\text{Selling price, }\$60} = 25\%$$

Variable expense ratio:

$$\frac{\text{Variable expense, }\$45}{\text{Selling price, }\$60} = 75\%$$

2.
$$\text{Sales} = \text{Variable expenses} + \text{Fixed expenses} + \text{Profits}$$
$$\$60Q = \$45Q + \$240,000 + \$0$$
$$\$15Q = \$240,000$$
$$Q = \$240,000 \div \$15 \text{ per unit}$$
$$Q = 16,000 \text{ units; or at } \$60 \text{ per unit, } \$960,000$$

Alternative solution:

$$X = 0.75X + \$240,000 + \$0$$
$$0.25X = \$240,000$$
$$X = \$240,000 \div 0.25$$
$$X = \$960,000; \text{ or at } \$60 \text{ per unit, } 16,000 \text{ units}$$

3.

Increase in sales	$400,000
Multiply by the CM ratio	× 25%
Expected increase in contribution margin	$100,000

Since the fixed expenses are not expected to change, net income will increase by the entire $100,000 increase in contribution margin computed above.

4. Equation method:

$$\text{Sales} = \text{Variable expenses} + \text{Fixed expenses} + \text{Profits}$$
$$\$60Q = \$45Q + \$240,000 + \$90,000$$
$$\$15Q = \$330,000$$
$$Q = \$330,000 \div \$15 \text{ per unit}$$
$$Q = 22,000 \text{ units}$$

Contribution margin method:

$$\frac{\text{Fixed expenses} + \text{Target profit}}{\text{Contribution margin per unit}} = \frac{\$240,000 + \$90,000}{\$15 \text{ per unit}} = 22,000 \text{ units}$$

5.

$$\text{Total sales} - \text{Break-even sales} = \text{Margin of safety in dollars}$$
$$\$1,200,000 - \$960,000 = \$240,000$$

$$\frac{\text{Margin of safety in dollars, } \$240,000}{\text{Total sales, } \$1,200,000} = 20\%$$

6. a.

$$\frac{\text{Contribution margin, } \$300,000}{\text{Net income, } \$60,000} = 5 \text{ (degree of operating leverage)}$$

b.

Expected increase in sales	8%
Degree of operating leverage	× 5
Expected increase in net income	40%

c. If sales increase by 8%, then 21,600 units (20,000 × 1.08 = 21,600) will be sold next year. The new income statement will be as follows:

	Total	Per Unit	Percent of Sales
Sales (21,600 units)	$1,296,000	$60	100%
Less variable expenses	972,000	45	75
Contribution margin	324,000	$15	25%
Less fixed expenses	240,000		
Net income	$ 84,000		

Thus, the $84,000 expected net income for next year represents a 40% increase over the $60,000 net income earned during the current year:

$$\frac{\$84,000 - \$60,000 = \$24,000}{\$60,000} = 40\% \text{ increase}$$

Note from the income statement above that the increase in sales from 20,000 to 21,600 units has resulted in increases in *both* total sales and total variable expenses. It is a common error to overlook the increase in variable expenses when preparing a projected income statement.

7. a. A 20% increase in sales would result in 24,000 units being sold next year: 20,000 units $\times$ 1.20 = 24,000 units.

	Total	Per Unit	Percent of Sales
Sales (24,000 units)	$1,440,000	$60	100%
Less variable expenses	1,152,000	48*	80
Contribution margin	288,000	$12	20%
Less fixed expenses	210,000†		
Net income	$ 78,000		

*$45 + $3 = $48; $48 ÷ $60 = 80%.
†$240,000 − $30,000 = $210,000.

Note that the change in per unit variable expenses results in a change in both the per unit contribution margin and the CM ratio.

b.
$$\frac{\text{Fixed expenses, \$210,000}}{\text{Contribution margin per unit, \$12}} = 17,500 \text{ units}$$

$$\frac{\text{Fixed expenses, \$210,000}}{\text{CM ratio, 20\%}} = \$1,050,000 \text{ break-even sales}$$

c. Yes, based on these data the changes should be made. The changes will increase the company's net income from the present $60,000 to $78,000 per year. Although the changes will also result in a higher break-even point (17,500 units as compared to the present 16,000 units), the company's margin of safety will actually be wider than before:

Total sales − Break-even sales = Margin of safety in dollars
$1,440,000 − $1,050,000 = $390,000

As shown in (5) above, the company's present margin of safety is only $240,000. Thus, several benefits will result from the proposed changes.

Glossary

Break-even point The level of sales at which profit is zero. The break-even point can also be defined as the point where total sales equals total expenses or as the point where total contribution margin equals total fixed expenses. (p. 232)

Contribution margin method A method of computing the break-even point in which the fixed expenses are divided by the contribution margin per unit. (p. 240)

Contribution margin ratio (CM ratio) The contribution margin as a percentage of total sales. (p. 233)

Cost-volume-profit (CVP) graph The relationships between revenues, costs, and level of activity in an organization presented in graphic form. (p. 241)

Degree of operating leverage A measure, at a given level of sales, of how a percentage change in sales volume will affect profits. The degree of operating leverage is computed by dividing contribution margin by net income. (p. 246)

Equation method A method of computing the break-even point that relies on the equation Sales = Variable expenses + Fixed expenses + Profits. (p. 238)

Incremental analysis An analytical approach that focuses only on those items of revenue, cost, and volume that will change as a result of a decision. (p. 235)

Margin of safety The excess of budgeted (or actual) sales over the break-even volume of sales. (p. 243)

Operating leverage A measure of how sensitive net income is to a given percentage change in sales. It is computed by dividing the contribution margin by net income. (p. 246)

Sales mix The relative proportions in which a company's products are sold. Sales mix is computed by expressing the sales of each product as a percentage of total sales. (p. 249)

Variable costing A method of determining unit product costs in which only the variable manufacturing costs are assigned to products and fixed manufacturing overhead costs are considered to be period expenses. (p. 252)

Questions

6–1   What is meant by a product's CM ratio? How is this ratio useful in planning business operations?

6–2   Often the most direct route to a business decision is to make an incremental analysis based on the information available. What is meant by an *incremental analysis?*

6–3   Company A's cost structure includes costs that are mostly variable, whereas Company B's cost structure includes costs that are mostly fixed. In a time of increasing sales, which company will tend to realize the most rapid increase in profits? Explain.

6–4   What is meant by the term *operating leverage?*

6–5   A 10% decrease in the selling price of a product will have the same impact on net income as a 10% increase in the variable expenses. Do you agree? Why or why not?

6–6   What is meant by the term *break-even point?*

6–7   Name three approaches to break-even analysis. Briefly explain how each approach works.

6–8   In response to a request from your immediate supervisor, you have prepared a CVP graph portraying the cost and revenue characteristics of your company's product and operations. Explain how the lines on the graph and the break-even point would change if (a) the selling price per unit decreased, (b) fixed costs increased throughout the entire range of activity portrayed on the graph, and (c) variable costs per unit increased.

6–9   Al's Auto Wash charges $4 to wash a car. The variable costs of washing a car are 15% of sales. Fixed expenses total $1,700 monthly. How many cars must be washed each month for Al to break even?

6–10   What is meant by the margin of safety?

6–11   What is meant by the term *sales mix?* What assumption is usually made concerning sales mix in CVP analysis?

6–12   Explain how a shift in the sales mix could result in both a higher break-even point and a lower net income.

6–13   How do absorption costing and variable costing differ in how they treat fixed manufacturing overhead costs?

Brief Exercises

BRIEF EXERCISE 6–1   Preparing a Contribution Margin Format Income Statement (LO1)
Whirly Corporation's most recent income statement is shown below:

	Total	Per Unit
Sales (10,000 units)	$350,000	$35.00
Less variable expenses	200,000	20.00
Contribution margin	150,000	$15.00
Less fixed expenses	135,000	
Net income	$ 15,000	

Required:

Prepare a new income statement under each of the following conditions (consider each case independently):

1. The sales volume increases by 100 units.
2. The sales volume decreases by 100 units.
3. The sales volume is 9,000 units.

BRIEF EXERCISE 6–2 Computing and Using the CM Ratio (LO2)

Last month when Holiday Creations, Inc., sold 50,000 units, total sales were $200,000, total variable expenses were $120,000, and total fixed expenses were $65,000.

Required:

1. What is the company's contribution margin (CM) ratio?
2. Estimate the change in the company's net income if it were to increase its total sales by $1,000.

BRIEF EXERCISE 6–3 Changes in Variable Costs, Fixed Costs, Selling Price, and Volume (LO3)

Data for Hermann Corporation are shown below:

	Per Unit	Percent of Sales
Sales price	$90	100%
Less variable expenses	63	70
Contribution margin	$27	30%

Fixed expenses are $30,000 per month and the company is selling 2,000 units per month.

Required:

1. The marketing manager argues that a $5,000 increase in the monthly advertising budget would increase monthly sales by $9,000. Should the advertising budget be increased?
2. Refer to the original data. Management is considering using higher-quality components that would increase the variable cost by $2 per unit. The marketing manager believes the higher-quality product would increase sales by 10% per month. Should the higher-quality components be used?

BRIEF EXERCISE 6–4 Compute the Break-Even Point (LO4)

Mauro Products has a single product, a woven basket whose selling price is $15 and whose variable cost is $12 per unit. The company's monthly fixed expenses are $4,200.

Required:

1. Solve for the company's break-even point in unit sales using the equation method.
2. Solve for the company's break-even point in sales dollars using the equation method and the CM ratio.
3. Solve for the company's break-even point in unit sales using the contribution margin method.
4. Solve for the company's break-even point in sales dollars using the contribution margin method and the CM ratio.

BRIEF EXERCISE 6–5 Prepare a Cost-Volume-Profit (CVP) Graph (LO5)

Karlik Enterprises has a single product whose selling price is $24 and whose variable cost is $18 per unit. The company's monthly fixed expense is $24,000.

Required:

1. Prepare a cost-volume-profit graph for the company up to a sales level of 8,000 units.
2. Estimate the company's break-even point in unit sales using your cost-volume-profit graph.

BRIEF EXERCISE 6–6 Compute the Level of Sales Required to Attain a Target Profit (LO6)

Lin Corporation has a single product whose selling price is $120 and whose variable cost is $80 per unit. The company's monthly fixed expense is $50,000.

Required:

1. Using the equation method, solve for the unit sales that are required to earn a target profit of $10,000.
2. Using the contribution margin approach, solve for the dollar sales that are required to earn a target profit of $15,000.

BRIEF EXERCISE 6–7   Compute the Margin of Safety (LO7)
Molander Corporation sells a sun umbrella used at resort hotels. Data concerning the next month's budget appear below:

Selling price	$ 30 per unit
Variable expense	$ 20 per unit
Fixed expense	$7,500 per month
Unit sales	1,000 units per month

Required:
1. Compute the company's margin of safety.
2. Compute the company's margin of safety as a percentage of its sales.

BRIEF EXERCISE 6–8   Compute and Use the Degree of Operating Leverage (LO8)
Engberg Company's most recent monthly income statement appears below:

	Amount	Percent of Sales
Sales	$80,000	100%
Less variable expenses	32,000	40
Contribution margin	48,000	60%
Less fixed expenses	38,000	
Net income	$10,000	

Required:
1. Compute the company's degree of operating leverage.
2. Using the degree of operating leverage, estimate the impact on net income of a 5% increase in sales.
3. Verify your estimate from part (2) above by constructing a new income statement for the company assuming a 5% increase in sales.

BRIEF EXERCISE 6–9   Compute the Break-Even Point for a Multi-product Company (LO9)
Lucido Products markets two computer games: Claimjumper and Makeover. A contribution margin income statement for a recent month for the two games appears below:

	Claimjumper	Makeover	Total
Sales	$30,000	$70,000	$100,000
Less variable expenses	20,000	50,000	70,000
Contribution margin	$10,000	$20,000	30,000
Less fixed expenses			24,000
Net income			$ 6,000

Required:
1. Compute the overall contribution margin (CM) ratio for the company.
2. Compute the overall break-even for the company in sales dollars.
3. Verify the overall break-even for the company by constructing an income statement showing the appropriate levels of sales for the two products.

Exercises

EXERCISE 6–1   Using a Contribution Margin Format Income Statement (LO1, LO3)
Miller Company's most recent income statement is shown below:

	Total	Per Unit
Sales (20,000 units)	$300,000	$15.00
Less variable expenses	180,000	9.00
Contribution margin	120,000	$ 6.00
Less fixed expenses	70,000	
Net income	$ 50,000	

Required:
Prepare a new income statement under each of the following conditions (consider each case independently):
1. The sales volume increases by 15%.
2. The selling price decreases by $1.50 per unit, and the sales volume increases by 25%.
3. The selling price increases by $1.50 per unit, fixed expenses increase by $20,000, and the sales volume decreases by 5%.
4. The selling price increases by 12%, variable expenses increase by 60 cents per unit, and the sales volume decreases by 10%.

EXERCISE 6–2   Break-Even and Target Profit Analysis (LO3, LO4, LO6)
Lindon Company is the exclusive distributor for an automotive product. The product sells for $40 per unit and has a CM ratio of 30%. The company's fixed expenses are $180,000 per year.

Required:
1. What are the variable expenses per unit?
2. Using the equation method:
   a. What is the break-even point in units and sales dollars?
   b. What sales level in units and in sales dollars is required to earn an annual profit of $60,000?
   c. Assume that by using a more efficient shipper, the company is able to reduce its variable expenses by $4 per unit. What is the company's new break-even point in units and sales dollars?
3. Repeat (2) above using the unit contribution method.

EXERCISE 6–3   Operating Leverage (LO1, LO8)
Magic Realm, Inc., has developed a new fantasy board game. The company sold 15,000 games last year at a selling price of $20 per game. Fixed costs associated with the game total $182,000 per year, and variable costs are $6 per game. Production of the game is entrusted to a printing contractor. Variable costs consist mostly of payments to this contractor.

Required:
1. Prepare an income statement for the game last year and compute the degree of operating leverage.
2. Management is confident that the company can sell 18,000 games next year (an increase of 3,000 games, or 20%, over last year). Compute:
   a. The expected percentage increase in net income for next year.
   b. The expected total dollar net income for next year. (Do not prepare an income statement; use the degree of operating leverage to compute your answer.)

EXERCISE 6–4   Break-Even Analysis and CVP Graphing (LO3, LO4, LO5)
The Hartford Symphony Guild is planning its annual dinner-dance. The dinner-dance committee has assembled the following expected costs for the event:

Dinner (per person)	$ 18
Favors and program (per person)	2
Band	2,800
Rental of ballroom	900
Professional entertainment during intermission ...	1,000
Tickets and advertising	1,300

The committee members would like to charge $35 per person for the evening's activities.

Required:

1. Compute the break-even point for the dinner-dance (in terms of the number of persons that must attend).
2. Assume that last year only 300 persons attended the dinner-dance. If the same number attend this year, what price per ticket must be charged in order to break even?
3. Refer to the original data ($35 ticket price per person). Prepare a CVP graph for the dinner-dance from a zero level of activity up to 700 tickets sold. Number of persons should be placed on the horizontal (X) axis, and dollars should be placed on the vertical (Y) axis.

EXERCISE 6–5 Break-Even Analysis, Target Profit Analysis, Margin of Safety, CM Ratio (LO2, LO4, LO6, LO7)

Menlo Company manufactures and sells a single product. The company's sales and expenses for last quarter follow:

	Total	Per Unit
Sales	$450,000	$30
Less variable expenses	180,000	12
Contribution margin	270,000	$18
Less fixed expenses	216,000	
Net income	$ 54,000	

Required:

1. What is the quarterly break-even point in units sold and in sales dollars?
2. Without resorting to computations, what is the total contribution margin at the break-even point?
3. How many units would have to be sold each quarter to earn a target profit of $90,000? Use the unit contribution method. Verify your answer by preparing a contribution income statement at the target level of sales.
4. Refer to the original data. Compute the company's margin of safety in both dollar and percentage terms.
5. What is the company's CM ratio? If sales increase by $50,000 per quarter and there is no change in fixed expenses, by how much would you expect quarterly net income to increase? (Do not prepare an income statement; use the CM ratio to compute your answer.)

EXERCISE 6–6 Break-Even and Target Profit Analysis (LO3, LO4, LO6)

Outback Outfitters manufactures and sells recreational equipment. One of the company's products, a small camp stove, sells for $50 per unit. Variable expenses are $32 per stove, and fixed expenses associated with the stove total $108,000 per month.

Required:

1. Compute the break-even point in number of stoves and in total sales dollars.
2. If the variable expenses per stove increase as a percentage of the selling price, will it result in a higher or a lower break-even point? Why? (Assume that the fixed expenses remain unchanged.)
3. At present, the company is selling 8,000 stoves per month. The sales manager is convinced that a 10% reduction in the selling price would result in a 25% increase in monthly sales of stoves. Prepare two contribution income statements, one under present operating conditions, and one as operations would appear after the proposed changes. Show both total and per unit data on your statements.
4. Refer to the data in (3) above. How many stoves would have to be sold at the new selling price to yield a minimum net income of $35,000 per month?

EXERCISE 6–7 Multiproduct Break-Even Analysis (LO1, LO9)

Olongapo Sports Corporation is the distributor in the Philippines of two premium golf balls—the Flight Dynamic and the Sure Shot. Monthly sales and the contribution margin ratios for the two products follow:

	Product		
	Flight Dynamic	Sure Shot	Total
Sales	P150,000	P250,000	P400,000
CM ratio	80%	36%	?

Fixed expenses total P183,750 per month. (The currency in the Philippines is the peso, which is denoted by P.)

Required:
1. Prepare an income statement for the company as a whole. Carry computations to one decimal place.
2. Compute the break-even point for the company based on the current sales mix.
3. If sales increase by P100,000 a month, by how much would you expect net income to increase? What are your assumptions?

EXERCISE 6–8   Interpretation of the CVP Graph (LO4, LO5)
A CVP graph such as the one shown below is a useful technique for showing relationships between costs, volume, and profits in an organization.

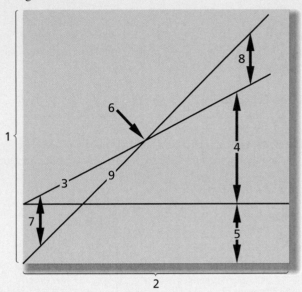

Required:
1. Identify the numbered components in the CVP graph.
2. State the effect of each of the following actions on line 3, line 9, and the break-even point. For line 3 and line 9, state whether the action will cause the line to:

> Remain unchanged.
> Shift upward.
> Shift downward.
> Have a steeper slope (i.e., rotate upward).
> Have a flatter slope (i.e., rotate downward).
> Shift upward *and* have a steeper slope.
> Shift upward *and* have a flatter slope.
> Shift downward *and* have a steeper slope.
> Shift downward *and* have a flatter slope.

In the case of the break-even point, state whether the action will cause the break-even point to:

> Remain unchanged.
> Increase.
> Decrease.
> Probably change, but the direction is uncertain.

Treat each case independently.

> *x. Example.*   Fixed costs are reduced by $5,000 per period.
>   *Answer* (see choices above): Line 3: Shift downward.
>   Line 9: Remain unchanged.
>   Break-even point: Decrease.

a. The unit selling price is increased from $18 to $20.
b. Unit variable costs are decreased from $12 to $10.
c. Fixed costs are increased by $3,000 per period.
d. Two thousand more units are sold during the period than were budgeted.

e. Due to paying salespersons a commission rather than a flat salary, fixed costs are reduced by $8,000 per period and unit variable costs are increased by $3.

f. Due to an increase in the cost of materials, both unit variable costs and the selling price are increased by $2.

g. Advertising costs are increased by $10,000 per period, resulting in a 10% increase in the number of units sold.

h. Due to automating an operation previously done by workers, fixed costs are increased by $12,000 per period and unit variable costs are reduced by $4.

Problems

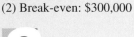

CHECK FIGURE
(2) Break-even: $300,000

PROBLEM 6–1   Basic CVP Analysis (LO1, LO2, LO3, LO4, LO6, LO8)

Feather Friends, Inc., makes a high-quality wooden birdhouse that sells for $20 per unit. Variable costs are $8 per unit, and fixed costs total $180,000 per year.

Required:

Answer the following independent questions:

1. What is the product's CM ratio?

2. Use the CM ratio to determine the break-even point in sales dollars.

3. Due to an increase in demand, the company estimates that sales will increase by $75,000 during the next year. By how much should net income increase (or net loss decrease) assuming that fixed costs do not change?

4. Assume that the operating results for last year were:

Sales	$400,000
Less variable expenses	160,000
Contribution margin	240,000
Less fixed expenses	180,000
Net income	$ 60,000

a. Compute the degree of operating leverage at the current level of sales.

b. The president expects sales to increase by 20% next year. By what percentage should net income increase?

5. Refer to the original data. Assume that the company sold 18,000 units last year. The sales manager is convinced that a 10% reduction in the selling price, combined with a $30,000 increase in advertising, would cause annual sales in units to increase by one-third. Prepare two contribution income statements, one showing the results of last year's operations and one showing the results of operations if these changes are made. Would you recommend that the company do as the sales manager suggests?

6. Refer to the original data. Assume again that the company sold 18,000 units last year. The president does not want to change the selling price. Instead, he wants to increase the sales commission by $1 per unit. He thinks that this move, combined with some increase in advertising, would increase annual sales by 25%. By how much could advertising be increased with profits remaining unchanged? Do not prepare an income statement; use the incremental analysis approach.

CHECK FIGURE
(3) Net loss: $6,000
(5a) Break even: 21,000 units

PROBLEM 6–2   Basic CVP Analysis; Cost Structure (LO2, LO3, LO4, LO6)

Due to erratic sales of its sole product—a high-capacity battery for laptop computers—PEM, Inc., has been experiencing difficulty for some time. The company's income statement for the most recent month is given below:

Sales (19,500 units × $30 per unit)	$585,000
Less variable expenses	409,500
Contribution margin	175,500
Less fixed expenses	180,000
Net loss	$ (4,500)

Required:

1. Compute the company's CM ratio and its break-even point in both units and dollars.
2. The president believes that a $16,000 increase in the monthly advertising budget, combined with an intensified effort by the sales staff, will result in an $80,000 increase in monthly sales. If the president is right, what will be the effect on the company's monthly net income or loss? (Use the incremental approach in preparing your answer.)
3. Refer to the original data. The sales manager is convinced that a 10% reduction in the selling price, combined with an increase of $60,000 in the monthly advertising budget, will cause unit sales to double. What will the new income statement look like if these changes are adopted?
4. Refer to the original data. The Marketing Department thinks that a fancy new package for the laptop computer battery would help sales. The new package would increase packaging costs by 75 cents per unit. Assuming no other changes, how many units would have to be sold each month to earn a profit of $9,750?
5. Refer to the original data. By automating certain operations, the company could reduce variable costs by $3 per unit. However, fixed costs would increase by $72,000 each month.
   a. Compute the new CM ratio and the new break-even point in both units and dollars.
   b. Assume that the company expects to sell 26,000 units next month. Prepare two income statements, one assuming that operations are not automated and one assuming that they are. (Show data on a per unit and percentage basis, as well as in total, for each alternative.)
   c. Would you recommend that the company automate its operations? Explain.

PROBLEM 6–3   Basic CVP Analysis; Graphing (LO2, LO3, LO4, LO5)

The Fashion Shoe Company operates a chain of women's shoe shops around the country. The shops carry many styles of shoes that are all sold at the same price. Sales personnel in the shops are paid a substantial commission on each pair of shoes sold (in addition to a small basic salary) in order to encourage them to be aggressive in their sales efforts.

The following cost and revenue data relate to Shop 48 and are typical of one of the company's many outlets:

CHECK FIGURE
(1) 12,500 pairs of shoes
(3) $6,000 loss

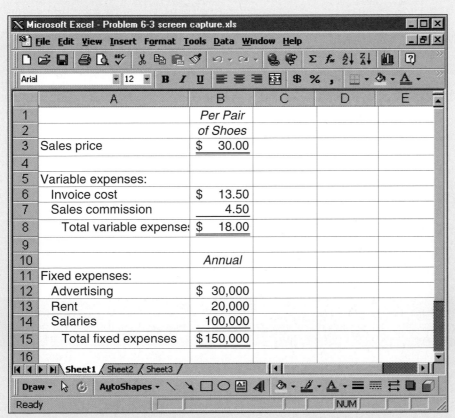

	Per Pair of Shoes
Sales price	$ 30.00
Variable expenses:	
Invoice cost	$ 13.50
Sales commission	4.50
Total variable expenses	$ 18.00
	Annual
Fixed expenses:	
Advertising	$ 30,000
Rent	20,000
Salaries	100,000
Total fixed expenses	$150,000

Required:

1. Calculate the annual break-even point in dollar sales and in unit sales for Shop 48.
2. Prepare a CVP graph showing cost and revenue data for Shop 48 from a zero level of activity up to 20,000 pairs of shoes sold each year. Clearly indicate the break-even point on the graph.

3. If 12,000 pairs of shoes are sold in a year, what would be Shop 48's net income or loss?
4. The company is considering paying the store manager of Shop 48 an incentive commission of 75 cents per pair of shoes (in addition to the salesperson's commission). If this change is made, what will be the new break-even point in dollar sales and in unit sales?
5. Refer to the original data. As an alternative to (4) above, the company is considering paying the store manager 50 cents commission on each pair of shoes sold in excess of the break-even point. If this change is made, what will be the shop's net income or loss if 15,000 pairs of shoes are sold?
6. Refer to the original data. The company is considering eliminating sales commissions entirely in its shops and increasing fixed salaries by $31,500 annually. If this change is made, what will be the new break-even point in dollar sales and in unit sales for Shop 48? Would you recommend that the change be made? Explain.

CHECK FIGURE
(a) Case 2 Variable
    expenses: $60,000
(b) Case 4 Fixed expenses:
    $185,000

PROBLEM 6–4   Multiproduct Break-Even Analysis (LO1, LO9)
Fill in the missing amounts in each of the eight case situations below. Each case is independent of the others. (Hint: One way to find the missing amounts would be to prepare a contribution income statement for each case, enter the known data, and then compute the missing items.)
a. Assume that only one product is being sold in each of the four following case situations:

Case	Units Sold	Sales	Variable Expenses	Contribution Margin per Unit	Fixed Expenses	Net Income (Loss)
1	15,000	$180,000	$120,000	$?	$ 50,000	$?
2	?	100,000	?	10	32,000	8,000
3	10,000	?	70,000	13	?	12,000
4	6,000	300,000	?	?	100,000	(10,000)

b. Assume that more than one product is being sold in each of the four following case situations:

Case	Sales	Variable Expenses	Average Contribution Margin (percent)	Fixed Expenses	Net Income (Loss)
1	$500,000	$?	20	$?	$ 7,000
2	400,000	260,000	?	100,000	?
3	?	?	60	130,000	20,000
4	600,000	420,000	?	?	(5,000)

CHECK FIGURE
(2) Break-even: B864,000

PROBLEM 6–5   Sales Mix; Multiproduct Break-Even Analysis (LO1, LO4, LO9)
Gold Star Rice, Ltd., of Thailand exports Thai rice throughout Asia. The company grows three varieties of rice—Fragrant, White, and Loonzain. (The currency in Thailand is the baht, which is denoted by B.) Budgeted sales by product and in total for the coming month are shown below:

Product								
	White		Fragrant		Loonzain		Total	
Percentage of total sales ..	20%		52%		28%		100%	
Sales	B150,000	100%	B390,000	100%	B210,000	100%	B750,000	100%
Less variable expenses ...	108,000	72	78,000	20	84,000	40	270,000	36
Contribution margin	B 42,000	28%	B312,000	80%	B126,000	60%	480,000	64%
Less fixed expenses							449,280	
Net income							B 30,720	

$$\text{Break-even sales:} \quad \frac{\text{Fixed expenses, B449,280}}{\text{CM ratio, 0.64}} = \text{B702,000}$$

As shown by these data, net income is budgeted at B30,720 for the month and break-even sales at B702,000.

Assume that actual sales for the month total B750,000 as planned. Actual sales by product are: White, B300,000; Fragrant, B180,000; and Loonzain, B270,000.

Required:

1. Prepare a contribution income statement for the month based on actual sales data. Present the income statement in the format shown above.
2. Compute the break-even sales for the month based on your actual data.
3. Considering the fact that the company met its B750,000 sales budget for the month, the president is shocked at the results shown on your income statement in (1) above. Prepare a brief memo for the president explaining why both the operating results and break-even sales are different from what was budgeted.

PROBLEM 6–6 Break-Even and Target Profit Analysis (LO4, LO6)

The Shirt Works sells a large variety of tee shirts and sweatshirts. Steve Hooper, the owner, is thinking of expanding his sales by hiring local high school students, on a commission basis, to sell sweatshirts bearing the name and mascot of the local high school.

These sweatshirts would have to be ordered from the manufacturer six weeks in advance, and they could not be returned because of the unique printing required. The sweatshirts would cost Mr. Hooper $8 each with a minimum order of 75 sweatshirts. Any additional sweatshirts would have to be ordered in increments of 75.

Since Mr. Hooper's plan would not require any additional facilities, the only costs associated with the project would be the costs of the sweatshirts and the costs of the sales commissions. The selling price of the sweatshirts would be $13.50 each. Mr. Hooper would pay the students a commission of $1.50 for each shirt sold.

CHECK FIGURE
(1) 300 sweatshirts

Required:

1. To make the project worthwhile, Mr. Hooper would require a $1,200 profit for the first three months of the venture. What level of sales in units and in dollars would be required to reach this target net income? Show all computations.
2. Assume that the venture is undertaken and an order is placed for 75 sweatshirts. What would be Mr. Hooper's break-even point in units and in sales dollars? Show computations and explain the reasoning behind your answer.

PROBLEM 6–7 Changes in Fixed and Variable Costs; Break-Even and Target Profit Analysis (LO3, LO4, LO6)

Neptune Company produces toys and other items for use in beach and resort areas. A small, inflatable toy has come onto the market that the company is anxious to produce and sell. Enough capacity exists in the company's plant to produce 16,000 units of the toy each month. Variable costs to manufacture and sell one unit would be $1.25, and fixed costs associated with the toy would total $35,000 per month.

The company's Marketing Department predicts that demand for the new toy will exceed the 16,000 units that the company is able to produce. Additional manufacturing space can be rented from another company at a fixed cost of $1,000 per month. Variable costs in the rented facility would total $1.40 per unit, due to somewhat less efficient operations than in the main plant. The new toy will sell for $3 per unit.

CHECK FIGURE
(1) Break-even:
21,000 units

Required:

1. Compute the monthly break-even point for the new toy in units and in total dollar sales. Show all computations in good form.
2. How many units must be sold each month to make a monthly profit of $12,000?
3. If the sales manager receives a bonus of 10 cents for each unit sold in excess of the break-even point, how many units must be sold each month to earn a return of 25% on the monthly investment in fixed costs?

PROBLEM 6–8 Sales Mix; Break-Even Analysis; Margin of Safety (LO1, LO4, LO7, LO9)

Island Novelties, Inc., of Palau makes two products, Hawaiian Fantasy and Tahitian Joy. Present revenue, cost, and sales data on the two products follow:

CHECK FIGURE
(1b) Break-even: $732,000
(2b) Margin of safety: 22%

	Hawaiian Fantasy	Tahitian Joy
Selling price per unit	$ 15	$ 100
Variable expenses per unit	9	20
Number of units sold annually	20,000	5,000

Fixed expenses total $475,800 per year. The Republic of Palau uses the U.S. dollar as its currency.

Required:

1. Assuming the sales mix given above, do the following:
   a. Prepare a contribution income statement as in Exhibit 6–3 showing both dollar and percent columns for each product and for the company as a whole.
   b. Compute the break-even point in dollars for the company as a whole and the margin of safety in both dollars and percent.
2. Another product, Samoan Delight, has just come onto the market. Assume that the company could sell 10,000 units at $45 each. The variable expenses would be $36 each. The company's fixed expenses would not change.
   a. Prepare another contribution income statement, including sales of Samoan Delight (sales of the other two products would not change). Carry percentage computations to one decimal place.
   b. Compute the company's new break-even point in dollars and the new margin of safety in both dollars and percent.
3. The president of the company examines your figures and says, "There's something strange here. Our fixed costs haven't changed and you show greater total contribution margin if we add the new product, but you also show our break-even point going up. With greater contribution margin, the break-even point should go down, not up. You've made a mistake somewhere." Explain to the president what has happened.

CHECK FIGURE
(1) Break even: 2,500 pairs
(5a) Leverage: 6

PROBLEM 6–9   Graphing; Incremental Analysis; Operating Leverage (LO3, LO4, LO5, LO6, LO8)
Angie Silva has recently opened The Sandal Shop in Brisbane, Australia, a store that specializes in fashionable sandals. Angie has just received a degree in business and she is anxious to apply the principles she has learned to her business. In time, she hopes to open a chain of sandal shops. As a first step, she has prepared the following analysis for her new store:

Sales price per pair of sandals	$40
Variable expenses per pair of sandals	16
Contribution margin per pair of sandals ...	$24
Fixed expenses per year:	
Building rental	$15,000
Equipment depreciation	7,000
Selling	20,000
Administrative	18,000
Total fixed expenses	$60,000

Required:

1. How many pairs of sandals must be sold each year to break even? What does this represent in total dollar sales?
2. Prepare a CVP graph for the store from a zero level of activity up to 5,000 pairs of sandals sold each year. Indicate the break-even point on your graph.
3. Angie has decided that she must earn at least $18,000 the first year to justify her time and effort. How many pairs of sandals must be sold to reach this target profit?
4. Angie now has two salespersons working in the store—one full time and one part time. It will cost her an additional $8,000 per year to convert the part-time position to a full-time position. Angie believes that the change would bring in an additional $25,000 in sales each year. Should she convert the position? Use the incremental approach (do not prepare an income statement).
5. Refer to the original data. During the first year, the store sold only 3,000 pairs of sandals and reported the following operating results:

Sales (3,000 pair)	$120,000
Less variable expenses	48,000
Contribution margin	72,000
Less fixed expenses	60,000
Net income	$ 12,000

a. What is the store's degree of operating leverage?
b. Angie is confident that with a more intense sales effort and with a more creative advertising program she can increase sales by 50% next year. What would be the expected percentage increase in net income? Use the degree of operating leverage to compute your answer.

Building Your Skills

ANALYTICAL THINKING (LO3, LO4, LO9)

Cheryl Montoya picked up the phone and called her boss, Wes Chan, the vice president of marketing at Piedmont Fasteners Corporation: "Wes, I'm not sure how to go about answering the questions that came up at the meeting with the president yesterday."

"What's the problem?"

"The president wanted to know each product's break-even, but I am having trouble figuring them out."

"I'm sure you can handle it, Cheryl. And, by the way, I need your analysis on my desk tomorrow morning at 8:00 sharp in time for the follow-up meeting at 9:00."

Piedmont Fasteners Corporation makes three different clothing fasteners in its manufacturing facility in North Carolina. Data concerning these products appear below:

	Velcro	Metal	Nylon
Normal annual sales volume	100,000	200,000	400,000
Unit selling price	$1.65	$1.50	$0.85
Variable cost per unit	$1.25	$0.70	$0.25

Total fixed expenses are $400,000 per year.

All three products are sold in highly competitive markets, so the company is unable to raise its prices without losing unacceptable numbers of customers.

The company has an extremely effective just-in-time manufacturing system, so there are no beginning or ending work in process or finished goods inventories.

Required:
1. What is the company's overall break-even in total sales dollars?
2. Of the total fixed costs of $400,000, $20,000 could be avoided if the Velcro product were dropped, $80,000 if the Metal product were dropped, and $60,000 if the Nylon product were dropped. The remaining fixed costs of $240,000 consist of common fixed costs such as administrative salaries and rent on the factory building that could be avoided only by going out of business entirely.
   a. What is the break-even quantity of each product?
   b. If the company sells exactly the break-even quantity of each product, what will be the overall profit of the company?

COMMUNICATING IN PRACTICE (LO3, LO4, LO6, LO8)

Pittman Company is a small but growing manufacturer of telecommunications equipment. The company has no sales force of its own; rather, it relies completely on independent sales agents to market its products. These agents are paid a commission of 15% of selling price for all items sold.

Barbara Cheney, Pittman's controller, has just prepared the company's budgeted income statement for next year. The statement follows:

CHECK FIGURE
(1a) Break-even:
$12,000,000

PITTMAN COMPANY
Budgeted Income Statement
For the Year Ended December 31

Sales		$16,000,000
Manufacturing costs:		
Variable	$7,200,000	
Fixed overhead	2,340,000	9,540,000
Gross margin		6,460,000
Selling and administrative costs:		
Commissions to agents	2,400,000	
Fixed marketing costs	120,000*	
Fixed administrative costs	1,800,000	4,320,000
Net operating income		2,140,000
Less fixed interest cost		540,000
Income before income taxes		1,600,000
Less income taxes (30%)		480,000
Net income		$ 1,120,000

*Primarily depreciation on storage facilities.

As Barbara handed the statement to Karl Vecci, Pittman's president, she commented, "I went ahead and used the agents' 15% commission rate in completing these statements, but we've just learned that they refuse to handle our products next year unless we increase the commission rate to 20%."

"That's the last straw," Karl replied angrily. "Those agents have been demanding more and more, and this time they've gone too far. How can they possibly defend a 20% commission rate?"

"They claim that after paying for advertising, travel, and the other costs of promotion, there's nothing left over for profit," replied Barbara.

"I say it's just plain robbery," retorted Karl. "And I also say it's time we dumped those guys and got our own sales force. Can you get your people to work up some cost figures for us to look at?"

"We've already worked them up," said Barbara. "Several companies we know about pay a 7.5% commission to their own salespeople, along with a small salary. Of course, we would have to handle all promotion costs, too. We figure our fixed costs would increase by $2,400,000 per year, but that would be more than offset by the $3,200,000 (20% × $16,000,000) that we would avoid on agents' commissions."

The breakdown of the $2,400,000 cost figure follows:

Salaries:	
Sales manager	$ 100,000
Salespersons	600,000
Travel and entertainment	400,000
Advertising	1,300,000
Total	$2,400,000

"Super," replied Karl. "And I note that the $2,400,000 is just what we're paying the agents under the old 15% commission rate."

"It's even better than that," explained Barbara. "We can actually save $75,000 a year because that's what we're having to pay the auditing firm now to check out the agents' reports. So our overall administrative costs would be less."

"Pull all of these numbers together and we'll show them to the executive committee tomorrow," said Karl. "With the approval of the committee, we can move on the matter immediately."

Required:
1. Compute Pittman Company's break-even point in sales dollars for next year assuming:
   a. That the agents' commission rate remains unchanged at 15%.
   b. That the agents' commission rate is increased to 20%.
   c. That the company employs its own sales force.

2. Assume that Pittman Company decides to continue selling through agents and pays the 20% commission rate. Determine the volume of sales that would be required to generate the same net income as contained in the budgeted income statement for next year.

3. Determine the volume of sales at which net income would be equal regardless of whether Pittman Company sells through agents (at a 20% commission rate) or employs its own sales force.

4. Compute the degree of operating leverage that the company would expect to have on December 31 at the end of next year assuming:
   a. That the agents' commission rate remains unchanged at 15%.
   b. That the agents' commission rate is increased to 20%.
   c. That the company employs its own sales force.
   Use income *before* income taxes in your operating leverage computation.

5. Based on the data in (1) through (4) above, draft a memorandum to Barbara Cheney that sets forth your recommendation as to whether the company should continue to use sales agents (at a 20% commission rate) or employ its own sales force. Give reasons for your recommendation.

(CMA, adapted)

CHECK FIGURE
(2) 15,820 patient-days

SKILLS CHALLENGER (LO4, LO6)

Wymont Hospital operates a general hospital with separate departments such as Pediatrics, Maternity, and Surgery. Wymont Hospital charges each separate department for services to its patients such as meals and laundry and for administrative services such as billing and collections. Space and bed charges are fixed for the year.

Last year, the Pediatrics Department at Wymont Hospital charged its patients an average of $65 per day, had a capacity of 80 beds, operated 24 hours per day for 365 days, and had total revenue of $1,138,800.

Expenses charged by the hospital to the Pediatrics Department for the year were as follows:

	Basis for Allocation	
	Patient-Days (variable)	Bed Capacity (fixed)
Dietary	$ 42,952	
Janitorial		$ 12,800
Laundry	28,000	
Laboratory	47,800	
Pharmacy	33,800	
Repairs and maintenance	5,200	7,140
General administrative services		131,760
Rent		275,320
Billings and collections	87,000	
Other	18,048	25,980
	$262,800	$453,000

The only personnel directly employed by the Pediatrics Department are supervising nurses, nurses, and aides. The hospital has minimum personnel requirements for Pediatrics based on total annual patient-days in Pediatrics. Hospital requirements, beginning at the minimum expected level of operation, follow:

Annual Patient-Days	Aides	Nurses	Supervising Nurses
10,000–14,000	21	11	4
14,001–17,000	22	12	4
17,001–23,725	22	13	4
23,726–25,550	25	14	5
25,551–27,375	26	14	5
27,376–29,200	29	16	6

These staffing levels represent full-time equivalents, and it should be assumed that the Pediatrics Department always employs only the minimum number of required full-time equivalent personnel.

Annual salaries for each class of employee are: supervising nurses, $18,000; nurses, $13,000; and aides, $5,000. Salary expense for last year was $72,000, $169,000, and $110,000 for supervising nurses, nurses, and aides, respectively.

Required:
1. Compute the following:
   a. The number of patient-days in the Pediatrics Department for last year. (Each day a patient is in the hospital is known as a *patient-day.*)
   b. The variable cost per patient-day for last year.
   c. The total fixed costs, including both allocated fixed costs and personnel costs, in the Pediatrics Department for each level of operation shown on page 271 (i.e., total fixed costs at the 10,000–14,000 patient-day level of operation, total fixed costs at the 14,001–17,000 patient-day level of operation, etc.).
2. Using the data computed in (1) above and any other data as needed, compute the *minimum* number of patient-days required for the Pediatrics Department to break even. You may assume that variable and fixed cost behavior and that revenue per patient-day will remain unchanged in the future.
3. Determine the minimum number of patient-days required for the Pediatrics Department to earn an annual "profit" of $200,000.

(CPA, adapted)

TAKING IT TO THE NET
As you know, the World Wide Web is a medium that is constantly evolving. Sites come and go and change without notice. To enable periodic update of site addresses, this problem has been posted to the textbook website (www.mhhe.com/folk1e). After accessing the site, enter the Student Center and select this chapter. Select and complete the Taking It to the Net problem.

TEAMWORK IN ACTION (LO1)
The cost structure of the airline industry can serve as the basis for a discussion of a number of different cost concepts. Airlines also provide an excellent illustration of the concept of operating leverage, the sensitivity of a firm's operating profits to changes in demand, and the opportunities and risks presented by such a cost structure. Airline profits and stock prices are among some of the most volatile on Wall Street. A recent study of the U.S. airline industry disclosed the following operating cost categories and their percentage of total operating cost:*

Uniform System of Accounts Required by the Department of Transportation	Mean Percentage of Operating Cost, 1981–85
Fuel and oil	24.3%
Flying operations labor (flight crews—pilots, copilots, navigators, and flight engineers)	8.6
Passenger service labor (flight attendants)	4.6
Aircraft traffic and servicing labor (personnel servicing aircraft and handling passengers at gates, baggage, and cargo)	8.9
Promotions and sales labor (reservations and sales agents, advertising and publicity)	9.0
Maintenance labor (maintenance of flight equipment and ground property and equipment)	7.0
Maintenance materials and overhead	2.1
Ground property and equipment (landing fees, and rental expenses and depreciation for ground property and equipment)	12.5
Flight equipment (rental expenses and depreciation on aircraft frames and engines)	8.4
General overhead (administrative personnel, utilities, insurance, communications, etc.)	14.6
Total	100.0%

*R. D. Banker and H. H. Johnson, "An Empirical Study of Cost Drivers in the U.S. Airline Industry," *The Accounting Review,* July 1993, pp. 576–601.

Required:

1. Your team should discuss and then write up a brief description of the objectives of airline cost accounting systems. All team members should agree with and understand the description.

2. Each member of the team should present an answer to one of the following questions to the other team members, who should confirm or correct the answer.

   a. For each of the accounts listed above, indicate whether the costs in the account are mainly fixed or variable with respect to the number of flights flown—irrespective of how many passengers are carried on the flights. For purposes of thinking about this assignment, assume that all flights always fly nearly full and the airline already operates out of the airport. Based on this analysis, estimate the percentage of costs that are fixed with respect to the number of flights flown.

   b. For each of the accounts listed above, indicate whether the costs in the account are mainly fixed or variable with respect to the number of passengers carried on a particular scheduled flight. Based on this analysis, estimate the percentage of costs that are fixed with respect to the number of passengers carried on a particular scheduled flight.

3. The team should discuss and then write up brief answers to the questions listed below. All team members should agree with and understand the answers.

   a. What conclusions do you draw about the nature of fixed and variable costs based on your analysis in question 2 above?

   b. Why are profits more sensitive (more variable) to changes in demand when the cost structure contains a high proportion of fixed costs? What is probably a more effective way to improve the profitability of an airline—increase the number of flights or increase the average number of passengers on flights the airline already flies?

Chapter Seven

Profit Planning

Decision Feature Survival 101

Budgets are perhaps even more important in small service organizations than they are in large manufacturing companies. The accounting firm of Carter, Young, Langford, and Roach in Nashville, Tennessee, is typical of many small firms that must keep a constant eye on their cash flows. Because of high fixed costs, small changes in revenues or a client delinquent in paying bills can have potentially disastrous effects on the firm's cash flows.

Lucy Carter, the managing partner of the firm, uses a formal budget for keeping cash flow on an even keel. She says, "I don't know how small CPA firms can survive without a budget in this business climate." The formal budget is based on estimated client billings (i.e., revenues) for the coming year. The annual budget is broken down into months, and each month the budget is compared to the actual financial results of the month. If the actuals fall short of the budget, adjustments may be necessary. For example, because of shortfalls in billings in one year, the firm reduced its staff by three staff accountants and added a part-time staff accountant. Because of the critical nature of client billings, Carter's staff prepares daily reports on billings that indicate how well actual billings compare to the budgeted billings on a month-to-date basis.

The firm provides accounting, auditing, tax, and consulting services to clients in the healthcare industry. The firm's website (www.cylr.com) includes detailed descriptions of the services offered, provides background information about each of the firm's six principals, lists articles recently published, and describes employment opportunities.

Sources: Carter, Young, Langford & Roach website, July 2000, and Gene R. Barrett, "How Small CPA Firms Manage Their Cash," *Journal of Accountancy*, August 1993, pp. 56–59. Copyright © 1993 from the *Journal of Accountancy* by the American Institute of Certified Public Accountants, Inc. Opinions of the authors are their own and do not necessarily reflect policies of the AICPA. Reprinted with permission.

Learning Objectives
After studying Chapter 7, you should be able to:

LO1 Understand why organizations budget and the processes they use to create budgets.

LO2 Prepare a sales budget, including a schedule of expected cash receipts.

LO3 Prepare a production budget.

LO4 Prepare a direct materials budget, including a schedule of expected cash disbursements for purchases of materials.

LO5 Prepare a direct labor budget.

LO6 Prepare a manufacturing overhead budget.

LO7 Prepare a selling and administrative expense budget.

LO8 Prepare a cash budget.

LO9 Prepare a budgeted income statement.

LO10 Prepare a budgeted balance sheet.

In this chapter, we focus on the steps taken by businesses to achieve their desired levels of profits—a process that is generally called *profit planning*. We shall see that profit planning is accomplished through the preparation of a number of budgets, which, when brought together, form an integrated business plan known as the *master budget*. The master budget is an essential management tool that communicates management's plans throughout the organization, allocates resources, and coordinates activities.

The Basic Framework of Budgeting

Learning Objective 1
Understand why organizations budget and the processes they use to create budgets.

A **budget** is a detailed plan for acquiring and using financial and other resources over a specified time period. It represents a plan for the future expressed in formal quantitative terms. The act of preparing a budget is called *budgeting*. The use of budgets to control a firm's activities is known as *budgetary control*.

The **master budget** is a summary of a company's plans that sets specific targets for sales, production, distribution, and financing activities. It generally culminates in a cash budget, a budgeted income statement, and a budgeted balance sheet. In short, it represents a comprehensive expression of management's plans for the future and how these plans are to be accomplished.

Personal Budgets

Nearly everyone budgets to some extent, even though many of the people who use budgets do not recognize what they are doing as budgeting. For example, most people make estimates of their income and plan expenditures for food, clothing, housing, and so on. As a result of this planning, people restrict their spending to some predetermined, allowable amount. While they may not be conscious of the fact, these people clearly go through a budgeting process. Income is estimated, expenditures are planned, and spending is restricted in accordance with the plan. Individuals also use budgets to forecast their future financial condition for purposes such as purchasing a home, financing college education, or setting aside funds for retirement. These budgets may exist only in the mind of the individual, but they are budgets nevertheless.

The budgets of a business firm serve much the same functions as the budgets prepared informally by individuals. Business budgets tend to be more detailed and to involve more work, but they are similar to the budgets prepared by individuals in most other respects. Like personal budgets, they assist in planning and controlling expenditures; they also assist in predicting operating results and financial condition in future periods.

Difference between Planning and Control

Concept 7–1

The terms *planning* and *control* are often confused, and occasionally these terms are used in such a way as to suggest that they mean the same thing. Actually, planning and control are two quite distinct concepts. **Planning** involves developing objectives and preparing various budgets to achieve these objectives. **Control** involves the steps taken by management to increase the likelihood that the objectives set down at the planning stage are attained and that all parts of the organization function in a manner consistent with organizational policies. To be completely effective, a good budgeting system must provide for *both* planning and control. Good planning without effective control is time wasted.

Advantages of Budgeting

Companies realize many benefits from a budgeting program. Among these benefits are the following:

1. Budgets provide a means of *communicating* management's plans throughout the organization.
2. Budgets force managers to *think about* and plan for the future. In the absence of the necessity to prepare a budget, too many managers would spend all of their time dealing with daily emergencies.
3. The budgeting process provides a means of *allocating resources* to those parts of the organization where they can be used most effectively.
4. The budgeting process can uncover potential *bottlenecks* before they occur.
5. Budgets *coordinate* the activities of the entire organization by *integrating* the plans of the various parts. Budgeting helps to ensure that everyone in the organization is pulling in the same direction.
6. Budgets define goals and objectives that can serve as *benchmarks* for evaluating subsequent performance.

A Looming Financial Crisis

The Repertory Theatre of St. Louis is a not-for-profit professional theater that is supported by contributions from donors and by ticket sales. Financially, the theater appeared to be doing well. However, a five-year budget revealed that within a few years, expenses would exceed revenues and the theater would be facing a financial crisis. Realistically, additional contributions from donors would not fill the gap. Cutting costs would not work because of the theater's already lean operations; cutting costs even more would jeopardize the quality of the theater's productions. Raising ticket prices was ruled out due to competitive pressures and to the belief that this would be unpopular with many donors. The solution was to build a second mainstage performing space that would allow the theater to put on more performances and thereby sell more tickets. By developing a long-range budget, the management of The Repertory Theatre of St. Louis was able to identify in advance a looming financial crisis and to develop a solution that would avert the crisis in time.

Source: Lawrence P. Carr, ed., "The Repertory Theatre of St. Louis (B): Strategic Budgeting," *Cases from Management Accounting Practice: Volumes 10 and 11,* Institute of Management Accountants, Montvale, NJ, 1997. Reprinted with permission from *Management Accounting.*

Responsibility Accounting

Most of what we say in this chapter and in the next three chapters centers on the concept of *responsibility accounting.* The basic idea behind **responsibility accounting** is that a manager should be held responsible for those items—and *only* those items—that the manager can actually control to a significant extent. Each line item (i.e., revenue or cost) in the budget is made the responsibility of a manager, and that manager is held responsible for subsequent deviations between budgeted goals and actual results. In effect, responsibility accounting *personalizes* accounting information by looking at costs from a *personal control* standpoint. This concept is central to any effective profit planning and control system. Someone must be held responsible for each cost or else no one will be responsible, and the cost will inevitably grow out of control.

Being held responsible for costs does not mean that the manager is penalized if the actual results do not measure up to the budgeted goals. However, the manager should take the initiative to correct any unfavorable discrepancies, should understand the source of significant favorable or unfavorable discrepancies, and should be prepared to explain the reasons for discrepancies to higher management. The point of an effective responsibility system is to make sure that nothing "falls through the cracks," that the organization reacts quickly and appropriately to deviations from its plans, and that the organization learns from the feedback it gets by comparing budgeted goals to actual results. The point is *not* to penalize individuals for missing targets.

Choosing a Budget Period

Operating budgets ordinarily cover the company's fiscal year. Many companies divide their budget year into four quarters. The first quarter is then subdivided into months, and monthly budgets are developed. The last three quarters are carried in the budget at quarterly totals only. As the year progresses, the figures for the second quarter are broken down into monthly amounts, then the third-quarter figures are broken down, and so forth. This approach has the advantage of requiring periodic review and reappraisal of budget data throughout the year.

In this chapter, we will focus on one-year operating budgets. However, using basically the same techniques, operating budgets can be prepared for periods that extend over many years. It may be difficult to accurately forecast sales and required data much beyond a year, but even rough estimates can be invaluable in uncovering potential problems and opportunities that would otherwise be overlooked. For example, as described in the box on page 277, as a result of preparing a five-year budget, management at The Repertory Theatre of St. Louis was able to identify an impending financial crisis.

in business | *today* Selling What We Make

Budgeting plays an important role in coordinating activities in large organizations. Jerome York, the chief financial officer at IBM, discovered at one budget meeting that "the division that makes AS/400 workstations planned to churn out 10,000 more machines than the marketing division was promising to sell. He asked nicely that the two divisions agree on how many they would sell for the sake of consistency (and to cut down on the inventory problem). The rival executives said it couldn't be done. Mr. York got tougher, saying it could. Ultimately, it was."

Source: Laurie Hays, "Blue Blood: IBM's Finance Chief, Ax in Hand, Scours Empire for Costs to Cut," *The Wall Street Journal,* January 26, 1994, pp. A1, A6.

The Self-Imposed Budget

The success of a budget program will be determined in large part by the way in which the budget is developed. In the most successful budget programs, managers with cost control responsibilities actively participate in preparing their own budgets. This is in contrast to the approach in which budgets are imposed from above. The participative approach to preparing budgets is particularly important if the budget is to be used to control and evaluate a manager's performance. If a budget is imposed on a manager from above, it will probably generate resentment and ill will rather than cooperation and commitment.

This budgeting approach in which managers prepare their own budget estimates—called a *self-imposed budget*—is generally considered to be the most effective method of budget preparation. A **self-imposed budget** or **participative budget** is a budget that is prepared with the full cooperation and participation of managers at all levels. Exhibit 7–1 illustrates this approach to budget preparation.

A number of advantages are commonly cited for such self-imposed budgets:

1. Individuals at all levels of the organization are recognized as members of the team whose views and judgments are valued by top management.
2. Budget estimates prepared by front-line managers can be more accurate and reliable than estimates prepared by top managers who are more remote from day-to-day activities and who have less intimate knowledge of markets and operating conditions.
3. Motivation is generally higher when an individual participates in setting his or her own goals than when management imposes the goals. Self-imposed budgets create commitment.

4. If a manager is not able to meet a budget that has been imposed from above, the manager can always say that the budget was unreasonable or unrealistic to start with, and therefore was impossible to meet. With a self-imposed budget, this excuse is not available.

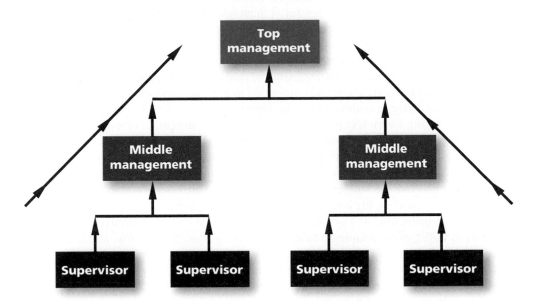

Exhibit 7–1
The Initial Flow of Budget Data in a Participative Budgeting System

The initial flow of budget data in a participative system is from lower levels of responsibility to higher levels of responsibility. Each person with responsibility for cost control will prepare his or her own budget estimates and submit them to the next higher level of management. These estimates are reviewed and consolidated as they move upward in the organization.

Once self-imposed budgets are prepared, are they subject to any kind of review? The answer is yes. Budget estimates prepared by lower-level managers cannot necessarily be accepted without question by higher levels of management. If no system of checks and balances is present, self-imposed budgets may be too loose and allow too much "budgetary slack." The result will be inefficiency and waste. Therefore, before budgets are accepted, they must be carefully reviewed by immediate superiors. If changes from the original budget seem desirable, the items in question are discussed and modified as necessary.

In essence, all levels of an organization should work together to produce the budget. Since top management is generally unfamiliar with detailed, day-to-day operations, it should rely on subordinates to provide detailed budget data. On the other hand, top management has a perspective on the company as a whole that is also vital. Each level of responsibility in an organization should contribute in the way that it best can in a *cooperative* effort to develop an integrated budget.

We have described an ideal budgetary process that involves self-imposed budgets prepared by the managers who are directly responsible for revenues and costs. Most companies deviate from this ideal. Typically, top managers initiate the budget process by issuing broad guidelines in terms of overall target profits or sales. Lower-level managers are directed to prepare budgets that meet those targets. The difficulty is that the targets set by top managers may be unrealistically high or may allow too much slack. If the targets are too high and employees know they are unrealistic, motivation will suffer. If the targets allow too much slack, waste will occur. And unfortunately top managers are often not in a position to know whether the targets they have set are appropriate. Admittedly, however, a pure self-imposed budgeting system may lack sufficient strategic direction and lower-level managers may be tempted to build into their budgets a great deal of budgetary slack. Nevertheless, because of the motivational advantages of self-imposed budgets, top managers should be cautious about setting inflexible targets.

The Matter of Human Relations

The success of a budget program also depends on: (1) the degree to which top management accepts the budget program as a vital part of the company's activities, and (2) the way in which top management uses budgeted data.

If a budget program is to be successful, it must have the complete acceptance and support of the persons who occupy key management positions. If lower or middle management personnel sense that top management is lukewarm about budgeting, or if they sense that top management simply tolerates budgeting as a necessary evil, then their own attitudes will reflect a similar lack of enthusiasm. Budgeting is hard work, and if top management is not enthusiastic about and committed to the budget program, then it is unlikely that anyone else in the organization will be either.

In administering the budget program, it is particularly important that top management not use the budget as a club to pressure employees or as a way to find someone to blame if something goes wrong. Using budgets in such negative ways will simply breed hostility, tension, and mistrust rather than greater cooperation and productivity. Unfortunately, research suggests that the budget is often used as a pressure device and that great emphasis is placed on "meeting the budget" under all circumstances.[1]

Rather than being used as a pressure device, the budget should be used as a positive instrument to assist in establishing goals, in measuring operating results, and in isolating areas that are in need of extra effort or attention. Any misgivings that employees have about a budget program can be overcome by meaningful involvement at all levels and by proper use of the program over time. Administration of a budget program requires a great deal of insight and sensitivity on the part of management. The budget program should be designed to be a positive aid in achieving both individual and company goals.

Management must keep clearly in mind that the human dimension in budgeting is of key importance. It is easy to become preoccupied with the technical aspects of the budget program to the exclusion of the human aspects. Indeed, the use of budget data in a rigid and inflexible manner is the greatest single complaint of persons whose performance is being evaluated using the budget process.[2] Management should remember that the purposes of the budget are to motivate employees and to coordinate efforts. Preoccupation with the dollars and cents in the budget, or being rigid and inflexible, can only lead to frustration of these purposes.

in business today **Hitting the Target**

In establishing a budget, how challenging should budget targets be? In practice, companies typically set their budgets either at a "stretch" level or a "highly achievable" level. A stretch-level budget is one that has only a small chance of being met by even the most capable managers. A highly achievable budget is one that is challenging, but is very likely to be met with reasonably hard work. Research shows that managers prefer highly achievable budgets. Such budgets are generally coupled with bonuses that are given when budget targets are met, along with added bonuses when these targets are exceeded. Highly achievable budgets are believed to build a manager's confidence and to generate greater commitment to the budget program.

Source: Kenneth A. Merchant, *Rewarding Results: Motivating Profit Center Managers* (Boston, MA: Harvard Business School Press, 1989). For further discussion of budget targets, see Kenneth A. Merchant, "How Challenging Should Profit Budget Targets Be?" *Management Accounting* 72, no. 5 (November 1990), pp. 46–48.

---

[1] Paul J. Carruth, Thurrell O. McClendon, and Milton R. Ballard, "What Supervisors Don't Like about Budget Evaluations," *Management Accounting* 64, no. 8 (February 1983), p. 42.

[2] Carruth et al., "What Supervisors Don't Like . . . ," p. 91.

Zero-Based Budgeting

In the traditional approach to budgeting, the manager starts with last year's budget and adds to it (or subtracts from it) according to anticipated needs. This is an incremental approach to budgeting in which the previous year's budget is taken for granted as a baseline.

Zero-based budgeting is an alternative approach that is sometimes used—particularly in the governmental and not-for-profit sectors of the economy. Under a **zero-based budget,** managers are required to justify *all* budgeted expenditures, not just changes in the budget from the previous year. The baseline is zero rather than last year's budget.

A zero-based budget requires considerable documentation. In addition to all of the schedules in the usual master budget, the manager must prepare a series of "decision packages" in which all of the activities of the department are ranked according to their relative importance and the cost of each activity is identified. Higher-level managers can then review the decision packages and cut back in those areas that appear to be less critical or whose costs do not appear to be justified.

Nearly everyone would agree that zero-based budgeting is a good idea. The only issue is the frequency with which a zero-based review is carried out. Under zero-based budgeting, the review is performed every year. Critics of zero-based budgeting charge that properly executed zero-based budgeting is too time-consuming and too costly to justify on an annual basis. In addition, it is argued that annual reviews soon become mechanical and that the whole purpose of zero-based budgeting is then lost.

Whether or not a company should use an annual review is a matter of judgment. In some situations, annual zero-based reviews may be justified; in other situations, they may not because of the time and cost involved. However, most managers would at least agree that on occasion zero-based reviews can be very helpful.

Baseline Budgeting

in business | *today*

All of the universities responding to a survey in the United Kingdom prepare budgets. The majority (60%) indicated that managers have the right amount of input into their budgets. Most of the respondents (84%) indicated that the prior year is used as a baseline when budgets are prepared.

Source: Paul Cropper and Colin Drury, "Management Accounting Practices in Universities," *Management Accounting: Magazine for Chartered Management Accountants*, February 1996, p. 28 (3 pages).

The Budget Committee

A standing **budget committee** will usually be responsible for overall policy matters relating to the budget program and for coordinating the preparation of the budget itself. This committee generally consists of the president; vice presidents in charge of various functions such as sales, production, and purchasing; and the controller. Difficulties and disputes between segments of the organization in matters relating to the budget are resolved by the budget committee. In addition, the budget committee approves the final budget and receives periodic reports on the progress of the company in attaining budgeted goals.

Disputes can (and do) erupt over budget matters. Because budgets allocate resources, the budgeting process to a large extent determines which departments get more resources and which get relatively less. Also, the budget sets the benchmarks by which managers and their departments will be at least partially evaluated. Therefore, it should not be surprising that managers take the budgeting process very seriously and invest considerable energy and even emotion in ensuring that their interests, and those of their departments, are protected. Because of this, the budgeting process can easily degenerate into an interoffice brawl in which the ultimate goal of working together toward common goals is forgotten.

Running a successful budgeting program that avoids interoffice battles requires considerable interpersonal skills in addition to purely technical skills. But even the best interpersonal skills will fail if, as discussed earlier, top management uses the budget process inappropriately as a club or as a way to find blame.

in business *today* **The Politics of Budgeting**

Budgeting is often an intensely political process in which managers jockey for resources and relaxed goals for the upcoming year. One group of consultants describes the process in this way: Annual budgets "have a particular urgency in that they provide the standard and most public framework against which managers are assessed and judged. It is, therefore, not surprising that budget-setting is taken seriously . . . Often budgets are a means for managers getting what they want. A relaxed budget will secure a relatively easy twelve months, a tight one means that their names will constantly be coming up in the monthly management review meeting. Far better to shift the burden of cost control and financial discipline to someone else. Budgeting is an intensely political exercise conducted with all the sharper managerial skills not taught at business school, such as lobbying and flattering superiors, forced haste, regretted delay, hidden truth, half-truths, and lies."

Source: Michael Morrow, ed., *Activity-Based Management* (New York: Woodhead-Faulkner, 1992), p. 91.

An Overview of the Master Budget

The master budget consists of a number of separate but interdependent budgets. Exhibit 7–2 provides an overview of the various parts of the master budget and how they are related.

Exhibit 7–2
The Master Budget
Interrelationships

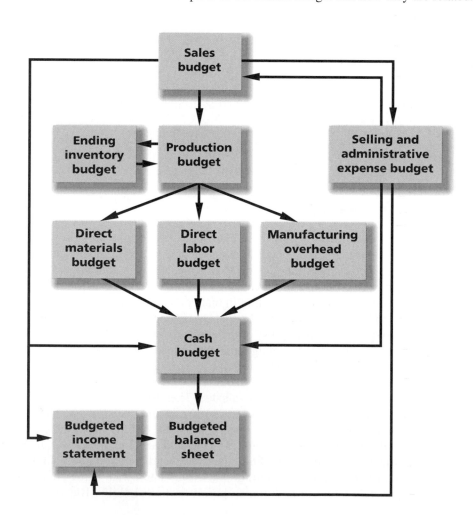

The Sales Budget A **sales budget** is a detailed schedule showing the expected sales for the budget period; typically, it is expressed in both dollars and units of product. An accurate sales budget is the key to the entire budgeting process. All of the other parts of the master budget are dependent on the sales budget in some way, as illustrated in Exhibit 7–2. Thus, if the sales budget is sloppily done, then the rest of the budgeting process is largely a waste of time.

The sales budget will help determine how many units will have to be produced. Thus, the production budget is prepared after the sales budget. The production budget in turn is used to determine the budgets for manufacturing costs including the direct materials budget, the direct labor budget, and the manufacturing overhead budget. These budgets are then combined with data from the sales budget and the selling and administrative expense budget to determine the cash budget. In essence, the sales budget triggers a chain reaction that leads to the development of the other budgets.

As shown in Exhibit 7–2, the selling and administrative expense budget is both dependent on and a determinant of the sales budget. This reciprocal relationship arises because sales will in part be determined by the funds committed for advertising and sales promotion.

The Cash Budget Once the operating budgets (sales, production, and so on) have been established, the cash budget and other financial budgets can be prepared. A **cash budget** is a detailed plan showing how cash resources will be acquired and used over some specified time period. Observe from Exhibit 7–2 that all of the operating budgets have an impact on the cash budget. In the case of the sales budget, the impact comes from the planned cash receipts to be received from sales. In the case of the other budgets, the impact comes from the planned cash expenditures within the budgets themselves.

Sales Forecasting—A Critical Step

The sales budget is usually based on the company's *sales forecast.* Sales from prior years are commonly used as a starting point in preparing the sales forecast. In addition, the manager may examine the company's unfilled back orders, the company's pricing policy and marketing plans, trends in the industry, and general economic conditions. Sophisticated statistical tools may be used to analyze the data and to build models that are helpful in predicting key factors influencing the company's sales. The accompanying feature on Virtual People suggests how some companies use computer simulations to enhance their marketing strategies and sales forecasts. We will not, however, go into the details of how sales forecasts are made. This is a subject that is more appropriately covered in marketing courses.

Virtual People   *in business* today

Some companies are turning to elaborate computer simulations for help in forecasting sales. In one emerging approach, software designers create a "virtual economy" containing "virtual people." "These 'people,' constructed of bits of computer code, are endowed with ages, incomes, domiciles, genders, and buying habits. [For example, some people] buy a new music CD as soon as it hits the stores; others, only after a certain number of their neighbors own it or a certain number of radio stations have played it. All these assumptions are based on real data . . . " The computer model may contain millions of these virtual people who then react—sometimes in unpredictable ways—to advertising, sales promotions, new product offerings, and so on. Managers can use such a model to plan their marketing strategy and to forecast sales.

Source: Rita Koselka, "Playing the Game of Life," *Forbes,* April 7, 1997, pp. 100–108.

You were recently hired as the sales manager for a company that designs and manufactures hard-soled casual and dress shoes for sale to department stores. The vice president of sales recently decided that the company will add athletic footwear to its catalog and asked you to prepare a sales budget for that product line for the coming year. How would you forecast sales for this product line?

Preparing the Master Budget

Managerial Accounting in Action

The Issue

Tom Wills is the majority stockholder and chief executive officer of Hampton Freeze, Inc., a company he started in 1998. The company makes premium popsicles using only natural ingredients and featuring exotic flavors such as tangy tangerine and minty mango. The company's business is highly seasonal, with most of the sales occurring in spring and summer.

In 1999, the company's second year of operations, a major cash crunch in the first and second quarters almost forced the company into bankruptcy. In spite of this cash crunch, 1999 turned out to be a very successful year in terms of both overall cash flow and net income. Partly as a result of that harrowing experience, Tom decided toward the end of 1999 to hire a professional financial manager. Tom interviewed several promising candidates for the job and settled on Larry Giano, who had considerable experience in the packaged foods industry. In the job interview, Tom questioned Larry about the steps he would take to prevent a recurrence of the 1999 cash crunch:

Tom: As I mentioned earlier, we are going to wind up 1999 with a very nice profit. What you may not know is that we had some very big financial problems this year.
Larry: Let me guess. You ran out of cash sometime in the first or second quarter.
Tom: How did you know?
Larry: Most of your sales are in the second and third quarter, right?
Tom: Sure, everyone wants to buy popsicles in the spring and summer, but nobody wants them when the weather turns cold.
Larry: So you don't have many sales in the first quarter?
Tom: Right.
Larry: And in the second quarter, which is the spring, you are producing like crazy to fill orders?
Tom: Sure.
Larry: Do your customers, the grocery stores, pay you the day you make your deliveries?
Tom: Are you kidding? Of course not.
Larry: So in the first quarter, you don't have many sales. In the second quarter, you are producing like crazy, which eats up cash, but you aren't paid by your customers until long after you have paid your employees and suppliers. No wonder you had a cash problem. I see this pattern all the time in food processing because of the seasonality of the business.
Tom: So what can we do about it?
Larry: The first step is to predict the magnitude of the problem before it occurs. If we can predict early in the year what the cash shortfall is going to be, we can go to the bank and arrange for credit before we really need it. Bankers tend to be leery of panicky people who show up begging for emergency loans. They are much more likely to make the loan if you look like you know what you are doing, you have done your homework, and you are in control of the situation.

Tom: How can we predict the cash shortfall?

Larry: You can put together a cash budget. While you're at it, you might as well do a master budget. You'll find it is well worth the effort.

Tom: I don't like budgets. They are too confining. My wife budgets everything at home, and I can't spend what I want.

Larry: Can I ask a personal question?

Tom: What?

Larry: Where did you get the money to start this business?

Tom: Mainly from our family's savings. I get your point. We wouldn't have had the money to start the business if my wife hadn't been forcing us to save every month.

Larry: Exactly. I suggest you use the same discipline in your business. It is even more important here because you can't expect your employees to spend your money as carefully as you would.

Tom: I'm sold. Welcome aboard.

With the full backing of Tom Wills, Larry Giano set out to create a master budget for the company for the year 2000. In his planning for the budgeting process, Larry drew up the following list of documents that would be a part of the master budget:

1. A sales budget, including a schedule of expected cash collections.
2. A production budget (a merchandise purchases budget would be used in a merchandising company).
3. A direct materials budget, including a schedule of expected cash disbursements for raw materials.
4. A direct labor budget.
5. A manufacturing overhead budget.
6. An ending finished goods inventory budget.
7. A selling and administrative expense budget.
8. A cash budget.
9. A budgeted income statement.
10. A budgeted balance sheet.

Larry felt it was important to have everyone's cooperation in the budgeting process, so he asked Tom to call a companywide meeting in which the budgeting process would be explained. At the meeting there was initially some grumbling, but Tom was able to convince nearly everyone of the necessity for planning and getting better control over spending. It helped that the cash crisis earlier in the year was still fresh in everyone's minds. As much as some people disliked the idea of budgets, they liked their jobs even more.

In the months that followed, Larry worked closely with all of the managers involved in the master budget, gathering data from them and making sure that they understood and fully supported the parts of the master budget that would affect them. In subsequent years, Larry hoped to turn the whole budgeting process over to the managers and to take a more advisory role.

The interdependent documents that Larry Giano prepared for Hampton Freeze are Schedules 1 through 10 of his company's master budget. In this section, we will study these schedules.

The Sales Budget

The sales budget is the starting point in preparing the master budget. As shown earlier in Exhibit 7–2, all other items in the master budget, including production, purchases, inventories, and expenses, depend on it in some way.

The sales budget is constructed by multiplying the budgeted sales in units by the selling price. Schedule 1 on the next page contains the sales budget for Hampton Freeze for the year 2000, by quarters. Notice from the schedule that the company plans to sell 100,000 cases of popsicles during the year, with sales peaking in the third quarter.

Learning Objective 2
Prepare a sales budget, including a schedule of expected cash receipts.

Schedule 1

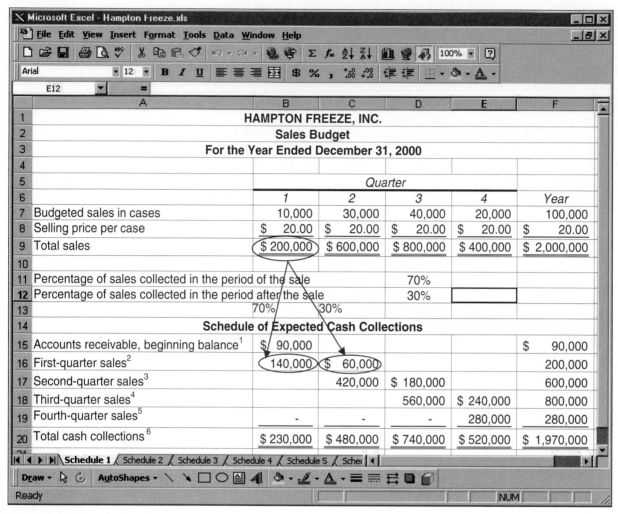

[1]Cash collections from last year's fourth-quarter sales. See the beginning-of-year balance sheet on page 296.

[2]$200,000 × 70%; $200,000 × 30%.

[3]$600,000 × 70%; $600,000 × 30%.

[4]$800,000 × 70%; $800,000 × 30%.

[5]$400,000 × 70%.

[6]Uncollected fourth-quarter sales appear as accounts receivable on the company's end-of-year balance sheet (see Schedule 10 on page 297).

A schedule of expected cash collections, such as the one that appears in Schedule 1 for Hampton Freeze, is prepared after the sales budget. This schedule will be needed later to prepare the cash budget. Cash collections consist of collections on sales made to customers in prior periods plus collections on sales made in the current budget period. At Hampton Freeze, experience has shown that 70% of sales are collected in the quarter in which the sale is made and the remaining 30% are collected in the following quarter. For example, 70% of the first quarter sales of $200,000 (or $140,000) are collected during the first quarter and 30% (or $60,000) are collected during the second quarter.

in business *today* A Controversial Approach to Setting Prices

Demand pricing, a nontraditional approach to the retail pricing of gasoline, is being tested in parts of Europe and explored in the United States. A computer model is used to forecast how consumers would respond to changes in prices throughout the day. For example, higher prices might be charged during the morning and evening rush hours when customers are not likely to shop around for a better price.

Late in 1999, Coca-Cola casually reported that it might use vending machines that have the ability to adjust the price of soft drinks as outdoor temperatures fluctuate. Obviously, consumers would pay higher prices on hotter days. The ensuing media coverage was negative, consumers complained of price gouging, and PepsiCo stepped in to take advantage of the situation by expressing its outrage.

Operators of retail gas outlets in the U.S. are naturally concerned about the backlash that might result if the demand pricing approach were used. Technology presents another obstacle that would need to be overcome before demand pricing could be implemented. Operating systems will not be able to effectively handle the price changes until signage, point-of-sale registers, and the accounting department are upgraded and fully integrated.

Source: Keith Reid, "The Pricing Equation: Which Price Is Right," *National Petroleum News*, February 2000, pp. 16–18.

The Production Budget

Learning Objective 3
Prepare a production budget.

The production budget is prepared after the sales budget. The **production budget** lists the number of units that must be produced during each budget period to meet sales needs and to provide for the desired ending inventory. Production needs can be determined as follows:

Concept 7–2

Budgeted sales in units	XXXX
Add desired ending inventory	XXXX
Total needs	XXXX
Less beginning inventory	XXXX
Required production	XXXX

Schedule 2 contains the production budget for Hampton Freeze.

Note that production requirements for a quarter are influenced by the desired level of the ending inventory. Inventories should be carefully planned. Excessive inventories tie up funds and create storage problems. Insufficient inventories can lead to lost sales or crash production efforts in the following period. At Hampton Freeze, management believes that an ending inventory equal to 20% of the next quarter's sales strikes the appropriate balance.

Inventory Purchases—Merchandising Firm

Hampton Freeze prepares a production budget, since it is a *manufacturing* firm. If it were a *merchandising* firm, it would prepare a **merchandise purchases budget** showing the amount of goods to be purchased from its suppliers during the period. The merchandise purchases budget follows the same basic format as the production budget, as shown below:

Budgeted cost of goods sold (in units or in dollars)	XXXXX
Add desired ending merchandise inventory	XXXXX
Total needs	XXXXX
Less beginning merchandise inventory	XXXXX
Required purchases (in units or in dollars)	XXXXX

A merchandising firm would prepare an inventory purchases budget such as the one above for each item carried in stock.

Schedule 2

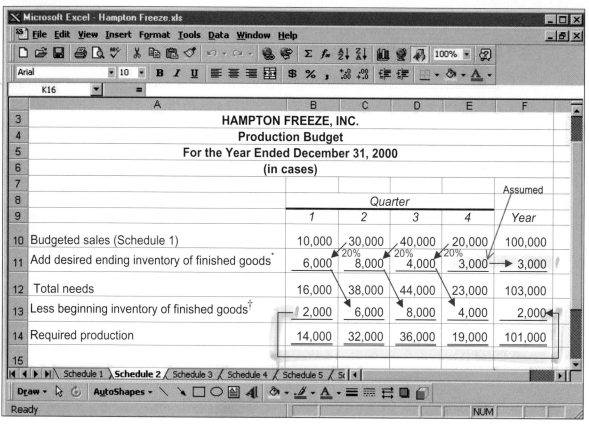

*Twenty percent of the next quarter's sales. The ending inventory of 3,000 cases is assumed.

†The beginning inventory in each quarter is the same as the prior quarter's ending inventory.

The Direct Materials Budget

Learning Objective 4

Prepare a direct materials budget, including a schedule of expected cash disbursements for purchases of materials.

Returning to Hampton Freeze, after the production requirements have been computed, a *direct materials budget* can be prepared. The **direct materials budget** details the raw materials that must be purchased to fulfill the production budget and to provide for adequate inventories. The required purchases of raw materials are computed as follows:

Raw materials needed to meet the production schedule	XXXXX
Add desired ending inventory of raw materials	XXXXX
Total raw materials needs	XXXXX
Less beginning inventory of raw materials	XXXXX
Raw materials to be purchased	XXXXX

Schedule 3 contains the direct materials budget for Hampton Freeze. The only raw material included in that budget is high fructose sugar, which is the major ingredient in pop-

Schedule 3

```
X Microsoft Excel - Hampton Freeze.xls                                    _ □ X
```
File Edit View Insert Format Tools Data Window Help   _ 日 X

Arial ... 10 ... **B** *I* U ... $ % , ... 92% ...

H30 =

	A	B	C	D	E	F	G
3	HAMPTON FREEZE, INC.						
4	Direct Materials Budget						
5	For the Year Ended December 31, 2000						
6						Assumed	
7				Quarter			
8		1	2	3	4	Year	
9	Required production in cases (Schedule 2)	14,000	32,000	36,000	19,000	101,000	
10	Raw materials needed per case (pounds)	15	15	15	15	15	
11	Production needs (pounds)	210,000	480,000	540,000	285,000	1,515,000	
12	Add desired ending inventory of raw materials[1]	48,000	54,000	28,500	22,500	22,500	
13	Total needs	258,000	534,000	568,500	307,500	1,537,500	
14	Less beginning inventory of raw materials	21,000	48,000	54,000	28,500	21,000	
15	Raw materials to be purchased	237,000	486,000	514,500	279,000	1,516,500	
16	Cost of raw materials per pound	$ 0.20	$ 0.20	$ 0.20	$ 0.20	$ 0.20	
17	Cost of raw materials to be purchased	$ 47,400	$ 97,200	$ 102,900	$ 55,800	$ 303,300	
18							
19	Percentage of purchases paid for in the period of the purchase			50%			
20	Percentage of purchases paid for in the period after purchase			50%			
21		50%	50%				
22	Schedule of Expected Cash Disbursements for Materials						
23							
24	Accounts payable, beginning balance[2]	$ 25,800				$ 25,800	
25	First-quarter purchases[3]	23,700	$ 23,700			47,400	
26	Second-quarter purchases[4]		48,600	$ 48,600		97,200	
27	Third-quarter purchases[5]			51,450	$ 51,450	102,900	
28	Fourth-quarter purchases[6]	-	-	-	27,900	27,900	
29	Total cash disbursements	$ 49,500	$ 72,300	$ 100,050	$ 79,350	$ 301,200	

◄ ◄ ► ►◄ Schedule 1 / Schedule 2 \ **Schedule 3** / Schedule 4 / Schedule 5 / Sche ◄

Draw ▾ ... AutoShapes ▾ \ ... □ ○ ... ... ▾ ... ▾ **A** ▾ ... ...

Ready   NUM

[1]Ten percent of the next quarter's production needs. For example, the second-quarter production needs are 480,000 pounds. Therefore, the desired ending inventory for the first quarter would be 10% × 480,000 pounds = 48,000 pounds. The ending inventory of 22,500 pounds for the quarter is assumed.

[2]Cash payments for last year's fourth-quarter material purchases. See the beginning-of-year balance sheet on page 296.

[3]$47,500 × 50%; $47,500 × 50%.

[4]$97,200 × 50%; $97,200 × 50%.

[5]$102,900 × 50%; $102,900 × 50%.

[6]$55,800 × 50%. Unpaid fourth-quarter purchases appear as accounts payable on the company's end-of-year balance sheet.

sicles other than water. The remaining raw materials are relatively insignificant and are included in variable manufacturing overhead. Notice that materials requirements are first determined in units (pounds, gallons, and so on) and then translated into dollars by multiplying by the appropriate unit cost. Also note that the management of Hampton Freeze desires to maintain ending inventories of sugar equal to 10% of the following quarter's production needs.

The direct materials budget is usually accompanied by a schedule of expected cash disbursements for raw materials. This schedule is needed to prepare the overall cash budget. Disbursements for raw materials consist of payments for purchases on account in prior periods plus any payments for purchases in the current budget period. Schedule 3 contains such a schedule of cash disbursements.

Schedule 4

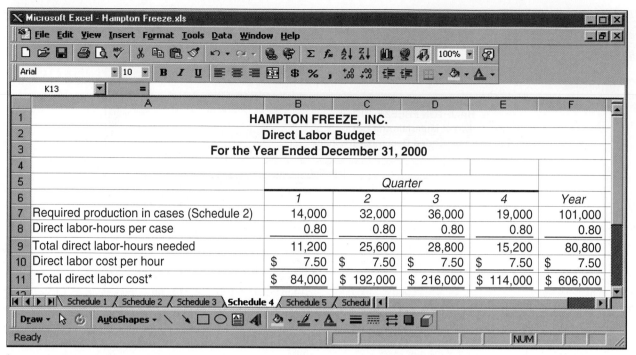

		Quarter			
	1	2	3	4	Year
Required production in cases (Schedule 2)	14,000	32,000	36,000	19,000	101,000
Direct labor-hours per case	0.80	0.80	0.80	0.80	0.80
Total direct labor-hours needed	11,200	25,600	28,800	15,200	80,800
Direct labor cost per hour	$ 7.50	$ 7.50	$ 7.50	$ 7.50	$ 7.50
Total direct labor cost*	$ 84,000	$ 192,000	$ 216,000	$ 114,000	$ 606,000

*This schedule assumes that the direct labor work force will be fully adjusted to the total direct labor-hours needed each quarter.

The Direct Labor Budget

The **direct labor budget** is also developed from the production budget. Direct labor requirements must be computed so that the company will know whether sufficient labor time is available to meet production needs. By knowing in advance just what will be needed in the way of labor time throughout the budget year, the company can develop plans to adjust the labor force as the situation may require. Firms that neglect to budget run the risk of facing labor shortages or having to hire and lay off at awkward times. Erratic labor policies lead to insecurity and inefficiency on the part of employees.

To compute direct labor requirements, the number of units of finished product to be produced each period (month, quarter, and so on) is multiplied by the number of direct labor-hours required to produce a single unit. The direct labor requirements can then be translated into expected direct labor costs. How this is done will depend on the labor policy of the firm. In Schedule 4, the management of Hampton Freeze has assumed that the direct labor force will be adjusted as the work requirements change from quarter to quarter. In that case, the total direct labor cost is computed by simply multiplying the direct labor-hour requirements by the direct labor rate per hour.

However, many companies have employment policies or contracts that prevent them from laying off and rehiring workers as needed. Suppose, for example, that Hampton Freeze has 50 workers who are classified as direct labor and each of them is guaranteed at least 480 hours of pay each quarter at a rate of $7.50 per hour. In that case, the minimum direct labor cost for a quarter would be as follows:

$$50 \text{ workers} \times 480 \text{ hours per worker} \times \$7.50 \text{ per hour} = \$180,000$$

Note that in Schedule 4 the direct labor costs for the first and fourth quarters would have to be increased to the $180,000 level if Hampton Freeze's labor policy did not allow it to adjust the work force.

The Manufacturing Overhead Budget

The **manufacturing overhead budget** provides a schedule of all costs of production other than direct materials and direct labor. Schedule 5 shows the manufacturing overhead

Schedule 5

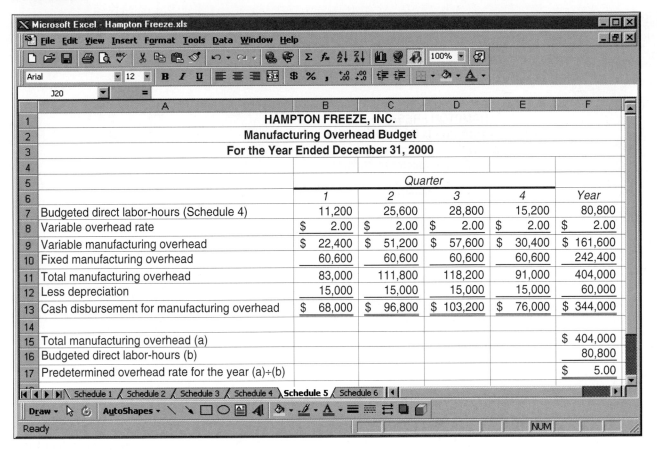

	Quarter				Year
	1	2	3	4	
Budgeted direct labor-hours (Schedule 4)	11,200	25,600	28,800	15,200	80,800
Variable overhead rate	$ 2.00	$ 2.00	$ 2.00	$ 2.00	$ 2.00
Variable manufacturing overhead	$ 22,400	$ 51,200	$ 57,600	$ 30,400	$ 161,600
Fixed manufacturing overhead	60,600	60,600	60,600	60,600	242,400
Total manufacturing overhead	83,000	111,800	118,200	91,000	404,000
Less depreciation	15,000	15,000	15,000	15,000	60,000
Cash disbursement for manufacturing overhead	$ 68,000	$ 96,800	$ 103,200	$ 76,000	$ 344,000
Total manufacturing overhead (a)					$ 404,000
Budgeted direct labor-hours (b)					80,800
Predetermined overhead rate for the year (a)÷(b)					$ 5.00

The title of the spreadsheet is **HAMPTON FREEZE, INC.** / **Manufacturing Overhead Budget** / **For the Year Ended December 31, 2000**

budget for Hampton Freeze. Note how the production costs are separated into variable and fixed components. The variable component is $2 per direct labor-hour. The fixed component is $60,600 per quarter.

Schedule 5 for Hampton Freeze shows its budgeted cash disbursements for manufacturing overhead. Since some of the overhead costs are not cash outflows, the total budgeted manufacturing overhead costs must be adjusted to determine the cash disbursements for manufacturing overhead. At Hampton Freeze, the only significant noncash manufacturing overhead cost is depreciation, which is $15,000 per quarter. These noncash depreciation charges are deducted from the total budgeted manufacturing overhead to determine the expected cash disbursements. Hampton Freeze pays all overhead costs involving cash disbursements in the quarter incurred. Note that the company's predetermined overhead rate for the year will be $5 per direct labor-hour.

The Ending Finished Goods Inventory Budget

After completing Schedules 1–5, Larry Giano had all of the data he needed to compute unit product costs. This computation was needed for two reasons: first, to determine cost of goods sold on the budgeted income statement; and second, to know what amount to put on the balance sheet inventory account for unsold units. The carrying cost of the unsold units is computed on the **ending finished goods inventory budget.**

Larry Giano considered using variable costing in preparing Hampton Freeze's budget statements, but he decided to use absorption costing instead since the bank would very likely require that absorption costing be used. He also knew that it would be easy to convert the absorption costing financial statements to a variable costing basis later. At this point, the primary concern was to determine what financing, if any, would be required in the year 2000 and then to arrange for that financing from the bank.

The unit product cost computations are shown in Schedule 6. For Hampton Freeze, the absorption costing unit product cost is $13 per case of popsicles—consisting of $3 of

Schedule 6

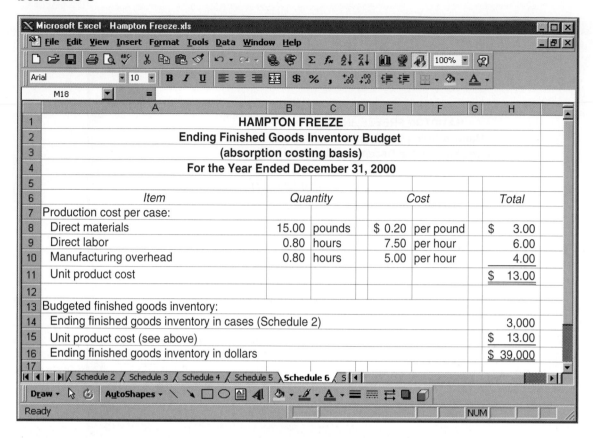

direct materials, $6 of direct labor, and $4 of manufacturing overhead. Manufacturing overhead is applied to units of product on the basis of direct labor-hours. The budgeted carrying cost of the expected ending inventory is $39,000.

The Selling and Administrative Expense Budget

Learning Objective 7

Prepare a selling and administrative expense budget.

The **selling and administrative expense budget** lists the budgeted expenses for areas other than manufacturing. In large organizations, this budget would be a compilation of many smaller, individual budgets submitted by department heads and other persons responsible for selling and administrative expenses. For example, the marketing manager in a large organization would submit a budget detailing the advertising expenses for each budget period.

Schedule 7 contains the selling and administrative expense budget for Hampton Freeze.

in business today **Brainwashed Consumers**

Marketing costs are in the range of 25% to 35% of sales in the automotive, consumer packaged goods, pharmaceutical, and telecommunications industries according to a recent PricewaterhouseCoopers survey. Evaluating the effectiveness of marketing costs is much harder than measuring the benefits of costs like direct materials. PricewaterhouseCoopers consultants suggest that a company's managerial accountants need to work closely with its marketing department to design a system for evaluating marketing costs. In addition to reviewing indicators such as the number of units sold, criteria might include the extent to which a brand dominates the minds of consumers.

Source: G. K. De Vriend, P. A. von der Heide and J. C. Steigstra, "Here's a Good Way to Tell If Your Marketing Efforts Are Working," *Strategic Finance*, March 2000, pp. 56–62.

Schedule 7

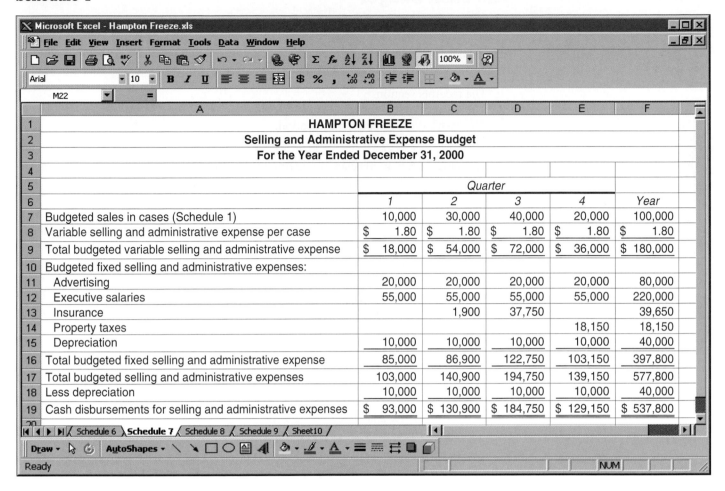

	A	B	C	D	E	F
1		HAMPTON FREEZE				
2		Selling and Administrative Expense Budget				
3		For the Year Ended December 31, 2000				
4						
5			Quarter			
6		1	2	3	4	Year
7	Budgeted sales in cases (Schedule 1)	10,000	30,000	40,000	20,000	100,000
8	Variable selling and administrative expense per case	$ 1.80	$ 1.80	$ 1.80	$ 1.80	$ 1.80
9	Total budgeted variable selling and administrative expense	$ 18,000	$ 54,000	$ 72,000	$ 36,000	$ 180,000
10	Budgeted fixed selling and administrative expenses:					
11	Advertising	20,000	20,000	20,000	20,000	80,000
12	Executive salaries	55,000	55,000	55,000	55,000	220,000
13	Insurance		1,900	37,750		39,650
14	Property taxes				18,150	18,150
15	Depreciation	10,000	10,000	10,000	10,000	40,000
16	Total budgeted fixed selling and administrative expense	85,000	86,900	122,750	103,150	397,800
17	Total budgeted selling and administrative expenses	103,000	140,900	194,750	139,150	577,800
18	Less depreciation	10,000	10,000	10,000	10,000	40,000
19	Cash disbursements for selling and administrative expenses	$ 93,000	$ 130,900	$ 184,750	$ 129,150	$ 537,800

Letting the Business Take Care of Itself

in business today

Harlan Accola turned his interests in flying and photography into a money-making pursuit by selling aerial photos of farms and homes. Sales were so good that what started out as a way to finance a hobby soon became a full-scale business. He paid an outside accountant to prepare financial statements, which he admits he didn't understand. "I didn't think it was important. I thought a financial statement was just something you had to give to the bank to keep your loan OK. So I took it, looked at the bottom line, and tossed it into a desk drawer."

Accola's casual approach worked for a while. However, within a few years he had lost control of his cash flows. Unpaid creditors were hounding him, and the Internal Revenue Service was demanding overdue taxes. The bank, alarmed by the cash flow situation, demanded to be repaid the $240,000 loan it had extended to the company. Accola confesses that "I thought if I made enough sales, everything else would take care of itself. But I confused profits with cash flow." The good news is that the company recovered from its near-brush with bankruptcy, instituted formal financial planning procedures, and is now very successful.

Source: Jay Finnegan, "Everything according to Plan," *Inc.,* March 1995, pp. 78–85.

The Cash Budget

Learning Objective 8
Prepare a cash budget.

As illustrated in Exhibit 7–2, the cash budget pulls together much of the data developed in the preceding steps. It is a good idea to restudy Exhibit 7–2 to get the big picture firmly in mind before moving on.

The cash budget is composed of four major sections:

1. The receipts section.
2. The disbursements section.
3. The cash excess or deficiency section.
4. The financing section.

The receipts section consists of a listing of all of the cash inflows, except for financing, expected during the budget period. Generally, the major source of receipts will be from sales.

The disbursements section consists of all cash payments that are planned for the budget period. These payments will include raw materials purchases, direct labor payments, manufacturing overhead costs, and so on, as contained in their respective budgets. In addition, other cash disbursements such as equipment purchases, dividends, and other cash withdrawals by owners are listed. For instance, we see in Schedule 8 that management plans to spend $130,000 during the budget period on equipment purchases and $32,000 on dividends to the owners. This is additional information that does not appear on any of the earlier schedules.

The cash excess or deficiency section is computed as follows:

Cash balance, beginning	XXXX
Add receipts	XXXX
Total cash available before financing	XXXX
Less disbursements	XXXX
Excess (deficiency) of cash available over disbursements	XXXX

If there is a cash deficiency during any budget period, the company will need to borrow funds. If there is a cash excess during any budget period, funds borrowed in previous periods can be repaid or the excess funds can be invested.

The financing section provides a detailed account of the borrowings and repayments projected to take place during the budget period. It also includes a detail of interest payments that will be due on money borrowed.[3]

Generally speaking, the cash budget should be broken down into time periods that are as short as feasible. Considerable fluctuations in cash balances may be hidden by looking at a longer time period. While a monthly cash budget is most common, many firms budget cash on a weekly or even daily basis. Larry Giano has prepared a quarterly cash budget for Hampton Freeze that can be further refined as necessary. This budget appears in Schedule 8. Larry has assumed in the budget that an open line of credit can be arranged with the bank that can be used as needed to bolster the company's cash position. He has also assumed that any loans taken out with this line of credit would carry an interest rate of 10% per year. Larry has assumed that all borrowings and repayments are in round $1,000 amounts and that all borrowing occurs at the beginning of a quarter and all repayments are made at the end of a quarter.

In the case of Hampton Freeze, all loans have been repaid by year-end. If all loans are not repaid and a budgeted income statement or balance sheet is being prepared, then interest must be accrued on the unpaid loans. This interest will *not* appear on the cash budget (since it has not yet been paid), but it will appear as part of interest expense on the budgeted income statement and as a liability on the budgeted balance sheet.

---

[3]The format for the statement of cash flows, which is discussed in Chapter 13, may also be used for the cash budget.

Schedule 8

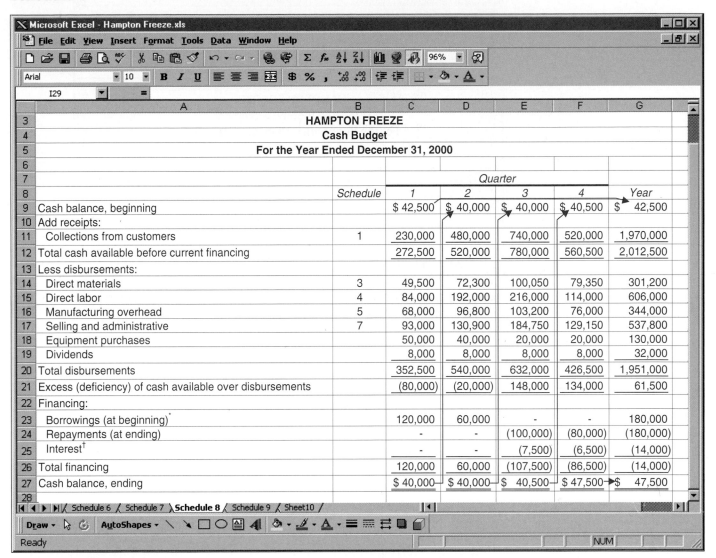

	Schedule	Quarter 1	Quarter 2	Quarter 3	Quarter 4	Year
HAMPTON FREEZE						
Cash Budget						
For the Year Ended December 31, 2000						
Cash balance, beginning		$ 42,500	$ 40,000	$ 40,000	$ 40,500	$ 42,500
Add receipts:						
Collections from customers	1	230,000	480,000	740,000	520,000	1,970,000
Total cash available before current financing		272,500	520,000	780,000	560,500	2,012,500
Less disbursements:						
Direct materials	3	49,500	72,300	100,050	79,350	301,200
Direct labor	4	84,000	192,000	216,000	114,000	606,000
Manufacturing overhead	5	68,000	96,800	103,200	76,000	344,000
Selling and administrative	7	93,000	130,900	184,750	129,150	537,800
Equipment purchases		50,000	40,000	20,000	20,000	130,000
Dividends		8,000	8,000	8,000	8,000	32,000
Total disbursements		352,500	540,000	632,000	426,500	1,951,000
Excess (deficiency) of cash available over disbursements		(80,000)	(20,000)	148,000	134,000	61,500
Financing:						
Borrowings (at beginning)*		120,000	60,000	-	-	180,000
Repayments (at ending)		-	-	(100,000)	(80,000)	(180,000)
Interest†		-	-	(7,500)	(6,500)	(14,000)
Total financing		120,000	60,000	(107,500)	(86,500)	(14,000)
Cash balance, ending		$ 40,000	$ 40,000	$ 40,500	$ 47,500	$ 47,500

*The company requires a minimum cash balance of $40,000. Therefore, borrowing must be sufficient to cover the cash deficiency of $80,000 in quarter 1 and to provide for the minimum cash balance of $40,000. All borrowings and repayments of principal are in round $1,000 amounts.

†The interest payments relate only to the principal being repaid at the time it is repaid. For example, the interest in quarter 3 relates only to the interest due on the $100,000 principal being repaid from quarter 1 borrowing: $100,000 × 10% per year × ¾ year = $7,500. The interest paid in quarter 4 is computed as follows:

$$\$20,000 \times 10\% \text{ per year} \times 1 \text{ year} \quad .... \quad \$2,000$$
$$\$60,000 \times 10\% \text{ per year} \times \tfrac{3}{4} \text{ year} \quad ... \quad \underline{4,500}$$
$$\text{Total interest paid} \quad .... \quad \underline{\underline{\$6,500}}$$

The Budgeted Income Statement

A budgeted income statement can be prepared from the data developed in Schedules 1–8. *The budgeted income statement is one of the key schedules in the budget process.* It shows the company's planned profit for the upcoming budget period, and it serves as a benchmark against which subsequent company performance can be measured.

Schedule 9 contains the budgeted income statement for Hampton Freeze.

Learning Objective 9
Prepare a budgeted income statement.

The Budgeted Balance Sheet

The budgeted balance sheet is developed by beginning with the current balance sheet and adjusting it for the data contained in the other budgets. Hampton Freeze's budgeted

Learning Objective 10
Prepare a budgeted balance sheet.

Schedule 9

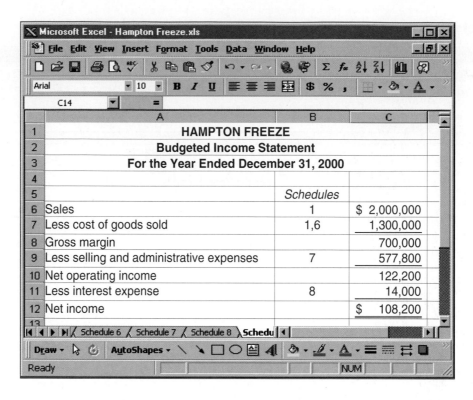

balance sheet is presented in Schedule 10. Some of the data on the budgeted balance sheet have been taken from the company's end-of-year balance sheet for 1999 which appears below:

HAMPTON FREEZE, INC.
Balance Sheet
December 31, 1999

Assets

Current assets:

Cash	$42,500	
Accounts receivable	90,000	
Raw materials inventory (21,000 pounds)	4,200	
Finished goods inventory (2,000 cases)	26,000	
Total current assets		$162,700

Plant and equipment:

Land	80,000	
Buildings and equipment	700,000	
Accumulated depreciation	(292,000)	
Plant and equipment, net		488,000
Total assets		$650,700

Liabilities and Stockholders' Equity

Current liabilities:

Accounts payable (raw materials)		$25,800

Stockholders' equity:

Common stock, no par	$175,000	
Retained earnings	449,900	
Total stockholders' equity		624,900
Total liabilities and stockholders' equity		$650,700

Schedule 10

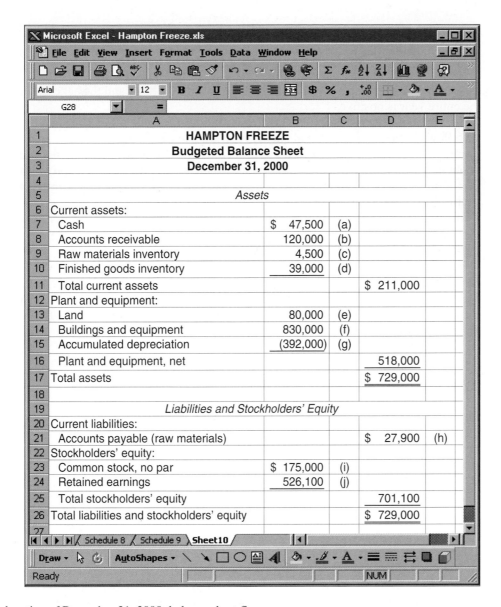

Explanation of December 31, 2000, balance sheet figures:

a. The ending cash balance, as projected by the cash budget in Schedule 8.

b. Thirty percent of fourth-quarter sales, from Schedule 1 ($400,000 × 30% = $120,000).

c. From Schedule 3, the ending raw materials inventory will be 22,500 pounds. This material costs $0.20 per pound. Therefore, the ending inventory in dollars will be 22,500 pounds × $0.20 per pound = $4,500.

d. From Schedule 6.

e. From the December 31, 1999, balance sheet (no change).

f. The December 31, 1999, balance sheet indicated a balance of $700,000. During 2000, $130,000 additional equipment will be purchased (see Schedule 8), bringing the December 31, 2000, balance to $830,000.

g. The December 31, 1999, balance sheet indicated a balance of $292,000. During 2000, $100,000 of depreciation will be taken ($60,000 on Schedule 5 and $40,000 on Schedule 7), bringing the December 31, 2000, balance to $392,000.

h. One-half of the fourth-quarter raw materials purchases, from Schedule 3.

i. From the December 31, 1999, balance sheet (no change).

j. December 31, 1999 balance $449,900

    Add net income, from Schedule 9 108,200

                                                      558,100

    Deduct dividends paid, from Schedule 8 32,000

    December 31, 2000, balance $526,100

Managerial Accounting in Action

The Wrap Up

After completing the master budget, Larry Giano took the documents to Tom Wills, chief executive officer of Hampton Freeze, for his review.

Larry: Here's the budget. Overall, the net income is excellent, and the net cash flow for the entire year is positive.

Tom: Yes, but I see on this cash budget that we have the same problem with negative cash flows in the first and second quarters that we had last year.

Larry: That's true. I don't see any way around that problem. However, there is no doubt in my mind that if you take this budget to the bank today, they'll approve an open line of credit that will allow you to borrow enough to make it through the first two quarters without any problem.

Tom: Are you sure? They didn't seem very happy to see me last year when I came in for an emergency loan.

Larry: Did you repay the loan on time?

Tom: Sure.

Larry: I don't see any problem. You won't be asking for an emergency loan this time. The bank will have plenty of warning. And with this budget, you have a solid plan that shows when and how you are going to pay off the loan. Trust me, they'll go for it.

Tom: Fantastic! It would sure make life a lot easier this year.

in business today The Great Huddle

Springfield Remanufacturing Corporation (SRC) rebuilds used engines. SRC was a failing division of International Harvester when it was purchased by Jack Stack and a group of employees. Mr. Stack, the CEO of the company, likens a successful business to a winning team on the playing field. He argues that in order to win:

- All team players must know the rules of the game.
- All team players must follow the action and know how to keep score.
- All team players must have a stake in the outcome.

At SRC, every employee is taught to understand the company's income statement, balance sheet, and statement of cash flows. Each Wednesday all managers attend "The Great Huddle" in which a projected income statement for the current month is filled in on a blank form. Managers report and discuss the numbers for which they are responsible. The managers then return to their departments and hold a series of "huddles" with employees in which the projected income statement is discussed and actions (called new plays) are planned. Employees are given a stake in the outcome by receiving bonuses if certain overall financial goals are met. In addition, an employee stock ownership program (ESOP) encourages employees to take a direct financial stake in the company.

The company has been very successful. Over the six years since leaving International Harvester, a share of stock in the company that was originally worth $63 has grown in value to $26,250.

Source: Olen L. Greer, Stevan K. Olson, and Mary Callison, "The Key to Real Teamwork: Understanding Numbers," *Management Accounting,* May 1992, pp. 37–44. Reprinted with permission from *Management Accounting.*

you decide A Fiscally Responsible Student

You are a new student who will be footing part of the bill for your education. You saved quite a bit of money but are sure that you will need to earn more to cover your expenses. Before you look for a part-time job, you need to decide how many hours per week you will work and what hourly wage you will need in order to pay your expenses. You decide to prepare a budget for your college education. How should you proceed?

Summary

LO1   Understand why organizations budget and the processes they use to create budgets.
The purpose in this chapter has been to present an overview of the budgeting process and to show how the various budgets relate to each other.

Organizations budget for a variety of reasons including to communicate management's plans through-out the organization, to force managers to think about and plan for the future, to allocate resources within the organization, to identify bottlenecks before they occur, to coordinate activities, and to provide bench-marks for evaluating subsequent performance.

Budgets should be developed with the full participation of all managers who will be subject to bud-getary controls.

LO2   Prepare a sales budget, including a schedule of expected cash receipts.
The sales budget forms the foundation for the master budget. It provides details concerning the anticipated unit and dollar sales for each budget period.

The schedule of expected cash receipts is based on the sales budget, the expected breakdown between cash and credit sales, and the expected pattern of collections on credit sales.

LO3   Prepare a production budget.
The production budget details how many units must be produced each budget period to satisfy expected sales and to provide for adequate levels of finished goods inventories.

LO4   Prepare a direct materials budget, including a schedule of expected cash disburse-ments for purchases of materials.
The direct materials budget shows the materials that must be purchased each budget period to meet antici-pated production requirements and to provide for adequate levels of materials inventories.

Cash disbursements for purchases of materials will depend on the amount of materials purchased in each budget period and the company's policies concerning payments to suppliers for materials acquired on credit.

LO5   Prepare a direct labor budget.
The direct labor budget shows the direct labor-hours that are required to meet the production schedule as detailed in the production budget. The direct labor-hour requirements are used to determine the direct la-bor cost in each budget period.

LO6   Prepare a manufacturing overhead budget.
Manufacturing overhead consists of both variable and fixed manufacturing overhead. The variable manu-facturing overhead usually depends on the number of units produced from the production budget or the di-rect labor hours from the direct labor budget. The variable and fixed manufacturing overheads are combined to determine the total manufacturing overhead. Any noncash manufacturing overhead such as depreciation is deducted from the total manufacturing overhead to determine the cash disbursements for manufacturing overhead.

LO7   Prepare a selling and administrative expense budget.
Like manufacturing overhead, selling and administrative expenses consist of both variable and fixed ex-penses. The variable expenses depend on the number of units sold or some other measure of activity. The variable and fixed expenses are combined to determine the total selling and administrative expense. Any noncash selling and administrative expenses such as depreciation are deducted from the total to determine the cash disbursements for selling and administrative expenses.

LO8   Prepare a cash budget.
The cash budget is a critical element of the master budget. It permits managers to anticipate and plan for cash shortfalls.

The cash budget is organized into a receipts section, a disbursements section, a cash excess or defi-ciency section, and a financing section. The cash budget draws on information taken from nearly all of the other budgets and schedules including the schedule of cash receipts, the schedule of cash disbursements for materials, the direct labor budget, the manufacturing overhead budget, and the selling and administrative expense budget.

LO9   Prepare a budgeted income statement.
The budgeted income statement is constructed using data from the sales budget, the ending finished goods budget, the manufacturing overhead budget, the selling and administrative budget, and the cash budget.

LO10   Prepare a budgeted balance sheet.
The budgeted balance sheet is constructed using data from virtually all of the other parts of the master budget.

Guidance Answers to Decision Maker and You Decide

SALES MANAGER (p. 284)
You probably cannot rely on the sales forecasts for casual and dress shoes to forecast the sales of athletic footwear. You should meet with the vice president of sales to become knowledgeable about the factors that were considered when the decision was made to add this product line. Hopefully, the decision-making process included an extensive analysis of that market. If not, such market research will need to be undertaken at this time. In either case, you should review the results of that research to gain a better understanding of the market for athletic footwear. In addition, you should meet with the marketing department to become familiar with their plans for promoting the product and any goals that have been set in terms of unit sales or market share. Because this is a new product line, you should carefully state the assumptions used to forecast the sales.

A FISCALLY RESPONSIBLE STUDENT (p. 298)
To prepare a personal budget, start by estimating your expenses. To ensure that you do not overlook any expenses, you can visit your college's financial aid office to request an estimate of student expenses for the coming school year. Your school might also offer a course designed to help students succeed in college. The textbooks for such courses often include strategies for managing money while in college and may include sample budgets. Consider sharing your list of expenses with someone knowledgeable (a faculty member, advisor, or adult relative) and asking for feedback. After you have estimated your expenses, you can determine the amount of income you will need in addition to the money you have saved. (Don't forget to set aside some of your savings for unforeseen emergencies.)

Many, if not most, college professors expect you to put in 2 to 3 hours outside of class per week for every hour that you are in class. If you find that the number of hours that you will need to work is excessive, you should consider restricting your spending in some areas. Keep in mind your long-term goal, which is to succeed in college!

Review Problem: Budget Schedules

Mylar Company manufactures and sells a product that has seasonal variations in demand, with peak sales coming in the third quarter. The following information concerns operations for Year 2—the coming year—and for the first two quarters of Year 3:

a. The company's single product sells for $8 per unit. Budgeted sales in units for the next six quarters are as follows:

	Year 2 Quarter				Year 3 Quarter	
	1	2	3	4	1	2
Budgeted sales in units . . .	40,000	60,000	100,000	50,000	70,000	80,000

b. Sales are collected in the following pattern: 75% in the quarter the sales are made, and the remaining 25% in the following quarter. On January 1, Year 2, the company's balance sheet showed $65,000 in accounts receivable, all of which will be collected in the first quarter of the year. Bad debts are negligible and can be ignored.

c. The company desires an ending inventory of finished units on hand at the end of each quarter equal to 30% of the budgeted sales for the next quarter. This requirement was met on December 31, Year 1, in that the company had 12,000 units on hand to start the new year.

d. Five pounds of raw materials are required to complete one unit of product. The company requires an ending inventory of raw materials on hand at the end of each quarter equal to 10% of the production needs of the following quarter. This requirement was met on December 31, Year 1, in that the company had 23,000 pounds of raw materials on hand to start the new year.

e. The raw material costs $0.80 per pound. Purchases of raw material are paid for in the following pattern: 60% paid in the quarter the purchases are made, and the remaining 40% paid in the following quarter. On January 1, Year 2, the company's balance sheet showed $81,500 in accounts payable for raw material purchases, all of which will be paid for in the first quarter of the year.

Required:
Prepare the following budgets and schedules for the year, showing both quarterly and total figures:
1. A sales budget and a schedule of expected cash collections.
2. A production budget.
3. A direct materials purchases budget and a schedule of expected cash payments for material purchases.

SOLUTION TO REVIEW PROBLEM
1. The sales budget is prepared as follows:

| | \multicolumn{4}{c}{Year 2 Quarter} | |
	1	2	3	4	Year
Budgeted sales in units ..	40,000	60,000	100,000	50,000	250,000
Selling price per unit	× $8	× $8	× $8	× $8	× $8
Total sales	$320,000	$480,000	$800,000	$400,000	$2,000,000

Based on the budgeted sales above, the schedule of expected cash collections is prepared as follows:

| | \multicolumn{4}{c}{Year 2 Quarter} | |
	1	2	3	4	Year
Accounts receivable, beginning balance	$ 65,000				$ 65,000
First-quarter sales ($320,000 × 75%, 25%)	240,000	$ 80,000			320,000
Second-quarter sales ($480,000 × 75%, 25%) ...		360,000	$120,000		480,000
Third-quarter sales ($800,000 × 75%, 25%)			600,000	$200,000	800,000
Fourth-quarter sales ($400,000 × 75%)				300,000	300,000
Total cash collections	$305,000	$440,000	$720,000	$500,000	$1,965,000

2. Based on the sales budget in units, the production budget is prepared as follows:

| | \multicolumn{4}{c}{Year 2 Quarter} | | \multicolumn{2}{c}{Year 3 Quarter} |
	1	2	3	4	Year	1	2
Budgeted sales (units)	40,000	60,000	100,000	50,000	250,000	70,000	80,000
Add desired ending inventory of finished goods* ..	18,000	30,000	15,000	21,000†	21,000	24,000	
Total needs	58,000	90,000	115,000	71,000	271,000	94,000	
Less beginning inventory of finished goods	12,000	18,000	30,000	15,000	12,000	21,000	
Required production	46,000	72,000	85,000	56,000	259,000	73,000	

*30% of the following quarter's budgeted sales in units.
†30% of the budgeted Year 3 first-quarter sales.

3. Based on the production budget figures, raw materials will need to be purchased as follows during the year:

	Year 2 Quarter					Year 3 Quarter
	1	2	3	4	Year 2	1
Required production (units)	46,000	72,000	85,000	56,000	259,000	73,000
Raw materials needed per unit (pounds)	× 5	× 5	× 5	× 5	× 5	× 5
Production needs (pounds)	230,000	360,000	425,000	280,000	1,295,000	365,000
Add desired ending inventory of raw materials (pounds)*	36,000	42,500	28,000	36,500†	36,500	
Total needs (pounds)	266,000	402,500	453,000	316,500	1,331,500	
Less beginning inventory of raw materials (pounds)	23,000	36,000	42,500	28,000	23,000	
Raw materials to be purchased (pounds)	243,000	366,500	410,500	288,500	1,308,500	

*Ten percent of the following quarter's production needs in pounds.
†Ten percent of the Year 3 first-quarter production needs in pounds.

Based on the raw material purchases above, expected cash payments are computed as follows:

	Year 2 Quarter				
	1	2	3	4	Year 2
Cost of raw materials to be purchased at $0.80 per pound	$194,400	$293,200	$328,400	$230,800	$1,046,800
Accounts payable, beginning balance	$ 81,500				$ 81,500
First-quarter purchases ($194,400 × 60%, 40%)	116,640	$ 77,760			194,400
Second-quarter purchases ($293,200 × 60%, 40%) ..		175,920	$117,280		293,200
Third-quarter purchases ($328,400 × 60%, 40%)			197,040	$131,360	328,400
Fourth-quarter purchases ($230,800 × 60%)				138,480	138,480
Total cash disbursements	$198,140	$253,680	$314,320	$269,840	$1,035,980

Glossary

Budget   A detailed plan for acquiring and using financial and other resources over a specified time period. (p. 276)

Budget committee   A group of key management persons who are responsible for overall policy matters relating to the budget program and for coordinating the preparation of the budget. (p. 281)

Cash budget   A detailed plan showing how cash resources will be acquired and used over some specific time period. (p. 283)

Control   Those steps taken by management to increase the likelihood that the objectives set down at the planning stage are attained and to ensure that all parts of the organization function in a manner consistent with organizational policies. (p. 276)

Direct labor budget   A detailed plan showing labor requirements over some specific time period. (p. 290)

Direct materials budget   A detailed plan showing the amount of raw materials that must be purchased during a period to meet both production and inventory needs. (p. 288)

Ending finished goods inventory budget   A budget showing the dollar amount of cost expected to appear on the balance sheet for unsold units at the end of a period. (p. 291)

Manufacturing overhead budget   A detailed plan showing the production costs, other than direct materials and direct labor, that will be incurred over a specified time period. (p. 290)

Master budget   A summary of a company's plans in which specific targets are set for sales, production, distribution, and financing activities and that generally culminates in a cash budget, budgeted income statement, and budgeted balance sheet. (p. 276)

Merchandise purchases budget   A budget used by a merchandising company that shows the amount of goods that must be purchased from suppliers during the period. (p. 287)

Participative budget   See *self-imposed budget.* (p. 278)

Planning   Developing objectives and preparing budgets to achieve these objectives. (p. 276)

Production budget   A detailed plan showing the number of units that must be produced during a period in order to meet both sales and inventory needs. (p. 287)

Responsibility accounting   A system of accountability in which managers are held responsible for those items of revenue and cost—and only those items—over which the manager can exert significant control. The managers are held responsible for differences between budgeted goals and actual results. (p. 277)

Sales budget   A detailed schedule showing the expected sales for coming periods; these sales are typically expressed in both dollars and units. (p. 283)

Self-imposed budget   A method of preparing budgets in which managers prepare their own budgets. These budgets are then reviewed by the manager's supervisor, and any issues are resolved by mutual agreement. (p. 278)

Selling and administrative expense budget   A detailed schedule of planned expenses that will be incurred in areas other than manufacturing during a budget period. (p. 292)

Zero-based budget   A method of budgeting in which managers are required to justify all costs as if the programs involved were being proposed for the first time. (p. 281)

Questions

7–1   What is a budget? What is budgetary control?

7–2   What are some of the major benefits to be gained from budgeting?

7–3   What is meant by the term *responsibility accounting?*

7–4   What is a master budget? Briefly describe its contents.

7–5   Why is the sales forecast the starting point in budgeting?

7–6   "As a practical matter, planning and control mean exactly the same thing." Do you agree? Explain.

7–7   What is a self-imposed budget? What are the major advantages of self-imposed budgets? What caution must be exercised in their use?

7–8   How can budgeting assist a firm in its employment policies?

7–9   "The principal purpose of the cash budget is to see how much cash the company will have in the bank at the end of the year." Do you agree? Explain.

Brief Exercises

BRIEF EXERCISE 7–1   Budget Process (LO1)

The following terms pertain to the budgeting process:

Benchmarks	Bottlenecks
Budget	Budget committee
Control	Imposed from above
Motivation	Planning
Responsibility accounting	Self-imposed budget

Required:

Fill in the blanks with the most appropriate word or phrase from the above list.

1. _____ is generally higher when an individual participates in setting his or her own goals than when the goals are imposed from above.

2. If a manager is not able to meet the budget and it has been _____, the manager can always say that the budget was unreasonable or unrealistic to start with, and therefore was impossible to meet.

3. A _____ is a detailed plan for acquiring and using financial and other resources over a specified time period.

4. _____ involves developing objectives and preparing various budgets to achieve those objectives.
5. The budgeting process can uncover potential _____ before they occur.
6. _____ involves the steps taken by management to increase the likelihood that the objectives set down at the planning stage are attained.
7. Budgets define goals and objectives that can serve as _____ for evaluating subsequent performance.
8. In _____ , a manager is held accountable for those items, and only those items, over which he or she has significant control.
9. A _____ is one that is prepared with the full cooperation and participation of managers at all levels of the organization.
10. A _____ is usually responsible for overall policy matters relating to the budget program and for coordinating the preparation of the budget itself.

BRIEF EXERCISE 7–2   Schedule of Expected Cash Collections (LO2)
Silver Company makes a product that is very popular as a Mother's Day gift. Thus, peak sales occur in May of each year. These peak sales are shown in the company's sales budget for the second quarter given below:

	April	May	June	Total
Budgeted sales	$300,000	$500,000	$200,000	$1,000,000

From past experience, the company has learned that 20% of a month's sales are collected in the month of sale, that another 70% is collected in the month following sale, and that the remaining 10% is collected in the second month following sale. Bad debts are negligible and can be ignored. February sales totaled $230,000, and March sales totaled $260,000.

Required:
1. Prepare a schedule of expected cash collections from sales, by month and in total, for the second quarter.
2. Assume that the company will prepare a budgeted balance sheet as of June 30. Compute the accounts receivable as of that date.

BRIEF EXERCISE 7–3   Production Budget (LO3)
Down Under Products, Ltd., of Australia has budgeted sales of its popular boomerang for the next four months as follows:

	Sales in Units
April	50,000
May	75,000
June	90,000
July	80,000

The company is now in the process of preparing a production budget for the second quarter. Past experience has shown that end-of-month inventory levels must equal 10% of the following month's sales. The inventory at the end of March was 5,000 units.

Required:
Prepare a production budget for the second quarter; in your budget, show the number of units to be produced each month and for the quarter in total.

BRIEF EXERCISE 7–4   Materials Purchases Budget (LO4)
Three grams of musk oil are required for each bottle of Mink Caress, a very popular perfume made by a small company in western Siberia. The cost of the musk oil is 150 roubles per gram. (Siberia is located in Russia, whose currency is the rouble.) Budgeted production of Mink Caress is given below by quarters for Year 2 and for the first quarter of Year 3.

	Year 2 Quarter				Year 3 Quarter
	First	Second	Third	Fourth	First
Budgeted production, in bottles ...	60,000	90,000	150,000	100,000	70,000

Musk oil has become so popular as a perfume base that it has become necessary to carry large inventories as a precaution against stock-outs. For this reason, the inventory of musk oil at the end of a quarter must be equal to 20% of the following quarter's production needs. Some 36,000 grams of musk oil will be on hand to start the first quarter of Year 2.

Required:
Prepare a materials purchases budget for musk oil, by quarter and in total, for Year 2. At the bottom of your budget, show the amount of purchases in roubles for each quarter and for the year in total.

BRIEF EXERCISE 7–5   Direct Labor Budget (LO5)
The production department of Rordan Corporation has submitted the following forecast of units to be produced by quarter for the upcoming fiscal year.

	1st Quarter	2nd Quarter	3rd Quarter	4th Quarter
Units to be produced	8,000	6,500	7,000	7,500

Each unit requires 0.35 direct labor-hours, and direct labor-hour workers are paid $12.00 per hour.

Required:
1. Construct the company's direct labor budget for the upcoming fiscal year, assuming that the direct labor work force is adjusted each quarter to match the number of hours required to produce the forecasted number of units produced.
2. Construct the company's direct labor budget for the upcoming fiscal year, assuming that the direct labor work force is not adjusted each quarter. Instead, assume that the company's direct labor work force consists of permanent employees who are guaranteed to be paid for at least 2,600 hours of work each quarter. If the number of required direct labor-hours is less than this number, the workers are paid for 2,600 hours anyway. Any hours worked in excess of 2,600 hours in a quarter are paid at the rate of 1.5 times the normal hourly rate for direct labor.

BRIEF EXERCISE 7–6   Manufacturing Overhead Budget (LO6)
The direct labor budget of Yuvwell Corporation for the upcoming fiscal year contains the following details concerning budgeted direct labor-hours.

	1st Quarter	2nd Quarter	3rd Quarter	4th Quarter
Budgeted direct labor-hours	8,000	8,200	8,500	7,800

The company's variable manufacturing overhead rate is $3.25 per direct labor-hour and the company's fixed manufacturing overhead is $48,000 per quarter. The only noncash item included in the fixed manufacturing overhead is depreciation, which is $16,000 per quarter.

Required:
1. Construct the company's manufacturing overhead budget for the upcoming fiscal year.
2. Compute the company's manufacturing overhead rate (including both variable and fixed manufacturing overhead) for the upcoming fiscal year. Round off to the nearest whole cent.

BRIEF EXERCISE 7–7   Selling and Administrative Budget (LO7)
The budgeted unit sales of Weller Company for the upcoming fiscal year are provided below:

	1st Quarter	2nd Quarter	3rd Quarter	4th Quarter
Budgeted unit sales	15,000	16,000	14,000	13,000

The company's variable selling and administrative expense per unit is $2.50. Fixed selling and administrative expenses include advertising expenses of $8,000 per quarter, executive salaries of $35,000 per quarter, and depreciation of $20,000 per quarter. In addition, the company makes insurance payments of $5,000 in the first quarter and $5,000 in the third quarter. Finally, property taxes of $8,000 are paid in the second quarter.

Required:
Prepare the company's selling and administrative expense budget for the upcoming fiscal year.

BRIEF EXERCISE 7–8 Cash Budget (LO8)

Garden Depot is a retailer that is preparing its budget for the upcoming fiscal year. Management has prepared the following summary of its budgeted cash flows:

	1st Quarter	2nd Quarter	3rd Quarter	4th Quarter
Total cash receipts	$180,000	$330,000	$210,000	$230,000
Total cash disbursements	$260,000	$230,000	$220,000	$240,000

The company's beginning cash balance for the upcoming fiscal year will be $20,000. The company requires a minimum cash balance of $10,000 and may borrow any amount needed from a local bank at an annual interest rate of 12%. The company may borrow any amount at the beginning of any quarter and may repay its loans, or any part of its loans, at the end of any quarter. Interest payments are due on any principal at the time it is repaid.

Required:
Prepare the company's cash budget for the upcoming fiscal year.

BRIEF EXERCISE 7–9 Budgeted Income Statement (LO9)

Gig Harbor Boating is the wholesale distributor of a small recreational catamaran sailboat. Management has prepared the following summary data to use in its annual budgeting process:

Budgeted sales (in units)	460
Selling price per unit	$1,950
Cost per unit	$1,575
Variable selling and administrative expenses (per unit)	$75
Fixed selling and administrative expenses (per year)	$105,000
Interest expense for the year	$14,000

Required:
Prepare the company's budgeted income statement.

BRIEF EXERCISE 7–10 Budgeted Balance Sheet (LO10)

The management of Mecca Copy, a photocopying center located on University Avenue, has compiled the following data to use in preparing its budgeted balance sheet for next year:

	Ending Balances
Cash	?
Accounts receivable	$ 8,100
Supplies inventory	3,200
Equipment	34,000
Accumulated depreciation	16,000
Accounts payable	1,800
Common stock	5,000
Retained earnings	?

The beginning balance of retained earnings was $28,000, net income is budgeted to be $11,500, and dividends are budgeted to be $4,800.

Required:
Prepare the company's budgeted balance sheet.

EXERCISE 7–1 Schedules of Expected Cash Collections and Disbursements (LO2, LO4, LO8)

You have been asked to prepare a December cash budget for Ashton Company, a distributor of exercise equipment. The following information is available about the company's operations:

a. The cash balance on December 1 will be $40,000.

b. Actual sales for October and November and expected sales for December are as follows:

	October	November	December
Cash sales	$ 65,000	$ 70,000	$ 83,000
Sales on account	400,000	525,000	600,000

Sales on account are collected over a three-month period in the following ratio: 20% collected in the month of sale, 60% collected in the month following sale, and 18% collected in the second month following sale. The remaining 2% is uncollectible.

c. Purchases of inventory will total $280,000 for December. Thirty percent of a month's inventory purchases are paid during the month of purchase. The accounts payable remaining from November's inventory purchases total $161,000, all of which will be paid in December.

d. Selling and administrative expenses are budgeted at $430,000 for December. Of this amount, $50,000 is for depreciation.

e. A new web server for the Marketing Department costing $76,000 will be purchased for cash during December, and dividends totaling $9,000 will be paid during the month.

f. The company must maintain a minimum cash balance of $20,000. An open line of credit is available from the company's bank to bolster the cash position as needed.

Required:

1. Prepare a schedule of expected cash collections for December.

2. Prepare a schedule of expected cash disbursements for materials during December to suppliers for inventory purchases.

3. Prepare a cash budget for December. Indicate in the financing section any borrowing that will be needed during the month.

EXERCISE 7–2 Sales and Production Budgets (LO2, LO3)

The marketing department of Jessi Corporation has submitted the following sales forecast for the upcoming fiscal year.

	1st Quarter	2nd Quarter	3rd Quarter	4th Quarter
Budgeted sales (units)	11,000	12,000	14,000	13,000

The selling price of the company's product is $18.00 per unit. Management expects to collect 65% of sales in the quarter in which the sales are made, 30% in the following quarter, and 5% of sales are expected to be uncollectible. The beginning balance of accounts receivable, all of which is expected to be collected in the first quarter, is $70,200.

The company expects to start the first quarter with 1,650 units in finished goods inventory. Management desires an ending finished goods inventory in each quarter equal to 15% of the next quarter's budgeted sales. The desired ending finished goods inventory for the fourth quarter is 1,850 units.

Required:

1. Prepare the company's sales budget and schedule of expected cash collections.

2. Prepare the company's production budget for the upcoming fiscal year.

EXERCISE 7–3 Production and Direct Materials Budgets (LO3, LO4)

The marketing department of Gaeber Industries has submitted the following sales forecast for the upcoming fiscal year.

	1st Quarter	2nd Quarter	3rd Quarter	4th Quarter
Budgeted sales (units)	8,000	7,000	6,000	7,000

The company expects to start the first quarter with 1,600 units in finished goods inventory. Management desires an ending finished goods inventory in each quarter equal to 20% of the next quarter's budgeted sales. The desired ending finished goods inventory for the fourth quarter is 1,700 units.

In addition, the beginning raw materials inventory for the first quarter is budgeted to be 3,120 pounds and the beginning accounts payable for the first quarter is budgeted to be $14,820.

Each unit requires 2 pounds of raw material that costs $4.00 per pound. Management desires to end each quarter with an inventory of raw materials equal to 20% of the following quarter's production needs. The desired ending inventory for the fourth quarter is 3,140 pounds. Management plans to pay for 75% of raw material purchases in the quarter acquired and 25% in the following quarter.

Required:

1. Prepare the company's production budget for the upcoming fiscal year.
2. Prepare the company's direct materials budget and schedule of expected cash disbursements for materials for the upcoming fiscal year.

EXERCISE 7–4   Direct Materials and Direct Labor Budgets (LO4, LO5)

The production department of Hareston Company has submitted the following forecast of units to be produced by quarter for the upcoming fiscal year.

	1st Quarter	2nd Quarter	3rd Quarter	4th Quarter
Units to be produced	7,000	8,000	6,000	5,000

In addition, the beginning raw materials inventory for the first quarter is budgeted to be 1,400 pounds and the beginning accounts payable for the first quarter is budgeted to be $2,940.

Each unit requires 2 pounds of raw material that costs $1.40 per pound. Management desires to end each quarter with an inventory of raw materials equal to 10% of the following quarter's production needs. The desired ending inventory for the fourth quarter is 1,500 pounds. Management plans to pay for 80% of raw material purchases in the quarter acquired and 20% in the following quarter. Each unit requires 0.60 direct labor-hours and direct labor-hour workers are paid $14.00 per hour.

Required:

1. Prepare the company's direct materials budget and schedule of expected cash disbursements for materials for the upcoming fiscal year.
2. Prepare the company's direct labor budget for the upcoming fiscal year, assuming that the direct labor work force is adjusted each quarter to match the number of hours required to produce the forecasted number of units produced.

EXERCISE 7–5   Direct Labor and Manufacturing Overhead Budgets (LO5, LO6)

The production department of Raredon Corporation has submitted the following forecast of units to be produced by quarter for the upcoming fiscal year.

	1st Quarter	2nd Quarter	3rd Quarter	4th Quarter
Units to be produced	12,000	14,000	13,000	11,000

Each unit requires 0.70 direct labor-hours, and direct labor-hour workers are paid $10.50 per hour.

In addition, the variable manufacturing overhead rate is $1.50 per direct labor-hour. The fixed manufacturing overhead is $80,000 per quarter. The only noncash element of manufacturing overhead is depreciation, which is $22,000 per quarter.

Required:

1. Prepare the company's direct labor budget for the upcoming fiscal year, assuming that the direct labor work force is adjusted each quarter to match the number of hours required to produce the forecasted number of units produced.
2. Prepare the company's manufacturing overhead budget.

EXERCISE 7–6   Cash Budget Relations (LO8)

A cash budget, by quarters, is given below for a retail company. Fill in the missing amounts (000 omitted). The company requires a minimum cash balance of at least $5,000 to start each quarter.

	1	2	3	4	Year
Cash balance, beginning	$ 6	$?	$?	$?	$?
Add collections from customers	?	?	96	?	323
Total cash available					
before current financing	71	?	?	?	?
Less disbursements:					
Purchase of inventory	35	45	?	35	?
Operating expenses	?	30	30	?	113
Equipment purchases	8	8	10	?	36
Dividends	2	2	2	2	?
Total disbursements	?	85	?	?	?
Excess (deficiency) of cash available					
over disbursements	(2)	?	11	?	?
Financing:					
Borrowings	?	15	—	—	?
Repayments (including interest)*	—	—	(?)	(17)	(?)
Total financing	?	?	?	?	?
Cash balance, ending	$?	$?	$?	$?	$?

*Interest will total $1,000 for the year.

Problems

PROBLEM 7–1   Schedule of Expected Cash Collections; Cash Budget (LO2, LO8)

Herbal Care Corp., a distributor of herb-based sunscreens, is ready to begin its third quarter, in which peak sales occur. The company has requested a $40,000, 90-day loan from its bank to help meet cash requirements during the quarter. Since Herbal Care has experienced difficulty in paying off its loans in the past, the loan officer at the bank has asked the company to prepare a cash budget for the quarter. In response to this request, the following data have been assembled:

a. On July 1, the beginning of the third quarter, the company will have a cash balance of $44,500.

b. Actual sales for the last two months and budgeted sales for the third quarter follow:

May (actual)	$250,000
June (actual)	300,000
July (budgeted)	400,000
August (budgeted)	600,000
September (budgeted)	320,000

Past experience shows that 25% of a month's sales are collected in the month of sale, 70% in the month following sale, and 3% in the second month following sale. The remainder is uncollectible.

c. Budgeted merchandise purchases and budgeted expenses for the third quarter are given below:

	July	August	September
Merchandise purchases	$240,000	$350,000	$175,000
Salaries and wages	45,000	50,000	40,000
Advertising	130,000	145,000	80,000
Rent payments	9,000	9,000	9,000
Depreciation	10,000	10,000	10,000

Merchandise purchases are paid in full during the month following purchase. Accounts payable for merchandise purchases on June 30, which will be paid during July, total $180,000.

d. Equipment costing $10,000 will be purchased for cash during July.

e. In preparing the cash budget, assume that the $40,000 loan will be made in July and repaid in September. Interest on the loan will total $1,200.

Required:

1. Prepare a schedule of expected cash collections for July, August, and September and for the quarter in total.
2. Prepare a cash budget, by month and in total, for the third quarter.
3. If the company needs a minimum cash balance of $20,000 to start each month, can the loan be repaid as planned? Explain.

CHECK FIGURE
(1) July: 36,000 units

PROBLEM 7–2   Production and Purchases Budgets (LO3, LO4)

Pearl Products Limited of Shenzhen, China, manufactures and distributes toys throughout Southeast Asia. Three cubic centimeters (cc) of solvent H300 are required to manufacture each unit of Supermix, one of the company's products. The company is now planning raw materials needs for the third quarter, the quarter in which peak sales of Supermix occur. To keep production and sales moving smoothly, the company has the following inventory requirements:

a. The finished goods inventory on hand at the end of each month must be equal to 3,000 units of Supermix plus 20% of the next month's sales. The finished goods inventory on June 30 is budgeted to be 10,000 units.

b. The raw materials inventory on hand at the end of each month must be equal to one-half of the following month's production needs for raw materials. The raw materials inventory on June 30 is budgeted to be 54,000 cc of solvent H300.

c. The company maintains no work in process inventories.

A sales budget for Supermix for the last six months of the year follows.

	Budgeted Sales in Units
July	35,000
August	40,000
September	50,000
October	30,000
November	20,000
December	10,000

Required:

1. Prepare a production budget for Supermix for the months July–October.
2. Examine the production budget that you prepared in (1) above. Why will the company produce more units than it sells in July and August, and fewer units than it sells in September and October?
3. Prepare a budget showing the quantity of solvent H300 to be purchased for July, August, and September, and for the quarter in total.

CHECK FIGURE
(1) May 31 cash balance: $8,900
(2) NI: $15,900

PROBLEM 7–3   Cash Budget; Income Statement; Balance Sheet (LO4, LO8, LO9, LO10)

Minden Company is a wholesale distributor of premium European chocolates. The company's balance sheet as of April 30 is given below:

MINDEN COMPANY
Balance Sheet
April 30

Assets

Cash	$ 9,000
Accounts receivable, customers	54,000
Inventory	30,000
Buildings and equipment, net of depreciation	207,000
Total assets	$300,000

Liabilities and Stockholders' Equity

Accounts payable, suppliers	$ 63,000
Note payable	14,500
Capital stock, no par	180,000
Retained earnings	42,500
Total liabilities and stockholders' equity	$300,000

The company is in the process of preparing budget data for May. A number of budget items have already been prepared, as stated below:

a. Sales are budgeted at $200,000 for May. Of these sales, $60,000 will be for cash; the remainder will be credit sales. One-half of a month's credit sales are collected in the month the sales are made, and the remainder is collected in the following month. All of the April 30 receivables will be collected in May.

b. Purchases of inventory are expected to total $120,000 during May. These purchases will all be on account. Forty percent of all purchases are paid for in the month of purchase; the remainder is paid in the following month. All of the April 30 accounts payable to suppliers will be paid during May.

c. The May 31 inventory balance is budgeted at $40,000.

d. Operating expenses for May are budgeted at $72,000, exclusive of depreciation. These expenses will be paid in cash. Depreciation is budgeted at $2,000 for the month.

e. The note payable on the April 30 balance sheet will be paid during May, with $100 in interest. (All of the interest relates to May.)

f. New refrigerating equipment costing $6,500 will be purchased for cash during May.

g. During May, the company will borrow $20,000 from its bank by giving a new note payable to the bank for that amount. The new note will be due in one year.

Required:

1. Prepare a cash budget for May. Support your budget with schedules showing budgeted cash receipts from sales and budgeted cash payments for inventory purchases.
2. Prepare a budgeted income statement for May. Use the traditional income statement format.
3. Prepare a budgeted balance sheet as of May 31.

PROBLEM 7–4   Integration of the Sales, Production, and Purchases Budgets (LO2, LO3, LO4)

Milo Company manufactures beach umbrellas. The company is now preparing detailed budgets for the third quarter and has assembled the following information to assist in the budget preparation:

a. The Marketing Department has estimated sales as follows for the remainder of the year (in units):

July	30,000	October	20,000
August	70,000	November	10,000
September	50,000	December	10,000

The selling price of the beach umbrellas is $12 per unit.

b. All sales are on account. Based on past experience, sales are collected in the following pattern:

> 30% in the month of sale
> 65% in the month following sale
> 5% uncollectible

Sales for June totaled $300,000.

c. The company maintains finished goods inventories equal to 15% of the following month's sales. This requirement will be met at the end of June.

d. Each beach umbrella requires 4 feet of Gilden, a material that is sometimes hard to get. Therefore, the company requires that the inventory of Gilden on hand at the end of each month be equal to 50% of the following month's production needs. The inventory of Gilden on hand at the beginning and end of the quarter will be:

> June 30 .... 72,000 feet
> September 30 ...... ? feet

CHECK FIGURE
(2) July: 36,000 units

e. The Gilden costs $0.80 per foot. One-half of a month's purchases of Gilden is paid for in the month of purchase; the remainder is paid for in the following month. The accounts payable on July 1 for purchases of Gilden during June will be $76,000.

Required:
1. Prepare a sales budget, by month and in total, for the third quarter. (Show your budget in both units and dollars.) Also prepare a schedule of expected cash collections, by month and in total, for the third quarter.
2. Prepare a production budget for each of the months July–October.
3. Prepare a materials purchases budget for Gilden, by month and in total, for the third quarter. Also prepare a schedule of expected cash payments for Gilden, by month and in total, for the third quarter.

CHECK FIGURE
(2a) May purchases:
     $574,000
 (3) June 30 cash balance:
     $57,100

PROBLEM 7–5   Cash Budget with Supporting Schedules (LO2, LO4, LO8)
Garden Sales, Inc., sells garden supplies. Management is planning its cash needs for the second quarter. The company usually has to borrow money during this quarter to support peak sales of lawn care equipment, which occur during May. The following information has been assembled to assist in preparing a cash budget for the quarter:
a. Budgeted monthly income statements for April–July are:

	April	May	June	July
Sales	$600,000	$900,000	$500,000	$400,000
Cost of goods sold	420,000	630,000	350,000	280,000
Gross margin	180,000	270,000	150,000	120,000
Less operating expenses:				
Selling expense	79,000	120,000	62,000	51,000
Administrative expense*	45,000	52,000	41,000	38,000
Total operating expenses	124,000	172,000	103,000	89,000
Net income	$ 56,000	$ 98,000	$ 47,000	$ 31,000

*Includes $20,000 depreciation each month.

b. Sales are 20% for cash and 80% on account.
c. Sales on account are collected over a three-month period in the following ratio: 10% collected in the month of sale; 70% collected in the first month following the month of sale; and the remaining 20% collected in the second month following the month of sale. February's sales totaled $200,000, and March's sales totaled $300,000.
d. Inventory purchases are paid for within 15 days. Therefore, 50% of a month's inventory purchases are paid for in the month of purchase. The remaining 50% is paid in the following month. Accounts payable at March 31 for inventory purchases during March total $126,000.
e. At the end of each month, inventory must be on hand equal to 20% of the cost of the merchandise to be sold in the following month. The merchandise inventory at March 31 is $84,000.
f. Dividends of $49,000 will be declared and paid in April.
g. Equipment costing $16,000 will be purchased for cash in May.
h. The cash balance at March 31 is $52,000; the company must maintain a cash balance of at least $40,000 at all times.
i. The company can borrow from its bank as needed to bolster the Cash account. Borrowings and repayments must be in multiples of $1,000. All borrowings take place at the beginning of a month, and all repayments are made at the end of a month. The annual interest rate is 12%. Compute interest on whole months ($\frac{1}{12}$, $\frac{2}{12}$, and so forth).

Required:
1. Prepare a schedule of expected cash collections from sales for each of the months April, May, and June, and for the quarter in total.
2. Prepare the following for merchandise inventory:
    a. An inventory purchases budget for each of the months April, May, and June.
    b. A schedule of expected cash disbursements for inventory for each of the months April, May, and June, and for the quarter in total.
3. Prepare a cash budget for the third quarter, by month as well as in total for the quarter. Show borrowings from the company's bank and repayments to the bank as needed to maintain the minimum cash balance.

PROBLEM 7–6   Cash Budget with Supporting Schedules (LO2, LO4, LO7, LO8)

Westex Products is a wholesale distributor of industrial cleaning products. When the treasurer of Westex Products approached the company's bank in late 1999 seeking short-term financing, he was told that money was very tight and that any borrowing over the next year would have to be supported by a detailed statement of cash receipts and disbursements. The treasurer also was told that it would be very helpful to the bank if borrowers would indicate the quarters in which they would be needing funds, as well as the amounts that would be needed, and the quarters in which repayments could be made.

Since the treasurer is unsure as to the particular quarters in which the bank financing will be needed, he has assembled the following information to assist in preparing a detailed cash budget:

a. Budgeted sales and merchandise purchases for the year 2000, as well as actual sales and purchases for the last quarter of 1999, are:

CHECK FIGURE
(2) First quarter net
payments: $75,000
(3) First quarter ending
cash balance: $12,000

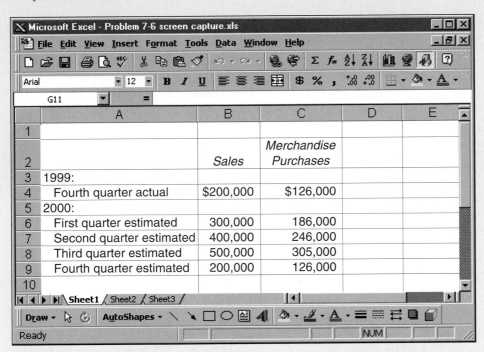

	Sales	Merchandise Purchases
1999:		
Fourth quarter actual	$200,000	$126,000
2000:		
First quarter estimated	300,000	186,000
Second quarter estimated	400,000	246,000
Third quarter estimated	500,000	305,000
Fourth quarter estimated	200,000	126,000

b. The company normally collects 65% of a quarter's sales before the quarter ends and another 33% in the following quarter. The remainder is uncollectible. This pattern of collections is now being experienced in the 1999 fourth-quarter actual data.

c. Eighty percent of a quarter's merchandise purchases are paid for within the quarter. The remainder is paid in the following quarter.

d. Operating expenses for the year 2000 are budgeted quarterly at $50,000 plus 15% of sales. Of the fixed amount, $20,000 each quarter is depreciation.

e. The company will pay $10,000 in dividends each quarter.

f. Equipment purchases of $75,000 will be made in the second quarter, and purchases of $48,000 will be made in the third quarter. These purchases will be for cash.

g. The Cash account contained $10,000 at the end of 1999. The treasurer feels that this represents a minimum balance that must be maintained.

h. Any borrowing will take place at the beginning of a quarter, and any repayments will be made at the end of a quarter at an annual interest rate of 10%. Interest is paid only when principal is repaid. All borrowings and all repayments of principal must be in round $1,000 amounts. Interest payments can be in any amount. (Compute interest on whole months, e.g., $^1\!/_{12}$, $^2\!/_{12}$.)

i. At present, the company has no loans outstanding.

Required:

1. Prepare the following by quarter and in total for the year 2000:
    a. A schedule of expected cash collections.
    b. A schedule of budgeted cash disbursements for merchandise purchases.

2. Compute the expected cash payments for operating expenses, by quarter and in total, for the year 2000.

3. Prepare a cash budget, by quarter and in total, for the year 2000. Show clearly in your budget the quarter(s) in which borrowing will be necessary and the quarter(s) in which repayments can be made, as requested by the company's bank.

PROBLEM 7–7   **Comprehensive Master Budget** (LO2, LO4, LO7, LO8, LO9, LO10)

Hillyard Company, an office supplies specialty store, prepares its master budget on a quarterly basis. The following data have been assembled to assist in preparation of the master budget for the first quarter:

a. As of December 31 (the end of the prior quarter), the company's general ledger showed the following account balances:

	Debits	Credits
Cash	$ 48,000	
Accounts Receivable	224,000	
Inventory	60,000	
Buildings and Equipment (net)	370,000	
Accounts Payable		$ 93,000
Capital Stock		500,000
Retained Earnings		109,000
	$702,000	$702,000

b. Actual sales for December and budgeted sales for the next four months are as follows:

December (actual)	$280,000
January	400,000
February	600,000
March	300,000
April	200,000

c. Sales are 20% for cash and 80% on credit. All payments on credit sales are collected in the month following sale. The accounts receivable at December 31 are a result of December credit sales.

d. The company's gross profit rate is 40% of sales.

e. Monthly expenses are budgeted as follows: salaries and wages, $27,000 per month: advertising, $70,000 per month; shipping, 5% of sales; depreciation, $14,000 per month; other expenses, 3% of sales.

f. At the end of each month, inventory is to be on hand equal to 25% of the following month's sales needs, stated at cost.

g. One-half of a month's inventory purchases is paid for in the month of purchase; the other half is paid for in the following month.

h. During February, the company will purchase a new copy machine for $1,700 cash. During March, other equipment will be purchased for cash at a cost of $84,500.

i. During January, the company will declare and pay $45,000 in cash dividends.

j. The company must maintain a minimum cash balance of $30,000. An open line of credit is available at a local bank for any borrowing that may be needed during the quarter. All borrowing is done at the beginning of a month, and all repayments are made at the end of a month. Borrowings and repayments of principal must be in multiples of $1,000. Interest is paid only at the time of payment of principal. The annual interest rate is 12%. (Figure interest on whole months, e.g., $\frac{1}{12}$, $\frac{2}{12}$.)

Required:

Using the data above, complete the following statements and schedules for the first quarter:

1. Schedule of expected cash collections:

	January	February	March	Quarter
Cash sales	$ 80,000			
Credit sales	224,000			
Total cash collections	$304,000			

2. a. Inventory purchases budget:

	January	February	March	Quarter
Budgeted cost of goods sold	$240,000*	$360,000		
Add desired ending inventory	90,000†			
Total needs	330,000			
Less beginning inventory	60,000			
Required purchases	$270,000			

*For January sales: $400,000 sales × 60% cost ratio = $240,000.
†$360,000 × 25% = $90,000.

b. Schedule of cash disbursements for purchases:

	January	February	March	Quarter
December purchases	$ 93,000			$ 93,000
January purchases ($270,000)	135,000	135,000		270,000
February purchases				
March purchases				
Total cash disbursements for purchases	$228,000			

3. Schedule of cash disbursements for expenses:

	January	February	March	Quarter
Salaries and wages	$ 27,000			
Advertising	70,000			
Shipping	20,000			
Other expenses	12,000			
Total cash disbursements for operating expenses	$129,000			

4. Cash budget:

	January	February	March	Quarter
Cash balance, beginning	$ 48,000			
Add cash collections	304,000			
Total cash available	352,000			
Less disbursements:				
Purchases of inventory	228,000			
Operating expenses	129,000			
Purchases of equipment	—			
Cash dividends	45,000			
Total disbursements	402,000			
Excess (deficiency) of cash	(50,000)			
Financing:				
Etc.				

5. Prepare an income statement for the quarter ending March 31 as shown in Schedule 9 in the chapter.
6. Prepare a balance sheet as of March 31.

PROBLEM 7–8   Comprehensive Master Budget (LO2, LO4, LO7, LO8, LO9, LO10)
Following is selected information relating to the operations of Shilow Company, a wholesale distributor:

Current assets as of March 31:	
Cash	$ 8,000
Accounts receivable	20,000
Inventory	36,000
Plant and equipment, net	120,000
Accounts payable	21,750
Capital stock	150,000
Retained earnings	12,250

a. Gross profit is 25% of sales.
b. Actual and budgeted sales data:

March (actual)	$50,000
April	60,000
May	72,000
June	90,000
July	48,000

c. Sales are 60% for cash and 40% on credit. Credit sales are collected in the month following sale. The accounts receivable at March 31 are a result of March credit sales.
d. At the end of each month, inventory is to be on hand equal to 80% of the following month's sales needs, stated at cost.
e. One-half of a month's inventory purchases is paid for in the month of purchase; the other half is paid for in the following month. The accounts payable at March 31 are a result of March purchases of inventory.
f. Monthly expenses are as follows: salaries and wages, 12% of sales; rent, $2,500 per month; other expenses (excluding depreciation), 6% of sales. Assume that these expenses are paid monthly. Depreciation is $900 per month (includes depreciation on new assets).
g. Equipment costing $1,500 will be purchased for cash in April.
h. The company must maintain a minimum cash balance of $4,000. An open line of credit is available at a local bank. All borrowing is done at the beginning of a month, and all repayments are made at the end of a month; borrowing must be in multiples of $1,000. The annual interest rate is 12%. Interest is paid only at the time of repayment of principal; figure interest on whole months ($\frac{1}{12}$, $\frac{2}{12}$, and so forth).

Required:
Using the data above:
1. Complete the following schedule:

Schedule of Expected Cash Collections

	April	May	June	Quarter
Cash sales	$36,000			
Credit sales	20,000	____	____	____
Total collections	$56,000			

2. Complete the following:

Inventory Purchases Budget

	April	May	June	Quarter
Budgeted cost of goods sold	$45,000*	$54,000		
Add desired ending inventory	43,200†			
Total needs	88,200	____	____	____
Less beginning inventory	36,000			
Required purchases	$52,200			

*For April sales: $60,000 sales × 75% cost ratio = $45,000.
†$54,000 × 80% = $43,200.

Schedule of Expected Cash Disbursements—Purchases

	April	May	June	Quarter
March purchases	$21,750			$21,750
April purchases	26,100	$26,100		52,200
May purchases				
June purchases				
Total disbursements	$47,850			

3. Complete the following:

Schedule of Expected Cash Disbursements—Operating Expenses

	April	May	June	Quarter
Salaries and wages	$ 7,200			
Rent	2,500			
Other expenses	3,600			
Total disbursements	$13,300			

4. Complete the following cash budget:

Cash Budget

	April	May	June	Quarter
Cash balance, beginning	$ 8,000			
Add cash collections	56,000			
Total cash available	64,000			
Less cash disbursements:				
For inventory	47,850			
For expenses	13,300			
For equipment	1,500			
Total cash disbursements	62,650			
Excess (deficiency) of cash	1,350			
Financing:				
Etc.				

5. Prepare an income statement for the quarter ended June 30. (Use the functional format in preparing your income statement, as shown in Schedule 9 in the text.)
6. Prepare a balance sheet as of June 30.

Building Your Skills

ANALYTICAL THINKING (LO2, LO4, LO8, LO9, LO10)

You have just been hired as a new management trainee by Earrings Unlimited, a distributor of earrings to various retail outlets located in shopping malls across the country. In the past, the company has done very little in the way of budgeting and at certain times of the year has experienced a shortage of cash.

Since you are well trained in budgeting, you have decided to prepare comprehensive budgets for the upcoming second quarter in order to show management the benefits that can be gained from an integrated budgeting program. To this end, you have worked with accounting and other areas to gather the information assembled below.

The company sells many styles of earrings, but all are sold for the same price—$10 per pair. Actual sales of earrings for the last three months and budgeted sales for the next six months follow (in pairs of earrings):

CHECK FIGURE
(1c) April purchases: 79,000 units
(2) June 30 cash balance: $94,700

January (actual)	20,000	June (budget)	50,000
February (actual)	26,000	July (budget)	30,000
March (actual)	40,000	August (budget)	28,000
April (budget)	65,000	September (budget)	25,000
May (budget)	100,000		

The concentration of sales before and during May is due to Mother's Day. Sufficient inventory should be on hand at the end of each month to supply 40% of the earrings sold in the following month.

Suppliers are paid $4 for a pair of earrings. One-half of a month's purchases is paid for in the month of purchase; the other half is paid for in the following month. All sales are on credit, with no discount, and payable within 15 days. The company has found, however, that only 20% of a month's sales are collected in the month of sale. An additional 70% is collected in the following month, and the remaining 10% is collected in the second month following sale. Bad debts have been negligible.

Monthly operating expenses for the company are given below:

Variable:	
Sales commissions	4% of sales
Fixed:	
Advertising	$200,000
Rent	18,000
Salaries	106,000
Utilities	7,000
Insurance expired	3,000
Depreciation	14,000

Insurance is paid on an annual basis, in November of each year.

The company plans to purchase $16,000 in new equipment during May and $40,000 in new equipment during June; both purchases will be for cash. The company declares dividends of $15,000 each quarter, payable in the first month of the following quarter.

A listing of the company's ledger accounts as of March 31 is given below:

Assets	
Cash	$ 74,000
Accounts receivable ($26,000 February sales;	
$320,000 March sales)	346,000
Inventory	104,000
Prepaid insurance	21,000
Property and equipment (net)	950,000
Total assets	$1,495,000

Liabilities and Stockholders' Equity	
Accounts payable	$ 100,000
Dividends payable	15,000
Capital stock	800,000
Retained earnings	580,000
Total liabilities and stockholders' equity	$1,495,000

Part of the use of the budgeting program will be to establish an ongoing line of credit at a local bank. Therefore, determine the borrowing that will be needed to maintain a minimum cash balance of $50,000. All borrowing will be done at the beginning of a month; any repayments will be made at the end of a month.

The annual interest rate will be 12%. Interest will be computed and paid at the end of each quarter on all loans outstanding during the quarter. Compute interest on whole months ($\frac{1}{12}$, $\frac{2}{12}$, and so forth).

Required:
Prepare a master budget for the three-month period ending June 30. Include the following detailed budgets:
1. a. A sales budget, by month and in total.
   b. A schedule of expected cash collections from sales, by month and in total.
   c. A merchandise purchases budget in units and in dollars. Show the budget by month and in total.
   d. A schedule of expected cash disbursements for merchandise purchases, by month and in total.
2. A cash budget. Show the budget by month and in total.
3. A budgeted income statement for the three-month period ending June 30. Use the contribution approach.
4. A budgeted balance sheet as of June 30.

COMMUNICATING IN PRACTICE (LO8)

Risky Rolling, Inc. is a rapidly expanding manufacturer of skateboards that have been modified for use on ski slopes during the off-season. This year's sales are considerably higher than last year's sales, and sales are expected to double next year. The unexpected growth in sales has presented numerous challenges to the company's management team and the stress is really starting to show. Laura Dennan, the company's president, believes that the management time required to prepare a cash budget should be devoted to other, more pressing matters.

Required:
Write a memorandum to the president that states why cash budgeting is particularly important to a rapidly expanding company such as Risky Rolling.

ETHICS CHALLENGE (LO1, LO2)

Norton Company, a manufacturer of infant furniture and carriages, is in the initial stages of preparing the annual budget for next year. Scott Ford has recently joined Norton's accounting staff and is interested to learn as much as possible about the company's budgeting process. During a recent lunch with Marge Atkins, sales manager, and Pete Granger, production manager, Ford initiated the following conversation.

Ford: Since I'm new around here and am going to be involved with the preparation of the annual budget, I'd be interested to learn how the two of you estimate sales and production numbers.
Atkins: We start out very methodically by looking at recent history, discussing what we know about current accounts, potential customers, and the general state of consumer spending. Then, we add that usual dose of intuition to come up with the best forecast we can.
Granger: I usually take the sales projections as the basis for my projections. Of course, we have to make an estimate of what this year's ending inventories will be, which is sometimes difficult.
Ford: Why does that present a problem? There must have been an estimate of ending inventories in the budget for the current year.
Granger: Those numbers aren't always reliable since Marge makes some adjustments to the sales number before passing them on to me.
Ford: What kind of adjustments?
Atkins: Well, we don't want to fall short of the sales projections so we generally give ourselves a little breathing room by lowering the initial sales projection anywhere from 5% to 10%.
Granger: So, you can see why this year's budget is not a very reliable starting point. We always have to adjust the projected production rates as the year progresses and, of course, this changes the ending inventory estimates. By the way, we make similar adjustments to expenses by adding at least 10% to the estimates; I think everyone around here does the same thing.

Required:
1. Marge Atkins and Pete Granger have described the use of what is sometimes called *budgetary slack*.
   a. Explain why Atkins and Granger behave in this manner and describe the benefits they expect to realize from the use of budgetary slack.
   b. Explain how the use of budgetary slack can adversely affect Atkins and Granger.
2. As a management accountant, Scott Ford believes that the behavior described by Marge Atkins and Pete Granger may be unethical. By referring to the Standards of Ethical Conduct for Practitioners of Management Accounting and Financial Management in Chapter 1, explain why the use of budgetary slack may be unethical.

(CMA, adapted)

TAKING IT TO THE NET

As you know, the World Wide Web is a medium that is constantly evolving. Sites come and go and change without notice. To enable periodic update of site addresses, this problem has been posted to the textbook web site (www.mhhe.com/folk1e). After accessing the site, enter the Student Center and select this chapter. Select and complete the Taking It to the Net problem.

TEAMWORK IN ACTION (LO1)

Tom Emory and Jim Morris strolled back to their plant from the administrative offices of Ferguson & Son Mfg. Company. Tom is manager of the machine shop in the company's factory; Jim is manager of the equipment maintenance department.

The men had just attended the monthly performance evaluation meeting for plant department heads. These meetings had been held on the third Tuesday of each month since Robert Ferguson, Jr., the president's son, had become plant manager a year earlier.

As they were walking, Tom Emory spoke: "Boy, I hate those meetings! I never know whether my department's accounting reports will show good or bad performance. I'm beginning to expect the worst. If the accountants say I saved the company a dollar, I'm called 'Sir,' but if I spend even a little too much—boy, do I get in trouble. I don't know if I can hold on until I retire."

Tom had just been given the worst evaluation he had ever received in his long career with Ferguson & Son. He was the most respected of the experienced machinists in the company. He had been with Ferguson & Son for many years and was promoted to supervisor of the machine shop when the company expanded and moved to its present location. The president (Robert Ferguson, Sr.) had often stated that the company's success was due to the high quality of the work of machinists like Tom. As supervisor, Tom stressed the importance of craftsmanship and told his workers that he wanted no sloppy work coming from his department.

When Robert Ferguson, Jr., became the plant manager, he directed that monthly performance comparisons be made between actual and budgeted costs for each department. The departmental budgets were intended to encourage the supervisors to reduce inefficiencies and to seek cost reduction opportunities. The company controller was instructed to have his staff "tighten" the budget slightly whenever a department attained its budget in a given month; this was done to reinforce the plant manager's desire to reduce costs. The young plant manager often stressed the importance of continued progress toward attaining the budget; he also made it known that he kept a file of these performance reports for future reference when he succeeded his father.

Tom Emory's conversation with Jim Morris continued as follows:

Emory: I really don't understand. We've worked so hard to get up to budget, and the minute we make it they tighten the budget on us. We can't work any faster and still maintain quality. I think my men are ready to quit trying. Besides, those reports don't tell the whole story. We always seem to be interrupting the big jobs for all those small rush orders. All that setup and machine adjustment time is killing us. And quite frankly, Jim, you were no help. When our hydraulic press broke down last month, your people were nowhere to be found. We had to take it apart ourselves and got stuck with all that idle time.

Morris: I'm sorry about that, Tom, but you know my department has had trouble making budget, too. We were running well behind at the time of that problem, and if we'd spent a day on that old machine, we would never have made it up. Instead we made the scheduled inspections of the forklift trucks because we knew we could do those in less than the budgeted time.

Emory: Well, Jim, at least you have some options. I'm locked into what the scheduling department assigns to me and you know they're being harassed by sales for those special orders. Incidentally, why didn't your report show all the supplies you guys wasted last month when you were working in Bill's department?

Morris: We're not out of the woods on that deal yet. We charged the maximum we could to other work and haven't even reported some of it yet.

Emory: Well, I'm glad you have a way of getting out of the pressure. The accountants seem to know everything that's happening in my department, sometimes even before I do. I thought all that budget and accounting stuff was supposed to help, but it just gets me into trouble. It's all a big pain. I'm trying to put out quality work; they're trying to save pennies.

Required:

The team should discuss and then respond to the following two questions. All team members should agree with and understand the answers and be prepared to explain the solutions in class. (Each teammate can assume responsibility for a different part of the presentation.)

1. Identify the problems that appear to exist in Ferguson & Son Mfg. Company's budgetary control system and explain how the problems are likely to reduce the effectiveness of the system.
2. Explain how Ferguson & Son Mfg. Company's budgetary control system could be revised to improve its effectiveness.

(CMA, adapted)

Chapter Eight

Standard Costs

A Look Back

We discussed the budgeting process in Chapter 7 and overviewed each of the budgets that constitute the master budget.

A Look at This Chapter

We begin a discussion of management control and performance measures by focusing on standard costing systems in Chapter 8. Management by exception and variance analysis are described, as are the computations of material, labor, and overhead variances.

A Look Ahead

We compare and contrast the static budget approach to a flexible budget approach in Chapter 9 and discuss the preparation of performance reports, using a flexible budget approach, to analyze overhead variances.

Chapter Outline

Decision Feature Setting A New Standard for the Restaurant Industry

In 1965, Alan Stillman, an unattached perfume salesman, came up with the ideal way to meet girls in his New York neighborhood. He bought and renovated a rundown neighborhood bar, and named his new restaurant T.G.I.F. (Thank Goodness It's Friday). "Friday's" was an instant success with $1 million in sales during its first year. In 1972, a group of Dallas businessmen surpassed the feat. Their Dallas T.G.I. Friday's® franchise earned revenues of $2 million in its first year. The two businesses merged and expanded. Today, the restaurant, with its red and white striped theme, wooden floors, booths with Tiffany lamps, authentic memorabilia, and blue exterior, is a common sight. By 2000, there were 438 T.G.I. Friday's® operating in the U.S. and 137 in 49 countries throughout the world. Approximately two-thirds of the restaurants are franchised; Carlson Restaurants Worldwide Inc. owns the rest.

Michael Hinkle-Morrison, vice president of knowledge technologies for Friday's Hospitality Worldwide (www.tgifridays.com), implemented two major technology initiatives in 1997. The first program enhanced the speed of service. Seating is managed by the use of touch screens and orders are displayed on monitors. The system can routinely generate reports such as a comparison of the sales of servers. The information generated by the system has helped the restaurants to operate more efficiently.

The second program was modeled after the standard costing systems commonly used by manufacturers. After establishing standards by studying the actual amount of time that it takes to perform each task in the restaurant, the company developed a straightforward spreadsheet program to measure actual performance against those standards. Restaurant managers are now able to recognize changes that need to be made to employee schedules in order to meet productivity goals. In addition, the system identifies those workers who are not meeting the company's standards.

Hinkle-Morrison's challenge is to avoid information-overload. He does not want managers to spend all of their time at their desks. Each manager needs to understand how well the restaurant is performing and keep focused on the dining experience of its customers.

Sources: Carlson Restaurants Worldwide Inc. website, July 2000; Hoover's Online website, July 2000; T.G.I. Friday's® website, July 2000; Alan Liddle, "Michael Hinkle-Morrison: Making Tech Work at Friday's Every Day," *Nation's Restaurant News,* May 19, 1997, p. 120.

In this chapter we begin our study of management control and performance measures. As explained in the following quotation, performance measurement serves a vital function in both personal life and in organizations:

> Imagine you want to improve your basketball shooting skill. You know that practice will help, so you [go] to the basketball court. There you start shooting toward the hoop, but as soon as the ball gets close to the rim your vision goes blurry for a second, so that you cannot observe where the ball ended up in relation to the target (left, right, in front, too far back, inside the hoop?). It would be pretty difficult to improve under those conditions. . . . (And by the way, how long would [shooting baskets] sustain your interest if you couldn't observe the outcome of your efforts?)
>
> Or imagine someone engaging in a weight loss program. A normal step in such programs is to purchase a scale to be able to track one's progress: Is this program working? Am I losing weight? A positive answer would be encouraging and would motivate me to keep up the effort, while a negative answer might lead me to reflect on the process: Am I working on the right diet and exercise program? Am I doing everything I am supposed to? etc. Suppose you don't want to set up a sophisticated measurement system and decide to forgo the scale. You would still have some idea of how well you are doing from simple methods such as clothes feeling looser, a belt that fastens at a different hole, or simply via observation in a mirror! Now, imagine trying to sustain a weight loss program without *any* feedback on how well you are doing.
>
> In these . . . examples, availability of quantitative measures of performance can yield two types of benefits: First, performance feedback can help improve the "production process" through a better understanding of what works and what doesn't; e.g., shooting this way works better than shooting that way. Secondly, feedback on performance can sustain motivation and effort, because it is encouraging and/or because it suggests that more effort is required for the goal to be met.[1]

In the same way, performance measurement can be helpful in an organization. It can provide feedback concerning what works and what does not work, and it can help motivate people to sustain their efforts.

Companies in highly competitive industries like Federal Express, Southwest Airlines, Dell Computer, Shell Oil, and Toyota must be able to provide high-quality goods and services at low cost. If they do not, they will perish. Stated in the starkest terms, managers must obtain inputs such as raw materials and electricity at the lowest possible prices and must use them as effectively as possible—while maintaining or increasing the quality of the output. If inputs are purchased at prices that are too high or more input is used than is really necessary, higher costs will result.

How do managers control the prices that are paid for inputs and the quantities that are used? They could examine every transaction in detail, but this obviously would be an inefficient use of management time. For many companies, the answer to this control problem lies at least partially in *standard costs*.

Standard Costs—Management by Exception

A *standard* is a benchmark or "norm" for measuring performance. Standards are found everywhere. Your doctor evaluates your weight using standards that have been set for individuals of your age, height, and gender. The food we eat in restaurants must be prepared under specified standards of cleanliness. The buildings we live in must conform to standards set in building codes. Standards are also widely used in managerial accounting where they relate to the *quantity* and *cost* of inputs used in manufacturing goods or providing services.

---

[1]Soumitra Dutta and Jean-François Manzoni, *Process Reengineering, Organizational Change and Performance Improvement* (New York: McGraw-Hill, 1999), Chapter IV.

Managers—often assisted by engineers and accountants—set quantity and cost standards for each major input such as raw materials and labor time. *Quantity standards* indicate how much of an input should be used in manufacturing a unit of product or in providing a unit of service. *Cost (price) standards* indicate what the cost, or purchase price, of the input should be. Actual quantities and actual costs of inputs are compared to these standards. If either the quantity or the cost of inputs departs significantly from the standards, managers investigate the discrepancy. The purpose is to find the cause of the problem and then eliminate it so that it does not recur. This process is called **management by exception.**

In our daily lives, we operate in a management by exception mode most of the time. Consider what happens when you sit down in the driver's seat of your car. You put the key in the ignition, you turn the key, and your car starts. Your expectation (standard) that the car will start is met; you do not have to open the car hood and check the battery, the connecting cables, the fuel lines, and so on. If you turn the key and the car does not start, then you have a discrepancy (variance). Your expectations are not met, and you need to investigate why. Note that even if the car starts after a second try, it would be wise to investigate anyway. The fact that the expectation was not met should be viewed as an opportunity to uncover the cause of the problem rather than as simply an annoyance. If the underlying cause is not discovered and corrected, the problem may recur and become much worse.

Who Uses Standard Costs?

Manufacturing, service, food, and not-for-profit organizations all make use of standards to some extent. Auto service centers like Firestone and Sears, for example, often set specific labor time standards for the completion of certain work tasks, such as installing a carburetor or doing a valve job, and then measure actual performance against these standards. Fast-food outlets such as McDonald's have exacting standards for the quantity of meat going into a sandwich, as well as standards for the cost of the meat. Hospitals have standard costs (for food, laundry, and other items) for each occupied bed per day, as well as standard time allowances for certain routine activities, such as laboratory tests. In short, you are likely to run into standard costs in virtually any line of business that you enter.

Manufacturing companies often have highly developed standard costing systems in which standards relating to materials, labor, and overhead are developed in detail for each separate product. These standards are listed on a **standard cost card** that provides the manager with a great deal of information concerning the inputs that are required to produce a unit and their costs. In the following section, we provide a detailed example of the setting of standard costs and the preparation of a standard cost card.

Setting Standard Costs

Setting price and quantity standards is more an art than a science. It requires the combined expertise of all persons who have responsibility over input prices and over the effective use of inputs. In a manufacturing setting, this might include accountants, purchasing managers, engineers, production supervisors, line managers, and production workers. Past records of purchase prices and of input usage can be helpful in setting standards. However, the standards should be designed to encourage efficient *future* operations, not a repetition of past inefficient operations.

Ideal versus Practical Standards

Should standards be attainable all of the time, should they be attainable only part of the time, or should they be so tight that they become, in effect, "the impossible dream"? Opinions among managers vary, but standards tend to fall into one of two categories— either ideal or practical.

Ideal standards are those that can be attained only under the best circumstances. They allow for no machine breakdowns or other work interruptions, and they call for a level of effort that can be attained only by the most skilled and efficient employees working at peak effort 100% of the time. Some managers feel that such standards have a motivational value. These managers argue that even though employees know they will rarely meet the standard, it is a constant reminder of the need for ever-increasing efficiency and effort. Few firms use ideal standards. Most managers feel that ideal standards tend to discourage even the most diligent workers. Moreover, variances from ideal standards are difficult to interpret. Large variances from the ideal are normal and it is difficult to "manage by exception."

Practical standards are defined as standards that are "tight but attainable." They allow for normal machine downtime and employee rest periods, and they can be attained through reasonable, though highly efficient, efforts by the average worker. Variances from such a standard represent deviations that fall outside of normal operating conditions and signal a need for management attention. Furthermore, practical standards can serve multiple purposes. In addition to signaling abnormal conditions, they can also be used in forecasting cash flows and in planning inventory. By contrast, ideal standards cannot be used in forecasting and planning; they do not allow for normal inefficiencies, and therefore they result in unrealistic planning and forecasting figures.

Throughout the remainder of this chapter, we will assume the use of practical rather than ideal standards.

you *decide*   **Baseball Coach**

During the summer, you coach a little league team in your neighborhood. One of the parents has approached you with a list of Major League records that he believes should be used as benchmarks or standards for performance for the kids. The parent suggests that players who meet the benchmarks be recognized and rewarded for their efforts. How do you respond?

The Colonial Pewter Company was organized a year ago. The company's only product is a reproduction of an 18th century pewter bookend. The bookend is made largely by hand, using traditional metal-working tools. Consequently, the manufacturing process is labor intensive and requires a high level of skill.

Colonial Pewter has recently expanded its work force to take advantage of unexpected demand for the bookends as gifts. The company started with a small cadre of experienced pewter workers but has had to hire less experienced workers as a result of the expansion. The president of the company, J. D. Wriston, has called a meeting to discuss production problems. Attending the meeting are Tom Kuchel, the production manager; Janet Warner, the purchasing manager; and Terry Sherman, the corporate controller.

J. D.: I've got a feeling that we aren't getting the production we should out of our new people.
Tom: Give us a chance. Some of the new people have been on board for less than a month.
Janet: Let me add that production seems to be wasting an awful lot of material—particularly pewter. That stuff is very expensive.
Tom: What about the shipment of defective pewter you bought a couple of months ago—the one with the iron contamination? That caused us major problems.
Janet: That's ancient history. How was I to know it was off-grade? Besides, it was a great deal.
J. D.: Calm down everybody. Let's get the facts before we start sinking our fangs into each other.
Tom: I agree. The more facts the better.
J. D.: Okay, Terry, it's your turn. Facts are the controller's department.
Terry: I'm afraid I can't provide the answers off the top of my head, but it won't take me too long to set up a system that can routinely answer questions relating to worker productivity, material waste, and input prices.
J. D.: How long is "not too long"?
Terry: I will need all of your cooperation, but how about a week from today?
J. D.: That's okay with me. What about everyone else?
Tom: Sure.
Janet: Fine with me.
J. D.: Let's mark it on our calendars.

Setting Direct Materials Standards

Terry Sherman's first task was to prepare price and quantity standards for the company's only significant raw material, pewter ingots. The **standard price per unit** for direct materials should reflect the final, delivered cost of the materials, net of any discounts taken. After consulting with purchasing manager Janet Warner, Terry prepared the following documentation for the standard price of a pound of pewter in ingot form:

Purchase price, top-grade pewter ingots, in 40-pound ingots	$3.60
Freight, by truck, from the supplier's warehouse	0.44
Receiving and handling	0.05
Less purchase discount	(0.09)
Standard price per pound	$4.00

Notice that the standard price reflects a particular grade of material (top grade), purchased in particular lot sizes (40-pound ingots), and delivered by a particular type of carrier (truck). Allowances have also been made for handling and discounts. If everything proceeds according to these expectations, the net cost of a pound of pewter should therefore be $4.00.

Managerial Accounting in Action

The Issue

Learning Objective 1
Explain how direct materials standards and direct labor standards are set.

The **standard quantity per unit** for direct materials should reflect the amount of material going into each unit of finished product, as well as an allowance for unavoidable waste, spoilage, and other normal inefficiencies. After consulting with the production manager, Tom Kuchel, Terry Sherman prepared the following documentation for the standard quantity of pewter in a pair of bookends:

Material requirements as specified in the bill of materials for a pair of bookends, in pounds	2.7
Allowance for waste and spoilage, in pounds	0.2
Allowance for rejects, in pounds	0.1
Standard quantity per pair of bookends, in pounds	3.0

A **bill of materials** is a list that shows the quantity of each type of material going into a unit of finished product. It is a handy source for determining the basic material input per unit, but it should be adjusted for waste and other factors, as shown above, when determining the standard quantity per unit of product. "Waste and spoilage" in the table above refers to materials that are wasted as a normal part of the production process or that spoil before they are used. "Rejects" refers to the direct material contained in units that are defective and must be scrapped.

in business today "Allowable" Waste

After many years of operating a standard cost system, a major wood products company reviewed the materials standards for its products by breaking each standard down into its basic elements. In doing so, the company discovered that there was a 20% waste factor built into the standard cost for every product. Management was dismayed to learn that the dollar amount of "allowable" waste was so large. Since the quantity standards had not been scrutinized for many years, management was unaware of the existence of this significant cost improvement potential in the company.

Source: James M. Reeve, "The Impact of Variation on Operating System Performance," *Performance Excellence* (Sarasota, FL: American Accounting Association, 1990), p. 77.

Although it is common to recognize allowances for waste, spoilage, and rejects when setting standard costs, this practice is now coming into question. Those involved in TQM (total quality management) and similar improvement programs argue that no amount of waste or defects should be tolerated. If allowances for waste, spoilage, and rejects are built into the standard cost, the levels of those allowances should be periodically reviewed and reduced over time to reflect improved processes, better training, and better equipment.

Once the price and quantity standards have been set, the standard cost of material per unit of finished product can be computed as follows:

$$3.0 \text{ pounds per unit} \times \$4.00 \text{ per pound} = \$12 \text{ per unit}$$

This $12 cost figure will appear as one item on the standard cost card of the product.

Setting Direct Labor Standards

Direct labor price and quantity standards are usually expressed in terms of a labor rate and labor-hours. The **standard rate per hour** for direct labor should include not only wages earned but also fringe benefits and other labor costs. Using last month's wage records and in consultation with the production manager, Terry determined the standard rate per hour at the Colonial Pewter Company as follows:

Basic wage rate per hour	$10
Employment taxes at 10% of the basic rate	1
Fringe benefits at 30% of the basic rate	3
Standard rate per direct labor-hour	$14

Many companies prepare a single standard rate for all employees in a department. This standard rate reflects the expected "mix" of workers, even though the actual wage rates may vary somewhat from individual to individual due to differing skills or seniority. A single standard rate simplifies the use of standard costs and also permits the manager to monitor the use of employees within departments. More is said on this point a little later. According to the standard computed above, the direct labor rate for Colonial Pewter should average $14 per hour.

The standard direct labor time required to complete a unit of product (generally called the **standard hours per unit**) is perhaps the single most difficult standard to determine. One approach is to divide each operation performed on the product into elemental body movements (such as reaching, pushing, and turning over). Published tables of standard times for such movements are available. These times can be applied to the movements and then added together to determine the total standard time allowed per operation. Another approach is for an industrial engineer to do a time and motion study, actually clocking the time required for certain tasks. As stated earlier, the standard time should include allowances for breaks, personal needs of employees, cleanup, and machine downtime. After consulting with the production manager, Terry prepared the following documentation for the standard hours per unit:

Basic labor time per unit, in hours	1.9
Allowance for breaks and personal needs	0.1
Allowance for cleanup and machine downtime	0.3
Allowance for rejects	0.2
Standard labor-hours per unit of product	2.5

Once the rate and time standards have been set, the standard labor cost per unit of product can be computed as follows:

$$\text{2.5 hours per unit} \times \text{\$14 per hour} = \text{\$35 per unit}$$

This $35 cost figure appears along with direct materials as one item on the standard cost card of the product.

Beating Standards

in business | *today*

Industrie Natuzzi SpA, founded and run by Pasquale Natuzzi, produces handmade leather furniture for the world market in Santaeramo Del Colle in southern Italy. Natuzzi is export-oriented and has, for example, about 25% of the U.S. leather furniture market. The company's furniture is handmade by craftsmen, each of whom has a computer terminal that is linked to a sophisticated computer network. The computer terminal provides precise instructions on how to accomplish a particular task in making a piece of furniture. And the computer keeps track of how quickly the craftsman completes the task. If the craftsman beats the standard time to complete the task, the computer adds a bonus to the craftsman's pay.

The company's computers know exactly how much thread, screws, foam, leather, labor, and so on, is required for every model. "Should the price of Argentinean hides or German dyes rise one day, employees in Santaeramo enter the new prices into the computer, and the costs for all sofas with that leather and those colors are immediately recalculated. 'Everything has to be clear for me,' says Natuzzi. 'Why this penny? Where is it going?'"

Source: Richard C. Morais, "A Methodical Man," *Forbes,* August 11, 1997, pp. 70–72.

Setting Variable Manufacturing Overhead Standards

As with direct labor, the price and quantity standards for variable manufacturing overhead are generally expressed in terms of rate and hours. The rate represents *the variable portion of the predetermined overhead rate* discussed in Chapter 2; the hours represent whatever hours base is used to apply overhead to units of product (usually machine-hours or direct labor-hours, as we learned in Chapter 2). At Colonial Pewter, the variable portion of the predetermined overhead rate is $3 per direct labor-hour. Therefore, the standard variable manufacturing overhead cost per unit is computed as follows:

$$\text{2.5 hours per unit} \times \text{\$3 per hour} = \text{\$7.50 per unit}$$

This $7.50 cost figure appears along with direct materials and direct labor as one item on the standard cost card in Exhibit 8–1. Observe that the **standard cost per unit** is computed by multiplying the standard quantity or hours by the standard price or rate.

Are Standards the Same as Budgets?

Standards and budgets are very similar. The major distinction between the two terms is that a standard is a *unit* amount, whereas a budget is a *total* amount. The standard cost for materials at Colonial Pewter is $12 per pair of bookends. If 1,000 pairs of bookends are to be manufactured during a budgeting period, then the budgeted cost of materials would be $12,000. In effect, *a standard can be viewed as the budgeted cost for one unit of product.*

A General Model for Variance Analysis

An important reason for separating standards into two categories—price and quantity—is that different managers are usually responsible for buying and for using inputs and these two activities occur at different points in time. In the case of raw materials, for example, the purchasing manager is responsible for the price, and this responsibility is exercised at the time of purchase. In contrast, the production manager is responsible for the amount of the raw material used, and this responsibility is exercised when the materials are used in production, which may be many weeks or months after the purchase date. It

Exhibit 8–1
Standard Cost Card—Variable Production Cost

Inputs	(1) Standard Quantity or Hours	(2) Standard Price or Rate	(3) Standard Cost (1) × (2)
Direct materials	3.0 pounds	$ 4.00	$12.00
Direct labor	2.5 hours	14.00	35.00
Variable manufacturing overhead	2.5 hours	3.00	7.50
Total standard cost per unit			$54.50

is important, therefore, that we cleanly separate discrepancies due to deviations from price standards from those due to deviations from quantity standards. Differences between *standard* prices and *actual* prices and *standard* quantities and *actual* quantities are called **variances.** The act of computing and interpreting variances is called *variance analysis.*

Price and Quantity Variances

A general model for computing standard cost variances for variable costs is presented in Exhibit 8–2. This model isolates price variances from quantity variances and shows how each of these variances is computed.[2] We will be using this model throughout the chapter to compute variances for direct materials, direct labor, and variable manufacturing overhead.

Three things should be noted from Exhibit 8–2. First, note that a price variance and a quantity variance can be computed for all three variable cost elements—direct materials, direct labor, and variable manufacturing overhead—even though the variance is not called by the same name in all cases. For example, a price variance is called a *materials price variance* in the case of direct materials but a *labor rate variance* in the case of direct labor and an *overhead spending variance* in the case of variable manufacturing overhead.

Second, note that even though a price variance may be called by different names, it is computed in exactly the same way regardless of whether one is dealing with direct materials, direct labor, or variable manufacturing overhead. The same is true with the quantity variance.

Third, note that variance analysis is actually a type of input-output analysis. The inputs represent the actual quantity of direct materials, direct labor, and variable manufacturing overhead used; the output represents the good production of the period, expressed in terms of the *standard quantity (or the standard hours) allowed for the actual output* (see column 3 in Exhibit 8–2). By **standard quantity allowed** or **standard hours allowed,** we mean the amount of direct materials, direct labor, or variable manufacturing overhead *that should have been used* to produce the actual output of the period. This could be more or could be less materials, labor, or overhead than was *actually* used, depending on the efficiency or inefficiency of operations. The standard quantity allowed is computed by multiplying the actual output in units by the standard input allowed per unit.

With this general model as a foundation, we will now examine the price and quantity variances in more detail.

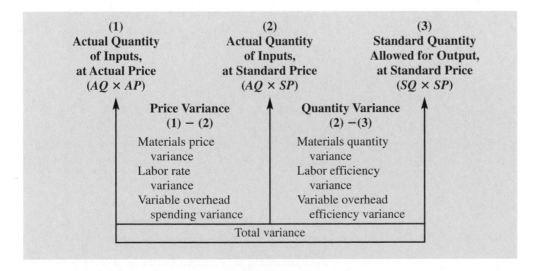

Exhibit 8–2
A General Model for Variance Analysis—Variable Production Costs

---

[2]Variance analysis of fixed costs is discussed in the next chapter.

Using Standard Costs—Direct Materials Variances

Concept 8–1

After determining Colonial Pewter Company's standard costs for direct materials, direct labor, and variable manufacturing overhead, Terry Sherman's next step was to compute the company's variances for June, the most recent month. As discussed in the preceding section, variances are computed by comparing standard costs to actual costs. To facilitate this comparison, Terry referred to the standard cost data contained in Exhibit 8–1. This exhibit shows that the standard cost of direct materials per unit of product is as follows:

$$3.0 \text{ pounds per unit} \times \$4.00 \text{ per pound} = \$12 \text{ per unit}$$

Colonial Pewter's purchasing records for June showed that 6,500 pounds of pewter were purchased at a cost of $3.80 per pound. This cost figure included freight and handling and was net of the quantity discount. All of the material purchased was used during June to manufacture 2,000 pairs of pewter bookends. Using these data and the standard costs from Exhibit 8–1, Terry computed the price and quantity variances shown in Exhibit 8–3.

The three arrows in Exhibit 8–3 point to three different total cost figures. The first, $24,700, refers to the actual total cost of the pewter that was purchased during June. The second, $26,000, refers to what the pewter would have cost if it had been purchased at the standard price of $4.00 a pound rather than the actual price of $3.80 a pound. The difference between these two figures, $1,300 ($26,000 − $24,700), is the price variance. It exists because the actual purchase price was $0.20 per pound less than the standard purchase price. Since 6,500 pounds were purchased, the total amount of the variance is $1,300 ($0.20 per pound × 6,500 pounds). This variance is labeled favorable (denoted by F), since the actual purchase price was less than the standard purchase price. A price variance is labeled unfavorable (denoted by U) if the actual price exceeds the standard price.

The third arrow in Exhibit 8–3 points to $24,000—the cost that the pewter would have been had it been purchased at the standard price and only the amount allowed by the standard quantity had been used. The standards call for 3 pounds of pewter per unit. Since 2,000 units were produced, 6,000 pounds of pewter should have been used. This is referred to as the standard quantity allowed for the output. If this 6,000 pounds of pewter had been purchased at the standard price of $4.00 per pound, the company would have spent $24,000. The difference between this figure, $24,000, and the figure at the end of the middle arrow in Exhibit 8–3, $26,000, is the quantity variance of $2,000.

To understand this quantity variance, note that the actual amount of pewter used in production was 6,500 pounds. However, the standard amount of pewter allowed for the

Exhibit 8–3
Variance Analysis—Direct Materials

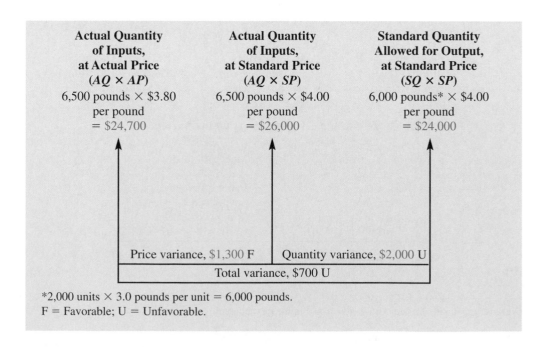

Actual Quantity of Inputs, at Actual Price ($AQ \times AP$)	Actual Quantity of Inputs, at Standard Price ($AQ \times SP$)	Standard Quantity Allowed for Output, at Standard Price ($SQ \times SP$)
6,500 pounds × $3.80 per pound = $24,700	6,500 pounds × $4.00 per pound = $26,000	6,000 pounds* × $4.00 per pound = $24,000

Price variance, $1,300 F   Quantity variance, $2,000 U

Total variance, $700 U

*2,000 units × 3.0 pounds per unit = 6,000 pounds.
F = Favorable; U = Unfavorable.

actual output is only 6,000 pounds. Therefore, a total of 500 pounds too much pewter was used to produce the actual output. To express this in dollar terms, the 500 pounds is multiplied by the standard price of $4.00 per pound to yield the quantity variance of $2,000. Why is the standard price, rather than the actual price, of the pewter used in this calculation? The production manager is ordinarily responsible for the quantity variance. If the actual price were used in the calculation of the quantity variance, the production manager would be held responsible for the efficiency or inefficiency of the purchasing manager. Apart from being unfair, fruitless arguments between the production manager and purchasing manager would occur every time the actual price of an input is above its standard price. To avoid these arguments, the standard price is used when computing the quantity variance.

The quantity variance in Exhibit 8–3 is labeled unfavorable (denoted by U). This is because more pewter was used to produce the actual output than is called for by the standard. A quantity variance is labeled unfavorable if the actual quantity exceeds the standard quantity and is labeled favorable if the actual quantity is less than the standard quantity.

The computations in Exhibit 8–3 reflect the fact that all of the material purchased during June was also used during June. How are the variances computed if a different amount of material is purchased than is used? To illustrate, assume that during June the company purchased 6,500 pounds of materials, as before, but that it used only 5,000 pounds of material during the month and produced only 1,600 units. In this case, the price variance and quantity variance would be as shown in Exhibit 8–4.

Most firms compute the materials price variance when materials *are purchased* rather than when the materials are placed into production.[3] This permits earlier isolation of the variance, since materials may remain in storage for many months before being used in production. Isolating the price variance when materials are purchased also permits the company to carry its raw materials in the inventory accounts at standard cost. This greatly simplifies assigning raw materials costs to work in process when raw materials are later placed into production.[4]

Note from the exhibit that the price variance is computed on the entire amount of material purchased (6,500 pounds), as before, whereas the quantity variance is computed

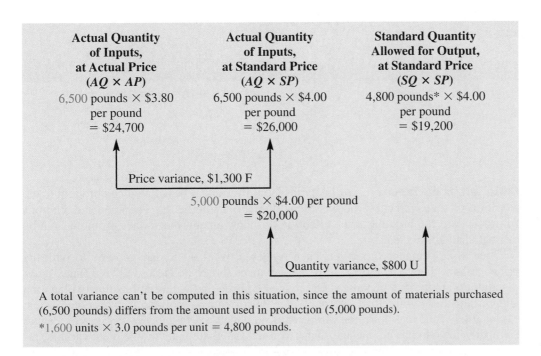

Exhibit 8–4
Variance Analysis—Direct Materials, When the Amount Purchased Differs from the Amount Used

Actual Quantity of Inputs, at Actual Price ($AQ \times AP$)	Actual Quantity of Inputs, at Standard Price ($AQ \times SP$)	Standard Quantity Allowed for Output, at Standard Price ($SQ \times SP$)
6,500 pounds × $3.80 per pound = $24,700	6,500 pounds × $4.00 per pound = $26,000	4,800 pounds* × $4.00 per pound = $19,200

Price variance, $1,300 F

5,000 pounds × $4.00 per pound = $20,000

Quantity variance, $800 U

A total variance can't be computed in this situation, since the amount of materials purchased (6,500 pounds) differs from the amount used in production (5,000 pounds).

*1,600 units × 3.0 pounds per unit = 4,800 pounds.

---

[3]Max Laudeman and F. W. Schaeberle, "The Cost Accounting Practices of Firms Using Standard Costs," *Cost and Management* 57, no. 4 (July–August 1983), p. 24.
[4]See Appendix 8A at the end of the chapter for an illustration of journal entries in a standard cost system.

only on the portion of this material used in production during the month (5,000 pounds). A quantity variance on the 1,500 pounds of material that was purchased during the month but *not* used in production (6,500 pounds purchased − 5,000 pounds used = 1,500 pounds unused) will be computed in a future period when these materials are drawn out of inventory and used in production. The situation illustrated in Exhibit 8–4 is common for companies that purchase materials well in advance of use and store the materials in warehouses while awaiting the production process.

Materials Price Variance—A Closer Look

A **materials price variance** measures the difference between what is paid for a given quantity of materials and what should have been paid according to the standard that has been set. From Exhibit 8–3, this difference can be expressed by the following formula:

$$\text{Materials price variance} = (AQ \times AP) - (AQ \times SP)$$

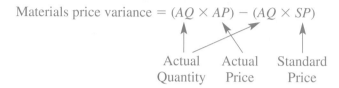

Actual	Actual	Standard
Quantity	Price	Price

The formula can be factored into simpler form as follows:

$$\text{Materials price variance} = AQ(AP - SP)$$

Some managers prefer this simpler formula, since it permits variance computations to be made very quickly. Using the data from Exhibit 8–3 in this formula, we have the following:

$$6{,}500 \text{ pounds } (\$3.80 \text{ per pound } - \$4.00 \text{ per pound}) = \$1{,}300 \text{ F}$$

Notice that the answer is the same as that yielded in Exhibit 8–3. If the company wanted to put these data into a performance report, the data might appear as follows:

COLONIAL PEWTER COMPANY Performance Report—Purchasing Department						
	(1)	**(2)**	**(3)**	**(4)** Difference in Price	**(5)** Total Price Variance	
Item Purchased	Quantity Purchased	Actual Price	Standard Price	(2) − (3)	(1) × (4)	Explanation
Pewter	6,500 pounds	$3.80	$4.00	$0.20	$1,300 F	Bargained for an especially favorable price

F = Favorable; U = Unfavorable.

Isolation of Variances   At what point should variances be isolated and brought to the attention of management? The answer is, the earlier the better. The sooner deviations from standard are brought to the attention of management, the sooner problems can be evaluated and corrected.

Once a performance report has been prepared, what does management do with the price variance data? The most significant variances should be viewed as "red flags," calling attention to the fact that an exception has occurred that will require some explanation and perhaps follow-up effort. Normally, the performance report itself will contain some explanation of the reason for the variance, as shown above. In the case of Colonial Pewter Company, the purchasing manager, Janet Warner, said that the favorable price variance resulted from bargaining for an especially favorable price.

Responsibility for the Variance   Who is responsible for the materials price variance? Generally speaking, the purchasing manager has control over the price paid for goods and is therefore responsible for any price variances. Many factors influence the prices paid for goods, including how many units are ordered in a lot, how the order is delivered, whether the order is a rush order, and the quality of materials purchased. A deviation in any of these factors from what was assumed when the standards were set can result in a price variance. For example, purchase of second-grade materials rather than top-grade materials may result in a favorable price variance, since the lower-grade materials would generally be less costly (but perhaps less suitable for production).

There may be times, however, when someone other than the purchasing manager is responsible for a materials price variance. Production may be scheduled in such a way, for example, that the purchasing manager must request express delivery. In these cases, the production manager would bear responsibility for the resulting price variances.

A word of caution is in order. Variance analysis should not be used as an excuse to conduct witch-hunts or as a means of beating line managers and workers over the head. The emphasis must be on the control function in the sense of *supporting* the line managers and *assisting* them in meeting the goals that they have participated in setting for the company. In short, the emphasis should be positive rather than negative. Excessive dwelling on what has already happened, particularly in terms of trying to find someone to blame, can destroy morale and kill any cooperative spirit.

Materials Quantity Variance—A Closer Look

The **materials quantity variance** measures the difference between the quantity of materials used in production and the quantity that should have been used according to the standard that has been set. Although the variance is concerned with the physical usage of materials, it is generally stated in dollar terms, as shown in Exhibit 8–3. The formula for the materials quantity variance is as follows:

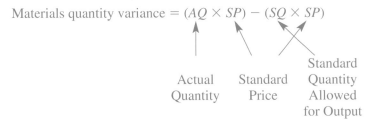

$$\text{Materials quantity variance} = (AQ \times SP) - (SQ \times SP)$$

Actual Quantity · Standard Price · Standard Quantity Allowed for Output

Again, the formula can be factored into simpler terms:

$$\text{Materials quantity variance} = SP(AQ - SQ)$$

Using the data from Exhibit 8–3 in the formula, we have the following:

$$\$4.00 \text{ per pound}(6,500 \text{ pounds} - 6,000 \text{ pounds}^*) = \$2,000 \text{ U}$$

*2,000 units × 3.0 pounds per unit = 6,000 pounds.

The answer, of course, is the same as that yielded in Exhibit 8–3. The data might appear as follows if a formal performance report were prepared:

COLONIAL PEWTER COMPANY Performance Report—Production Department						
Type of Materials	(1) Standard Price	(2) Actual Quantity	(3) Standard Quantity Allowed	(4) Difference in Quantity (2) − (3)	(5) Total Quantity Variance (1) × (4)	Explanation
Pewter	$4.00	6,500 pounds	6,000 pounds	500 pounds	$2,000 U	Second-grade materials unsuitable for production

F = Favorable; U = Unfavorable.

The materials quantity variance is best isolated at the time that materials are placed into production. Materials are drawn for the number of units to be produced, according to the standard bill of materials for each unit. Any additional materials are usually drawn with an excess materials requisition slip, which is different in color from the normal requisition slips. This procedure calls attention to the excessive usage of materials *while production is still in process* and provides an opportunity for early control of any developing problem.

Excessive usage of materials can result from many factors, including faulty machines, inferior quality of materials, untrained workers, and poor supervision. Generally speaking, it is the responsibility of the production department to see that material usage is kept in line with standards. There may be times, however, when the *purchasing* department may be responsible for an unfavorable materials quantity variance. If the purchasing department obtains inferior quality materials in an effort to economize on price, the materials may be unsuitable for use and may result in excessive waste. Thus, purchasing rather than production would be responsible for the quantity variance. At Colonial Pewter, the production manager, Tom Kuchel, said that second-grade materials were the cause of the unfavorable materials quantity variance for June.

Using Standard Costs—Direct Labor Variances

Learning Objective 3
Compute the direct labor rate and efficiency variances and explain their significance.

Concept 8–2

Terry's next step in determining Colonial Pewter's variances for June was to compute the direct labor variances for the month. Recall from Exhibit 8–1 that the standard direct labor cost per unit of product is $35, computed as follows:

$$2.5 \text{ hours per unit} \times \$14.00 \text{ per hour} = \$35 \text{ per unit}$$

During June, the company paid its direct labor workers $74,250, including employment taxes and fringe benefits, for 5,400 hours of work. This was an average of $13.75 per hour. Using these data and the standard costs from Exhibit 8–1, Terry computed the direct labor rate and efficiency variances that appear in Exhibit 8–5.

Notice that the column headings in Exhibit 8–5 are the same as those used in the prior two exhibits, except that in Exhibit 8–5 the terms *hours* and *rate* are used in place of the terms *quantity* and *price*.

Exhibit 8–5
Variance Analysis—Direct Labor

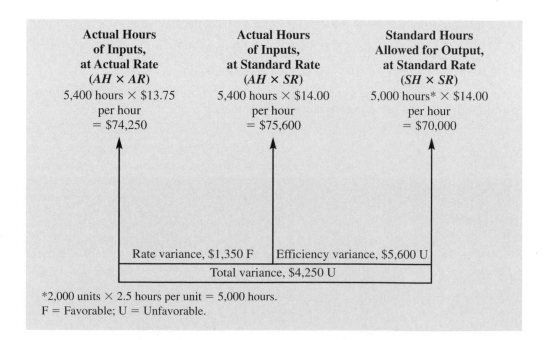

*2,000 units × 2.5 hours per unit = 5,000 hours.
F = Favorable; U = Unfavorable.

Controlling the Costs of Visual Effects

in business today

Special effects, such as the computed-generated action shots of dinosaurs in Jurassic Park, are expensive to produce. A single visual effect, lasting three to seven seconds, can cost up to $50,000, and a high-profile film may contain hundreds of these shots. Since visual effects are produced under fixed-price contracts, visual-effects companies must carefully estimate their costs. Once a bid has been accepted, costs must be zealously monitored to make sure they do not spin out of control.

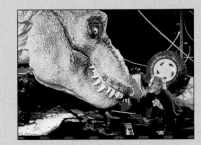

Buena Vista Visual Effects, a part of Walt Disney Studios, uses a standard cost system to estimate and control costs. A "storyboard" is created for each special effects shot. The storyboard sketches the visual effect, details the length of the shot, which is measured in frames (24 frames equals one second of film), and describes the work that will need to be done to create the effect. A detailed budget is then prepared using standard costs. As the project progresses, actual costs are compared to the standard cost, and significant cost overruns are investigated.

Source: Ray Scalice, "Lights! Cameras! . . . Accountants," *Management Accounting,* June 1996, pp. 42–46. Reprinted with permission from *Management Accounting.*

Labor Rate Variance—A Closer Look

As explained earlier, the price variance for direct labor is commonly termed a **labor rate variance.** This variance measures any deviation from standard in the average hourly rate paid to direct labor workers. The formula for the labor rate variance is expressed as follows:

$$\text{Labor rate variance} = (AH \times AR) - (AH \times SR)$$

Actual Hours   Actual Rate   Standard Rate

The formula can be factored into simpler form as follows:

$$\text{Labor rate variance} = AH(AR - SR)$$

Using the data from Exhibit 8–5 in the formula, we have the following:

$$5{,}400 \text{ hours } (\$13.75 \text{ per hour} - \$14.00 \text{ per hour}) = \$1{,}350 \text{ F}$$

In most firms, the rates paid to workers are quite predictable. Nevertheless, rate variances can arise through the way labor is used. Skilled workers with high hourly rates of pay may be given duties that require little skill and call for low hourly rates of pay. This will result in unfavorable labor rate variances, since the actual hourly rate of pay will exceed the standard rate specified for the particular task being performed. A reverse situation exists when unskilled or untrained workers are assigned to jobs that require some skill or training. The lower pay scale for these workers will result in favorable rate variances, although the workers may be inefficient. Finally, unfavorable rate variances can arise from overtime work at premium rates if any portion of the overtime premium is added to the direct labor account.

Who is responsible for controlling the labor rate variance? Since rate variances generally arise as a result of how labor is used, supervisors bear responsibility for seeing that labor rate variances are kept under control.

Labor Efficiency Variance—A Closer Look

The quantity variance for direct labor, more commonly called the **labor efficiency variance,** measures the productivity of labor time. No variance is more closely watched by management, since it is widely believed that increasing the productivity of direct labor time is vital to reducing costs. The formula for the labor efficiency variance is expressed as follows:

$$\text{Labor efficiency variance} = (AH \times SR) - (SH \times SR)$$

		Standard
Actual	Standard	Hours
Hours	Rate	Allowed
		for Output

Factored into simpler terms, the formula is as follows:

$$\text{Labor efficiency variance} = SR(AH - SH)$$

Using the data from Exhibit 8–5 in the formula, we have the following:

$$\$14.00 \text{ per hour } (5{,}400 \text{ hours} - 5{,}000 \text{ hours*}) = \$5{,}600 \text{ U}$$

*2,000 units × 2.5 hours per unit = 5,000 hours.

Possible causes of an unfavorable labor efficiency variance include poorly trained or motivated workers; poor quality materials, requiring more labor time in processing; faulty equipment, causing breakdowns and work interruptions; poor supervision of workers; and inaccurate standards. The managers in charge of production would generally be responsible for control of the labor efficiency variance. However, the variance might be chargeable to purchasing if the acquisition of poor materials resulted in excessive labor processing time.

When the labor force is essentially fixed in the short term, another important cause of an unfavorable labor efficiency variance is insufficient demand for the output of the factory. In some firms, the actual labor-hours worked is basically fixed—particularly in the short term. It is difficult, and perhaps even unwise, to constantly adjust the work force in response to changes in the work load. Therefore, the only way a work center manager can avoid an unfavorable labor efficiency variance in such firms is by keeping everyone busy all of the time. The option of reducing the number of workers on hand is not available.

Thus, if customer orders are insufficient to keep the workers busy, the work center manager has two options—either accept an unfavorable labor efficiency variance or build inventory.[5] A central lesson of just-in-time (JIT) is that building inventory with no immediate prospect of sale is a bad idea. Inventory—particularly work in process inventory—leads to high defect rates, obsolete goods, and generally inefficient operations. As a consequence, when the work force is basically fixed in the short term, managers must be cautious about how labor efficiency variances are used. Some managers advocate dispensing with labor efficiency variances entirely in such situations—at least for the purposes of motivating and controlling workers on the shop floor.

decision | *maker*   **Department Resources Manager**

You are the manager of the computer-generated special effects department for a company that produces special effects for high-profile films. You receive a copy of this month's performance report for your department and discover a large labor efficiency variance that is unfavorable. What factors might have contributed to this unfavorable variance?

Using Standard Costs—Variable Manufacturing Overhead Variances

The final step in Terry's analysis of Colonial Pewter's variances for June was to compute the variable manufacturing overhead variances. The variable portion of manufacturing

---

[5]For further discussion, see Eliyahu M. Goldratt and Jeff Cox, *The Goal,* 2nd rev. ed. (Croton-on-Hudson, NY: North River Press, 1992).

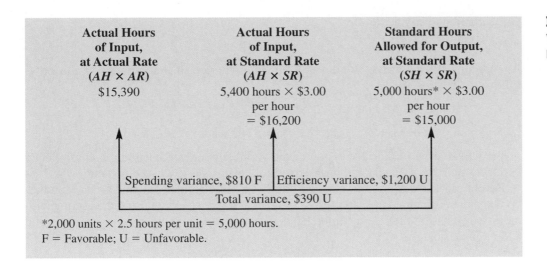

Exhibit 8–6
Variance Analysis—Variable
Manufacturing Overhead

overhead can be analyzed using the same basic formulas that are used to analyze direct materials and direct labor. Recall from Exhibit 8–1 that the standard variable manufacturing overhead is $7.50 per unit of product, computed as follows:

$$2.5 \text{ hours per unit} \times \$3.00 \text{ per hour} = \$7.50 \text{ per unit}$$

Colonial Pewter's cost records showed that the total actual variable manufacturing overhead cost for June was $15,390. Recall from the earlier discussion of the direct labor variances that 5,400 hours of direct labor time were recorded during the month and that the company produced 2,000 pairs of bookends. Terry's analysis of this overhead data appears in Exhibit 8–6.

Notice the similarities between Exhibits 8–5 and 8–6. These similarities arise from the fact that direct labor-hours are being used as a base for allocating overhead cost to units of product; thus, the same hourly figures appear in Exhibit 8–6 for variable manufacturing overhead as in Exhibit 8–5 for direct labor. The main difference between the two exhibits is in the standard hourly rate being used, which in this company is much lower for variable manufacturing overhead.

Learning Objective 4
Compute the variable manufacturing overhead spending and efficiency variances.

Manufacturing Overhead Variances—A Closer Look

The formula for the **variable overhead spending variance** is expressed as follows:

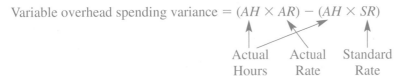

Or, factored into simpler terms:

$$\text{Variable overhead spending variance} = AH(AR - SR)$$

Using the data from Exhibit 8–6 in the formula, we have the following:

$$5,400 \text{ hours } (\$2.85 \text{ per hour}^* - \$3.00 \text{ per hour}) = \$810 \text{ F}$$

*$15,390 ÷ 5,400 hours = $2.85 per hour.

The formula for the **variable overhead efficiency variance** is expressed as follows:

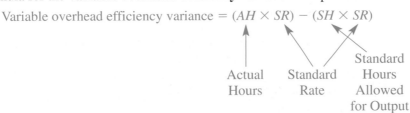

Or, factored into simpler terms:

Variable overhead efficiency variance = $SR(AH - SH)$

Again using the data from Exhibit 8–6, the computation of the variance would be as follows:

$3.00 per hour (5,400 hours − 5,000 hours*) = $1,200 U

*2,000 units × 2.5 hours per unit = 5,000 hours.

We will reserve further discussion of the variable overhead spending and efficiency variances until the next chapter, where overhead analysis is discussed in depth.

Before proceeding further, we suggest that you pause at this point and go back and review the data contained in Exhibits 8–1 through 8–6. These exhibits and the accompanying text discussion provide a comprehensive, integrated illustration of standard setting and variance analysis.

Managerial Accounting in Action

The Wrap-Up

In preparation for the scheduled meeting to discuss his analysis of Colonial Pewter's standard costs and variances, Terry distributed Exhibits 8–1 through 8–6, with supporting explanations, to the management group of Colonial Pewter. This included J. D. Wriston, the president of the company; Tom Kuchel, the production manager; and Janet Warner, the purchasing manager. J. D. Wriston opened the meeting with the following question:

J. D.: Terry, I think I understand the report you distributed, but just to make sure, would you mind summarizing the highlights of what you found?

Terry: As you can see, the biggest problems are the unfavorable materials quantity variance of $2,000 and the unfavorable labor efficiency variance of $5,600.

J. D.: Tom, you're the production boss. What do you think is responsible for the unfavorable labor efficiency variance?

Tom: It pretty much has to be the new production workers. Our experienced workers shouldn't have much problem meeting the standard of 2.5 hours per unit. We all knew that there would be some inefficiency for a while as we brought new people on board.

J. D.: No one is disputing that, Tom. However, $5,600 is a lot of money. Is this problem likely to go away very soon?

Tom: I hope so. If we were to contrast the last two weeks of June with the first two weeks, I'm sure we would see some improvement.

J. D.: I don't want to beat up on you, Tom, but this is a significant problem. Can you do something to accelerate the training process?

Tom: Sure. I could pair up each of the new guys with one of our old-timers and have them work together for a while. It would slow down our older guys a bit, but I'll bet the new workers would learn a lot.

J. D.: Let's try it. Now, what about that $2,000 unfavorable materials quantity variance?

Tom: Are you asking me?

J. D.: Well, I would like someone to explain it.

Tom: Don't look at me. It's that iron-contaminated pewter that Janet bought on her "special deal."

Janet: We got rid of that stuff months ago.

J. D.: Hold your horses. We're not trying to figure out who to blame here. I just want to understand what happened. If we can understand what happened, maybe we can fix it.

Terry: Tom, are the new workers generating a lot of scrap?

Tom: Yeah, I guess so.

J. D.: I think that could be part of the problem. Can you do anything about it?

Tom: I can watch the scrap real closely for a few days to see where it's being generated. If it is the new workers, I can have the old-timers work with them on the problem when I team them up.

J. D.: Good. Let's reconvene in a few weeks and see what has happened. Hopefully, we can get those unfavorable variances under control.

Variance Analysis and Management by Exception

Variance analysis and performance reports are important elements of *management by exception*. Simply put, management by exception means that the manager's attention should be directed toward those parts of the organization where plans are not working out for one reason or another. Time and effort should not be wasted attending to those parts of the organization where things are going smoothly.

The budgets and standards discussed in this chapter and in the preceding chapter reflect management's plans. If all goes according to plan, there will be little difference between actual results and the results that would be expected according to the budgets and standards. If this happens, managers can concentrate on other issues. However, if actual results do not conform to the budget and to standards, the performance reporting system sends a signal to the manager that an "exception" has occurred. This signal is in the form of a variance from the budget or standards.

However, are all variances worth investigating? The answer is no. Differences between actual results and what was expected will almost always occur. If every variance were investigated, management would waste a great deal of time tracking down nickel-and-dime differences. Variances may occur for any of a variety of reasons—only some of which are significant and warrant management attention. For example, hotter-than-normal weather in the summer may result in higher-than-expected electrical bills for air conditioning. Or, workers may work slightly faster or slower on a particular day. Because of unpredictable random factors, one can expect that virtually every cost category will produce a variance of some kind.

How should managers decide which variances are worth investigating? One clue is the size of the variance. A variance of $5 is probably not big enough to warrant attention, whereas a variance of $5,000 might well be worth tracking down. Another clue is the size of the variance relative to the amount of spending involved. A variance that is only 0.1% of spending on an item is likely to be well within the bounds one would normally expect due to random factors. On the other hand, a variance of 10% of spending is much more likely to be a signal that something is basically wrong.

In addition to watching for unusually large variances, the pattern of the variances should be monitored. For example, a run of steadily mounting variances should trigger an investigation even though none of the variances is large enough by itself to warrant investigation.

Evaluation of Controls Based on Standard Costs

Advantages of Standard Costs

Standard cost systems have a number of advantages.

1. As stated earlier, the use of standard costs is a key element in a management by exception approach. So long as costs remain within the standards, managers can focus on other issues. When costs fall significantly outside the standards, managers are alerted that there may be problems requiring attention. This approach helps managers focus on important issues.
2. So long as standards are viewed as reasonable by employees, they can promote economy and efficiency. They provide benchmarks that individuals can use to judge their own performance.
3. Standard costs can greatly simplify bookkeeping. Instead of recording actual costs for each job, the standard costs for materials, labor, and overhead can be charged to jobs.
4. Standard costs fit naturally in an integrated system of "responsibility accounting." The standards establish what costs should be, who should be responsible for them, and whether actual costs are under control.

Potential Problems with the Use of Standard Costs

The use of standard costs can present a number of potential problems. Most of these problems result from improper use of standard costs and the management by exception principle or from using standard costs in situations in which they are not appropriate.

1. Standard cost variance reports are usually prepared on a monthly basis and often are released days or even weeks after the end of the month. As a consequence, the information in the reports may be so stale that it is almost useless. Timely, frequent reports that are approximately correct are better than infrequent reports that are very precise but out of date by the time they are released. Some companies are now reporting variances and other key operating data daily or even more frequently.

2. If managers are insensitive and use variance reports as a club, morale may suffer. Employees should receive positive reinforcement for work well done. Management by exception, by its nature, tends to focus on the negative. If variances are used as a club, subordinates may be tempted to cover up unfavorable variances or take actions that are not in the best interests of the company to make sure the variances are favorable. For example, workers may put on a crash effort to increase output at the end of the month to avoid an unfavorable labor efficiency variance. In the rush to produce output, quality may suffer.

3. Labor quantity standards and efficiency variances make two important assumptions. First, they assume that the production process is labor-paced; if labor works faster, output will go up. However, output in many companies is no longer determined by how fast labor works; rather, it is determined by the processing speed of machines. Second, the computations assume that labor is a variable cost. However, direct labor may be essentially fixed. If labor is fixed, then an undue emphasis on labor efficiency variances creates pressure to build excess work in process and finished goods inventories.

4. In some cases, a "favorable" variance can be as bad or worse than an "unfavorable" variance. For example, McDonald's has a standard for the amount of hamburger meat that should be in a Big Mac. A "favorable" variance means that less meat was used than the standard specifies. The result is a substandard Big Mac and possibly a dissatisfied customer.

5. There may be a tendency with standard cost reporting systems to emphasize meeting the standards to the exclusion of other important objectives such as maintaining and improving quality, on-time delivery, and customer satisfaction. This tendency can be reduced by using supplemental performance measures that focus on these other objectives.

6. Just meeting standards may not be sufficient; continual improvement may be necessary to survive in the current competitive environment. For this reason, some companies focus on the trends in the standard cost variances—aiming for continual improvement rather than just meeting the standards. In other companies, engineered standards are being replaced either by a rolling average of actual costs, which is expected to decline, or by very challenging target costs.

In sum, managers should exercise considerable care in their use of a standard cost system. It is particularly important that managers go out of their way to focus on the positive, rather than just on the negative, and to be aware of possible unintended consequences.

Nevertheless, standard costs are still found in the vast majority of manufacturing companies and in many service companies, although their use is changing. For evaluating performance, standard cost variances may be supplanted in the future by a particularly interesting development known as the *balanced scorecard,* which is discussed in the next section. While the balanced scorecard concept is new in most of the world, it has been eagerly embraced by a wide variety of organizations including Analog Devices, KPMG Peat Marwick, Tenneco, Allstate, AT&T, Elf Atochem, Conair-Franklin, Chemical Bank, 3COM, Rockwater, Apple Computer, Advanced Micro Devices (AMD), FMC, the Bank of Montreal, and the Massachusetts Special Olympics.

Correcting the Motivation

In an article about the big three auto makers in North America, *The Wall Street Journal* reported the following:

> General Motors is wrestling with how to change a way of life in a sprawling, hidebound bureaucracy . . . That's why GM has spent more than a year overhauling how it measures success.
>
> "Traditionally, we measured labor efficiency in the plants," Mr. Hoglund [a GM executive vice president] says, to elicit greater output per unit of labor. "Then we found out it drove all the wrong behaviors—people got rewarded for higher and higher volumes, but there was no incentive for quality." Moreover, all the comparisons were internal. Now, he says, the key measures are customer satisfaction and how various processes stack up against the best of the competition.

Source: "Tooling Along: With Auto Profits Up, Big Three Again Get a Major Opportunity," *The Wall Street Journal*, May 4, 1994, pp. A1, A11.

Balanced Scorecard

A **balanced scorecard** consists of an integrated set of performance measures that are derived from the company's strategy and that support the company's strategy throughout the organization.[6, 7] A strategy is essentially a theory about how to achieve the organization's goals. For example, Southwest Airlines' strategy is to offer passengers low prices and fun on short-haul jet service. The low prices result from the absence of costly frills such as meals, assigned seating, and interline baggage checking. The fun is provided by flight attendants who go out of their way to entertain passengers with their antics. This is an interesting strategy. Southwest Airlines consciously hires people who have a sense of humor and who enjoy their work. Hiring and retaining such employees probably costs no more—and may cost less—than retaining grumpy flight attendants who view their jobs as a chore. Southwest Airlines' strategy is to build loyal customers through a combination of "fun"—which does not cost anything to provide—and low prices that are possible because of the lack of costly frills offered by competing airlines. The theory is that low prices and fun will lead to loyal customers, which, in combination with low costs, will lead to high profits. So far, this theory has worked.

Under the balanced scorecard approach, top management translates its strategy into performance measures that employees can understand and can do something about. For example, the amount of time passengers have to wait in line to have their baggage checked might be a performance measure for the supervisor in charge of the Southwest Airlines check-in counter at the Phoenix airport. This performance measure is easily understood by the supervisor and can be improved by the supervisor's actions. The details of the balanced scorecard approach are covered in more advanced texts.

---

[6]The balanced scorecard concept was developed by Robert Kaplan and David Norton. For further details, see their articles "The Balanced Scorecard—Measures that Drive Performance," *Harvard Business Review,* January/February 1992, pp. 71–79; "Using the Balanced Scorecard as a Strategic Management System," *Harvard Business Review,* January/February 1996, pp. 75–85; "Why Does a Business Need a Balanced Scorecard?" *Journal of Cost Management,* May/June 1997, pp. 5–10; and their book *Translating Strategy into Action: The Balanced Scorecard* (Boston, MA: Harvard Business School Press, 1996).

[7]In the 1960s, the French developed a concept similar to the balanced scorecard called Tableau de Bord or "dashboard." For details, see Michel Lebas, "Managerial Accounting in France: Overview of Past Tradition and Current Practice," *The European Accounting Review,* 1994, 3, no. 3, pp. 471–487; and Marc Epstein and Jean-François Manzoni, "The Balanced Scorecard and the Tableau de Bord: Translating Strategy into Action," *Management Accounting,* August 1997, pp. 28–36.

Hilton Hotels is committed to meeting the expectations of its guests. Recently, Hilton, which operates in a decentralized fashion, undertook a study to determine whether customers were satisfied with the performance of individual hotels. The study revealed that the level of service was inconsistent throughout the chain. Hilton responded by adopting a balanced scorecard approach. The company discovered that customers really do not value any of the other services offered by a hotel if they are not able to relax in rooms that are clean and quiet. After assessing how each hotel can improve its performance in this regard, Hilton established goals for each property. The company also designed tools to ensure that property managers understand and are able to respond to measures of their performance. For example, in addition to providing numerical performance measures, color-coded charts communicate whether each measure is below, at, or above each goal set for the property.

Source: Dieter Huckstein and Robert Duboff, "Hilton Hotels: A Comprehensive Approach to Delivering Value for All Stakeholders," *Cornell Hotel & Restaurant Administration Quarterly,* August 1999, p. 28.

Summary

LO1   Explain how direct materials standards and direct labor standards are set.

Each direct cost has both a price and a quantity standard. The standard price for an input is the price that should be paid for a single unit of the input. In the case of direct materials, the price should include shipping and receiving costs and should be net of quantity and other discounts. In the case of direct labor, the standard rate should include wages, fringe benefits, and employment taxes.

LO2   Compute the direct materials price and quantity variances and explain their significance.

The materials price variance is the difference between the actual price paid for materials and the standard price, multiplied by the quantity purchased. An unfavorable variance occurs whenever the actual price exceeds the standard price. A favorable variance occurs when the actual price is less than the standard price for the input.

The materials quantity variance is the difference between the amount of materials actually used and the amount that should have been used to produce the actual good output of the period, multiplied by the standard price per unit of the input. An unfavorable materials quantity variance occurs when the amount of materials actually used exceeds the amount that should have been used according to the materials quantity standard. A favorable variance occurs when the amount of materials actually used is less than the amount that should have been used according to the standard.

LO3   Compute the direct labor rate and efficiency variances and explain their significance.

The direct labor rate variance is the difference between the actual wage rate paid and the standard wage rate, multiplied by the hours worked. An unfavorable variance occurs whenever the actual wage rate exceeds the standard wage rate. A favorable variance occurs when the actual wage rate is less than the standard wage rate.

The labor efficiency variance is the difference between the hours actually worked and the hours that should have been used to produce the actual good output of the period, multiplied by the standard wage rate. An unfavorable labor efficiency variance occurs when the hours actually worked exceed the hours allowed for the actual output. A favorable variance occurs when the hours actually worked are less than hours allowed for the actual output.

LO4   Compute the variable manufacturing overhead spending and efficiency variances.

The variable manufacturing overhead spending variance is the difference between the actual variable manufacturing overhead cost incurred and the actual hours worked multiplied by the variable manufacturing overhead rate. The variable manufacturing overhead efficiency variance is the difference between the hours actually worked and the hours that should have been used to produce the actual good output of the period, multiplied by the standard variable manufacturing overhead rate.

Guidance Answers to You Decide and Decision Maker

BASEBALL COACH (p. 326)

Major League records would be similar to ideal standards. They call for levels of effort and skill that have been attained only by professional baseball players under the best circumstances. Even though such standards might have a motivational value to someone like Sammy Sosa, they would probably tend to discourage the players on your Little League team if you told them that they needed to meet those expectations to receive recognition.

Practical standards are tight but can be attained through reasonable, though highly efficient, efforts by the average worker. Practical standards might motivate your players to do their best on the field and might help you to identify problems requiring additional coaching or practice. Given the differing athletic abilities and skill levels among the players on your team, it might be best to start with each player's statistics from last season and then make adjustments to create benchmarks for each player.

After acknowledging your gratitude for the parent's interest in the team, you might remind the parents that the kids are playing on the team to have fun and develop their skills and self-confidence. Then, after explaining the pros and cons of each of the two types of standards, you can address how you set benchmarks for the players.

DEPARTMENT RESOURCES MANAGER (p. 338)

An unfavorable labor efficiency variance in the computer-generated special effects department might have been caused by inexperienced, poorly trained, or unmotivated employees, faulty hardware and/or software that may have caused work interruptions, and/or poor supervision of the employees in this department. In addition, it is possible that there was insufficient demand for the output of this department—resulting in idle time—or that the standard (or benchmark) for this department is inaccurate.

Review Problem: Standard Costs

Xavier Company produces a single product. Variable manufacturing overhead is applied to products on the basis of direct labor-hours. The standard costs for one unit of product are as follows:

Direct material: 6 ounces at $0.50 per ounce	$ 3
Direct labor: 1.8 hours at $10 per hour	18
Variable manufacturing overhead: 1.8 hours at $5 per hour	9
Total standard variable cost per unit	$30

During June, 2,000 units were produced. The costs associated with June's operations were as follows:

Material purchased: 18,000 ounces at $0.60 per ounce	$10,800
Material used in production: 14,000 ounces	—
Direct labor: 4,000 hours at $9.75 per hour	39,000
Variable manufacturing overhead costs incurred	20,800

Required:
Compute the materials, labor, and variable manufacturing overhead variances.

SOLUTION TO THE REVIEW PROBLEM
Materials Variances

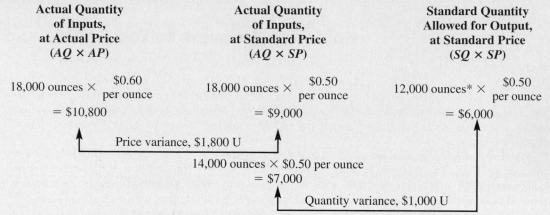

Actual Quantity of Inputs, at Actual Price ($AQ \times AP$)	Actual Quantity of Inputs, at Standard Price ($AQ \times SP$)	Standard Quantity Allowed for Output, at Standard Price ($SQ \times SP$)
18,000 ounces × $0.60 per ounce = $10,800	18,000 ounces × $0.50 per ounce = $9,000	12,000 ounces* × $0.50 per ounce = $6,000

Price variance, $1,800 U

14,000 ounces × $0.50 per ounce = $7,000

Quantity variance, $1,000 U

A total variance can't be computed in this situation, since the amount of materials purchased (18,000 ounces) differs from the amount of materials used in production (14,000 ounces).

*2,000 units × 6 ounces per unit = 12,000 ounces.

Using the formulas in the chapter, the same variances would be computed as:

$$\text{Materials price variance} = AQ(AP - SP)$$
$$18,000 \text{ ounces } (\$0.60 \text{ per ounce} - \$0.50 \text{ per ounce}) = \$1,800 \text{ U}$$

$$\text{Materials quantity variance} = SP(AQ - SQ)$$
$$\$0.50 \text{ per ounce } (14,000 \text{ ounces} - 12,000 \text{ ounces}) = \$1,000 \text{ U}$$

Labor Variances

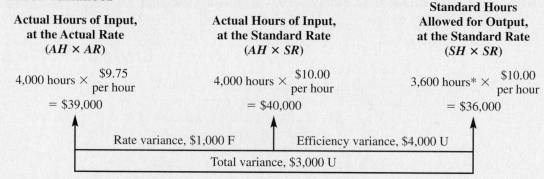

Actual Hours of Input, at the Actual Rate ($AH \times AR$)	Actual Hours of Input, at the Standard Rate ($AH \times SR$)	Standard Hours Allowed for Output, at the Standard Rate ($SH \times SR$)
4,000 hours × $9.75 per hour = $39,000	4,000 hours × $10.00 per hour = $40,000	3,600 hours* × $10.00 per hour = $36,000

Rate variance, $1,000 F   Efficiency variance, $4,000 U

Total variance, $3,000 U

*2,000 units × 1.8 hours per unit = 3,600 hours.

Using the formulas in the chapter, the same variances would be computed as:

$$\text{Labor rate variance} = AH(AR - SR)$$
$$4,000 \text{ hours } (\$9.75 \text{ per hour} - \$10.00 \text{ per hour}) = \$1,000 \text{ F}$$

$$\text{Labor efficiency variance} = SR(AH - SH)$$
$$\$10.00 \text{ per hour } (4,000 \text{ hours} - 3,600 \text{ hours}) = \$4,000 \text{ U}$$

Variable Manufacturing Overhead Variances

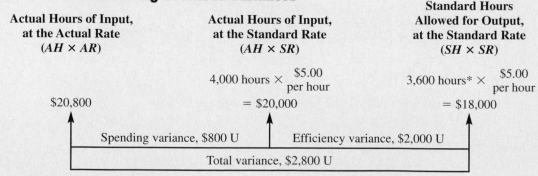

Actual Hours of Input, at the Actual Rate ($AH \times AR$)	Actual Hours of Input, at the Standard Rate ($AH \times SR$)	Standard Hours Allowed for Output, at the Standard Rate ($SH \times SR$)
$20,800	4,000 hours × $5.00 per hour = $20,000	3,600 hours* × $5.00 per hour = $18,000

Spending variance, $800 U   Efficiency variance, $2,000 U

Total variance, $2,800 U

*2,000 units × 1.8 hours per unit = 3,600 hours.

Using the formulas in the chapter, the same variances would be computed as:

$$\text{Variable overhead spending variance} = AH(AR - SR)$$
$$4{,}000 \text{ hours } (\$5.20 \text{ per hour}^* - \$5.00 \text{ per hour}) = \$800 \text{ U}$$

$$^*\$20{,}800 \div 4{,}000 \text{ hours} = \$5.20 \text{ per hour.}$$

$$\text{Variable overhead efficiency variance} = SR(AH - SH)$$
$$\$5.00 \text{ per hour } (4{,}000 \text{ hours} - 3{,}600 \text{ hours}) = \$2{,}000 \text{ U}$$

Glossary

Balanced scorecard   An integrated set of performance measures that is derived from and supports the organization's strategy. (p. 343)

Bill of materials   A listing of the quantity of each type of material required to manufacture a unit of product. (p. 328)

Ideal standards   Standards that allow for no machine breakdowns or other work interruptions and that require peak efficiency at all times. (p. 326)

Labor efficiency variance   A measure of the difference between the actual hours taken to complete a task and the standard hours allowed, multiplied by the standard hourly labor rate. (p. 337)

Labor rate variance   A measure of the difference between the actual hourly labor rate and the standard rate, multiplied by the number of hours worked during the period. (p. 337)

Management by exception   A system of management in which standards are set for various operating activities, with actual results then compared to these standards. Any differences that are deemed significant are brought to the attention of management as "exceptions." (p. 325)

Materials price variance   A measure of the difference between the actual unit price paid for an item and the standard price, multiplied by the quantity purchased. (p. 334)

Materials quantity variance   A measure of the difference between the actual quantity of materials used in production and the standard quantity allowed, multiplied by the standard price per unit of materials. (p. 335)

Practical standards   Standards that allow for normal machine downtime and other work interruptions and that can be attained through reasonable, though highly efficient, efforts by the average worker. (p. 326)

Standard cost card   A detailed listing of the standard amounts of materials, labor, and overhead that should go into a unit of product, multiplied by the standard price or rate that has been set for each cost element. (p. 325)

Standard cost per unit   The standard cost of a unit of product as shown on the standard cost card; it is computed by multiplying the standard quantity or hours by the standard price or rate for each cost element. (p. 330)

Standard hours allowed   The time that should have been taken to complete the period's output as computed by multiplying the actual number of units produced by the standard hours per unit. (p. 331)

Standard hours per unit   The amount of labor time that should be required to complete a single unit of product, including allowances for breaks, machine downtime, cleanup, rejects, and other normal inefficiencies. (p. 329)

Standard price per unit   The price that should be paid for a single unit of materials, including allowances for quality, quantity purchased, shipping, receiving, and other such costs, net of any discounts allowed. (p. 327)

Standard quantity allowed   The amount of materials that should have been used to complete the period's output as computed by multiplying the actual number of units produced by the standard quantity per unit. (p. 331)

Standard quantity per unit   The amount of materials that should be required to complete a single unit of product, including allowances for normal waste, spoilage, rejects, and similar inefficiencies. (p. 328)

Standard rate per hour   The labor rate that should be incurred per hour of labor time, including employment taxes, fringe benefits, and other such labor costs. (p. 328)

Variable overhead efficiency variance   The difference between the actual activity (direct labor-hours, machine-hours, or some other base) of a period and the standard activity allowed, multiplied by the variable part of the predetermined overhead rate. (p. 339)

Variable overhead spending variance   The difference between the actual variable overhead cost incurred during a period and the standard cost that should have been incurred based on the actual activity of the period. (p. 339)

Variance   The difference between standard prices and quantities on the one hand and actual prices and quantities on the other hand. (p. 331)

Appendix 8A | *General Ledger Entries to Record Variances*

Learning Objective 5

Prepare journal entries to record standard costs and variances.

Although standard costs and variances can be computed and used by management without being formally entered into the accounting records, most organizations prefer to make formal entries. Formal entry tends to give variances a greater emphasis than informal, off-the-record computations. This emphasis gives a clear signal of management's desire to keep costs within the limits that have been set. In addition, formal use of standard costs simplifies the bookkeeping process enormously. Inventories and cost of goods sold can be valued at their standard costs—eliminating the need to keep track of the actual cost of each unit.

Direct Materials Variances

To illustrate the general ledger entries needed to record standard cost variances, we will return to the data contained in the review problem at the end of the chapter. The entry to record the purchase of direct materials would be as follows:

Raw Materials (18,000 ounces at $0.50 per ounce)	9,000	
Materials Price Variance (18,000 ounces at $0.10 per ounce U)	1,800	
Accounts Payable (18,000 ounces at $0.60 per ounce)		10,800

Notice that the price variance is recognized when purchases are made, rather than when materials are actually used in production. This permits the price variance to be isolated early, and it also permits the materials to be carried in the inventory account at standard cost. As direct materials are later drawn from inventory and used in production, the quantity variance is isolated as follows:

Work in Process (12,000 ounces at $0.50 per ounce)	6,000	
Materials Quantity Variance (2,000 ounces U at $0.50 per ounce)	1,000	
Raw Materials (14,000 ounces at $0.50 per ounce)		7,000

Thus, direct materials enter into the Work in Process account at standard cost, in terms of both price and quantity.

Notice that both the price variance and the quantity variance above are unfavorable and are debit entries. If these variances had been favorable, they would have appeared as credit entries, as in the case of the direct labor rate variance below.

Direct Labor Variances

Referring again to the cost data in the review problem at the end of the chapter, the general ledger entry to record the incurrence of direct labor cost would be:

Work in Process (3,600 hours at $10.00 per hour)	36,000	
Labor Efficiency Variance (400 hours U at $10.00 per hour)	4,000	
Labor Rate Variance (4,000 hours at $0.25 per hour F)		1,000
Wages Payable (4,000 hours at $9.75 per hour)		39,000

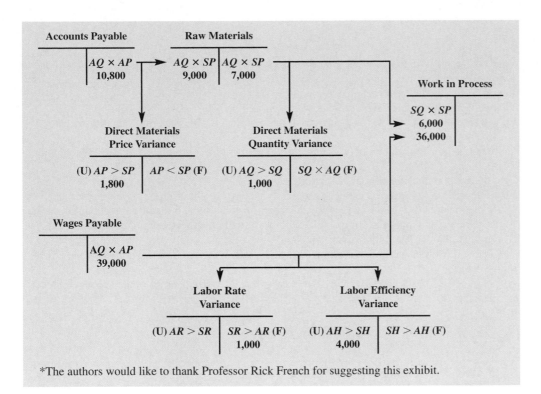

*The authors would like to thank Professor Rick French for suggesting this exhibit.

Thus, as with direct materials, direct labor costs enter into the Work in Process account at standard, both in terms of the rate and in terms of the hours allowed for the actual production of the period.

Variable Manufacturing Overhead Variances

Variable manufacturing overhead variances generally are not recorded in the accounts separately but rather are determined as part of the general analysis of overhead, which is discussed in the next chapter.

Cost Flows in a Standard Cost System

The flows of costs through the company's accounts are illustrated in Exhibit 8A–1. Note that entries into the various inventory accounts are made at standard cost—not actual cost. The differences between actual and standard costs are entered into special accounts that accumulate the various standard cost variances. Ordinarily, these standard cost variance accounts are closed out to Cost of Goods Sold at the end of the period. Unfavorable variances increase Cost of Goods Sold, and favorable variances decrease Cost of Goods Sold.

Summary for Appendix 8A

LO5   **(Appendix 8A) Prepare journal entries to record standard costs and variances.**
Raw materials and work in process and finished goods inventories are all carried at their standard costs. Differences between actual and standard costs are recorded as variances. Favorable variances are credit entries and unfavorable variances are debit entries.

Questions

8–1 What is a quantity standard? What is a price standard?

8–2 Distinguish between ideal and practical standards.

8–3 What is meant by the term *variance*?

8–4 What is meant by the term *management by exception*?

8–5 Who is generally responsible for the materials price variance? The materials quantity variance? The labor efficiency variance?

8–6 The materials price variance can be computed at what two different points in time? Which point is better? Why?

8–7 What dangers lie in using standards as punitive tools?

8–8 What effect, if any, would you expect poor quality materials to have on direct labor variances?

8–9 If variable manufacturing overhead is applied to production on the basis of direct labor-hours and the direct labor efficiency variance is unfavorable, will the variable overhead efficiency variance be favorable or unfavorable, or could it be either? Explain.

8–10 Why can undue emphasis on labor efficiency variances lead to excess work in process inventories?

8–11 (Appendix 8A) What are the advantages of making formal journal entries in the accounting records for variances?

Brief Exercises

BRIEF EXERCISE 8–1   Setting Standards (LO1)

Victoria Chocolates, Ltd., makes premium handcrafted chocolate confections in London. The owner of the company is setting up a standard cost system and has collected the following data for one of the company's products, the Empire Truffle. This product is made with the finest white chocolate and various fillings. The data below pertain only to the white chocolate used in the product:

Material requirements, kilograms of white chocolate per dozen truffles . .	0.70	kilograms
Allowance for waste, kilograms of white chocolate per dozen truffles . . .	0.03	kilograms
Allowance for rejects, kilograms of white chocolate per dozen truffles . .	0.02	kilograms
Purchase price, finest grade white chocolate	£7.50	per kilogram
Purchase discount	8%	of purchase price
Shipping cost from the supplier in Belgium	£0.30	per kilogram
Receiving and handling cost	£0.04	per kilogram

Required:
1. Determine the standard price of a kilogram of white chocolate.
2. Determine the standard quantity of white chocolate for a dozen truffles.
3. Determine the standard cost of the white chocolate in a dozen truffles.

BRIEF EXERCISE 8–2   Materials Variance (LO2)

Bandar Industries Berhad of Malaysia manufactures sporting equipment. One of the company's products, a football helmet for the North American market, requires a special plastic. During the quarter ending June 30, the company manufactured 35,000 helmets, using 22,500 kilograms of plastic in the process. The plastic cost the company RM 171,000. (The currency in Malaysia is the ringgit, which is denoted here by RM.)

According to the standard cost card, each helmet should require 0.6 kilograms of plastic, at a cost of RM 8 per kilogram.

Required:
1. What cost for plastic should have been incurred in the manufacture of the 35,000 helmets? How much greater or less is this than the cost that was incurred?
2. Break down the difference computed in (1) above into a materials price variance and a materials quantity variance.

BRIEF EXERCISE 8–3   Direct Labor Variances (LO3)

SkyChefs, Inc., prepares in-flight meals for a number of major airlines. One of the company's products is grilled salmon in dill sauce with baby new potatoes and spring vegetables. During the most recent week, the company prepared 4,000 of these meals using 960 direct labor-hours. The company paid these direct labor workers a total of $9,600 for this work, or $10.00 per hour.

According to the standard cost card for this meal, it should require 0.25 direct labor-hours at a cost of $9.75 per hour.

Required:
1. What direct labor cost should have been incurred to prepare the 4,000 meals? How much greater or less is this than the direct labor cost that was incurred?
2. Break down the difference computed in (1) above into a labor rate variance and a labor efficiency variance.

BRIEF EXERCISE 8–4   Variable Overhead Variances (LO4)

Logistics Solutions provides order fulfillment services for dot.com merchants. The company maintains warehouses that stock items carried by its dot.com clients. When a client receives an order from a customer, the order is forwarded to Logistics Solutions, which pulls the item from storage, packs it, and ships it to the customer. The company uses a predetermined variable overhead rate based on direct labor-hours.

In the most recent month, 120,000 items were shipped to customers using 2,300 direct labor-hours. The company incurred a total of $7,360 in variable overhead costs.

According to the company's standards, 0.02 direct labor-hours are required to fulfill an order for one item and the variable overhead rate is $3.25 per direct labor-hour.

Required:
1. What variable overhead cost should have been incurred to fill the orders for the 120,000 items? How much greater or less is this than the variable overhead cost that was incurred?
2. Break down the difference computed in (1) above into a variable overhead spending variance and a variable overhead efficiency variance.

BRIEF EXERCISE 8–5   Recording Variances in the General Ledger (LO5)

(Appendix 8A) Bliny Corporation makes a product with the following standard costs for direct material and direct labor:

Direct material: 2.00 meters at $3.25 per meter	$6.50
Direct labor: 0.40 hours at $12.00 per hour	$4.80

During the most recent month, 5,000 units were produced. The costs associated with the month's production of this product were as follows:

Material purchased: 12,000 meters at $3.15 per meter	$37,800
Material used in production: 10,500 meters	—
Direct labor: 1,975 hours at $12.20 per hour	$24,095

The standard cost variances for direct material and direct labor have been computed to be:

Materials price variance: 12,000 meters at $0.10 per meter F	$1,200 F
Materials quantity variance: 500 meters at $3.25 per meter U	$1,625 U
Labor rate variance: 1,975 hours at $0.20 per hour U	$395 U
Labor efficiency variance: 25 hours at $12.00 per hour F	$300 F

Required:
1. Prepare the general ledger entry to record the purchase of materials on account for the month.
2. Prepare the general ledger entry to record the use of materials for the month.
3. Prepare the general ledger entry to record the incurrence of direct labor cost for the month.

Exercises

EXERCISE 8–1   Setting Standards; Preparing a Standard Cost Card (LO1)

Martin Company manufactures a powerful cleaning solvent. The main ingredient in the solvent is a raw material called Echol. Information on the purchase and use of Echol follows:

Purchase of Echol   Echol is purchased in 15-gallon containers at a cost of $115 per container. A discount of 2% is offered by the supplier for payment within 10 days, and Martin Company takes all discounts. Shipping costs, which Martin Company must pay, amount to $130 for an average shipment of 100 15-gallon containers of Echol.

Use of Echol   The bill of materials calls for 7.6 quarts of Echol per bottle of cleaning solvent. (There are four quarts in a gallon.) About 5% of all Echol used is lost through spillage or evaporation (the 7.6 quarts above is the *actual* content per bottle). In addition, statistical analysis has shown that every 41st bottle is rejected at final inspection because of contamination.

Required:
1. Compute the standard purchase price for one quart of Echol.
2. Compute the standard quantity of Echol (in quarts) per salable bottle of cleaning solvent.
3. Using the data from (1) and (2) above, prepare a standard cost card showing the standard cost of Echol per bottle of cleaning solvent.

EXERCISE 8–2   Material and Labor Variances (LO2, LO3)
Huron Company produces a commercial cleaning compound known as Zoom. The direct materials and direct labor standards for one unit of Zoom are given below:

	Standard Quantity or Hours	Standard Price or Rate	Standard Cost
Direct materials	4.6 pounds	$ 2.50 per pound	$11.50
Direct labor	0.2 hours	12.00 per hour	2.40

During the most recent month, the following activity was recorded:
a. Twenty thousand pounds of material were purchased at a cost of $2.35 per pound.
b. All of the material purchased was used to produce 4,000 units of Zoom.
c. A total of 750 hours of direct labor time was recorded at a total labor cost of $10,425.

Required:
1. Compute the direct materials price and quantity variances for the month.
2. Compute the direct labor rate and efficiency variances for the month.

EXERCISE 8–3   Material Variances (LO2)
Refer to the data in Exercise 8–2. Assume that instead of producing 4,000 units during the month, the company produced only 3,000 units, using 14,750 pounds of material in the production process. (The rest of the material purchased remained in inventory.)

Required:
Compute the direct materials price and quantity variances for the month.

EXERCISE 8–4   Labor and Variable Overhead Variances (LO3, LO4)
Erie Company manufactures a small cassette player called the Jogging Mate. The company uses standards to control its costs. The labor standards that have been set for one Jogging Mate cassette player are as follows:

Standard Hours	Standard Rate per Hour	Standard Cost
18 minutes	$12.00	$3.60

During August, 5,750 hours of direct labor time were recorded in the manufacture of 20,000 units of the Jogging Mate. The direct labor cost totaled $73,600 for the month.

Required:
1. What direct labor cost should have been incurred in the manufacture of the 20,000 units of the Jogging Mate? By how much does this differ from the cost that was incurred?
2. Break down the difference in cost from (1) above into a labor rate variance and a labor efficiency variance.

3. The budgeted variable manufacturing overhead rate is $4 per direct labor-hour. During August, the company incurred $21,850 in variable manufacturing overhead cost. Compute the variable overhead spending and efficiency variances for the month.

EXERCISE 8–5   Materials and Labor Variances (LO2, LO3)

Dawson Toys, Ltd., produces a toy called the Maze. The company has recently established a standard cost system to help control costs and has established the following standards for the Maze toy:

> Direct materials: 6 microns per toy at $0.50 per micron
> Direct labor: 1.3 hours per toy at $8 per hour

During July, the company produced 3,000 Maze toys. Production data for the month on the toy follow:

> Direct materials: 25,000 microns were purchased for use in production at a cost of $0.48 per micron. Some 5,000 of these microns were still in inventory at the end of the month.
> Direct labor: 4,000 direct labor-hours were worked at a cost of $36,000.

Required:
1. Compute the following variances for July:
    a. Direct materials price and quantity variances.
    b. Direct labor rate and efficiency variances.
2. Prepare a brief explanation of the significance and possible causes of each variance.

EXERCISE 8–6   Material and Labor Variances; Journal Entries (LO2, LO3, LO5)

(Appendix 8A) Genola Fashions began production of a new product on June 1. The company uses a standard cost system and has established the following standards for one unit of the new product:

	Standard Quantity or Hours	Standard Price or Rate	Standard Cost
Direct materials	2.5 yards	$14 per yard	$35.00
Direct labor	1.6 hours	8 per hour	12.80

During June, the following activity was recorded relative to the new product:
a. Purchasing acquired 10,000 yards of material at a cost of $13.80 per yard.
b. Production used 8,000 yards of the material to manufacture 3,000 units of the new product.
c. Production reported 5,000 hours of labor time worked directly on the new product; the cost of this labor time was $43,000.

Required:
1. For materials:
    a. Compute the direct materials price and quantity variances.
    b. Prepare journal entries to record the purchase of materials and the use of materials in production.
2. For direct labor:
    a. Compute the direct labor rate and efficiency variances.
    b. Prepare a journal entry to record the incurrence of direct labor cost for the month.
3. Post the entries you have prepared to the following T-accounts:

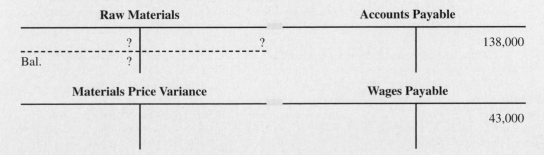

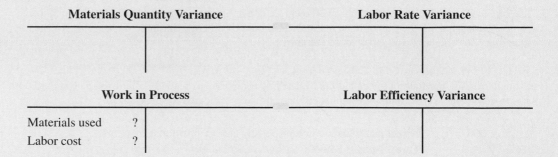

Materials Quantity Variance		Labor Rate Variance

Work in Process		Labor Efficiency Variance
Materials used ?		
Labor cost ?		

Problems

PROBLEM 8–1   Variance Analysis in a Hospital (LO2, LO3, LO4)

John Fleming, chief administrator for Valley View Hospital, is concerned about costs for tests in the hospital's lab. Charges for lab tests are consistently higher at Valley View than at other hospitals and have resulted in many complaints. Also, because of strict regulations on amounts reimbursed for lab tests, payments received from insurance companies and governmental units have not been high enough to provide an acceptable level of profit for the lab.

Mr. Fleming has asked you to evaluate costs in the hospital's lab for the past month. The following information is available:

a. Basically, two types of tests are performed in the lab—blood tests and smears. During the past month, 1,800 blood tests and 2,400 smears were performed in the lab.

b. Small glass plates are used in both types of tests. During the past month, the hospital purchased 12,000 plates at a cost of $28,200. This cost is net of a 6% quantity discount. Some 1,500 of these plates were still on hand unused at the end of the month; there were no plates on hand at the beginning of the month.

c. During the past month, 1,150 hours of labor time were recorded in the lab. The cost of this labor time was $13,800.

d. Variable overhead cost last month in the lab for utilities and supplies totaled $7,820.

Valley View Hospital has never used standard costs. By searching industry literature, however, you have determined the following nationwide averages for hospital labs:

Plates: Two plates are required per lab test. These plates cost $2.50 each and are disposed of after the test is completed.

Labor: Each blood test should require 0.3 hours to complete, and each smear should require 0.15 hours to complete. The average cost of this lab time is $14 per hour.

Overhead: Overhead cost is based on direct labor-hours. The average rate for variable overhead is $6 per hour.

Mr. Fleming would like a complete analysis of the cost of plates, labor, and overhead in the lab for the last month so that he can get to the root of the lab's cost problem.

Required:

1. Compute a materials price variance for the plates purchased last month and a materials quantity variance for the plates used last month.

2. For labor cost in the lab:
    a. Compute a labor rate variance and a labor efficiency variance.
    b. In most hospitals, one-half of the workers in the lab are senior technicians and one-half are assistants. In an effort to reduce costs, Valley View Hospital employs only one-fourth senior technicians and three-fourths assistants. Would you recommend that this policy be continued? Explain.

3. Compute the variable overhead spending and efficiency variances. Is there any relationship between the variable overhead efficiency variance and the labor efficiency variance? Explain.

PROBLEM 8–2   Basic Variance Analysis (LO2, LO3, LO4)

Becton Labs, Inc., produces various chemical compounds for industrial use. One compound, called Fludex, is prepared by means of an elaborate distilling process. The company has developed standard costs for one unit of Fludex, as follows:

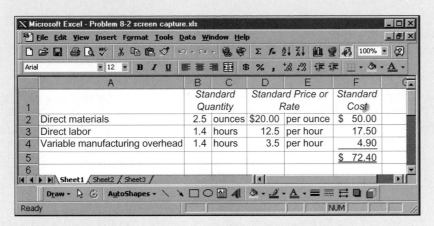

	A	B	C	D	E	F
1		Standard Quantity		Standard Price or Rate		Standard Cost
2	Direct materials	2.5	ounces	$20.00	per ounce	$ 50.00
3	Direct labor	1.4	hours	12.5	per hour	17.50
4	Variable manufacturing overhead	1.4	hours	3.5	per hour	4.90
5						$ 72.40
6						

During November, the following activity was recorded by the company relative to production of Fludex:

a. Materials purchased, 12,000 ounces at a cost of $225,000.
b. There was no beginning inventory of materials on hand to start the month; at the end of the month, 2,500 ounces of material remained in the warehouse unused.
c. The company employs 35 lab technicians to work on the production of Fludex. During November, each worked an average of 160 hours at an average rate of $12 per hour.
d. Variable manufacturing overhead is assigned to Fludex on the basis of direct labor-hours. Variable manufacturing overhead costs during November totaled $18,200.
e. During November, 3,750 good units of Fludex were produced.

The company's management is anxious to determine the efficiency of the activities surrounding the production of Fludex.

Required:
1. For materials used in the production of Fludex:
   a. Compute the price and quantity variances.
   b. The materials were purchased from a new supplier who is anxious to enter into a long-term purchase contract. Would you recommend that the company sign the contract? Explain.
2. For direct labor employed in the production of Fludex:
   a. Compute the rate and efficiency variances.
   b. In the past, the 35 technicians employed in the production of Fludex consisted of 20 senior technicians and 15 assistants. During November, the company experimented with only 15 senior technicians and 20 assistants in order to save costs. Would you recommend that the new labor mix be continued? Explain.
3. Compute the variable overhead spending and efficiency variances. What relationship can you see between this efficiency variance and the labor efficiency variance?

PROBLEM 8–3   Comprehensive Variance Analysis (LO2, LO3, LO4)
Miller Toy Company manufactures a plastic swimming pool at its Westwood Plant. The plant has been experiencing problems for some time as shown by its June income statement below:

CHECK FIGURE
(1a) Materials price
variance: $3,000 F
(2) Net variance:
$16,290 U

	Budgeted	Actual
Sales (15,000 pools)	$450,000	$450,000
Less variable expenses:		
Variable cost of goods sold*	180,000	196,290
Variable selling expenses	20,000	20,000
Total variable expenses	200,000	216,290
Contribution margin	250,000	233,710
Less fixed expenses:		
Manufacturing overhead	130,000	130,000
Selling and administrative	84,000	84,000
Total fixed expenses	214,000	214,000
Net income	$ 36,000	$ 19,710

*Contains direct materials, direct labor, and variable manufacturing overhead.

Janet Dunn, who has just been appointed general manager of the Westwood Plant, has been given instructions to "get things under control." Upon reviewing the plant's income statement, Ms. Dunn has concluded that the major problem lies in the variable cost of goods sold. She has been provided with the following standard cost per swimming pool:

	Standard Quantity or Hours	Standard Price or Rate	Standard Cost
Direct materials	3.0 pounds	$2.00 per pound	$ 6.00
Direct labor	0.8 hours	6.00 per hour	4.80
Variable manufacturing overhead	0.4 hours*	3.00 per hour	1.20
Total standard cost			$12.00

*Based on machine-hours.

Ms. Dunn has determined that during June the plant produced 15,000 pools and incurred the following costs:

a. Purchased 60,000 pounds of materials at a cost of $1.95 per pound.
b. Used 49,200 pounds of materials in production. (Finished goods and work in process inventories are insignificant and can be ignored.)
c. Worked 11,800 direct labor-hours at a cost of $7.00 per hour.
d. Incurred variable manufacturing overhead cost totaling $18,290 for the month. A total of 5,900 machine-hours was recorded.

It is the company's policy to close all variances to cost of goods sold on a monthly basis.

Required:
1. Compute the following variances for June:
   a. Direct materials price and quantity variances.
   b. Direct labor rate and efficiency variances.
   c. Variable overhead spending and efficiency variances.
2. Summarize the variances that you computed in (1) above by showing the net overall favorable or unfavorable variance for the month. What impact did this figure have on the company's income statement? Show computations.
3. Pick out the two most significant variances that you computed in (1) above. Explain to Ms. Dunn possible causes of these variances.

CHECK FIGURE
(2a) Labor rate variance:
   $3,200 U
(3) Variable overhead
   efficiency variance:
   $2,000 F

PROBLEM 8–4 Comprehensive Variance Analysis; Journal Entries (LO2, LO3, LO4, LO5)
(Appendix 8A) Trueform Products, Inc., produces a broad line of sports equipment and uses a standard cost system for control purposes. Last year the company produced 8,000 of its varsity footballs. The standard costs associated with this football, along with the actual costs incurred last year, are given below (per football):

	Standard Cost	Actual Cost
Direct materials:		
Standard: 3.7 feet at $5.00 per foot	$18.50	
Actual: 4.0 feet at $4.80 per foot		$19.20
Direct labor:		
Standard: 0.9 hours at $7.50 per hour	6.75	
Actual: 0.8 hours at $8.00 per hour		6.40
Variable manufacturing overhead:		
Standard: 0.9 hours at $2.50 per hour	2.25	
Actual: 0.8 hours at $2.75 per hour		2.20
Total cost per football	$27.50	$27.80

The president was elated when he saw that actual costs exceeded standard costs by only $0.30 per football. He stated, "I was afraid that our unit cost might get out of hand when we gave out those raises last year in order to stimulate output. But it's obvious our costs are well under control."

There was no inventory of materials on hand to start the year. During the year, 32,000 feet of materials were purchased and used in production.

Required:
1. For direct materials:
   a. Compute the price and quantity variances for the year.
   b. Prepare journal entries to record all activity relating to direct materials for the year.
2. For direct labor:
   a. Compute the rate and efficiency variances.
   b. Prepare a journal entry to record the incurrence of direct labor cost for the year.
3. Compute the variable overhead spending and efficiency variances.
4. Was the president correct in his statement that "our costs are well under control"? Explain.
5. State possible causes of each variance that you have computed.

CHECK FIGURE
(1) Nyclyn: 18.0 kgs.
(3) Standard cost: $97.20

PROBLEM 8–5   Setting Standards (LO1)

Danson Company is a chemical manufacturer that supplies various products to industrial users. The company plans to introduce a new chemical solution, called Nysap, for which it needs to develop a standard product cost. The following information is available on the production of Nysap:

a. Nysap is made by combining a chemical compound (nyclyn) and a solution (salex), and boiling the mixture. A 20% loss in volume occurs for both the salex and the nyclyn during boiling. After boiling, the mixture consists of 9.6 liters of salex and 12 kilograms of nyclyn per 10-liter batch of Nysap.
b. After the boiling process is complete, the solution is cooled slightly before 5 kilograms of protet are added per 10-liter batch of Nysap. The addition of the protet does not affect the total liquid volume. The resulting solution is then bottled in 10-liter containers.
c. The finished product is highly unstable, and one 10-liter batch out of six is rejected at final inspection. Rejected batches have no commercial value and are thrown out.
d. It takes a worker 35 minutes to process one 10-liter batch of Nysap. Employees work an eight-hour day, including one hour per day for rest breaks and cleanup.

Required:
1. Determine the standard quantity for each of the raw materials needed to produce an acceptable 10-liter batch of Nysap.
2. Determine the standard labor time to produce an acceptable 10-liter batch of Nysap.
3. Assuming the following purchase prices and costs, prepare a standard cost card for materials and labor for one acceptable 10-liter batch of Nysap:

Salex	$1.50 per liter
Nyclyn	2.80 per kilogram
Protet	3.00 per kilogram
Direct labor cost	9.00 per hour

(CMA, adapted)

CHECK FIGURE
(1) Actual hours: 145

PROBLEM 8–6   Working Backwards from Labor Variances (LO3)

The auto repair shop of Quality Motor Company uses standards to control the labor time and labor cost in the shop. The standard labor cost for a motor tune-up is given below:

Job	Standard Hours	Standard Rate	Standard Cost
Motor tune-up	2.5	$9	$22.50

The record showing the time spent in the shop last week on motor tune-ups has been misplaced. However, the shop supervisor recalls that 50 tune-ups were completed during the week, and the controller recalls the following variance data relating to tune-ups:

Labor rate variance	$87 F
Total labor variance	93 U

Required:
1. Determine the number of actual labor-hours spent on tune-ups during the week.
2. Determine the actual hourly rate of pay for tune-ups last week.

(Hint: A useful way to proceed would be to work from known to unknown data either by using the variance formulas or by using the columnar format shown in Exhibit 8–5.)

CHECK FIGURE
(1) Standard cost: $31.50
(3) 2.8 yards

PROBLEM 8–7 Comprehensive Variance Problem (LO1, LO2, LO3, LO4)
Highland Company produces a lightweight backpack that is popular with college students. Standard variable costs relating to a single backpack are given below:

	Standard Quantity or Hours	Standard Price or Rate	Standard Cost
Direct materials	?	$6 per yard	$?
Direct labor	?	?	?
Variable manufacturing overhead	?	$3 per hour	?
Total standard cost			$?

During March, 1,000 backpacks were manufactured and sold. Selected information relating to the month's production is given below:

	Materials Used	Direct Labor	Variable Manufacturing Overhead
Total standard cost allowed*	$16,800	$10,500	$4,200
Actual costs incurred	15,000	?	3,600
Materials price variance	?		
Materials quantity variance	1,200 U		
Labor rate variance		?	
Labor efficiency variance		?	
Variable overhead spending variance			?
Variable overhead efficiency variance			?

*For the month's production.

The following additional information is available for March's production:

Actual direct labor-hours	1,500
Standard overhead rate per hour	$3.00
Standard price of one yard of materials	6.00
Difference between standard and actual cost per backpack produced during March	0.15 F

Overhead is applied to production on the basis of direct labor-hours.

Required:
1. What is the standard cost of a single backpack?
2. What was the actual cost per backpack produced during March?
3. How many yards of material are required at standard per backpack?
4. What was the materials price variance for March?
5. What is the standard direct labor rate per hour?
6. What was the labor rate variance for March? The labor efficiency variance?
7. What was the variable overhead spending variance for March? The variable overhead efficiency variance?
8. Prepare a standard cost card for one backpack.

PROBLEM 8–8 Computations from Incomplete Data (LO2, LO3)

CHECK FIGURE
(1a) Actual cost: $5.30/ft.
(2a) Standard labor rate: $8

Sharp Company manufactures a product for which the following standards have been set:

	Standard Quantity or Hours	Standard Price or Rate	Standard Cost
Direct materials	3 feet	$5 per foot	$15
Direct labor	? hours	? per hour	?

During March, the company purchased direct materials at a cost of $55,650, all of which were used in the production of 3,200 units of product. In addition, 4,900 hours of direct labor time were worked on the product during the month. The cost of this labor time was $36,750. The following variances have been computed for the month:

Materials quantity variance	$4,500 U
Total labor variance	1,650 F
Labor efficiency variance	800 U

Required:
1. For direct materials:
   a. Compute the actual cost per foot for materials for March.
   b. Compute the materials price variance and a total variance for materials.
2. For direct labor:
   a. Compute the standard direct labor rate per hour.
   b. Compute the standard hours allowed for the month's production.
   c. Compute the standard hours allowed per unit of product.

(Hint: In completing the problem, it may be helpful to move from known to unknown data either by using the columnar format shown in Exhibits 8–3 and 8–5 or by using the variance formulas.)

PROBLEM 8–9 Variance Analysis with Multiple Lots (LO2, LO3)

CHECK FIGURE
(2b) Total quantity variance: $216 U
(4b) Total labor efficiency variance: $3,900 U

Hillcrest Leisure Wear, Inc., manufactures men's clothing. The company has a single line of slacks that is produced in lots, with each lot representing an order from a customer. As a lot is completed, the customer's store label is attached to the slacks before shipment.

Hillcrest has a standard cost system and has established the following standards for a dozen slacks:

	Standard Quantity or Hours	Standard Price or Rate	Standard Cost
Direct materials	32 yards	$2.40 per yard	$76.80
Direct labor	6 hours	7.50 per hour	45.00

During October, Hillcrest worked on three orders for slacks. The company's job cost records for the month reveal the following:

Lot	Units in Lot (dozens)	Materials Used (yards)	Hours Worked
48	1,500	48,300	8,900
49	950	30,140	6,130
50	2,100	67,250	10,270

The following additional information is available:

a. Hillcrest purchased 180,000 yards of material during October at a cost of $424,800.
b. Direct labor cost incurred during the month for production of slacks amounted to $192,280.
c. There was no work in process inventory on October 1. During October, lots 48 and 49 were completed, and lot 50 was 100% complete as to materials and 80% complete as to labor.

Required:
1. Compute the materials price variance for the materials purchased during October.
2. Determine the materials quantity variance for October in both yards and dollars:
   a. For each lot worked on during the month.
   b. For the company as a whole.
3. Compute the labor rate variance for October.
4. Determine the labor efficiency variance for the month in both hours and dollars:
   a. For each lot worked on during the month.
   b. For the company as a whole.
5. In what situations might it be better to express variances in units (hours, yards, and so on) rather than in dollars? In dollars rather than in units?

(CPA, adapted)

CHECK FIGURE
(1a) Materials price
    variance: $6,000 F
(3) Variable overhead
    spending variance:
    $1,650 F

PROBLEM 8–10   Comprehensive Variance Analysis with Incomplete Data; Journal Entries
(LO1, LO2, LO3, LO4, LO5)
(Appendix 8A) Maple Products, Ltd., manufactures a hockey stick that is used worldwide. The standard cost of one hockey stick is:

	Standard Quantity or Hours	Standard Price or Rate	Standard Cost
Direct materials	? feet	$3.00 per foot	$?
Direct labor	2 hours	? per hour	?
Variable manufacturing overhead	? hours	1.30 per hour	?
Total standard cost			$27.00

Last year, 8,000 hockey sticks were produced and sold. Selected cost data relating to last year's operations follow:

	Dr.	Cr.
Direct materials purchased (60,000 feet)	$174,000	
Wages payable (? hours)		$79,200*
Work in process—direct materials	115,200	
Direct labor rate variance		3,300
Variable overhead efficiency variance	650	

*Relates to the actual direct labor cost for the year.

The following additional information is available for last year's operations:

a. No materials were on hand at the start of last year. Some of the materials purchased during the year were still on hand in the warehouse at the end of the year.
b. The variable manufacturing overhead rate is based on direct labor-hours. Total actual variable manufacturing overhead cost for last year was $19,800.
c. Actual direct materials usage for last year exceeded the standard by 0.2 feet per stick.

Required:
1. For direct materials:
   a. Compute the price and quantity variances for last year.
   b. Prepare journal entries to record all activities relating to direct materials for last year.
2. For direct labor:
   a. Verify the rate variance given above and compute the efficiency variance for last year.
   b. Prepare a journal entry to record activity relating to direct labor for last year.
3. Compute the variable overhead spending variance for last year and verify the variable overhead efficiency variance given above.
4. State possible causes of each variance that you have computed.
5. Prepare a completed standard cost card for one hockey stick.

PROBLEM 8–11   Developing Standard Costs (LO1)
ColdKing Company is a small producer of fruit-flavored frozen desserts. For many years, ColdKing's products have had strong regional sales on the basis of brand recognition; however, other companies have begun marketing similar products in the area, and price competition has become increasingly important. John Wakefield, the company's controller, is planning to implement a standard cost system for ColdKing and has gathered considerable information from his co-workers on production and material requirements for Cold-King's products. Wakefield believes that the use of standard costing will allow ColdKing to improve cost control and make better pricing decisions.

ColdKing's most popular product is raspberry sherbet. The sherbet is produced in 10-gallon batches, and each batch requires 6 quarts of good raspberries. The fresh raspberries are sorted by hand before they enter the production process. Because of imperfections in the raspberries and normal spoilage, 1 quart of berries is discarded for every 4 quarts of acceptable berries. Three minutes is the standard direct labor time for the sorting that is required to obtain 1 quart of acceptable raspberries. The acceptable raspberries are then blended with the other ingredients; blending requires 12 minutes of direct labor time per batch. After blending, the sherbet is packaged in quart containers. Wakefield has gathered the following pricing information:

a. ColdKing purchases raspberries at a cost of $0.80 per quart. All other ingredients cost a total of $0.45 per gallon of sherbert.
b. Direct labor is paid at the rate of $9.00 per hour.
c. The total cost of material and labor required to package the sherbet is $0.38 per quart.

Required:
1. Develop the standard cost for the direct cost components (materials, labor, and packaging) of a 10-gallon batch of raspberry sherbet. The standard cost should identify the standard quantity, standard rate, and standard cost per batch for each direct cost component of a batch of raspberry sherbet.
2. As part of the implementation of a standard cost system at ColdKing, John Wakefied plans to train those responsible for maintaining the standards on how to use variance analysis. Wakefield is particularly concerned with the causes of unfavorable variances.
   a. Discuss possible causes of unfavorable materials price variances and identify the individual(s) who should be held responsible for these variances.
   b. Discuss possible causes of unfavorable labor efficiency variances and identify the individual(s) who should be held responsible for these variances.

(CMA, adapted)

Building Your Skills

ANALYTICAL THINKING (LO2, LO3, LO4, LO5)
(Appendix 8A) You are employed by Olster Company, which manufactures products for the senior citizen market. As a rising young executive in the company, you are scheduled to make a presentation in a few hours to your superior. This presentation relates to last week's production of Maxitol, a popular health tonic that is manufactured by Olster Company. Unfortunately, while studying ledger sheets and variance summaries by poolside in the company's fitness area, you were bumped and dropped the papers into the pool. In desperation, you fished the papers from the water, but you have discovered that only the following fragments are readable:

Maxitol—Standard Cost Card

	Standard Quantity or Hours	Standard Price or Rate	Standard Cost
Material A	6 gallons	$8 per gall	$
Material B		per pou	
Direct labor		per ho	0
Standard cost per batc			$99.50

Maxitol—General Ledger Accounts

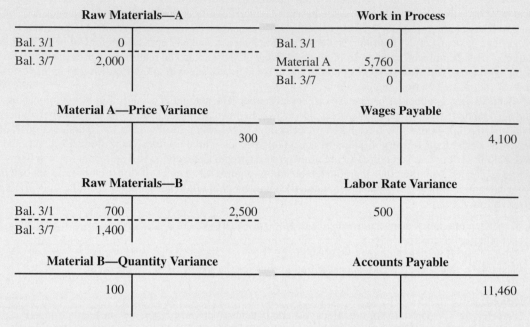

Raw Materials—A		
Bal. 3/1	0	
Bal. 3/7	2,000	

Work in Process		
Bal. 3/1	0	
Material A	5,760	
Bal. 3/7	0	

Material A—Price Variance	
	300

Wages Payable	
	4,100

Raw Materials—B		
Bal. 3/1	700	2,500
Bal. 3/7	1,400	

Labor Rate Variance	
500	

Material B—Quantity Variance	
100	

Accounts Payable	
	11,460

You remember that the accounts payable are for purchases of both material A and material B. You also remember that only 10 direct labor workers are involved in the production of Maxitol and that each worked 40 hours last week. The wages payable above are for wages earned by these workers.

You realize that to be ready for your presentation, you must reconstruct all data relating to Maxitol very quickly. As a start, you have called purchasing and found that 1,000 gallons of material A and 800 pounds of material B were purchased last week.

Required:
1. How many batches of Maxitol were produced last week? (This is a key figure; be sure it's right before going on.)
2. For material A:
    a. What was the cost of material A purchased last week?
    b. How many gallons were used in production last week?
    c. What was the quantity variance?
    d. Prepare journal entries to record all activity relating to material A for last week.
3. For material B:
    a. What is the standard cost per pound for material B?
    b. How many pounds of material B were used in production last week? How many pounds should have been used at standard?
    c. What is the standard quantity of material B per batch?
    d. What was the price variance for material B last week?
    e. Prepare journal entries to record all activity relating to material B for last week.
4. For direct labor:
    a. What is the standard rate per direct labor-hour?
    b. What are the standard hours per batch?
    c. What were the standard hours allowed for last week's production?
    d. What was the labor efficiency variance for last week?
    e. Prepare a journal entry to record all activity relating to direct labor for last week.
5. Complete the standard cost card shown above for one batch of Maxitol.

COMMUNICATING IN PRACTICE (LO1)
Make an appointment to meet with the manager of an auto repair shop that uses standards. In most cases, this would be an auto repair shop that is affiliated with a national chain such as Firestone or Sears or the service department of a new-car dealer.

Required:
At the scheduled meeting, find out the answers to the following questions and write a memo to your instructor describing the information obtained during your meeting.
1. How are standards set?

2. Are standards practical or ideal?
3. Is the actual time taken to complete a task compared to the standard time?
4. What are the consequences of unfavorable variances? Of favorable variances?
5. Do the standards and variances create any potential problems?

ETHICS CHALLENGE (LO1)

Stacy Cummins, the newly hired controller at Merced Home Products, Inc., was disturbed by what she had discovered about the standard costs at the Home Security Division. In looking over the past several years of quarterly earnings reports at the Home Security Division, she noticed that the first-quarter earnings were always poor, the second-quarter earnings were slightly better, the third-quarter earnings were again slightly better, and then the fourth quarter and the year always ended with a spectacular performance in which the Home Security Division always managed to meet or exceed its target profit for the year. She also was concerned to find letters from the company's external auditors to top management warning about an unusual use of standard costs at the Home Security Division.

When Ms. Cummins ran across these letters, she asked the assistant controller, Gary Farber, if he knew what was going on at the Home Security Division. Gary said that it was common knowledge in the company that the vice president in charge of the Home Security Division, Preston Lansing, had rigged the standards at the Home Security Division in order to produce the same quarterly earnings pattern every year. According to company policy, variances are taken directly to the income statement as an adjustment to cost of goods sold.

Favorable variances have the effect of increasing net income, and unfavorable variances have the effect of decreasing net income. Lansing had rigged the standards so that there were always large favorable variances. Company policy was a little vague about when these variances have to be reported on the divisional income statements. While the intent was clearly to recognize variances on the income statement in the period in which they arise, nothing in the company's accounting manuals explicitly required this. So for many years Lansing had followed a practice of saving up the favorable variances and using them to create a nice smooth pattern of earnings growth in the first three quarters, followed by a big "Christmas present" of an extremely good fourth quarter. (Financial reporting regulations forbid carrying variances forward from one year to the next on the annual audited financial statements, so all of the variances must appear on the divisional income statement by the end of the year.)

Ms. Cummins was concerned about these revelations and attempted to bring up the subject with the president of Merced Home Products but was told that "we all know what Lansing's doing, but as long as he continues to turn in such good reports, don't bother him." When Ms. Cummins asked if the board of directors was aware of the situation, the president somewhat testily replied, "Of course they are aware."

Required:
1. How did Preston Lansing probably "rig" the standard costs—are the standards set too high or too low? Explain.
2. Should Preston Lansing be permitted to continue his practice of managing reported earnings?
3. What should Stacy Cummins do in this situation?

TAKING IT TO THE NET

As you know, the World Wide Web is a medium that is constantly evolving. Sites come and go and change without notice. To enable periodic update of site addresses, this problem has been posted to the textbook website (www.mhhe.com/folk1e). After accessing the site, enter the Student Center and select this chapter. Select and complete the Taking It to the Net problem.

TEAMWORK IN ACTION (LO1)

Terry Travers is the manufacturing supervisor of Aurora Manufacturing Company, which produces a variety of plastic products. Some of these products are standard items that are listed in the company's catalog, while others are made to customer specifications. Each month, Travers receives a performance report showing the budget for the month, the actual activity, and the variance between budget and actual. Part of Travers' annual performance evaluation is based on his department's performance against budget. Aurora's purchasing manager, Sally Christensen, also receives monthly performance reports and she, too, is evaluated in part on the basis of these reports.

The monthly reports for June had just been distributed when Travers met Christensen in the hallway outside their offices. Scowling, Travers began the conversation, "I see we have another set of monthly performance reports hand-delivered by that not very nice junior employee in the budget office. He seemed pleased to tell me that I'm in trouble with my performance again."

Christensen: I got the same treatment. All I ever hear about are the things I haven't done right. Now I'll have to spend a lot of time reviewing the report and preparing explanations. The worst part is that it's now the 21st of July so the information is almost a month old, and we have to spend all this time on history.

Travers: My biggest gripe is that our production activity varies a lot from month to month, but we're given an annual budget that's written in stone. Last month we were shut down for three days when a strike delayed delivery of the basic ingredient used in our plastic formulation, and we had already exhausted our inventory. You know about that problem, though, because we asked you to call all over the country to find an alternate source of supply. When we got what we needed on a rush basis, we had to pay more than we normally do.

Christensen: I expect problems like that to pop up from time to time—that's part of my job—but now we'll both have to take a careful look at our reports to see where the charges are reflected for that rush order. Every month I spend more time making sure I should be charged for each item reported than I do making plans for my department's daily work. It's really frustrating to see charges for things I have no control over.

Travers: The way we get information doesn't help, either. I don't get copies of the reports you get, yet a lot of what I do is affected by your department, and by most of the other departments we have. Why do the budget and accounting people assume that I should only be told about my operations even though the president regularly gives us pep talks about how we all need to work together as a team?

Christensen: I seem to get more reports than I need, and I am never asked to comment on them until top management calls me on the carpet about my department's shortcomings. Do you ever hear comments when your department shines?

Travers: I guess they don't have time to review the good news. One of my problems is that all the reports are in dollars and cents. I work with people, machines, and materials. I need information to help me *this* month to solve *this* month's problems—not another report of the dollars expended *last* month or the month before.

Required:

Your team should discuss and then respond to the following questions. All team members should agree with and understand the answers and be prepared to report on those answers in class. (Each teammate can assume responsibility for a different part of the presentation.)

1. Based on the conversation between Terry Travers and Sally Christensen, describe the likely motivation and behavior of these two employees as a result of the standard cost and variance reporting system that is used by Aurora Manufacturing Company.

2. List the recommendations that your team would make to Aurora Manufacturing Company to enhance employee motivation as it relates to the company's standard cost and variance reporting system.

(CMA, adapted)

Chapter Nine

Flexible Budgets and Overhead Analysis

Chapter Outline

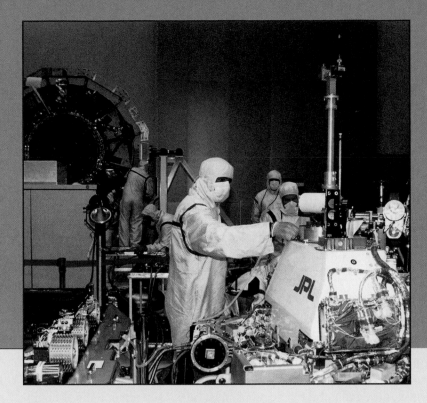

Decision Feature NASA Reduces Its Overhead Costs

NASA (www.nasa.gov) is the civilian agency responsible for all aeronautical and space activities sponsored by the United States other than those that are the responsibility of the Department of Defense (DOD). An online newsletter (today@nasa.gov) provides daily updates about the activities of NASA.

During the six-year period from 1994 to 2000, NASA's budget decreased from $14.5 billion to $13.6 billion. This trend will most likely reverse if NASA's budget request of $14.1 billion for fiscal 2001 is approved. NASA administrator Daniel Goldin is pleased that Congress has agreed to reinvest the cost savings that have resulted from NASA's "faster, cheaper, better" approach. Comparing fiscal 1990 through 1994 to fiscal 1995 through 1999, the average spacecraft development cost declined by 65%, the average development time decreased from 8 to 5 years, and the number of flights per year has increased from 2 to 7.

NASA was able to achieve more with less during the 1990s by significantly reducing its overhead costs. By way of illustration, Goldin compared the size of the mission operations staff for the Viking and Pathfinder missions. It took a crew of 1,000 to send Viking to Mars. Just under 20 years later, a crew of 50 sent the Pathfinder to Mars. Part of NASA's success can be attributed to its decision to outsource support activities. Contractors aggressively bid against each other to perform the work. This example of NASA's determination to control its overhead costs relates to a cost management program that was instituted by NASA in 1995.

The multiyear initiative encompasses NASA's management, budgeting, and accounting processes. In part, the program is expected to reduce the cost of missions, inspire the agency's managers to perform efficiently, benchmark activities, support the decision-making process, provide justification for NASA's budget requests, and further enhance NASA's accountability to the taxpayers. Even as a review of the cost management program in 1998 highlighted the efficiencies that have resulted, NASA continues to analyze and refine its cost management policies and procedures.

Source: NASA website, July 2000; John Rhea, "Cutting the Fat: DOD Can Learn How from NASA," *Military & Aerospace Electronics,* March 1998, p. 3 (3 pages). Courtesy of *Military & Aerospace Electronics Magazine.*

Learning Objectives
After studying Chapter 9, you should be able to:

LO1 Prepare a flexible budget and explain the advantages of the flexible budget approach over the static budget approach.

LO2 Prepare a performance report for both variable and fixed overhead costs using the flexible budget approach.

LO3 Use the flexible budget to prepare a variable overhead performance report containing only a spending variance.

LO4 Use the flexible budget to prepare a variable overhead performance report containing both a spending and an efficiency variance.

LO5 Compute the predetermined overhead rate and apply overhead to products in a standard cost system.

LO6 Compute and interpret the fixed overhead budget and volume variances.

Controlling overhead costs is a major preoccupation of managers in business, in government, and in not-for-profit organizations. Overhead is a major cost, if not *the* major cost, in most large organizations. It costs Microsoft very little to download copies of its software onto hard disks and to provide purchasers with software manuals; almost all of Microsoft's costs are in research and development and marketing—elements of overhead. Or consider Disney World. The only direct cost of serving a particular guest is the cost of the food the guest consumes at the park; virtually all of the other costs of running the amusement park are overhead. Boeing has huge amounts of overhead in the form of engineering salaries, buildings, insurance, administrative salaries, and marketing costs.

in business *today* **Reducing Overhead Costs**

Overhead costs now account for as much as 66% of the total costs incurred by companies in service industries and up to 37% of the total costs of manufacturers. Because of the magnitude of these costs, overhead cost reduction is now a recurring goal for many organizations. However, the extent of the reductions must be considered in light of competitive pressures to improve fundamental services to customers and product quality. Managers must take care not to cut costs that add value to the company.

Source: Nick Develin, "Unlocking Overhead Value," *Management Accounting,* December 1999, pp. 22–24. Reprinted with permission from *Management Accounting.*

Controlling overhead costs poses special problems. Costs like direct materials and direct labor are often easier to understand, and therefore to control, than overhead, which can include everything from the disposable coffee cup in the visitor's waiting area to the president's salary. Overhead is usually made up of many separate costs—many of which may be small. This makes it impractical to control them in the same way that costs such as direct materials and direct labor are controlled. And some overhead costs are variable, some are fixed, and some are a mixture of fixed and variable. These particular problems can be largely overcome by the use of flexible budgets—a topic that was briefly discussed in Chapter 7. In this chapter, we study flexible budgets in greater detail and learn how they can be used to control costs. We also expand the study of overhead variances that we started in Chapter 8.

Flexible Budgets

Learning Objective 1
Prepare a flexible budget and explain the advantages of the flexible budget approach over the static budget approach.

Characteristics of a Flexible Budget

The budgets that we studied in Chapter 7 were *static budgets.* A **static budget** is prepared for only the planned level of activity. This approach is suitable for planning purposes, but it is inadequate for evaluating how well costs are controlled. If the actual activity during a period differs from what was planned, it would be misleading to simply compare actual costs to the static budget. If activity is higher than expected, the variable costs should be higher than expected; and if activity is lower than expected, the variable costs should be lower than expected.

Flexible budgets take into account changes in costs that should occur as a consequence of changes in activity. A **flexible budget** provides estimates of what costs should be for any level of activity within a specified range. When a flexible budget is used in performance evaluation, actual costs are compared to what the *costs should have been for the*

Exhibit 9–1

RICK'S HAIRSTYLING Static Budget For the Month Ended March 31	
Budgeted number of client-visits	5,000
Budget variable overhead costs:	
Hairstyling supplies	$ 6,000
Client gratuities	20,000
Electricity	1,000
Total variable overhead cost	27,000
Budgeted fixed overhead costs:	
Support staff wages and salaries	8,000
Rent	12,000
Insurance	1,000
Utilities other than electricity	500
Total fixed overhead cost	21,500
Total budgeted overhead cost	$48,500

actual level of activity during the period rather than to the budgeted costs from the original budget. This is a very important distinction—particularly for variable costs. If adjustments for the level of activity are not made, it is very difficult to interpret discrepancies between budgeted and actual costs.

Deficiencies of the Static Budget

To illustrate the difference between a static budget and a flexible budget, we will consider the case of Rick's Hairstyling, a tony hairstyling salon located in Beverly Hills that is owned and managed by Rick Manzi. The salon has very loyal customers—many of whom are associated with the film industry. Despite the glamour associated with his salon, Rick is a very shrewd businessman. Recently he has been attempting to get better control over his overhead, and at the urging of his accounting and business adviser Victoria Kho, he has begun to prepare monthly budgets. Victoria Kho is a certified public accountant and certified management accountant in independent practice who specializes in small service-oriented businesses like Rick's Hairstyling.

At the end of February, Rick carefully prepared the March budget for overhead items that appears in Exhibit 9–1. Rick believes that the number of customers served in a month is the best way to measure the overall level of activity in his salon. Rick refers to these visits as client-visits. A customer who comes into the salon and has his or her hair styled is counted as one client-visit. After some discussion with Victoria Kho, Rick identified three major categories of variable overhead costs—hairstyling supplies, client gratuities, and electricity—and four major categories of fixed costs—support staff wages and salaries, rent, insurance, and utilities other than electricity. Client gratuities consist of flowers, candies, and glasses of champagne that Rick gives to his customers while they are in the salon. Rick considers electricity to be a variable cost, since almost all of the electricity in the salon is consumed in running blow-dryers, curling irons, and other hairstyling equipment.

To develop the budget for variable overhead, Rick estimated that the average cost per client-visit should be $1.20 for hairstyling supplies, $4.00 for client gratuities, and $0.20 for electricity. Based on his estimate of 5,000 client-visits in March, Rick budgeted for $6,000 ($1.20 per client-visit × 5,000 client-visits) in hairstyling supplies, $20,000 ($4.00 per client-visit × 5,000 client-visits) in client gratuities, and $1,000 ($0.20 per client-visit × 5,000 client-visits) in electricity.

Exhibit 9–2

RICK'S HAIRSTYLING
Static Budget Performance Report
For the Month Ended March 31

	Actual	Budgeted	Variance
Client-visits	5,200	5,000	200 F
Variable overhead costs:			
Hairstyling supplies	$ 6,400	$ 6,000	$ 400 U*
Client gratuities	22,300	20,000	2,300 U*
Electricity	1,020	1,000	20 U*
Total variable overhead cost	29,720	27,000	2,720 U*
Fixed overhead costs:			
Support staff wages and salaries	8,100	8,000	100 U
Rent	12,000	12,000	-0-
Insurance	1,000	1,000	-0-
Utilities other than electricity	470	500	30 F
Total fixed overhead cost	21,570	21,500	70 U
Total overhead cost	$51,290	$48,500	$2,790 U*

*The cost variances for variable costs and for total overhead are useless for evaluating how well costs were controlled since they have been derived by comparing actual costs at one level of activity to budgeted costs at a different level of activity.

The budget for fixed overhead items was based on Rick's records of how much he had spent on these items in the past. The budget included $8,000 for support staff wages and salaries, $12,000 for rent, $1,000 for insurance, and $500 for utilities other than electricity.

At the end of March, Rick prepared a report comparing actual to budgeted costs. That report appears in Exhibit 9–2. The problem with that report, as Rick immediately realized, is that it compares costs at one level of activity (5,200 client-visits) to costs at a different level of activity (5,000 client-visits). Since Rick had 200 more client-visits than expected, his variable costs *should* be higher than budgeted. The static budget performance report confuses control over activity and control over costs. From Rick's standpoint, the increase in activity was good and should be counted as a favorable variance, but the increase in activity has an apparently negative impact on the costs in the report. Rick knew that something would have to be done to make the report more meaningful, but he was unsure of what to do. So he made an appointment to meet with Victoria Kho to discuss the next step.

Managerial Accounting in Action

The Issue

RICK'S
hairstyling salon

Victoria: How is the budgeting going?

Rick: Pretty well. I didn't have any trouble putting together the overhead budget for March. I also made out a report comparing the actual costs for March to the budgeted costs, but that report isn't giving me what I really want to know.

Victoria: Because your actual level of activity didn't match your budgeted activity?

Rick: Right. I know that shouldn't affect my fixed costs, but we had a lot more client-visits than I had expected and that had to affect my variable costs.

Victoria: So you want to know whether the actual costs are justified by the actual level of activity you had in March?

Rick: Precisely.

Victoria: If you leave your reports and data with me, I can work on it later today, and by tomorrow I'll have a report to show to you. Actually, I have a styling appointment for later this week. Why don't I move my appointment up to tomorrow, and I will bring along the analysis so we can discuss it.

Rick: That's great.

Exhibit 9–3
Illustration of the Flexible Budgeting Concept

	Cost Formula (per client-visit)	Activity (in client-visits)			
RICK'S HAIRSTYLING **Flexible Budget** **For the Month Ended March 31**					
Budgeted number of client-visits	5,000				
Overhead Costs		**4,900**	**5,000**	**5,100**	**5,200**
Variable overhead costs:					
Hairstyling supplies	$1.20	$ 5,880	$ 6,000	$ 6,120	$ 6,240
Client gratuities	4.00	19,600	20,000	20,400	20,800
Electricity (variable)	0.20	980	1,000	1,020	1,040
Total variable overhead cost	$5.40	26,460	27,000	27,540	28,080
Fixed overhead costs:					
Support staff wages and salaries		8,000	8,000	8,000	8,000
Rent		12,000	12,000	12,000	12,000
Insurance		1,000	1,000	1,000	1,000
Utilities other than electricity		500	500	500	500
Total fixed overhead cost		21,500	21,500	21,500	21,500
Total overhead cost		$47,960	$48,500	$49,040	$49,580

How a Flexible Budget Works

The basic idea of the flexible budget approach is that a budget does not have to be static. Depending on the actual level of activity, a budget can be adjusted to show what costs *should be* for that specific level of activity. A master budget summarizes a company's plans and indicates how the plans will be accomplished. To simplify the discussion of the budgeting process, only one level of activity was assumed when each of the components of the master budget was illustrated in Chapter 7. However, a master budget can also be developed using a flexible budget approach. Because management places a great deal of significance on the control of overhead costs, the overhead budget is used in this chapter to illustrate the concept of flexible budgeting. However, the flexible budget approach is equally applicable to each of the components of the master budget.

To illustrate how flexible budgets work, Victoria wrote a report for Rick that is simple to prepare (Exhibit 9–3). It shows how overhead costs can be expected to change, depending on the monthly level of activity. Within the activity range of 4,900 to 5,200 client-visits, the fixed costs are expected to remain the same. For the variable overhead costs, Victoria multiplied Rick's per client costs ($1.20 for hairstyling supplies, $4.00 for client gratuities, and $0.20 for electricity) by the appropriate number of client-visits in each column. For example, the $1.20 cost of hairstyling supplies was multiplied by 4,900 client-visits to give the total cost of $5,880 for hairstyling supplies at that level of activity.

Learning Objective 2
Prepare a performance report for both variable and fixed overhead costs using the flexible budget approach.

Using the Flexible Budgeting Concept in Performance Evaluation

To get a better idea of how well Rick's variable overhead costs were controlled in March, Victoria applied the flexible budgeting concept to create a new performance report. (Exhibit 9–4). Using the flexible budget approach, Victoria constructed a budget based on the

Exhibit 9–4

	RICK'S HAIRSTYLING Flexible Budget Performance Report For the Month Ended March 31			
Budgeted number of client-visits	5,000			
Actual number of client-visits	5,200			

Overhead Costs	Cost Formula (per client-visit)	Actual Costs Incurred for 5,200 Client-Visits	Budget Based on 5,200 Client-Visits	Variance
Variable overhead costs:				
Hairstyling supplies	$1.20	$ 6,400	$ 6,240	$ 160 U
Client gratuities	4.00	22,300	20,800	1,500 U
Electricity (variable)	0.20	1,020	1,040	20 F
Total variable overhead cost	$5.40	29,720	28,080	1,640 U
Fixed overhead costs:				
Support staff wages and salaries		8,100	8,000	100 U
Rent		12,000	12,000	-0-
Insurance		1,000	1,000	-0-
Utilities other than electricity		470	500	30 F
Total fixed overhead cost		21,570	21,500	70 U
Total overhead cost		$51,290	$49,580	$1,710 U

actual number of client-visits for the month. The budget is prepared by multiplying the actual level of activity by the cost formula for each of the variable cost categories. For example, using the $1.20 per client-visit for hairstyling supplies, the total cost for this item *should be* $6,240 for 5,200 client-visits ($1.20 × 5,200). Since the actual cost for hairstyling supplies was $6,400, the unfavorable variance was $160.

Contrast the performance report in Exhibit 9–4 with the static budget approach in Exhibit 9–2. The variance for hairstyling supplies was $400 unfavorable using the static budget approach. In that exhibit, apples were being compared to oranges in the case of the variable cost items. Actual costs at one level of activity were being compared to budgeted costs at a different level of activity. Because actual activity was higher by 200 client-visits than budgeted activity, the total cost of hairstyling supplies *should* have been $240 ($1.20 per client-visit × 200 client-visits) higher than budgeted. As a result, $240 of the $400 "unfavorable" variance in the static budget performance report in Exhibit 9–2 was spurious.

In contrast, the flexible budget performance report in Exhibit 9–4 provides a more valid assessment of performance. Apples are compared to apples. Actual costs are compared to what costs should have been at the actual level of activity. When this is done, we see that the variance is $160 unfavorable rather than $400 unfavorable as it was in the original static budget performance report. In some cases, as with electricity in Rick's report, an unfavorable variance may be transformed into a favorable variance when an increase in activity is properly taken into account in a performance report.

Managerial Accounting in Action

The Wrap-Up

The following discussion took place the next day at Rick's salon.

Victoria: Let me show you what I've got. [Victoria shows the report contained in Exhibit 9–4.] All I did was multiply the costs per client-visit by the number of client-visits you actually had in March for the variable costs. That allowed me to come up with a better benchmark for what the variable costs should have been.

Rick: That's what you labeled the "budget based on 5,200 client-visits"?

Victoria: That's right. Your original budget was based on 5,000 client-visits, so it understated what the variable overhead costs should be when you actually serve 5,200 customers.

Rick: That's clear enough. These variances aren't quite as shocking as the variances on my first report.

Victoria: Yes, but you still have an unfavorable variance of $1,500 for client gratuities.

Rick: I know how that happened. In March there was a big Democratic Party fundraising dinner that I forgot about when I prepared the March budget. Everyone in the film industry was there.

Victoria: Even Arnold Schwarzeneger?

Rick: Well, all the Democrats were there. At any rate, to fit all of our regular clients in, we had to push them through here pretty fast. Everyone still got top-rate service, but I felt pretty bad about not being able to spend as much time with each customer. I wanted to give my customers a little extra something to compensate them for the less personal service, so I ordered a lot of flowers which I gave away by the bunch.

Victoria: With the prices you charge, Rick, I am sure the gesture was appreciated.

Rick: One thing bothers me about the report. Why are some of my actual fixed costs different from what I budgeted? Doesn't fixed mean that they are not supposed to change?

Victoria: We call these costs *fixed* because they shouldn't be affected by *changes in the level of activity.* However, that doesn't mean that they can't change for other reasons. For example, your utilities bill, which includes natural gas for heating, varies with the weather.

Rick: I can see that. March was warmer than normal, so my utilities bill was lower than I had expected.

Victoria: The use of the term *fixed* also suggests to people that the cost can't be controlled, but that isn't true. It is often easier to control fixed costs than variable costs. For example, it would be fairly easy for you to change your insurance bill by adjusting the amount of insurance you carry. It would be much more difficult for you to have much of an impact on the variable electric bill, which is a necessary part of serving customers.

Rick: I think I understand, but it *is* confusing.

Victoria: Just remember that a cost is called variable if it is proportional to activity; it is called fixed if it does not depend on the level of activity. However, fixed costs can change for reasons having nothing to do with changes in the level of activity. And controllability has little to do with whether a cost is variable or fixed. Fixed costs are often more controllable than variable costs.

Using the flexible budget approach, Rick Manzi now has a much better way of assessing whether overhead costs are under control. The analysis is not so simple, however, in companies that provide a variety of products and services. The number of units produced or customers served may not be an adequate measure of overall activity. For example, does it make sense to count a Sony floppy diskette, worth only a few dollars, as equivalent to a large-screen Sony TV? If the number of units produced is used as a measure of overall activity, then the floppy diskette and the large-screen TV would be counted as equivalent. Clearly, the number of units produced (or customers served) may not be appropriate as an overall measure of activity when the organization has a variety of products or services; a common denominator may be needed.

The Measure of Activity—A Critical Choice

What should be used as the measure of activity when the company produces a variety of products and services? At least three factors are important in selecting an activity base for an overhead flexible budget:

1. There should be a causal relationship between the activity base and variable overhead costs. Changes in the activity base should cause, or at least be highly correlated with,

changes in the variable overhead costs in the flexible budget. Ideally, the variable overhead costs in the flexible budget should vary in direct proportion to changes in the activity base. For example, in a carpentry shop specializing in handmade wood furniture, the costs of miscellaneous supplies such as glue, wooden dowels, and sandpaper can be expected to vary with the number of direct labor-hours. Direct labor-hours would therefore be a good measure of activity to use in a flexible budget for the costs of such supplies.

2. The activity base should not be expressed in dollars or other currency. For example, direct labor cost is usually a poor choice for an activity base in flexible budgets. Changes in wage rates affect the activity base but do not usually result in a proportionate change in overhead. For example, we would not ordinarily expect to see a 5% increase in the consumption of glue in a carpentry shop if the workers receive a 5% increase in pay. Therefore, it is normally best to use physical rather than financial measures of activity in flexible budgets.

3. The activity base should be simple and easily understood. A base that is not easily understood will probably result in confusion and misunderstanding. It is difficult to control costs if people don't understand the reports or do not accept them as valid.

in business today Gas Stations

Generally, convenience store and car wash sales are directly related to the volume of gas sold by a gas station. Consequently, the gas sales budget would be the starting point for the entire budgeting process. Factors that should be considered when forecasting gas sales might include: the prior year's sales, changes in the volume of traffic in the area, changes in the environment that impact access to the station (for example, road construction or the installation of median barriers that impede access), and changes in the number or type of gas stations that are operating in the immediate vicinity.

When a flexible budgeting approach is used, the manager of a gas station might choose to prepare one overhead budget or separate overhead budgets for each of its segments (gas station, convenience store, and car wash). The decision would be based on whether or not the same activity base could be used for the three segments.

Source: Steven P. Smalley, "Measuring the Convenience of Gas Stations," *Appraisal Journal*, October 1999, p. 339. Reprinted with permission from *The Appraisal Journal*, October 1999. © 1999 by the Appraisal Institute, Chicago, Illinois.

Variable Overhead Variances—A Closer Look

Concept 9–2

A special problem arises when the flexible budget is based on *hours* of activity (such as direct labor-hours) rather than on units of product or number of customers served. The problem relates to whether actual hours or standard hours should be used to develop the flexible budget on the performance report.

The Problem of Actual versus Standard Hours

The nature of the problem can best be seen through a specific example. MicroDrive Corporation is an automated manufacturer of precision personal computer disk-drive motors. Data concerning the company's variable manufacturing overhead costs are shown in Exhibit 9–5.

MicroDrive Corporation uses machine-hours as the activity base in its flexible budget. Based on the budgeted production of 25,000 motors and the standard of 2 machine-hours per motor, the budgeted level of activity was 50,000 machine-hours. However, actual production for the year was only 20,000 motors, and 42,000 hours of machine time were used to produce these motors. According to the standard, only 40,000 hours of machine time should have been used (40,000 hours = 2 hours per motor × 20,000 motors).

Exhibit 9–5
MicroDrive Corporation Data

Budgeted production	25,000	motors
Actual production	20,000	motors
Standard machine-hours per motor	2	machine-hours per motor
Budgeted machine-hours (2 × 25,000)	50,000	machine-hours
Standard machine-hours allowed for the actual production (2 × 20,000)	40,000	machine-hours
Actual machine-hours	42,000	machine-hours

Variable overhead costs per machine-hour:		
Indirect labor	$0.80	per machine-hour
Lubricants	0.30	per machine-hour
Power	0.40	per machine-hour

Actual total variable overhead costs:	
Indirect labor	$36,000
Lubricants	11,000
Power	24,000
Total actual variable overhead cost	$71,000

In preparing an overhead performance report for the year, MicroDrive could use the 42,000 machine-hours actually worked during the year *or* the 40,000 machine-hours that should have been worked according to the standard. If the actual hours are used, only a spending variance will be computed. If the standard hours are used, both a spending *and* an efficiency variance will be computed. Both of these approaches are illustrated in the following sections.

Spending Variance Alone

If MicroDrive Corporation bases its overhead performance report on the 42,000 machine-hours actually worked during the year, then the performance report will show only a spending variance for variable overhead. A performance report prepared in this way is shown in Exhibit 9–6.

Learning Objective 3
Use the flexible budget to prepare a variable overhead performance report containing only a spending variance.

The formula for the spending variance was introduced in the preceding chapter. That formula is:

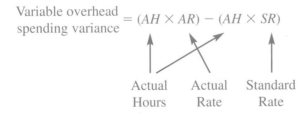

$$\begin{array}{c}\text{Variable overhead} \\ \text{spending variance}\end{array} = (AH \times AR) - (AH \times SR)$$

Actual   Actual   Standard
Hours   Rate   Rate

Or, in factored form:

$$\begin{array}{c}\text{Variable overhead} \\ \text{spending variance}\end{array} = AH\,(AR - SR)$$

The report in Exhibit 9–6 is structured around the first, or unfactored, format.

Interpreting the Spending Variance   The variable overhead spending variance is useful only if the cost driver for variable overhead really is the actual hours worked. Then the flexible budget based on the actual hours worked is a valid benchmark that tells us

Exhibit 9–6

MICRODRIVE CORPORATION
Variable Overhead Performance Report
For the Year Ended December 31

Budget allowances are based on 42,000 machine-hours actually worked

Comparing the budget against actual overhead cost yields only a spending variance

Budgeted machine-hours	50,000
Actual machine-hours	42,000
Standard machine-hours allowed	40,000

Overhead Costs	Cost Formula (per machine-hour)	Actual Costs Incurred 42,000 Machine-Hours (AH × AR)	Budget Based on 42,000 Machine-Hours (AH × SR)	Spending Variance
Variable overhead costs:				
Indirect labor	$0.80	$36,000	$33,600*	$2,400 U
Lubricants	0.30	11,000	12,600	1,600 F
Power................................	0.40	24,000	16,800	7,200 U
Total variable overhead cost	$1.50	$71,000	$63,000	$8,000 U

*42,000 machine-hours × $0.80 per machine-hour = $33,600. Other budget allowances are computed in the same way.

how much *should* have been spent in total on variable overhead items during the period. The actual overhead costs would be larger than this benchmark, resulting in an unfavorable variance, if either (1) the variable overhead items cost more to purchase than the standards allow or (2) more variable overhead items were used than the standards allow. So the spending variance includes both price and quantity variances. In principle, these variances could be separately reported, but this is seldom done. Ordinarily, the price element in this variance will be small, so the variance will mainly be influenced by how efficiently variable overhead resources such as production supplies are used.

in business today Exchanging Pallets

Large wooden pallets are used in the food service industry to ship and store goods. This may seem like a trivial item, but suppliers to the food service industry annually pay out an average of $1.4 million for these pallets, while distributors in the industry average $114,000. To attempt to reduce these costs, a voluntary exchange program was developed to recycle used pallets. However, recipients of pallets in an exchange often complain that they need to spend money repairing or replacing the pallets they receive.

Efficient Foodservice Response, an alliance of trade organizations in the industry, has recommended that companies come together to address the problems inherent in the voluntary exchange program. In addition, food service companies have been encouraged to improve the handling of goods in warehouses. Goods are often stacked and then restacked, which increases handling costs, but not the value of the product.

Source: Ken Cottrill, "Platform for Change," *Traffic World, The Logistics News Weekly,* March 13, 2000, pp. 17–19.

Exhibit 9-7

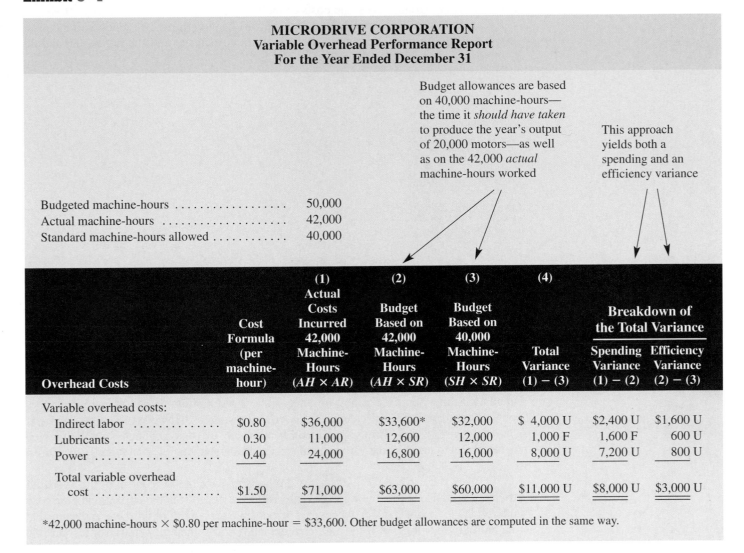

MICRODRIVE CORPORATION
Variable Overhead Performance Report
For the Year Ended December 31

Budget allowances are based on 40,000 machine-hours—the time it *should have taken* to produce the year's output of 20,000 motors—as well as on the 42,000 *actual* machine-hours worked

This approach yields both a spending and an efficiency variance

Budgeted machine-hours	50,000	
Actual machine-hours	42,000	
Standard machine-hours allowed	40,000	

		(1)	(2)	(3)	(4)		
		Actual Costs	Budget	Budget		Breakdown of the Total Variance	
	Cost Formula (per machine-hour)	Incurred 42,000 Machine-Hours	Based on 42,000 Machine-Hours	Based on 40,000 Machine-Hours	Total Variance	Spending Variance	Efficiency Variance
Overhead Costs		$(AH \times AR)$	$(AH \times SR)$	$(SH \times SR)$	$(1) - (3)$	$(1) - (2)$	$(2) - (3)$
Variable overhead costs:							
Indirect labor	$0.80	$36,000	$33,600*	$32,000	$ 4,000 U	$2,400 U	$1,600 U
Lubricants	0.30	11,000	12,600	12,000	1,000 F	1,600 F	600 U
Power	0.40	24,000	16,800	16,000	8,000 U	7,200 U	800 U
Total variable overhead cost	$1.50	$71,000	$63,000	$60,000	$11,000 U	$8,000 U	$3,000 U

*42,000 machine-hours × $0.80 per machine-hour = $33,600. Other budget allowances are computed in the same way.

Both Spending and Efficiency Variances

If management of MicroDrive Corporation wants both a spending and an efficiency variance for variable overhead, then it should compute budget allowances for *both* the 40,000 machine-hour and the 42,000 machine-hour levels of activity. A performance report prepared in this way is shown in Exhibit 9–7.

Note from Exhibit 9–7 that the spending variance is the same as the spending variance shown in Exhibit 9–6. The performance report in Exhibit 9–7 has simply been expanded to include an efficiency variance as well. Together, the spending and efficiency variances make up the total variance.

Interpreting the Efficiency Variance   Like the variable overhead spending, the variable overhead efficiency variance is useful only if the cost driver for variable overhead really is the actual hours worked. Then any increase in hours actually worked should result in additional variable overhead costs. Consequently, if too many hours were used to create the actual output, this is likely to result in an increase in variable overhead. The variable overhead efficiency variance is an estimate of the effect on variable overhead costs of inefficiency in the use of the base (i.e., hours). In a sense, the term *variable overhead efficiency variance* is a misnomer. It seems to suggest that it measures the efficiency

> **Learning Objective 4**
> Use the flexible budget to prepare a variable overhead performance report containing both a spending and an efficiency variance.

with which variable overhead resources were used. It does not. It is an estimate of the indirect effect on variable overhead costs of inefficiency in the use of the activity base.

Recall from the preceding chapter that the variable overhead efficiency variance is a function of the difference between the actual hours incurred and the hours that should have been used to produce the period's output:

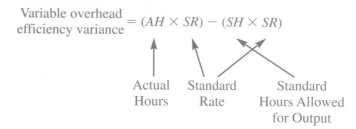

$$\frac{\text{Variable overhead}}{\text{efficiency variance}} = (AH \times SR) - (SH \times SR)$$

Actual Hours   Standard Rate   Standard Hours Allowed for Output

Or, in factored form:

$$\frac{\text{Variable overhead}}{\text{efficiency variance}} = SR(AH - SH)$$

If more hours are worked than are allowed at standard, then the overhead efficiency variance will be unfavorable. However, as discussed above, the inefficiency is not in the use of overhead *but rather in the use of the base itself.*

This point can be illustrated by looking again at Exhibit 9–7. Two thousand more machine-hours were used during the period than should have been used to produce the period's output. Each of these hours presumably required the incurrence of $1.50 of variable overhead cost, resulting in an unfavorable variance of $3,000 (2,000 hours × $1.50 = $3,000). Although this $3,000 variance is called an overhead efficiency variance, it could better be called a machine-hours efficiency variance, since it results from using too many machine-hours rather than from inefficient use of overhead resources. However, the term *overhead efficiency variance* is so firmly ingrained in day-to-day use that a change is unlikely. Even so, be careful to interpret the variance with a clear understanding of what it really measures.

Control of the Efficiency Variance   Who is responsible for control of the overhead efficiency variance? Since the variance really reflects efficiency in the utilization of the base underlying the flexible budget, whoever is responsible for control of this base is responsible for control of the variance. If the base is direct labor-hours, then the supervisor responsible for the use of labor time will be responsible for any overhead efficiency variance.

Activity-Based Costing and the Flexible Budget

It is unlikely that all of the variable overhead in a complex organization is driven by a single factor such as the number of units produced or the number of labor-hours or machine-hours. Activity-based costing provides a way of recognizing a variety of overhead cost drivers and thereby increasing the accuracy of the costing system. In activity-based costing, each overhead cost pool has its own measure of activity. The actual spending in each overhead cost pool can be independently evaluated using the techniques discussed in this chapter. The only difference is that the cost formulas for variable overhead costs will be stated in terms of different kinds of activities instead of all being stated in terms of units or a common measure of activity such as direct labor-hours or machine-hours. If done properly, activity-based costing can greatly enhance the usefulness of overhead performance reports by recognizing multiple causes of overhead costs. But the usefulness of overhead performance reports depends on how carefully the reports are done. In particular, managers must take care to separate the variable from the fixed costs in the flexible budgets.[1]

---

[1]See Mak and Roush, "Managing Activity Costs with Flexible Budgeting and Variance Analysis," *Accounting Horizons,* September 1996, pp. 141–146, for an insightful discussion of activity-based costing and overhead variance analysis.

Pools within Pools

Caterpillar, Inc., a manufacturer of heavy equipment and a pioneering company in the development and use of activity-based costing, divides its overhead costs into three large pools—the logistics cost pool, the manufacturing cost pool, and the general cost pool. In turn, these three cost pools are subdivided into scores of activity centers, with each center having its own flexible budget from which variable and fixed overhead rates are developed. In an article describing the company's cost system, the systems manager stated that "the many manufacturing cost center rates are the unique elements that set Caterpillar's system apart from simple cost systems."

Source: Lou F. Jones, "Product Costing at Caterpillar," *Management Accounting* 72, no. 8 (February 1991), p. 39. Reprinted with permission from *Management Accounting*.

Overhead Rates and Fixed Overhead Analysis

The detailed analysis of fixed overhead differs considerably from the analysis of variable overhead, simply because of the difference in the nature of the costs involved. To provide a background for our discussion, we will first review briefly the need for, and computation of, predetermined overhead rates. This review will be helpful, since the predetermined overhead rate plays a major role in fixed overhead analysis. We will then show how fixed overhead variances are computed and make some observations as to their usefulness to managers.

Flexible Budgets and Overhead Rates

Fixed costs come in large, indivisible pieces that by definition do not change with changes in the level of activity within the relevant range. This creates a problem in product costing, since a given level of fixed overhead cost spread over a small number of units will result in a higher cost per unit than if the same amount of cost is spread over a large number of units. Consider the data in the following table:

> **Learning Objective 5**
> Compute the predetermined overhead rate and apply overhead to products in a standard cost system.

Month	(1) Fixed Overhead Cost	(2) Number of Units Produced	(3) Unit Cost (1) ÷ (2)
January	$6,000	1,000	$6.00
February	6,000	1,500	4.00
March	6,000	800	7.50

Notice that the large number of units produced in February results in a low unit cost ($4.00), whereas the small number of units produced in March results in a high unit cost ($7.50). This problem arises only in connection with the fixed portion of overhead, since by definition the variable portion of overhead remains constant on a per unit basis, rising and falling in total proportionately with changes in the activity level. Most managers feel that the fixed portion of unit cost should be stabilized so that a single unit cost figure can be used throughout the year. As we learned in Chapter 2, this stability can be accomplished through use of the predetermined overhead rate.

Throughout the remainder of this chapter, we will be analyzing the fixed overhead costs of MicroDrive Corporation. To assist us in that task, the flexible budget of the company—including fixed costs—is displayed in Exhibit 9–8. Note that the total fixed overhead costs amount to $300,000 within the range of activity in the flexible budget.

Exhibit 9–8

MICRODRIVE CORPORATION Flexible Budgets at Various Levels of Activity					
Overhead Costs	Cost Formula (per machine-hour)	Activity (in machine-hours)			
		40,000	45,000	50,000	55,000
Variable overhead costs:					
Indirect labor	$0.80	$ 32,000	$ 36,000	$ 40,000	$ 44,000
Lubricants	0.30	12,000	13,500	15,000	16,500
Power	0.40	16,000	18,000	20,000	22,000
Total variable overhead cost	$1.50	60,000	67,500	75,000	82,500
Fixed overhead costs:					
Depreciation		100,000	100,000	100,000	100,000
Supervisory salaries		160,000	160,000	160,000	160,000
Insurance		40,000	40,000	40,000	40,000
Total fixed overhead cost		300,000	300,000	300,000	300,000
Total overhead cost		$360,000	$367,500	$375,000	$382,500

Denominator Activity   The formula that we used in Chapter 2 to compute the predetermined overhead rate is given below

$$\text{Predetermined overhead rate} = \frac{\text{Estimated total manufacturing overhead cost}}{\text{Estimated total units in the base (MH, DLH, etc.)}}$$

The estimated total units in the base in the formula for the predetermined overhead rate is called the **denominator activity.** Recall from our discussion in Chapter 2 that once an estimated activity level (denominator activity) has been chosen, it remains unchanged throughout the year, even if the actual activity turns out to be different from what was estimated. The reason for not changing the denominator is to maintain stability in the amount of overhead applied to each unit of product regardless of when it is produced during the year.

Computing the Overhead Rate   When we discussed predetermined overhead rates in Chapter 2, we didn't explain how the estimated total manufacturing cost was determined. This figure can be derived from the flexible budget. Once the denominator level of activity has been chosen, the flexible budget can be used to determine the total amount of overhead cost that should be incurred at that level of activity. The predetermined overhead rate can then be computed using the following variation on the basic formula for the predetermined overhead rate:

$$\text{Predetermined overhead rate} = \frac{\text{Overhead from the flexible budget at the denominator level of activity}}{\text{Denominator level of activity}}$$

To illustrate, refer to MicroDrive Corporation's flexible budget for manufacturing overhead in Exhibit 9–8. Suppose that the budgeted activity level for the year is 50,000 machine-hours and that this will be used as the denominator activity in the formula for the predetermined overhead rate. The numerator in the formula is the estimated total overhead cost of $375,000 when the activity is 50,000 machine-hours. This figure is taken from the flexible budget in Exhibit 9–8. In sum, the predetermined overhead rate for MicroDrive Corporation will be computed as follows:

$$\frac{\$375,000}{50,000 \text{ MHs}} = \$7.50 \text{ per machine-hour}$$

Or the company can break its predetermined overhead rate down into variable and fixed elements rather than using a single combined figure:

$$\text{Variable element: } \frac{\$75,000}{50,000 \text{ MHs}} = \$1.50 \text{ per machine-hour (MH)}$$

$$\text{Fixed element: } \frac{\$300,000}{50,000 \text{ MHs}} = \$6 \text{ per machine-hour (MH)}$$

For every standard machine-hour of operation, work in process will be charged with $7.50 of overhead, of which $1.50 will be variable overhead and $6.00 will be fixed overhead. If a disk-drive motor should take two machine-hours to complete, then its cost will include $3 variable overhead and $12 fixed overhead, as shown on the following standard cost card:

Standard Cost Card—Per Motor

Direct materials (assumed)	$14
Direct labor (assumed)	6
Variable overhead (2 machine-hours at $1.50 per machine-hour)	3
Fixed overhead (2 machine-hours at $6 per machine-hour)	12
Total standard cost per motor	$35

In sum, the flexible budget provides the estimated overhead cost needed to compute the predetermined overhead rate. Thus, the flexible budget plays a key role in determining the amount of fixed and variable overhead cost that will be charged to units of product.

Overhead Application in a Standard Cost System

To understand the fixed overhead variances, it is necessary first to understand how overhead is applied to work in process in a standard cost system. In Chapter 2, recall that we applied overhead to work in process on the basis of actual hours of activity (multiplied by the predetermined overhead rate). This procedure was correct, since at the time we were dealing with a normal cost system.[2] However, we are now dealing with a standard cost system. In such a system, overhead is applied to work in process on the basis of the *standard hours allowed for the output of the period* rather than on the basis of the actual number of hours worked. This point is illustrated in Exhibit 9–9. In a standard cost system, every unit of product moving along the production line bears the same amount of

Normal Cost System Manufacturing Overhead		Standard Cost System Manufacturing Overhead	
Actual overhead costs incurred	Applied overhead costs: Actual hours × Predetermined overhead rate	Actual overhead costs incurred	Applied overhead costs: Standard hours allowed for output × Predetermined overhead rate
Under- or overapplied overhead		Under- or overapplied overhead	

Exhibit 9–9
Applied Overhead Costs: Normal Cost System versus Standard Cost System

---

[2]Normal cost systems are discussed in Chapter 2.

overhead cost, regardless of any variations in efficiency that may have been involved in its production.

The Fixed Overhead Variances

To illustrate the computation of fixed overhead variances, we will refer again to the data for MicroDrive Corporation.

Denominator activity in machine-hours	50,000
Budgeted fixed overhead costs	$300,000
Fixed portion of the predetermined overhead rate (computed earlier)	$6 per machine-hour

Let us assume that the following actual operating results were recorded for the year:

Actual machine-hours	42,000
Standard machine-hours allowed*	40,000
Actual fixed overhead costs:	
Depreciation	$100,000
Supervisory salaries	172,000
Insurance	36,000
Total actual cost	$308,000

*For the actual production of the year.

From these data, two variances can be computed for fixed overhead—a *budget variance* and a *volume variance*. The variances are shown in Exhibit 9–10.

Notice from the exhibit that overhead has been applied to work in process on the basis of 40,000 standard hours allowed for the output of the year rather than on the basis of 42,000 actual hours worked. As stated earlier, this keeps unit costs from being affected by any variations in efficiency.

The Budget Variance—A Closer Look

The **budget variance** is the difference between the actual fixed overhead costs incurred during the period and the budgeted fixed overhead costs as contained in the flexible budget. It can be computed as shown in Exhibit 9–10 or by using the following formula:

$$\frac{\text{Budget}}{\text{variance}} = \frac{\text{Actual fixed}}{\text{overhead cost}} - \frac{\text{Flexible budget}}{\text{fixed overhead cost}}$$

Applying this formula to MicroDrive Corporation, the budget variance would be as follows:

$$\$308,000 - \$300,000 = \$8,000 \text{ U}$$

The variances computed for the fixed costs at Rick's Hairstyling in Exhibit 9–4 are all budget variances, since they represent the difference between the actual fixed overhead cost and the budgeted fixed overhead cost from the flexible budget.

An expanded overhead performance report for MicroDrive Corporation appears in Exhibit 9–11. This report now includes the budget variances for fixed overhead as well as the spending variances for variable overhead that were in Exhibit 9–6.

The budget variances for fixed overhead can be very useful, since they represent the difference between how much *should* have been spent (according to the flexible budget) and how much was actually spent. For example, supervisory salaries has a $12,000 unfavorable variance. There should be some explanation for this large variance. Was it due to an increase in salaries? Was it due to overtime? Was another supervisor hired? If so, why

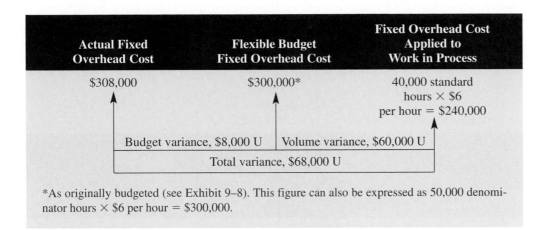

Exhibit 9–10
Computation of the Fixed
Overhead Variances

was another supervisor hired?—this was not included in the budget when activity for the year was planned.

The Value of Safety

in business today

Companies in the trucking industry have an average profit margin of only about 2%. Safety Solutions, Inc., a company that provides loss prevention and safety consulting services, claims that trucking companies can increase their profit margins to 5% by incurring *additional* overhead costs. How can this be?

Safety Solutions, Inc., claims that trucking companies with effective safety programs are less likely to receive large fines and often incur lower insurance costs. In addition, drivers are more likely to remain with companies with safer records, thus reducing hiring and training costs. Further, a reputation for safety may attract additional customers. Safety Solutions recommends investing in a formal safety program. In addition to ensuring ongoing compliance with government regulations, the safety program should include monitoring equipment and extensive preventative maintenance.

Source: "The Operating Margin of Safety (Safety in the Trucking Industry)," *Oregon Business*, August 1999, p. 22.

The Volume Variance—A Closer Look

The **volume variance** is a measure of utilization of plant facilities. The variance arises whenever the standard hours allowed for the output of a period are different from the denominator activity level that was planned when the period began. It can be computed as shown in Exhibit 9–10 or by means of the following formula:

$$\text{Volume variance} = \begin{pmatrix} \text{Fixed portion of} \\ \text{the predetermined} \\ \text{overhead rate} \end{pmatrix} \times \begin{pmatrix} \text{Denominator} \\ \text{hours} \end{pmatrix} - \begin{pmatrix} \text{Standard hours} \\ \text{allowed} \end{pmatrix}$$

Applying this formula to MicroDrive Corporation, the volume variance would be computed as follows:

$$\$6 \text{ per MH } (50,000 \text{ MH} - 40,000 \text{ MH}) = \$60,000 \text{ U}$$

Note that this computation agrees with the volume variance as shown in Exhibit 9–10. As stated earlier, the volume variance is a measure of utilization of available plant facilities. An unfavorable variance, as above, means that the company operated at an activity level *below* that planned for the period. A favorable variance would mean that the company operated at an activity level *greater* than that planned for the period.

Exhibit 9–11
Fixed Overhead Costs on the
Overhead Performance Report

MICRODRIVE CORPORATION
Overhead Performance Report
For the Year Ended December 31

Budgeted machine-hours	50,000			
Actual machine-hours	42,000			
Standard machine-hours allowed	40,000			

Overhead Costs	Cost Formula (per machine-hour)	Actual Costs 42,000 Machine-Hours	Budget Based on 42,000 Machine-Hours	Spending or Budget Variance
Variable overhead costs:				
Indirect labor	$0.80	$ 36,000	$ 33,600	$ 2,400 U
Lubricants	0.30	11,000	12,600	1,600 F
Power	0.40	24,000	16,800	7,200 U
Total variable overhead cost	$1.50	71,000	63,000	8,000 U
Fixed overhead costs:				
Depreciation		100,000	100,000	—
Supervisory salaries		172,000	160,000	12,000 U
Insurance		36,000	40,000	4,000 F
Total fixed overhead cost		308,000	300,000	8,000 U
Total overhead cost		$379,000	$363,000	$16,000 U

It is important to note that the volume variance does not measure over- or underspending. A company normally would incur the same dollar amount of fixed overhead cost regardless of whether the period's activity was above or below the planned (denominator) level. In short, the volume variance is an activity-related variance. It is explainable only by activity and is controllable only through activity.

To summarize:

1. If the denominator activity and the standard hours allowed for the output of the period are the same, then there is no volume variance.
2. If the denominator activity is greater than the standard hours allowed for the output of the period, then the volume variance is unfavorable, signifying an underutilization of available facilities.
3. If the denominator activity is less than the standard hours allowed for the output of the period, then the volume variance is favorable, signifying a higher utilization of available facilities than was planned.

decision | *maker* **Vice President of Production**

One of the company's factories produces a single product. The factory recently reported a significant unfavorable volume variance for the year. Sales for that product were less than anticipated. What should you do?

Graphic Analysis of Fixed Overhead Variances

Some insights into the budget and volume variances can be gained through graphic analysis. A graph containing these variances is presented in Exhibit 9–12.

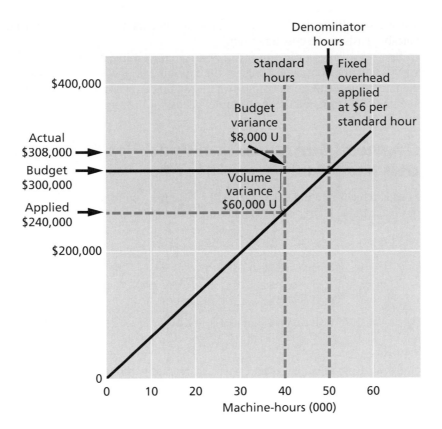

Exhibit 9–12
Graphic Analysis of Fixed
Overhead Variances

As shown in the graph, fixed overhead cost is applied to work in process at the predetermined rate of $6 for each standard hour of activity. (The applied-cost line is the upward-sloping line on the graph.) Since a denominator level of 50,000 machine-hours was used in computing the $6 rate, the applied-cost line crosses the budget-cost line at exactly the 50,000 machine-hour point. Thus, if the denominator hours and the standard hours allowed for the output are the same, there can be no volume variance, since the applied-cost line and the budget-cost line will exactly meet on the graph. It is only when the standard hours differ from the denominator hours that a volume variance can arise.

In the case at hand, the standard hours allowed for the actual output (40,000 hours) are less than the denominator hours (50,000 hours); the result is an unfavorable volume variance, since less cost was applied to production than was originally budgeted. If the situation had been reversed and the standard hours allowed for the actual output had exceeded the denominator hours, then the volume variance on the graph would have been favorable.

Cautions in Fixed Overhead Analysis

The reason we get a volume variance for fixed overhead is that the total fixed cost does not depend on activity; yet when applying the costs to work in process, we act *as if* the fixed costs were variable and depended on activity. This point can be seen from the graph in Exhibit 9–12. Notice from the graph that the fixed overhead costs are applied to work in process at a rate of $6 per hour *as if* they were variable. Treating these costs as if they were variable is necessary for product costing purposes, but there are some real dangers here. The manager can easily become misled and start thinking of the fixed costs as if they were *in fact* variable.

The manager must keep clearly in mind that fixed overhead costs come in large, indivisible pieces. Expressing fixed costs on a unit or per hour basis, though necessary for product costing for external reports, is artificial. Increases or decreases in activity in fact have no effect on total fixed costs within the relevant range of activity. Even though fixed costs are expressed on a unit or per hour basis, they are *not* proportional to activity. In a sense, the volume variance is the error that occurs as a result of treating fixed costs as variable costs in the costing system.

Because of the confusion that can arise concerning the interpretation of the volume variance, some companies present the volume variance in physical units (hours) rather than in dollars. These companies feel that stating the variance in physical units gives management a clearer signal concerning the cause of the variance.

Overhead Variances and Under- or Overapplied Overhead Cost

Four variances relating to overhead cost have been computed for MicroDrive Corporation in this chapter. These four variances are as follows:

Variable overhead spending variance (p. 376)	$ 8,000 U
Variable overhead efficiency variance (p. 377)	3,000 U
Fixed overhead budget variance (p. 383)	8,000 U
Fixed overhead volume variance (p. 383)	60,000 U
Total overhead variance	$79,000 U

Recall from Chapter 2 that under- or overapplied overhead is the difference between the amount of overhead applied to products and the actual overhead costs incurred during a period. Basically, the overhead variances we have computed in this chapter break the under- or overapplied overhead down into variances that can be used by managers for control purposes. Consequently, *the sum of the overhead variances equals the under- or overapplied overhead cost for a period.*

Furthermore, in a standard cost system, unfavorable variances are equivalent to underapplied overhead and favorable variances are equivalent to overapplied overhead. Unfavorable variances occur because more was spent on overhead than the standards allow. Underapplied overhead occurs when more was spent on overhead than was applied to products during the period. But in a standard costing system, the standard amount of overhead allowed is exactly the same amount of overhead applied to products. Therefore, in a standard costing system, unfavorable variances and underapplied overhead are the same thing, as are favorable variances and overapplied overhead.

For MicroDrive Corporation, the total overhead variance was $79,000 unfavorable. Therefore, its overhead cost was underapplied by $79,000 for the year. To solidify this point in your mind, *carefully study the review problem at the end of the chapter!* This review problem provides a comprehensive summary of overhead analysis, including the computation of under- or overapplied overhead cost in a standard cost system.

---

you *decide*   **Budget Analyst**

Your company is in the process of implementing an activity-based costing program and plans to use the flexible approach to budgeting. To aid in the analysis of the factory overhead once these plans are in place, how should the under- or overapplied overhead be analyzed? Who should be held responsible for each of the variances?

Summary

LO1   **Prepare a flexible budget and explain the advantages of the flexible budget approach over the static budget approach.**

A flexible budget shows what costs should be as a function of the level of activity. A flexible budget provides a better benchmark for evaluating how well costs have been controlled than the static budget approved at the beginning of the period. Some costs should be different from the amounts budgeted at the beginning of the period simply because the level of activity is different from what was expected. The flexible budget takes this fact into account, whereas the static budget does not.

LO2 Prepare a performance report for both variable and fixed overhead costs using the flexible budget approach.

A flexible budget performance report compares actual costs to what the costs should have been, given the actual level of activity for the period. Variable costs are flexed (i.e., adjusted) for the actual level of activity. This is done by multiplying the cost per unit of activity by the actual level of activity. Fixed costs, at least within the relevant range, are not adjusted for the level of activity. The total cost for a fixed cost item is carried over from the static budget without adjustment.

LO3 Use the flexible budget to prepare a variable overhead performance report containing only a spending variance.

The spending variance for a variable overhead item is computed by comparing the actual cost incurred to the amount that should have been spent, based on the actual direct labor-hours or machine-hours of the period.

LO4 Use the flexible budget to prepare a variable overhead performance report containing both a spending and an efficiency variance.

As stated above, the spending variance for a variable overhead item is computed by comparing the actual cost incurred to the amount that should have been spent, based on the actual direct labor-hours or machine-hours of the period. The efficiency variance is computed by comparing the cost that should have been incurred for the actual direct labor-hours or machine-hours of the period to the cost that should have been incurred for the actual level of *output* of the period.

LO5 Compute the predetermined overhead rate and apply overhead to products in a standard cost system.

In a standard cost system, overhead is applied to products based on the standard hours allowed for the actual output of the period. This differs from a normal cost system in which overhead is applied to products based on the actual hours of the period.

LO6 Compute and interpret the fixed overhead budget and volume variances.

The fixed overhead budget variance is the difference between the actual total fixed overhead costs incurred for the period and the budgeted total fixed overhead costs. This variance measures how well fixed overhead costs were controlled.

The fixed overhead volume variance is the difference between the fixed overhead applied to production using the predetermined overhead rate and the budgeted total fixed overhead. A favorable variance occurs when the standard hours allowed for the actual output exceed the hours assumed when the predetermined overhead rate was computed. An unfavorable variance occurs when the standard hours allowed for the actual output is less than the hours assumed when the predetermined overhead rate was computed.

Guidance Answers to You Decide and Decision Maker

VICE PRESIDENT OF PRODUCTION (p. 384)
An unfavorable fixed overhead volume variance means that the factory is operating at an activity level below the level that was planned for the year. You should meet with the vice president of sales to determine why demand was less than planned. Was production part of the problem? Were orders delivered late? Were customers quoted lead times that were too long? Could production help increase demand by improving the quality of the product and the services provided to customers? If sales are declining and are not expected to rebound, you should consider how to make use of the excess capacity in this factory. You might consider whether the factory could be reconfigured to produce another product or if a section of the factory could be leased to another company.

BUDGET ANALYST (p. 386)
The under- or overapplied overhead should be broken into its four components: (1) the variable overhead spending variance, (2) the variable overhead efficiency variance, (3) the fixed overhead budget variance, and (4) the fixed overhead volume variance.

The person who purchases the variable overhead items (such as lubricants) and the supervisor(s) who directs and/or controls the employees who are classified as indirect labor are responsible for the variable overhead spending variance. Whoever is responsible for the control of the activity base that is used to apply overhead should be responsible for the control of the variable overhead efficiency variance. The person(s) responsible for negotiating the purchase of the fixed overhead items (such as rent and insurance) and the supervisor(s) who directs and/or controls the support staff are responsible for the fixed overhead budget variance. The fixed overhead volume variance does not indicate that the company has overspent or underspent; it is a measure of utilization of available plant facilities. As such, the person responsible for determining the level of activity for the plant would be responsible for this variance.

Review Problem: Overhead Analysis

(This problem provides a comprehensive review of Chapter 9, including the computation of under- or over-applied overhead and its breakdown into the four overhead variances.)

Data for the manufacturing overhead of Aspen Company are given below:

Overhead Costs	Cost Formula (per machine-hour)	Machine-Hours		
		5,000	6,000	7,000
Variable overhead costs:				
Supplies	$0.20	$ 1,000	$ 1,200	$ 1,400
Indirect labor	0.30	1,500	1,800	2,100
Total variable overhead cost	$0.50	2,500	3,000	3,500
Fixed overhead costs:				
Depreciation		4,000	4,000	4,000
Supervision		5,000	5,000	5,000
Total fixed overhead cost		9,000	9,000	9,000
Total overhead cost		$11,500	$12,000	$12,500

Five hours of machine time are required per unit of product. The company has set denominator activity for the coming period at 6,000 machine-hours (or 1,200 units). The computation of the predetermined overhead rate would be as follows:

$$\text{Total:} \ \frac{\$12,000}{6,000 \text{ MHs}} = \$2.00 \text{ per machine-hour}$$

$$\text{Variable element:} \ \frac{\$3,000}{6,000 \text{ MHs}} = \$0.50 \text{ per machine-hour}$$

$$\text{Fixed element:} \ \frac{\$9,000}{6,000 \text{ MHs}} = \$1.50 \text{ per machine-hour}$$

Assume the following *actual* results for the period:

Number of units produced	1,300 units
Actual machine-hours	6,800 machine-hours
Standard machine-hours allowed*	6,500 machine-hours
Actual variable overhead cost	$4,200
Actual fixed overhead cost	9,400

*1,300 units × 5 machine-hours per unit.

Therefore, the company's Manufacturing Overhead account would appear as follows at the end of the period:

Manufacturing Overhead

Actual overhead costs	13,600*	13,000†	Applied overhead costs

| Underapplied overhead | 600 | | |

*$4,200 variable + $9,400 fixed = $13,600.
†6,500 standard machine-hours × $2 per machine-hour = $13,000.
In a standard cost system, overhead is applied on the basis of standard hours, not actual hours.

Required:

Analyze the $600 underapplied overhead in terms of:

1. A variable overhead spending variance.
2. A variable overhead efficiency variance.
3. A fixed overhead budget variance.
4. A fixed overhead volume variance.

SOLUTION TO REVIEW PROBLEM

Variable Overhead Variances

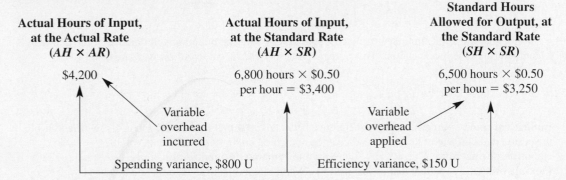

Actual Hours of Input, at the Actual Rate (AH × AR)	Actual Hours of Input, at the Standard Rate (AH × SR)	Standard Hours Allowed for Output, at the Standard Rate (SH × SR)
$4,200	6,800 hours × $0.50 per hour = $3,400	6,500 hours × $0.50 per hour = $3,250

Variable overhead incurred   Variable overhead applied

Spending variance, $800 U   Efficiency variance, $150 U

These same variances in the alternative format would be as follows:

Variable overhead spending variance:

$$\text{Spending variance} = (AH \times AR) - (AH \times SR)$$
$$(\$4,200^*) - (6,800 \text{ hours} \times \$0.50 \text{ per hour}) = \$800 \text{ U}$$

*$AH \times AR$ equals the total actual cost for the period.

Variable overhead efficiency variance:

$$\text{Efficiency variance} = SR(AH - SH)$$
$$\$0.50 \text{ per hour} (6,800 \text{ hours} - 6,500 \text{ hours}) = \$150 \text{ U}$$

Fixed Overhead Variances

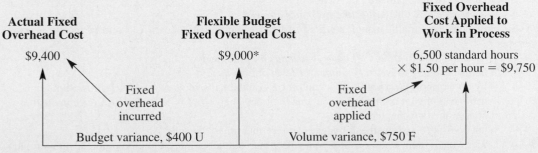

Actual Fixed Overhead Cost	Flexible Budget Fixed Overhead Cost	Fixed Overhead Cost Applied to Work in Process
$9,400	$9,000*	6,500 standard hours × $1.50 per hour = $9,750

Fixed overhead incurred   Fixed overhead applied

Budget variance, $400 U   Volume variance, $750 F

*Can be expressed as: 6,000 denominator hours × $1.50 per hour = $9,000.

These same variances in the alternative format would be as follows:
  Fixed overhead budget variance:

$$\text{Budget variance} = \text{Actual fixed overhead cost} - \text{Flexible budget fixed overhead cost}$$
$$\$9,400 - \$9,000 = \$400 \text{ U}$$

  Fixed overhead volume variance:

$$\text{Volume variance} = \text{Fixed portion of the predetermined overhead rate} \times \left(\text{Denominator hours} - \text{Standard hours}\right)$$
$$\$1.50 \text{ per hour } (6,000 \text{ hours} - 6,500 \text{ hours}) = \$750 \text{ F}$$

Summary of Variances

A summary of the four overhead variances is given below:

Variable overhead:	
Spending variance	$800 U
Efficiency variance	150 U
Fixed overhead:	
Budget variance	400 U
Volume variance	750 F
Underapplied overhead	$600

Notice that the $600 summary variance figure agrees with the underapplied balance in the company's Manufacturing Overhead account. This agreement verifies the accuracy of our variance analysis.

Glossary

Budget variance   A measure of the difference between the actual fixed overhead costs incurred during the period and budgeted fixed overhead costs as contained in the flexible budget. (p. 382)
Denominator activity   The activity figure used to compute the predetermined overhead rate. (p. 380)
Flexible budget   A budget that is designed to cover a range of activity and that can be used to develop budgeted costs at any point within that range to compare to actual costs incurred. (p. 368)
Static budget   A budget designed for only one level of activity. (p. 368)
Volume variance   The variance that arises whenever the standard hours allowed for the output of a period are different from the denominator activity level that was used to compute the predetermined overhead rate. (p. 383)

Questions

9–1   What is a static budget?
9–2   What is a flexible budget and how does it differ from a static budget?
9–3   In comparing flexible budget data with actual data in a performance report for variable overhead, what variance(s) will be produced if the flexible budget data are based on actual hours worked? On both actual hours worked and standard hours allowed?
9–4   What is meant by the term *standard hours allowed?*
9–5   How does the variable manufacturing overhead spending variance differ from the materials price variance?
9–6   Why is the term *overhead efficiency variance* a misnomer?
9–7   What is meant by the term *denominator level of activity?*
9–8   Why do we apply overhead to work in process on the basis of standard hours allowed in this chapter when we applied it on the basis of actual hours in Chapter 2? What is the difference in costing systems between the two chapters?
9–9   What does the fixed overhead budget variance measure?
9–10   Under what circumstances would you expect the volume variance to be favorable? Unfavorable? Does the variance measure deviations in spending for fixed overhead items? Explain.

9–11   In Chapter 2, you became acquainted with the concept of under- or overapplied overhead. The under- or overapplied overhead can be broken down into what four variances?

9–12   If factory overhead is overapplied for August, would you expect the total of the overhead variances to be favorable or unfavorable?

Brief Exercises

BRIEF EXERCISE 9–1   Preparing a Flexible Budget (LO1)

An incomplete flexible budget is given below for Lavage Rapide, a Swiss company that owns and operates a large automatic carwash facility near Geneva. The Swiss currency is the Swiss franc, which is denoted by SFr.

LAVAGE RAPIDE Flexible Budget For the Month Ended August 31				
Overhead Costs	**Cost Formula (per car)**	**Activity (cars)**		
		8,000	**9,000**	**10,000**
Variable overhead costs:				
Cleaning supplies	?	?	7,200 SFr	?
Electricity	?	?	2,700	?
Maintenance	?	?	1,800	?
Total variable overhead cost	?	?	?	?
Fixed overhead costs:				
Operator wages		?	9,000	?
Depreciation		?	6,000	?
Rent		?	8,000	?
Total fixed overhead cost		?	?	?
Total overhead cost		?	?	?

Required:

Fill in the missing data.

BRIEF EXERCISE 9–2   Prepare a Static Budget (LO1)

Refer to the data in Brief Exercise 9–1. Lavage Rapide's owner-manager would like to prepare a budget for August assuming an activity level of 8,800 cars.

Required:

Prepare a static budget for August. Use Exhibit 9–1 in the chapter as your guide.

BRIEF EXERCISE 9–3   Flexible Budget Performance Report (LO2)

Refer to the data in Brief Exercise 9–1. Lavage Rapide's actual level of activity during August was 8,900 cars, although the owner had constructed his static budget for the month assuming the level of activity would be 8,800 cars. The actual overhead costs incurred during August are given below:

	Actual Costs Incurred for 8,900 Cars
Variable overhead costs:	
Cleaning supplies	7,080 SFr
Electricity	2,460
Maintenance	1,550
Fixed overhead costs:	
Operator wages	9,100
Depreciation	7,000
Rent	8,000

Required:
Prepare a flexible budget performance report for both the variable and fixed overhead costs for August. Use Exhibit 9 4 in the chapter as your guide.

BRIEF EXERCISE 9–4   Variable Overhead Performance Report with Just a Spending Variance (LO3)
Yung Corporation bases its variable overhead performance report on the actual direct labor-hours of the period. Data concerning the most recent year that ended on December 31 appear below:

Budgeted direct labor-hours	38,000
Actual direct labor-hours	34,000
Standard direct labor-hours allowed	35,000

Cost formula (per direct labor-hour):

Indirect labor	$0.60
Supplies	0.10
Electricity	0.05

Actual costs incurred:

Indirect labor	$21,200
Supplies	3,200
Electricity	1,600

Required:
Prepare a variable overhead performance report using the format in Exhibit 9–6. Compute just the variable overhead spending variances (do not compute the variable overhead efficiency variances).

BRIEF EXERCISE 9–5   Variable Overhead Performance Report with Both Spending and Efficiency Variances (LO4)
Refer to the data for Yung Corporation in Brief Exercise 9–4. Management would like to compute both spending and efficiency variances for variable overheads in the company's variable overhead performance report.

Required:
Prepare a variable overhead performance report using the format in Exhibit 9–7. Compute both the variable overhead spending variances and the overhead efficiency variances.

BRIEF EXERCISE 9–6   Applying Overhead in a Standard Costing System (LO5)
Privack Corporation has a standard cost system in which it applies overhead to products based on the standard direct labor-hours allowed for the actual output of the period. Data concerning the most recent year appear below:

Variable overhead cost per direct labor-hour	$2.00
Total fixed overhead cost per year	$250,000
Budgeted standard direct labor-hours (denominator level of activity)	40,000
Actual direct labor-hours	39,000
Standard direct labor-hours allowed for the actual output	38,000

Required:
1. Compute the predetermined overhead rate for the year.
2. Determine the amount of overhead that would be applied to the output of the period.

BRIEF EXERCISE 9–7   Fixed Overhead Variances (LO6)

Primara Corporation has a standard cost system in which it applies overhead to products based on the standard direct labor-hours allowed for the actual output of the period. Data concerning the most recent year appear below:

Total budgeted fixed overhead cost for the year	$250,000
Actual fixed overhead cost for the year	$254,000
Budgeted standard direct labor-hours (denominator level of activity)	25,000
Actual direct labor-hours	27,000
Standard direct labor-hours allowed for the actual output	26,000

Required:

1. Compute the fixed portion of the predetermined overhead rate for the year.
2. Compute the fixed overhead budget variance and volume variance.

Exercises

EXERCISE 9–1   Prepare a Flexible Budget (LO1)

The cost formulas for Emory Company's manufacturing overhead costs are given below. These cost formulas cover a relevant range of 15,000 to 25,000 machine-hours each year.

Overhead Costs	Cost Formula
Utilities	$0.30 per machine-hour
Indirect labor	$52,000 plus $1.40 per machine-hour
Supplies	$0.20 per machine-hour
Maintenance	$18,000 plus $0.10 per machine-hour
Depreciation	$90,000

Required:

Prepare a flexible budget in increments of 5,000 machine-hours. Include all costs in your budget.

EXERCISE 9–2   Variable Overhead Performance Report (LO2, LO3)

The variable portion of Murray Company's flexible budget for manufacturing overhead is given below:

Variable Overhead Costs	Cost Formula (per machine-hour)	Machine-Hours		
		10,000	12,000	14,000
Supplies	$0.20	$ 2,000	$ 2,400	$ 2,800
Maintenance	0.80	8,000	9,600	11,200
Utilities	0.10	1,000	1,200	1,400
Rework time	0.40	4,000	4,800	5,600
Total variable overhead cost	$1.50	$15,000	$18,000	$21,000

During a recent period, the company recorded 11,500 machine-hours of activity. The variable overhead costs incurred were:

Supplies	$2,400
Maintenance	8,000
Utilities	1,100
Rework time	5,300

The budgeted activity for the period had been 12,000 machine-hours.

Required:

1. Prepare a variable overhead performance report for the period. Indicate whether variances are favorable (F) or unfavorable (U). Show only a spending variance on your report.
2. Discuss the significance of the variances. Might some variances be the result of others? Explain.

EXERCISE 9–3   Variable Overhead Variances with Performance Report (LO2, LO4)

The check-clearing office of Columbia National Bank is responsible for processing all checks that come to the bank for payment. Managers at the bank believe that variable overhead costs are essentially proportional to the number of labor-hours worked in the office, so labor-hours is used as the activity base for budgeting and for performance reports for variable overhead costs in the department. Data for September, the most recent month, appear below:

Budgeted labor-hours 3,080
Actual labor-hours 3,100
Standard labor-hours allowed for the actual
    number of checks processed 3,200

	Cost Formula (per labor-hour)	Actual Costs Incurred in September
Variable overhead costs:		
Office supplies	$0.10	$ 365
Staff coffee lounge	0.20	520
Indirect labor	0.90	2,710
Total variable overhead cost	$1.20	$3,595

Required:

Prepare a variable overhead performance report for September for the check-clearing office that includes both spending and efficiency variances. Use Exhibit 9–7 as a guide.

EXERCISE 9–4   Predetermined Overhead Rates (LO5)

Operating at a normal level of 30,000 direct labor-hours, Lasser Company produces 10,000 units of product each period. The direct labor wage rate is $6 per hour. Two and one-half yards of direct materials go into each unit of product; the material costs $8.60 per yard. The flexible budget used to plan and control manufacturing overhead costs is given below (in condensed form):

Overhead Costs	Cost Formula (per direct labor-hour)	Direct Labor-Hours		
		20,000	30,000	40,000
Variable costs	$1.90	$ 38,000	$ 57,000	$ 76,000
Fixed costs		168,000	168,000	168,000
Total overhead cost		$206,000	$225,000	$244,000

Required:

1. Using 30,000 direct labor-hours as the denominator activity, compute the predetermined overhead rate and break it down into variable and fixed elements.
2. Complete the standard cost card below for one unit of product:

Direct materials, 2.5 yards at $8.60 per yard $21.50
Direct labor,   ? ....   ?
Variable overhead,   ? ....   ?
Fixed overhead,   ? ....   ?
Total standard cost per unit .... $?

EXERCISE 9–5   Predetermined Overhead Rates and Overhead Variances (LO4, LO5, LO6)

Norwall Company's flexible budget for manufacturing overhead (in condensed form) is given below:

Overhead Costs	Cost Formula (per machine-hour)	Machine-Hours 50,000	Machine-Hours 60,000	Machine-Hours 70,000
Variable costs	$3	$150,000	$180,000	$210,000
Fixed costs		300,000	300,000	300,000
Total overhead cost		$450,000	$480,000	$510,000

The following information is available for a recent period:

a. A denominator activity of 60,000 machine-hours is used to compute the predetermined overhead rate.

b. At the 60,000 standard machine-hours level of activity, the company should produce 40,000 units of product.

c. The company's actual operating results were:

Number of units produced	42,000
Actual machine-hours	64,000
Actual variable overhead costs	$185,600
Actual fixed overhead costs	302,400

Required:

1. Compute the predetermined overhead rate and break it down into variable and fixed cost elements.
2. Compute the standard hours allowed for the actual production.
3. Compute the variable overhead spending and efficiency variances and the fixed overhead budget and volume variances.

EXERCISE 9–6 Fixed Overhead Variances (LO6)

Selected operating information on three different companies for a recent year is given below:

	Company A	Company B	Company C
Full-capacity machine-hours	10,000	18,000	20,000
Budgeted machine-hours*	9,000	17,000	20,000
Actual machine-hours	9,000	17,800	19,000
Standard machine-hours allowed for actual production	9,500	16,000	20,000

*Denominator activity for computing the predetermined overhead rate.

Required:

For each company, state whether the company would have a favorable or unfavorable volume variance and why.

EXERCISE 9–7   Variable Overhead Performance Report (LO2, LO4)

The cost formulas for variable overhead costs in a machining operation are given below:

Variable Overhead Costs	Cost Formula (per machine-hour)
Power	$0.30
Setup time	0.20
Polishing wheels	0.16
Maintenance	0.18
Total variable overhead cost	$0.84

During August, the machining operation was scheduled to work 11,250 machine-hours and to produce 4,500 units of product. The standard machine time per unit of product is 2.5 hours. A strike near the end of the month forced a cutback in production. Actual results for the month were:

Actual machine-hours worked	9,250
Actual number of units produced	3,600

Actual costs for the month were:

Variable Overhead Costs	Total Actual Costs	Per Machine-Hour
Power	$2,405	$0.26
Setup time	2,035	0.22
Polishing wheels	1,110	0.12
Maintenance	925	0.10
Total variable overhead cost	$6,475	$0.70

Required:

Prepare an overhead performance report for the machining operation for August. Use column headings in your report as shown below:

Overhead Item	Cost Formula (per machine-hour)	Actual Costs Incurred 9,250 Machine-Hours	Budget Based on ? Machine-Hours	Budget Based on ? Machine-Hours	Total Variance	Breakdown of the Total Variance	
						Spending Variance	Efficiency Variance

Problems

CHECK FIGURE
(3) Total of spending and
budget variances:
$5,700 U

PROBLEM 9–1 Preparing a Performance Report (LO2, LO3, LO6)

Several years ago, Westmont Company developed a comprehensive budgeting system for profit planning and control purposes. The line supervisors have been very happy with the system and with the reports being prepared on their performance, but both middle and upper management have expressed considerable dissatisfaction with the information being generated by the system. A typical manufacturing overhead performance report for a recent period is shown below:

WESTMONT COMPANY Overhead Performance Report—Assembly Department For the Quarter Ended March 31			
	Actual	**Budget**	**Variance**
Machine-hours	35,000	40,000	
Variable overhead costs:			
Indirect materials	$ 29,700	$ 32,000	$2,300 F
Rework time	7,900	8,000	100 F
Utilities	51,800	56,000	4,200 F
Machine setup	11,600	12,000	400 F
Total variable overhead cost	101,000	108,000	7,000 F
Fixed overhead costs:			
Maintenance	79,200	80,000	800 F
Inspection	60,000	60,000	—
Total fixed overhead cost	139,200	140,000	800 F
Total overhead cost	$240,200	$248,000	$7,800 F

After receiving a copy of this overhead performance report, the supervisor of the Assembly Department stated, "These reports are super. It makes me feel really good to see how well things are going in my department. I can't understand why those people upstairs complain so much."

The budget data above are for the original planned level of activity for the quarter.

Required:
1. The company's vice president is uneasy about the performance reports being prepared and would like you to evaluate their usefulness to the company.
2. What changes, if any, would you recommend be made in the overhead performance report above in order to give better insight into how well the supervisor is controlling costs?
3. Prepare a new overhead performance report for the quarter, incorporating any changes you suggested in (2) above. (Include both the variable and the fixed costs in your report.)

PROBLEM 9–2 Preparing a Performance Report (LO2, LO3)

The St. Lucia Blood Bank, a private charity partly supported by government grants, is located on the Caribbean island of St. Lucia. The Blood Bank has just finished its operations for September, which was a particularly busy month due to a powerful hurricane that hit neighboring islands causing many injuries. The hurricane largely bypassed St. Lucia, but residents of St. Lucia willingly donated their blood to help people on other islands. As a consequence, the blood bank collected and processed over 20% more blood than had been originally planned for the month.

A report prepared by a government official comparing actual costs to budgeted costs for the Blood Bank appears below. (The currency on St. Lucia is the East Caribbean dollar.) Continued support from the government depends on the Blood Bank's ability to demonstrate control over their costs.

CHECK FIGURE
(1) Flexible budget total cost at 620 liters: $32,290

ST. LUCIA BLOOD BANK
Cost Control Report
For the Month Ended September 30

	Actual	Budget	Variance
Liters of blood collected	620	500	120 F
Variable costs:			
Medical supplies	$ 9,350	$ 7,500	$1,850 U
Lab tests	6,180	6,000	180 U
Refreshments for donors	1,340	1,000	340 U
Administrative supplies	400	250	150 U
Total variable cost	17,270	14,750	2,520 U
Fixed costs:			
Staff salaries	10,000	10,000	—
Equipment depreciation	2,800	2,500	300 U
Rent	1,000	1,000	—
Utilities	570	500	70 U
Total fixed cost	14,370	14,000	370 U
Total cost	$31,640	$28,750	$2,890 U

The managing director of the Blood Bank was very unhappy with this report, claiming that his costs were higher than expected due to the emergency on the neighboring islands. He also pointed out that the additional costs had been fully covered by payments from grateful recipients on the other islands. The government official who prepared the report countered that all of the figures had been submitted by the Blood Bank to the government; he was just pointing out that actual costs were a lot higher than promised in the budget.

Required:
1. Prepare a new performance report for September using the flexible budget approach. (Note: Even though some of these costs might be classified as direct costs rather than as overhead, the flexible budget approach can still be used to prepare a flexible budget performance report.)
2. Do you think any of the variances in the report you prepared should be investigated? Why?

PROBLEM 9–3   Comprehensive Standard Cost Variances (LO4, LO6)

Flandro Company uses a standard cost system and sets predetermined overhead rates on the basis of direct labor-hours. The following data are taken from the company's budget for the current year:

Denominator activity (direct labor-hours)	10,000
Variable manufacturing overhead cost	$25,000
Fixed manufacturing overhead cost	59,000

The standard cost card for the company's only product is given below:

Direct materials, 3 yards at $4.40	$13.20
Direct labor, 2 hours at $6	12.00
Manufacturing overhead, 140% of direct labor cost	16.80
Standard cost per unit	$42.00

During the year, the company produced 6,000 units of product and incurred the following costs:

Materials purchased, 24,000 yards at $4.80	$115,200
Materials used in production (in yards)	18,500
Direct labor cost incurred, 11,600 hours at $6.50	$ 75,400
Variable manufacturing overhead cost incurred	29,580
Fixed manufacturing overhead cost incurred	60,400

Required:

1. Redo the standard cost card in a clearer, more usable format by detailing the variable and fixed overhead cost elements.
2. Prepare an analysis of the variances for materials and labor for the year.
3. Prepare an analysis of the variances for variable and fixed overhead for the year.
4. What effect, if any, does the choice of a denominator activity level have on unit standard costs? Is the volume variance a controllable variance from a spending point of view? Explain.

PROBLEM 9–4   Applying Overhead; Overhead Variances (LO4, LO5, LO6)

Chilczuk, S.A., of Gdansk, Poland, is a major producer of classic Polish sausage. The company uses a standard cost system to help in the control of costs. Overhead is applied to production on the basis of labor-hours. According to the company's flexible budget, the following manufacturing overhead costs should be incurred at an activity level of 35,000 labor-hours (the denominator activity level):

Variable overhead costs	PZ 87,500
Fixed overhead costs	210,000
Total overhead cost	PZ297,500

The currency in Poland is the zloty, which is denoted here by PZ.

During the most recent year, the following operating results were recorded:

Activity:	
Actual labor-hours worked	30,000
Standard labor-hours allowed for output	32,000
Cost:	
Actual variable overhead cost incurred	PZ 78,000
Actual fixed overhead cost incurred	209,400

At the end of the year, the company's Manufacturing Overhead account contained the following data:

Manufacturing Overhead

Actual	287,400	Applied	272,000
	15,400		

Management would like to determine the cause of the PZ15,400 underapplied overhead.

Required:
1. Compute the predetermined overhead rate. Break the rate down into variable and fixed cost elements.
2. Show how the PZ272,000 applied figure in the Manufacturing Overhead account was computed.
3. Analyze the PZ15,400 underapplied overhead figure in terms of the variable overhead spending and efficiency variances and the fixed overhead budget and volume variances.
4. Explain the meaning of each variance that you computed in (3) above.

PROBLEM 9–5   Comprehensive Standard Cost Variances (LO4, LO6)

"Wonderful! Not only did our salespeople do a good job in meeting the sales budget this year, but our production people did a good job in controlling costs as well," said Kim Clark, president of Martell Company. "Our $18,000 overall manufacturing cost variance is only 1.5% of the $1,200,000 standard cost of products sold during the year. That's well within the 3% parameter set by management for acceptable variances. It looks like everyone will be in line for a bonus this year."

The company produces and sells a single product. A standard cost card for the product follows:

CHECK FIGURE
(3a) Efficiency variance:
$7,500 U
(3b) Volume variance:
$42,000 F

[handwritten] 18,000 over/expected cost

Standard Cost Card—Per Unit of Product

Direct materials, 2 feet at $8.45 per foot	$16.90
Direct labor, 1.4 hours at $8 per hour	11.20
Variable overhead, 1.4 hours at $2.50 per hour	3.50
Fixed overhead, 1.4 hours at $6 per hour	8.40
Standard cost per unit	$40.00

The following additional information is available for the year just completed:
a. The company manufactured 30,000 units of product during the year.
b. A total of 64,000 feet of material was purchased during the year at a cost of $8.55 per foot. All of this material was used to manufacture the 30,000 units. There were no beginning or ending inventories for the year.
c. The company worked 45,000 direct labor-hours during the year at a cost of $7.80 per hour.
d. Overhead is applied to products on the basis of direct labor-hours. Data relating to manufacturing overhead costs follow:

Denominator activity level (direct labor-hours)	35,000
Budgeted fixed overhead costs (from the overhead flexible budget)	$210,000
Actual variable overhead costs incurred	108,000
Actual fixed overhead costs incurred	211,800

Required:
1. Compute the direct materials price and quantity variances for the year.
2. Compute the direct labor rate and efficiency variances for the year.
3. For manufacturing overhead compute:
   a. The variable overhead spending and efficiency variances for the year.
   b. The fixed overhead budget and volume variances for the year.
4. Total the variances you have computed, and compare the net amount with the $18,000 mentioned by the president. Do you agree that bonuses should be given to everyone for good cost control during the year? Explain.

PROBLEM 9–6   Using Fixed Overhead Variances (LO6)

The standard cost card for the single product manufactured by Cutter, Inc., is given below:

Standard Cost Card—Per Unit

Direct materials, 3 yards at $6 per yard	$18
Direct labor, 4 hours at $7.75 per hour	31
Variable overhead, 4 hours at $1.50 per hour	6
Fixed overhead, 4 hours at $5 per hour	20
Total standard cost per unit	$75

Manufacturing overhead is applied to production on the basis of direct labor-hours. During the year, the company worked 37,000 hours and manufactured 9,500 units of product. Selected data relating to the company's fixed manufacturing overhead cost for the year are shown below:

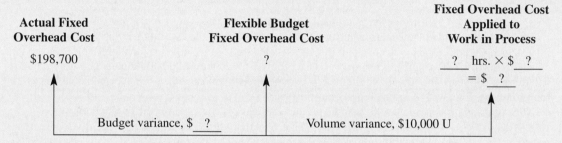

Actual Fixed Overhead Cost	Flexible Budget Fixed Overhead Cost	Fixed Overhead Cost Applied to Work in Process
$198,700	?	? hrs. × $? = $?

Budget variance, $?   Volume variance, $10,000 U

Required:
1. What were the standard hours allowed for the year's production?
2. What was the amount of fixed overhead cost contained in the flexible budget for the year?
3. What was the fixed overhead budget variance for the year?
4. What denominator activity level did the company use in setting the predetermined overhead rate for the year?

PROBLEM 9–7   Relations among Fixed Overhead Variances (LO6)

Selected information relating to Yost Company's operations for the most recent year is given below:

Activity:	
Denominator activity (machine-hours)	45,000
Standard hours allowed per unit	3
Number of units produced	14,000
Costs:	
Actual fixed overhead costs incurred	$267,000
Fixed overhead budget variance	3,000 F

The company applies overhead cost to products on the basis of machine-hours.

Required:
1. What were the standard hours allowed for the actual production?
2. What was the fixed portion of the predetermined overhead rate?
3. What was the volume variance?

PROBLEM 9–8 Flexible Budget and Overhead Performance Report (LO1, LO2, LO4)

You have just been hired by FAB Company, the manufacturer of a revolutionary new garage door opening device. John Foster, the president, has asked that you review the company's costing system and "do what you can to help us get better control of our manufacturing overhead costs." You find that the company has never used a flexible budget, and you suggest that preparing such a budget would be an excellent first step in overhead planning and control.

After much effort and analysis, you are able to determine the following cost formulas for the company's normal operating range of 20,000 to 30,000 machine-hours each month:

Overhead Costs	Cost Formula
Utilities	$0.90 per machine-hour
Maintenance	$1.60 per machine-hour plus $40,000 per month
Machine setup	$0.30 per machine-hour
Indirect labor	$0.70 per machine-hour plus $130,000 per month
Depreciation	$70,000 per month

To show the president how the flexible budget concept works, you have gathered the following actual cost data for the most recent month, March, in which the company worked 26,000 machine-hours and produced 15,000 units:

Utilities	$ 24,200
Maintenance	78,100
Machine setup	8,400
Indirect labor	149,600
Depreciation	71,500
Total cost	$331,800

The only variance in the fixed costs for the month was with depreciation, which was increased as a result of a purchase of new equipment.

The company had originally planned to work 30,000 machine-hours during March.

Required:
1. Prepare a flexible budget for the company in increments of 5,000 hours.
2. Prepare an overhead performance report for the company for March. (Use the format illustrated in Exhibit 9–11.)
3. What additional information would you need to compute an overhead efficiency variance for the company?

PROBLEM 9–9 Overhead Performance Report (LO2, LO4)

Frank Western, supervisor of the Machining Department for Freemont Company, was visibly upset after being reprimanded for his department's poor performance over the prior month. The department's performance report is given below:

CHECK FIGURE
(2) Total variance: $6,500 F

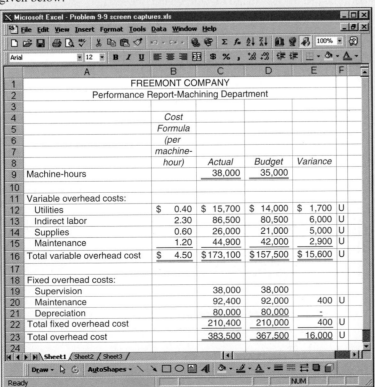

	A	B	C	D	E	F
1		FREEMONT COMPANY				
2		Performance Report-Machining Department				
3						
4		*Cost*				
5		*Formula*				
6		*(per*				
7		*machine-*				
8		*hour)*	*Actual*	*Budget*	*Variance*	
9	Machine-hours		38,000	35,000		
10						
11	Variable overhead costs:					
12	Utilities	$ 0.40	$ 15,700	$ 14,000	$ 1,700 U	
13	Indirect labor	2.30	86,500	80,500	6,000 U	
14	Supplies	0.60	26,000	21,000	5,000 U	
15	Maintenance	1.20	44,900	42,000	2,900 U	
16	Total variable overhead cost	$ 4.50	$173,100	$157,500	$ 15,600 U	
17						
18	Fixed overhead costs:					
19	Supervision		38,000	38,000		
20	Maintenance		92,400	92,000	400 U	
21	Depreciation		80,000	80,000	-	
22	Total fixed overhead cost		210,400	210,000	400 U	
23	Total overhead cost		383,500	367,500	16,000 U	
24						

"I just can't understand all the red ink," said Western to Sarah Mason, supervisor of another department. "When the boss called me in, I thought he was going to give me a pat on the back because I know for a fact that my department worked more efficiently last month than it has ever worked before. Instead, he tore me apart. I thought for a minute that it might be over the supplies that were stolen out of our warehouse last month. But they only amounted to a couple of thousand dollars, and just look at this report. *Everything* is unfavorable, and I don't even know why."

The budget for the Machining Department had called for production of 14,000 units last month, which is equal to a budgeted activity level of 35,000 machine-hours (at a standard time of 2.5 hours per unit). Actual production in the Machining Department for the month was 16,000 units.

Required:
1. Evaluate the overhead performance report given above and explain why the variances are all unfavorable.
2. Prepare a new overhead performance report that will help Mr. Western's superiors assess efficiency and cost control in the Machining Department. (Hint: Exhibit 9–7 may be helpful in structuring your report; however, the report you prepare should include both variable and fixed costs.)
3. Would the supplies stolen out of the warehouse be included as part of the variable overhead spending variance or as part of the variable overhead efficiency variance for the month? Explain.

CHECK FIGURE
(2) Standard cost: $45
(4) Volume variance:
    $24,000 F

PROBLEM 9–10 Applying Overhead; Overhead Variances (LO4, LO5, LO6)

Lane Company manufactures a single product that requires a great deal of hand labor. Overhead cost is applied on the basis of direct labor-hours. The company's condensed flexible budget for manufacturing overhead is given below:

Overhead Costs	Cost Formula (per direct labor-hour)	Direct Labor-Hours		
		45,000	60,000	75,000
Variable costs	$2	$ 90,000	$120,000	$150,000
Fixed costs		480,000	480,000	480,000
Total overhead cost		$570,000	$600,000	$630,000

The company's product requires 3 pounds of material that has a standard cost of $7 per pound and 1.5 hours of direct labor time that has a standard rate of $6 per hour.

The company planned to operate at a denominator activity level of 60,000 direct labor-hours and to produce 40,000 units of product during the most recent year. Actual activity and costs for the year were as follows:

Number of units produced	42,000
Actual direct labor-hours worked	65,000
Actual variable overhead cost incurred	$123,500
Actual fixed overhead cost incurred	483,000

Required:
1. Compute the predetermined overhead rate for the year. Break the rate down into variable and fixed elements.
2. Prepare a standard cost card for the company's product; show the details for all manufacturing costs on your standard cost card.
3. Do the following:
   a. Compute the standard hours allowed for the year's production.
   b. Complete the following Manufacturing Overhead T-account for the year:

Manufacturing Overhead

?	?
?	?

4. Determine the reason for any under- or overapplied overhead for the year by computing the variable overhead spending and efficiency variances and the fixed overhead budget and volume variances.

5. Suppose the company had chosen 65,000 direct labor-hours as the denominator activity rather than 60,000 hours. State which, if any, of the variances computed in (4) above would have changed, and explain how the variance(s) would have changed. No computations are necessary.

Building Your Skills

ANALYTICAL THINKING (LO4, LO5, LO6)

A company that uses a standard cost system has provided the following data. The company's flexible budget for manufacturing overhead is based on standard machine-hours.

CHECK FIGURE
(5) $210,000 fixed
(14) $1.75/hour

1. Denominator activity in hours	?
2. Standard hours allowed for units produced	32,000
3. Actual hours worked	30,000
4. Flexible budget variable overhead per machine-hour	$?
5. Flexible budget fixed overhead (total)	?
6. Actual variable overhead cost incurred	54,000
7. Actual fixed overhead cost incurred	209,400
8. Variable overhead cost applied to production*	?
9. Fixed overhead cost applied to production*	192,000
10. Variable overhead spending variance	?
11. Variable overhead efficiency variance	3,500 F
12. Fixed overhead budget variance	?
13. Fixed overhead volume variance	18,000 U
14. Variable portion of the predetermined overhead rate	?
15. Fixed portion of the predetermined overhead rate	?
16. Underapplied (or overapplied) overhead	?

*Based on standard hours allowed for units produced.

Required:

Compute the unknown amounts. (Hint: One way to proceed would be to use the format for variance analysis found in Exhibit 8–6 for variable overhead and in Exhibit 9–10 for fixed overhead.)

COMMUNICATING IN PRACTICE   (LO1)

Use an online yellow pages directory such as www.comfind.com, or www.athand.com to find a manufacturer in your area that has a website. Make an appointment with the controller or chief financial officer of the company. Before your meeting, find out as much as you can about the organization's operations from its website.

Required:

After asking the following questions, write a brief memorandum to your instructor that summarizes the information obtained from the company's website and addresses what you found out during your interview.

1. Are actual overhead costs compared to a static budget, to a flexible budget, or to something else?

2. Does the organization distinguish between variable and fixed overhead costs in its performance reports?

3. What are the consequences of unfavorable variances? Of favorable variances?

ETHICS CHALLENGE   (LO2)

Tom Kemper is the controller of the Wichita manufacturing facility of Prudhom Enterprises, Incorporated. Among the many reports that must be filed with corporate headquarters is the annual overhead performance report. The report covers an entire fiscal year, which ends on December 31, and is due at corporate headquarters shortly after the beginning of the New Year. Kemper does not like putting work off to the last minute, so just before Christmas he put together a preliminary draft of the overhead performance report. Some adjustments would be required for transactions that occur between Christmas and New Year's Day, but there are generally very few of these. A copy of the preliminary draft report, which Kemper completed on December 21, follows:

WICHITA MANUFACTURING FACILITY
Overhead Performance Report
December 21 Preliminary Draft

Budgeted machine-hours   200,000
Actual machine-hours   180,000

Overhead Costs	Cost Formula (per machine-hour)	Actual Costs 180,000 Machine-Hours	Budget Based on 180,000 Machine-Hours	Spending or Budget Variance
Variable overhead costs:				
Power	$0.10	$ 19,750	$ 18,000	$ 1,750 U
Supplies	0.25	47,000	45,000	2,000 U
Abrasives	0.30	58,000	54,000	4,000 U
Total variable overhead cost	$0.65	124,750	117,000	7,750 U
Fixed overhead costs:				
Depreciation		345,000	332,000	13,000 U
Supervisory salaries		273,000	275,000	2,000 F
Insurance		37,000	37,000	—
Industrial engineering		189,000	210,000	21,000 F
Factory building lease		60,000	60,000	—
Total fixed overhead cost		904,000	914,000	10,000 F
Total overhead cost		$1,028,750	$1,031,000	$ 2,250 F

     Melissa Ilianovitch, the general manager at the Wichita facility, asked to see a copy of the preliminary draft report at 4:45 P.M. on December 23. Kemper carried a copy of the report to her office where the following discussion took place:

Ilianovitch: Ouch! Almost all of the variances on the report are unfavorable. The only thing that looks good at all are the favorable variances for supervisory salaries and for industrial engineering. How did we have an unfavorable variance for depreciation?

Kemper: Do you remember that milling machine that broke down because the wrong lubricant was used by the machine operator?

Ilianovitch: Only vaguely.

Kemper: It turned out we couldn't fix it. We had to scrap the machine and buy a new one.

Ilianovitch: This report doesn't look good. I was raked over the coals last year when we had just a few unfavorable variances.

Kemper: I'm afraid the final report is going to look even worse.

Ilianovitch: Oh?

Kemper: The line item for industrial engineering on the report is for work we hired Ferguson Engineering to do for us on a contract basis. The original contract was for $210,000, but we asked them to do some additional work that was not in the contract. Under the terms of the contract, we have to reimburse Ferguson Engineering for the costs of the additional work. The $189,000 in actual costs that appear on the preliminary draft report reflects only their billings up through December 21. The last bill they had sent us was on November 28, and they completed the project just last week. Yesterday I got a call from Laura Sunder over at Ferguson and she said they would be sending us a final bill for the project before the end of the year. The total bill, including the reimbursements for the additional work, is going to be . . .

Ilianovitch: I am not sure I want to hear this.

Kemper: $225,000.

Ilianovitch: Ouch! Ouch! Ouch!

Kemper: The additional work we asked them to do added $15,000 to the cost of the project.

Ilianovitch: No way can I turn in a performance report with an overall unfavorable variance. They'll kill me at corporate headquarters. Call up Laura at Ferguson and ask her not to send the bill until after the first of the year. We have to have that $21,000 favorable variance for industrial engineering on the performance report.

Required:
What should Tom Kemper do? Explain.

TAKING IT TO THE NET

As you know, the World Wide Web is a medium that is constantly evolving. Sites come and go and change without notice. To enable periodic update of site addresses, this problem has been posted to the textbook website (www.mhhe.com/folk1e). After accessing the site, enter the Student Center and select this chapter. Select and complete the Taking It to the Net problem.

TEAMWORK IN ACTION   (LO1, LO3, LO5)

Boyne University offers an extensive continuing education program in many cities throughout the state. For the convenience of its faculty and administrative staff and to save costs, the university employs a supervisor to operate a motor pool. The motor pool operated with 20 vehicles until February, when an additional automobile was acquired. The motor pool furnishes gasoline, oil, and other supplies for its automobiles. A mechanic does routine maintenance and minor repairs. Major repairs are done at a nearby commercial garage.

Each year, the supervisor prepares an operating budget that informs the university administration of the funds needed for operating the motor pool. Depreciation (straight line) on the automobiles is recorded in the budget in order to determine the cost per mile of operating the vehicles.

The following performance report was prepared by a budget analyst who was recently hired by the university. It presents the operating budget for the current year, which was approved by the university. The performance report also shows actual operating costs for March of the current year compared to one-twelfth of the annual operating budget.

UNIVERSITY MOTOR POOL Performance Report for March				
	Annual Operating Budget	Monthly Budget*	March Actual	(Over) Under Budget
Gasoline	$ 42,000	$ 3,500	$ 4,300	$(800)
Oil, minor repairs, parts	3,600	300	380	(80)
Outside repairs	2,700	225	50	175
Insurance	6,000	500	525	(25)
Salaries and benefits	30,000	2,500	2,500	—
Depreciation of vehicles	26,400	2,200	2,310	(110)
Total costs	$110,700	$ 9,225	$10,065	$(840)
Total miles	600,000	50,000	63,000	
Cost per mile	$0.1845	$0.1845	$0.1598	
Number of automobiles in use . . .	20	20	21	

*Annual operating budget ÷ 12 months.

The annual operating budget was constructed on the following assumptions:

a. Twenty automobiles in the motor pool.
b. Thirty thousand miles driven per year per automobile.
c. Fifteen miles per gallon per automobile.
d. $1.05 per gallon of gasoline.
e. $0.006 cost per mile for oil, minor repairs, and parts.
f. $135 cost per automobile per year for outside repairs.
g. $300 cost per automobile per year for insurance.

The supervisor of the motor pool is unhappy with the monthly performance report comparing budget and actual costs for March, claiming it presents an unfair picture of performance.

Required:

1. Using a flexible budgeting approach, prepare a new performance report for March showing budgeted costs, actual costs, and variances. All team members should understand how the revised performance report was prepared.
2. The team should discuss and then write up brief answers to the questions listed below. All team members should agree with and understand the answers.
   a. What are the deficiencies in the performance report that was prepared by the budget analyst?
   b. How does the revised performance report, which was prepared using a flexible budget approach, overcome these deficiencies?

(CMA, adapted)

Chapter Ten

Decentralization

Chapter Outline

Decision Feature **Centralizing Communications**

Ingersoll-Rand, a global conglomerate, traces its roots to the early 1870s. After receiving a patent for his steam-powered rock drill in 1871, Simon Ingersoll formed the Ingersoll Rock Drill Company. Over 125 years have passed since Ingersoll's invention laid the foundation for this international powerhouse. During that period, the company has grown and diversified by forming new subsidiaries and acquiring other companies. Its presence was first felt overseas with the formation of Ingersoll-Rand (India) Private Ltd. in 1921. Some of its many acquisitions include Schlage Lock Company in 1974, Clark Equipment Company (including the Bobcat product line) in 1995, the manufacturer of Steelcraft doors in 1996, Thermo King in 1997, and Hussman International in 2000. Ingersoll-Rand now operates over 100 manufacturing facilities worldwide.

The company earned approximately $545 million on sales of almost $7.7 billion during the year ended December 31, 1999. Expenditures for wages, salaries, and benefits exceeded $1.9 billion for its 46,000 employees during that same period. Ingersoll-Rand was the *Industryweek* Best Managed Company in 1997, 1998, and 1999, and has received numerous other recognitions and awards. Even so, in 1999 the company decided that it needed to restructure its organization to compete effectively in today's economy.

Previously comprised of 8 autonomous companies, Ingersoll-Rand now operates as 13 separate business units. To improve communications, its outdated, stand-alone computer systems are being replaced with integrated systems that can provide information to managers and headquarters in real time. The company continues to operate in a decentralized fashion. Even though many of its functions have been centralized, such as purchasing, payroll, and accounts receivable and payable, decision-making is still spread throughout the organization. For example, factory managers continue to be responsible for deciding what must be purchased. However, instead of issuing purchase orders to vendors, the requisitions are communicated to headquarters, which then issues the purchase orders. As a result of this centralized approach to purchasing, the company has been able to negotiate better discounts with suppliers.

Analysts estimate the cost of the restructuring at $50 million. Don Janson, director of common administrative resources implementations at Ingersoll-Rand, predicts that the changes will pay for themselves within three years.

Source: Ingersoll-Rand Company website, July 2000; Steve Konicki, "A Company Merges Its Many Units—Successfully," *Informationweek*, May 8, 2000, pp. 174–178.

Learning Objectives
After studying Chapter 10, you should be able to:

LO1 Understand the role of cost, profit, and investment centers in a decentralized organization.

LO2 Compute the return on investment (ROI).

LO3 Show how changes in sales, expenses, and assets affect an organization's ROI.

LO4 Compute residual income and understand the strengths and weaknesses of this method of measuring performance.

Once an organization grows beyond a few people, it becomes impossible for the top manager to make decisions about everything. For example, the CEO of the Hyatt Hotel chain cannot be expected to decide whether a particular hotel guest at the Hyatt Hotel on Maui should be allowed to check out later than the normal checkout time. To some degree, managers have to delegate decisions to those who are at lower levels in the organization. However, the degree to which decisions are delegated varies from organization to organization.

Decentralization in Organizations

A **decentralized organization** is one in which decision-making is not confined to a few top executives but rather is spread throughout the organization, with managers at various levels making key operating decisions relating to their sphere of responsibility. Decentralization is a matter of degree, since all organizations are decentralized to some extent out of necessity. At one extreme, a strongly decentralized organization is one in which there are few, if any, constraints on the freedom of even the lowest-level managers and employees to make decisions. At the other extreme, in a strongly centralized organization, lower-level managers have little freedom to make a decision. Although most organizations fall somewhere between these two extremes, there is a pronounced trend toward more and more decentralization.

Advantages and Disadvantages of Decentralization

Decentralization has many benefits, including:

1. Top management is relieved of much day-to-day problem solving and is left free to concentrate on strategy, on higher-level decision-making, and on coordinating activities.
2. Decentralization provides lower-level managers with vital experience in making decisions. Without such experience, they would be ill-prepared to make decisions when they are promoted into higher-level positions.
3. Added responsibility and decision-making authority often result in increased job satisfaction. It makes the job more interesting and provides greater incentives for people to put out their best efforts.
4. Lower-level managers generally have more detailed and up-to-date information about conditions in their own area of responsibility than top managers. Therefore, the decisions of lower-level managers are often based on better information.
5. It is difficult to evaluate a manager's performance if the manager is not given much latitude in what he or she can do.

Decentralization has four major disadvantages:

1. Lower-level managers may make decisions without fully understanding the "big picture." While top-level managers typically have less detailed information about operations than the lower-level managers, they usually have more information about the company as a whole and may have a better understanding of the company's strategy.
2. In a truly decentralized organization, there may be a lack of coordination among autonomous managers. This problem can be reduced by clearly defining the company's strategy and communicating it effectively throughout the organization.
3. Lower-level managers may have objectives that are different from the objectives of the entire organization. For example, some managers may be more interested in

increasing the sizes of their departments than in increasing the profits of the company.[1] To some degree, this problem can be overcome by designing performance evaluation systems that motivate managers to make decisions that are in the best interests of the company.

4. In a strongly decentralized organization, it may be more difficult to effectively spread innovative ideas. Someone in one part of the organization may have a terrific idea that would benefit other parts of the organization, but without strong central direction the idea may not be shared with, and adopted by, other parts of the organization.

Decentralization and Segment Reporting

Effective decentralization requires *segmental reporting*. In addition to the companywide income statement, reports are needed for individual segments of the organization. A **segment** is a part or activity of an organization about which managers would like cost, revenue, or profit data. Examples of segments include divisions of a company, sales territories, individual stores, service centers, manufacturing plants, marketing departments, individual customers, and product lines. A company's operations can be segmented in many ways. For example, a grocery store chain like Safeway or Kroger's can segment their businesses by geographic region, by individual store, by the nature of the merchandise (i.e., green groceries, canned goods, paper goods), by brand name, and so on.

A Friend

decision maker

One of your friends from college started a business that designs web pages, which has become a wildly successful startup. On the way to meet your friend for lunch, you think about how great it would be to be your own boss—to be able to come and go as you please. At lunch, you hardly recognize her. She's tired and stressed, complains a lot about the hours she's been putting in to supervise various projects, and is puzzled by the high turnover that she has experienced at the manager level. After all, as she notes, she keeps her hand in all of the major projects. What advice do you have for her?

Cost, Profit, and Investment Centers

Decentralized companies typically categorize their business segments into cost centers, profit centers, and investment centers—depending on the responsibilities of the managers of the segments.[2]

Cost Center   A **cost center** is a business segment whose manager has control over costs but not over revenue or investment funds. Service departments such as accounting,

---

[1]There is a similar problem with top-level managers as well. The shareholders of the company have, in effect, decentralized by delegating their decision-making authority to the top managers. Unfortunately, top managers may abuse that trust by spending too much company money on palatial offices, rewarding themselves and their friends too generously, and so on. The issue of how to ensure that top managers act in the best interests of the owners of the company continues to puzzle experts. To a large extent, the owners rely on performance evaluation using return on investment and residual income measures as discussed later in the chapter and on bonuses and stock options. The stock market is also an important disciplining mechanism. If top managers squander the company's resources, the price of the company's stock will almost surely fall—resulting in a loss of prestige, bonuses, and possibly a job.

[2]Some companies classify business segments that are responsible mainly for generating revenue, such as an insurance sales office, as *revenue centers*. Other companies would consider this to be just another type of profit center, since costs of some kind (salaries, rent, utilities) are usually deducted from the revenues in the segment's income statement.

finance, general administration, legal, personnel, and so on, are usually considered to be cost centers. In addition, manufacturing facilities are often considered to be cost centers. The managers of cost centers are expected to minimize cost while providing the level of services or the amount of products demanded by the other parts of the organization. For example, the manager of a production facility would be evaluated at least in part by comparing actual costs to how much the costs should have been for the actual number of units produced during the period.

Profit Center   In contrast to a cost center, a **profit center** is any business segment whose manager has control over both cost and revenue. Like a cost center, however, a profit center generally does not have control over investment funds. For example, the manager in charge of one of the Six Flags amusement parks would be responsible for both the revenues and costs, and hence the profits, of the amusement park but may not have control over major investments in the park. Profit center managers are often evaluated by comparing actual profit to targeted or budgeted profit.

Investment Center   An **investment center** is any segment of an organization whose manager has control over cost, revenue, and investments in operating assets. For example, the vice president of the Truck Division at General Motors would have a great deal of discretion over investments in the division. The vice president of the Truck Division would be responsible for initiating investment proposals, such as funding research into more fuel-efficient engines for sport-utility vehicles. Once the proposal has been approved by the top level of managers at General Motors and the board of directors, the vice president of the Truck Division would then be responsible for making sure that the investment pays off. Investment center managers are usually evaluated using return on investment or residual income measures as discussed later in the chapter.

Responsibility Centers

Responsibility center is broadly defined as any part of an organization whose manager has control over cost, revenue, or investment funds. Cost centers, profit centers, and investment centers are *all* known as responsibility centers.

A partial organization chart for Universal Foods Corporation, a company in the snack food and beverage industry, appears in Exhibit 10–1. This partial organization chart indicates how the various business segments of the company are classified in terms of responsibility. Note that the cost centers are the departments and work centers that do not generate significant revenues by themselves. These are staff departments such as finance, legal, and personnel, and operating units such as the bottling plant, warehouse, and beverage distribution center. The profit centers are business segments that generate revenues and include the beverage, salty snacks, and confections product segments. The vice president of operations oversees allocation of investment funds across the product segments and is responsible for revenues and costs and so it is treated as an investment center. And finally, corporate headquarters is an investment center, since it is responsible for all revenues, costs, and investments.

Traceable and Common Fixed Costs

Performance reports are often compiled for a part of the organization, or segment, such as an investment center. In such segment reports, a distinction should be drawn between *traceable fixed costs* and *common fixed costs*. A **traceable fixed cost** of a segment is a fixed cost that is incurred because of the existence of the segment and if the segment were eliminated, the fixed cost would disappear. Examples of traceable fixed costs include the following:

- The salary of the Fritos product manager at PepsiCo is a traceable fixed cost of the Fritos business segment of PepsiCo.

Exhibit 10–1

Business Segments Classified as Cost, Profit, and Investment Centers

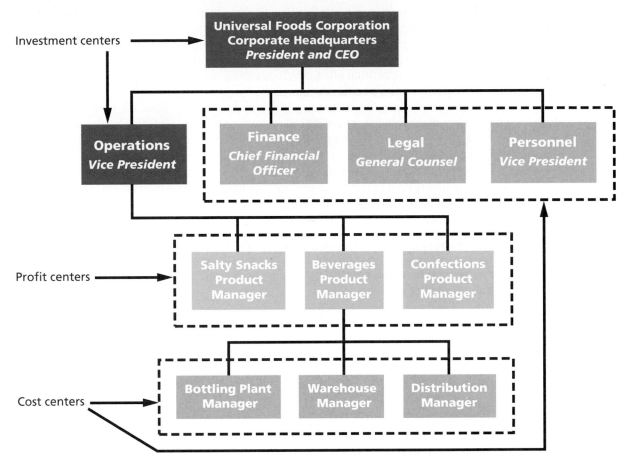

- The maintenance cost for the building in which Boeing 747s are assembled is a traceable fixed cost of the 747 business segment of Boeing.
- The liability insurance at Disney World is a traceable fixed cost of the Disney World business segment of the Disney Corporation.

A **common fixed cost** is a fixed cost that supports the operations of more than one segment, but is not traceable in whole or in part to any one segment. Even if the segment were entirely eliminated, there would be no change in a common fixed cost. Examples of common fixed costs include the following:

- The salary of the CEO of General Motors is a common fixed cost of the various divisions of General Motors.
- The cost of the checkout equipment at a Safeway or Kroger grocery store is a common fixed cost of the various departments—such as groceries, produce, bakery—in the store.
- The cost of the receptionist's salary at an office shared by a number of doctors is a common fixed cost of the doctors. The cost is traceable to the office, but not to any one of the doctors individually.

In general, traceable costs should be assigned to segments, but common fixed costs should not be assigned to segments—to do so would overstate the costs that are actually caused by the segments and that could be avoided by eliminating the segments. The details of how to deal with traceable and common fixed costs in segment reports are covered in more advanced texts. For example, see Chapter 12 of Ray Garrison and Eric Noreen, *Managerial Accounting*, 9th edition, Irwin/McGraw-Hill, 2000.

Rate of Return for Measuring Managerial Performance

When a company is truly decentralized, managers are given a great deal of autonomy. So great is this autonomy that the various profit and investment centers are often viewed as being virtually independent businesses, with their managers having about the same control over decisions as if they were in fact running their own independent firms. With this autonomy, fierce competition often develops among managers, with each striving to make his or her segment the "best" in the company.

Competition between investment centers is particularly keen for investment funds. How do top managers in corporate headquarters go about deciding who gets new investment funds as they become available, and how do these managers decide which investment centers are most profitably using the funds that have already been entrusted to their care? One of the most popular ways of making these judgments is to measure the rate of return that investment center managers are able to generate on their assets. This rate of return is called the *return on investment (ROI)*.

The Return on Investment (ROI) Formula

Concept 10–1

The **return on investment (ROI)** is defined as net operating income divided by average operating assets:

$$ROI = \frac{\text{Net operating income}}{\text{Average operating assets}}$$

There are some issues about how to measure net operating income and average operating assets, but this formula seems clear enough. The higher the return on investment (ROI) of a business segment, the greater the profit generated per dollar invested in the segment's operating assets.

Net Operating Income and Operating Assets Defined

Note that *net operating income,* rather than net income, is used in the ROI formula. **Net operating income** is income before interest and taxes and is sometimes referred to as EBIT (earnings before interest and taxes). The reason for using net operating income in the formula is that the income figure used should be consistent with the base to which it is applied. Notice that the base (i.e., denominator) consists of *operating assets.* Thus, to be consistent we use net operating income in the numerator.

Operating assets include cash, accounts receivable, inventory, plant and equipment, and all other assets held for productive use in the organization. Examples of assets that would not be included in the operating assets category, (i.e., examples of nonoperating assets) would include land held for future use, an investment in another company, or a factory building rented to someone else. The operating assets base used in the formula is typically computed as the average of the operating assets between the beginning and the end of the year.

Plant and Equipment: Net Book Value or Gross Cost?

A major issue in ROI computations is the dollar amount of plant and equipment that should be included in the operating assets base. To illustrate the problem involved, assume that a company reports the following amounts for plant and equipment on its balance sheet:

Plant and equipment	$3,000,000
Less accumulated depreciation	900,000
Net book value	$2,100,000

What dollar amount of plant and equipment should the company include with its operating assets in computing ROI? One widely used approach is to include only the plant and equipment's *net book value*—that is, the plant's original cost less accumulated depreciation ($2,100,000 in the example above). A second approach is to ignore depreciation and include the plant's entire *gross cost* in the operating assets base ($3,000,000 in the example above). Both of these approaches are used in actual practice, even though they will obviously yield very different operating asset and ROI figures.

The following arguments can be raised for using net book value to measure operating assets and for using gross cost to measure operating assets in ROI computations:

Arguments for Using Net Book Value to Measure Operating Assets in ROI Computations:

1. The net book value method is consistent with how plant and equipment are reported on the balance sheet (i.e., cost less accumulated depreciation to date).
2. The net book value method is consistent with the computation of operating income, which includes depreciation as an operating expense.

Arguments for Using Gross Cost to Measure Operating Assets in ROI Computations:

1. The gross cost method eliminates both the age of equipment and the method of depreciation as factors in ROI computations. (Under the net book value method, ROI will tend to increase over time as net book value declines due to depreciation.)
2. The gross cost method does not discourage replacement of old, worn-out equipment. (Under the net book value method, replacing fully depreciated equipment with new equipment can have a dramatic, adverse effect on ROI.)

Managers generally view consistency as the most important of the considerations above. As a result, a majority of companies use the net book value approach in ROI computations. In this text, we will also use the net book value approach unless a specific exercise or problem directs otherwise.

Controlling the Rate of Return

> **Learning Objective 3**
> Show how changes in sales, expenses, and assets affect an organization's ROI.

When we first defined the return on investment, we used the following formula:

$$\text{ROI} = \frac{\text{Net operating income}}{\text{Average operating assets}}$$

We can modify this formula slightly by introducing sales as follows:

$$\text{ROI} = \frac{\text{Net operating income}}{\text{Sales}} \times \frac{\text{Sales}}{\text{Average operating assets}}$$

The first term on the right-hand side of the equation is the *margin*, which is defined as follows:

$$\text{Margin} = \frac{\text{Net operating income}}{\text{Sales}}$$

The **margin** is a measure of management's ability to control operating expenses in relation to sales. The lower the operating expenses per dollar of sales, the higher the margin earned.

The second term on the right-hand side of the preceding equation is *turnover* which is defined as follows:

$$\text{Turnover} = \frac{\text{Sales}}{\text{Average operating assets}}$$

Turnover is a measure of the sales that are generated for each dollar invested in operating assets.

Exhibit 10–2
Elements of
Return on
Investment
(ROI)

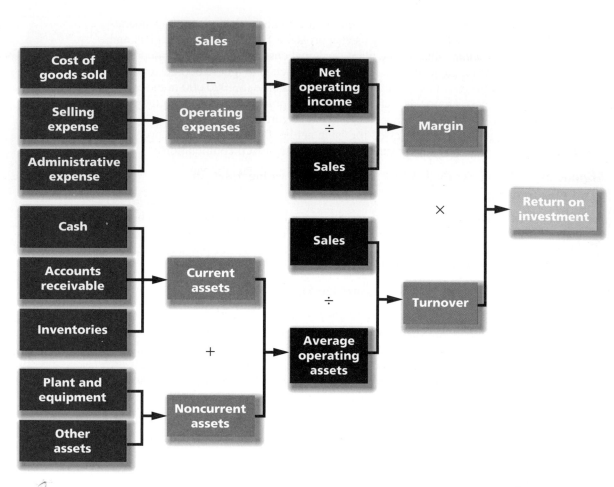

The following alternative form of the ROI formula, which we will use most frequently, combines margin and turnover:

$$\text{ROI} = \text{Margin} \times \text{Turnover}$$

Which formula for ROI should be used—the original one stated in terms of net operating income and average operating assets or this one stated in terms of margin and turnover? Either can be used—they will always give the same answer. However, the margin and turnover formulation provides some additional insights.

Some managers tend to focus too much on margin and ignore turnover. To some degree at least, the margin can be a valuable indicator of a manager's performance. Standing alone, however, it overlooks one very crucial area of a manager's responsibility—the investment in operating assets. Excessive funds tied up in operating assets, which depresses turnover, can be just as much of a drag on profitability as excessive operating expenses, which depresses margin. One of the advantages of ROI as a performance measure is that it forces the manager to control the investment in operating assets as well as to control expenses and the margin.

Du Pont pioneered the ROI concept and recognized the importance of looking at both margin and turnover in assessing the performance of a manager. The ROI formula is now widely used as the key measure of the performance of an investment center. The ROI formula blends together many aspects of the manager's responsibilities into a single figure that can be compared to the returns of competing investment centers, the returns of other firms in the industry, and to the past returns of the investment center itself.

Du Pont also developed the diagram that appears in Exhibit 10–2. This exhibit helps managers understand how they can control ROI. An investment center manager can increase ROI in basically three ways:

1. Increase sales.
2. Reduce expenses.
3. Reduce assets.

To illustrate how the rate of return can be improved by each of these three actions, consider how the manager of the Monthaven Burger Grill is evaluated. Burger Grill is a small chain of upscale casual restaurants that has been rapidly adding outlets via franchising. The Monthaven franchise is owned by a group of local surgeons who have little time to devote to management and little expertise in business matters. Therefore, they delegate operating decisions—including decisions concerning investment in operating assets such as inventories—to a professional manager they have hired. The manager is evaluated largely based on the ROI the franchise generates.

The following data represent the results of operations for the most recent month:

Net operating income	$10,000
Sales	100,000
Average operating assets	50,000

The rate of return generated by the Monthaven Burger Grill investment center is as follows:

$$\text{ROI} = \text{Margin} \times \text{Turnover}$$

$$= \frac{\text{Net operating income}}{\text{Sales}} \times \frac{\text{Sales}}{\text{Average operating assets}}$$

$$= \frac{\$10,000}{\$100,000} \times \frac{\$100,000}{\$50,000}$$

$$= 10\% \times 2 = 20\%$$

As we stated above, to improve the ROI figure, the manager can (1) increase sales, (2) reduce expenses, or (3) reduce the operating assets.

Approach 1: Increase Sales   Assume that the manager of the Monthaven Burger Grill is able to increase sales from $100,000 to $110,000. Assume further that either because of good cost control or because some costs in the company are fixed, the net operating income increases even more rapidly, going from $10,000 to $12,000 per period. Assume that the operating assets remain constant. Then the new ROI would be:

$$\text{ROI} = \frac{\$12,000}{\$110,000} \times \frac{\$110,000}{\$50,000}$$

$$= 10.91\% \times 2.2 = 24\% \text{ (as compared to 20\% above)}$$

Approach 2: Reduce Expenses   Assume that the manager of the Monthaven Burger Grill is able to reduce expenses by $1,000 so that net operating income increases from $10,000 to $11,000. Assume that both sales and operating assets remain constant. Then the new ROI would be:

$$\text{ROI} = \frac{\$11,000}{\$100,000} \times \frac{\$100,000}{\$50,000}$$

$$= 11\% \times 2 = 22\% \text{ (as compared to 20\% above)}$$

Approach 3: Reduce Assets   Assume that the manager of the Monthaven Burger Grill is able to reduce operating assets from $50,000 to $40,000, but that sales and net operating income remain unchanged. Then the new ROI would be:

$$\text{ROI} = \frac{\$10,000}{\$100,000} \times \frac{\$100,000}{\$40,000}$$

$$= 10\% \times 2.5 = 25\% \text{ (as compared to 20\% above)}$$

A clear understanding of these three approaches to improving the ROI figure is critical to the effective management of an investment center. We will now look at each approach in more detail.

Increase Sales

When first looking at the ROI formula, one is inclined to think that the sales figure is neutral, since it appears as the denominator in the margin computation and as the numerator in the turnover computation. We *could* cancel out the sales figure, but we don't do so for two reasons. First, this would tend to draw attention away from the fact that the rate of return is a function of *two* variables, margin and turnover. And second, it would tend to conceal the fact that a change in sales can affect both the margin and the turnover in an organization. A change in sales can affect the *margin* if expenses increase or decrease at a different rate than sales. For example, a company may be able to keep a tight control on its costs as its sales go up, with the result that net operating income increases more rapidly than sales and increases the margin. Or a company may have fixed expenses that remain constant as sales go up, resulting in an increase in the net operating income and in the margin. Either (or both) of these factors could have been responsible for the increase in the margin percentage from 10% to 10.91% illustrated in approach 1 above.

Further, a change in sales can affect the *turnover* if sales either increase or decrease without a proportionate increase or decrease in the operating assets. In the first approach above, for example, sales increased from $100,000 to $110,000, but the operating assets remained unchanged. As a result, the turnover increased from 2 to 2.2 for the period.

Reduce Expenses

Often the easiest route to increased profitability and to a stronger ROI figure is to simply cut the "fat" out of an organization through a concerted effort to control expenses. When margins begin to be squeezed, this is generally the first line of attack by a manager. Discretionary fixed costs (that is, fixed costs that arise from annual decisions by management to spend in certain fixed cost areas) usually come under scrutiny first, and various programs are either curtailed or eliminated in an effort to cut costs. Managers must be careful, however, not to cut out muscle and bone along with the fat. Also, they must remember that frequent cost-cutting binges can destroy morale. Most managers now agree that it is best to stay "lean and mean" all of the time.

Reduce Operating Assets

Managers have always been sensitive to the need to control sales, operating expenses, and operating margins. However, they have not always been equally sensitive to the need to control investment in operating assets. Firms that have adopted the ROI approach to measuring managerial performance report that one of the first reactions of investment center managers is to trim their investment in operating assets. Managers soon realize that an excessive investment in operating assets reduces turnover and hurts the ROI. As these managers reduce their investment in operating assets, funds are released that can be used elsewhere in the organization.

How can an investment center manager control the investment in operating assets? One approach is to eliminate unneeded inventory. JIT purchasing and JIT manufacturing have been extremely helpful in reducing inventories of all types, with the result that ROI figures have improved dramatically in some companies. Another approach is to devise various methods of speeding up the collection of receivables. For example, many firms now employ the lockbox technique by which customers in distant states send their payments directly to post office boxes in their area. The funds are received and deposited by a local bank on behalf of the payee firm. This speeds up the collection process, since the payments are not delayed in the postal system. As a result of the speedup in collection, the accounts receivable balance is reduced and the asset turnover is increased.

ROI and the Balanced Scorecard

Simply exhorting managers to increase ROI is not sufficient. Managers who are told to increase ROI will naturally wonder how this is to be accomplished. The Du Pont scheme, which is illustrated in Exhibit 10–2, provides managers with *some* guidance. Generally speaking, ROI can be increased by increasing sales, decreasing costs, and/or decreasing investments in operating assets. However, it may not be obvious to managers how they are supposed to increase sales, decrease costs, and decrease investments in a way that is consistent with the company's strategy. For example, a manager who is given inadequate guidance may cut back on investments that are critical to implementing the company's strategy.

For that reason, as discussed in Chapter 8, when managers are evaluated based on ROI, a balanced scorecard approach is advised. And indeed, ROI, or residual income (discussed below), is typically included as one of the financial performance measures on a company's balanced scorecard. As briefly discussed in Chapter 8, the balanced scorecard provides a way of communicating a company's strategy to managers throughout the organization. The scorecard indicates *how* the company intends to improve its financial performance. A well-constructed balanced scorecard should answer questions like: "What internal business processes should be improved?" and "Which customer should be targeted and how will they be attracted and retained at a profit?" In short, a well-constructed balanced scorecard can provide managers with a road map that indicates how the company intends to increase its ROI. In the absence of such a road map of the company's strategy, managers may have difficulty understanding what they are supposed to do to increase ROI and they may work at cross-purposes rather than in harmony with the overall strategy of the company.

Criticisms of ROI

Although ROI is widely used in evaluating performance, it is not a perfect tool. The method is subject to the following criticisms:

1. Just telling managers to increase ROI may not be enough. Managers may not know how to increase ROI; they may increase ROI in a way that is inconsistent with the company's strategy; or they may take actions that increase ROI in the short run but harm the company in the long run (such as cutting back on research and development). This is why ROI is best used as part of a balanced scorecard as discussed above. A balanced scorecard can provide concrete guidance to managers, make it more likely that actions taken are consistent with the company's strategy, and reduce the likelihood that short-run performance will be enhanced at the expense of long-term performance.
2. A manager who takes over a business segment typically inherits many committed costs over which the manager has no control. These committed costs make it difficult to fairly assess the performance of the manager relative to other managers.
3. As discussed in the next section, a manager who is evaluated based on ROI may reject investment opportunities that are profitable for the company as a whole.

Store Manager

you decide

You were recently hired as the manager of a chain of jewelry stores that are located in downtown Chicago. You are excited about the high level of autonomy that you have been given to run the stores but are nervous because you've heard rumors that the previous manager was let go because the return on investment (ROI) of the stores was unacceptable. What steps should you consider to improve ROI?

Residual Income—Another Measure of Performance

Concept 10–2

Another approach to measuring an investment center's performance focuses on a concept known as *residual income*. **Residual income** is the net operating income that an investment center earns above the minimum required return on its operating assets. **Economic value added (EVA)** is a similar concept that differs in some details from residual income.[3] For example, under the economic value added concept, funds used for research and development are treated as investments rather than as expenses.[4] However, for our purposes, we will not draw any distinction between residual income and economic value added.

When residual income or economic value added is used to measure performance, the objective is to maximize the total amount of residual income or economic value added, not to maximize overall ROI. Organizations as diverse as Coca-Cola, Quaker Oats, the United States Postal Service, Varity Corporation, and Husky Injection Molding have embraced some version of residual income in recent years.

in business today Rankings Based on EVA

Economic value added (EVA) can be used to evaluate the performance of entire companies as well as segments of companies, such as divisions. *Fortune* magazine publishes an annual ranking of companies based on EVA. In the 1999 ranking, the companies with the largest EVA were Philip Morris, General Electric, Intel, and Merck—each with economic value added in excess of $4 billion for the year. In contrast, the biggest wealth destroyer was General Motors, with a *negative* economic value added for the year of more than $5.5 billion. A similar study carried out by *CFO Asia* magazine for Asian companies found that EVA ranged from a high of $764 million at CLP Holdings to a low of negative $988 million at Cheung Kong Holdings.

Sources: Shawn Tully, "America's Wealth Creators," *Fortune*, November 22, 1999, pp. 275–284; and Tom Leander, "Value Champs," *CFO Asia*, November 1999, pp. 26–37.

For purposes of illustration, consider the following data for an investment center—the Ketchican Division of Alaskan Marine Services Corporation.

ALASKAN MARINE SERVICES CORPORATION
Ketchican Division
Basic Data for Performance Evaluation

Average operating assets	$100,000
Net operating income	$ 20,000
Minimum required rate of return	15%

Alaskan Marine Services Corporation has long had a policy of evaluating investment center managers based on ROI, but it is considering a switch to residual income. The con-

---

[3]The basic idea underlying residual income and economic value added has been around for over 100 years. In recent years, economic value added has been popularized and trademarked by the consulting firm Stern, Stewart & Co.

[4]Over 100 different adjustments could be made for deferred taxes, LIFO reserves, provisions for future liabilities, mergers and acquisitions, gains or losses due to changes in accounting rules, operating leases, and other accounts, but most companies make only a few. For further details, see John O'Hanlon and Ken Peasnell, "Wall Street's Contribution to Management Accounting: The Stern Stewart EVA® Financial Management System," *Management Accounting Research* 9, 1998, pp. 421–444.

troller of the company, who is in favor of the change to residual income, has provided the following table that shows how the performance of the division would be evaluated under each of the two methods:

ALASKAN MARINE SERVICES CORPORATION Ketchican Division	Alternative Performance Measures	
	ROI	**Residual Income**
Average operating assets (a)	$100,000	$100,000
Net operating income (b)	$ 20,000	$ 20,000
ROI, (b) ÷ (a)	20%	
Minimum required return (15% × $100,000)		15,000
Residual income		$ 5,000

The reasoning underlying the residual income calculation is straightforward. The company is able to earn a rate of return of at least 15% on its investments. Since the company has invested $100,000 in the Ketchican Division in the form of operating assets, the company should be able to earn at least $15,000 (15% × $100,000) on this investment. Since the Ketchican Division's net operating income is $20,000, the residual income above and beyond the minimum required return is $5,000. If residual income is adopted as the performance measure to replace ROI, the manager of the Ketchican Division would be evaluated based on the growth from year to year in residual income.

Flocking to EVA

in business today

According to *Fortune* magazine, "Managers who run their businesses according to the precepts of EVA have hugely increased the value of their companies. Investors who know about EVA, and know which companies are employing it, have grown rich. Little wonder that highly regarded major corporations—Coca-Cola, AT&T, Quaker Oats, Briggs & Stratton, CSX, and many others—are flocking to the concept . . . Here's how Coca-Cola CEO Roberto Goizueta, a champion wealth creator, explained it: 'We raise capital to make concentrate, and sell it at an operating profit. Then we pay the cost of capital. Shareholders pocket the difference.'"

Source: Shawn Tully, "The Real Key to Creating Wealth," *Fortune,* September 20, 1993, pp. 38–50. Copyright © 1993 Time Inc. Reprinted by permission.

Reacting to the Use of EVA

in business today

One study of a sample of companies adopting economic value added as a performance measure found that, relative to companies that did not adopt EVA, these companies "(1) increased their dispositions of assets and decreased their new investment, (2) increased their payouts to shareholders through share repurchases, and (3) used their assets more intensively. These actions are consistent with the strong rate of return discipline associated with the capital charge in residual income-based measures."

Source: James S. Wallace, "Adopting Residual Income-Based Compensation Plans: Do You Get What You Pay For?" *Journal of Accounting and Economics* 24, 1997, pp. 275–300.

Motivation and Residual Income

One of the primary reasons why the controller of Alaskan Marine Services Corporation would like to switch from ROI to residual income has to do with how managers view new investments under the two performance measurement schemes. The residual income approach encourages managers to make investments that are profitable for the entire company but that would be rejected by managers who are evaluated by the ROI formula.

To illustrate this problem, suppose that the manager of the Ketchican Division is considering purchasing a computerized diagnostic machine to aid in servicing marine diesel engines. The machine would cost $25,000 and is expected to generate additional operating income of $4,500 a year. From the standpoint of the company, this would be a good investment since it promises a rate of return of 18% ($4,500 ÷ $25,000), which is in excess of the company's minimum required rate of return of 15%.

If the manager of the Ketchican Division is evaluated based on residual income, she would be in favor of the investment in the diagnostic machine as shown below:

ALASKAN MARINE SERVICES CORPORATION
Ketchican Division
Performance Evaluated Using Residual Income

	Present	New Project	Overall
Average operating assets	$100,000	$25,000	$125,000
Net operating income	$ 20,000	$ 4,500	$ 24,500
Minimum required return	15,000	3,750*	18,750
Residual income	$ 5,000	$ 750	$ 5,750

*$25,000 × 15% = $3,750.

Since the project would increase the residual income of the Ketchican Division, the manager would want to invest in the new diagnostic machine.

Now suppose that the manager of the Ketchican Division is evaluated based on ROI. The effect of the diagnostic machine on the division's ROI is computed below:

ALASKAN MARINE SERVICES CORPORATION
Ketchican Division
Performance Evaluated Using ROI

	Present	New Project	Overall
Average operating assets (a)	$100,000	$25,000	$125,000
Net operating income (b)	$20,000	$4,500	$24,500
ROI, (b) ÷ (a)	20%	18%	19.6%

The new project reduces the division's ROI from 20% to 19.6%. This happens because the 18% rate of return on the new diagnostic machine, while above the company's 15% minimum rate of return, is below the division's present ROI of 20%. Therefore, the new diagnostic machine would drag the division's ROI down even though it would be a good investment from the standpoint of the company as a whole. If the manager of the division is evaluated based on ROI, she will be reluctant to even propose such an investment.

Basically, a manager who is evaluated based on ROI will reject any project whose rate of return is below the division's current ROI even if the rate of return on the project is above the minimum required rate of return for the entire company. In contrast, any project whose rate of return is above the minimum required rate of return for the company will result in an increase in residual income. Since it is in the best interests of the company as a whole to accept any project whose rate of return is above the minimum required rate of return, managers who are evaluated based on residual income will tend to make better decisions concerning investment projects than managers who are evaluated based on ROI.

Shoring Up Return on Capital

in business today

Manitowic Co. is located in Manitowic, Wisconsin, a town on the shores of Lake Michigan. The company makes construction cranes, ice machines, and Great Lakes shipping vessels. Over the past four years, the company's share price has increased over 500%. Part of this increase is attributed to the company's adoption of EVA. The company has slashed headquarters staff from 127 to 30 people. Inventories have been cut by $50 million—from $84 million down to $34 million. Divisions that fail to cut excess assets get no bonus. Before the adoption of EVA, the company's return on total capital was 10.5%. It is now 22%.

Source: Michelle Conlin, "Hoisting Job," *Forbes*, April 19, 1999, pp. 152, 156.

Trimming Inventories with EVA

in business today

Quaker Oats provides an example of how use of EVA can change the way a company operates. "Until Quaker adopted the concept [of EVA] in 1991, its businesses had one overriding goal—increasing quarterly earnings. To do it, they guzzled capital. They offered sharp price discounts at the end of each quarter, so plants ran overtime turning out huge shipments of Gatorade, Rice-A-Roni, 100% Natural Cereal, and other products. Managers led the late rush, since their bonuses depended on raising operating profits each quarter . . . Pumping up sales requires many warehouses (capital) to hold vast temporary inventories (more capital). But who cared? Quaker's operating businesses paid no charge for capital in internal accounting, so they barely noticed. It took EVA to spotlight the problem . . . One plant has trimmed inventories from $15 million to $9 million, even though it is producing much more, and Quaker has closed 5 of 15 warehouses, saving $6 million a year in salaries and capital costs."

Source: Shawn Tully, "The Real Key to Creating Wealth," *Fortune,* September 20, 1993, pp. 38–50. Copyright © 1993 Time Inc. Reprinted by permission.

Divisional Comparison and Residual Income

The residual income approach has one major disadvantage. It can't be used to compare the performance of divisions of different sizes. You would expect larger divisions to have more residual income than smaller divisions, not necessarily because they are better managed but simply because of the bigger numbers involved.

As an example, consider the following residual income computations for Division X and Division Y:

	Division	
	X	Y
Average operating assets (a)	$1,000,000	$250,000
Net operating income	$ 120,000	$ 40,000
Minimum required return: 10% × (a)	100,000	25,000
Residual income	$ 20,000	$ 15,000

Observe that Division X has slightly more residual income than Division Y, but that Division X has $1,000,000 in operating assets as compared to only $250,000 in operating assets for Division Y. Thus, Division X's greater residual income is probably more a result of its size than the quality of its management. In fact, it appears that the smaller division is better managed, since it has been able to generate nearly as much residual income with only one-fourth as much in operating assets to work with. This problem can be reduced to some degree by focusing on the percentage change in residual income from year to year rather than on the absolute amount of the residual income.

Transfer Prices

A problem arises in evaluating segments of a company when one segment provides a good or service to another segment. For example, the truck division of Ford provides trucks to other Ford divisions to use in their operations such as the division that markets passenger cars. If both the truck and passenger car divisions are evaluated based on their profits, disputes are likely to arise over the *transfer price* charged for the trucks used by the passenger car division. A **transfer price** is the price charged when one segment of an organization provides a good or service to another segment in the organization. The selling segment, in this case the truck division, would naturally like the transfer price to be as high as possible whereas the buying segment, in this case the passenger car division, would like the price to be as low as possible.

   The question of what transfer price to charge is one of the most difficult problems in managerial accounting. The objective in transfer pricing should be to motivate the segment managers to do what is in the best interests of the overall organization. For example, if we want the manager of the passenger car division of Ford to make decisions that are in the best interests of the overall organization, the transfer price charged to the passenger car division for trucks must be the cost incurred by the entire organization up to the point of transfer—including any opportunity costs. If the transfer price is less than this cost, then the manager of the passenger car division will think that the cost of the trucks is lower than it really is and will tend to demand more trucks than would be optimal for the entire company. If the transfer price is greater than the cost incurred by the entire organization up to the point of the transfer, then the passenger car division manager will think the cost of the trucks is higher than it really is and will tend to demand fewer trucks than would be optimal for the entire organization. While this principle may seem clear-cut, as a practical matter, implementing it is very difficult for a variety of reasons. In practice, companies usually adopt a simplified transfer pricing policy based on variable cost, absorption cost, or market prices. All of these approaches have flaws, which are covered in more advanced texts.

Summary

LO1   Understand the role of cost, profit, and investment centers in a decentralized organization.

A segment is a part of an organization. Segments are often classified as cost, profit, or investment centers. The manager of a cost center has control over cost, but not over revenue or the use of investment funds. The manager of a profit center has control over cost and revenue, but not over the use of investment funds. The manager of an investment center has control over cost, revenue, and the use of investment funds.

LO2   Compute the return on investment (ROI).

Return on investment (ROI) is defined to be net operating income divided by average operating assets. Alternatively, it can be defined as the product of margin and turnover, where margin is net operating income divided by sales and turnover is sales divided by average operating assets.

LO3   Show how changes in sales, expenses, and assets affect an organization's ROI.

The relations among sales, expenses, assets, and ROI are complex. The effect of a change in any one variable on the others will depend on the specific circumstances. Nevertheless, an increase in sales often leads to an increase in ROI via the effect of sales on net income. If the organization has significant fixed costs, then a given percentage increase in sales is likely to have an even larger percentage effect on net operating income.

LO4   Compute residual income and understand the strengths and weaknesses of this method of measuring performance.

Residual income is the difference between net operating income and the minimum required return on average operating assets. The minimum required return on average operating assets is computed by applying the minimum rate of return to the average operating assets.

The major advantage of residual income over ROI is that it does not discourage investment in projects whose rates of return are above the minimum required rate of return for the entire organization, but below the segment's current ROI.

Guidance Answers to You Decide and Decision Maker

A FRIEND (p. 409)

It sounds like your friend's business is strongly centralized; that is, she makes all major decisions and takes responsibility for all of the major projects. Not only is your friend spreading herself too thin and burning out as a result, her managers seem to have little, if any, freedom. You might propose that she consider decentralizing the organization.

A strongly decentralized organization in which even the lowest-level managers and employees are free to make decisions may not be the answer, but some degree of decentralization would help the current situation. She would be relieved of much of the daily problem solving and could use the time to concentrate on strategy, higher-level decision-making, and coordinating the activities of her managers. Not only would her managers become more skilled at making effective decisions, they would probably enjoy their jobs more and should be more willing to remain with the company. If your friend is reluctant to make changes, you might suggest that she interview the managers who have left the company. Their comments may help point your friend in the right direction.

STORE MANAGER (p. 417)

Three approaches can be used to increase ROI:

1. Increase sales—An increase in sales will positively impact the margin if expenses increase less than sales. An increase in sales will also affect turnover if there is not a proportionate increase in operating assets.
2. Reduce expenses—This approach is often the first path selected by managers to increase profitability and ROI. You should start by reviewing the stores' discretionary fixed costs (such as advertising). It may be possible to cut some discretionary fixed costs with minimal damage to the long-run goals of the organization. You should also investigate whether there are adequate physical controls over the inventory of jewelry items. Thefts result in an increase in cost of goods sold without a corresponding increase in sales!
3. Reduce operating assets—An excessive investment in operating assets (such as inventory) reduces turnover and hurts ROI. Given the nature of the operations of retail jewelry stores, inventory must be in sufficient quantities at specific times during the year (such as Christmas, Valentine's Day, and Mother's Day) or sales will suffer. However, those levels do not need to be maintained throughout the year.

Review Problem: Return on Investment (ROI) and Residual Income

The Magnetic Imaging Division of Medical Diagnostics, Inc., has reported the following results for last year's operations:

Sales	$25 million
Net operating income	3 million
Average operating assets	10 million

Required:

1. Compute the margin, turnover, and ROI for the Magnetic Imaging Division.
2. Top management of Medical Diagnostics, Inc., has set a minimum required rate of return on average operating assets of 25%. What is the Magnetic Imaging Division's residual income for the year?

SOLUTION TO REVIEW PROBLEM

1. The required calculations appear below:

$$\text{Margin} = \frac{\text{Net operating income, } \$3,000,000}{\text{Sales, } \$25,000,000}$$

$$= 12\%$$

$$\text{Turnover} = \frac{\text{Sales, } \$25,000,000}{\text{Average operating assets, } \$10,000,000}$$

$$= 2.5$$

$$\text{ROI} = \text{Margin} \times \text{Turnover}$$

$$= 12\% \times 2.5$$

$$= 30\%$$

2. The residual income for the Magnetic Imaging Division is computed as follows:

Average operating assets	$10,000,000
Net operating income	$ 3,000,000
Minimum required return (25% × $10,000,000)	2,500,000
Residual income	$ 500,000

Glossary

Common fixed cost   A fixed cost that supports more than one business segment, but is not traceable in whole or in part to any one of the business segments. (p. 411)

Cost center   A business segment whose manager has control over cost but has no control over revenue or the use of investment funds. (p. 409)

Decentralized organization   An organization in which decision-making is not confined to a few top executives but rather is spread throughout the organization. (p. 408)

Economic value added (EVA)   A concept similar to residual income. (p. 418)

Investment center   A business segment whose manager has control over cost and over revenue and that also has control over the use of investment funds. (p. 410)

Margin Net operating income divided by sales. (p. 413)

Net operating income   Income before interest and income taxes have been deducted. (p. 412)

Operating assets   Cash, accounts receivable, inventory, plant and equipment, and all other assets held for productive use in an organization. (p. 412)

Profit center   A business segment whose manager has control over cost and revenue but has no control over the use of investment funds. (p. 410)

Residual income   The net operating income that an investment center earns above the required return on its operating assets. (p. 418)

Responsibility center   Any business segment whose manager has control over cost, revenue, or the use of investment funds. (p. 410)

Return on investment (ROI)   Net operating income divided by average operating assets. It also equals margin multiplied by turnover. (p. 412)

Segment   Any part or activity of an organization about which the manager seeks cost, revenue, or profit data. (p. 409)

Traceable fixed cost   A fixed cost that is incurred because of the existence of a particular business segment. (p. 410)

Transfer price   The price charged when one division or segment provides goods or services to another division or segment of an organization. (p. 422)

Turnover   The amount of sales generated in an investment center for each dollar invested in operating assets. It is computed by dividing sales by the average operating assets figure. (p. 413)

10–1 What is meant by the term *decentralization?*
10–2 What benefits result from decentralization?
10–3 Distinguish between a cost center, a profit center, and an investment center.
10–4 Define a segment of an organization. Give several examples of segments.
10–5 What is meant by the terms *margin* and *turnover?*
10–6 What are the three basic approaches to improving return on investment (ROI)?
10–7 What is meant by residual income?
10–8 In what way can the use of ROI as a performance measure for investment centers lead to bad decisions? How does the residual income approach overcome this problem?
10–9 What is meant by the term *transfer price,* and why are transfer prices needed?

Brief Exercises

BRIEF EXERCISE 10–1   Principles of Decentralization (LO1)
Listed below are a number of terms that are associated with decentralization in organizations.

Cost center	Profit center
Segment	Investment center
Responsibility center	Transfer price
Job satisfaction	

Required:
Fill in the appropriate terms from the above list in the blanks provided.
1. A(n) _____ is a part or activity of an organization about which managers would like cost, revenue, or profit data.
2. Added responsibility and decision-making authority often result in increased _____ .
3. A(n) _____ is a business segment whose manager has control over both cost and revenue, but not over investment funds.
4. When one segment, such as a division of a company, provides goods or services to another segment of the company, the _____ will determine how much revenue the segment recognizes on the transaction.
5. A(n) _____ is a business segment whose manager has control over costs, but not over revenue or investment funds.
6. A(n) _____ is any segment of an organization whose manager has control over cost, revenue, or investment funds.
7. A(n) _____ is a business segment whose manager has control over cost, revenue, and investments in operating assets.

BRIEF EXERCISE 10–2   Compute the Return on Investment (ROI) (LO2)
Alyeska Services Company, a division of a major oil company, provides various services to the operators of the North Slope oil field in Alaska. Data concerning the most recent year appear below:

Sales	$7,500,000
Net operating income	600,000
Average operating assets	5,000,000

Required:
1. Compute the margin for Alyeska Services Company.
2. Compute the turnover for Alyeska Services Company.
3. Compute the return on investment (ROI) for Alyeska Services Company.

BRIEF EXERCISE 10–3   Effects of Changes in Sales, Expenses, and Assets on ROI (LO3)
CommercialServices.com Corporation provides business-to-business services on the Internet. Data concerning the most recent year appear below:

Sales	$3,000,000
Net operating income	150,000
Average operating assets	750,000

Required:

Consider each question below independently. Carry out all computations to two decimal places.
1. Compute the company's return on investment (ROI).
2. The entrepreneur who founded the company is convinced that sales will increase next year by 50% and that net operating income would increase as a result by 200%, with no increase in average operating assets. What would be the company's ROI?
3. The chief financial officer of the company believes a more realistic scenario would be a $1,000,000 increase in sales, requiring a $250,000 increase in average operating assets, with a resulting $200,000 increase in net operating income. What would be the company's ROI in this scenario?

BRIEF EXERCISE 10–4   Residual income (LO4)

Juniper Design Ltd. of Manchester, England, is a company specializing in providing design services to residential developers. Last year the company had net operating income of £600,000 on sales of £3,000,000. The company's average operating assets for the year were £2,800,000 and its minimum required rate of return was 18%. (The currency used in England is the pound sterling, denoted by £.)

Required:

Compute the company's residual income for the year.

Exercises

EXERCISE 10–1   Computing and Interpreting Return on Investment (ROI) (LO2)

Selected operating data for two divisions of Outback Brewing, Ltd., of Australia are given below:

	Division	
	Queensland	New South Wales
Sales	$4,000,000	$7,000,000
Average operating assets	2,000,000	2,000,000
Net operating income	360,000	420,000
Property, plant, and equipment (net)	950,000	800,000

Required:

1. Compute the rate of return for each division using the return on investment (ROI) formula stated in terms of margin and turnover.
2. So far as you can tell from the data, which divisional manager seems to be doing the better job? Why?

EXERCISE 10–2   Contrasting Return on Investment (ROI) and Residual Income (LO2, LO4)

Meiji Isetan Corp. of Japan has two regional divisions with headquarters in Osaka and Yokohama. Selected data on the two divisions follow (in millions of yen, denoted by ¥):

	Division	
	Osaka	Yokohama
Sales	¥3,000,000	¥9,000,000
Net operating income	210,000	720,000
Average operating assets	1,000,000	4,000,000

Required:

1. For each division, compute the return on investment (ROI) in terms of margin and turnover. Where necessary, carry computations to two decimal places.

2. Assume that the company evaluates performance by use of residual income and that the minimum required return for any division is 15%. Compute the residual income for each division.
3. Is Yokohama's greater amount of residual income an indication that it is better managed? Explain.

EXERCISE 10–3   Evaluating New Investments with Return on Investment (ROI) and Residual Income (LO2, LO4)

Selected sales and operating data for three divisions of a multinational structural engineering firm are given below:

	Division		
	Asia	Europe	North America
Sales	$12,000,000	$14,000,000	$25,000,000
Average operating assets	3,000,000	7,000,000	5,000,000
Net operating income	600,000	560,000	800,000
Minimum required rate of return ...	14%	10%	16%

Required:
1. Compute the return on investment (ROI) for each division using the formula stated in terms of margin and turnover.
2. Compute the residual income for each division.
3. Assume that each division is presented with an investment opportunity that would yield a 15% rate of return.
   a. If performance is being measured by ROI, which division or divisions will probably accept the opportunity? Reject? Why?
   b. If performance is being measured by residual income, which division or divisions will probably accept the opportunity? Reject? Why?

EXERCISE 10–4   Effects of Changes in Profits and Assets on Return on Investment (ROI) (LO3)

Pecs Alley is a regional chain of health clubs. The managers of the clubs, who have authority to make investments as needed, are evaluated based largely on return on investment (ROI). The Springfield Club reported the following results for the past year:

Sales	$1,400,000
Net operating income	70,000
Average operating assets	350,000

Required:
The following questions are to be considered independently. Carry out all computations to two decimal places.
1. Compute the club's return on investment (ROI).
2. Assume that the manager of the club is able to increase sales by $70,000 and that, as a result, net operating income increases by $18,200. Further assume that this is possible without any increase in operating assets. What would be the club's return on investment (ROI)?
3. Assume that the manager of the club is able to reduce expenses by $14,000 without any change in sales or operating assets. What would be the club's return on investment (ROI)?
4. Assume that the manager of the club is able to reduce operating assets by $70,000 without any change in sales or net operating income. What would be the club's return on investment (ROI)?

EXERCISE 10–5   Cost-Volume Profit Analysis and Return on Investment (ROI) (LO3)

Posters.com is a small Internet retailer of high-quality posters. The company has $1,000,000 in operating assets and fixed expenses of $150,000 per year. With this level of operating assets and fixed expenses, the company can support sales of up to $3,000,000 per year. The company's contribution margin ratio is 25%, which means that an additional dollar of sales results in additional contribution margin, and net operating income, of 25 cents.

Required:
1. Complete the following table showing the relation between sales and return on investment (ROI).

Sales	Net Operating Income	Average Operating Assets	ROI
$2,500,000	$475,000	$1,000,000	?
2,600,000	?	1,000,000	?
2,700,000	?	1,000,000	?
2,800,000	?	1,000,000	?
2,900,000	?	1,000,000	?
3,000,000	?	1,000,000	?

2. What happens to the company's return on investment (ROI) as the sales increase? Explain.

Problems

CHECK FIGURE
Bravo: 2.5 Turnover

PROBLEM 10–1   Return on Investment (ROI) Relations (LO2)
Provide the missing data in the following tabulation:

	Division		
	Alpha	**Bravo**	**Charlie**
Sales	$?	$11,500,000	$?
Net operating income	?	920,000	210,000
Average operating assets	800,000	?	?
Margin	4%	?	7%
Turnover	5	?	?
Return on investment (ROI)	?	20%	14%

CHECK FIGURE
Company B residual
income: ($40,000)

PROBLEM 10–2   Return on Investment (ROI) and Residual Income Relations (LO2, LO4)
A family friend has asked your help in analyzing the operations of three anonymous companies. Supply the missing data in the tabulation below:

	Company		
	A	**B**	**C**
Sales	$9,000,000	$7,000,000	$4,500,000
Net operating income	?	280,000	?
Average operating assets	3,000,000	?	1,800,000
Return on investment (ROI)	18%	14%	?
Minimum required rate of return:			
Percentage	16%	?	15%
Dollar amount	?	320,000	?
Residual income	?	?	90,000

CHECK FIGURE
(2) Company A margin:
14%

PROBLEM 10–3   Comparison of Performance Using Return on Investment (ROI) (LO2)
Comparative data on three companies in the same industry are given below:

	Company		
	A	**B**	**C**
Sales	$600,000	$500,000	$?
Net operating income	84,000	70,000	?
Average operating assets	300,000	?	1,000,000
Margin	?	?	3.5%
Turnover	?	?	2
ROI	?	7%	?

Required:
1. What advantages can you see in breaking down the ROI computation into two separate elements, margin and turnover?
2. Fill in the missing information above, and comment on the relative performance of the three companies in as much detail as the data permit. Make *specific recommendations* on steps to be taken to improve the return on investment, where needed.

(Adapted from National Association of Accountants, *Research Report No. 35,* p. 34)

PROBLEM 10–4   Return on Investment (ROI) and Residual Income (LO2, LO4)
Financial data for Joel de Paris, Inc., for last year follow:

CHECK FIGURE
(1) ROI, 25%

JOEL DE PARIS, INC.
Balance Sheet

	Ending Balance	Beginning Balance
Assets		
Cash	$ 120,000	$ 140,000
Accounts receivable	530,000	450,000
Inventory	380,000	320,000
Plant and equipment, net	620,000	680,000
Investment in Buisson, S.A.	280,000	250,000
Land (undeveloped)	170,000	180,000
Total assets	$2,100,000	$2,020,000
Liabilities and Stockholders' Equity		
Accounts payable	$ 310,000	$ 360,000
Long-term debt	1,500,000	1,500,000
Stockholders' equity	290,000	160,000
Total liabilities and stockholders' equity	$2,100,000	$2,020,000

JOEL DE PARIS, INC.
Income Statement

Sales		$4,050,000
Less operating expenses		3,645,000
Net operating income		405,000
Less interest and taxes:		
Interest expense	$ 150,000	
Tax expense	110,000	260,000
Net income		$ 145,000

The company paid dividends of $15,000 last year. The "Investment in Buisson, S.A.," on the balance sheet represents an investment in the stock of another company.

Required:
1. Compute the company's margin, turnover, and ROI for last year.
2. The board of directors of Joel de Paris, Inc., has set a minimum required return of 15%. What was the company's residual income last year?

PROBLEM 10–5   Return on Investment (ROI) and Residual Income (LO2, LO4)
"I know headquarters wants us to add on that new product line," said Dell Havasi, manager of Billings Company's Office Products Division. "But I want to see the numbers before I make any move. Our division has led the company for three years, and I don't want any letdown."

Billings Company is a decentralized organization with five autonomous divisions. The divisions are evaluated on the basis of the return that they are able to generate on invested assets, with year-end bonuses given to the divisional managers who have the highest ROI figures. Operating results for the company's Office Products Division for the most recent year are given below:

CHECK FIGURE
(1b) Total ROI: 19.2%

Sales	$10,000,000
Less variable expenses	6,000,000
Contribution margin	4,000,000
Less fixed expenses	3,200,000
Net operating income	$ 800,000
Divisional operating assets	$ 4,000,000

The company had an overall ROI of 15% last year (considering all divisions). The Office Products Division has an opportunity to add a new product line that would require an additional investment in operating assets of $1,000,000. The cost and revenue characteristics of the new product line per year would be:

Sales	$2,000,000
Variable expenses	60% of sales
Fixed expenses	$640,000

Required:
1. Compute the Office Products Division's ROI for the most recent year; also compute the ROI as it will appear if the new product line is added.
2. If you were in Dell Havasi's position, would you be inclined to accept or reject the new product line? Explain.
3. Why do you suppose headquarters is anxious for the Office Products Division to add the new product line?
4. Suppose that the company views a return of 12% on invested assets as being the minimum that any division should earn and that performance is evaluated by the residual income approach.
   a. Compute the Office Products Division's residual income for the most recent year; also compute the residual income as it will appear if the new product line is added.
   b. Under these circumstances, if you were in Dell Havasi's position, would you accept or reject the new product line? Explain.

CHECK FIGURE
(3) ROI: 19.6%
(6) ROI: 16.3%

PROBLEM 10–6   Return on Investment (ROI) Analysis (LO2, LO3)
The income statement for Huerra Company for last year is given below:

	Total	Unit
Sales	$4,000,000	$80.00
Less variable expenses	2,800,000	56.00
Contribution margin	1,200,000	24.00
Less fixed expenses	840,000	16.80
Net operating income	360,000	7.20
Less income taxes @ 30%	108,000	2.16
Net income	$ 252,000	$ 5.04

The company had average operating assets of $2,000,000 during the year.

Required:
1. Compute the company's ROI for the period using the ROI formula stated in terms of margin and turnover.

For each of the following questions, indicate whether the margin and turnover will increase, decrease, or remain unchanged as a result of the events described, and then compute the new ROI figure. Consider each question separately, starting in each case from the data used to compute the original ROI in (1) above.

2. By use of just-in-time (JIT), the company is able to reduce the average level of inventory by $400,000. (The released funds are used to pay off short-term creditors.)
3. The company achieves a cost savings of $32,000 per year by using less costly materials.
4. The company issues bonds and uses the proceeds to purchase $500,000 in machinery and equipment. Interest on the bonds is $60,000 per year. Sales remain unchanged. The new, more efficient equipment reduces production costs by $20,000 per year.
5. As a result of a more intense effort by salespeople, sales are increased by 20%; operating assets remain unchanged.
6. Obsolete items of inventory carried on the records at a cost of $40,000 are scrapped and written off as a loss since they are unsalable.
7. The company uses $200,000 of cash (received on accounts receivable) to repurchase and retire some of its common stock.

PROBLEM 10–7   Return on Investment (ROI); Residual Income; Decentralization (LO1, LO2, LO4)

CHECK FIGURE
(1b) Residual income:
$499,200

Raddington Industries produces tool and die machinery for manufacturers. The company expanded vertically several years ago by acquiring Reigis Steel Company, one of its suppliers of alloy steel plates. Raddington decided to maintain Reigis' separate identity and therefore established the Reigis Steel Division as one of its investment centers.

Raddington evaluates its divisions on the basis of ROI. Management bonuses are also based on ROI. All investments in operating assets are expected to earn a minimum rate of return of 11%.

Reigis' ROI has ranged from 14% to 17% since it was acquired by Raddington. During the past year, Reigis had an investment opportunity that would yield an estimated rate of return of 13%. Reigis' management decided against the investment because it believed the investment would decrease the division's overall ROI.

Last year's income statement for Reigis Steel Division is given below. The division's operating assets employed were $12,960,000 at the end of the year, which represents an 8% increase over the previous year-end balance.

REIGIS STEEL DIVISION Divisional Income Statement For the Year Ended December 31		
Sales		$31,200,000
Cost of goods sold		16,500,000
Gross margin		14,700,000
Less operating expenses:		
Selling expenses	$5,620,000	
Administrative expenses	7,208,000	12,828,000
Net operating income		$1,872,000

Required:
1. Compute the following performance measures for the Reigis Steel Division:
   a. ROI. (Remember, ROI is based on the *average* operating assets, computed from the beginning-of-year and end-of-year balances.) State ROI in terms of margin and turnover.
   b. Residual income.
2. Would the management of Reigis Steel Division have been more likely to accept the investment opportunity it had last year if residual income were used as a performance measure instead of ROI? Explain.
3. The Reigis Steel Division is a separate investment center within Raddington Industries. Identify the items Reigis must be free to control if it is to be evaluated fairly by either the ROI or residual income performance measures.

(CMA, adapted)

Building Your Skills

CHECK FIGURE
(1) Margin: 7%
(4) Total ROI: 16.4%

ANALYTICAL THINKING (LO2, LO3, LO4)

The Valve Division of Bendix, Inc., produces a small valve that is used by various companies as a component part in their products. Bendix, Inc., operates its divisions as autonomous units, giving its divisional managers great discretion in pricing and other decisions. Each division is expected to generate a rate of return of at least 14% on its operating assets. The Valve Division has average operating assets of $700,000. The valves are sold for $5 each. Variable costs are $3 per valve, and fixed costs total $462,000 per year. The division has a capacity of 300,000 valves each year.

Required:
1. How many valves must the Valve Division sell each year to generate the desired rate of return on its assets?
   a. What is the margin earned at this level of sales?
   b. What is the turnover at this level of sales?
2. Assume that the Valve Division's current ROI is just equal to the minimum required 14%. In order to increase the division's ROI, the divisional manager wants to increase the selling price per valve by 4%. Market studies indicate that an increase in the selling price would cause sales to drop by 20,000 units each year. However, operating assets could be reduced by $50,000 due to decreased needs for accounts receivable and inventory. Compute the margin, turnover, and ROI if these changes are made.
3. Refer to the original data. Assume again that the Valve Division's current ROI is just equal to the minimum required 14%. Rather than increase the selling price, the sales manager wants to reduce the selling price per valve by 4%. Market studies indicate that this would fill the plant to capacity. In order to carry the greater level of sales, however, operating assets would increase by $50,000. Compute the margin, turnover, and ROI if these changes are made.
4. Refer to the original data. Assume that the normal volume of sales is 280,000 valves each year at a price of $5 per valve. Another division of the company is currently purchasing 20,000 valves each year from an overseas supplier, at a price of $4.25 per valve. The manager of the Valve Division has adamantly refused to meet this price, pointing out that it would result in a loss for his division:

Selling price per valve		$4.25
Cost per valve:		
Variable	$3.00	
Fixed ($462,000 ÷ 300,000 valves)	1.54	4.54
Net loss per valve		$(0.29)

The manager of the Valve Division also points out that the normal $5 selling price barely allows his division the required 14% rate of return. "If we take on some business at only $4.25 per unit, then our ROI is obviously going to suffer," he reasons, "and maintaining that ROI figure is the key to my future. Besides, taking on these extra units would require us to increase our operating assets by at least $50,000 due to the larger inventories and receivables we would be carrying." If the manager of the Valve Division accepts the transfer price of $4.25 for 20,000 units, how would that decision impact the Valve Division's ROI? Should the manager of the Valve Division accept the price of $4.25 per valve? Why or why not?

COMMUNICATING IN PRACTICE (LO1, LO4)

How do the performance measurement and compensation systems of service firms compare with those of manufacturers? To study one well-run service-oriented business, ask the manager of your local McDonald's if he or she could spend some time discussing the performance measures that the company uses to evaluate store managers and how the performance measures tie in with their compensation.

Required:
After asking the following questions, write a brief memorandum to your instructor that summarizes what you discovered during your interview with the manager of the franchise.
1. What are McDonald's goals, that is, the broad, long-range plans of the company (e.g., to increase market share)?
2. What performance measures are used to help motivate the store managers and monitor progress toward achieving the corporation's goals?
3. Are the performance measures consistent with the store manager's compensation plan?

TAKING IT TO THE NET

As you know, the World Wide Web is a medium that is constantly evolving. Sites come and go, and change without notice. To enable periodic update of site addresses, this problem has been posted to the textbook website (www.mhhe.com/folk1e). After accessing the site, enter the Student Center and select this chapter. Select and complete the Taking It to the Net problem.

TEAMWORK IN ACTION (LO4)

Residual income and economic value added are becoming increasingly popular as useful approaches to measuring an investment center's performance. Why?

Required:

Break into teams and discuss the primary reason that companies would change from ROI to a residual income approach. Ensure that all members of the team understand and agree with the team's consensus. Each and every member of the team should be prepared to present the team's conclusion in a class discussion.

Chapter Eleven

Relevant Costs for Decision Making

Chapter Outline

Decision Feature **Getting the Customer Involved**

Special orders are one-time orders. Generally, managers agree to accept special orders that generate additional profits (referred to as incremental net operating income in this chapter) and reject special orders that do not. However, managers sometimes accept a special order that is unprofitable if they believe that the special order will lead to additional future sales of normal items to a customer. This is often the case for book retailers, who can usually afford to stock only a small percentage of the books that are in print.

Processing a special book order requires a lot of work—an employee must locate and order the book from a publisher and then call the customer when it arrives. Special orders are also costly because they often require special shipping and quantity discounts are not available. Moreover, special orders are risky since the customer may never come in to pick up and pay for a book that was ordered. Even so, many book retailers take special orders because they count on an increase in customer loyalty. Canada's leading bookseller, Chapters Inc. (www.chaptersinc.com), has taken a different approach.

Chapters Inc. operates more than 200 traditional bookstores (averaging 2,700 square feet in size) and 70 superstores (ranging in size from 16,000 to 46,000 square feet) across Canada. The company also owns 70% of Chapters Online (www.chapters.ca), an online e-tailer of books and related products. In addition, realizing that many customers do not have Internet access and/or prefer the experience of visiting a bookstore, Chapters has installed e-commerce kiosks in each of its superstores in cooperation with Chapters Online.

Chapters' customers are now able to check the availability of a book using the in-store kiosks, which access a real-time database. If the title is in the store, the customer is directed to the appropriate shelf. If the book is not in stock, the customer can order the book at the kiosk. The kiosks overcome two of the major problems relating to special orders of books discussed above. First, the process is no longer labor-intensive. Customers special order their own books, which are shipped directly to them. Second, rather than being risky, special orders at the kiosks immediately generate cash for the company. The customer either pays online at the kiosk using a credit card or at the register using cash at the time the order is placed. The decision to accept or reject special orders is no longer the issue it once was for the managers of the Chapters superstores and Rick Segal, president and chief operating officer of Chapters Online, claims that the costs of the kiosks were recovered within six months.

Source: Chapters Inc. website, August 2000; John Berry, "Kiosks Take Special Orders," *Internetweek*, May 8, 2000, p. 51 (3 pages). Used with permission, CMP Media Inc.

Making decisions is one of the basic functions of a

manager. Managers are constantly faced with problems of deciding what products to sell, what production methods to use, whether to make or buy component parts, what prices to charge, what channels of distribution to use, whether to accept special orders at special prices, and so forth. Decision-making is often a difficult task that is complicated by the existence of numerous alternatives and massive amounts of data, only some of which may be relevant.

Every decision involves choosing from among at least two alternatives. In making a decision, the costs and benefits of one alternative must be compared to the costs and benefits of other alternatives. Costs that differ between alternatives are called **relevant costs.** Distinguishing between relevant and irrelevant cost and benefit data is critical for two reasons. First, irrelevant data can be ignored and need not be analyzed. This can save decision makers tremendous amounts of time and effort. Second, bad decisions can easily result from erroneously including irrelevant cost and benefit data when analyzing alternatives. To be successful in decision-making, managers must be able to tell the difference between relevant and irrelevant data and must be able to correctly use the relevant data in analyzing alternatives. The purpose of this chapter is to develop these skills by illustrating their use in a wide range of decision-making situations. We hasten to add that these decision-making skills are as important in your personal life as they are to managers. After completing your study of the material in this chapter, you should be able to think more clearly about decisions in all facets of your life.

Cost Concepts for Decision-Making

Four cost terms discussed in Chapter 1 are particularly applicable to this chapter. These terms are *differential costs, incremental costs, opportunity costs,* and *sunk costs.* You may find it helpful to turn back to Chapter 1 and refresh your memory concerning these terms before reading on.

Identifying Relevant Costs and Benefits

Only those costs and benefits that differ in total between alternatives are relevant in a decision. If a cost will be the same regardless of the alternative selected, then the decision has no effect on the cost and it can be ignored. For example, if you are trying to decide whether to go to a movie or to rent a videotape for the evening, the rent on your apartment is irrelevant. Whether you go to a movie or rent a videotape, the rent on your apartment will be exactly the same and is therefore irrelevant in the decision. On the other hand, the cost of the movie ticket and the cost of renting the videotape would be relevant in the decision since they are *avoidable costs.*

An **avoidable cost** is a cost that can be eliminated in whole or in part by choosing one alternative over another. By choosing the alternative of going to the movie, the cost of renting the videotape can be avoided. By choosing the alternative of renting the videotape, the cost of the movie ticket can be avoided. Therefore, the cost of the movie ticket and the cost of renting the videotape are both avoidable costs. On the other hand, the rent on the apartment is not an avoidable cost of either alternative. You would continue to rent your apartment under either alternative. Avoidable costs are relevant costs. Unavoidable costs are irrelevant costs.

Two broad categories of costs are never relevant in decisions. These irrelevant costs are:

1. Sunk costs.
2. Future costs that do not differ between the alternatives.

As we learned in Chapter 1, a **sunk cost** is a cost that has already been incurred and that cannot be avoided regardless of what a manager decides to do. Sunk costs are always the same, no matter what alternatives are being considered, and they are therefore always irrelevant and should be ignored. On the other hand, future costs that do differ between alternatives *are* relevant. For example, when deciding whether to go to a movie or rent a videotape, the cost of buying a movie ticket and the cost of renting a videotape have not yet been incurred. These are future costs that differ between alternatives when the decision is being made and therefore are relevant.

Along with sunk cost, the term **differential cost** was introduced in Chapter 1. In managerial accounting, the terms *avoidable cost, differential cost, incremental cost,* and *relevant cost* are often used interchangeably. To identify the costs that are avoidable (differential) in a particular decision situation and are therefore relevant, these steps can be followed:

1. Eliminate costs and benefits that do not differ between alternatives. These irrelevant costs consist of (a) sunk costs and (b) future costs that do not differ between alternatives.
2. Use the remaining costs and benefits that do differ between alternatives in making the decision. The costs that remain are the differential, or avoidable, costs.

Different Costs for Different Purposes

We need to recognize from the outset of our discussion that costs that are relevant in one decision situation are not necessarily relevant in another. Simply put, this means that *the manager needs different costs for different purposes.* For one purpose, a particular group of costs may be relevant; for another purpose, an entirely different group of costs may be relevant. Thus, in *each* decision situation the manager must examine the data at hand and isolate the relevant costs. Otherwise, the manager runs the risk of being misled by irrelevant data.

The concept of "different costs for different purposes" is basic to managerial accounting; we shall see its application frequently in the pages that follow.

Sunk Costs Are Not Relevant Costs

One of the most difficult conceptual lessons that managers have to learn is that sunk costs are never relevant in decisions. The temptation to include sunk costs in the analysis is especially strong in the case of book value of old equipment. We focus on book value of old equipment below, and then we consider other kinds of sunk costs in other parts of the chapter. We shall see that regardless of the kind of sunk cost involved, the conclusion is always the same—sunk costs are not avoidable, and therefore they should be ignored in decisions.

SoaringWings, Inc., is a small manufacturer of high-quality hang gliders. The most critical component of a hang glider is its metal frame, which must be very strong and yet very light. The frames are made by brazing together tubes of high-strength, but lightweight, metal alloys. Most of the brazing must be done by hand, but some can be done in an automated process by machine. Pete Kronski, the production manager of SoaringWings, Inc., has been trying to convince J. J. Marker, the company's president, to purchase a new brazing machine from Furimoro Industries. This machine would replace an old brazing machine from Bryston, Inc., that generates a large amount of scrap and waste.

On a recent blustery morning, Pete and J. J. happened to drive into the company's parking lot at the same time. The following conversation occurred as they walked together into the building.

Managerial Accounting in Action

The Issue

SOARING WINGS, INC.

Pete: Morning, J. J. Have you had a chance to look at the specifications on the new brazing machine from Furimoro Industries that I gave you last week?

J. J.: Are you still bugging me about the brazing machine?

Pete: You know it's almost impossible to keep that old Bryston brazing machine working within tolerances.

J. J.: I know, I know. But we're carrying the Bryston machine on the books for $140,000.

Pete: That's right. But I've done some investigating, and we could sell it for $90,000 to a plumbing company in town that doesn't require as tight tolerances as we do.

J. J.: Pete, that's just brilliant! You want me to sell a $140,000 machine for $90,000 and take a loss of $50,000. Do you have any other great ideas this morning?

Pete: J. J., I know it sounds far-fetched, but we would actually save money buying the new machine.

J. J.: I'm skeptical. However, if you can show me the hard facts, I'll listen.

Pete: Fair enough. I'll do it.

Book Value of Old Equipment

Pete first gathered the following data concerning the old machine and the proposed new machine:

Old Machine		Proposed New Machine	
Original cost	$175,000	List price new	$200,000
Remaining book value	140,000	Expected life	4 years
Remaining life	4 years	Disposal value in four years	$ –0–
Disposal value now	$ 90,000	Annual variable expenses	
Disposal value in four years	–0–	to operate	300,000
Annual variable expenses		Annual revenue from sales	500,000
to operate	345,000		
Annual revenue from sales	500,000		

Should the old machine be disposed of and the new machine purchased? The first reaction of SoaringWings' president was to say no, since disposal of the old machine would result in a "loss" of $50,000:

Old Machine	
Remaining book value	$140,000
Disposal value now	90,000
Loss if disposed of now	$ 50,000

Given this potential loss if the old machine is sold, a manager may reason, "We've already made an investment in the old machine, so now we have no choice but to use it until our investment has been fully recovered." A manager may tend to think this way even though the new machine is clearly more efficient than the old machine. An error made in the past cannot be corrected by simply *using* the machine. The investment that has been made in the old machine is a sunk cost. The portion of this investment that remains on the company's books (the book value of $140,000) should not be considered in a decision about whether to buy the new machine. Pete Kronski verified the irrelevance of the book value of the old machine by the following analysis:[1]

---

[1]The computations involved in this example are taken one step further in Chapter 12 where we discuss the time value of money and the use of present value in decision-making.

	Total Cost and Revenues—Four Years		
	Keep Old Machine	Purchase New Machine	Differential Costs and Benefits
Sales	$ 2,000,000	$ 2,000,000	$ –0–
Variable expenses	(1,380,000)	(1,200,000)	180,000
Cost (depreciation) of the new machine	—	(200,000)	(200,000)
Depreciation of the old machine or book value write-off	(140,000)	(140,000)*	–0–
Disposal value of the old machine	—	90,000*	90,000
Total net operating income over the four years	$ 480,000	$ 550,000	$ 70,000

*For external reporting purposes, the $140,000 remaining book value of the old machine and the $90,000 disposal value would be netted together and deducted as a single $50,000 "loss" figure.

Looking at all four years together, notice that the firm will be $70,000 better off by purchasing the new machine. Also notice that the $140,000 book value of the old machine had *no effect* on the outcome of the analysis. Since this book value is a sunk cost, it must be absorbed by the firm regardless of whether the old machine is kept and used or whether it is sold. If the old machine is kept and used, then the $140,000 book value is deducted in the form of depreciation. If the old machine is sold, then the $140,000 book value is deducted in the form of a lump-sum write-off. Either way, the company bears the same $140,000 cost and the differential cost is zero.

Focusing on Relevant Costs   What costs in the example above are relevant in the decision concerning the new machine? Looking at the original cost data, we should eliminate (1) the sunk costs and (2) the future costs and benefits that do not differ between the alternatives at hand.

1. The sunk costs:
   a. The remaining book value of the old machine ($140,000).
2. The future costs and benefits that do not differ:
   a. The sales revenue ($500,000 per year).
   b. The variable expenses (to the extent of $300,000 per year).

The costs and benefits that remain will form the basis for a decision. The analysis is as follows:

	Differential Costs and Benefits— Four Years
Reduction in variable expense promised by the new machine ($45,000* per year × 4 years)	$ 180,000
Cost of the new machine	(200,000)
Disposal value of the old machine	90,000
Net advantage of the new machine	$ 70,000

*$345,000 − $300,000 = $45,000.

Note that the items above are the same as those in the last column of the earlier analysis and represent those costs and benefits that differ between the two alternatives. Armed with this analysis, Pete felt confident that he would be able to explain the financial advantages of the new machine to the president of the company.

in business | *today* Hazardous Computers

Disposing of old equipment can be difficult—particularly when environmental regulations are involved. For example, computer equipment often contains lead and other substances that could contaminate the air, soil, or groundwater. Cindy Brethauer, the network administrator for 1st Choice Bank, in Greeley, Colorado, was faced with the mounting problem of storing old monitors, printers, and personal computers that could not be simply thrown away. These bulky items were constantly being shuttled back and forth from one storage space to another. For help, she turned to Technology Recycling LLC, which hauls away old computers and peripherals for $35 per component. Technology LLC employs disabled people to strip the machines. Many of the materials taken from the machines are recycled, while the environmentally sensitive materials are taken to disposal facilities approved by the Environmental Protection Agency. Technology LLC handles the complicated paperwork for its customers. One benefit for customers of finally disposing of the old equipment is a reduction in personal property taxes.

Source: Jill Hecht Maxwell, *Inc. Tech,* 2000, no. 1, p. 25.

Managerial Accounting in Action

The Wrap-Up

SOARING WINGS, INC.

Pete Kronski took his analysis to the office of J. J. Marker, the president of SoaringWings, where the following conversation took place.

Pete: J. J., do you remember that discussion we had about the proposed new brazing machine?

J. J. Sure I remember. Did you find out that I'm right?

Pete: Not exactly. Here's the analysis where I compare the profit with the old machine over the next four years to the profit with the new machine.

J. J.: I see you're claiming the profit is $70,000 higher with the new machine. Are you assuming higher sales with the new machine?

Pete: No, I have assumed total sales of $2,000,000 over the four years in either situation. The real advantage comes with the reduction in variable expenses of $180,000.

J. J.: Where are those reductions going to come from?

Pete: The new brazing machine should cut our scrap and rework rate at least in half. That results in substantial savings in materials and labor costs.

J. J.: What about the $50,000 loss on the old machine?

Pete: What really matters is the $200,000 cost of the new machine and the $90,000 salvage value of the old machine. The book value of the old machine is irrelevant. No matter what we do, that cost will eventually flow through the income statement as a charge in one form or another.

J. J.: I find that hard to accept, but it is difficult to argue with your analysis.

Pete: The analysis actually understates the advantages of the new machine. We don't catch all of the defects caused by the old machine, and defective products are sometimes sold to customers. With the new machine, I expect our warranty costs to decrease and our repeat sales to increase. And I would hate to be held responsible for any accidents caused by defective brazing by our old machine.

J. J.: Okay, I'm convinced. Put together a formal proposal, and we'll present it at the next meeting of the board of directors.

Future Costs that Do Not Differ Are Not Relevant Costs

We stated above that people often have difficulty accepting the idea that sunk costs are never relevant in a decision. Some people also have difficulty accepting the principle that future costs that do not differ between alternatives are never relevant in a decision. An example will help illustrate how future costs *should* be handled in a decision.

Future Labor Costs that Don't Differ   *in business* | *today*

In the early 1990s, General Motors Corp. laid off tens of thousands of its hourly workers who would nevertheless continue to receive full pay under union contracts. GM entered into an agreement with one of its suppliers, Android Industries, Inc., to use laid-off GM workers. GM agreed to pay the wages of the workers who would be supervised by Android Industries. In return, Android subtracted the wages from the bills it submitted to GM under their current contract. This reduction in contract price is pure profit to GM, since GM would have had to pay the laid-off workers in any case.

Source: GM Agrees to Allow a Parts Supplier to Use Some of Its Idled Employees," *The Wall Street Journal,* November 30, 1992, p. B3.

An Example of Irrelevant Future Costs

A company is contemplating the purchase of a new labor-saving machine that will cost $30,000 and have a 10-year useful life. Data concerning the company's annual sales and costs with and without the new machine are shown below:

	Current Situation	Situation with the New Machine
Units produced and sold	5,000	5,000
Selling price per unit	$ 40	$ 40
Direct materials cost per unit	14	14
Direct labor cost per unit	8	5
Variable overhead cost per unit	2	2
Fixed costs, other	62,000	62,000
Fixed costs, new machine	—	3,000

The new machine promises a saving of $3 per unit in direct labor costs ($8 − $5 = $3), but it will increase fixed costs by $3,000 per year. All other costs, as well as the total number of units produced and sold, will remain the same. Following the steps outlined earlier, the analysis is as follows:

1. Eliminate the sunk costs. (No sunk costs are included in this example.)
2. Eliminate the future costs and benefits that do not differ between the alternatives.
   a. The selling price per unit and the number of units sold do not differ between the alternatives. (Therefore, total future sales revenues will not differ.)
   b. The direct materials cost per unit, the variable overhead cost per unit, and the number of units produced do not differ between the alternatives. (Therefore, total future direct materials costs and variable overhead costs will not differ.)
   c. The "Fixed costs, other" do not differ between the alternatives.

The remaining costs—direct labor costs and the fixed costs associated with the new machine—are the only relevant costs.

Savings in direct labor costs ($5,000 units at a cost saving of $3 per unit)	$15,000
Less increase in fixed costs	3,000
Net annual cost savings promised by the new machine	$12,000

Exhibit 11–1
Differential Cost Analysis

	5,000 Units Produced and Sold		
	Current Situation	Situation with New Machine	Differential Costs and Benefits
Sales	$200,000	$200,000	$ –0–
Variable expenses:			
Direct materials	70,000	70,000	–0–
Direct labor	40,000	25,000	15,000
Variable overhead	10,000	10,000	–0–
Total variable expenses	120,000	105,000	
Contribution margin	80,000	95,000	
Less fixed expenses:			
Other	62,000	62,000	–0–
New machine	–0–	3,000	(3,000)
Total fixed expenses	62,000	65,000	
Net operating income	$ 18,000	$ 30,000	$12,000

This solution can be verified by looking at *all* of the cost data (both those that are relevant and those that are not) under the two alternatives. This is done in Exhibit 11–1. Notice from the exhibit that the net advantage in favor of buying the machine is $12,000—the same answer we obtained by focusing on just the relevant costs. Thus, we can see that future costs that do not differ between alternatives are indeed irrelevant in the decision-making process and can be safely eliminated from the analysis.

Why Isolate Relevant Costs?

In the preceding example, we used two different approaches to analyze the alternatives. First, we considered only the relevant costs; and second, we considered all costs, both those that were relevant and those that were not. We obtained the same answer under both approaches. It would be natural to ask, "Why bother to isolate relevant costs when total costs will do the job just as well?" Isolating relevant costs is desirable for at least two reasons.

First, only rarely will enough information be available to prepare a detailed income statement for both alternatives. Assume, for example, that you are called on to make a decision relating to a *single operation* of a multidepartmental, multiproduct firm. Under these circumstances, it would be virtually impossible to prepare an income statement of any type. You would have to rely on your ability to recognize which costs are relevant and which are not in order to assemble that data necessary to make a decision.

Second, mingling irrelevant costs with relevant costs may cause confusion and distract attention from the matters that are really critical. Furthermore, the danger always exists that an irrelevant piece of data may be used improperly, resulting in an incorrect decision. The best approach is to ignore irrelevant data and base the decision entirely on the relevant data.

Relevant cost analysis, combined with the contribution approach to the income statement, provides a powerful tool for making decisions. We will investigate various uses of this tool in the remaining sections of this chapter.

in business *today* **Environmental Costs**

A decision analysis can be flawed by incorrectly including irrelevant costs such as sunk costs and future costs that do not differ between alternatives. It can also be flawed by omitting future costs that *do* differ between alternatives. This is particularly a problem with environmental costs that have dramatically increased in recent years and about which many managers have little knowledge.

Consider the environmental complications posed by a decision of whether to install a solvent-based or powder-based system for spray-painting parts. In a solvent painting system, parts are sprayed as they move along a conveyor. The paint that misses the part is swept away by a wall of water, called a water curtain. The excess paint accumulates in a pit as sludge that must be removed each month. Environmental regulations classify this sludge as hazardous waste. As a result, the company must obtain a permit to produce the waste and must maintain meticulous records of how the waste is transported, stored, and disposed of. The annual costs of complying with these regulations can easily exceed $140,000 in total for a painting facility that initially costs only $400,000 to build. The costs of complying with environmental regulations include the following:

- The waste sludge must be hauled to a special disposal site. The typical disposal fee is about $300 per barrel, or $55,000 per year for a modest solvent-based painting system.
- Workers must be specially trained to handle the paint sludge.
- The company must carry special insurance.
- The company must pay substantial fees to the state for releasing pollutants (i.e., the solvent) into the air.
- The water in the water curtain must be specially treated to remove contaminants. This cost can run into tens of thousands of dollars per year.

In contrast, a powder-based painting system avoids almost all of these environmental costs. Excess powder used in the painting process can be recovered and reused without creating a hazardous waste. Additionally, the powder-based system does not release contaminants into the atmosphere. Therefore, even though the cost of building a powder-based system may be higher than the cost of building a solvent-based system, over the long run the costs of the powder-based system may be far lower due to the high environmental costs of a solvent-based system. Managers need to be aware of such environmental costs and take them fully into account when making decisions.

Source: Germain Böer, Margaret Curtin, and Louis Hoyt, "Environmental Cost Management," *Management Accounting,* September 1998, pp. 28–38. Reprinted with permission.

Adding and Dropping Product Lines and Other Segments

Decisions relating to whether old product lines or other segments of a company should be dropped and new ones added are among the most difficult that a manager has to make. In such decisions, many qualitative and quantitative factors must be considered. Ultimately, however, any final decision to drop an old segment or to add a new one is going to hinge primarily on the impact the decision will have on net operating income. To assess this impact, it is necessary to make a careful analysis of the costs involved.

Learning Objective 3
Prepare an analysis showing whether a product line or other organizational segment should be dropped or retained.

Southwest Airlines announced that Buffalo would become its 57th destination beginning October 2000. Although the company did not service any cities in the Northeast prior to 1993, four of its last five new destinations are in that part of the country. With an average one-way fare of $79 made possible by offering frequent, no-frills service using only Boeing 737s, cities are begging for consideration as Southwest continues to expand.

Source: David Field, "Southwest Continues Northeast Expansion," *USA Today*, June 21, 2000, p. 12B, Copyright 2000, Reprinted with permission.

Exhibit 11–2
Discount Drug Company
Product Lines

	Total	Product Line		
		Drugs	Cosmetics	Housewares
Sales	$250,000	$125,000	$75,000	$50,000
Less variable expenses	105,000	50,000	25,000	30,000
Contribution margin	145,000	75,000	50,000	20,000
Less fixed expenses:				
Salaries	50,000	29,500	12,500	8,000
Advertising	15,000	1,000	7,500	6,500
Utilities	2,000	500	500	1,000
Depreciation—fixtures	5,000	1,000	2,000	2,000
Rent	20,000	10,000	6,000	4,000
Insurance	3,000	2,000	500	500
General administrative	30,000	15,000	9,000	6,000
Total fixed expenses	125,000	59,000	38,000	28,000
Net operating income (loss) ...	$ 20,000	$ 16,000	$12,000	$ (8,000)

Concept 11–1

An Illustration of Cost Analysis

Consider the three major product lines of the Discount Drug Company—drugs, cosmetics, and housewares. Sales and cost information for the preceding month for each separate product line and for the store in total are given in Exhibit 11–2.

What can be done to improve the company's overall performance? One product line—housewares—shows a net operating loss for the month. Perhaps dropping this line would cause profits in the company as a whole to improve. In deciding whether the line should be dropped, management should reason as follows:

If the housewares line is dropped, then the company will lose $20,000 per month in contribution margin. By dropping the line, however, it may be possible to avoid some fixed costs. It may be possible, for example, to discharge certain employees, or it may be possible to reduce advertising costs. If by dropping the housewares line the company is able to avoid more in fixed costs than it loses in contribution margin, then it will be better off if the line is eliminated, since overall net income should improve. On the other hand, if the company is not able to avoid as much in fixed costs as it loses in contribution margin, then the housewares line should be retained. In short, the manager should ask, "What costs can I avoid if I drop this product line?"

As we have seen from our earlier discussion, not all costs are avoidable. For example, some of the costs associated with a product line may be sunk costs. Other costs may be allocated fixed costs that will not differ in total regardless of whether the product line is dropped or retained.

To show how the manager should proceed in a product-line analysis, suppose that the management of the Discount Drug Company has analyzed the costs being charged to the three product lines and has determined the following:

1. The salaries expense represents salaries paid to employees working directly in each product-line area. All of the employees working in housewares would be discharged if the line is dropped.
2. The advertising expense represents direct advertising of each product line and is avoidable if the line is dropped.
3. The utilities expense represents utilities costs for the entire company. The amount charged to each product line is an allocation based on space occupied and is not avoidable if the product line is dropped.
4. The depreciation expense represents depreciation on fixtures used for display of the various product lines. Although the fixtures are nearly new, they are custom-built and will have little resale value if the housewares line is dropped.

5. The rent expense represents rent on the entire building housing the company; it is allocated to the product lines on the basis of sales dollars. The monthly rent of $20,000 is fixed under a long-term lease agreement.

6. The insurance expense represents insurance carried on inventories within each of the three product-line areas.

7. The general administrative expense represents the costs of accounting, purchasing, and general management, which are allocated to the product lines on the basis of sales dollars. Total administrative costs will not change if the housewares line is dropped.

With this information, management can identify costs that can and cannot be avoided if the product line is dropped:

	Total Cost	Not Avoidable*	Avoidable
Salaries	$ 8,000		$ 8,000
Advertising	6,500		6,500
Utilities	1,000	$ 1,000	
Depreciation—fixtures	2,000	2,000	
Rent	4,000	4,000	
Insurance	500		500
General administrative	6,000	6,000	
Total fixed expenses	$28,000	$13,000	$15,000

*These costs represent either (1) sunk costs or (2) future costs that will not change whether the housewares line is retained or discontinued.

To determine how dropping the line will affect the overall profits of the company, we can compare the contribution margin that will be lost to the costs that can be avoided if the line is dropped:

Contribution margin lost if the housewares line is discontinued (see Exhibit 11–2)	$(20,000)
Less fixed costs that can be avoided if the housewares line is discontinued (see above)	15,000
Decrease in overall company net operating income	$ (5,000)

In this case, the fixed costs that can be avoided by dropping the product line are less than the contribution margin that will be lost. Therefore, based on the data given, the housewares line should not be discontinued unless a more profitable use can be found for the floor and counter space that it is occupying.

Selling More by Selling Less

in business today

IBM recently realized it was offering too many different products to its customers. After preparing a cost analysis for each of the features offered on its PCs, the company discovered that only 200 of the features were profitable. The company reacted by trimming its PC catalog from 3,000 different models to 180. In addition to selling more units by offering fewer choices to its customers, the company realized labor savings in excess of 15% and was able to reduce its inventory of parts by 65%.

Source: Tom Andel, "Communication of Technical Information," *Transportation & Distribution*, February 1998, p. 97.

Exhibit 11–3
A Comparative Format for
Product-Line Analysis

	Keep Housewares	Drop Housewares	Difference: Net Income Increase or (Decrease)
Sales	$50,000	$ –0–	$(50,000)
Less variable expenses	30,000	–0–	30,000
Contribution margin	20,000	–0–	(20,000)
Less fixed expenses:			
Salaries	8,000	–0–	8,000
Advertising	6,500	–0–	6,500
Utilities	1,000	1,000	–0–
Depreciation—fixtures	2,000	2,000	–0–
Rent	4,000	4,000	–0–
Insurance	500	–0–	500
General administrative	6,000	6,000	–0–
Total fixed expenses	28,000	13,000	15,000
Net operating income (loss)	$ (8,000)	$(13,000)	$ (5,000)

A Comparative Format

Some managers prefer to approach decisions of this type by preparing comparative income statements showing the effects on the company as a whole of either keeping or dropping the product line in question. A comparative analysis of this type for the Discount Drug Company is shown in Exhibit 11–3.

As shown by column 3 in the exhibit, overall company net operating income will decrease by $5,000 each period if the housewares line is dropped. This is the same answer, of course, as we obtained in our earlier analysis.

Beware of Allocated Fixed Costs

Our conclusion that the housewares line should not be dropped seems to conflict with the data shown earlier in Exhibit 11–2. Recall from the exhibit that the housewares line is showing a loss rather than a profit. Why keep a line that is showing a loss? The explanation for this apparent inconsistency lies at least in part with the *common fixed costs* that are being allocated to the product lines. A **common fixed cost** is a fixed cost that supports the operations of more than one segment of an organization and is not avoidable in whole or in part by eliminating any one segment. For example, the salary of the CEO of a company ordinarily would not be cut if any one product line were dropped, so it is a common fixed cost of the product lines. In fact, if dropping a product line is a good idea that results in higher profits for the company, the compensation of the CEO is likely to increase, rather than decrease, as a result of dropping the product line. One of the great dangers in allocating common fixed costs is that such allocations can make a product line (or other segment of a business) *look* less profitable than it really is. By allocating the common fixed costs among all product lines, the housewares line has been made to *look* as if it were unprofitable, whereas, in fact, dropping the line would result in a decrease in overall company net operating income. This point can be seen clearly if we recast the data in Exhibit 11–2 and eliminate the allocation of the common fixed costs. This recasting of data is shown in Exhibit 11–4.

Notice that the common fixed expenses have not been allocated to the product lines in Exhibit 11–4. Only the fixed expenses that are traceable to the product lines and that could be avoided by dropping the product lines are assigned to them. For example, the fixed expenses of advertising the housewares product line can be traced to that product line and can be eliminated if that product line is dropped. However, the general administrative

Exhibit 11–4
Discount Drug Company Product
Lines—Recast in Contribution
Format (from Exhibit 11–2)

	Total	Product Line		
		Drugs	**Cosmetics**	**Housewares**
Sales	$250,000	$125,000	$75,000	$50,000
Less variable expenses	105,000	50,000	25,000	30,000
Contribution margin	145,000	75,000	50,000	20,000
Less traceable fixed expenses:				
Salaries	50,000	29,500	12,500	8,000
Advertising	15,000	1,000	7,500	6,500
Depreciation—fixtures	5,000	1,000	2,000	2,000
Insurance	3,000	2,000	500	500
Total traceable fixed expenses	73,000	33,500	22,500	17,000
Product-line segment margin .	72,000	$ 41,500	$27,500	$ 3,000*
Less common fixed expenses:				
Utilities	2,000			
Rent	20,000			
General administrative	30,000			
Total common fixed expenses	52,000			
Net operating income	$ 20,000			

*If the housewares line is dropped, this $3,000 in segment margin will be lost to the company. In addition, we have seen that the $2,000 depreciation on the fixtures is a sunk cost that cannot be avoided. The sum of these two figures ($3,000 + $2,000 = $5,000) would be the decrease in the company's overall profits if the housewares line were discontinued.

expenses, such as the CEO's salary, cannot be traced to the individual product lines and would not be eliminated if any one product line were dropped. Consequently, these common fixed expenses are not allocated to the product lines in Exhibit 11–4 as they were in Exhibit 11–2. The allocations in Exhibit 11–2 provide a misleading picture that suggests that portions of the fixed common expenses can be eliminated by dropping individual product lines—which is not the case.

Exhibit 11–4 gives us a much different perspective of the housewares line than does Exhibit 11–2. As shown in Exhibit 11–4, the housewares line is covering all of its own traceable fixed costs and is generating a $3,000 *segment margin* toward covering the common fixed costs of the company. The **segment margin** is the difference between the revenue generated by a segment and its own traceable costs. Unless another product line can be found that will generate more than a $3,000 segment margin, the company would be better off keeping the housewares line. By keeping the line, the company's overall net operating income will be higher than if the product line were dropped.

Additionally, we should note that managers may choose to retain an unprofitable product line if the line is necessary to the sale of other products or if it serves as a "magnet" to attract customers. Bread, for example, is not an especially profitable line in food stores, but customers expect it to be available, and many would undoubtedly shift their buying elsewhere if a particular store decided to stop carrying it.

The Trap Laid by Fully Allocated Costs

in business | *today*

A bakery distributed its products through route salespersons, each of whom loaded a truck with an assortment of products in the morning and spent the day calling on customers in an assigned territory. Believing that some items were more profitable than others, management asked for an analysis of product costs and sales. The accountants to whom the task was assigned allocated all manufacturing and marketing costs to products to obtain a net profit for each product. The resulting figures indicated that some of the products were being sold at a loss, and management discontinued these products. However, when this change was put into effect, the company's overall profit declined. It was then seen that by dropping some products, sales revenues had been reduced without commensurate reduction in costs because the common manufacturing costs and route sales costs had to be continued in order to make and sell the remaining products.

The Make or Buy Decision

Learning Objective 4

Prepare a well-organized make or buy analysis.

A decision on whether to produce a fabricated part internally rather than to buy the part externally from a supplier is called a **make or buy decision.** To provide an illustration of a make or buy decision, consider Mountain Goat Cycles. The company is now producing the heavy-duty gear shifters used in its most popular line of mountain bikes. The company's Accounting Department reports the following costs of producing the shifter internally:

Concept 11–2

	Per Unit	8,000 Units
Direct materials	$ 6	$ 48,000
Direct labor	4	32,000
Variable overhead	1	8,000
Supervisor's salary	3	24,000
Depreciation of special equipment	2	16,000
Allocated general overhead	5	40,000
Total cost	$21	$168,000

in business | *today* **The Role of Expert Suppliers**

Sometimes, qualitative factors dictate that a company buy rather than make certain parts. Cummins Engine Company, a manufacturer of diesel engines, faced the problem of developing much more advanced piston designs in order to meet mandated emissions standards. Pistons are the "guts" of the engine, so management was reluctant to outsource these parts. However, advanced pistons could already be acquired from several outside suppliers whose cumulative volumes of piston production were many times larger than that of Cummins. This volume had allowed the suppliers to invest 20 times as much as Cummins in research and development and to build advanced manufacturing processes. Consequently, the suppliers were far ahead of Cummins and were likely to remain so without substantial investments that would be difficult to justify. Therefore, management decided to outsource the production of pistons.

Source: Ravi Venkatesan, "Strategic Sourcing: To Make or Not to Make," *Harvard Business Review,* November–December 1992, p. 104.

An outside supplier has offered to sell Mountain Goat Cycles 8,000 shifters a year at a price of only $19 each. Should the company stop producing the shifters internally and start purchasing them from the outside supplier? To approach the decision from a financial

Exhibit 11–5
Mountain Goat Cycles Make or
Buy Analysis

	Production "Cost" per Unit	Per Unit Differential Costs		Total Differential Costs—8,000 Units	
		Make	Buy	Make	Buy
Direct materials	$ 6	$ 6		$ 48,000	
Direct labor	4	4		32,000	
Variable overhead	1	1		8,000	
Supervisor's salary	3	3		24,000	
Depreciation of special equipment	2	—		—	
Allocated general overhead . .	5	—		—	
Outside purchase price			$19		$152,000
Total cost	$21	$14	$19	$112,000	$152,000
Difference in favor of continuing to make		$ 5		$40,000	

point of view, the manager should again focus on the differential costs. As we have seen, the differential costs can be obtained by eliminating those costs that are not avoidable—that is, by eliminating (1) the sunk costs and (2) the future costs that will continue regardless of whether the shifters are produced internally or purchased outside. The costs that remain after making these eliminations are the costs that are avoidable to the company by purchasing outside. If these avoidable costs are less than the outside purchase price, then the company should continue to manufacture its own shifters and reject the outside supplier's offer. That is, the company should purchase outside only if the outside purchase price is less than the costs that can be avoided internally as a result of stopping production of the shifters.

Looking at the cost data for producing the shifter internally, note first that depreciation of special equipment is listed as one of the costs of producing the shifters internally. Since the equipment has already been purchased, this depreciation is a sunk cost and is therefore irrelevant. If the equipment could be sold, its salvage value would be relevant. Or if the machine could be used to make other products, this could be relevant as well. However, we will assume that the equipment has no salvage value and that it has no other use except making the heavy-duty gear shifters.

Also note that the company is allocating a portion of its general overhead costs to the shifters. Any portion of this general overhead cost that would actually be eliminated if the gear shifters were purchased rather than made would be relevant in the analysis. However, it is likely that the general overhead costs allocated to the gear shifters are in fact common to all items produced in the factory and would continue unchanged even if the shifters are purchased from the outside. Such allocated common costs are not differential costs (since they do not differ between the make or buy alternatives) and should be eliminated from the analysis along with the sunk costs.

The variable costs of producing the shifters (materials, labor, and variable overhead) are differential costs, since they can be avoided by buying the shifters from the outside supplier. If the supervisor can be discharged and his or her salary avoided by buying the shifters, then it too will be a differential cost and relevant to the decision. Assuming that both the variable costs and the supervisor's salary can be avoided by buying from the outside supplier, then the analysis takes the form shown in Exhibit 11–5.

Since it costs $5 less per unit to continue to make the shifters, Mountain Goat Cycles should reject the outside supplier's offer. However, there is one additional factor that the company may wish to consider before coming to a final decision. This factor is the opportunity cost of the space now being used to produce the shifters.

The Matter of Opportunity Cost

If the space now being used to produce the shifters *would otherwise be idle,* then Mountain Goat Cycles should continue to produce its own shifters and the supplier's offer should be rejected, as stated above. Idle space that has no alternative use has an opportunity cost of zero.

But what if the space now being used to produce shifters could be used for some other purpose? In that case, the space would have an opportunity cost that would have to be considered in assessing the desirability of the supplier's offer. What would this opportunity cost be? It would be the segment margin that could be derived from the best alternative use of the space.

To illustrate, assume that the space now being used to produce shifters could be used to produce a new cross-country bike that would generate a segment margin of $60,000 per year. Under these conditions, Mountain Goat Cycles would be better off to accept the supplier's offer and to use the available space to produce the new product line:

	Make	Buy
Differential cost per unit (see prior example)	$ 14	$ 19
Number of units needed annually	× 8,000	× 8,000
Total annual cost	112,000	152,000
Opportunity cost—segment margin forgone on a potential new product line	60,000	
Total cost	$172,000	$152,000
Difference in favor of purchasing from the outside supplier		$ 20,000

Opportunity costs are not recorded in accounts of an organization. They do not represent actual dollar outlays. Rather, they represent economic benefits that are *forgone* as a result of pursuing some course of action. The opportunity costs of Mountain Goat Cycles are sufficiently large in this case to make continued production of the shifters very costly from an economic point of view.

decision | maker   **Vice President of Production**

You are faced with a make or buy decision. The company currently makes a component for one of its products but is considering whether it should instead purchase the component. If the offer from an outside supplier were accepted, the company would no longer need to rent the machinery that is currently being used to manufacture the component. You realize that the annual rental cost is a fixed cost, but recall some sort of warning about fixed costs. Is the annual rental cost relevant to this make or buy decision?

Special Orders

Managers often must evaluate whether a *special order* should be accepted, and if the order is accepted, the price that should be charged. A **special order** is a one-time order that is not considered part of the company's normal ongoing business. To illustrate, Mountain Goat Cycles has just received a request from the Seattle Police Department to produce 100 specially modified mountain bikes at a price of $179 each. The bikes would be used to patrol some of the more densely populated residential sections of the city. Mountain Goat Cycles can easily modify its City Cruiser model to fit the specifications of the

Seattle Police. The normal selling price of the City Cruiser bike is $249, and its unit product cost is $182 as shown below:

Direct materials	$ 86
Direct labor	45
Manufacturing overhead	51
Unit product cost	$182

The variable portion of the above manufacturing overhead is $6 per unit. The order would have no effect on the company's total fixed manufacturing overhead costs.

The modifications to the bikes consist of welded brackets to hold radios, nightsticks, and other gear. These modifications would require $17 in incremental variable costs. In addition, the company would have to pay a graphics design studio $1,200 to design and cut stencils that would be used for spray painting the Seattle Police Department's logo and other identifying marks on the bikes.

This order should have no effect on the company's other sales. The production manager says that she can handle the special order without disrupting any of the regular scheduled production.

What effect would accepting this order have on the company's net operating income?

Only the incremental costs and benefits are relevant. Since the existing fixed manufacturing overhead costs would not be affected by the order, they are not incremental costs and are therefore not relevant. The incremental net operating income can be computed as follows:

	Per Unit	Total 100 Bikes
Incremental revenue	$179	$17,900
Incremental costs:		
Variable costs:		
Direct materials	86	8,600
Direct labor	45	4,500
Variable manufacturing overhead	6	600
Special modifications	17	1,700
Total variable cost	$154	15,400
Fixed cost:		
Purchase of stencils		1,200
Total incremental cost		16,600
Incremental net operating income		$ 1,300

Therefore, even though the price on the special order ($179) is below the normal unit product cost ($182) and the order would require incurring additional costs, the order would result in an increase in net operating income. In general, a special order is profitable as long as the incremental revenue from the special order exceeds the incremental costs of the order. We must note, however, that it is important to make sure that there is indeed idle capacity and that the special order does not cut into normal sales. For example, if the company was operating at capacity, opportunity costs would have to be taken into account as well as the incremental costs that have already been detailed above.

Pricing New Products

When offering a new product or service for the first time, a company must decide on its selling price. A cost-based approach has often been followed in practice. In this approach, the product is first designed and produced, then its cost is determined and its price is computed by adding a mark-up to the cost. This *cost-plus* approach to pricing suffers from a number of drawbacks—the most obvious being that customers may not be willing to pay the price set by the company. If the price is too high, customers may decide to purchase a similar product from a competitor or, if no similar competing product exists, they may decide not to buy the product at all.

Target costing provides an alternative, market-based approach to pricing new products. In the **target costing** approach, management estimates how much the market will be willing to pay for the new product even before the new product has been designed. The company's required profit margin is subtracted from the estimated selling price to determine the target cost for the new product. A cross-functional team consisting of designers, engineers, cost accountants, marketing personnel, and production personnel is charged with the responsibility of ensuring that the cost of the product is ultimately less than the target cost. If at some point in the product development process it becomes clear that it will not be possible to meet the target cost, the new product is abandoned.

The target costing approach to pricing has a number of advantages over the cost-plus approach. First, the target costing approach is focused on the market and the customer. A product is not made unless the company is reasonably confident that customers will be willing to buy the product at a price that provides the company with an adequate profit. Second, the target costing approach instills a much higher level of cost-consciousness than the cost-plus approach and probably results in less expensive products that are more attractive to customers. The target cost lid creates relentless pressure to drive out unnecessary costs. In the cost-plus approach, there is little pressure to control costs since whatever the costs turn out to be, the price will be higher. This allows designers and engineers to create products with expensive features that customers may not actually be willing to pay for. Because of these advantages, more and more companies are abandoning the cost-plus approach to new product pricing in favor of the target costing approach.

you *decide*   **Tutor**

Your financial accounting instructor has suggested that you should consider working with selected students in her class as a tutor. Should you adopt a cost-plus or target costing approach to setting your hourly fee?

Utilization of a Constrained Resource

Managers are routinely faced with the problem of deciding how constrained resources are going to be utilized. A department store, for example, has a limited amount of floor space and therefore cannot stock every product that may be available. A manufacturing firm has a limited number of machine-hours and a limited number of direct labor-hours at its disposal. When a limited resource of some type restricts the company's ability to satisfy demand, the company is said to have a **constraint.** Because of the constrained resource, the company cannot fully satisfy demand, so the manager must decide how the constrained resource should be used. Fixed costs are usually unaffected by such choices, so the manager should select the course of action that will maximize the firm's *total* contribution margin.

Learning Objective 6
Determine the most profitable use of a constrained resource.

Contribution in Relation to a Constrained Resource

To maximize total contribution margin, a firm should not necessarily promote those products that have the highest *unit* contribution margins. Rather, total contribution margin will be maximized by promoting those products or accepting those orders that provide the highest unit contribution margin *in relation to the constrained resource.* To illustrate, Mountain Goat Cycles makes a line of paniers—a saddlebag for bicycles. There are two models of paniers—a touring model and a mountain model. Cost and revenue data for the two models of paniers are given below:

| | Model | |
	Mountain Panier	Touring Panier
Selling price per unit	$25	$30
Variable cost per unit	10	18
Contribution margin per unit	$15	$12
Contribution margin (CM) ratio	60%	40%

The mountain panier appears to be much more profitable than the touring panier. It has a $15 per unit contribution margin as compared to only $12 per unit for the touring model, and it has a 60% CM ratio as compared to only 40% for the touring model.

But now let us add one more piece of information—the plant that makes the paniers is operating at capacity. Ordinarily this does not mean that every machine and every person in the plant is working at the maximum possible rate. Because machines have different capacities, some machines will be operating at less than 100% of capacity. However, if the plant as a whole cannot produce any more units, some machine or process must be operating at capacity. The machine or process that is limiting overall output is called the **bottleneck**—it is the constraint.

At Mountain Goat Cycles, the bottleneck is a particular stitching machine. The mountain panier requires 2 minutes of stitching time, and each unit of the touring panier requires 1 minute of stitching time. Since this stitching machine already has more work than it can handle, something will have to be cut back. In this situation, which product is more profitable? To answer this question, the manager should look at the *contribution margin per unit of the constrained resource.* This figure is computed by dividing the contribution margin by the amount of the constrained resource a unit of product requires. These calculations are carried out below for the mountain and touring paniers.

	Model	
	Mountain Panier	**Touring Panier**
Contribution margin per unit (above) (a)	$15.00	$12.00
Time on the stitching machine required to produce one unit (b)	2 min.	1 min.
Contribution margin per unit of the constrained resource, (a) ÷ (b)	$7.50/min.	$12.00/min.

It is now easy to decide which product is less profitable and should be deemphasized. Each minute of processing time on the stitching machine that is devoted to the touring panier results in an increase of $12 in contribution margin and profits. The comparable figure for the mountain panier is only $7.50 per minute. Therefore, the touring model should be emphasized. Even though the mountain model has the larger per unit contribution margin and the larger CM ratio, the touring model provides the larger contribution margin in relation to the constrained resource.

To verify that the touring model is indeed the more profitable product, suppose an hour of additional stitching time is available and that there are unfilled orders for both products. The additional hour on the stitching machine could be used to make either 30 mountain paniers (60 minutes ÷ 2 minutes) or 60 touring paniers (60 minutes ÷ 1 minute), with the following consequences:

	Model	
	Mountain Panier	**Touring Panier**
Contribution margin per unit (above)	$ 15	$ 12
Additional units that can be processed in one hour	× 30	× 60
Additional contribution margin	$450	$720

This example clearly shows that looking at unit contribution margins alone is not enough; the contribution margin must be viewed in relation to the amount of the constrained resource each product requires.

Managing Constraints

Profits can be increased by effectively managing the organization's constraints. One aspect of managing constraints is to decide how to best utilize them. As discussed above, if the constraint is a bottleneck in the production process, the manager should select the product mix that maximizes the total contribution margin. In addition, the manager should take an active role in managing the constraint itself. Management should focus efforts on increasing the efficiency of the bottleneck operation and on increasing its capacity. Such efforts directly increase the output of finished goods and will often pay off in an almost immediate increase in profits.

It is often possible for a manager to effectively increase the capacity of the bottleneck, which is called **relaxing (or elevating) the constraint.** For example, the stitching machine operator could be asked to work overtime. This would result in more available stitching time and hence more finished goods that can be sold. The benefits from relaxing the constraint in such a manner are often enormous and can be easily quantified. The manager should first ask, "What would I do with additional capacity at the bottleneck if it were available?" In the example, if there are unfilled orders for both the touring and mountain paniers, the additional capacity would be used to process more touring paniers, since that would be a better use of the additional capacity. In that situation, the additional capacity would be worth $12 per minute or $720 per hour. This is because adding an hour of capacity would generate an additional $720 of contribution margin if it would be used solely to process more touring paniers. Since overtime pay for the operator is likely to be much less than $720 per hour, running the stitching machine on overtime would be an excellent way to increase the profits of the company while at the same time satisfying customers.

To reinforce this concept, suppose that making touring paniers has already been given top priority and consequently there are only unfilled orders for the mountain panier. How much would it be worth to the company to run the stitching machine overtime in this situation? Since the additional capacity would be used to make the mountain panier, the value of that additional capacity would drop to $7.50 per minute or $450 per hour. Nevertheless, the value of relaxing the constraint would still be quite high.

These calculations indicate that managers should pay great attention to bottleneck operations. If a bottleneck machine breaks down or is ineffectively utilized, the losses to the company can be quite large. In our example, for every minute the stitching machine is down due to breakdowns or setups, the company loses between $7.50 and $12.00. The losses on an hourly basis are between $450 and $720! In contrast, there is no such loss of contribution margin if time is lost on a machine that is not a bottleneck—such machines have excess capacity anyway.

The implications are clear. Managers should focus much of their attention on managing bottlenecks. As we have discussed, managers should emphasize products that most profitably utilize the constrained resource. They should also make sure that products are processed smoothly through the bottlenecks, with minimal lost time due to breakdowns and setups. And they should try to find ways to increase the capacity at the bottlenecks.

The capacity of a bottleneck can be effectively increased in a number of ways, including:

- Working overtime on the bottleneck.
- Subcontracting some of the processing that would be done at the bottleneck.
- Investing in additional machines at the bottleneck.
- Shifting workers from processes that are not bottlenecks to the process that is a bottleneck.
- Focusing business process improvement efforts such as TQM and Business Process Reengineering on the bottleneck.
- Reducing defective units. Each defective unit that is processed through the bottleneck and subsequently scrapped takes the place of a good unit that could be sold.

The last three methods of increasing the capacity of the bottleneck are particularly attractive, since they are essentially free and may even yield additional cost savings.

The Real Cost of Setups   *in business* | *today*

The bottleneck at Southwestern Ohio Steel is the blanking line. On the blanking line, large rolls of steel up to 60 inches wide are cut into flat sheets. Setting up the blanking line between jobs takes an average of 2.5 hours, and during this time, the blanking line is shut down.

Management estimates the opportunity cost of lost sales at $225 per hour, which is the contribution margin per hour of the blanking line for a typical order. Under these circumstances, a new loading device with an annual fixed cost of $36,000 that would save 720 setup hours per year looked like an excellent investment. The new loading device would have an average cost of only $50 per hour ($36,000 ÷ 720 hours = $50) compared to the $225 per hour the company would generate in added contribution margin.

Source: Robert J. Campbell, "Steeling Time with ABC or TOC," *Management Accounting,* January 1995, pp. 31–36. Reprinted with permission.

in business today **Solving the Real Problem**

It is often possible to elevate the constraint at very low cost. Western Textile Products makes pockets, waistbands, and other clothing components. The constraint at the company's plant in Greenville, South Carolina, was the slitting machines. These large machines slit huge rolls of textiles into appropriate widths for use on other machines. Management was contemplating adding a second shift to elevate the constraint. However, investigation revealed that the slitting machines were actually being run only one hour in a nine-hour shift. "The other eight hours were required to get materials, load and unload the machine, and do setups. Instead of adding a second shift, a second person was assigned to each machine to fetch materials and do as much of the setting up as possible off-line while the machine was running." This approach resulted in increasing the run time to four hours. If another shift had been added without any improvement in how the machines were being used, the cost would have been much higher and there would have been only a one-hour increase in run time.

Source: Eric Noreen, Debra Smith, and James T. Mackey, *The Theory of Constraints and Its Implications for Management Accounting* (Croton-on-Hudson, NY: The North River Press, 1995), pp. 84–85.

Summary

LO1   Distinguish between relevant and irrelevant costs in decisions.

Every decision involves a choice from among at least two alternatives. Only those costs and benefits that differ between alternatives are relevant; costs and benefits that are the same for all alternatives are not affected by the decision and can be ignored. Only future costs that differ between alternatives are relevant. Costs that have already been incurred are sunk costs and are always irrelevant. Future costs that do not differ between alternatives are not relevant.

LO2   Prepare an analysis showing whether to keep or replace old equipment.

Decisions concerning the replacement of old equipment should focus on the differences in costs and benefits between the old and new equipment. It is particularly important to realize that the original cost and net book value of the old equipment are irrelevant in making such a decision, although the disposal value of the old equipment is relevant.

LO3   Prepare an analysis showing whether a product line or other organizational segment should be dropped or retained.

A decision of whether a product line or other segment should be dropped should focus on the differences in the costs and benefits between dropping or retaining the product line or segment. Caution should be exercised when using reports in which common fixed costs have been allocated among segments. If these common fixed costs are unaffected by the decision of whether to drop or retain the segment, they are irrelevant and should be removed before determining the real profitability of a segment.

LO4   Prepare a well-organized make or buy analysis.

A make or buy decision should focus on the costs and benefits that differ between the alternatives of making or buying a component. As in other decisions, sunk costs—such as the depreciation on old equipment—should be ignored. Future costs that do not differ between alternatives—such as allocations of common fixed costs like general overhead—should be ignored.

LO5   Prepare an analysis showing whether a special order should be accepted.

When deciding whether to accept or reject a special order, the analyst should focus on the benefits and costs that differ between those two alternatives. Specifically, a special order should be accepted when the incremental revenue from the sale exceeds the incremental cost. As always, sunk costs and future costs that do not differ between the alternatives are irrelevant.

LO6   Determine the most profitable use of a constrained resource.

When demand for a company's products and services exceeds its ability to supply them, the company has a bottleneck. The bottleneck, whether it is a particular material, skilled labor, or a specific machine, is a constrained resource. Since the company is unable to make everything it could sell, managers must decide what the company will make and what the company will not make. In this situation, the profitability of a product is best measured by its contribution margin per unit of the constrained resource. The products with the highest contribution margin per unit of the constrained resource should be favored.

Managers should focus their attention on effectively managing the constraint. This involves making the best use possible of the constrained resource and increasing the amount of the constrained resource that is available.

Guidance Answers to You Decide and Decision Maker

VICE PRESIDENT OF PRODUCTION (p. 450)

The warning that you recall about fixed costs in decisions relates to *allocated* fixed costs. Allocated fixed costs often make a product line or other segment of a business appear less profitable than it really is. However, in this situation, the annual rental cost for the machinery is an *avoidable* fixed cost rather than an allocated fixed cost. An avoidable fixed cost is a cost that can be eliminated in whole or in part by choosing one alternative over another. Because the annual rental cost of the machinery can be avoided if the company purchases the components from an outside supplier, it is relevant to this decision.

TUTOR (p. 452)

Individuals who provide services to others often struggle to decide how to charge for their services. As a tutor, you probably will not incur any significant costs, unless you agree to provide the supplies (such as paper, pencils, calculators, or study guides) or software that might be required to assist the students you will be tutoring. As such, a cost-plus approach may not be a practical way to set the hourly fee (or price) for your services. On the other hand, if you use a target costing approach, you would estimate how much the market (that is, other students who require tutoring services) would be willing to pay for the tutoring services. How would you obtain this information? You probably should ask your instructor. If your institution offers tutoring services to its students, you should inquire about the fee that is charged by that office or department. You should check the student newspaper (or local newspapers) to determine the going rate for tutors. If you plan to tutor instead of working at a part-time job, you should consider the opportunity cost (that is, the hourly rate that you will be forgoing).

Review Problem: Relevant Costs

Charter Sports Equipment manufactures round, rectangular, and octagonal trampolines. Data on sales expenses for the past month follow:

		Trampoline		
	Total	**Round**	**Rectangular**	**Octagonal**
Sales	$1,000,000	$140,000	$500,000	$360,000
Less variable expenses	410,000	60,000	200,000	150,000
Contribution margin	590,000	80,000	300,000	210,000
Less fixed expenses:				
Advertising—traceable	216,000	41,000	110,000	65,000
Depreciation of special equipment	95,000	20,000	40,000	35,000
Line supervisors' salaries ...	19,000	6,000	7,000	6,000
General factory overhead* ..	200,000	28,000	100,000	72,000
Total fixed expenses	530,000	95,000	257,000	178,000
Net operating income (loss) ...	$ 60,000	$(15,000)	$ 43,000	$ 32,000

*A common cost that is allocated on the basis of sales dollars.

Management is concerned about the continued losses shown by the round trampolines and wants a recommendation as to whether or not the line should be discontinued. The special equipment used to produce the trampolines has no resale value. If the round trampoline model is dropped, the two line supervisors assigned to the model would be discharged.

Required:
1. Should production and sale of the round trampolines be discontinued? You may assume that the company has no other use for the capacity now being used to produce the round trampolines. Show computations to support your answer.
2. Recast the above data in a format that would be more usable to management in assessing the long-run profitability of the various product lines.

SOLUTION TO REVIEW PROBLEM
1. No, production and sale of the round trampolines should not be discontinued. Computations to support this answer follow:

Contribution margin lost if the round trampolines are discontinued ...		$(80,000)
Less fixed costs that can be avoided:		
Advertising—traceable	$41,000	
Line supervisors' salaries	6,000	47,000
Decrease in net operating income for the company as a whole		$(33,000)

The depreciation of the special equipment represents a sunk cost, and therefore it is not relevant to the decision. The general factory overhead is allocated and will presumably continue regardless of whether or not the round trampolines are discontinued; thus, it also is not relevant to the decision.

ALTERNATIVE SOLUTION TO QUESTION 1

	Keep Round Tramps	Drop Round Tramps	Difference: Net Income Increase or (Decrease)
Sales	$140,000	$ –0–	$(140,000)
Less variable expenses	60,000	–0–	60,000
Contribution margin	80,000	–0–	(80,000)
Less fixed expenses:			
Advertising—traceable	41,000	–0–	41,000
Depreciation of special equipment	20,000	20,000	–0–
Line supervisors' salaries	6,000	–0–	6,000
General factory overhead	28,000	28,000	–0–
Total fixed expenses	95,000	48,000	47,000
Net operating income (loss)	$ (15,000)	$(48,000)	$ (33,000)

2. If management wants a clear picture of the profitability of the segments, the general factory overhead should not be allocated. It is a common cost and therefore should be deducted from the total product-line segment margin, as shown in Exhibit 11–4. A more useful income statement format would be as follows:

	Total	Trampoline		
		Round	Rectangular	Octagonal
Sales	$1,000,000	$140,000	$500,000	$360,000
Less variable expenses	410,000	60,000	200,000	150,000
Contribution margin	590,000	80,000	300,000	210,000
Less traceable fixed expenses:				
Advertising—traceable	216,000	41,000	110,000	65,000
Depreciation of special equipment	95,000	20,000	40,000	35,000
Line supervisors' salaries	19,000	6,000	7,000	6,000
Total traceable fixed expenses . . .	330,000	67,000	157,000	106,000
Product-line segment margin	260,000	$ 13,000	$143,000	$104,000
Less common fixed expenses	200,000			
Net operating income (loss)	$ 60,000			

Glossary

Avoidable cost   Any cost that can be eliminated (in whole or in part) by choosing one alternative over another in a decision-making situation. In managerial accounting, this term is synonymous with *relevant cost* and *differential cost*. (p. 436)

Bottleneck   A machine or process that limits total output because it is operating at capacity. (p. 453)

Common fixed cost   A fixed cost that supports the operations of more than one segment of an organization and is not avoidable in whole or in part by eliminating any one segment. (p. 446)

Constraint   A limitation under which a company must operate, such as limited machine time available or limited raw materials available that restricts the company's ability to satisfy demand. (p. 453)

Differential cost   Any cost that differs between alternatives in a decision-making situation. In managerial accounting, this term is synonymous with *avoidable cost* and *relevant cost*. (p. 437)

Make or buy decision   A decision as to whether an item should be produced internally or purchased from an outside supplier. (p. 448)

Relaxing (or elevating) the constraint   An action that increases the capacity of a bottleneck. (p. 454)

Relevant cost   A cost that differs between alternatives in a particular decision. In managerial accounting, this term is synonymous with *avoidable cost* and *differential cost*. (p. 436)

Segment margin   The difference between the revenue generated by a segment and its own traceable cost. (p. 447)

Special order   A one-time order that is not considered part of the company's normal ongoing business. (p. 450)

Sunk cost   Any cost that has already been incurred and that cannot be changed by any decision made now or in the future. (p. 437)

Target costing   Before launching a new product, management estimates how much the market will be willing to pay for the product and then takes steps to ensure that the cost of the product will be low enough to provide an adequate profit margin. (p. 452)

Questions

11–1   What is a *relevant cost?*

11–2   Define the following terms: *incremental cost, opportunity cost,* and *sunk cost.*

11–3   Are variable costs always relevant costs? Explain.

11–4   The original cost of a machine the company already owns is irrelevant in decision-making. Explain why this is so.

11–5   "Sunk costs are easy to spot—they're simply the fixed costs associated with a decision." Do you agree? Explain.

11–6   "Variable costs and differential costs mean the same thing." Do you agree? Explain.

11–7   "All future costs are relevant in decision-making." Do you agree? Why?

11–8   Prentice Company is considering dropping one of its product lines. What costs of the product line would be relevant to this decision? Irrelevant?

11–9   "If a product line is generating a loss, then that's pretty good evidence that the product line should be discontinued." Do you agree? Explain.

11–10   What is the danger in allocating common fixed costs among product lines or other segments of an organization?

11–11   How does opportunity cost enter into the make or buy decision?

11–12   Give four examples of possible constraints.

11–13   How will relating product contribution margins to the constrained resource they require help a company ensure that profits will be maximized?

11–14   Airlines sometimes offer reduced rates during certain times of the week to members of a businessperson's family if they accompany him or her on trips. How does the concept of relevant costs enter into the decision to offer reduced rates of this type?

Brief Exercises

BRIEF EXERCISE 11–1   Identifying Relevant Costs (LO1)

Listed below are a number of costs that may be relevant in decisions faced by the management of Svahn, AB, a Swedish manufacturer of sailing yachts:

Item	Case 1 Relevant	Case 1 Not Relevant	Case 2 Relevant	Case 2 Not Relevant
a. Sales revenue				
b. Direct materials				
c. Direct labor				
d. Variable manufacturing overhead				
e. Depreciation—Model B100 machine				
f. Book value—Model B100 machine				
g. Disposal value—Model B100 machine				
h. Market value—Model B300 machine (cost)				
i. Depreciation—Model B300 machine				
j. Fixed manufacturing overhead (general)				
k. Variable selling expense				
l. Fixed selling expense				
m. General administrative overhead				

Required:

Copy the information above onto your answer sheet and place an X in the appropriate column to indicate whether each item is relevant or not relevant in the following situations (requirement 1 relates to Case 1 above, and requirement 2 relates to Case 2):

1. Management is considering purchasing a Model B300 machine to use in addition to the company's present Model B100 machine. This will increase the company's production and sales. The increase in volume will be large enough to require increases in fixed selling expenses and in general administrative overhead, but not in the fixed manufacturing overhead.

2. Management is instead considering replacing its present Model B100 machine with a new Model B300 machine. The Model B100 machine would be sold. This change will have no effect on production or sales, other than some savings in direct materials costs due to less waste.

BRIEF EXERCISE 11–2   Equipment Replacement Decision (LO2)

Waukee Railroad is considering the purchase of a powerful, high-speed wheel grinder to replace a standard wheel grinder that is now in use. Selected information on the two machines is given below:

	Standard Wheel Grinder	High-Speed Wheel Grinder
Original cost new	$20,000	$30,000
Accumulated depreciation to date	6,000	—
Current salvage value	9,000	—
Estimated cost per year to operate	15,000	7,000
Remaining years of useful life	5 years	5 years

Required:

Prepare a computation covering the five-year period that will show the net advantage or disadvantage of purchasing the high-speed wheel grinder. Use only relevant costs in your analysis.

BRIEF EXERCISE 11–3   Dropping or Retaining a Segment (LO3)

Bed & Bath, a retailing company, has two departments, Hardware and Linens. A recent monthly income statement for the company follows:

	Total	Department	
		Hardware	Linens
Sales	$4,000,000	$3,000,000	$1,000,000
Less variable expenses	1,300,000	900,000	400,000
Contribution margin	2,700,000	2,100,000	600,000
Less fixed expenses	2,200,000	1,400,000	800,000
Net operating income (loss)	$ 500,000	$ 700,000	$ (200,000)

A study indicates that $340,000 of the fixed expenses being charged to Linens are sunk costs or allocated costs that will continue even if the Linens Department is dropped. In addition, the elimination of the Linens Department will result in a 10% decrease in the sales of the Hardware Department. If the Linens Department is dropped, what will be the effect on the net operating income of the company as a whole?

BRIEF EXERCISE 11–4   Make or Buy a Component (LO4)

For many years Futura Company has purchased the starters that it installs in its standard line of farm tractors. Due to a reduction in output of certain of its products, the company has idle capacity that could be used to produce the starters. The chief engineer has recommended against this move, however, pointing out that the cost to produce the starters would be greater than the current $8.40 per unit purchase price:

	Per Unit	Total
Direct materials	$3.10	
Direct labor	2.70	
Supervision	1.50	$60,000
Depreciation	1.00	40,000
Variable manufacturing overhead	0.60	
Rent	0.30	12,000
Total production cost	$9.20	

A supervisor would have to be hired to oversee production of the starters. However, the company has sufficient idle tools and machinery that no new equipment would have to be purchased. The rent charge above is based on space utilized in the plant. The total rent on the plant is $80,000 per period. Depreciation is due to obsolescence rather than wear and tear. Prepare computations to show the dollar advantage or disadvantage per period of making the starters.

BRIEF EXERCISE 11–5   Special Order (LO5)

Delta Company produces a single product. The cost of producing and selling a single unit of this product at the company's normal activity level of 60,000 units per year is:

Direct materials	$5.10
Direct labor	3.80
Variable manufacturing overhead	1.00
Fixed manufacturing overhead	4.20
Variable selling and administrative expense	1.50
Fixed selling and administrative expense	2.40

The normal selling price is $21 per unit. The company's capacity is 75,000 units per year. An order has been received from a mail-order house for 15,000 units at a special price of $14 per unit. This order would not affect regular sales.

Required:
1. If the order is accepted, by how much will annual profits be increased or decreased? (The order will not change the company's total fixed costs.)
2. Assume the company has 1,000 units of this product left over from last year that are vastly inferior to the current model. The units must be sold through regular channels at reduced prices. What unit cost figure is relevant for establishing a minimum selling price for these units? Explain.

BRIEF EXERCISE 11–6   Utilization of a Constrained Resource (LO6)

Benoit Company produces three products, A, B, and C. Data concerning the three products follow (per unit):

	Product		
	A	B	C
Selling price	$80	$56	$70
Less variable expenses:			
Direct materials	24	15	9
Other variable expenses	24	27	40
Total variable expenses	48	42	49
Contribution margin	$32	$14	$21
Contribution margin ratio	40%	25%	30%

Demand for the company's products is very strong, with far more orders each month than the company has raw materials available to produce. The same material is used in each product. The material costs $3 per pound with a maximum of 5,000 pounds available each month. Which orders would you advise the company to accept first, those for A, for B, or for C? Which orders second? Third?

Exercises

EXERCISE 11–1   Identifying Relevant Costs (LO1)

Bill has just returned from a duck hunting trip. He has brought home eight ducks. Bill's friend, John, disapproves of duck hunting, and to discourage Bill from further hunting, John has presented him with the following cost estimate per duck:

Camper and equipment:	
Cost, $12,000; usable for eight seasons; 10 hunting trips per season	$150
Travel expense (pickup truck):	
100 miles at $0.12 per mile (gas, oil, and tires—$0.07 per mile: depreciation	
and insurance—$0.05 per mile)	12
Shotgun shells (two boxes)	20
Boat:	
Cost, $2,320, usable for eight seasons; 10 hunting trips per season	29
Hunting license:	
Cost, $30 for the season; 10 hunting trips per season	3
Money lost playing poker:	
Loss, $18 (Bill plays poker every weekend)	18
A fifth of Old Grandad:	
Cost, $8 (used to ward off the cold)	8
Total cost	$240
Cost per duck ($240 ÷ 8 ducks)	$ 30

Required:
1. Assuming that the duck hunting trip Bill has just completed is typical, what costs are relevant to a decision as to whether Bill should go duck hunting again this season?
2. Suppose that Bill gets lucky on his next hunting trip and shoots 10 ducks in the amount of time it took him to shoot 8 ducks on his last trip. How much would it have cost him to shoot the last two ducks?
3. Which costs are relevant in a decision of whether Bill should give up hunting? Explain.

EXERCISE 11–2   Identification of Relevant Costs; Equipment Replacement (LO1, LO2)

Hollings Company sells office furniture in the Rocky Mountain area. As part of its service, it delivers furniture to customers.

The costs associated with the acquisition and annual operation of a delivery truck are given below:

Insurance	$1,600
Licenses	250
Taxes (vehicle)	150
Garage rent for parking (per truck)	1,200
Depreciation ($9,000 ÷ 5 years)	1,800*
Gasoline, oil, tires, and repairs	0.07 per mile

*Based on obsolescence rather than on wear and tear.

Required:

1. Assume that Hollings Company has purchased one truck and that the truck has been driven 50,000 miles during the first year. Compute the average cost per mile of owning and operating the truck.

2. At the beginning of the second year, Hollings Company is unsure whether to use the truck or leave it parked in the garage and have all hauling done commercially. (The state requires the payment of vehicle taxes even if the vehicle isn't used.) What costs from the previous list are relevant to this decision? Explain.

3. Assume that the company decides to use the truck during the second year. Near year-end an order is received from a customer over 1,000 miles away. What costs from the previous list are relevant in a decision between using the truck to make the delivery and having the delivery done commercially? Explain.

4. Occasionally, the company could use two trucks at the same time. For this reason, some thought is being given to purchasing a second truck. The total miles driven would be the same as if only one truck were owned. What costs from the previous list are relevant to a decision over whether to purchase the second truck? Explain.

EXERCISE 11–3   Dropping or Retaining a Segment (LO3)

Thalassines Kataskeves, S.A., of Greece makes marine equipment. The company has been experiencing losses on its bilge pump product line for several years. The most recent quarterly income statement for the bilge pump product line is given below:

THALASSINES KATASKEVES, S.A.
Income Statement—Bilge Pump
For the Quarter Ended March 31

Sales		€850,000
Less variable expenses:		
Variable manufacturing expenses	€330,000	
Sales commissions	42,000	
Shipping	18,000	
Total variable expenses		390,000
Contribution margin		460,000
Less fixed expenses:		
Advertising	270,000	
Depreciation of equipment (no resale value)	80,000	
General factory overhead	105,000*	
Salary of product-line manager	32,000	
Insurance on inventories	8,000	
Purchasing department expenses	45,000†	
Total fixed expenses		540,000
Net operating loss		€(80,000)

*Common costs allocated on the basis of machine-hours.
†Common costs allocated on the basis of sales dollars.

The currency in Greece is the euro, denoted by €. The discontinuance of the bilge pump product line would not affect sales of other product lines and would have no noticeable effect on the company's total general factory overhead or total Purchasing Department expenses.

Required:

Would you recommend that the bilge pump product line be discontinued? Support your answer with appropriate computations.

EXERCISE 11–4   Make or Buy a Component (LO4)

Han Products manufactures 30,000 units of part S-6 each year for use on its production line. At this level of activity, the cost per unit for part S-6 is as follows:

Direct materials	$ 3.60
Direct labor	10.00
Variable overhead	2.40
Fixed overhead	9.00
Total cost per part	$25.00

An outside supplier has offered to sell 30,000 units of part S-6 each year to Han Products for $21 per part. If Han Products accepts this offer, the facilities now being used to manufacture part S-6 could be rented to another company at an annual rental of $80,000. However, Han Products has determined that two-thirds of the fixed overhead being applied to part S-6 would continue even if part S-6 were purchased from the outside supplier.

Required:

Prepare computations to show the net dollar advantage or disadvantage of accepting the outside supplier's offer.

EXERCISE 11–5   Evaluating a Special Order (LO5)

Imperial Jewelers is considering a special order for 20 handcrafted gold bracelets for a major upscale wedding. The gold bracelets are to be given as gifts to members of the wedding party. The normal selling price of a gold bracelet is $189.95 and its unit product cost is $149.00 as shown below:

Materials	$ 84.00
Direct labor	45.00
Manufacturing overhead	20.00
Unit product cost	$149.00

The manufacturing overhead is largely fixed and unaffected by variations in how much jewelry is produced in any given period. However, $4.00 of the overhead is variable with respect to the number of bracelets produced. The customer who is interested in the special bracelet order would like special filigree applied to the bracelets. This filigree would require additional materials costing $2.00 per bracelet and would also require acquisition of a special tool costing $250 that would have no other use once the special order is completed. This order would have no effect on the company's regular sales and the order could be fulfilled using the company's existing capacity without affecting any other order.

Required:

What effect would accepting this order have on the company's net operating income if a special price of $169.95 is offered per bracelet for this order? Should the special order be accepted at this price?

EXERCISE 11–6   Utilization of a Constrained Resource (LO6)

Barlow Company manufactures three products: A, B, and C. The selling price, variable costs, and contribution margin for one unit of each product follow:

	Product		
	A	**B**	**C**
Selling price	$180	$270	$240
Less variable expenses:			
Direct materials	24	72	32
Other variable expenses	102	90	148
Total variable expenses	126	162	180
Contribution margin	$ 54	$108	$ 60
Contribution margin ratio	30%	40%	25%

The same raw material is used in all three products. Barlow Company has only 5,000 pounds of material on hand and will not be able to obtain any more material for several weeks due to a strike in its supplier's plant. Management is trying to decide which product(s) to concentrate on next week in filling its backlog of orders. The material costs $8 per pound.

Required:
1. Compute the amount of contribution margin that will be obtained per pound of material used in each product.
2. Which orders would you recommend that the company work on next week—the orders for product A, product B, or product C? Show computations.
3. A foreign supplier could furnish Barlow with additional stocks of the raw material at a substantial premium over the usual price. If there is unfilled demand for all three products, what is the highest price that Barlow Company should be willing to pay for an additional pound of materials?

Problems

PROBLEM 11–1 Equipment Replacement Decision (LO2)
Murl Plastics, Inc., purchased a new machine one year ago at a cost of $60,000. Although the machine operates well, the president of Murl Plastics is wondering if the company should replace it with a new electronically operated machine that has just come on the market. The new machine would slash annual operating costs by two-thirds, as shown in the comparative data below:

CHECK FIGURE
(2) Net advantage: $60,000

	Present Machine	Proposed New Machine
Purchase cost new	$60,000	$90,000
Estimated useful life new	6 years	5 years
Annual operating costs	$42,000	$14,000
Annual straight-line depreciation	10,000	18,000
Remaining book value	50,000	—
Salvage value now	10,000	—
Salvage value in 5 years	–0–	–0–

In trying to decide whether to purchase the new machine, the president has prepared the following analysis:

Book value of the old machine	$50,000
Less salvage value	10,000
Net loss from disposal	$40,000

"Even though the new machine looks good," said the president, "we can't get rid of that old machine if it means taking a huge loss on it. We'll have to use the old machine for at least a few more years."

Sales are expected to be $200,000 per year, and selling and administrative expenses are expected to be $126,000 per year, regardless of which machine is used.

Required:

1. Prepare a summary income statement covering the next five years, assuming:
   a. That the new machine is not purchased.
   b. That the new machine is purchased.
2. Determine the desirability of purchasing the new machine using only relevant costs in your analysis.

CHECK FIGURE
(1) Discontinuing the racing bikes would decrease net operating income by $11,000

PROBLEM 11–2 Dropping or Retaining a Product (LO3)

The Regal Cycle Company manufactures three types of bicycles—a dirt bike, a mountain bike, and a racing bike. Data on sales and expenses for the past quarter follow:

	Total	Dirt Bikes	Mountain Bikes	Racing Bikes
Sales	$300,000	$90,000	$150,000	$60,000
Less variable manufacturing and selling expenses	120,000	27,000	60,000	33,000
Contribution margin	180,000	63,000	90,000	27,000
Less fixed expenses:				
Advertising, traceable	30,000	10,000	14,000	6,000
Depreciation of special equipment	23,000	6,000	9,000	8,000
Salaries of product-line managers	35,000	12,000	13,000	10,000
Common allocated costs*	60,000	18,000	30,000	12,000
Total fixed expenses	148,000	46,000	66,000	36,000
Net operating income (loss)	$ 32,000	$17,000	$ 24,000	$ (9,000)

*Allocated on the basis of sales dollars.

Management is concerned about the continued losses shown by the racing bikes and wants a recommendation as to whether or not the line should be discontinued. The special equipment used to produce racing bikes has no resale value and does not wear out.

Required:

1. Should production and sale of the racing bikes be discontinued? Show computations to support your answer.
2. Recast the above data in a format that would be more usable to management in assessing the long-run profitability of the various product lines.

CHECK FIGURE
(1) Decrease in profits: $3,200

PROBLEM 11–3 Discontinuing a Flight (LO3)

Profits have been decreasing for several years at Pegasus Airlines. In an effort to improve the company's performance, consideration is being given to dropping several flights that appear to be unprofitable.

A typical income statement for one such flight (flight 482) is given below (per flight):

Ticket revenue (175 seats × 40% occupancy × $200 ticket price)	$14,000	100.0%
Less variable expenses ($15 per person)	1,050	7.5
Contribution margin	12,950	92.5%
Less flight expenses:		
Salaries, flight crew	1,800	
Flight promotion	750	
Depreciation of aircraft	1,550	
Fuel for aircraft	6,800	
Liability insurance	4,200	
Salaries, flight assistants	500	
Baggage loading and flight preparation	1,700	
Overnight costs for flight crew and assistants at destination	300	
Total flight expenses	17,600	
Net operating loss	$ (4,650)	

The following additional information is available about flight 482:

a. Members of the flight crew are paid fixed annual salaries, whereas the flight assistants are paid by the flight.

b. One-third of the liability insurance is a special charge assessed against flight 482 because in the opinion of the insurance company, the destination of the flight is in a "high-risk" area. The remaining two-thirds would be unaffected by a decision to drop flight 482.

c. The baggage loading and flight preparation expense is an allocation of ground crews' salaries and depreciation of ground equipment. Dropping flight 482 would have no effect on the company's total baggage loading and flight preparation expenses.

d. If flight 482 is dropped, Pegasus Airlines has no authorization at present to replace it with another flight.

e. Depreciation of aircraft is due entirely to obsolescence. Depreciation due to wear and tear is negligible.

f. Dropping flight 482 would not allow Pegasus Airlines to reduce the number of aircraft in its fleet or the number of flight crew on its payroll.

Required:

1. Prepare an analysis showing what impact dropping flight 482 would have on the airline's profits.

2. The airline's scheduling officer has been criticized because only about 50% of the seats on Pegasus' flights are being filled compared to an average of 60% for the industry. The scheduling officer has explained that Pegasus' average seat occupancy could be improved considerably by eliminating about 10% of the flights, but that doing so would reduce profits. Explain how this could happen.

PROBLEM 11–4   Make or Buy a Component (LO4)

CHECK FIGURE
(1) The part can be made
inside the company
for $6 less per unit

Troy Engines, Ltd., manufactures a variety of engines for use in heavy equipment. The company has always produced all of the necessary parts for its engines, including all of the carburetors. An outside supplier has offered to produce and sell one type of carburetor to Troy Engines, Ltd., for a cost of $35 per unit. To evaluate this offer, Troy Engines, Ltd., has gathered the following information relating to its own cost of producing the carburetor internally:

	Per Unit	15,000 Units per Year
Direct materials	$14	$210,000
Direct labor	10	150,000
Variable manufacturing overhead	3	45,000
Fixed manufacturing overhead, traceable	6*	90,000
Fixed manufacturing overhead, allocated	9	135,000
Total cost	$42	$630,000

*One-third supervisory salaries; two-thirds depreciation of special equipment (no resale value).

Required:

1. Assuming that the company has no alternative use for the facilities that are now being used to produce the carburetors, should the outside supplier's offer be accepted? Show all computations.

2. Suppose that if the carburetors were purchased, Troy Engines, Ltd., could use the freed capacity to launch a new product. The segment margin of the new product would be $150,000 per year. Should Troy Engines, Ltd., accept the offer to buy the carburetors for $35 per unit? Show all computations.

PROBLEM 11–5   Accept or Reject a Special Order (LO5)

CHECK FIGURE
(1) Net increase in profits:
$65,000

Polaski Company manufactures and sells a single product called a Ret. Operating at capacity, the company can produce and sell 30,000 Rets per year. Costs associated with this level of production and sales are given below:

	Unit	Total
Direct materials	$15	$ 450,000
Direct labor	8	240,000
Variable manufacturing overhead	3	90,000
Fixed manufacturing overhead	9	270,000
Variable selling expense	4	120,000
Fixed selling expense	6	180,000
Total cost	$45	$1,350,000

The Rets normally sell for $50 each. Fixed manufacturing overhead is constant at $270,000 per year within the range of 25,000 through 30,000 Rets per year.

Required:

1. Assume that due to a recession, Polaski Company expects to sell only 25,000 Rets through regular channels next year. A large retail chain has offered to purchase 5,000 Rets if Polaski is willing to accept a 16% discount off the regular price. There would be no sales commissions on this order; thus, variable selling expenses would be slashed by 75%. However, Polaski Company would have to purchase a special machine to engrave the retail chain's name on the 5,000 units. This machine would cost $10,000. Polaski Company has no assurance that the retail chain will purchase additional units any time in the future. Determine the impact on profits next year if this special order is accepted.

2. Refer to the original data. Assume again that Polaski Company expects to sell only 25,000 Rets through regular channels next year. The U.S. Army would like to make a one-time-only purchase of 5,000 Rets. The Army would pay a fixed fee of $1.80 per Ret, and in addition it would reimburse Polaski Company for all costs of production (variable and fixed) associated with the units. Since the Army would pick up the Rets with its own trucks, there would be no variable selling expenses of any type associated with this order. If Polaski Company accepts the order, by how much will profits be increased or decreased for the year?

3. Assume the same situation as that described in (2) above, except that the company expects to sell 30,000 Rets through regular channels next year. Thus, accepting the U.S. Army's order would require giving up regular sales of 5,000 Rets. If the Army's order is accepted, by how much will profits be increased or decreased from what they would be if the 5,000 Rets were sold through regular channels?

CHECK FIGURE
(2) 140,000 total hours

PROBLEM 11–6   Utilization of a Constrained Resource (LO6)

The Walton Toy Company manufactures a line of dolls and a doll dress sewing kit. Demand for the dolls is increasing, and management requests assistance from you in determining an economical sales and production mix for the coming year. The company has provided the following information:

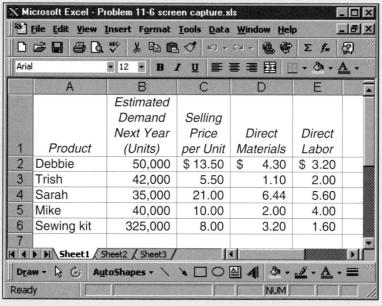

Product	Estimated Demand Next Year (Units)	Selling Price per Unit	Direct Materials	Direct Labor
Debbie	50,000	$ 13.50	$ 4.30	$ 3.20
Trish	42,000	5.50	1.10	2.00
Sarah	35,000	21.00	6.44	5.60
Mike	40,000	10.00	2.00	4.00
Sewing kit	325,000	8.00	3.20	1.60

The following additional information is available:

a. The company's plant has a capacity of 130,000 direct labor-hours per year on a single-shift basis. The company's present employees and equipment can produce all five products.
b. The direct labor rate is $8 per hour; this rate is expected to remain unchanged during the coming year.
c. Fixed costs total $520,000 per year. Variable overhead costs are $2 per direct labor-hour.
d. All of the company's nonmanufacturing costs are fixed.
e. The company's present inventory of finished products is negligible and can be ignored.

Required:

1. Determine the contribution margin per direct labor-hour expended on each product.
2. Prepare a schedule showing the total direct labor-hours that will be required to produce the units estimated to be sold during the coming year.
3. Examine the data you have computed in (1) and (2) above. Indicate how much of each product should be made so that total production time is equal to the 130,000 hours available.

4. What is the highest price, in terms of a rate per hour, that Walton Toy Company would be willing to pay for additional capacity (that is, for added direct labor time)?
5. Assume again that the company does not want to reduce sales of any product. Identify ways in which the company could obtain the additional output.

(CPA, heavily adapted)

CHECK FIGURE
(1) fl 36,000 advantage
to buy

PROBLEM 11–7   Make or Buy Analysis; Equipment Replacement Decision (LO2, LO4)
"In my opinion, we ought to stop making our own drums and accept that outside supplier's offer," said Wim Niewindt, managing director of Antilles Refining, N.V., of Aruba. "At a price of 18 florins per drum, we would be paying 5 florins less than it costs us to manufacture the drums in our own plant. (The currency in Aruba is the florin, denoted below by fl.) Since we use 60,000 drums a year, that would be an annual cost savings of 300,000 florins." Antilles Refining's present cost to manufacture one drum is given below (based on 60,000 drums per year):

Direct material	fl 10.35
Direct labor	6.00
Variable overhead	1.50
Fixed overhead (fl 2.80 general company overhead, fl 1.60 depreciation and, fl 0.75 supervision)	5.15
Total cost per drum	fl 23.00

A decision about whether to make or buy the drums is especially important at this time since the equipment being used to make the drums is completely worn out and must be replaced. The choices facing the company are:

Alternative 1: Purchase new equipment and continue to make the drums. The equipment would cost fl 810,000; it would have a six-year useful life and no salvage value. The company uses straight-line depreciation.
Alternative 2: Purchase the drums from an outside supplier at fl 18 per drum under a six-year contract.

The new equipment would be more efficient than the equipment that Antilles Refining has been using and, according to the manufacturer, would reduce direct labor and variable overhead costs by 30%. The old equipment has no resale value. Supervision cost (fl 45,000 per year) and direct materials cost per drum would not be affected by the new equipment. The new equipment's capacity would be 90,000 drums per year. The company has no other use for the space being used to produce the drums.
The company's total general company overhead would be unaffected by this decision.

Required:
1. To assist the managing director in making a decision, prepare an analysis showing what the total cost and the cost per drum would be under each of the two alternatives given above. Assume that 60,000 drums are needed each year. Which course of action would you recommend to the managing director?
2. Would your recommendation in (1) above be the same if the company's needs were: (a) 75,000 drums per year or (b) 90,000 drums per year? Show computations to support your answer, with costs presented on both a total and a per unit basis.
3. What other factors would you recommend that the company consider before making a decision?

CHECK FIGURE
(1) $40,000 disadvantage
to close

PROBLEM 11–8   Shutting Down or Continuing to Operate a Plant (LO3)
(Note: This type of decision is similar to that of dropping a product line.)
Birch Company normally produces and sells 30,000 units of RG-6 each month. RG-6 is a small electrical relay used in the automotive industry as a component part in various products. The selling price is $22 per unit, variable costs are $14 per unit, fixed manufacturing overhead costs total $150,000 per month, and fixed selling costs total $30,000 per month.
Employment-contract strikes in the companies that purchase the bulk of the RG-6 units have caused Birch Company's sales to temporarily drop to only 8,000 units per month. Birch Company estimates that the strikes will last for about two months, after which time sales of RG-6 should return to normal. Due to the current low level of sales, however, Birch Company is thinking about closing down its own plant during the two months that the strikes are on. If Birch Company does close down its plant, it is estimated that fixed manufacturing overhead costs can be reduced to $105,000 per month and that fixed selling costs can be reduced by 10%. Start-up costs at the end of the shutdown period would total $8,000. Since Birch Company uses just-in-time (JIT) production methods, no inventories are on hand.

Required:

1. Assuming that the strikes continue for two months, as estimated, would you recommend that Birch Company close its own plant? Show computations in good form.
2. At what level of sales (in units) for the two-month period should Birch Company be indifferent between closing the plant or keeping it open? Show computations. (Hint: This is a type of break-even analysis, except that the fixed cost portion of your break-even computation should include only those fixed costs that are relevant [i.e., avoidable] over the two-month period.)

PROBLEM 11–9   Relevant Cost Analysis in a Variety of Situations (LO3, LO4, LO5)

Andretti Company has a single product called a Dak. The company normally produces and sells 60,000 Daks each year at a selling price of $32 per unit. The company's unit costs at this level of activity are given below:

Direct materials	$10.00	
Direct labor	4.50	
Variable manufacturing overhead ...	2.30	
Fixed manufacturing overhead	5.00	($300,000 total)
Variable selling expenses	1.20	
Fixed selling expenses	3.50	($210,000 total)
Total cost per unit	$26.50	

A number of questions relating to the production and sale of Daks follow. Each question is independent.

Required:

1. Assume that Andretti Company has sufficient capacity to produce 90,000 Daks each year without any increase in fixed manufacturing overhead costs. The company could increase its sales by 25% above the present 60,000 units each year if it were willing to increase the fixed selling expenses by $80,000. Would the increased fixed expenses be justified?
2. Assume again that Andretti Company has sufficient capacity to produce 90,000 Daks each year. A customer in a foreign market wants to purchase 20,000 Daks. Import duties on the Daks would be $1.70 per unit, and costs for permits and licenses would be $9,000. The only selling costs that would be associated with the order would be $3.20 per unit shipping cost. You have been asked by the president to compute the per unit break-even price on this order.
3. The company has 1,000 Daks on hand that have some irregularities and are therefore considered to be "seconds." Due to the irregularities, it will be impossible to sell these units at the normal price through regular distribution channels. What unit cost figure is relevant for setting a minimum selling price?
4. Due to a strike in its supplier's plant, Andretti Company is unable to purchase more material for the production of Daks. The strike is expected to last for two months. Andretti Company has enough material on hand to continue to operate at 30% of normal levels for the two-month period. As an alternative, Andretti could close its plant down entirely for the two months. If the plant were closed, fixed overhead costs would continue at 60% of their normal level during the two-month period; the fixed selling costs would be reduced by 20% while the plant was closed. What would be the dollar advantage or disadvantage of closing the plant for the two-month period?
5. An outside manufacturer has offered to produce Daks for Andretti Company and to ship them directly to Andretti's customers. If Andretti Company accepts this offer, the facilities that it uses to produce Daks would be idle; however, fixed overhead costs would be reduced by 75% of their present level. Since the outside manufacturer would pay for all the costs of shipping, the variable selling costs would be only two-thirds of their present amount. Compute the unit cost figure that is relevant for comparison to whatever quoted price is received from the outside manufacturer.

Building Your Skills

ANALYTICAL THINKING   (LO3)

Tracey Douglas is the owner and managing director of Heritage Garden Furniture, Ltd., a South African company that makes museum-quality reproductions of antique outdoor furniture. Ms. Douglas would like advice concerning the advisability of eliminating the model C3 lawnchair. These lawnchairs have been among the company's best-selling products, but they seem to be unprofitable.

A condensed statement of operating income for the company and for the model C3 lawnchair for the quarter ended June 30 follows:

	All Products	Model C3 Lawnchair
Sales	R2,900,000	R300,000
Cost of sales:		
Direct materials	759,000	122,000
Direct labor	680,000	72,000
Fringe benefits (20% of direct labor)	136,000	14,400
Variable manufacturing overhead	28,000	3,600
Building rent and maintenance	30,000	4,000
Depreciation	75,000	19,100
Total cost of sales	1,708,000	235,100
Gross margin	1,192,000	64,900
Selling and administrative expenses:		
Product managers' salaries	75,000	10,000
Sales commissions (5% of sales)	145,000	15,000
Fringe benefits (20% of salaries and commissions)	44,000	5,000
Shipping	120,000	10,000
General administrative expenses	464,000	48,000
Total selling and administrative expenses	848,000	88,000
Net operating income (loss)	R344,000	R(23,100)

The currency in South Africa is the rand, denoted here by R.

The following additional data have been supplied by the company:

a. Direct labor is a variable cost at Heritage Garden Furniture.
b. All of the company's products are manufactured in the same facility and use the same equipment. Building rent and maintenance and depreciation are allocated to products using various bases. The equipment does not wear out through use; it eventually becomes obsolete.
c. There is ample capacity to fill all orders.
d. Dropping the model C3 lawnchair would have no effect on sales of other product lines.
e. Inventories of work in process or finished goods are insignificant.
f. Shipping costs are traced directly to products.
g. General administrative expenses are allocated to products on the basis of sales dollars. There would be no effect on the total general administrative expenses if the model C3 lawnchair were dropped.
h. If the model C3 lawnchair were dropped, the product manager would be laid off.

Required:
1. Given the current level of sales, would you recommend that the model C3 lawnchair be dropped? Prepare appropriate computations to support your answer.
2. What would sales of the model C3 lawnchair have to be, at minimum, in order to justify retaining the product? (Hint: Set this up as a break-even problem but include only the relevant costs from (1) above.)

COMMUNICATING IN PRACTICE   (LO4)

Silven Industries, which manufactures and sells a highly successful line of summer lotions and insect repellents, has decided to diversify in order to stabilize sales throughout the year. A natural area for the company to consider is the production of winter lotions and creams to prevent dry and chapped skin.

After considerable research, a winter products line has been developed. However, Bob Murdock, Silven's president, has decided to introduce only one of the new products for this coming winter. If the product is a success, further expansion in future years will be initiated.

The product selected (called Chap-Off) is a lip balm that will be sold in a lipstick-type tube. The product will be sold to wholesalers in boxes of 24 tubes for $8 per box. Because of excess capacity, no additional fixed overhead costs will be incurred to produce the product. However, a $90,000 charge for fixed overhead will be absorbed by the product under the company's absorption costing system.

Using the production and sales estimates of 100,000 boxes of Chap-Off, the Accounting Department has developed the following cost per box:

CHECK FIGURE
(1) $0.20 savings per box to make

Direct material	$3.60
Direct labor	2.00
Manufacturing overhead	1.40
Total cost	$7.00

The costs above include costs for producing both the lip balm and the tube into which the lip balm is to be placed. As an alternative to making the tubes, Silven has approached a supplier to discuss the possibility of purchasing the tubes for Chap-Off. The purchase price of the empty tubes from the supplier would be $1.35 per box of 24 tubes. If Silven Industries accepts the purchase proposal, it is predicted that direct labor and variable manufacturing overhead costs per box of Chap-Off would be reduced by 10% and that direct materials costs would be reduced by 25%.

Required:

Write a memorandum to the president that answers the following questions. Use headings to organize the information presented in the memorandum. Include computations to support your answers where appropriate.

1. Should Silven Industries make the tubes for the lip balm or buy them from the supplier? How much would be saved by making this decision?
2. What is the maximum purchase price that would be acceptable to Silven Industries if the tubes for the lip balm were bought from a supplier?
3. As noted above, the Accounting Department assumed that 100,000 boxes of Chap-Off would be produced and sold. However, the vice president of sales estimates that 120,000 boxes of Chap-Off can be sold. This higher volume would require additional equipment at an annual rental of $40,000. Assuming the company buys the tubes from the supplier at $1.35 per box of 24 tubes and that the supplier will not accept an order for less than 100,000 boxes of tubes, should Silven Industries make the tubes for the lip balm or buy them from the supplier? What are the total costs of producing 120,000 boxes of Chap-Off assuming that the company makes the tubes? What are the total costs assuming that the company buys the tubes? How much would be saved by buying the tubes rather than making them internally?
4. Refer to the information in (3) above. Assume that a different supplier will accept an order of any size for the tubes at $1.35 per box of 24 tubes. Should Silven Industries make the tubes for the lip balm or buy them from the supplier?
5. What qualitative factors should be considered in this make or buy decision?

(CMA, heavily adapted)

ETHICS CHALLENGE (LO3)

Haley Romeros had just been appointed vice president of the Rocky Mountain Region of the Bank Services Corporation (BSC). The company provides check processing services for small banks. The banks send checks presented for deposit or payment to BSC, which records the data on each check in a computerized database. BSC then sends the data electronically to the nearest Federal Reserve Bank check-clearing center where the appropriate transfers of funds are made between banks. The Rocky Mountain Region has three check processing centers, which are located in Billings, Montana; Great Falls, Montana; and Clayton, Idaho. Prior to her promotion to vice president, Ms. Romeros had been the manager of a check processing center in New Jersey.

Immediately upon assuming her new position, Ms. Romeros requested a complete financial report for the just-ended fiscal year from the region's controller, John Littlebear. Ms. Romeros specified that the financial report should follow the standardized format required by corporate headquarters for all regional performance reports. That report follows:

BANK SERVICES CORPORATION (BSC)
Rocky Mountain Region
Financial Performance

		Check Processing Centers		
	Total	**Billings**	**Great Falls**	**Clayton**
Sales	$50,000,000	$20,000,000	$18,000,000	$12,000,000
Operating expenses:				
Direct labor	32,000,000	12,500,000	11,000,000	8,500,000
Variable overhead	850,000	350,000	310,000	190,000
Equipment depreciation ..	3,900,000	1,300,000	1,400,000	1,200,000
Facility expense	2,800,000	900,000	800,000	1,100,000
Local administrative expense*	450,000	140,000	160,000	150,000
Regional administrative expense†	1,500,000	600,000	540,000	360,000
Corporate administrative expense‡	4,750,000	1,900,000	1,710,000	1,140,000
Total operating expense	46,250,000	17,690,000	15,920,000	12,640,000
Net operating income	$ 3,750,000	$ 2,310,000	$ 2,080,000	$ (640,000)

*Local administrative expenses are the administrative expenses incurred at the check processing centers.
†Regional administrative expenses are allocated to the check processing centers based on sales.
‡Corporate administrative expenses are charged to segments of the company such as the Rocky Mountain Region and the check processing centers at the rate of 9.5% of their sales.

Upon seeing this report, Ms. Romeros summoned John Littlebear for an explanation.

Romeros: What's the story on Clayton? It didn't have a loss the previous year did it?
Littlebear: No, the Clayton facility has had a nice profit every year since it was opened six years ago, but Clayton lost a big contract this year.
Romeros: Why?
Littlebear: One of our national competitors entered the local market and bid very aggressively on the contract. We couldn't afford to meet the bid. Clayton's costs—particularly their facility expenses—are just too high. When Clayton lost the contract, we had to lay off a lot of employees, but we could not reduce the fixed costs of the Clayton facility.
Romeros: Why is Clayton's facility expense so high? It's a smaller facility than either Billings or Great Falls and yet its facility expense is higher.
Littlebear: The problem is that we are able to rent suitable facilities very cheaply at Billings and Great Falls. No such facilities were available at Clayton; we had them built. Unfortunately, there were big cost overruns. The contractor we hired was inexperienced at this kind of work and in fact went bankrupt before the project was completed. After hiring another contractor to finish the work, we were way over budget. The large depreciation charges on the facility didn't matter at first because we didn't have much competition at the time and could charge premium prices.
Romeros: Well we can't do that anymore. The Clayton facility will obviously have to be shut down. Its business can be shifted to the other two check processing centers in the region.
Littlebear: I would advise against that. The $1,200,000 in depreciation at the Clayton facility is misleading. That facility should last indefinitely with proper maintenance. And it has no resale value; there is no other commercial activity around Clayton.
Romeros: What about the other costs at Clayton?
Littlebear: If we shifted Clayton's business over to the other two processing centers in the region, we wouldn't save anything on direct labor or variable overhead costs. We might save $90,000 or so in local administrative expense, but we would not save any regional administrative expense and corporate headquarters would still charge us 9.5% of our sales as corporate administrative expense.
In addition, we would have to rent more space in Billings and Great Falls in order to handle the work transferred from Clayton; that would probably cost us at least $600,000 a year. And don't forget that it

will cost us something to move the equipment from Clayton to Billings and Great Falls. And the move will disrupt service to customers.

Romeros: I understand all of that, but a money-losing processing center on my performance report is completely unacceptable.

Littlebear: And if you shut down Clayton, you are going to throw some loyal employees out of work.

Romeros: That's unfortunate, but we have to face hard business realities.

Littlebear: And you would have to write off the investment in the facilities at Clayton.

Romeros: I can explain a write-off to corporate headquarters; hiring an inexperienced contractor to build the Clayton facility was my predecessor's mistake. But they'll have my head at headquarters if I show operating losses every year at one of my processing centers. Clayton has to go. At the next corporate board meeting, I am going to recommend that the Clayton facility be closed.

Required:

1. From the standpoint of the company as a whole, should the Clayton processing center be shut down and its work redistributed to other processing centers in the region? Explain.
2. Do you think Haley Romeros's decision to shut down the Clayton facility is ethical? Explain.
3. What influence should the depreciation on the facilities at Clayton have on prices charged by Clayton for its services?

TAKING IT TO THE NET

As you know, the World Wide Web is a medium that is constantly evolving. Sites come and go and change without notice. To enable periodic update of site addresses, this problem has been posted to the textbook website (www.mhhe.com/folk1e). After accessing the site, enter the Student Center and select this chapter. Select and complete the Taking It to the Net problem.

TEAMWORK IN ACTION   (LO4, LO6)

Sportway, Inc., is a wholesale distributor supplying a wide range of moderately priced sporting equipment to large chain stores. About 60% of Sportway's products are purchased from other companies while the remainder of the products are manufactured by Sportway. The company has a Plastics Department that is currently manufacturing molded fishing tackle boxes. Sportway is able to manufacture and sell 8,000 tackle boxes annually, making full use of its direct labor capacity at available workstations. Presented below are the selling price and costs associated with Sportway's tackle boxes.

Selling price per box		$86.00
Cost per box:		
Molded plastic	$ 8.00	
Hinges, latches, handle	9.00	
Direct labor ($15 per hour)	18.75	
Manufacturing overhead	12.50	
Selling and administrative cost	17.00	65.25
Net operating income per box		$20.75

Because Sportway believes it could sell 12,000 tackle boxes if it had sufficient manufacturing capacity, the company has looked into the possibility of purchasing the tackle boxes for distribution. Maple Products, a steady supplier of quality products, would be able to provide up to 9,000 tackle boxes per year at a price of $68 per box delivered to Sportway's facility.

Traci Kader, Sportway's production manager, has suggested that the company could make better use of its Plastics Department by manufacturing skateboards. To support her position, Traci has a market study that indicates an expanding market for skateboards. Traci believes that Sportway could expect to sell 17,500 skateboards annually at a price of $45 per skateboard. Traci's estimate of the costs to manufacture the skateboards is presented below.

Selling price per skateboard		$45.00
Cost per skateboard:		
Molded plastic	$5.50	
Wheels, hardware	7.00	
Direct labor ($15 per hour)	7.50	
Manufacturing overhead	5.00	
Selling and administrative cost	9.00	34.00
Net operating income per skateboard		$11.00

In the Plastics Department, Sportway uses direct labor-hours as the application base for manufacturing overhead. Included in the manufacturing overhead for the current year is $50,000 of fixed overhead costs, of which 40% is traceable to the Plastics Department and 60% is allocated factorywide manufacturing overhead cost. The remaining manufacturing overhead cost is variable with respect to direct labor-hours. The skateboards could be produced with existing equipment and personnel in the Plastics Department.

For each unit of product that Sportway sells, regardless of whether the product has been purchased or is manufactured by Sportway, there is an allocated $6 fixed cost per unit for distribution. This $6 per unit is included in the selling and administrative cost for all products. The remaining amount of selling and administrative cost for all products—purchased or manufactured—is variable. The total selling and administrative cost figure for the purchased tackle boxes would be $10 per unit.

Required:
Your team should discuss and then respond to the following questions. All team members should agree with and understand the answers (including the calculations supporting the answers) and be prepared to report to the class. (Each teammate can assume responsibility for a different part of the presentation.)

1. Determine the number of direct labor-hours per year being used to manufacture tackle boxes.
2. Compute the contribution margin per unit for:
   a. Purchased tackle boxes.
   b. Manufactured tackle boxes.
   c. Manufactured skateboards.
3. Determine the number of tackle boxes (if any) that Sportway should purchase and the number of tackle boxes and/or skateboards that it should manufacture, and compute the improvement in net income that will result from this product mix over current operations.

(CMA, adapted)

Chapter Twelve

Capital Budgeting Decisions

Chapter Outline

Decision Feature Funding Only the Best Projects

Steven Burd became the CEO of Safeway, now one of the largest food and drug retailers in North America, in 1992. At the time, Safeway was operating approximately 1,100 stores, which occupied approximately 39 million square feet of retail space. Burd immediately slashed annual capital spending from $550 million to $290 million. He justified the decision as follows: "We had projects that were not returning the cost of money. So we cut spending back, which made the very best projects come to the surface."

Safeway set a minimum 22.5% pretax return on investment in all new store and remodeling projects. In addition to opening new stores, Burd felt that the company should emphasize expanding existing stores that are in excellent locations so as to pump up sales. With its new approach to capital budgeting firmly in place, Safeway started to steadily increase its capital spending on both new stores and remodeling projects.

Eight years after implementing the new decision-making process, Safeway's 1,665 stores now occupy 70.8 million square feet of retail space. The company's capital budget approached $1.5 billion in 1999, when it opened 67 and remodeled 251 stores. It plans to spend another $1.6 billion to open 70 to 75 stores and remodel 250 others in 2000. Safeway's approach to capital budgeting projects relating to its stores has continued to result in strong returns on investment.

Safeway recently decided to make a significant investment in a different type of capital project. Analysts had been critical of the company's reluctance to enter the online marketplace, but during June 2000, the company announced that it was investing $30 million in GroceryWorks.com, an online grocer. Customers will be able to access the GroceryWorks.com online website via Safeway's home page (www.safeway.com). Safeway's management stressed that they had felt the need to complete a comprehensive analysis of any project of this nature before proceeding. Given the problems that have plagued Peapod.com and Webvan, two major online grocers, Safeway's diligent approach to its decision-making process is being praised.

Sources: Safeway, Inc., website, August 2000; Jessica Materna, "Safeway Rolls into the Web through Online Deliverer," *San Francisco Business Times,* June 23, 2000, p. 26 © *San Francisco Business Times.* Reprinted with the permission of the *San Francisco Business Times.* Robert Berner, "Safeway's Resurgence Is Built on Attention to Detail," *The Wall Street Journal,* October 2, 1998, p. B4.

Learning Objectives
After studying Chapter 12, you should be able to:

LO1 Determine the acceptability of an investment project using the net present value method.

LO2 Prepare a net present value analysis of two competing investment projects using either the incremental-cost approach or the total-cost approach.

LO3 Rank investment projects in order of preference using the profitability index.

LO4 Determine the payback period for an investment.

LO5 Compute the simple rate of return for an investment.

LO6 (Appendix 12A) Explain the concept of present value and make present value computations.

The term **capital budgeting** is used to describe how managers plan significant outlays on projects that have long-term implications, such as the purchase of new equipment and the introduction of new products. Most companies have many more potential projects than can actually be funded. Hence, managers must carefully select those projects that promise the greatest future return. How well managers make these capital budgeting decisions is a critical factor in the long-run profitability of the company.

Capital budgeting involves *investment*—a company must commit funds now in order to receive a return in the future. Investments are not limited to stocks and bonds. Purchase of inventory or equipment is also an investment. For example, Tri-Con Global Restaurants Inc. makes an investment when it opens a new Pizza Hut restaurant. L. L. Bean makes an investment when it installs a new computer to handle customer billing. DaimlerChrysler makes an investment when it redesigns a product such as the Jeep Eagle and must retool its production lines. Merck & Co. invests in medical research. Amazon.com makes an investment when it redesigns its website. All of these investments are characterized by a commitment of funds today in the expectation of receiving a return in the future in the form of additional cash inflows or reduced cash outflows.

Capital Budgeting—Planning Investments

Typical Capital Budgeting Decisions

The types of business decisions that require capital budgeting analysis are virtually any decisions that involve an outlay now in order to obtain some return (increase in revenue or reduction in costs) in the future. Typical capital budgeting decisions include:

1. Cost reduction decisions: Should new equipment be purchased to reduce costs?
2. Expansion decisions: Should a new plant, warehouse, or other facility be acquired to increase capacity and sales?
3. Equipment selection decisions: Which of several available machines would be the most cost effective to purchase?
4. Lease or buy decisions: Should new equipment be leased or purchased?
5. Equipment replacement decisions: Should old equipment be replaced now or later?

in business *today* **The Yukon Goes Online**

Canada's Yukon Territory, which is two-thirds the size of Texas, has only 31,000 residents. Two-thirds of those live in Whitehorse, the territory's capital. All are about to get higher-speed Internet access as part of an ambitious Canadian government program to connect the Yukon with the rest of the world. To date, the Yukon's physical isolation has precluded economic growth in the area. The Internet may change all that. In some ways, it already has. A variety of organizations in the Yukon have made significant outlays on Internet projects that will have long-term implications.

After struggling to stay in business with annual sales of only $10,000, Herbie Croteau, the founder of Midnight Sun Plant Food, spent $1,600 to build a website for the company (www.midnightsunplantfood.com). Just two years later, sales are expected to exceed $65,000. Croteau is in the process of spending another $2,000 to redesign the company's website.

The town of Haines Junction is spending $10,000 to redesign its website. The town's chief administrative officer estimates that printing costs for tourist brochures will drop by

75% since tourist information can now be obtained online at www.yukon.com/community/kluane/hj.html.

Four years ago, Roland and Susan Shaver started Bear North Adventures to provide guided snowmobile tours. To date, their biggest investment (other than for snowmobiles) has been the $2,000 they spent to create a website packed with photos at www.bearnorth.yukon.net.

Source: David H. Freedman, "Cold Comfort," *Forbes ASAP*, May 29, 2000, pp. 174–182.

Capital budgeting decisions tend to fall into two broad categories—*screening decisions* and *preference decisions*. **Screening decisions** are those relating to whether a proposed project meets some preset standard of acceptance. For example, a firm may have a policy of accepting projects only if they promise a return of, say, 20% on the investment. The required rate of return is the minimum rate of return a project must yield to be acceptable.

Preference decisions, by contrast, relate to selecting from among several *competing* courses of action. To illustrate, a firm may be considering several different machines to replace an existing machine on the assembly line. The choice of which machine to purchase is a *preference* decision.

In this chapter, we initially discuss ways of making screening decisions. Preference decisions are discussed toward the end of the chapter.

The Time Value of Money

As stated earlier, business investments commonly involve returns that extend over fairly long periods of time. Therefore, in approaching capital budgeting decisions, it is necessary to employ techniques that recognize the *time value of money*. A dollar today is worth more than a dollar a year from now. The same concept applies in choosing between investment projects. Those projects that promise returns earlier in time are preferable to those that promise returns later in time.

The capital budgeting techniques that recognize the above two characteristics of business investments most fully are those that involve *discounted cash flows*. We will spend most of this chapter illustrating the use of discounted cash flow methods in making capital budgeting decisions. If you are not already familiar with discounting and the use of present value tables, you should read Appendix 12A, The Concept of Present Value, at the end of this chapter before proceeding any further.

Several approaches can be used to evaluate investments using discounted cash flows. The easiest method to use is the *net present value method*, which is the subject of the next several sections.

The Net Present Value Method

Under the net present value method, the present value of a project's cash inflows is compared to the present value of the project's cash outflows. The difference between the present value of these cash flows, called the **net present value,** determines whether or not the project is an acceptable investment. To illustrate, let us assume the following data:

EXAMPLE A
Harper Company is contemplating the purchase of a machine capable of performing certain operations that are now performed manually. The machine will cost $5,000, and it will last for five years. At the end of the five-year period, the machine will have a zero scrap value.

Learning Objective 1
Determine the acceptability of an investment project using the net present value method.

Concept 12–1   **479**

Exhibit 12–1

Net Present Value Analysis of a
Proposed Project

Initial cost			$5,000
Life of the project (years)			5
Annual cost savings			$1,800
Salvage value			–0–
Required rate of return			20%

Item	Year(s)	Amount of Cash Flow	20% Factor	Present Value of Cash Flows
Annual cost savings	1–5	$ 1,800	2.991*	$5,384
Initial investment	Now	(5,000)	1.000	(5,000)
Net present value				$ 384

*From Table 12B-4 in Appendix 12B at the end of this chapter.

Use of the machine will reduce labor costs by $1,800 per year. Harper Company requires a minimum return of 20% before taxes on all investment projects.[1]

Should the machine be purchased? Harper Company must determine whether a cash investment now of $5,000 can be justified if it will result in an $1,800 reduction in cost each year over the next five years. It may appear that the answer is obvious since the total cost savings is $9,000 (5 × $1,800). However, the company can earn a 20% return by investing its money elsewhere. It is not enough that the cost reductions cover just the original cost of the machine; they must also yield at least a 20% return or the company would be better off investing the money elsewhere.

To determine whether the investment is desirable, the stream of annual $1,800 cost savings is discounted to its present value and then compared to the cost of the new machine. Since Harper Company requires a minimum return of 20% on all investment projects, this rate is used in the discounting process. Exhibit 12–1 shows how this analysis is done.

According to the analysis, Harper Company should purchase the new machine. The present value of the cost savings is $5,384, as compared to a present value of only $5,000 for the investment required (cost of the machine). Deducting the present value of the investment required from the present value of the cost savings gives a *net present value* of $384. Whenever the net present value is zero or greater, as in our example, an investment project is acceptable. Whenever the net present value is negative (the present value of the cash outflows exceeds the present value of the cash inflows), an investment project is not acceptable. In sum:

If the Net Present Value Is . . .	Then the Project Is . . .
Positive	Acceptable, since it promises a return greater than the required rate of return.
Zero	Acceptable, since it promises a return equal to the required rate of return.
Negative	Not acceptable, since it promises a return less than the required rate of return.

A full interpretation of the solution would be as follows: The new machine promises more than the required 20% rate of return. This is evident from the positive net present value of $384. Harper Company could spend up to $5,384 for the new machine and still obtain the minimum required 20% rate of return. The net present value of $384, therefore, shows the amount of "cushion" or "margin of error." One way to look at this is that the

---

[1]For simplicity, we ignore taxes and inflation.

company could underestimate the cost of the new machine by up to $384, or overestimate the net present value of the future cash savings by up to $384, and the project would still be financially attractive.

Emphasis on Cash Flows

In capital budgeting decisions, the focus is on cash flows and not on accounting net income. The reason is that accounting net income is based on accrual concepts that ignore the timing of cash flows into and out of an organization. From a capital budgeting standpoint, the timing of cash flows is important, since a dollar received today is more valuable than a dollar received in the future. Therefore, even though the accounting net income figure is useful for many things, it is not ordinarily used in discounted cash flow analysis.[2] Instead of determining accounting net income, the manager concentrates on identifying the specific cash flows of the investment project.

What kinds of cash flows should the manager look for? Although they will vary from project to project, certain types of cash flows tend to recur as explained in the following paragraphs.

Typical Cash Outflows Most projects will have an immediate cash outflow in the form of an initial investment in equipment or other assets. Any salvage value realized from the sale of old equipment can be recognized as a cash inflow or as a reduction in the required investment. In addition, some projects require that a company expand its working capital. **Working capital** is current assets (cash, accounts receivable, and inventory) less current liabilities. When a company takes on a new project, the balances in the current asset accounts will often increase. For example, opening a new Nordstrom's department store would require additional cash in sales registers, increased accounts receivable for new customers, and more inventory to stock the shelves. These additional working capital needs should be treated as part of the initial investment in a project. Also, many projects require periodic outlays for repairs and maintenance and for additional operating costs. These should all be treated as cash outflows for capital budgeting purposes.

Typical Cash Inflows On the cash inflow side, a project will normally either increase revenues or reduce costs. Either way, the amount involved should be treated as a cash inflow for capital budgeting purposes. *A reduction in costs is equivalent to an increase in revenues.* Cash inflows are also frequently realized from salvage of equipment when a project ends. In addition, any working capital that was tied up in the project can be released for use elsewhere at the end of the project and should be treated as a cash inflow. Working capital is released, for example, when a company sells off its inventory or collects its receivables.

In summary, the following types of cash flows are common in business investment projects:

Cash outflows:
    Initial investment (including installation costs).
    Increased working capital needs.
    Repairs and maintenance.
    Incremental operating costs.
Cash inflows:
    Incremental revenues.
    Reduction in costs.
    Salvage value.
    Release of working capital.

---

[2]Under certain conditions, capital budgeting decisions can be correctly made by discounting appropriately defined accounting net income. However, this approach requires advanced techniques that are beyond the scope of this book.

Simplifying Assumptions

Two simplifying assumptions are usually made in net present value analysis.

The first assumption is that all cash flows other than the initial investment occur at the end of periods. This is somewhat unrealistic in that cash flows typically occur *throughout* a period. The purpose of this assumption is just to simplify computations.

The second assumption is that all cash flows generated by an investment project are immediately reinvested at a rate of return equal to the discount rate. Unless these conditions are met, the net present value computed for the project will not be accurate.

in business today **A Return on Investment of 100%**

During negotiations to build a replacement for the old Fenway Park in Boston, the Red Sox offered the city approximately $2 million per year over 30 years in exchange for an investment of $150 million by the city for land acquisition and cleanup. In May 2000, after denying his lack of support for the project, Boston Mayor Thomas M. Menino stated that his goal is a 100% rate of return on any investment that is made by the city. Some doubt that the Red Sox would be able to pay players' salaries if the team were required to meet the mayor's goal. The mayor has countered with a list of suggestions for raising private funds (such as selling shares to the public, as the Celtics did in 1986). Private funds would reduce the investment that would need to be made by the city and, as a result, reduce the future payments made to the city by the Red Sox. Negotiations continue.

Source: Meg Vaillancourt, "Boston Mayor Wants High Return on Investment in New Ballpark," *Knight-Ridder/Tribune Business News,* May 11, 2000, pITEM00133018. Reprinted with permission of Knight Ridder/Tribune Information Services.

Choosing a Discount Rate

A positive net present value means that the project's return exceeds the discount rate. A negative net present value means that the project's return is less than the discount rate. Therefore, if the company's minimum required rate of return is used as the discount rate, a project with a positive net present value is acceptable and a project with a negative net present value is unacceptable.

What is a company's minimum required rate of return? The company's *cost of capital* is usually regarded as the minimum required rate of return. The **cost of capital** is the average rate of return the company must pay to its long-term creditors and to shareholders for the use of their funds. The cost of capital is the minimum required rate of return because if a project's rate of return is less than the cost of capital, the company does not earn enough of a return to compensate its creditors and shareholders. Therefore, any project with a rate of return less than the cost of capital should not be accepted.

The cost of capital serves as a *screening device* in net present value analysis. When the cost of capital is used as the discount rate, any project with a negative net present value does not cover the company's cost of capital and should be discarded as unacceptable.

decision maker **Negotiator for the Red Sox**

As stated above, Boston Mayor Thomas M. Menino's goal is a 100% rate of return on any investment that is made by the city to build a new park for the Red Sox. How would you respond to the mayor?

An Extended Example of the Net Present Value Method

To conclude our discussion of the net present value method, we present below an extended example of how it is used to analyze an investment proposal. This example will also help to tie together (and to reinforce) many of the ideas developed thus far.

Exhibit 12–2
The Net Present Value Method—An Extended Example

Sales revenues	$200,000
Less cost of goods sold	125,000
Less out-of-pocket costs for salaries, advertising, etc.	35,000
Annual net cash inflows	$ 40,000

Item	Year(s)	Amount of Cash Flows	20% Factor	Present Value of Cash Flows
Purchase of equipment	Now	$ (60,000)	1.000	$ (60,000)
Working capital needed	Now	(100,000)	1.000	(100,000)
Overhaul of equipment	4	(5,000)	0.482*	(2,410)
Annual net cash inflows from sales of the product line	1–5	40,000	2.991†	119,640
Salvage value of the equipment	5	10,000	0.402*	4,020
Working capital released	5	100,000	0.402*	40,200
Net present value				$ 1,450

*From Table 12B-3 in Appendix 12B.
†From Table 12B-4 in Appendix 12B.

EXAMPLE B

Under a special licensing arrangement, Swinyard Company has an opportunity to market a new product in the western United States for a five-year period. The product would be purchased from the manufacturer, with Swinyard Company responsible for all costs of promotion and distribution. The licensing arrangement could be renewed at the end of the five-year period at the option of the manufacturer. After careful study, Swinyard Company has estimated the following costs and revenues for the new product:

Cost of equipment needed	$ 60,000
Working capital needed	100,000
Overhaul of the equipment in four years	5,000
Salvage value of the equipment in five years	10,000
Annual revenues and costs:	
Sales revenues	200,000
Cost of goods sold	125,000
Out-of-pocket operating costs (for salaries, advertising, and other direct costs)	35,000

At the end of the five-year period, the working capital would be released for investment elsewhere if the manufacturer decided not to renew the licensing arrangement. Swinyard Company's discount rate and cost of capital is 20%. Would you recommend that the new product be introduced?

This example involves a variety of cash inflows and cash outflows. The solution is given in Exhibit 12–2.

Notice particularly how the working capital is handled in this exhibit. It is counted as a cash outflow at the beginning of the project and as a cash inflow when it is released at the end of the project. Also notice how the sales revenues, cost of goods sold, and out-of-pocket costs are handled. **Out-of-pocket costs** are actual cash outlays for salaries, advertising, and other operating expenses. Depreciation would not be an out-of-pocket cost, since it involves no current cash outlay.

Since the overall net present value is positive, the new product should be added assuming the company has no better use for the investment funds.

Expanding the Net Present Value Method

So far, our examples have involved only a single investment alternative. We will now expand the net present value method to include two alternatives. In addition, we will integrate the concept of relevant costs into the discounted cash flow analysis.

The net present value method can be used to compare competing investment projects in two ways. One is the *total-cost approach,* and the other is the *incremental-cost approach.* Each approach is illustrated below.

The Total-Cost Approach

The total-cost approach is the most flexible method for comparing projects. To illustrate the mechanics of the approach, let us assume the following data:

EXAMPLE C
Harper Ferry Company provides a ferry service across the Mississippi River. One of its ferryboats is in poor condition. This ferry can be renovated at an immediate cost of $20,000. Further repairs and an overhaul of the motor will be needed five years from now at a cost of $8,000. In all, the ferry will be usable for 10 years if this work is done. At the end of 10 years, the ferry will have to be scrapped at a salvage value of approximately $6,000. The scrap value of the ferry right now is $7,000. It will cost $30,000 each year to operate the ferry, and revenues will total $40,000 annually.

As an alternative, Harper Ferry Company can purchase a new ferryboat at a cost of $36,000. The new ferry will have a life of 10 years, but it will require some repairs at the end of 5 years. It is estimated that these repairs will amount to $3,000. At the end of 10 years, it is estimated that the ferry will have a scrap value of $6,000. It will cost $21,000 each year to operate the ferry, and revenues will total $40,000 annually.

Harper Ferry Company requires a return of at least 18% before taxes on all investment projects.

Should the company purchase the new ferry or renovate the old ferry? Exhibit 12–3 gives the solution using the total-cost approach.

Two points should be noted from the exhibit. First, observe that *all* cash inflows and *all* cash outflows are included in the solution under each alternative. No effort has been made to isolate those cash flows that are relevant to the decision and those that are not relevant. The inclusion of all cash flows associated with each alternative gives the approach its name—the *total-cost* approach.

Second, notice that a net present value figure is computed for each of the two alternatives. This is a distinct advantage of the total-cost approach in that an unlimited number of alternatives can be compared side by side to determine the best action. For example, another alternative for Harper Ferry Company would be to get out of the ferry business entirely. If management desired, the net present value of this alternative could be computed to compare with the alternatives shown in Exhibit 12–3. Still other alternatives might be open to the company. Once management has determined the net present value of each alternative, it can select the course of action that promises to be the most profitable. In the case at hand, given only the two alternatives, the best alternative is to purchase the new ferry.[3]

The Incremental-Cost Approach

When only two alternatives are being considered, the incremental-cost approach offers a simpler and more direct route to a decision. Unlike the total-cost approach, it focuses only

---

[3]The alternative with the highest net present value is not always the best choice, although it is the best choice in this case. For further discussion, see the section Preference Decisions—The Ranking of Investment Projects.

Exhibit 12–3

The Total-Cost Approach to Project Selection

			New Ferry	Old Ferry
Annual revenues			$40,000	$40,000
Annual cash operating costs			21,000	30,000
Net annual cash inflows			$19,000	$10,000

Item	Year(s)	Amount of Cash Flows	18% Factor*	Present Value of Cash Flows
Buy the new ferry:				
Initial investment	Now	$(36,000)	1.000	$(36,000)
Repairs in five years	5	(3,000)	0.437	(1,311)
Net annual cash inflows	1–10	19,000	4.494	85,386
Salvage of the old ferry	Now	7,000	1.000	7,000
Salvage of the new ferry	10	6,000	0.191	1,146
Net present value				56,221
Keep the old ferry:				
Initial repairs	Now	(20,000)	1.000	(20,000)
Repairs in five years	5	(8,000)	0.437	(3,496)
Net annual cash inflows	1–10	10,000	4.494	44,940
Salvage of the old ferry	10	6,000	0.191	1,146
Net present value				22,590
Net present value in favor of buying the new ferry				$ 33,631

*All factors are from Tables 12B-3 and 12B-4 in Appendix 12B.

on differential costs.[4] The procedure is to include in the discounted cash flow analysis only those costs and revenues that *differ* between the two alternatives being considered. To illustrate, refer again to the data in Example C relating to Harper Ferry Company. The solution using only differential costs is presented in Exhibit 12–4.

Two things should be noted from the data in this exhibit. First, notice that the net present value in favor of buying the new ferry of $33,631 shown in Exhibit 12–4 agrees with the net present value shown under the total-cost approach in Exhibit 12–3. This agreement should be expected, since the two approaches are just different roads to the same destination.

Second, notice that the costs used in Exhibit 12–4 are just the differences between the costs shown for the two alternatives in the prior exhibit. For example, the $16,000 incremental investment required to purchase the new ferry in Exhibit 12–4 is the difference between the $36,000 cost of the new ferry and the $20,000 cost required to renovate the old ferry from Exhibit 12–3. The other figures in Exhibit 12–4 have been computed in the same way.

Least-Cost Decisions

Revenues are not directly involved in some decisions. For example, a company that does not charge for delivery service may need to replace an old delivery truck, or a company

---

[4]Technically, the incremental-cost approach is misnamed, since it focuses on differential costs (that is, on both cost increases and decreases) rather than just on incremental costs. As used here, the term *incremental costs* should be interpreted broadly to include both cost increases and cost decreases.

Exhibit 12–4

The Incremental-Cost Approach to Project Selection

Item	Year(s)	Amount of Cash Flows	18% Factor*	Present Value of Cash Flows
Incremental investment required to purchase the new ferry	Now	$(16,000)	1.000	$(16,000)
Repairs in five years avoided	5	5,000	0.437	2,185
Increased net annual cash inflows	1–10	9,000	4.494	40,446
Salvage of the old ferry	Now	7,000	1.000	7,000
Difference in salvage value in 10 years	10	–0–	—	–0–
Net present value in favor of buying the new ferry				$ 33,631

*All factors are from Tables 12B-3 and 12B-4 in Appendix 12B.

may be trying to decide whether to lease or to buy its fleet of executive cars. In situations such as these, where no revenues are involved, the most desirable alternative will be the one that promises the *least total cost* from the present value perspective. Hence, these are known as least-cost decisions. To illustrate a least-cost decision, assume the following data:

EXAMPLE D

Val-Tek Company is considering the replacement of an old threading machine. A new threading machine is available that could substantially reduce annual operating costs. Selected data relating to the old and the new machines are presented below:

	Old Machine	New Machine
Purchase cost when new	$20,000	$25,000
Salvage value now	3,000	—
Annual cash operating costs	15,000	9,000
Overhaul needed immediately	4,000	—
Salvage value in six years	–0–	5,000
Remaining life	6 years	6 years

Val-Tek Company's cost of capital is 10%.

Exhibit 12–5 provides an analysis of the alternatives using the total-cost approach.

As shown in the exhibit, the new machine has the lowest total cost when the present value of the net cash outflows is considered. An analysis of the two alternatives using the incremental-cost approach is presented in Exhibit 12–6. As before, the data in this exhibit represent the differences between the alternatives as shown under the total-cost approach.

Preference Decisions—The Ranking of Investment Projects

Learning Objective 3

Rank investment projects in order of preference using the profitability index.

Recall that when considering investment opportunities, managers must make two types of decisions—screening decisions and preference decisions. Screening decisions pertain to whether or not some proposed investment is acceptable. Preference decisions come *after* screening decisions and attempt to answer the following question: "How do the remaining investment proposals, all of which have been screened and provide an acceptable rate of return, rank in terms of preference? That is, which one(s) would be *best* for the firm to accept?"

Preference decisions are more difficult to make than screening decisions because investment funds are usually limited. This often requires that some (perhaps many) otherwise very profitable investment opportunities must be passed up.

Exhibit 12–5

The Total-Cost Approach (Least-Cost Decision)

Item	Year(s)	Amount of Cash Flows	10% Factor*	Present Value of Cash Flows
Buy the new machine:				
Initial investment	Now	$(25,000)	1.000	$(25,000)†
Salvage of the old machine	Now	3,000	1.000	3,000†
Annual cash operating costs	1–6	(9,000)	4.355	(39,195)
Salvage of the new machine	6	5,000	0.564	2,820
Present value of net cash outflows				(58,375)
Keep the old machine:				
Overhaul needed now	Now	(4,000)	1.000	(4,000)
Annual cash operating costs	1–6	(15,000)	4.355	(65,325)
Present value of net cash outflows				(69,325)
Net present value in favor of buying the new machine				$ 10,950

*All factors are from Tables 12B-3 and 12B-4 in Appendix 12B.
†These two items could be netted into a single $22,000 incremental-cost figure ($25,000 − $3,000 = $22,000).

Exhibit 12–6

The Incremental-Cost Approach (Least-Cost Decision)

Item	Year(s)	Amount of Cash Flows	10% Factor*	Present Value of Cash Flows
Incremental investment required to purchase the new machine	Now	$(21,000)	1.000	$(21,000)†
Salvage of the old machine	Now	3,000	1.000	3,000†
Savings in annual cash operating costs	1–6	6,000	4.355	26,130
Difference in salvage value in six years ...	6	5,000	0.564	2,820
Net present value in favor of buying the new machine				$ 10,950

*All factors are from Tables 12B-3 and 12B-4 in Appendix 12B.
†These two items could be netted into a single $18,000 incremental-cost figure ($21,000 −$3,000 = $18,000).

Sometimes preference decisions are called rationing decisions or ranking decisions because they ration limited investment funds among many competing alternatives, or there may be many alternatives that must be ranked.

If the net present value method is used to rank projects, the net present value of one project cannot be compared directly to the net present value of another project unless the investments in the projects are of equal size. For example, assume that a company is considering two competing investments, as shown below:

	Investment	
	A	B
Investment required	$(80,000)	$(5,000)
Present value of cash inflows	81,000	6,000
Net present value	$ 1,000	$ 1,000

Each project has a net present value of $1,000, but the projects are not equally desirable. The project requiring an investment of only $5,000 is much more desirable when funds are limited than the project requiring an investment of $80,000. To compare the two projects on a valid basis, the present value of the cash inflows should be divided by the investment required. The result is called the **profitability index.** The formula for the profitability index follows:

$$\text{Profitability index} = \frac{\text{Present value of cash inflows}}{\text{Investment required}} \quad (1)$$

The profitability indexes for the two investments above would be computed as follows:

	Investment	
	A	B
Present value of cash inflows (a)	$81,000	$6,000
Investment required (b)	$80,000	$5,000
Profitability index, (a) ÷ (b)	1.01	1.20

When using the profitability index to rank competing investment projects, the preference rule is: *The higher the profitability index, the more desirable the project.* Applying this rule to the two investments above, investment B should be chosen over investment A.

The profitability index is an application of the techniques for utilizing scarce resources discussed in Chapter 11. In this case, the scarce resource is the limited funds available for investment, and the profitability index is similar to the contribution margin per unit of the scarce resource.

A few details should be clarified with respect to the computation of the profitability index. The "Investment required" refers to any cash outflows that occur at the beginning of the project, reduced by any salvage value recovered from the sale of old equipment. The "Investment required" also includes any investment in working capital that the project may need. Finally, we should note that the "Present value of cash inflows" is net of all *out*flows that occur after the project starts.

in business today Managing the Financial Risks of Drug Research

Several different techniques can be used to take into account uncertainties about future cash flows in capital budgeting. The uncertainties are particularly apparent in the drug business where it costs an average of $359 million and 10 years to bring a new drug through the governmental approval process and to market. And once on the market, 7 out of 10 products fail to return the company's cost of capital.

Merck & Co. manages the financial risks and uncertainties of drug research using a Research Planning Model they have developed. The model, which produces net present value estimates and other key statistics, is based on a wide range of scientific and financial variables—most of which are uncertain. For example, the future selling price of any drug resulting from current research is usually highly uncertain, but managers at Merck & Co. can at least specify a range within which the selling price is likely to fall.

The computer is used to draw a value at random, within the permissible range, for each of the variables in the model. The model then computes a net present value. This process is repeated many times, and each time a new value of each of the variables is drawn at random. In this way, Merck is able to produce a probability distribution for the net present value. This can be used, for example, to estimate the probability that the project's net present value will exceed a certain level. "What are the payoffs of all this sophistication? In short, better decisions."

Source: Nancy A. Nichols, "Scientific Management at Merck: An Interview with CFO Judy Lewent," *Harvard Business Review,* January–February 1994, pp. 89–99.

The Internal Rate of Return Method

The *internal rate of return* method is a popular alternative to the net present value method. The **internal rate of return** is the rate of return promised by an investment over its useful life. It is computed by finding the discount rate at which the net present value of the investment is zero. The internal rate of return can be used to either screen projects or to rank them. Any project whose internal rate of return is less than the cost of capital is rejected and in general, the higher the rate of return of a project, the more desirable it is considered to be.

For technical reasons that are discussed in more advanced texts, the net present value method is generally considered to be more reliable than the internal rate of return method for both screening and ranking projects.

The Net Present Value Method and Income Taxes

Our discussion of the net present value method has assumed that there are no income taxes. In most countries—including the United States—income taxes, both on individual income and on business income, are a fact of life.

Income taxes affect net present value analysis in two ways. First, income taxes affect the cost of capital in that the cost of capital should reflect the *after-tax* cost of long-term debt and of equity. Second, net present value analysis should focus on *after-tax cash flows*. The effects of income taxes on both revenues and expenses should be fully reflected in the analysis. This includes taking into account the tax deductibility of depreciation. Whereas depreciation is not itself a cash flow, it reduces taxable income and therefore income taxes, which *are* a cash flow. The techniques for adjusting the cost of capital and cash flows for income taxes are beyond the scope of this book and are covered in more advanced texts.

Other Approaches to Capital Budgeting Decisions

The net present value and internal rate of return methods have gained widespread acceptance as decision-making tools. Other methods of making capital budgeting decisions are also used, however, and are preferred by some managers. In this section, we discuss two such methods known as *payback* and *simple rate of return*. Both methods have been in use for many years, but have been declining in popularity as primary tools for project evaluation.

The Payback Method

The payback method focuses on the *payback period*. The **payback period** is the length of time that it takes for a project to recoup its initial cost out of the cash receipts that it generates. This period is sometimes referred to as "the time that it takes for an investment to pay for itself." The basic premise of the payback method is that the more quickly the cost of an investment can be recovered, the more desirable is the investment.

The payback period is expressed in years. *When the net annual cash inflow is the same every year,* the following formula can be used to compute the payback period:

$$\text{Payback period} = \frac{\text{Investment required}}{\text{Net annual cash inflow}^*} \qquad (2)$$

*If new equipment is replacing old equipment, this becomes incremental net annual cash inflow.

To illustrate the payback method, assume the following data:

Learning Objective 4
Determine the payback period for an investment.

Concept 12–2

EXAMPLE E
York Company needs a new milling machine. The company is considering two machines: machine A and machine B. Machine A costs $15,000 and will reduce operating costs by $5,000 per year. Machine B costs only $12,000 but will also reduce operating costs by $5,000 per year.

Required:
Which machine should be purchased according to the payback method?

$$\text{Machine A payback period} = \frac{\$15,000}{\$5,000} = 3.0 \text{ years}$$

$$\text{Machine B payback period} = \frac{\$12,000}{\$5,000} = 2.4 \text{ years}$$

According to the payback calculations, York Company should purchase machine B, since it has a shorter payback period than machine A.

Evaluation of the Payback Method

The payback method is not a true measure of the profitability of an investment. Rather, it simply tells the manager how many years will be required to recover the original investment. Unfortunately, a shorter payback period does not always mean that one investment is more desirable than another.

To illustrate, consider again the two machines used in the example above. Since machine B has a shorter payback period than machine A, it *appears* that machine B is more desirable than machine A. But if we add one more piece of data, this illusion quickly disappears. Machine A has a projected 10-year life, and machine B has a projected 5-year life. It would take two purchases of machine B to provide the same length of service as would be provided by a single purchase of machine A. Under these circumstances, machine A would be a much better investment than machine B, even though machine B has a shorter payback period. Unfortunately, the payback method has no inherent mechanism for highlighting differences in useful life between investments. Such differences can be very important, and relying on payback alone may result in incorrect decisions.

A further criticism of the payback method is that it does not consider the time value of money. A cash inflow to be received several years in the future is weighed equally with a cash inflow to be received right now. To illustrate, assume that for an investment of $8,000 you can purchase either of the two following streams of cash inflows:

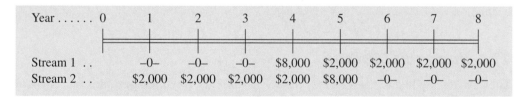

Year	0	1	2	3	4	5	6	7	8
Stream 1 ..		–0–	–0–	–0–	$8,000	$2,000	$2,000	$2,000	$2,000
Stream 2 ..		$2,000	$2,000	$2,000	$2,000	$8,000	–0–	–0–	–0–

Which stream of cash inflows would you prefer to receive in return for your $8,000 investment? Each stream has a payback period of 4.0 years. Therefore, if payback alone were relied on in making the decision, you would be forced to say that the streams are equally desirable. However, from the point of view of the time value of money, stream 2 is much more desirable than stream 1.

On the other hand, under certain conditions the payback method can be very useful. For one thing, it can help identify which investment proposals are in the "ballpark." That is, it can be used as a screening tool to help answer the question, "Should I consider this proposal further?" If a proposal doesn't provide a payback within some specified period, then there may be no need to consider it further. In addition, the payback period is often of great importance to new firms that are "cash poor." When a firm is cash poor, a project with a short payback period but a low rate of return might be preferred over another project with a high rate of return but a long payback period. The reason is that the company may simply need a faster return of its cash investment. And finally, the payback method is sometimes used in industries where products become obsolete very rapidly—such as consumer electronics. Since products may last only a year or two, the payback period on investments must be very short.

Capital Budgeting at U.K. Universities

in business | today

Capital budgeting techniques are widely used in large nonprofit organizations. A survey of universities in the United Kingdom revealed that 41% use the net present value method, 23% use the internal rate of return method, 29% use the payback method, and 11% use the accounting rate of return method. (Some universities use more than one method.) Furthermore, the central Funding Council of the United Kingdom requires that the net present value method be used for projects whose lifespans exceed 20 years.

Source: Paul Cooper, "Management Accounting Practices in Universities," *Management Accounting (U.K.)*, February 1996, pp. 28–30.

An Extended Example of Payback

As shown by formula (2) given earlier, the payback period is computed by dividing the investment in a project by the net annual cash inflows that the project will generate. If new equipment is replacing old equipment, then any salvage to be received on disposal of the old equipment should be deducted from the cost of the new equipment, and only the *incremental* investment should be used in the payback computation. In addition, any depreciation deducted in arriving at the project's net income must be added back to obtain the project's expected net annual cash inflow. To illustrate, assume the following data:

EXAMPLE F

Goodtime Fun Centers, Inc., operates many outlets in the eastern states. Some of the vending machines in one of its outlets provide very little revenue, so the company is considering removing the machines and installing equipment to dispense soft ice cream. The equipment would cost $80,000 and have an eight-year useful life. Incremental annual revenues and costs associated with the sale of ice cream would be as follows:

Sales	$150,000
Less cost of ingredients	90,000
Contribution margin	60,000
Less fixed expenses:	
Salaries	27,000
Maintenance	3,000
Depreciation	10,000
Total fixed expenses	40,000
Net income	$ 20,000

    The vending machines can be sold for a $5,000 scrap value. The company will not purchase equipment unless it has a payback of three years or less. Should the equipment to dispense ice cream be purchased?

    An analysis of the payback period of the proposed equipment is given in Exhibit 12–7. Several things should be noted from the data in this exhibit. First, notice that depreciation is added back to net income to obtain the net annual cash inflow from the new equipment. As stated earlier in the chapter, depreciation is not a cash outlay; thus, it must be added back to net income to adjust net income to a cash basis. Second, notice in the payback

Exhibit 12–7
Computation of the Payback
Period

Step 1: *Compute the net annual cash inflow.* Since the net annual cash inflow is not
given, it must be computed before the payback period can be determined:

Net income (given above)	$20,000
Add: Noncash deduction for depreciation	10,000
Net annual cash flow	$30,000

Step 2: *Compute the payback period.* Using the net annual cash inflow figure from
above, the payback period can be determined as follows:

Cost of the new equipment	$80,000
Less salvage value of old equipment	5,000
Investment required	$75,000

$$\text{Payback period} = \frac{\text{Investment required}}{\text{Net annual cash inflow}}$$

$$= \frac{\$75,000}{\$30,000} = 2.5 \text{ years}$$

computation that the salvage value from the old machines has been deducted from the
cost of the new equipment, and that only the incremental investment has been used in
computing the payback period.

Since the proposed equipment has a payback period of less than three years, the company's payback requirement has been met.

in business today Rapid Obsolescence

Intel Corporation invests a billion to a billion and a half dollars in plants to fabricate computer processor chips such as the Pentium IV. But the fab plants can only be used to make
state-of-the-art chips for about two years. By that time, the equipment is obsolete and the
plant must be converted to making less complicated chips. Under such conditions of rapid
obsolescence, the payback method may be the most appropriate way to evaluate investments. If the project does not pay back within a few years, it may never pay back its initial investment.

Source: "Pentium at a Glance," *Forbes ASAP*, February 26, 1996, p. 66.

Payback and Uneven Cash Flows

When the cash flows associated with an investment project change from year to year, the
simple payback formula that we outlined earlier is no longer usable, and the computations
involved in deriving the payback period can be fairly complex. Consider the following data:

Year	Investment	Cash Inflow
1	$4,000	$1,000
2		–0–
3		2,000
4	2,000	1,000
5		500
6		3,000
7		2,000
8		2,000

Year	(1) Beginning Unrecovered Investment	(2) Investment	(3) Cash Inflow	(4) Ending Unrecovered Investment (1) + (2) − (3)
1	$ 0	$4,000	$1,000	$3,000
2	3,000		–0–	3,000
3	3,000		2,000	1,000
4	1,000	2,000	1,000	2,000
5	2,000		500	1,500
6	1,500		3,000	–0–
7	–0–		2,000	–0–
8	–0–		2,000	–0–

Exhibit 12–8
Payback and Uneven Cash Flows

What is the payback period on this investment? The answer is 5.5 years, but to obtain this figure it is necessary to track the unrecovered investment year by year. The steps involved in this process are shown in Exhibit 12–8. By the middle of the sixth year, sufficient cash inflows will have been realized to recover the entire investment of $6,000 ($4,000 + $2,000).

The Simple Rate of Return Method

The **simple rate of return** method is another capital budgeting technique that does not involve discounted cash flows. The method is also known as the accounting rate of return, the unadjusted rate of return, and the financial statement method.

Learning Objective 5
Compute the simple rate of return for an investment.

Unlike the other capital budgeting methods that we have discussed, the simple rate of return method does not focus on cash flows. Rather, it focuses on accounting net income. The approach is to estimate the revenues that will be generated by a proposed investment and then to deduct from these revenues all of the projected operating expenses associated with the project. This net income figure is then related to the initial investment in the project, as shown in the following formula:

$$\text{Simple rate of return} = \frac{\overset{\text{Incremental}}{\text{revenues}} - \overset{\text{Incremental expenses,}}{\text{including deprciation}} = \overset{\text{Incremental}}{\text{net income}}}{\text{Intial investment*}} \quad (3)$$

*The investment should be reduced by any salvage from the sale of old equipment.

Or, if a cost reduction project is involved, formula (3) becomes:

$$\text{Simple rate of return} = \frac{\overset{\text{Cost}}{\text{savings}} - \overset{\text{Depreciation on}}{\text{new equipment}}}{\text{Initial investment*}} \quad (4)$$

*The investment should be reduced by any salvage from the sale of old equipment.

EXAMPLE G
Brigham Tea, Inc., is a processor of a low acid tea. The company is contemplating purchasing equipment for an additional processing line. The additional processing line would increase revenues by $90,000 per year. Incremental cash operating expenses would be $40,000 per year. The equipment would cost $180,000 and have a nine-year life. No salvage value is projected.

Required:
Compute the simple rate of return.

SOLUTION:
By applying the formula for the simple rate of return found in equation (3), we can compute the simple rate of return:

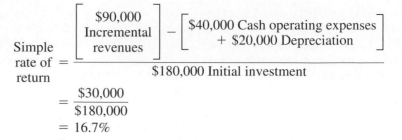

$$\text{Simple rate of return} = \frac{\left[\begin{array}{c}\$90,000\\ \text{Incremental}\\ \text{revenues}\end{array}\right] - \left[\begin{array}{c}\$40,000 \text{ Cash operating expenses}\\ + \$20,000 \text{ Depreciation}\end{array}\right]}{\$180,000 \text{ Initial investment}}$$

$$= \frac{\$30,000}{\$180,000}$$

$$= 16.7\%$$

EXAMPLE H

Midwest farms, Inc., hires people on a part-time basis to sort eggs. The cost of this hand-sorting process is $30,000 per year. The company is investigating the purchase of an egg-sorting machine that would cost $90,000 and have a 15-year useful life. The machine would have negligible salvage value, and it would cost $10,000 per year to operate and maintain. The egg-sorting equipment currently being used could be sold now for a scrap value of $2,500.

Required:

Compute the simple rate of return on the new egg-sorting machine.

SOLUTION:

A cost reduction project is involved in this situation. By applying the formula for the simple rate of return found in equation (4), we can compute the simple rate of return as follows:

$$\text{Simple rate of return} = \frac{\begin{array}{c}\$20,000\text{* Cost}\\ \text{savings}\end{array} - \begin{array}{c}\$6,000^\dagger \text{ Depreciation}\\ \text{on new equipment}\end{array}}{\$90,000 - \$2,500}$$

$$= 16.0\%$$

*$30,000 − $10,000 = $20,000 cost savings.
†$90,000 ÷ 15 years = $6,000 depreciation.

Criticisms of the Simple Rate of Return

The most damaging criticism of the simple rate of return method is that it does not consider the time value of money. A dollar received 10 years from now is viewed as being just as valuable as a dollar received today. Thus, the manager can be misled if the alternatives being considered have different cash flow patterns.

Additionally, many projects do not have uniform cash flows and incremental revenues and expenses over their useful lives. As a result, the simple rate of return will fluctuate from year to year, with the possibility that a project may appear to be desirable in some years and undesirable in other years. In contrast, the net present value method provides a single figure that summarizes all of the cash flows over the entire useful life of the project.

Postaudit of Investment Projects

A **postaudit** of an investment project involves a follow-up after the project has been approved to see whether or not expected results are actually realized. This is a key part of the capital budgeting process that provides an opportunity to see if realistic data are being submitted to support capital budgeting proposals. It also provides an opportunity to reinforce successful projects as needed, to strengthen or perhaps salvage projects that are encountering difficulty, to terminate unsuccessful projects before losses become too great, and to improve the overall quality of future investment proposals.

In performing a postaudit, the same technique should be used as was used in the original approval process. That is, if a project was approved on the basis of a net present value analysis, then the same procedure should be used in performing the postaudit. However, the data used in the postaudit analysis should be *actual observed data* rather than estimated data. This affords management with an opportunity to make a side-by-side comparison to see how well the project has worked out. It also helps assure that estimated data received on future proposals will be carefully prepared, since the persons submitting the data will know that their estimates will be given careful scrutiny in the postaudit process. Actual results that are far out of line with original estimates should be carefully reviewed by management. Those managers responsible for the original estimates should be required to provide a full explanation of any major differences between estimated and actual results.[5]

Investor

you decide

Each of the following situations is independent. Work out your own solution to each situation, and then check it against the solution provided.
1. John has just reached age 58. In 12 years, he plans to retire. Upon retiring, he would like to take an extended vacation, which he expects will cost at least $4,000. What lump-sum amount must he invest now to have the needed $4,000 at the end of 12 years if the rate of return is:
    a. Eight percent?
    b. Twelve percent?
2. The Morgans would like to send their daughter to an expensive music camp at the end of each of the next five years. The camp costs $1,000 a year. What lump-sum amount would have to be invested now to have the $1,000 at the end of each year if the rate of return is:
    a. Eight percent?
    b. Twelve percent?
3. You have just received an inheritance from a relative. You can invest the money and either receive a $20,000 lump-sum amount at the end of 10 years or receive $1,400 at the end of each year for the next 10 years. If your minimum desired rate of return is 12%, which alternative should you select?

Summary

LO1   Determine the acceptability of an investment project using the net present value method.

Investment decisions should take into account the time value of money since a dollar today is more valuable than a dollar received in the future. In the net present value method, future cash flows are discounted to their present value so that they can be compared on a valid basis with current cash outlays. The difference between the present value of the cash inflows and the present value of the cash outflows is called the project's net present value. If the net present value of the project is negative, the project is rejected. The company's cost of capital is often used as the discount rate in the net present value method.

LO2   Prepare a net present value analysis of two competing investment projects using either the incremental-cost approach or the total-cost approach.

When comparing two projects, the project with the highest net present value is the most desirable. The project with the highest net present value can be determined either by taking the net present value of the cash flows for each project or by taking the net present value of the differences in the cash flows between the two projects.

LO3   Rank investment projects in order of preference using the profitability index.

After screening out projects whose net present values are negative, the company may still have more projects than can be supported with available funds. The remaining projects can be ranked using the profitability index, which is computed by dividing the present value of the project's future net cash inflows by the required initial investment.

[5]For further discussion, see Lawrence A. Gordon and Mary D. Myers, "Postauditing Capital Projects," *Management Accounting* 72, no. 7 (January 1991), pp. 39–42. This study of 282 large U.S. companies states that "an increasing number of firms are recognizing the importance of the postaudit stage" (p. 41).

LO4   **Determine the payback period for an investment.**

The payback period is the number of periods that are required to recover the investment in a project from the project's cash inflows. The payback period is most useful for projects whose useful lives are short and uncertain. It is not, however, a generally reliable method for evaluating investment opportunities since it ignores the time value of money and all cash flows that occur after the investment has been recovered.

LO5   **Compute the simple rate of return for an investment.**

The simple rate of return is determined by dividing a project's accounting net income by the initial investment in the project. The simple rate of return is not a reliable guide for evaluating potential projects since it ignores the time value of money and its value may fluctuate from year to year.

Guidance Answers to Decision Maker and You Decide

A RETURN ON INVESTMENT OF 100% (p. 482)

Apparently, the mayor is suggesting that 100% is the appropriate rate of return for discounting the cash flows that would be received by the city to their net present value. You might respond by pointing out that an organization's cost of capital is usually regarded as the minimum required rate of return. Because the City of Boston does not have shareholders, its cost of capital might be considered the average rate of return that must be paid to its long-term creditors. It is highly unlikely that the city pays interest of 100% on its long-term debt.

Note that it is very possible that the term return on investment is being misused either by the mayor, the media, or both in this situation. The mayor's goal might actually be a 100% recovery of the city's investment from the Red Sox. Rather than expecting a 100% return *on* investment, the mayor may simply want a 100% return *of* investment. Taking the time to clarify the mayor's intent might change the course of negotiations.

INVESTOR (p. 495)

The solutions to the three questions are presented below. If you did not know how to approach these problems or did not arrive at the correct answers, you should study Appendix 12A, The Concept of Present Value, at the end of the chapter.

1. a. The amount that must be invested now would be the present value of the $4,000, using a discount rate of 8%. From Table 12B-3 in Appendix 12B, the factor for a discount rate of 8% for 12 periods is 0.397. Multiplying this discount factor by the $4,000 needed in 12 years will give the amount of the present investment required: $4,000 × 0.397 = $1,588.
    b. We will proceed as we did in (a) above, but this time we will use a discount rate of 12%. From Table 12B-3 in Appendix 12B, the factor for a discount rate of 12% for 12 periods is 0.257. Multiplying this discount factor by the $4,000 needed in 12 years will give the amount of the present investment required: $4,000 × 0.257 = $1,028.
        Notice that as the discount rate (desired rate of return) increases, the present value decreases.
2. This part differs from (1) above in that we are now dealing with an annuity rather than with a single future sum. The amount that must be invested now will be the present value of the $1,000 needed at the end of each year for five years. Since we are dealing with an annuity, or a series of annual cash flows, we must refer to Table 12B-4 in Appendix 12B for the appropriate discount factor.
    a. From Table 12B-4 in Appendix 12B, the discount factor for 8% for five periods is 3.993. Therefore, the amount that must be invested now to have $1,000 available at the end of each year for five years is $1,000 × 3.993 = $3,993.
    b. From Table 12B-4 in Appendix 12B, the discount factor for 12% for five periods is 3.605. Therefore, the amount that must be invested now to have $1,000 available at the end of each year for five years is $1,000 × 3.605 = $3,605.
        Again, notice that as the discount rate (desired rate of return) increases, the present value decreases. At a higher rate of return we can invest less than would have been needed if a lower rate of return were being earned.
3. For this part we will need to refer to both Tables 12B-3 and 12B-4 in Appendix 12B. From Table 12B-3, we will need to find the discount factor for 12% for 10 periods, then apply it to the $20,000 lump sum to be received in 10 years. From Table 12B-4, we will need to find the discount factor for 12% for 10 periods, then apply it to the series of $1,400 payments to be received over the 10-year period. Whichever alternative has the higher present value is the one that should be selected.

$$\$20,000 \times 0.322 = \$6,440$$
$$\$1,400 \times 5.650 = \$7,910$$

Thus, you would prefer to receive the $1,400 per year for 10 years rather than the $20,000 lump sum.

Review Problem: Comparison of Capital Budgeting Methods

Lamar Company is studying a project that would have an eight-year life and require a $1,600,000 investment in equipment. At the end of eight years, the project would terminate and the equipment would have no salvage value. The project would provide net income each year as follows:

Sales		$3,000,000
Less variable expenses		1,800,000
Contribution margin		1,200,000
Less fixed expenses:		
Advertising, salaries, and other		
fixed out-of-pocket costs	$700,000	
Depreciation	200,000	
Total fixed expenses		900,000
Net income		$ 300,000

The company's discount rate is 18%.

Required:
1. Compute the net annual cash inflow from the project.
2. Compute the project's net present value. Is the project acceptable?
3. Compute the project's payback period. If the company requires a maximum payback of three years, is the project acceptable?
4. Compute the project's simple rate of return.

SOLUTION TO REVIEW PROBLEM

1. The net annual cash inflow can be computed by deducting the cash expenses from sales:

Sales	$3,000,000
Less variable expenses	1,800,000
Contribution margin	1,200,000
Less advertising, salaries, and other fixed	
out-of-pocket costs	700,000
Net annual cash inflow	$ 500,000

Or it can be computed by adding depreciation back to net income:

Net income	$300,000
Add: Noncash deduction for depreciation	200,000
Net annual cash inflow	$500,000

2. The net present value can be computed as follows:

Item	Year(s)	Amount of Cash Flows	18% Factor	Present Value of Cash Flows
Cost of new equipment	Now	$(1,600,000)	1.000	$(1,600,000)
Net annual cash inflow	1–8	500,000	4.078	2,039,000
Net present value				$ 439,000

Yes, the project is acceptable since it has a positive net present value.

3. The formula for the payback period is:

$$\text{Payback period} = \frac{\text{Investment required}}{\text{Net annual cash inflow}}$$

$$= \frac{\$1,600,000}{\$500,000}$$

$$= 3.2 \text{ years}$$

No, the project is not acceptable when measured by the payback method. The 3.2 years payback period is greater than the maximum 3 years set by the company.

4. The formula for the simple rate of return is:

$$\text{Simple rate of return} = \frac{\overset{\text{Incremental}}{\text{revenues}} - \overset{\text{Incremental expenses,}}{\text{including depreciation}} = \overset{\text{Net}}{\text{income}}}{\text{Initial investment}}$$

$$= \frac{\$300,000}{\$1,600,000}$$

$$= 18.75\%$$

Glossary

Capital budgeting   The process of planning significant outlays on projects that have long-term implications such as the purchase of new equipment or the introduction of a new product. (p. 478)

Cost of capital   The average rate of return the company must pay to its long-term creditors and to shareholders for the use of their funds. (p. 482)

Internal rate of return   The discount rate at which the net present value of an investment project is zero; thus, the internal rate of return represents the return promised by a project over its useful life. (p. 489)

Net present value   The difference between the present value of the cash inflows and the present value of the cash outflows of an investment project. (p. 479)

Out-of-pocket costs   Actual cash outlays for salaries, advertising, repairs, and similar costs. (p. 483)

Payback period   The length of time that it takes for a project to recover its initial cost out of the cash receipts that it generates. (p. 489)

Postaudit   The follow-up after a project has been approved and implemented to determine whether expected results are actually realized. (p. 494)

Preference decision   A decision as to which of several competing acceptable investment proposals is best. (p. 479)

Profitability index   The ratio of the present value of a project's cash inflows to the investment required. (p. 488)

Screening decision   A decision as to whether a proposed investment meets some preset standard of acceptance. (p. 479)

Simple rate of return   The rate of return computed by dividing a project's annual accounting net income by the initial investment required. (p. 493)

Working capital   The excess of current assets over current liabilities. (p. 481)

Appendix 12A: The Concept of Present Value

A dollar received today is more valuable than a dollar received a year from now for the simple reason that if you have a dollar today, you can put it in the bank and have more than a dollar a year from now. Since dollars today are worth more than dollars in the future, we need some means of weighting cash flows that are received at different times so that they can be compared. The theory of interest provides us with the means of making such comparisons. With a few simple calculations, we can adjust the value of a dollar received any number of years from now so that it can be compared with the value of a dollar in hand today.

Learning Objective 6
Explain the concept of present value and make present value computations.

The Theory of Interest

If a bank pays 5% interest, then a deposit of $100 today will be worth $105 one year from now. This can be expressed in mathematical terms by means of the following equation:

$$F_1 = P(1 + r) \qquad (5)$$

where F_1 = the amount to be received in one period, P = the amount invested now, and r = the rate of interest per period.

If the investment made now is $100 deposited in a bank savings account that is to earn interest at 5%, then $P = \$100$ and $r = 0.05$. Under these conditions, $F_1 = \$105$, the amount to be received in one year.

The $100 present outlay is called the **present value** of the $105 amount to be received in one year. It is also known as the *discounted value* of the future $105 receipt. The $100 figure represents the value in present terms of $105 to be received a year from now when the interest rate is 5%.

Compound Interest   What if the $105 is left in the bank for a second year? In that case, by the end of the second year the original $100 deposit will have grown to $110.25:

Original deposit	$100.00
Interest for the first year: $100 × 0.05	5.00
Amount at the end of the first year	105.00
Interest for the second year: $105 × 0.05	5.25
Amount at the end of the second year	$110.25

Notice that the interest for the second year is $5.25, as compared to only $5 for the first year. The reason for the greater interest earned during the second year is that during the second year, interest is being paid *on interest*. That is, the $5 interest earned during the first year has been left in the account and has been added to the original $100 deposit when computing interest for the second year. This is known as **compound interest.** The compounding we have done is annual compounding. Interest can be compounded on a

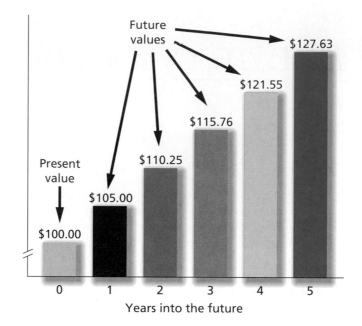

semiannual, quarterly, or even more frequent basis. The more frequently compounding is done, the more rapidly the balance will grow.

We can determine the balance in an account after n periods using the following equation:

$$F_n = P(1 + r)^n \qquad (6)$$

where n = the number of periods.

If $n = 2$ years and the interest rate is 5% per year, then our computation of the value of F in two years will be as follows:

$$F_2 = \$100(1 + 0.05)^2$$

$$F_2 = \$110.25$$

Present Value and Future Value   Exhibit 12A–1 shows the relationship between present value and future value as expressed in the theory of interest equations. As shown in the exhibit, if $100 is deposited in a bank at 5% interest, it will grow to $127.63 by the end of five years if interest is compounded annually.

Computation of Present Value

An investment can be viewed in two ways. It can be viewed either in terms of its future value or in terms of its present value. We have seen from our computations above that if we know the present value of a sum (such as our $100 deposit), it is a relatively simple task to compute the sum's future value in n years by using equation (6). But what if the tables are reversed and we know the *future* value of some amount but we do not know its present value?

For example, assume that you are to receive $200 two years from now. You know that the future value of this sum is $200, since this is the amount that you will be receiving in two years. But what is the sum's present value—what is it worth *right now?* The present value of any sum to be received in the future can be computed by turning equation (6) around and solving for P:

$$P = \frac{F_n}{(1 + r)^n} \qquad (7)$$

In our example, $F = \$200$ (the amount to be received in the future), $r = 0.05$ (the rate of interest), and $n = 2$ (the number of years in the future that the amount is to be received).

Year	Factor at 12% (Table 12B–3)	Interest Received	Present Value
1	0.893	$15,000	$13,395
2	0.797	15,000	11,955
3	0.712	15,000	10,680
4	0.636	15,000	9,540
5	0.567	15,000	8,505
			$54,075

$$P = \frac{\$200}{(1 + 0.05)^2}$$

$$P = \frac{\$200}{1.1025}$$

$$P = \$181.40$$

As shown by the computation above, the present value of a $200 amount to be received two years from now is $181.40 if the interest rate is 5%. In effect, $181.40 received *right now* is equivalent to $200 received two years from now if the rate of return is 5%. The $181.40 and the $200 are just two ways of looking at the same thing.

The process of finding the present value of a future cash flow, which we have just completed, is called **discounting.** We have *discounted* the $200 to its present value of $181.40. The 5% interest figure that we have used to find this present value is called the **discount rate.** Discounting future sums to their present value is a common practice in business, particularly in capital budgeting decisions.

If you have a power key (y^x) on your calculator, the above calculations are fairly easy. However, some of the present value formulas we will be using are more complex and difficult to use. Fortunately, tables are available in which many of the calculations have already been done for you. For example, Table 12B–3 in Appendix 12B shows the discounted present value of $1 to be received at various periods in the future at various interest rates. The table indicates that the present value of $1 to be received two periods from now at 5% is 0.907. Since in our example we want to know the present value of $200 rather than just $1, we need to multiply the factor in the table by $200:

$$\$200 \times 0.907 = \$181.40$$

This answer is the same as we obtained earlier using the formula in equation (7).

Present Value of a Series of Cash Flows

Although some investments involve a single sum to be received (or paid) at a single point in the future, other investments involve a *series* of cash flows. A series (or stream) of identical cash flows is known as an **annuity.** To provide an example, assume that a firm has just purchased some government bonds in order to temporarily invest funds that are being held for future plant expansion. The bonds will yield interest of $15,000 each year and will be held for five years. What is the present value of the stream of interest receipts from the bonds? As shown in Exhibit 12A–2, the present value of this stream is $54,075 if we assume a discount rate of 12% compounded annually. The discount factors used in this exhibit were taken from Table 12B–3 in Appendix 12B.

Two points are important in connection with Exhibit 12A–2. First, notice that the farther we go forward in time, the smaller is the present value of the $15,000 interest receipt. The present value of $15,000 received a year from now is $13,395, as compared to only $8,505 for the $15,000 interest payment to be received five years from now. This point simply underscores the fact that money has a time value.

The second point is that the computations in Exhibit 12A–2 involved unnecessary work. The same present value of $54,075 could have been obtained more easily by referring to Table 12B–4 in Appendix 12B. Table 12B–4 contains the present value of $1 to be received each year over a *series* of years at various interest rates. Table 12B–4 has been derived by simply adding together the factors from Table 12B–3. To illustrate, we used the factors below from Table 12B–3 in the computations in Exhibit 12A–2:

Year	Table 12B–3 Factors at 12%
1	0.893
2	0.797
3	0.712
4	0.636
5	0.567
	3.605

The sum of the five factors above is 3.605. Notice from Table 12B–4 that the factor for $1 to be received each year for five years at 12% is also 3.605. If we use this factor and multiply it by the $15,000 annual cash inflow, then we get the same $54,075 present value that we obtained earlier in Exhibit 12A–2.

$$\$15,000 \times 3.605 = \$54,075$$

Therefore, when computing the present value of a series (or stream) of equal cash flows, Table 12B–4 should be used.

To summarize, the present value tables in Appendix 12B should be used as follows:

Table 12B–3: This table should be used to find the present value of a single cash flow (such as a single payment or receipt) occurring in the future.

Table 12B–4: This table should be used to find the present value of a series (or stream) of identical cash flows beginning at the end of the current year and continuing into the future.

The use of both of these tables is illustrated in various exhibits in the main body of the chapter. *When a present value factor appears in an exhibit, you should take the time to trace it back into either Table 12B–3 or Table 12B–4 to get acquainted with the tables and how they work.*

Glossary (Appendix 12A)

Annuity   A series, or stream, of identical cash flows. (p. 501)
Compound interest   The process of paying interest on interest in an investment. (p. 499)
Discount rate   The rate of return that is used to find the present value of a future cash flow. (p. 501)
Discounting   The process of finding the present value of a future cash flow. (p. 501)
Present value   The value now of an amount that will be received in some future period. (p. 499)

Appendix 12B: Future Value and Present Value Tables

Periods	4%	6%	8%	10%	12%	14%	20%
1	1.040	1.060	1.080	1.100	1.120	1.140	1.200
2	1.082	1.124	1.166	1.210	1.254	1.300	1.440
3	1.125	1.191	1.260	1.331	1.405	1.482	1.728
4	1.170	1.263	1.361	1.464	1.574	1.689	2.074
5	1.217	1.338	1.469	1.611	1.762	1.925	2.488
6	1.265	1.419	1.587	1.772	1.974	2.195	2.986
7	1.316	1.504	1.714	1.949	2.211	2.502	3.583
8	1.369	1.594	1.851	2.144	2.476	2.853	4.300
9	1.423	1.690	1.999	2.359	2.773	3.252	5.160
10	1.480	1.791	2.159	2.594	3.106	3.707	6.192
11	1.540	1.898	2.332	2.853	3.479	4.226	7.430
12	1.601	2.012	2.518	3.139	3.896	4.818	8.916
13	1.665	2.133	2.720	3.452	4.364	5.492	10.699
14	1.732	2.261	2.937	3.798	4.887	6.261	12.839
15	1.801	2.397	3.172	4.177	5.474	7.138	15.407
20	2.191	3.207	4.661	6.728	9.646	13.743	38.338
30	3.243	5.744	10.063	17.450	29.960	50.950	237.376
40	4.801	10.286	21.725	45.260	93.051	188.884	1469.772

Exhibit 12B–1
Future Value of $1;
$F_n = P(1 + r)^n$

Periods	4%	6%	8%	10%	12%	14%	20%
1	1.000	1.000	1.000	1.000	1.000	1.000	1.000
2	2.040	2.060	2.080	2.100	2.120	2.140	2.200
3	3.122	3.184	3.246	3.310	3.374	3.440	3.640
4	4.247	4.375	4.506	4.641	4.779	4.921	5.368
5	5.416	5.637	5.867	6.105	6.353	6.610	7.442
6	6.633	6.975	7.336	7.716	8.115	8.536	9.930
7	7.898	8.394	8.923	9.487	10.089	10.730	12.916
8	9.214	9.898	10.637	11.436	12.300	13.233	16.499
9	10.583	11.491	12.488	13.580	14.776	16.085	20.799
10	12.006	13.181	14.487	15.938	17.549	19.337	25.959
11	13.486	14.972	16.646	18.531	20.655	23.045	32.150
12	15.026	16.870	18.977	21.385	24.133	27.271	39.580
13	16.627	18.882	21.495	24.523	28.029	32.089	48.497
14	18.292	21.015	24.215	27.976	32.393	37.581	59.196
15	20.024	23.276	27.152	31.773	37.280	43.842	72.035
20	29.778	36.786	45.762	57.276	75.052	91.025	186.688
30	56.085	79.058	113.283	164.496	241.333	356.787	1181.882
40	95.026	154.762	259.057	442.593	767.090	1342.025	7343.858

Exhibit 12B–2
Future Value of an Annuity of $1 in Arrears;
$$F_n = \frac{(1 + r)^n - 1}{r}$$

Exhibit 12B–3

Present Value of $1; $P = \dfrac{F_n}{(1 + r)^n}$

Period	4%	5%	6%	8%	10%	12%	14%	16%	18%	20%	22%	24%	26%	28%	30%	40%
1	0.962	0.952	0.943	0.926	0.909	0.893	0.877	0.862	0.847	0.833	0.820	0.806	0.794	0.781	0.769	0.714
2	0.925	0.907	0.890	0.857	0.826	0.797	0.769	0.743	0.718	0.694	0.672	0.650	0.630	0.610	0.592	0.510
3	0.889	0.864	0.840	0.794	0.751	0.712	0.675	0.641	0.609	0.579	0.551	0.524	0.500	0.477	0.455	0.364
4	0.855	0.823	0.792	0.735	0.683	0.636	0.592	0.552	0.516	0.482	0.451	0.423	0.397	0.373	0.350	0.260
5	0.822	0.784	0.747	0.681	0.621	0.567	0.519	0.476	0.437	0.402	0.370	0.341	0.315	0.291	0.269	0.186
6	0.790	0.746	0.705	0.630	0.564	0.507	0.456	0.410	0.370	0.335	0.303	0.275	0.250	0.227	0.207	0.133
7	0.760	0.711	0.665	0.583	0.513	0.452	0.400	0.354	0.314	0.279	0.249	0.222	0.198	0.178	0.159	0.095
8	0.731	0.677	0.627	0.540	0.467	0.404	0.351	0.305	0.266	0.233	0.204	0.179	0.157	0.139	0.123	0.068
9	0.703	0.645	0.592	0.500	0.424	0.361	0.308	0.263	0.225	0.194	0.167	0.144	0.125	0.108	0.094	0.048
10	0.676	0.614	0.558	0.463	0.386	0.322	0.270	0.227	0.191	0.162	0.137	0.116	0.099	0.085	0.073	0.035
11	0.650	0.585	0.527	0.429	0.350	0.287	0.237	0.195	0.162	0.135	0.112	0.094	0.079	0.066	0.056	0.025
12	0.625	0.557	0.497	0.397	0.319	0.257	0.208	0.168	0.137	0.112	0.092	0.076	0.062	0.052	0.043	0.018
13	0.601	0.530	0.469	0.368	0.290	0.229	0.182	0.145	0.116	0.093	0.075	0.061	0.050	0.040	0.033	0.013
14	0.577	0.505	0.442	0.340	0.263	0.205	0.160	0.125	0.099	0.078	0.062	0.049	0.039	0.032	0.025	0.009
15	0.555	0.481	0.417	0.315	0.239	0.183	0.140	0.108	0.084	0.065	0.051	0.040	0.031	0.025	0.020	0.006
16	0.534	0.458	0.394	0.292	0.218	0.163	0.123	0.093	0.071	0.054	0.042	0.032	0.025	0.019	0.015	0.005
17	0.513	0.436	0.371	0.270	0.198	0.146	0.108	0.080	0.060	0.045	0.034	0.026	0.020	0.015	0.012	0.003
18	0.494	0.416	0.350	0.250	0.180	0.130	0.095	0.069	0.051	0.038	0.028	0.021	0.016	0.012	0.009	0.002
19	0.475	0.396	0.331	0.232	0.164	0.116	0.083	0.060	0.043	0.031	0.023	0.017	0.012	0.009	0.007	0.002
20	0.456	0.377	0.312	0.215	0.149	0.104	0.073	0.051	0.037	0.026	0.019	0.014	0.010	0.007	0.005	0.001
21	0.439	0.359	0.294	0.199	0.135	0.093	0.064	0.044	0.031	0.022	0.015	0.011	0.008	0.006	0.004	0.001
22	0.422	0.342	0.278	0.184	0.123	0.083	0.056	0.038	0.026	0.018	0.013	0.009	0.006	0.004	0.003	0.001
23	0.406	0.326	0.262	0.170	0.112	0.074	0.049	0.033	0.022	0.015	0.010	0.007	0.005	0.003	0.002	
24	0.390	0.310	0.247	0.158	0.102	0.066	0.043	0.028	0.019	0.013	0.008	0.006	0.004	0.003	0.002	
25	0.375	0.295	0.233	0.146	0.092	0.059	0.038	0.024	0.016	0.010	0.007	0.005	0.003	0.002	0.001	
26	0.361	0.281	0.220	0.135	0.084	0.053	0.033	0.021	0.014	0.009	0.006	0.004	0.002	0.002	0.001	
27	0.347	0.268	0.207	0.125	0.076	0.047	0.029	0.018	0.011	0.007	0.005	0.003	0.002	0.001	0.001	
28	0.333	0.255	0.196	0.116	0.069	0.042	0.026	0.016	0.010	0.006	0.004	0.002	0.002	0.001	0.001	
29	0.321	0.243	0.185	0.107	0.063	0.037	0.022	0.014	0.008	0.005	0.003	0.002	0.001	0.001		
30	0.308	0.231	0.174	0.099	0.057	0.033	0.020	0.012	0.007	0.004	0.003	0.002	0.001	0.001		
40	0.208	0.142	0.097	0.046	0.022	0.011	0.005	0.003	0.001	0.001						

Exhibit 12B-4

Present Value of an Annuity of $1 in Arrears; $P_n = \dfrac{1}{r}\left[1 - \dfrac{1}{(1+r)^n}\right]$

Period	4%	5%	6%	8%	10%	12%	14%	16%	18%	20%	22%	24%	26%	28%	30%	40%
1	0.962	0.952	0.943	0.926	0.909	0.893	0.877	0.862	0.847	0.833	0.820	0.806	0.794	0.781	0.769	0.714
2	1.886	1.859	1.833	1.783	1.736	1.690	1.647	1.605	1.566	1.528	1.492	1.457	1.424	1.392	1.361	1.224
3	2.775	2.723	2.673	2.577	2.487	2.402	2.322	2.246	2.174	2.106	2.042	1.981	1.923	1.868	1.816	1.589
4	3.630	3.546	3.465	3.312	3.170	3.037	2.914	2.798	2.690	2.589	2.494	2.404	2.320	2.241	2.166	1.879
5	4.452	4.330	4.212	3.993	3.791	3.605	3.433	3.274	3.127	2.991	2.864	2.745	2.635	2.532	2.436	2.035
6	5.242	5.076	4.917	4.623	4.355	4.111	3.889	3.685	3.498	3.326	3.167	3.020	2.885	2.759	2.643	2.168
7	6.002	5.786	5.582	5.206	4.868	4.564	4.288	4.039	3.812	3.605	3.416	3.242	3.083	2.937	2.802	2.263
8	6.733	6.463	6.210	5.747	5.335	4.968	4.639	4.344	4.078	3.837	3.619	3.421	3.241	3.076	2.925	2.331
9	7.435	7.108	6.802	6.247	5.759	5.328	4.946	4.607	4.303	4.031	3.786	3.566	3.366	3.184	3.019	2.379
10	8.111	7.722	7.360	6.710	6.145	5.650	5.216	4.833	4.494	4.192	3.923	3.662	3.465	3.269	3.092	2.414
11	8.760	8.306	7.887	7.139	6.495	5.938	5.453	5.029	4.656	4.327	4.035	3.776	3.544	3.335	3.147	2.438
12	9.385	8.863	8.384	7.536	6.814	6.194	5.660	5.197	4.793	4.439	4.127	3.851	3.606	3.387	3.190	2.456
13	9.986	9.394	8.853	7.904	7.103	6.424	5.842	5.342	4.910	4.533	4.203	3.912	3.656	3.427	3.223	2.468
14	10.563	9.899	9.295	8.244	7.367	6.628	6.002	5.468	5.008	4.611	4.265	3.962	3.695	3.459	3.249	2.477
15	11.118	10.380	9.712	8.559	7.606	6.811	6.142	5.575	5.092	4.675	4.315	4.001	3.726	3.483	3.268	2.484
16	11.652	10.838	10.106	8.851	7.824	6.974	6.265	5.669	5.162	4.730	4.357	4.033	3.751	3.503	3.283	2.489
17	12.166	11.274	10.477	9.122	8.022	7.120	6.373	5.749	5.222	4.775	4.391	4.059	3.771	3.518	3.295	2.492
18	12.659	11.690	10.828	9.372	8.201	7.250	6.467	5.818	5.273	4.812	4.419	4.080	3.786	3.529	3.304	2.494
19	13.134	12.085	11.158	9.604	8.365	7.366	6.550	5.877	5.316	4.844	4.442	4.097	3.799	3.539	3.311	2.496
20	13.590	12.462	11.470	9.818	8.514	7.469	6.623	5.929	5.353	4.870	4.460	4.110	3.808	3.546	3.316	2.497
21	14.029	12.821	11.764	10.017	8.649	7.562	6.687	5.973	5.384	4.891	4.476	4.121	3.816	3.551	3.320	2.498
22	14.451	13.163	12.042	10.201	8.772	7.645	6.743	6.011	5.410	4.909	4.488	4.130	3.822	3.556	3.323	2.498
23	14.857	13.489	12.303	10.371	8.883	7.718	6.792	6.044	5.432	4.925	4.499	4.137	3.827	3.559	3.325	2.499
24	15.247	13.799	12.550	10.529	8.985	7.784	6.835	6.073	5.451	4.937	4.507	4.143	3.831	3.562	3.327	2.499
25	15.622	14.094	12.783	10.675	9.077	7.843	6.873	6.097	5.467	4.948	4.514	4.147	3.834	3.564	3.329	2.499
26	15.983	14.375	13.003	10.810	9.161	7.896	6.906	6.118	5.480	4.956	4.520	4.151	3.837	3.566	3.330	2.500
27	16.330	14.643	13.211	10.935	9.237	7.943	6.935	6.136	5.492	4.964	4.525	4.154	3.839	3.567	3.331	2.500
28	16.663	14.898	13.406	11.051	9.307	7.984	6.961	6.152	5.502	4.970	4.528	4.157	3.840	3.568	3.331	2.500
29	16.984	15.141	13.591	11.158	9.370	8.022	6.983	6.166	5.510	4.975	4.531	4.159	3.841	3.569	3.332	2.500
30	17.292	15.373	13.765	11.258	9.427	8.055	7.003	6.177	5.517	4.979	4.534	4.160	3.842	3.569	3.332	2.500
40	19.793	17.159	15.046	11.925	9.779	8.244	7.105	6.234	5.548	4.997	4.544	4.166	3.846	3.571	3.333	2.500

Questions

12–1   What is the difference between capital budgeting screening decisions and capital budgeting preference decisions?

12–2   What is meant by the term *time value of money?*

12–3   What is meant by the term *discounting?*

12–4   Why is the net present value method of making capital budgeting decisions superior to other methods such as the payback and simple rate of return methods?

12–5   What is net present value? Can it ever be negative? Explain.

12–6   If a firm has to pay interest of 14% on long-term debt, then its cost of capital is 14%. Do you agree? Explain.

12–7   What is meant by an investment project's internal rate of return? How is the internal rate of return computed?

12–8   Explain how the cost of capital serves as a screening tool when dealing with the net present value method.

12–9   As the discount rate increases, the present value of a given future cash flow also increases. Do you agree? Explain.

12–10   Refer to Exhibit 12–2. Is the return on this investment proposal exactly 20%, slightly more than 20%, or slightly less than 20%? Explain.

12–11   Why are preference decisions sometimes called *rationing* decisions?

12–12   How is the profitability index computed, and what does it measure?

12–13   What is the preference rule for ranking investment projects under the net present value method?

12–14   Can an investment with a profitability index of less than 1.00 be an acceptable investment? Explain.

12–15   What is meant by the term *payback period?* How is the payback period determined?

12–16   How can the payback method be useful to the manager?

12–17   What is the major criticism of the payback and simple rate of return methods of making capital budgeting decisions?

Brief Exercises

BRIEF EXERCISE 12–1   Net Present Value Method (LO1)

The management of Kunkel Company is considering the purchase of a machine that would reduce operating costs. The machine will cost $40,000, and it will last for eight years. At the end of the eight-year period, the machine will have zero scrap value. Use of the machine will reduce operating costs by $7,000 per year. The company requires a minimum return of 12% before taxes on all investment projects.

Required:

1. Determine the net present value of the investment in the machine.
2. What is the difference between the total, undiscounted cash inflows and cash outflows over the entire life of the machine?

BRIEF EXERCISE 12–2   Net Present Value Analysis of Competing Projects (LO2)

Labeau Products, Ltd., of Perth, Australia, has $35,000 to invest. The company is trying to decide between two alternative uses for the funds. The alternatives are:

	Invest in Project X	Invest in Project Y
Investment required	$35,000	$ 35,000
Annual cash inflows	9,000	—
Single cash inflow at the end of 10 years	—	150,000
Life of the project	10 years	10 years

The company's discount rate is 18%.

Required:

Which alternative would you recommend that the company accept? Show all computations using the net present value approach. Prepare a separate computation for each project.

BRIEF EXERCISE 12–3   Profitability Index (LO3)
Information on four investment proposals is given below:

	Investment Proposal			
	A	**B**	**C**	**D**
Investment required	$(90,000)	$(100,000)	$(70,000)	$(120,000)
Present value of cash inflows . .	126,000	90,000	105,000	160,000
Net present value	$ 36,000	$ (10,000)	$ 35,000	$ 40,000
Life of the project	5 years	7 years	6 years	6 years

Required:
1. Compute the profitability index for each investment proposal.
2. Rank the proposals in terms of preference.

BRIEF EXERCISE 12–4   Payback Method (LO4)
The management of Unter Corporation is considering an investment with the following characteristics:

Year	Investment	Cash Inflow
1	$15,000	$1,000
2	8,000	2,000
3	—	2,500
4	—	4,000
5	—	5,000
6	—	6,000
7	—	5,000
8	—	4,000
9	—	3,000
10	—	2,000

Required:
1. Determine the payback period of the investment.
2. Would the payback period be affected if the cash inflow in the last year were several times as large?

BRIEF EXERCISE 12–5   Simple Rate of Return Method (LO5)
The management of Ballard MicroBrew is considering the purchase of an automated bottling machine for $120,000. The machine would replace an old piece of equipment that costs $30,000 per year to operate. The new machine would have a useful life of 10 years with no salvage value. The new machine would cost $12,000 per year to operate. The old machine currently in use could be sold now for a scrap value of $40,000.

Required:
Compute the simple rate of return on the new automated bottling machine.

BRIEF EXERCISE 12–6   (Appendix 12A) Present Value Concepts (LO6)
Each of the following parts is independent.
1. The Atlantic Medical Clinic can purchase a new computer system that will save $7,000 annually in billing costs. The computer system will last for eight years and have no salvage value. What is the maximum purchase price that the Atlantic Medical Clinic should be willing to pay for the new computer system if the clinic's required rate of return is:
   a. Sixteen percent?
   b. Twenty percent?
2. The Caldwell *Herald* newspaper reported the following story:

   Frank Ormsby of Caldwell is the state's newest millionaire. By choosing the six winning numbers on last week's state lottery, Mr. Ormsby has won the week's grand prize totaling $1.6 million. The

State Lottery Commission has indicated that Mr. Ormsby will receive his prize in 20 annual installments of $80,000 each.

   a. If Mr. Ormsby can invest money at a 12% rate of return, what is the present value of his winnings?
   b. Is it correct to say that Mr. Ormsby is the "state's newest millionaire"? Explain your answer.
3. Fraser Company will need a new warehouse in five years. The warehouse will cost $500,000 to build. What lump-sum amount should the company invest now to have the $500,000 available at the end of the five-year period? Assume that the company can invest money at:
   a. Ten percent.
   b. Fourteen percent.

Exercises

EXERCISE 12–1   Net Present Value Analysis (LO1)
Windhoek Mines, Ltd., of Namibia, is contemplating the purchase of equipment to exploit a mineral deposit that is located on land to which the company has mineral rights. An engineering and cost analysis has been made, and it is expected that the following cash flows would be associated with opening and operating a mine in the area:

Cost of new equipment and timbers	R275,000
Working capital required	100,000
Net annual cash receipts	120,000*
Cost to construct new roads in three years	40,000
Salvage value of equipment in four years	65,000

*Receipts from sales of ore, less out-of-pocket costs for salaries, utilities, insurance, and so forth.

The currency in Namibia is the rand, here denoted by R.

   It is estimated that the mineral deposit would be exhausted after four years of mining. At that point, the working capital would be released for reinvestment elsewhere. The company's discount rate is 20%.

Required:
Determine the net present value of the proposed mining project. Should the project be accepted? Explain.

EXERCISE 12–2   Net Present Value Analysis of Competing Projects (LO2)
Perrot Industries has $100,000 to invest. The company is trying to decide between two alternative uses of the funds. The alternatives are:

	Project	
	A	B
Cost of equipment required	$100,000	—
Working capital investment required	—	$100,000
Annual cash inflows	21,000	16,000
Salvage value of equipment in six years	8,000	—
Life of the project	6 years	6 years

The working capital needed for project B will be released at the end of six years for investment elsewhere. Perrot Industries' discount rate is 14%.

Required:
Which investment alternative (if either) would you recommend that the company accept? Show all computations using the net present value format. Prepare a separate computation for each project.

EXERCISE 12–3   Profitability Index (LO3)
The management of Revco Products is exploring five different investment opportunities. Information on the five projects under study is given below:

	Project Number				
	1	2	3	4	5
Investment required	$(270,000)	$(450,000)	$(400,000)	$(360,000)	$(480,000)
Present value of cash inflows at a 10% discount rate	336,140	522,970	379,760	433,400	567,270
Net present value	$ 66,140	$ 72,970	$ (20,240)	$ 73,400	$ 87,270
Life of the project	6 years	3 years	5 years	12 years	6 years

The company's required rate of return is 10%; thus, a 10% discount rate has been used in the present value computations above. Limited funds are available for investment, so the company can't accept all of the available projects.

Required:
1. Compute the profitability index for each investment project.
2. Rank the five projects according to preference, in terms of:
   a. Net present value.
   b. Profitability index.
3. Which ranking do you prefer? Why?

EXERCISE 12–4 Payback and Simple Rate of Return Methods (LO4, LO5)

A piece of laborsaving equipment has just come onto the market that Mitsui Electronics, Ltd., could use to reduce costs in one of its plants in Japan. Relevant data relating to the equipment follow (currency is in thousands of yen, denoted by ¥):

Purchase cost of the equipment	¥432,000
Annual cost savings that will be provided by the equipment	¥90,000
Life of the equipment	12 years

Required:
1. Compute the payback period for the equipment. If the company requires a payback period of four years or less, would the equipment be purchased?
2. Compute the simple rate of return on the equipment. Use straight-line depreciation based on the equipment's useful life. Would the equipment be purchased if the company requires a rate of return of at least 14%?

EXERCISE 12–5 Basic Present Value Concepts (LO2)

Kathy Myers frequently purchases stocks and bonds, but she is uncertain how to determine the rate of return that she is earning. For example, three years ago she paid $13,000 for 200 shares of the common stock of Malti Company. She received a $420 cash dividend on the stock at the end of each year for three years. At the end of three years, she sold the stock for $16,000. Kathy would like to earn a return of at least 14% on all of her investments. She is not sure whether the Malti Company stock provided a 14% return and would like some help with the necessary computations.

Required:
Using the net present value method, determine whether or not the Malti Company stock provided a 14% return. Round all computations to the nearest whole dollar.

Problems

PROBLEM 12–1 Basic Net Present Value Analysis (LO1)

The Sweetwater Candy Company would like to buy a new machine that would automatically "dip" chocolates. The dipping operation is currently done largely by hand. The machine the company is considering costs $120,000. The manufacturer estimates that the machine would be usable for 12 years but would require the replacement of several key parts at the end of the sixth year. These parts would cost $9,000, including installation. After 12 years, the machine could be sold for about $7,500.

CHECK FIGURE
(1) $32,000 annual cash flows

The company estimates that the cost to operate the machine will be only $7,000 per year. The present method of dipping chocolates costs $30,000 per year. In addition to reducing costs, the new machine will increase production by 6,000 boxes of chocolates per year. The company realizes a contribution margin of $1.50 per box. A 20% rate of return is required on all investments.

Required:

1. What are the net annual cash inflows that will be provided by the new dipping machine?
2. Compute the new machine's net present value. Use the incremental cost approach and round all dollar amounts to the nearest whole dollar.

CHECK FIGURE
(1) $31,650 annual cash receipts

PROBLEM 12–2   Net Present Value Analysis (LO1)

In eight years, Kent Duncan will retire. He has $150,000 to invest, and he is exploring the possibility of opening a self-service auto wash. The auto wash could be managed in the free time he has available from his regular occupation, and it could be closed easily when he retires. After care .l study, Mr. Duncan has determined the following:

a. A building in which an auto wash could be installed is available under an eight-year lease at a cost of $1,700 per month.
b. Purchase and installation costs of equipment would total $150,000. In eight years the equipment could be sold for about 10% of its original cost.
c. An investment of an additional $2,000 would be required to cover working capital needs for cleaning supplies, change funds, and so forth. After eight years, this working capital would be released for investment elsewhere.
d. Both an auto wash and a vacuum service would be offered with a wash costing $1.50 and the vacuum costing 25 cents per use.
e. The only variable costs associated with the operation would be 23 cents per wash for water and 10 cents per use of the vacuum for electricity.
f. In addition to rent, monthly costs of operation would be: cleaning, $450; insurance, $75; and maintenance, $500.
g. Gross receipts from the auto wash would be about $1,350 per week. According to the experience of other auto washes, 70% of the customers using the wash would also use the vacuum.

Mr. Duncan will not open the auto wash unless it provides at least a 10% return, since this is the amount that could be earned by simply placing the $150,000 in high-grade securities.

Required:

1. Assuming that the auto wash will be open 52 weeks a year, compute the expected net annual cash receipts (gross cash receipts less cash disbursements) from its operation. (Do not include the cost of the equipment, the working capital, or the salvage value in these computations.)
2. Would you advise Mr. Duncan to open the car wash? Show computations using the net present value method of investment analysis. Round all dollar figures to the nearest whole dollar.

CHECK FIGURE
(1) $2,119 NPV in favor of new truck

PROBLEM 12–3   Total-Cost and Incremental-Cost Approaches (LO2)

Bilboa Freightlines, S.A., of Panama, has a small truck that it uses for intracity deliveries. The truck is in bad repair and must be either overhauled or replaced with a new truck. The company has assembled the following information. (Panama uses the U.S. dollar as its currency):

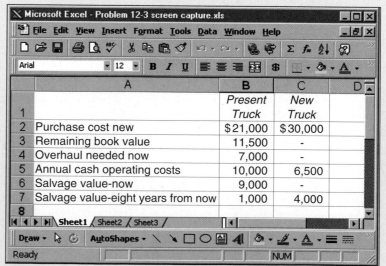

	Present Truck	New Truck
Purchase cost new	$21,000	$30,000
Remaining book value	11,500	-
Overhaul needed now	7,000	-
Annual cash operating costs	10,000	6,500
Salvage value-now	9,000	-
Salvage value-eight years from now	1,000	4,000

If the company keeps and overhauls its present delivery truck, then the truck will be usable for eight more years. If a new truck is purchased, it will be used for eight years, after which it will be traded in on another truck. The new truck would be diesel-operated, resulting in a substantial reduction in annual operating costs, as shown above.

The company computes depreciation on a straight-line basis. All investment projects are evaluated using a 16% discount rate.

Required:
1. Should Bilboa Freightlines keep the old truck or purchase the new one? Use the total-cost approach to net present value in making your decision. Round to the nearest whole dollar.
2. Redo (1) above, this time using the incremental-cost approach.

PROBLEM 12–4   Keep or Sell Property (LO2)

CHECK FIGURE
Keep the property alternative: $309,402 PV of cash flows

Raul Martinas, professor of languages at Eastern University, owns a small office building adjacent to the university campus. He acquired the property 10 years ago at a total cost of $530,000—$50,000 for the land and $480,000 for the building. He has just received an offer from a realty company that wants to purchase the property; however, the property has been a good source of income over the years, so Professor Martinas is unsure whether he should keep it or sell it. His alternatives are:

Keep the property. Professor Martinas' accountant has kept careful records of the income realized from the property over the past 10 years. These records indicate the following annual revenues and expenses:

Rental receipts		$140,000
Less building expenses:		
Utilities	$25,000	
Depreciation of building	16,000	
Property taxes and insurance	18,000	
Repairs and maintenance	9,000	
Custodial help and supplies	40,000	108,000
Net operating income		$ 32,000

Professor Martinas makes a $12,000 mortgage payment each year on the property. The mortgage will be paid off in eight more years. He has been depreciating the building by the straight-line method, assuming a salvage value of $80,000 for the building which he still thinks is an appropriate figure. He feels sure that the building can be rented for another 15 years. He also feels sure that 15 years from now the land will be worth three times what he paid for it.

Sell the property. A realty company has offered to purchase the property by paying $175,000 immediately and $26,500 per year for the next 15 years. Control of the property would go to the realty company immediately. To sell the property, Professor Martinas would need to pay the mortgage off, which could be done by making a lump-sum payment of $90,000.

Required:
Assume that Professor Martinas requires a 12% rate of return. Would you recommend he keep or sell the property? Show computations using the total-cost approach to net present value.

PROBLEM 12–5   Ranking of Projects (LO3)

CHECK FIGURE
(1) Project B profitability index: 1.31

Oxford Company has limited funds available for investment and must ration the funds among five competing projects. Selected information on the five projects follows:

Project	Investment Required	Net Present Value	Life of the Project (years)
A	$160,000	$44,323	7
B	135,000	42,000	12
C	100,000	35,035	7
D	175,000	38,136	3
E	150,000	(8,696)	6

The net present values above have been computed using a 10% discount rate. The company wants your assistance in determining which project to accept first, which to accept second, and so forth.

Required:
1. Compute the profitability index for each project.
2. In order of preference, rank the five projects in terms of:
   a. Net present value.
   b. Profitability index.
3. Which ranking do you prefer? Why?

CHECK FIGURE
(2) 15.0% return

PROBLEM 12–6   Simple Rate of Return and Payback Methods (LO4, LO5)
Sharkey's Fun Center contains a number of electronic games as well as a miniature golf course and various rides located outside the building. Paul Sharkey, the owner, would like to construct a water slide on one portion of his property. Mr. Sharkey has gathered the following information about the slide:

a. Water slide equipment could be purchased and installed at a cost of $330,000. According to the manufacturer, the slide would be usable for 12 years after which it would have no salvage value.
b. Mr. Sharkey would use straight-line depreciation on the slide equipment.
c. To make room for the water slide, several rides would be dismantled and sold. These rides are fully depreciated, but they could be sold for $60,000 to an amusement park in a nearby city.
d. Mr. Sharkey has concluded that about 50,000 more people would use the water slide each year than have been using the rides. The admission price would be $3.60 per person (the same price that the Fun Center has been charging for the rides).
e. Based on experience at other water slides, Mr. Sharkey estimates that incremental operating expenses each year for the slide would be: salaries, $85,000; insurance, $4,200; utilities, $13,000; and maintenance, $9,800.

Required:
1. Prepare an income statement showing the expected incremental net income each year from the water slide.
2. Compute the simple rate of return expected from the water slide. Based on this computation, would the water slide be constructed if Mr. Sharkey requires a simple rate of return of at least 14% on all investments?
3. Compute the payback period for the water slide. If Mr. Sharkey requires a payback period of five years or less, would the water slide be constructed?

CHECK FIGURE
(1b) 12.5% return

PROBLEM 12–7   Simple Rate of Return and Payback Analyses of Two Machines (LO4, LO5)
Westwood Furniture Company is considering the purchase of two different items of equipment, as described below:

Machine A. A compacting machine has just come onto the market that would permit Westwood Furniture Company to compress sawdust into various shelving products. At present the sawdust is disposed of as a waste product. The following information is available on the machine:

a. The machine would cost $420,000 and would have a 10% salvage value at the end of its 12–year useful life. The company uses straight-line depreciation and considers salvage value in computing depreciation deductions.
b. The shelving products manufactured from use of the machine would generate revenues of $300,000 per year. Variable manufacturing costs would be 20% of sales.
c. Fixed expenses associated with the new shelving products would be (per year): advertising, $40,000: salaries, $110,000; utilities, $5,200; and insurance, $800.

Machine B. A second machine has come onto the market that would allow Westwood Furniture Company to automate a sanding process that is now done largely by hand. The following information is available:

a. The new sanding machine would cost $234,000 and would have no salvage value at the end of its 13-year useful life. The company would use straight-line depreciation on the new machine.
b. Several old pieces of sanding equipment that are fully depreciated would be disposed of at a scrap value of $9,000.
c. The new sanding machine would provide substantial annual savings in cash operating costs. It would require an operator at an annual salary of $16,350 and $5,400 in annual maintenance costs. The current, hand-operated sanding procedure costs the company $78,000 per year in total.

Westwood Furniture Company requires a simple rate of return of 15% on all equipment purchases. Also, the company will not purchase equipment unless the equipment has a payback period of 4.0 years or less.

Required:

1. For machine A:
   a. Prepare an income statement showing the expected net income each year from the new shelving products. Use the contribution format.
   b. Compute the simple rate of return.
   c. Compute the payback period.
2. For machine B:
   a. Compute the simple rate of return.
   b. Compute the payback period.
3. According to the company's criteria, which machine, if either, should the company purchase?

PROBLEM 12–8   Net Present Value Analysis of Securities (LO2)

Linda Clark received $175,000 from her mother's estate. She placed the funds into the hands of a broker, who purchased the following securities on Linda's behalf:

a. Common stock was purchased at a cost of $95,000. The stock paid no dividends, but it was sold for $160,000 at the end of three years.
b. Preferred stock was purchased at its par value of $30,000. The stock paid a 6% dividend (based on par value) each year for three years. At the end of three years, the stock was sold for $27,000.
c. Bonds were purchased at a cost of $50,000. The bonds paid $3,000 in interest every six months. After three years, the bonds were sold for $52,700. (Note: In discounting a cash flow that occurs semiannually, the procedure is to halve the discount rate and double the number of periods. Use the same procedure in discounting the proceeds from the sale.)

The securities were all sold at the end of three years so that Linda would have funds available to open a new business venture. The broker stated that the investments had earned more than a 16% return, and he gave Linda the following computation to support his statement:

Common stock:	
Gain on sale ($160,000 − $95,000)	$65,000
Preferred stock:	
Dividends paid (6% × $30,000 × 3 years)	5,400
Loss on sale ($27,000 − $30,000)	(3,000)
Bonds:	
Interest paid ($3,000 × 6 periods)	18,000
Gain on sale ($52,700 − $50,000)	2,700
Net gain on all investments	$88,100

$$\frac{\$88,100 \div 3 \text{ years}}{\$175,000} = 16.8\%$$

Required:

1. Using a 16% discount rate, compute the net present value of *each* of the three investments. On which investment(s) did Linda earn a 16% rate of return? (Round computations to the nearest whole dollar.)
2. Considering all three investments together, did Linda earn a 16% rate of return? Explain.
3. Linda wants to use the $239,700 proceeds ($160,000 + $27,000 + $52,700 = $239,700) from sale of the securities to open a retail store under a 12–year franchise contract. What net annual cash inflow must the store generate for Linda to earn a 14% return over the 12-year period? Round computations to the nearest whole dollar.

Building Your Skills

ANALYTICAL THINKING   (LO2)

Top-Quality Stores, Inc., owns a nationwide chain of supermarkets. The company is going to open another store soon, and a suitable building site has been located in an attractive and rapidly growing area. In discussing how the company can acquire the desired building and other facilities needed to open the new store, Sam Watkins, the company's vice president in charge of sales, stated, "I know most of our competitors are starting to lease facilities rather than buy, but I just can't see the economics of it. Our development people tell me that we can buy the building site, put a building on it, and get all the store fixtures we need for just $850,000. They also say that property taxes, insurance, and repairs would run $20,000 a year. When you figure that we plan to keep a site for 18 years, that's a total cost of $1,210,000. But then when you realize that the property will be worth at least a half million in 18 years, that's a net cost to us of only $710,000. What would it cost to lease the property?"

"I understand that Beneficial Insurance Company is willing to purchase the building site, construct a building and install fixtures to our specifications, and then lease the facility to us for 18 years at an annual lease payment of $120,000," replied Lisa Coleman, the company's executive vice president.

"That's just my point," said Sam. "At $120,000 a year, it would cost us a cool $2,160,000 over the 18 years. That's three times what it would cost to buy, and what would we have left at the end? Nothing! The building would belong to the insurance company!"

"You're overlooking a few things," replied Lisa. "For one thing, the treasurer's office says that we could only afford to put $350,000 down if we buy the property, and then we would have to pay the other $500,000 off over four years at $175,000 a year. So there would be some interest involved on the purchase side that you haven't figured in."

"But that little bit of interest is nothing compared to over 2 million bucks for leasing," said Sam. "Also, if we lease I understand we would have to put up an $8,000 security deposit that we wouldn't get back until the end. And besides that, we would still have to pay all the yearly repairs and maintenance costs just like we owned the property. No wonder those insurance companies are so rich if they can swing deals like this."

"Well, I'll admit that I don't have all the figures sorted out yet," replied Lisa. "But I do have the operating cost breakdown for the building, which includes $7,500 annually for property taxes, $8,000 for insurance, and $4,500 for repairs and maintenance. If we lease, Beneficial will handle its own insurance costs and of course the owner will have to pay the property taxes. I'll put all this together and see if leasing makes any sense with our required rate of return of 16%. The president wants a presentation and recommendation in the executive committee meeting tomorrow. Let's see, development said the first lease payment would be due now and the remaining ones due in years 1–17. Development also said that this store should generate a net cash inflow that's well above the average for our stores."

Required:

1. Using the net present value approach, determine whether Top-Quality Stores, Inc., should lease or buy the new facility. Assume that you will be making your presentation before the company's executive committee, and remember that the president detests sloppy, disorganized reports.
2. What reply will you make in the meeting if Sam Watkins brings up the issue of the building's future sales value?

COMMUNICATING IN PRACTICE   (LO1, LO4, LO5)

Use an online yellow pages directory such as www.comfind.com, or www.athand.com to find a manufacturer in your area that has a website. Make an appointment with the controller or chief financial officer of the company. Before your meeting, find out as much as you can about the organization's operations from its website.

Required:

After asking the following questions about a capital budgeting decision that was made by the management of the company, write a brief memorandum to your instructor that summarizes the information obtained from the company's website and addresses what you found out during your interview.

1. What was the nature of the capital project?
2. What was the total cost of the capital project?
3. Did the project costs stay within budget (or estimate)?
4. What financial criteria were used to evaluate the project?

TAKING IT TO THE NET

As you know, the World Wide Web is a medium that is constantly evolving. Sites come and go and change without notice. To enable periodic update of site addresses, this problem has been posted to the textbook website (www.mhhe.com/folk1e). After accessing the site, enter the Student Center and select this chapter. Select and complete the Taking It to the Net problem.

CHECK FIGURE
(1) $30,046 NPV in favor of the model 400 machine

TEAMWORK IN ACTION   (LO1, LO2, LO3)

Kingsley Products, Ltd., is using a model 400 shaping machine to make one of its products. The company is expecting to have a large increase in demand for the product and is anxious to expand its productive capacity. Two possibilities are under consideration:

Alternative 1. Purchase another model 400 shaping machine to operate along with the currently owned model 400 machine.

Alternative 2. Purchase a model 800 shaping machine and use the currently owned model 400 machine as standby equipment. The model 800 machine is a high-speed unit with double the capacity of the model 400 machine.

The following additional information is available on the two alternatives:

a. Both the model 400 machine and the model 800 machine have a 10-year life from the time they are first used in production. The scrap value of both machines is negligible and can be ignored. Straight-line depreciation is used.

b. The cost of a new model 800 machine is $300,000.

c. The model 400 machine now in use cost $160,000 three years ago. Its present book value is $112,000, and its present market value is $90,000.

d. A new model 400 machine costs $170,000 now. If the company decides not to buy the model 800 machine, then the currently owned model 400 machine will have to be replaced in seven years at a cost of $200,000. The replacement machine will be sold at the end of the tenth year for $140,000.

e. Production over the next 10 years is expected to be:

Year	Production in Units
1	40,000
2	60,000
3	80,000
4–10	90,000

f. The two models of machines are not equally efficient. Comparative variable costs per unit are:

	Model	
	400	**800**
Materials per unit	$0.25	$0.40
Direct labor per unit	0.49	0.16
Supplies and lubricants per unit	0.06	0.04
Total variable cost per unit	$0.80	$0.60

g. The model 400 machine is less costly to maintain than the model 800 machine. Annual repairs and maintenance costs on a model 400 machine are $2,500.

h. Repairs and maintenance costs on a model 800 machine, with a model 400 machine used as standby, would total $3,800 per year.

i. No other factory costs will change as a result of the decision between the two machines.

j. Kingsley Products requires a 20% rate of return on all investments.

Required:

The team should discuss and then respond to the following. All team members should agree with and understand the answers (including the calculations supporting the answers) and be prepared to report the information developed in class. (Each teammate can assume responsibility for a different part of the presentation.)

1. Which alternative should the company choose? Use the net present value approach.

2. Suppose that the cost of labor increases by 10%. Would this make the model 800 machine more or less desirable? Explain. No computations are needed.

3. Suppose that the cost of materials doubles. Would this make the model 800 machine more or less desirable? Explain. No computations are needed.

Chapter Thirteen

"How Well Am I Doing?" Statement of Cash Flows

A Look Back

Decisions relating to capital budgeting involve significant outlays on long-term projects. Various techniques used for capital budgeting decisions were overviewed and illustrated in Chapter 12.

A Look at This Chapter

The statement of cash flows provides information that cannot be obtained from the balance sheet or income statement. After addressing the classification of various types of cash inflows and outflows, we illustrate techniques for preparing the statement of cash flows and discuss the interpretation of the information reported on this financial statement.

A Look Ahead

The use of financial statements to assess the financial health of a company is covered in Chapter 14. The focus in that chapter is on analysis of trends and on the use of financial ratios.

Chapter Outline

The Basic Approach to a Statement of Cash Flows
- Definition of Cash
- Constructing the Statement of Cash Flows Using Changes in Noncash Balance Sheet Accounts

An Example of a Simplified Statement of Cash Flows
- Constructing a Simplified Statement of Cash Flows
- The Need for a More Detailed Statement

Organization of the Full-Fledged Statement of Cash Flows
- Operating Activities
- Investing Activities
- Financing Activities

Other Issues in Preparing the Statement of Cash Flows
- Cash Flows: Gross or Net?
- Operating Activities: Direct or Indirect Method?
- Direct Exchange Transactions

An Example of a Full-Fledged Statement of Cash Flows

- Eight Basic Steps to Preparing the Statement of Cash Flows
- Setting Up the Worksheet (Steps 1–4)
- Adjustments to Reflect Gross, Rather than Net, Amounts (Step 5)
- Classifying Entries as Operating, Investing, or Financing Activities (Step 6)
- The Completed Statement of Cash Flows (Steps 7and 8)
- Interpretation of the Statement of Cash Flows
- Depreciation, Depletion, and Amortization

Appendix 13A: The Direct Method of Determining the "Net Cash Provided by Operating Activities"
- Similarities and Differences in the Handling of Data
- Special Rules—Direct and Indirect Methods

Appendix 13B: The T-Account Approach to Preparing the Statement of Cash Flows
- The T-Account Approach
- Preparing the Statement of Cash Flows from the Completed T-Accounts

Decision Feature **Is the Party Over?**

There was a time when many thought that e-tailers (e-retailers) might wipe out traditional retailers. Now investors wonder if e-tailers will be able to survive. It all boils down to cash flows. Unable to generate the cash needed to support their ongoing operations, the dot-coms are having a hard time raising money. The traditional sources of funds are venture capitalists, Wall Street investors, and banks. Venture capitalists, who often made the initial cash investments required to finance the start-up operations of many e-tailers, are unwilling to invest additional cash. After snatching up the initial public offering of almost any dot-com during the late 1990s, Wall Street investors are now guarded. Banks, quite willing to provide financing to established companies with histories of profitability, are reluctant to loan money to e-tailers because the risk of default is high.

Typically, a potential investor would start with a company's financial statements. The balance sheet provides information about the company's financial condition, and the income statement indicates whether or not a company is profitable, but neither helps to predict whether a company will generate cash. Users of financial statements look to the statement of cash flows for that information.

Market Guide, a Wall Street research firm, analyzed the statements of cash flows of selected e-tailers. Focusing only on the fourth quarter, Market Guide added the cash that was used for operations and the amount that was used to acquire equipment, and then divided that amount into the amount of cash that was on hand at the end of the quarter. Their approach estimates how long it will take for a given company to burn through its available cash. Matt Krantz, a *USA Today* reporter, updated the information by considering funds that the e-tailers were able to secure during the first quarter of 2000. During August 2000, Krantz warned that 5 of the 15 companies included in the *USA Today* "Internet 100" could run out of cash by mid-2001. The five companies cited were Drugstore.com, Egghead.com, EMusic, EToys, and Travelocity. Officials at each of the companies responded by noting that cost-cutting measures would improve their situations. Whether or not these companies can survive a cash crunch remains to be seen.

Sources: Matt Krantz, "Dot-Coms Could Run Out of Cash," *USA Today,* August 18, 2000, 1B; Matt Krantz, "E-Retailers Run Low on Fuel," *USA Today,* April 26, 2000, 1B. Copyright 2000, *USA Today.* Reprinted with permission.

Learning Objectives
After studying Chapter 13, you should be able to:

LO1 Know how to classify changes in noncash balance sheet accounts as sources or uses of cash.

LO2 State the general rules for determining whether transactions should be classified as operating activities, investing activities, or financing activities.

LO3 Prepare a statement of cash flows using the indirect method to determine the net cash provided by operating activities.

LO4 (Appendix 13A) Use the direct method to determine the net cash provided by operating activities.

LO5 (Appendix 13B) Prepare a statement of cash flows using the T-account approach.

Three major financial statements are ordinarily required for external reports—an income statement, a balance sheet, and a statement of cash flows. The purpose of the **statement of cash flows** is to highlight the major activities that directly and indirectly impact cash flows and hence affect the overall cash balance. Managers focus on cash for a very good reason—without sufficient cash at the right times, a company may miss golden opportunities or may even fall into bankruptcy.

The statement of cash flows answers questions that cannot be answered by the income statement and balance sheet. For example, the statement of cash flows can be used to answer questions like the following: Where did Delta Airlines get the cash to pay a dividend of nearly $140 million in a year in which, according to its income statement, it lost more than $1 billion? How was The Walt Disney Company able to invest nearly $800 million in expansion of its theme parks, including a major renovation of Epcot Center, despite a loss of more than $500 million on its investment in EuroDisney? Where did Wendy's International, Inc., get $125 million to expand its chain of fast-food restaurants in a year in which its net income was only $79 million and it did not raise any new debt? To answer such questions, familiarity with the statement of cash flows is required.

The statement of cash flows is a valuable analytical tool for managers as well as for investors and creditors, although managers tend to be more concerned with *prospective* statements of cash flows that are prepared as part of the budgeting process. The statement of cash flows can be used to answer crucial questions such as the following:

1. Is the company generating sufficient positive cash flows from its ongoing operations to remain viable?
2. Will the company be able to repay its debts?
3. Will the company be able to pay its usual dividend?
4. Why is there a difference between net income and net cash flow for the year?
5. To what extent will the company have to borrow money in order to make needed investments?

In this chapter, our focus is on the development of the statement of cash flows and on its use as a tool for assessing the well-being of a company.

The Basic Approach to a Statement of Cash Flows

Learning Objective 1
Know how to classify changes in noncash balance sheet accounts as sources or uses of cash.

For the statement of cash flows to be useful to managers and others, it is important that companies employ a common definition of cash. It is also important that the statement be constructed using consistent guidelines for identifying activities that are *sources* of cash and *uses* of cash. The proper definition of cash and the guidelines to use in identifying sources and uses of cash are discussed in this section.

Definition of Cash

In preparing a statement of cash flows, the term *cash* is broadly defined to include both cash and cash equivalents. **Cash equivalents** consist of short-term, highly liquid investments such as Treasury bills, commercial paper, and money market funds. Such investments are made solely for the purpose of generating a return on funds that are temporarily idle. Instead of simply holding cash, most companies invest their excess cash reserves in these types of interest-bearing assets that can be easily converted into cash. These short-term, liquid assets are usually included in *marketable securities* on the balance sheet. Since such assets are equivalent to cash, they are included with cash in preparing a statement of cash flows.

Is Cash King?

in business today

A survey of 2,359 stockholders across the United States supports the conclusion that investors find the statement of cash flows to be a very useful source of financial data. The survey found that investors use the statement of cash flows more and the income statement less than previously.

Source: Marc Epstein and Moses Pava, "How Useful Is the Statement of Cash Flows?" *Management Accounting*, July 1992, pp. 52–55. Reprinted with permission from *Management Accounting*.

Constructing the Statement of Cash Flows Using Changes in Noncash Balance Sheet Accounts

While not the recommended procedure, a type of statement of cash flows could be constructed by simply summarizing all of the debits and credits to the Cash and Cash Equivalents accounts during a period. However, this approach would overlook all of the transactions in which there is an implicit exchange of cash. For example, when a company purchases inventory on credit, there is an implicit exchange of cash. In essence, the supplier loans the company cash, which the company then uses to acquire inventory from the supplier. Rather than just looking at the transactions that explicitly involve cash, financial statement users are interested in all of the transactions that implicitly or explicitly involve cash. When inventory is purchased on credit, the Inventory account increases, which is an implicit *use* of cash. At the same time, Accounts Payable increases, which is an implicit *source* of cash. In general, increases in the Inventory account can be classified as uses of cash and increases in the Accounts Payable account can be classified as sources of cash. This suggests that analyzing changes in balance sheet accounts, such as Inventory and Accounts Payable, will uncover both the explicit and implicit sources and uses of cash. And this is indeed the basic approach taken in the statement of cash flows. The logic underlying this approach is demonstrated in Exhibit 13–1.

Exhibit 13–1 requires some explanation. The exhibit shows how net cash flow can be explained in terms of net income, dividends, and changes in balance sheet accounts. The

Exhibit 13–1

Explaining Net Cash Flow by Analysis of the Noncash Balance Sheet Accounts

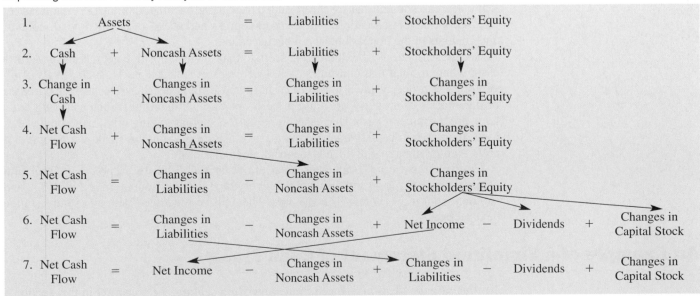

Exhibit 13–2

Classifications of Sources and
Uses of Cash

	Sources (i.e., credits)	Uses (i.e., debits)	
Net income	Always		
Net loss		Always	
Changes in noncash assets	Decreases	Increases	
Changes in liabilities*	Increases	Decreases	
Changes in capital stock accounts ..	Increases	Decreases	
Dividends paid to stockholders		Always	
	Total sources −	Total uses =	Net cash flow

*Contra asset accounts, such as the Accumulated Depreciation and Amortization account, follow
the rules for liabilities.

first line in the exhibit consists of the balance sheet equation: Assets = Liabilities +
Stockholders' Equity. The first step is to recognize that assets consist of cash and noncash assets. This is shown in the second line of the exhibit. The third line in the exhibit
recognizes that if the account balances are always equal, then the changes in the account
balances must be equal too. The next step is simply to note that the change in cash for a
period is by definition the company's net cash flow, which yields line 4 in the exhibit.
The only difference between line 4 and line 5 is that the changes in noncash assets is
moved from the left-hand side of the equation to the right-hand side. This is done because we are attempting to explain net cash flow, so it should be by itself on the left-hand
side of the equation. To get from line 5 to line 6, we need to remember that stockholders' equity is affected by net income, dividends, and changes in capital stock. Net income
increases stockholders' equity, while dividends reduce stockholders' equity. To get from
line 6 of the exhibit to line 7, a few terms on the right-hand side of the equation are
rearranged.

According to equation 7 in Exhibit 13–1, the net cash flow for a period can be determined by starting with net income, then deducting changes in noncash assets, adding
changes in liabilities, deducting dividends paid to stockholders, and finally adding
changes in capital stock. It is important to realize that changes in accounts can be either
increases (positive) or decreases (negative), and this affects how we should interpret
equation 7 in Exhibit 13–1. For example, increases in liabilities are added back to net income, whereas decreases in liabilities are deducted from net income to arrive at the net
cash flow. On the other hand, increases in noncash assets are deducted from net income
while decreases in noncash assets are added back to net income. Exhibit 13–2 summarizes
the appropriate classifications—in terms of sources and uses—of net income, dividends,
and changes in the noncash balance sheet accounts.

The classifications in Exhibit 13–2 seem to make sense. Positive net income generates
cash, whereas a net loss consumes cash. Decreases in noncash assets, such as sale of inventories or property, are a source of cash. Increases in noncash assets, such as purchase
of inventories or property, are a use of cash. Increases in liabilities, such as taking out a
loan, are a source of cash. Decreases in liabilities, such as paying off a loan, are a use of
cash. Increases in capital stock accounts, such as sale of common stock, are a source of
cash. And payments of dividends to stockholders use cash.

Constructing a simple statement of cash flows is a straightforward process. Begin with
net income (or net loss) and then add to it everything listed as sources in Exhibit 13–2 and
subtract from it everything listed as uses. This will be illustrated with an example in the
next section.

An Example of a Simplified Statement of Cash Flows

To illustrate the ideas introduced in the preceding section, we construct in this section a
simplified statement of cash flows for Nordstrom, Inc., one of the leading fashion retail-

Exhibit 13–3

NORDSTROM, INC.[*]
Income Statement
(dollars in millions)

Net sales	$3,638
Less cost of sales	2,469
Gross margin	1,169
Less operating expenses	941
Net operating income	228
Nonoperating items:	
Gain on sale of store	3
Income before taxes	231
Less income taxes	91
Net income	$ 140

[*]This statement is loosely based on an actual income statement published by Nordstrom. Among other differences, there was no "Gain on sale of store" in the original statement. This "gain" has been included here to illustrate how to handle gains and losses on a statement of cash flows.

ers in the United States. This simplified statement does not follow the format required by the FASB for external financial reports, but it shows where the numbers come from in a statement of cash flows and how they fit together. In later sections, we will show how the same basic data can be used to construct a full-fledged statement of cash flows that would be acceptable for external reports.

Constructing a Simplified Statement of Cash Flows

According to Exhibit 13–2, to construct a statement of cash flows we need the company's net income or loss, the changes in each of its balance sheet accounts, and the dividends paid to stockholders for the year. We can obtain this information from the Nordstrom financial statements that appear in Exhibits 13–3, 13–4, and 13–5. In a few instances, the actual statements have been simplified for ease of computation and discussion.

Note that changes between the beginning and ending balances have been computed for each of the balance sheet accounts in Exhibit 13–4, and each change has been classified as a source or use of cash. For example, accounts receivable decreased by $17 million. And, according to Exhibit 13–2, a decrease in such an asset account is classified as a source of cash.

A *simplified* statement of cash flows appears in Exhibit 13–6. This statement was constructed by gathering together all of the entries listed as sources in Exhibit 13–4 and all of the entries listed as uses. The sources exceeded the uses by $62 million. This is the net cash flow for the year and is also, by definition, the change in cash and cash equivalents for the year. (Trace this $62 million figure back to Exhibit 13–4.)

The Need for a More Detailed Statement

While the simplified statement of cash flows in Exhibit 13–6 is not difficult to construct, it is not acceptable for external financial reports and is not as useful as it could be for internal reports. The FASB requires that the statement of cash flows follow a different format and that a few of the entries be modified. Nevertheless, almost all of the entries on a full-fledged statement of cash flows are the same as the entries on the simplified statement of cash flows—they are just in a different order.

In the following sections, we will discuss the modifications to the simplified statement that are necessary to conform to external reporting requirements.

Exhibit 13–4

NORDSTROM, INC.*
Comparative Balance Sheet
(dollars in millions)

	Ending Balance	Beginning Balance	Change	Source or Use?
Assets				
Current assets:				
Cash and cash equivalents	$ 91	$ 29	$ +62	
Accounts receivable	637	654	−17	Source
Merchandise inventory	586	537	+49	Use
Total current assets	1,314	1,220		
Property, buildings, and equipment ..	1,517	1,394	+123	Use
Less accumulated depreciation and amortization	654	561	+93	Source
Net property, buildings, and equipment	863	833		
Total assets	$2,177	$2,053		
Liabilities and Stockholders' Equity				
Current liabilities:				
Accounts payable	$ 264	$ 220	+44	Source
Accrued wages and salaries payable	193	190	+3	Source
Accrued income taxes payable	28	22	+6	Source
Notes payable	40	38	+2	Source
Total current liabilities	525	470		
Long-term debt	439	482	−43	Use
Deferred income taxes	47	49	−2	Use
Total liabilities	1,011	1,001		
Stockholders' equity:				
Common stock	157	155	+2	Source
Retained earnings	1,009	897	+112	†
Total stockholders' equity	1,166	1,052		
Total liabilities and stockholders' equity	$2,177	$2,053		

*This statement differs from the actual statement published by Nordstrom.
†The change in retained earnings of $112 million equals the net income of $140 million less the cash dividends paid to stockholders of $28 million. Net income is classified as a source and dividends as a use.

Exhibit 13–5

NORDSTROM, INC.*
Statement of Retained Earnings
(dollars in millions)

Retained earnings, beginning balance	$ 897
Add: Net income	140
	1,037
Deduct: Dividends paid	28
Retained earnings, ending balance	$1,009

*This statement differs in a few details from the actual statement published by Nordstrom.

Exhibit 13–6

NORDSTROM, INC.
Simplified Statement of Cash Flows
(dollars in millions)

Note: This simplified statement is for illustration purposes only. It should *not* be used to complete end-of-chapter homework assignments or for preparing an actual statement of cash flows. See Exhibit 13–12 for the proper format for a statement of cash flows.

Sources

Net income	$140	
Decreases in noncash assets:		
Decrease in accounts receivable	17	
Increases in liabilities (and contra asset accounts):		
Increase in accumulated depreciation and amortization	93	
Increase in accounts payable	44	
Increase in accrued wages and salaries	3	
Increase in accrued income taxes	6	
Increase in notes payable	2	
Increases in capital stock accounts:		
Increase in common stock	2	
Total sources		$307

Uses

Increases in noncash assets:		
Increase in merchandise inventory	49	
Increase in property, buildings, and equipment	123	
Decreases in liabilities:		
Decrease in long-term debt	43	
Decrease in deferred income taxes	2	
Dividends	28	
Total uses		245
Net cash flow		$ 62

Organization of the Full-Fledged Statement of Cash Flows

To make it easier to compare statements of cash flows from different companies, the Financial Accounting Standards Board (FASB) requires that companies follow prescribed rules for preparing the statement of cash flows. Most companies follow these rules for internal reports as well as for external financial statements.

One of the FASB requirements is that the statement of cash flows be divided into three sections: *operating activities, investing activities,* and *financing activities.* The guidelines to be followed in classifying transactions under these three heads are summarized in Exhibit 13–7 and discussed below.

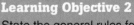

Learning Objective 2
State the general rules for determining whether transactions should be classified as operating activities, investing activities, or financing activities.

Operating Activities

Generally, **operating activities** are those activities that enter into the determination of net income. Technically, however, the FASB defines operating activities as all the transactions that are not classified as investing or financing activities. Generally speaking, this includes all transactions affecting current assets. It also includes all transactions affecting current liabilities except for issuing and repaying a note payable. Operating activities also include changes in noncurrent balance sheet accounts that directly affect net income such as the Accumulated Depreciation and Amortization account.

Concept 13–1

Exhibit 13–7
Guidelines for Classifying
Transactions as Operating,
Investing, and Financing
Activities

Operating activities:
- Net income
- Changes in current assets
- Changes in noncurrent assets that affect net income (e.g., depreciation)
- Changes in current liabilities (except for debts to lenders and dividends payable)
- Changes in noncurrent liabilities that affect net income

Investing activities:
- Changes in noncurrent assets that are not included in net income

Financing activities:
- Changes in the current liabilities that are debts to lenders rather than obligations to suppliers, employees, or the government
- Changes in noncurrent liabilities that are not included in net income
- Changes in capital stock accounts
- Dividends

Investing Activities

Generally speaking, transactions that involve acquiring or disposing of noncurrent assets are classified as **investing activities.** These transactions include acquiring or selling property, plant, and equipment; acquiring or selling securities held for long-term investment, such as bonds and stocks of other companies; and lending money to another entity (such as a subsidiary) and the subsequent collection of the loan. However, as previously discussed, changes in noncurrent assets that directly affect net income such as depreciation and amortization charges are classified as operating activities.

Financing Activities

As a general rule, borrowing from creditors or repaying creditors as well as transactions with the company's owners are classified as **financing activities.** For example, when a company borrows money by issuing a bond, the transaction is classified as a financing activity. However, transactions with creditors that affect net income are classified as operating activities. For example, interest on the company's debt is included in operating activities rather than financing activities because interest is deducted as an expense in computing net income. In contrast, dividend payments to owners do not affect net income and therefore are classified as financing rather than operating activities.

Most changes in current liabilities are considered to be operating activities unless the transaction involves borrowing money directly from a lender, as with a note payable, or repaying such a debt. Transactions involving accounts payable, wages payable, and taxes payable are included in operating activities rather than financing activities, since these transactions occur on a routine basis and involve the company's suppliers, employees, and the government rather than lenders.

Other Issues in Preparing the Statement of Cash Flows

We must consider several other issues before we can illustrate the preparation of a statement of cash flows that would be acceptable for external financial reports. These issues are (1) whether amounts on the statement should be presented gross or net, (2) whether operating activities should be presented using the direct or indirect method, and (3) whether direct exchanges should be reported on the statement.

Cash Flows: Gross or Net?

For both financing and investing activities, items on the statement of cash flows should be presented in gross amounts rather than in net amounts. To illustrate, suppose that

Macy's Department Stores purchases $50 million in property during the year and sells other property for $30 million. Instead of showing the net change of $20 million, the company must show the gross amounts of both the purchases and the sales. The purchases would be recorded as a use of cash, and the sales would be recorded as a source of cash. In like manner, if Alcoa receives $80 million from the issue of long-term bonds and then pays out $30 million to retire other bonds, the two transactions must be reported separately on the statement of cash flows rather than being netted against each other.

The gross method of reporting does *not* extend to operating activities, where debits and credits to an account are ordinarily netted against each other on the statement of cash flows. For example, if Sears adds $600 million to its accounts receivable as a result of sales during the year and $520 million of receivables is collected, only the net increase of $80 million would be reported on the statement of cash flows.

Operating Activities: Direct or Indirect Method?

The net result of the cash inflows and outflows arising from operating activities is known formally as the **net cash provided by operating activities.** This figure can be computed by either the direct or the indirect method.

Under the **direct method,** the income statement is reconstructed on a cash basis from top to bottom. For example, in the direct method, cash collected from customers is used instead of revenue, and payments to suppliers is used instead of cost of sales. In essence, cash receipts are counted as revenues and cash disbursements are counted as expenses. The difference between the cash receipts and cash disbursements is the net cash provided by operating activities for the period.

Under the **indirect method,** the operating activities section of the statement of cash flows is constructed by starting with net income and adjusting it to a cash basis. That is, rather than directly computing cash sales, cash expenses, and so forth, these amounts are arrived at *indirectly* by removing from net income any items that do not affect cash flows. The indirect method has an advantage over the direct method in that it shows the reasons for any differences between net income and the net cash provided by operating activities. The indirect method is also known as the **reconciliation method.**

Which method should be used for constructing the operating activities section of the statement of cash flows—the direct method or the indirect method? Both methods will result in exactly the same figure for the net cash provided by operating activities. However, for external reporting purposes, the FASB *recommends* and *encourages* the use of the direct method. But there is a catch. If the direct method is used, there must be a supplementary reconciliation of net income with operating cash flows. In essence, if a company chooses to use the direct method, it must also go to the trouble to construct a statement in which a form of the indirect method is used. However, if a company chooses to use the indirect method for determining the net cash flows from operating activities, there is no requirement that it also report the results of using the direct method.

The Popularity of the Indirect Method   *in business* | *today*

Not surprisingly, a survey of 600 companies revealed that only 7, or 1.2%, use the direct method to construct the statement of cash flows for external reports. The remaining 98.8% probably use the indirect method because it is simply less work.

Source: American Institute of Certified Public Accountants, *Accounting Trends and Techniques: 1999*, Jersey City, NJ, 1999, p. 499. Reprinted with permission from *Accounting Trends and Techniques*. © 1999 by American Institute of Certified Public Accountants, Inc.

While there are some good reasons for using the direct method, we use the indirect method in this chapter because it is by far the most popular method. The direct method is discussed and illustrated in Appendix 13A at the end of the chapter.

Loan Officer

You met recently with a prospective customer who would like to apply for a loan from your bank. The customer owns a small business and called to ask which method (direct or indirect) should be used to prepare the statement of cash flows. As a loan officer, which method would you prefer? Why?

Direct Exchange Transactions

Companies sometimes enter into **direct exchange transactions** in which noncurrent balance sheet items are swapped. For example, a company might issue common stock that is directly exchanged for property. Or a company might induce its creditors to swap their long-term debt for common stock of the company. Or a company might acquire equipment under a long-term lease contract offered by the seller.

Direct exchange transactions are not reported on the statement of cash flows. However, such direct exchanges are disclosed in a separate schedule that accompanies the statement.

An Example of a Full-Fledged Statement of Cash Flows

Learning Objective 3

Prepare a statement of cash flows using the indirect method to determine the net cash provided by operating activities.

In this section, we apply the FASB rules to construct a statement of cash flows for Nordstrom that would be acceptable for external reporting. The approach we take is based on an analysis of changes in balance sheet accounts, as in our earlier discussion of the simplified statement of cash flows. Indeed, as you will see, the full-fledged statement of cash flows is for the most part just a reorganized form of the simplified statement that appears in Exhibit 13–6.

The format for the operating activities part of the statement of cash flows is shown in Exhibit 13–8. For example, consider the effect of an increase in the Accounts Receivable account on the net cash provided by operating activities. Since the Accounts Receivable account is a noncash asset, we know from Exhibit 13–2 that increases in this account are treated as *uses* of cash. In other words, increases in Accounts Receivable are deducted when determining net cash flows. Intuitive explanations for this and other adjustments are sometimes slippery, but commonly given explanations are listed in Exhibit 13–9 for some of these adjustments. For example, Exhibit 13–9 suggests that an increase in Accounts Receivable is deducted from net income because sales have been recorded for which no cash has been collected. Therefore, to adjust net income to a cash basis, the increase in the Accounts Receivable account must be deducted from net income to show that cash-basis sales are less than reported sales. However, we can more simply state that an increase in Accounts Receivable is deducted when computing net cash flows because, according to the logic of Exhibits 13–1 and 13–2, increases in all noncash assets must be deducted.

Eight Basic Steps to Preparing the Statement of Cash Flows

A number of techniques have been developed to help prepare the statement of cash flows. Preparing a statement of cash flows can be confusing, and important details can be easily overlooked without such aids. We recommend that you use a worksheet, such as the one in Exhibit 13–10, to prepare a statement of cash flows. Another technique relies on the use of T-accounts. The use of the T-account approach to prepare the statement of cash flows is discussed and illustrated in Appendix 13B at the end of the chapter. You may find it helpful to review the illustration of the T-account approach in Appendix 13B even if your instructor does not cover this appendix in class.

	Add (+) or Deduct (−) to Adjust Net Income
Net income	$XXX
Adjustments needed to convert net income to a cash basis:	
Depreciation, depletion, and amortization charges	+
Add (deduct) changes in current asset accounts affecting revenue or expense:*	
Increase in the account	−
Decrease in the account	+
Add (deduct) changes in current liability accounts affecting revenue or expense:†	
Increase in the account	+
Decrease in the account	−
Add (deduct) gains or losses on sales of assets:	
Gain on sales of assets	−
Loss on sales of assets	+
Add (deduct) changes in the Deferred Income Taxes account:	
Increase in the account	+
Decrease in the account	−
Net cash provided by operating activities	$XXX

*Examples include accounts receivable, accrued receivables, inventory, and prepaid expenses.
†Examples include accounts payable, accrued liabilities, and taxes payable.

Exhibit 13–8
General Model: Indirect Method of Determining the "Net Cash Provided by Operating Activities"

As noted above, we will use the worksheet approach to illustrate the preparation of the statement of cash flows in this chapter. The worksheet in Exhibit 13–10 and statement of cash flows can be prepared using the eight steps that follow. This brief summary of the steps will be followed by more detailed explanations later.

1. Copy onto the worksheet the title of each account appearing on the comparative balance sheet except for cash and cash equivalents and retained earnings. To avoid confusion, contra asset accounts such as the Accumulated Depreciation and Amortization account should be listed with the liabilities. Contra asset accounts are treated the same way as liabilities on the statement of cash flows.
2. Compute the change from the beginning balance to the ending balance in each balance sheet account. Break the change in retained earnings down into net income and dividends paid to stockholders.
3. Using Exhibit 13–2 as a guide, code each entry on the worksheet as a source or a use.
4. Under the Cash Flow Effect column, write sources as positive numbers and uses as negative numbers.
5. Make any necessary adjustments to reflect gross, rather than net, amounts involved in transactions—including adjustments for gains and losses. Some of these adjustments may require adding new entries to the bottom of the worksheet. The net effect of all such adjusting entries must be zero.
6. Classify each entry on the worksheet as an operating activity, investing activity, or financing activity according to the FASB's criteria, as given in Exhibit 13–7.
7. Copy the data from the worksheet to the statement of cash flows section by section, starting with the operating activities section.
8. At the bottom of the statement of cash flows prepare a reconciliation of the beginning and ending balances of cash and cash equivalents. The net change in cash and cash equivalents shown at the bottom of this statement should equal the change in the Cash and Cash Equivalents accounts during the year.

Exhibit 13-9

Explanation of Adjustments for Changes in Current Asset and Current Liability Accounts (see Exhibit 13–8)

	Change in the Account	This Change Means That...	Therefore, to Adjust to a Cash Basis under the Indirect Method, We Must...
Accounts Receivable and Accrued Receivables	Increase	Sales (revenues) have been reported for which no cash has been collected.	Deduct the amount from net income to show that cash-basis sales are less than reported sales (revenues).
	Decrease	Cash has been collected for which no sales (revenues) have been reported for the current period.	Add the amount to net income to show that cash-basis sales are greater than reported sales (revenues).
Inventory	Increase	Goods have been purchased that are not included in cost of goods sold (COGS).	Deduct the amount from net income to show that cash-basis COGS is greater than reported COGS.
	Decrease	Goods have been included in COGS that were purchased in a prior period.	Add the amount to net income to show that cash-basis COGS is less than reported COGS.
Prepaid Expenses	Increase	More cash has been paid out for services than has been reported as expense.	Deduct the amount from net income to show that cash-basis expenses are greater than reported expenses.
	Decrease	More has been reported as expense for services than has been paid out in cash.	Add the amount to net income to show that cash-basis expenses are less than reported expenses.
Accounts Payable and Accrued Liabilities	Increase	More has been reported as expense for goods and services than has been paid out in cash.	Add the amount to net income to show that cash-basis expenses for goods and services are less than reported expenses.
	Decrease	More cash has been paid out for goods and services than has been reported as expense.	Deduct the amount from net income to show that cash-basis expenses for goods and services are greater than reported expenses.
Taxes Payable	Increase	More income tax expense has been reported than has been paid out in cash.	Add the amount to net income to show that cash-basis expenses are less than reported expenses.
	Decrease	More cash has been paid to the tax authorities than has been reported as income tax expense.	Deduct the amount from net income to show that cash-basis expenses are greater than reported expenses.

On the following pages we will apply these eight steps to the data contained in the comparative balance sheet for Nordstrom, Inc., found in Exhibit 13–4. *As we discuss each step, refer to Exhibit 13–4 and trace the data from this exhibit into the worksheet in Exhibit 13–10.*

Setting Up the Worksheet (Steps 1–4)

As indicated above, step 1 in preparing the worksheet is to simply list all of the relevant account titles from the company's balance sheet. Note that we have done this for Nordstrom, Inc., on the worksheet in Exhibit 13–10. (The titles of Nordstrom's accounts have been taken from the company's comparative balance sheet, which is found in Exhibit 13–4.) The only significant differences between Nordstrom's balance sheet accounts and

Exhibit 13–10

	(1) Change	(2) Source or Use?	(3) Cash Flow Effect	(4) Adjust- ments	(5) Adjusted Effect (3) + (4)	(6) Classi- fication*
NORDSTROM, INC. **Statement of Cash Flows Worksheet** **(dollars in millions)**						
Assets (except cash and cash equivalents)						
Current assets:						
Accounts receivable	$ −17	Source	$ +17		$ +17	Operating
Merchandise inventory	+49	Use	−49		−49	Operating
Noncurrent assets:						
Property, buildings, and equipment	+123	Use	−123	$−15	−138	Investing
Contra Assets, Liabilities, and **Stockholders' Equity**						
Contra assets:						
Accumulated depreciation and amortization . . .	+93	Source	+93	+10	+103	Operating
Current liabilities:						
Accounts payable	+44	Source	+44		+44	Operating
Accrued wages and salaries payable	+3	Source	+3		+3	Operating
Accrued income taxes payable	+6	Source	+6		+6	Operating
Notes payable	+2	Source	+2		+2	Financing
Noncurrent liabilities:						
Long-term debt	−43	Use	−43		−43	Financing
Deferred income taxes	−2	Use	−2		−2	Operating
Stockholders' equity:						
Common stock	+2	Source	+2		+2	Financing
Retained earnings:						
Net income	+140	Source	+140		+140	Operating
Dividends	−28	Use	−28		−28	Financing
Additional Entries						
Proceeds from sale of store				+8	+8	Investing
Gain on sale of store				−3	−3	Operating
Total (net cash flow)			$ +62	$ 0	$ +62	

*See Exhibit 13–11 (page 532) for the reasons for these classifications.

the worksheet listing are that (1) the Accumulated Depreciation and Amortization account has been moved down with the liabilities on the worksheet, (2) the Cash and Cash Equivalents accounts have been omitted, and (3) the change in retained earnings has been broken down into net income and dividends.

As stated in step 2, the change in each account's balance during the year is listed in the first column of the worksheet. We have entered these changes for Nordstrom's accounts onto the worksheet in Exhibit 13–10. (Refer to Nordstrom's comparative balance sheet in Exhibit 13–4 to see how these changes were computed.)

Then, as indicated in step 3, each change on the worksheet is classified as either a source or a use of cash. Whether a change is a source or a use can be determined by referring back to Exhibit 13–2, where we first discussed these classifications. For example, Nordstrom's Merchandise Inventory account increased by $49 million during the year. According to Exhibit 13–2, increases in noncash asset accounts are classified as uses of cash, so an entry has been made to that effect in the second column of the worksheet for the Merchandise Inventory account.

So far, nothing is new. All of this was done already in Exhibit 13–4 in preparation for constructing the simplified statement of cash flows. Step 4 is mechanical, but it helps prevent careless errors. Sources are coded as positive changes and uses as negative changes in the Cash Flow Effect column on the worksheet.

Adjustments to Reflect Gross, Rather than Net, Amounts (Step 5)

As discussed earlier, the FASB requires that gross, rather than net, amounts be disclosed in the investing and financing sections. This rule requires special treatment of gains and losses. To illustrate, suppose that Nordstrom decided to sell an old store and move its retail operations to a new location. Assume that the original cost of the old store was $15 million, its accumulated depreciation was $10 million, and that it was sold for $8 million in cash. The journal entry to record this transaction (in millions) appears below:

Cash	8	
Accumulated Depreciation and Amortization	10	
Property, Buildings, and Equipment		15
Gain on Sale		3

The $3 million gain is reflected in the income statement in Exhibit 13–3.

We can reconstruct the gross additions to the Property, Buildings, and Equipment account and the gross charges to the Accumulated Depreciation and Amortization account with the help of T-accounts:

Property, Buildings, and Equipment				Accumulated Depreciation and Amortization			
Bal.	1,394					561	Bal.
Additions	138	15	Disposal	Disposal	10	103	Depreciation
(plug*)			of store	of store			charges (plug)
Bal.	1,517					654	Bal.

*By *plug* we mean the balancing figure in the account.

According to the FASB rules, the gross additions of $138 million to the Property, Buildings, and Equipment account should be disclosed on the statement of cash flows rather than the net change in the account of $123 million ($1,517 million − $1,394 million = $123 million). Likewise, the gross depreciation charges of $103 million should be disclosed rather than the net change in the Accumulated Depreciation and Amortization account of $93 million ($654 million − $561 million = $93 million). And the cash proceeds of $8 million from sale of the building should also be disclosed on the statement of cash flows. All of this is accomplished, while preserving the correct overall net cash flows on the statement, by using the above journal entry to make adjusting entries on the worksheet. As indicated in Exhibit 13–2, the debits are recorded as positive adjustments, and the credits are recorded as negative adjustments. These adjusting entries are recorded under the Adjustments column in Exhibit 13–10.

It may not be clear why the gain on the sale is *deducted* in the operating activities section of the statement of cash flows. The company's $140 million net income, which is part of the operating activities section, includes the $3 million gain on the sale of the store. But this $3 million gain must be reported in the *investing* activities section of the statement of cash flows as part of the $8 million proceeds from the sale transaction. Therefore, to avoid double counting, the $3 million gain is deducted from net income in the operating activities section of the statement. The adjustments we have made on the worksheet accomplish this. The $3 million gain will be deducted in the operating activities section, and all $8 million of the sale proceeds will be shown as an investing item. As a result, all of the gain will be included in the investing section of the statement of cash flows and none of it will be in the operating activities section. There will be no double-counting of the gain.

In the case of a loss on the sale of an asset, we do the opposite. The loss is added back to the net income figure in the operating activities section of the statement of cash flows. Whatever cash proceeds are received from the sale of the asset are reported in the investing activities section.

Before turning to step 6 in the process of building the statement of cash flows, one small step is required. Add the Adjustments in column (4) to the Cash Flow Effect in column (3) to arrive at the Adjusted Effect in column (5).

Classifying Entries as Operating, Investing, or Financing Activities (Step 6)

In step 6, each entry on the worksheet is classified as an operating, investing, or financing activity using the guidelines in Exhibit 13–7. These classifications are entered directly on the worksheet in Exhibit 13–10 and are explained in Exhibit 13–11. Most of these classifications are straightforward, but the classification of the change in the Deferred Income Taxes account may require some additional explanation. Because of the way income tax expense is determined for financial reporting purposes, the expense that appears on the income statement often differs from the taxes that are actually owed to the government. Usually, the income tax expense overstates the company's actual income tax liability for the year. When this happens, the journal entry to record income taxes includes a credit to Deferred Income Taxes:

Income Tax Expense	XXX	
Income Taxes Payable		XXX
Deferred Income Taxes (plug)		XXX

Since deferred income taxes arise directly from the computation of an expense, the change in the Deferred Income Taxes account is included in the operating activities section of the statement of cash flows.

In the case of Nordstrom, the Deferred Income Taxes account decreased during the year, so income tax expense was apparently less than the company's income tax liability for the year by $2 million. In other words, for some reason Nordstrom had to pay the government $2 million more than the income tax expense recorded on the income statement, and therefore this additional cash outflow must be deducted to convert net income to a cash basis. Or, looking back again to Exhibit 13–2, Deferred Income Taxes is a liability account for Nordstrom's. Since this liability account decreased during the year, the change is counted as a use of cash and is deducted in determining net cash flow for the year.

Owner   *decision* | *maker*

You are the owner of a small manufacturing company. The company has developed an international market for its products, which has resulted in a very significant increase in sales revenue and net income during the last two months of the year. The operating activities section of the company's statement of cash flows shows a negative number (that is, cash was *used* rather than *provided* by operations). Would you be concerned?

The Completed Statement of Cash Flows (Steps 7 and 8)

Once the worksheet is completed, it is easy to complete step 7 by constructing an actual statement of cash flows. Nordstrom's statement of cash flows appears in Exhibit 13–12. Trace each item from the worksheet into this statement.

Exhibit 13–11

Classifications of Entries on Nordstrom's Statement of Cash Flows

Entry	Classification	Reason
• Changes in Accounts Receivable and Merchandise Inventory	Operating activity	Changes in current assets are included in operating activities.
• Change in Property, Buildings, and Equipment	Investing activity	Changes in noncurrent assets that do not directly affect net income are included in investing activities.
• Change in Accumulated Depreciation and Amortization	Operating activity	Depreciation and amortization directly affect net income and are therefore included in operating activities.
• Changes in Accounts Payable, Accrued Wages and Salaries Payable, and Accrued Income Taxes Payable	Operating activity	Changes in current liabilities (except for notes payable) are included in operating activities.
• Change in Notes Payable	Financing activity	Issuing or repaying notes payable is classified as a financing activity.
• Change in Long-Term Debt	Financing activity	Changes in noncurrent liabilities that do not directly affect net income are included in financing activities.
• Change in Deferred Income Taxes	Operating activity	Deferred income taxes result from income tax expense that directly affects net income. Therefore, this entry is included in operating activities.
• Change in Common Stock	Financing activity	Changes in capital stock accounts are always included in financing activities.
• Net Income	Operating activity	Net income is always included in operating activities.
• Dividends	Financing activity	Dividends paid to stockholders are always included in financing activities.
• Proceeds from sale of store	Investing activity	The gross amounts received on disposal of noncurrent assets are included in investing activities.
• Gains from sale of store	Operating activity	Gains and losses directly affect net income and are therefore included in operating activities.

Concept 13–2

The operating activities section of the statement follows the format laid out in Exhibit 13–8, beginning with net income. The other entries in the operating activities section are considered to be adjustments required to convert net income to a cash basis. The sum of all of the entries under the operating activities section is called the "net cash provided by operating activities."

The investing activities section comes next on the statement of cash flows. The worksheet entries that have been classified as investing activities are recorded in this section in any order. The sum of all the entries in this section is called the "net cash used for investing activities."

The financing activities section of the statement follows the investing activities section. The worksheet entries that have been classified as financing activities are recorded in this section in any order. The sum of all of the entries in this section is called the "net cash provided by financing activities."

Finally, for step 8, the bottom of the statement of cash flows contains a reconciliation of the beginning and ending balances of cash and cash equivalents.

Exhibit 13–12

NORDSTROM, INC.*
Statement of Cash Flows—Indirect Method
(dollars in millions)

Operating Activities

Net income	$ 140
Adjustments to convert net income to a cash basis:	
Depreciation and amortization charges	103
Decrease in accounts receivable	17
Increase in merchandise inventory	(49)
Increase in accounts payable	44
Increase in accrued wages and salaries payable	3
Increase in accrued income taxes payable	6
Decrease in deferred income taxes	(2)
Gain on sale of store	(3)
Net cash provided by operating activities	259

Investing Activities

Additions to property, buildings, and equipment	(138)
Proceeds from sale of store	8
Net cash used in investing activities	(130)

Financing Activities

Increase in notes payable	2
Decrease in long-term debt	(43)
Increase in common stock	2
Cash dividends paid	(28)
Net cash used in financing activities	(67)
Net increase in cash and cash equivalents	62
Cash and cash equivalents at beginning of year	29
Cash and cash equivalents at end of year	$ 91

*This statement differs from the actual statement published by Nordstrom.

Reconciliation of the beginning and ending cash balances

Taking It Week-by-Week

in business today

Media experts have touted the advantages of online journalism, which does not suffer from the space limitations of traditional media. For more than one year, APBNews.com captured the attention of web surfers by reporting the news online and won awards for its coverage. Then, in June 2000, the company's 140 employees were shocked to learn that the company had filed for bankruptcy and they had been fired. Not only had ABP-News.com spent all of the $20 million of funding that it started with, it was $7 million in debt. "Unfortunately, awards don't pay back creditors," Mark Sauter, the company's co-founder, lamented. Three weeks later, the company announced that it had been able to secure an undisclosed amount of short-term funding and was rehiring 24 of its employees. "We still think we can pull it off, but it's definitely week-to-week now," warned Sauter.

Source: Marco R. della Cava, "Wanted: Cash for Online Journalism," *USA Today*, July 20, 2000, p. 3D. Copyright 2000, *USA Today*. Reprinted with permission.

Interpretation of the Statement of Cash Flows

The completed statement of cash flows in Exhibit 13–12 provides a very favorable picture of Nordstrom's cash flows. The net cash flow from operations is a healthy $259 million.

This positive cash flow permitted the company to make substantial additions to its property, buildings, and equipment and to pay off a substantial portion of its long-term debt. If similar conditions prevail in the future, the company can continue to finance substantial growth from its own cash flows without the necessity of raising debt or selling stock.

When interpreting a statement of cash flows, it is particularly important to scrutinize the net cash provided by operating activities. This figure provides a measure of how successful the company is in generating cash on a continuing basis. A negative cash flow from operations would usually be a sign of fundamental difficulties. A positive cash flow from operations is necessary to avoid liquidating assets or borrowing money just to sustain day-to-day operations.

Depreciation, Depletion, and Amortization

There are a few pitfalls that the unwary can fall into when reading a statement of cash flows. Perhaps the most common is to misinterpret the nature of the depreciation charges on the statement of cash flows. Since depreciation is added back to net income, there is a tendency to think that all you have to do to increase net cash flow is to increase depreciation charges. This is false. In a merchandising company like Nordstrom, increasing the depreciation charge by X dollars would decrease net income by X dollars because of the added expense taken. Adding back the depreciation charge to net income on the statement of cash flows simply cancels out the reduction in net income caused by the depreciation charge. Referring back to Exhibit 13–2, depreciation, depletion, and amortization charges are added back to net income on the statement of cash flows because they are a decrease in an asset (or, an increase in a contra asset)—not because they generate cash.

Summary

LO1   Know how to classify changes in noncash balance sheet accounts as sources or uses of cash.

The statement of cash flows is one of the three major financial statements prepared by organizations. It explains how cash was generated and how it was used during the period. The statement of cash flows is widely used as a tool for assessing the financial health of organizations. In general, sources of cash include net income, decreases in assets, increases in liabilities, and increases in stockholders' capital accounts. Uses of cash include increases in assets, decreases in liabilities, decreases in stockholders' capital accounts, and dividends. A simplified form of the statement of cash flows can be easily constructed using just these definitions and a comparative balance sheet.

LO2   State the general rules for determining whether transactions should be classified as operating activities, investing activities, or financing activities.

For external reporting purposes, the statement of cash flows must be organized in terms of operating, investing, and financing activities. While there are some exceptions, operating activities include net income and changes in current assets and current liabilities. And, with a few exceptions, changes in noncurrent assets are generally included in investing activities and changes in noncurrent liabilities are generally included in financing activities.

LO3   Prepare a statement of cash flows using the indirect method to determine the net cash provided by operating activities.

The operating activities section of the statement of cash flows can be constructed using the indirect method (discussed in the main body of the chapter) or the direct method (discussed in Appendix 13A). Although the FASB prefers the use of the direct method, most companies use the indirect method, which is easier. Both methods report the same amount of net cash provided by operating activities.

When the indirect method is used, the operating activities section of the statement of cash flows starts with net income and shows the adjustments required to adjust net income to a cash basis. A worksheet can be used to construct the statement of cash flows. After determining the change in each balance sheet account, adjustments are made to reflect gross, rather than net, amounts involved in selected transactions, and each entry on the worksheet is labeled as an operating, investing, or financing activity. The data from the worksheet is then used to prepare each section of the statement of cash flows, beginning with the operating activities section.

Guidance Answers to Decision Maker and You Decide

LOAN OFFICER (p. 526)

Either method can be used to prepare the operating activities section of the statement of cash flows. Both methods result in exactly the same figure for the net cash provided by operating activities. A loan officer would probably prefer that the direct method be used because more information is disclosed. The major cash inflows arising from and outflows relating to the company's operations are separately reported in the operating activities section when the direct method is used. A loan officer might find this approach easier to follow than the indirect method, which reconciles net income to the amount of net cash provided by operating activities by presenting the required adjustments. Further, companies that use the direct method must also present the indirect method in a separate schedule accompanying the statement of cash flows. As a result, the loan officer would still have access to that information.

OWNER (p. 531)

Even though the company reported positive net income, the net effect of the company's operations was to *consume* rather than *generate* cash during the year. Cash disbursements relating to the company's operations exceeded the amount of cash receipts from operations. If the company generated a significant amount of sales just before the end of the year, it is quite possible that cash has not yet been received from the customers. In fact, given that the additional sales were international, a longer collection period would be expected. Nevertheless, as owner, you probably would want to ensure that the company's credit-granting policies and procedures were adhered to when these sales were made, and you should also monitor the trend in the average collection period. If additional information (such as a copy of the statement of cash flows) were available, other factors might be identified that would require further investigation.

Review Problem

Rockford Company's comparative balance sheet for 2001 and the company's income statement for the year follow:

ROCKFORD COMPANY
Comparative Balance Sheet
December 31, 2001, and 2000
(dollars in millions)

	2001	2000
Assets		
Cash	$ 26	$ 10
Accounts receivable	180	270
Inventory	205	160
Prepaid expenses	17	20
Plant and equipment	430	309
Less accumulated depreciation	(218)	(194)
Long-term investments	60	75
Total assets	$ 700	$ 650
Liabilities and Stockholders' Equity		
Accounts payable	$ 230	$ 310
Accrued liabilities	70	60
Bonds payable	135	40
Deferred income taxes	15	8
Common stock	140	140
Retained earnings	110	92
Total liabilities and stockholders' equity	$ 700	$ 650

ROCKFORD COMPANY
Income Statement
For the Year Ended December 31, 2001
(dollars in millions)

Sales	$1,000
Less cost of sales	530
Gross margin	470
Less operating expenses	352
Net operating income	118
Nonoperating items:	
Loss on sale of equipment	(4)
Income before taxes	114
Less income taxes	48
Net income	$ 66

Notes: Dividends of $48 million were paid in 2001. The loss on sale of equipment of $4 million reflects a transaction in which equipment with an original cost of $12 million and accumulated depreciation of $5 million was sold for $3 million in cash.

Required:
Using the indirect method, determine the net cash provided by operating activities for 2001 and construct a statement of cash flows for the year.

SOLUTION TO REVIEW PROBLEM
A worksheet for Rockford Company appears below. Using the worksheet, it is a simple matter to construct the statement of cash flows, including the net cash provided by operating activities.

ROCKFORD COMPANY
Statement of Cash Flows Worksheet
For the Year Ended December 31, 2001
(dollars in millions)

	(1) Change	(2) Source or Use?	(3) Cash Flow Effect	(4) Adjust- ments	(5) Adjusted Effect (3) + (4)	(6) Classi- fication
Assets (except cash and cash equivalents)						
Current assets:						
Accounts receivable	$ −90	Source	$ +90		$ +90	Operating
Inventory	+45	Use	−45		−45	Operating
Prepaid expenses	−3	Source	+3		+3	Operating
Noncurrent assets:						
Property, buildings, and equipment	+121	Use	−121	$−12	−133	Investing
Long-term investments	−15	Source	+15		+15	Investing
Contra Assets, Liabilities, and Stockholders' Equity						
Contra assets:						
Accumulated depreciation	+24	Source	+24	+5	+29	Operating
Current liabilities:						
Accounts payable	−80	Use	−80		−80	Operating
Accrued liabilities	+10	Source	+10		+10	Operating
Noncurrent liabilities:						
Bonds payable	+95	Source	+95		+95	Financing
Deferred income taxes	+7	Source	+7		+7	Operating
Stockholders' equity:						
Common stock	+0	—	+0		+0	Financing
Retained earnings:						
Net income	+66	Source	+66		+66	Operating
Dividends	−48	Use	−48		−48	Financing

continued

	(1) Change	(2) Source or Use?	(3) Cash Flow Effect	(4) Adjust-ments	(5) Adjusted Effect (3) + (4)	(6) Classi-fication
Additional Entries						
Proceeds from sale of equipment				+3	+3	Investing
Loss on sale of equipment				+4	+4	Operating
Total (net cash flow)			$ +16	$ 0	$ +16	

ROCKFORD COMPANY
Statement of Cash Flows—Indirect Method
For the Year Ended December 31, 2001
(dollars in millions)

Operating Activities

Net income	$ 66
Adjustments to convert net income to a cash basis:	
Depreciation and amortization charges	29
Decrease in accounts receivable	90
Increase in inventory	(45)
Decrease in prepaid expenses	3
Decrease in accounts payable	(80)
Increase in accrued liabilities	10
Increase in deferred income taxes	7
Loss on sale of equipment	4
Net cash provided by operating activities	84

Investing Activities:

Additions to property, buildings, and equipment	(133)
Decrease in long-term investments	15
Proceeds from sale of equipment	3
Net cash used in investing activities	(115)

Financing Activities:

Increase in bonds payable	95
Cash dividends paid	(48)
Net cash provided by financing activities	47
Net increase in cash and cash equivalents	16
Cash and cash equivalents at beginning of year	10
Cash and cash equivalents at end of year	$ 26

Note that the $16 increase in cash and cash equivalents agrees with the $16 increase in the company's Cash account shown in the balance sheet, and it agrees with the total in column (5) in the above worksheet.

Glossary

Cash equivalents   Short-term, highly liquid investments such as Treasury bills, commercial paper, and money market funds that are made solely for the purpose of generating a return on funds that are temporarily idle. (p. 518)

Direct exchange transactions   Transactions involving only noncurrent balance sheet accounts. For example, a company might issue common stock that is directly exchanged for property. (p. 526)

Direct method   A method of computing the cash provided by operating activities in which the income statement is reconstructed on a cash basis from top to bottom. (p. 525)

Financing activities   All transactions (other than payment of interest) involving borrowing from creditors or repaying creditors as well as transactions with the company's owners (except stock dividends and stock splits). (p. 524)

Indirect method   A method of computing the cash provided by operating activities that starts with net income and adjusts it to a cash basis. It is also known as the *reconciliation method.* (p. 525)

Investing activities   Transactions that involve acquiring or disposing of noncurrent assets. (p. 524)

Net cash provided by operating activities   The net result of the cash inflows and outflows arising from day-to-day operations. (p. 525)

Operating activities   Transactions that enter into the determination of net income. (p. 523)

Reconciliation method   See *Indirect method.* (p. 525)

Statement of cash flows   A financial statement that highlights the major activities that directly and indirectly impact cash flows and hence affect the overall cash balance. (p. 518)

As stated in the main body of the chapter, to compute the "Net cash provided by operating activities" under the direct method, we must reconstruct the income statement on a cash basis from top to bottom. A model is presented in Exhibit 13A–1 that shows the adjustments that must be made to adjust sales, expenses, and so forth, to a cash basis. To illustrate, we have included in the exhibit the Nordstrom data from the chapter.

Note that the "Net cash provided by operating activities" figure ($259 million) agrees with the amount computed in the chapter by the indirect method. The two amounts agree, since the direct and indirect methods are just different roads to the same destination. The investing and financing activities sections of the statement will be exactly the same as shown for the indirect method in Exhibit 13–12. The only difference between the indirect and direct methods is in the operating activities section.

Similarities and Differences in the Handling of Data

Although we arrive at the same destination under either the direct or the indirect methods, not all data are handled in the same way in the adjustment process. Stop for a moment, flip back to the general model for the indirect method in Exhibit 13–8 and compare the adjustments made in that exhibit to the adjustments made for the direct method in Exhibit 13A–1. The adjustments for accounts that affect revenue are the same in the two methods. In either case, increases in the account are deducted and decreases in the accounts are added. The adjustments for accounts that affect expenses, however, are handled in *opposite* ways in the indirect and direct methods. This is because under the indirect method the adjustments are made to *net income,* whereas under the direct method the adjustments are made to the *expense accounts* themselves.

To illustrate this difference, note the handling of prepaid expenses and depreciation in the indirect and direct methods. Under the indirect method (Exhibit 13–8), an increase in the Prepaid Expenses account is *deducted* from net income in computing the amount of cash provided by operations. Under the direct method (Exhibit 13A–1), an increase in Prepaid Expenses is *added* to operating expenses. The reason for the difference can be explained as follows: An increase in Prepaid Expenses means that more cash has been paid out for items such as insurance than has been included as expense for the period. Therefore, to adjust net income to a cash basis, we must either deduct this increase from net income (indirect method) or we must add this increase to operating expenses (direct method). Either way, we will end up with the same figure for cash provided by operations. In like manner, depreciation is added to net income under the indirect method to cancel out its effect (Exhibit 13–8), whereas it is deducted from operating expenses under the direct method to cancel out its effect (Exhibit 13A–1). These differences in the handling of data are true for all other expense items in the two methods.

In the matter of gains and losses on sales of assets, no adjustments are needed at all under the direct method. These gains and losses are simply ignored, since they are not part

Revenue or Expense Item	Add (+) or Deduct (−) to Adjust to a Cash Basis	Illustration— Nordstrom (in millions)	
Sales revenue (as reported)		$3,638	
Adjustments to a cash basis:			
1. Increase in accounts receivable	−		
2. Decrease in accounts receivable	+	+17	
Total			$3,655
Cost of goods sold (as reported)		2,469	
Adjustments to a cash basis:			
3. Increase in merchandise inventory	+	+49	
4. Decrease in merchandise inventory	−		
5. Increase in accounts payable	−	−44	
6. Decrease in accounts payable	+		
Total			2,474
Operating expenses (as reported)		941	
Adjustments to a cash basis:			
7. Increase in prepaid expenses	+		
8. Decrease in prepaid expenses	−		
9. Increase in accrued liabilities	−	−3	
10. Decrease in accrued liabilities	+		
11. Period's depreciation, depletion, and amortization charges	−	−103	
Total			835
Income tax expense (as reported)		91	
Adjustments to a cash basis:			
12. Increase in accrued taxes payable	−	−6	
13. Decrease in accrued taxes payable	+		
14. Increase in deferred income taxes	−		
15. Decrease in deferred income taxes	+	+2	
Total			87
Net cash provided by operating activities			$ 259

of sales, cost of goods sold, operating expenses, or income taxes. Observe that in Exhibit 13A–1, Nordstrom's $3 million gain on the sale of the store is not listed as an adjustment in the operating activities section.

Special Rules—Direct and Indirect Methods

As stated earlier, when the direct method is used, the FASB requires a reconciliation between net income and the net cash provided by operating activities, as determined by the indirect method. Thus, *when a company elects to use the direct method, it must also present the indirect method* in a separate schedule accompanying the statement of cash flows.

On the other hand, if a company elects to use the indirect method to compute the net cash provided by operating activities, then it must also provide a special breakdown of data. The company must provide a separate disclosure of the amount of interest and the amount of income taxes paid during the year. The FASB requires this separate disclosure so that users can take the data provided by the indirect method and make estimates of what the amounts for sales, income taxes, and so forth, would have been if the direct method had been used instead.

Summary

LO4 **(Appendix 13A) Use the direct method to determine the net cash provided by operating activities.**

When the direct method is used to determine the net cash provided by operating activities, the income statement is reconstructed on a cash basis. A worksheet, which starts with the major components of the company's income statement (such as sales revenue, cost of goods sold, operating expenses, and income tax expense), can be used to organize the data. Each of the income statement components is adjusted to a cash basis by reference to the changes in the related balance sheet account. (For example, the amount of sales revenue reported on the income statement is converted to the amount of cash received from customers by subtracting the increase, or adding the decrease, in accounts receivable during the period.) Special disclosure rules apply when a company uses the direct method.

Appendix 13B | The T-Account Approach to Preparing the Statement of Cash Flows

A worksheet approach was used to prepare the statement of cash flows in the chapter. The T-account approach is an alternative technique that is sometimes used to prepare the statement of cash flows. To illustrate the T-account approach, we will again use the data for Nordstrom, Inc. (the same company used to illustrate the worksheet approach).

Learning Objective 5
Prepare a statement of cash flows using the T-account approach.

The T-Account Approach

Note from Nordstrom's comparative balance sheet in Exhibit 13–4 that cash and cash equivalents increased from $29 million to $91 million, an increase of $62 million during the year. To determine the reasons for this change we will again prepare a statement of cash flows. As before, our basic approach will be to analyze the changes in the various balance sheet accounts. However, in this appendix we will use T-accounts rather than a worksheet.

Exhibit 13B–1 contains a T-account, titled "Cash," which we will use to accumulate the cash "Provided" and the cash "Used." The exhibit also includes T-accounts with the beginning and ending account balances for each of the other accounts on Nordstrom's balance sheet. *Before proceeding, refer to Nordstrom's comparative balance sheet in Exhibit 13–4 in the main body of the chapter, and trace the data from this exhibit to the T-accounts in Exhibit 13B–1.*

As we analyze each balance sheet account, we will post the related entry(s) directly to the T-accounts. To the extent that these changes have affected cash, we will also post an appropriate entry to the T-account representing Cash. *As you progress through this appendix, trace each entry to the T-accounts in Exhibit 13B–2. Pay special attention to the placement and description of the entries affecting the T-account representing Cash.*

Observe that in the Cash T-account in Exhibit 13B–2, all operating items are near the top of the Cash T-account, clustered around the net income figure. Also note that the T-account includes a subtotal titled "Net cash provided by operating activities." If the amounts in the "Used" column exceeded the amounts in the "Provided" column, the subtotal would be on the credit side of the T-account and would be labeled "Net cash *used* in operating activities." Also note that all investing and financing items have been placed below the subtotal in the lower portion of the Cash T-account. At the bottom of the T-account is a total titled "Net increase in cash and cash equivalents." If the amounts in the "Used" column exceeded the amounts in the "Provided" column, this total would be on the credit side of the T-account and would be labeled "Net *decrease* in cash and cash equivalents." The entries in the Cash T-account contain all of the entries needed for the statement of cash flows.

Retained Earnings The Retained Earnings account is generally the most useful starting point when developing a statement of cash flows. Details of the change in Nordstrom's

541

Exhibit 13B–1

T-Accounts Showing Changes in Account Balances—Nordstrom, Inc. (in millions)

Cash		
	Provided	**Used**
Net cash provided by operating activities		
Net increase in cash and cash equivalents		

Accounts Receivable			Merchandise Inventory			Property, Buildings, and Equipment			Accumulated Depreciation	
Bal.	654		Bal.	537		Bal.	1,394		561	Bal.
Bal.	637		Bal.	586		Bal.	1,517		654	Bal.

Accounts Payable			Accrued Wages and Salaries Payable			Accrued Income Taxes Payable			Notes Payable	
	220	Bal.		190	Bal.		22	Bal.	38	Bal.
	264	Bal.		193	Bal.		28	Bal.	40	Bal.

Long-Term Debt			Deferred Income Taxes			Common Stock			Retained Earnings	
	482	Bal.		49	Bal.		155	Bal.	897	Bal.
	439	Bal.		47	Bal.		157	Bal.	1,009	Bal.

Retained Earnings account are presented in Exhibit 13–5. Note from the exhibit that net income of $140 million was added to Retained Earnings and dividends of $28 million were charged against Retained Earnings during the year. The entries to record these changes and their effects on Cash are shown below. (The dollar amounts are in millions.)

The entry to record net income and the effect on Cash would be:

(1)

Cash—Provided	140	
Retained Earnings		140

Exhibit 13B–2
T-Accounts after Posting of Account Changes—Nordstrom, Inc. (in millions)

Cash

	Provided			Used	
Net income	(1)	140	(4)	49	Increase in merchandise inventory
Decrease in accounts receivable	(3)	17	(5)	3	Gain on sale of store
Depreciation and amortization charges	(7)	103	(13)	2	Decrease in deferred income taxes
Increase in accounts payable	(8)	44			
Increase in accrued wages and salaries payable	(9)	3			
Increase in accrued income taxes payable	(10)	6			
Net cash provided by operating activities		259			
Proceeds from sale of store	(5)	8	(2)	28	Cash dividends paid
Increase in notes payable	(11)	2	(6)	138	Additions to property, buildings, and equipment
Increase in common stock	(14)	2	(12)	43	Decrease in long-term debt
Net increase in cash and cash equivalents		62			

Accounts Receivable				Merchandise Inventory				Property, Buildings, and Equipment					Accumulated Depreciation			
Bal.	654			Bal.	537			Bal.	1,394					561	Bal.	
		17	(3)	(4)	49			(6)	138	15	(5)	(5)	10	103	(7)	
Bal.	637			Bal.	586			Bal.	1,517					654	Bal.	

Accounts Payable				Accrued Wages and Salaries Payable				Accrued Income Taxes Payable				Notes Payable			
	220	Bal.			190	Bal.			22	Bal.			38	Bal.	
	44	(8)			3	(9)			6	(10)			2	(11)	
	264	Bal.			193	Bal.			28	Bal.			40	Bal.	

Long-Term Debt				Deferred Income Taxes				Common Stock				Retained Earnings			
	482	Bal.			49	Bal.			155	Bal.			897	Bal.	
(12)	43			(13)	2				2	(14)	(2)	28	140	(1)	
	439	Bal.			47	Bal.			157	Bal.			1,009	Bal.	

Recall that net income is converted to a cash basis when the indirect method is used to prepare the operating activities section of the statement of cash flows. Since net income is the starting point, the cash effect is included in the upper portion of the Cash T-account.

The entry to record the dividends paid and the effect on Cash would be:

(2)

Retained Earnings	28	
Cash—Used		28

Since the payment of cash dividends is classified as an investing activity, the cash effect is included in the lower portion of the Cash T-account along with the other investing and financing items.

Once posted to the Retained Earnings T-account in Exhibit 13B–2, these two entries fully explain the change that took place in the Retained Earnings account during the year. We can now proceed through the remainder of the balance sheet accounts in Exhibit 13B–1, analyzing the change between the beginning and ending balances in each account, and recording the appropriate entries in the T-accounts.

Current Asset Accounts   Each of the current asset accounts is examined to determine the change that occurred during the year. The change is then recorded as a debit if the account balance increased or as a credit if the account balance decreased. The offsetting entry in the case of an increase in the account balance is "Cash—Used;" the offsetting entry in the case of a decrease in the account balance is "Cash—Provided."

To demonstrate, note that Nordstrom's Accounts Receivable decreased by $17 million during the year. The entry to record this change and its effect on Cash would be:

(3)

Cash—Provided	17	
Accounts Receivable		17

The merchandise inventory account increased by $49 million during the year. The entry to record this change and its effect on Cash would be:

(4)

Merchandise Inventory	49	
Cash—Used		49

Note that these two entries result in the correct adjusting entries in the current asset T-accounts so as to reconcile the beginning and ending balances. Also note that the changes in these two current asset accounts are included in the upper portion of the Cash T-account. This is because changes in current assets are considered part of operations and therefore are used to convert net income to a cash basis in the operating activities section of the statement of cash flows.

Property, Buildings, and Equipment and Accumulated Depreciation   The activity in the Property, Buildings, and Equipment account and the Accumulated Depreciation account is analyzed in the chapter beginning on page 530. *Reread the analysis of these accounts before proceeding.* Nordstrom sold a store, purchased property, buildings, and equipment, and recorded depreciation expense during the year. The entries in this case for the T-account analysis are more complex than for current assets. These entries are presented below. You should carefully trace each of these entries to the T-accounts in Exhibit 13B–2.

The entry to record the sale of the store and its effect on Cash would be:

(5)

Cash—Provided	8	
Accumulated Depreciation	10	
Property, Buildings, and Equipment		15
Gain on Sale		3

Since the sale of property, buildings, and equipment is classified as an investing activity, the cash effect is included in the lower portion of the Cash T-account along with the other investing and financing items. The proceeds from the sale, which will be reported in the investing activities section of the statement of cash flows, includes the gain that was recognized on the sale of the store. However, this gain was reported on Nordstrom's income statement in Exhibit 13–3 as part of the net income figure, which is the starting point for the operating activities section. As a result, to avoid double counting, the gain must be subtracted (or removed) from net income in the operating activities section of the statement of cash flows. Accordingly, the gain is recorded in the "Used" column in the upper portion of the Cash T-account along with the other operating items.

The entry to record the purchase of property, buildings, and equipment and its effect on Cash would be:

(6)

Property, Buildings, and Equipment	138	
Cash—Used		138

Since the purchase of property, buildings, and equipment is classified as an investing activity, the cash effect is included in the lower portion of the Cash T-account along with the other investing and financing items. Entry (6), along with entry (5) above, explains the change in the Property, Buildings, and Equipment account during the year.

The entry to record depreciation and amortization expense for the year would be:

(7)

Cash—Provided	103	
Accumulated Depreciation		103

Note that depreciation and amortization expense does not involve an actual outflow of cash. Consequently, depreciation and amortization expense must be added to net income to convert it to a cash basis in the operating activities section of the statement of cash flows. Note that the depreciation and amortization expense is recorded in the "Provided" column in the upper portion of the Cash T-account along with the other operating items. Entry (7), along with entry (5) above, explains the change in the Accumulated Depreciation account during the year.

Current Liabilities The T-accounts in Exhibit 13B–1 show that Nordstrom has four current liability accounts. Three of the four current liability accounts (Accounts Payable, Accrued Wages and Salaries Payable, and Accrued Income Taxes Payable) relate to the company's operating activities. In the entries that follow, increases in current liabilities are recorded as credits, with the offsetting entry being "Cash—Provided." Decreases in current liabilities are recorded as debits, with the offsetting entry being "Cash—Used."

Accounts Payable increased by $44 million during the year. The entry to record this change and its effect on Cash would be:

(8)

Cash—Provided	44	
Accounts Payable		44

The Accrued Wages and Salaries Payable account increased by $3 million during the year. The entry to record this change and its effect on Cash would be:

(9)

Cash—Provided	3	
Accrued Wages and Salaries Payable		3

The Accrued Income Taxes Payable account increased by $6 million during the year. The entry to record this change and its effect on Cash would be:

(10)

Cash—Provided	6	
Accrued Income Taxes Payable		6

Since the changes in these three current liability accounts are considered to be part of operations, their cash effects are included in the upper portion of the Cash T-account along with the other operating items.

The Notes Payable account increased by $2 million during the year. Nordstrom's financial statements give no indication that payments were made on the notes payable during the year. Therefore, we must assume that the increase represents an issuance of notes payable for cash. The entry to record the issuance and its effect on Cash would be:

(11)

Cash—Provided	2	
Notes Payable		2

Since transactions involving notes payable are classified as financing activities, their cash effects are included in the lower portion of the Cash T-account along with the other investing and financing items.

Long-Term Debt   Nordstrom's Long-Term Debt account decreased by $43 million during the year. Nordstrom's financial statements give no indication of any additional long-term borrowings during the year. Therefore, we must assume that the decrease represents retirements of long-term debt using cash. The entry to record the retirement and its effect on Cash would be:

(12)

Long-Term Debt	43	
Cash—Used		43

Since transactions involving long-term debt are classified as financing activities, their cash effects are included in the lower portion of the Cash T-account along with the other investing and financing items.

Deferred Income Taxes   The activity in Deferred Income Taxes is analyzed in the chapter beginning on page 531. *Reread the analysis of this account before proceeding.* The entry to record the activity in this account and its effect on Cash would be:

(13)

Deferred Income Taxes	2	
Cash—Used		2

Since changes in the Deferred Income Taxes account are classified as part of operations, its cash effects are included in the upper portion of the Cash T-account along with the other operating items.

Common Stock   The Common Stock account increased by $2 million. Since we have no information to the contrary, we must assume that the increase represents an issuance of common stock for cash. The entry to record the change and its effect on Cash would be:

(14)

Cash—Provided	2	
Common Stock		2

With this entry, our analysis of changes in Nordstrom's balance sheet accounts is complete. At this point, the subtotal titled "Net cash provided by operating activities" can be computed. To ensure that all activity has been properly recorded in the Cash T-account, the total titled "Net increase in cash and cash equivalents" should also be computed (by adding the investing and financing items in the lower portion of the Cash T-account to the subtotal of the upper portion). The $62 million net increase in cash and cash equivalents that is detailed in the Cash T-account in Exhibit 13A–2 equals the increase in cash and cash equivalents shown on Nordstrom's comparative balance sheet in Exhibit 13–4.

Preparing the Statement of Cash Flows from the Completed T-Accounts

The Cash T-account in Exhibit 13B–2 now contains the entries for those transactions that have affected Nordstrom's cash position during the year. Our only remaining task is to organize these data into a formal statement of cash flows. The statement is easy to prepare since the data relating to the operating activities are grouped in the upper portion of the Cash T-account and the data relating to investing and financing activities are grouped in the lower portion of the account.

The technique used to gather and organize data for the preparation of a statement of cash flows does not affect the preparation of the statement itself. The end result is the same. The statement of cash flows for Nordstrom, Inc. is presented in the chapter in Exhibit 13–12. *Refer to the Cash T-account in Exhibit 13B–2, and trace the entries in this T-account to Nordstrom's statement of cash flows in Exhibit 13–12.* Note that the subtotal, "Net cash provided by operating activities," and the total, "Net increase in cash and cash equivalents," in the Cash T-account match the amounts reported on Nordstrom's statement of cash flows.

Summary

LO5   (Appendix 13B) Prepare a statement of cash flows using the T-account approach.
The T-account approach is an alternative technique that can be used to gather and organize the data required to prepare a statement of cash flows. T-accounts are created for each balance sheet account. Each of these accounts is analyzed, and the related entries are posted directly to the T-accounts. The offsetting entry in most cases is Cash. Debits to Cash are labeled "Cash—Provided" and credits are labeled "Cash—Used." Operating items are listed near the top of the Cash T-account and investing and financing items are listed in the lower portion of the Cash T-account. The completed Cash T-account is used to prepare each section of the statement of cash flows, beginning with the operating activities section.

Questions

13–1   What is the purpose of a statement of cash flows?
13–2   What are *cash equivalents,* and why are they included with cash on a statement of cash flows?
13–3   What are the three major sections on a statement of cash flows, and what are the general rules that determine the transactions that should be included in each section?
13–4   Why is interest paid on amounts borrowed from banks and other lenders considered to be an operating activity when the amounts borrowed are financing activities?
13–5   If an asset is sold at a gain, why is the gain deducted from net income when computing the cash provided by operating activities under the indirect method?
13–6   Why aren't transactions involving accounts payable considered to be financing activities?
13–7   Give an example of a direct exchange and explain how such exchanges are handled when preparing a statement of cash flows.
13–8   Assume that a company repays a $300,000 loan from its bank and then later in the same year borrows $500,000. What amount(s) would appear on the statement of cash flows?

13–9 How do the direct and the indirect methods differ in their approach to computing the cash provided by operating activities?

13–10 A business executive once stated, "Depreciation is one of our biggest sources of cash." Do you agree that depreciation is a source of cash? Explain.

13–11 If the balance in Accounts Receivable increases during a period, how will this increase be handled under the indirect method when computing the cash provided by operating activities?

13–12 (Appendix 13A) If the balance in Accounts Payable decreases during a period, how will this decrease be handled under the direct method in computing the cash provided by operating activities?

13–13 During the current year, a company declared and paid a $60,000 cash dividend and a 10% stock dividend. How will these two items be treated on the current year's statement of cash flows?

13–14 Would a sale of equipment for cash be considered a financing activity or an investing activity? Why?

13–15 (Appendix 13A) A merchandising company showed $250,000 in cost of goods sold on its income statement. The company's beginning inventory was $75,000, and its ending inventory was $60,000. The accounts payable balance was $50,000 at the beginning of the year and $40,000 at the end of the year. Using the direct method, adjust the company's cost of goods sold to a cash basis.

Brief Exercises

BRIEF EXERCISE 13–1   Classifying Transactions as Sources or Uses (LO1)
Below are transactions that took place in Placid Company during the past year:

a. Equipment was purchased.
b. A cash dividend was declared and paid.
c. Accounts receivable decreased.
d. Short-term investments were purchased.
e. Equipment was sold.
f. Preferred stock was sold to investors.
g. Interest was paid to long-term creditors.
h. Salaries and wages payable decreased.
i. Stock of another company was purchased.
j. Bonds were issued that will be due in 10 years.
k. Rent was received from subleasing of space, reducing rents receivable.
l. Common stock was repurchased and retired.

Required:
For each of the above transactions, indicate whether it would be classified as a source or a use (or neither) on a simplified statement of cash flows.

BRIEF EXERCISE 13–2   Classifying Transactions as Operating, Investing, or Financing (LO2)
Refer to the transactions for Placid Company listed in Brief Exercise 13–1.

Required:
For each of the transactions in Brief Exercise 13–1, indicate whether it would be classified as an operating, investing, or financing activity (or would not be reported) on the statement of cash flows.

BRIEF EXERCISE 13–3   Cash Provided by Operating Activities (Indirect Method) (LO3)
For the just completed year, Hanna Company reported a net income of $35,000. Balances in the company's current asset and current liability accounts at the beginning and end of the year were:

	End of Year	Beginning of Year
Current assets:		
Cash	$ 30,000	$ 40,000
Accounts receivable	125,000	106,000
Inventory	213,000	180,000
Prepaid expenses	6,000	7,000
Current liabilities:		
Accounts payable	210,000	195,000
Accrued liabilities	4,000	6,000

The Deferred Income Taxes liability account on the balance sheet increased by $4,000 during the year, and depreciation charges were $20,000.

Required:
Using the indirect method, determine the cash provided by operating activities for the year.

BRIEF EXERCISE 13–4   Cash Provided by Operating Activities (Direct Method) (LO4)
(Appendix 13A) Refer to the data for Hanna Company in Brief Exercise 13–3. The company's income statement for the year appears below:

Sales	$350,000
Less cost of goods sold	140,000
Gross margin	210,000
Less operating expenses	160,000
Income before taxes	50,000
Less income taxes (30%)	15,000
Net income	$ 35,000

Required:
Using the direct method (and the data from Brief Exercise 13–3), convert the company's income statement to a cash basis.

BRIEF EXERCISE 13–5   Posting Account Changes to Cash T-Account (LO5)
Refer to the data for Hanna Company in Brief Exercise 13–3.

Required:
Using the indirect method (and the data from Brief Exercise 13–3), post the account changes to a Cash T-account to determine the cash provided by operating activities for the year.

Exercises

EXERCISE 13–1   Converting Net Income to a Cash Basis (Indirect Method) (LO3)
Changes in various accounts and gains and losses on sales of assets during the year for Argon Company are given below:

Item	Amount
Accounts Receivable	$ 90,000 decrease
Accrued Interest Receivable	4,000 increase
Inventory	120,000 increase
Prepaid Expenses	3,000 decrease
Accounts Payable	65,000 decrease
Accrued Liabilities	8,000 increase
Deferred Income Taxes Liability	12,000 increase
Sale of equipment	7,000 gain
Sale of long-term investments	10,000 loss

Required:
Prepare an answer sheet using the following column headings:

Item	Amount	Add	Deduct

On your answer sheet, enter the items and amounts. For each item, place an X in the Add or Deduct column to indicate whether the dollar amount should be added to or deducted from net income under the indirect method when computing the cash provided by operating activities for the year.

EXERCISE 13–2   Prepare a Statement of Cash Flows (Indirect Method) (LO3)

Comparative financial statement data for Carmono Company follow:

	2001	2000
Cash	$ 3	$ 6
Accounts receivable	22	24
Inventory	50	40
Plant and equipment	240	200
Less accumulated depreciation	(65)	(50)
Total assets	$250	$220
Accounts payable	$ 40	$ 36
Common stock	150	145
Retained earnings	60	39
Total liabilities and stockholders' equity	$250	$220

For 2001, the company reported net income as follows:

Sales	$275
Cost of goods sold	150
Gross margin	125
Operating expenses	90
Net income	$ 35

Dividends of $14 were declared and paid during 2001.

Required:

Using the indirect method, prepare a statement of cash flows for 2001.

EXERCISE 13–3   Convert Income Statement to a Cash Basis (Direct Method) (LO4)

(Appendix 13A) Refer to the data for Carmono Company in Exercise 13–2.

Required:

Using the direct method, convert the company's income statement to a cash basis.

EXERCISE 13–4   Prepare a Statement of Cash Flows (Indirect Method) (LO3)

The following changes took place during the year in Pavolik Company's balance sheet accounts:

Cash	$ 5	D	Accounts Payable	$ 35	I
Accounts Receivable	110	I	Accrued Liabilities	4	D
Inventory	70	D	Bonds Payable	150	I
Prepaid Expenses	9	I	Deferred Income Taxes		
Long-Term Investments	6	D	Liability	8	I
Plant and Equipment	200	I	Common Stock	80	D
Accumulated Depreciation	(60)	I	Retained Earnings	54	I
Land	15	D			

D = Decrease; I = Increase.

Long-term investments that had cost the company $6 were sold during the year for $16, and land that had cost $15 was sold for $9. In addition, the company declared and paid $30 in cash dividends during the year. No sales or retirements of plant and equipment took place during the year.

The company's income statement for the year follows:

Sales	$700
Less cost of goods sold	400
Gross margin	300
Less operating expenses	184
Net operating income	116
Nonoperating items:	
Gain on sale of investments $10	
Loss on sale of land 6	4
Income before taxes	120
Less income taxes	36
Net income	$ 84

The company's beginning cash balance was $90, and its ending balance was $85.

Required:
1. Use the indirect method to determine the cash provided by operating activities for the year.
2. Prepare a statement of cash flows for the year.

EXERCISE 13–5   Convert Income Statement to Cash Basis (Direct Method) (LO4)
(Appendix 13A) Refer to the data for Pavolik Company in Exercise 13–4.

Required:
Use the direct method to convert the company's income statement to a cash basis.

Problems

PROBLEM 13–1   Classifying Transactions on a Statement of Cash Flows (LO1, LO2)
Below are a number of transactions that took place in Seneca Company during the past year:

a. Common stock was sold for cash.
b. Interest was paid on a note, decreasing Interest Payable.
c. Bonds were retired.
d. A long-term loan was made to a subsidiary.
e. Interest was received on the loan in (d) above, reducing Interest Receivable.
f. A stock dividend was declared and issued on common stock.
g. A building was acquired by issuing shares of common stock.
h. Equipment was sold for cash.
i. Short-term investments were sold.
j. Cash dividends were declared and paid.
k. Preferred stock was converted into common stock.
l. Deferred Income Taxes, a long-term liability, was reduced.
m. Dividends were received on stock of another company held as an investment.
n. Equipment was purchased by giving a long-term note to the seller.

Required:
Prepare an answer sheet with the following column headings:

		Activity			Reported in	
Transaction	Source, Use, or Neither	Operating	Investing	Financing	a Separate Schedule	Not on the Statement

Enter the letter of the transaction in the left column and indicate whether the transaction would be a source, use, or neither. Then place an X in the appropriate column to show the proper classification of the transaction on the statement of cash flows, or to show if it would not appear on the statement at all.

PROBLEM 13–2   Prepare a Statement of Cash Flows (Indirect Method) (LO3)
Joyner Company has provided the following spreadsheet containing the balances in its balance sheet accounts for Year 1 and Year 2.

CHECK FIGURE
(1) Net cash used for investing activities: $172,000

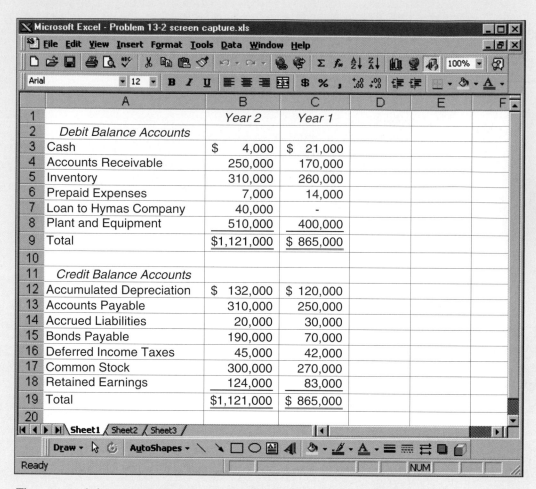

The company's income statement for Year 2 follows:

Sales	$900,000
Less cost of goods sold	500,000
Gross margin	400,000
Less operating expenses	328,000
Net operating income	72,000
Gain on sale of equipment	8,000
Income before taxes	80,000
Less income taxes	24,000
Net income	$ 56,000

Equipment that had cost $40,000 and on which there was accumulated depreciation of $30,000 was sold during Year 2 for $18,000. Cash dividends totaling $15,000 were declared and paid during Year 2.

Required:
1. Using the indirect method, compute the cash provided by operating activities for Year 2.
2. Prepare a statement of cash flows for Year 2.
3. Prepare a brief explanation as to why cash declined so sharply during the year.

CHECK FIGURE
(1) Net cash provided by
    operating activities:
    $20,000

PROBLEM 13–3   Prepare and Interpret a Statement of Cash Flows (Direct Method) (LO4)
(Appendix 13A) Refer to the financial statement data for Joyner Company in Problem 13–2. Sam Conway, president of the company, considers $15,000 to be a minimum cash balance for operating purposes. As can be seen from the balance sheet data, only $4,000 in cash was available at the end of the current year. The sharp decline is puzzling to Mr. Conway, particularly since sales and profits are at a record high.

Required:
1. Using the direct method, adjust the company's income statement to a cash basis for Year 2.
2. Using the data from (1) above and other data from the problem as needed, prepare a statement of cash flows for Year 2.
3. Explain to Mr. Conway why cash declined so sharply during the year.

CHECK FIGURE
(1) Net cash provided by operating activities: $104

PROBLEM 13–4   Prepare a Statement of Cash Flows (Indirect Method) (LO3)
Comparative financial statements for Weaver Company follow:

WEAVER COMPANY
Comparative Balance Sheet
December 31, 2001, and 2000

	2001	2000
Assets		
Cash	$ 9	$ 15
Accounts receivable	340	240
Inventory	125	175
Prepaid expenses	10	6
Plant and equipment	610	470
Less accumulated depreciation	(93)	(85)
Long-term investments	16	19
Total assets	$1,017	$840
Liabilities and Stockholders' Equity		
Accounts payable	$ 310	$230
Accrued liabilities	60	72
Bonds payable	290	180
Deferred income taxes	40	34
Common stock	210	250
Retained earnings	107	74
Total liabilities and stockholders' equity	$1,017	$840

WEAVER COMPANY
Income Statement
For the Year Ended December 31, 2001

Sales		$800
Less cost of goods sold		500
Gross margin		300
Less operating expenses		213
Net operating income		87
Nonoperating items:		
Gain on sale of investments	$7	
Loss on sale of equipment	4	3
Income before taxes		90
Less income taxes		27
Net income		$ 63

During 2001, the company sold some equipment for $20 that had cost $40 and on which there was accumulated depreciation of $16. In addition, the company sold long-term investments for $10 that had cost $3 when purchased several years ago. Cash dividends totaling $30 were paid during 2001.

Required:

1. Using the indirect method, determine the cash provided by operating activities for 2001.
2. Use the information in (1) above, along with an analysis of the remaining balance sheet accounts, and prepare a statement of cash flows for 2001.

PROBLEM 13–5　Prepare a Statement of Cash Flows (Direct Method) (LO4)

(Appendix 13A) Refer to the financial statement data for Weaver Company in Problem 13–4.

Required:

1. Using the direct method, adjust the company's income statement for 2001 to a cash basis.
2. Use the information obtained in (1) above, along with an analysis of the remaining balance sheet accounts, and prepare a statement of cash flows for 2001.

PROBLEM 13–6　Prepare and Interpret a Statement of Cash Flows (Indirect Method) (LO3)

Mary Walker, president of Rusco Products, considers $14,000 to be the minimum cash balance for operating purposes. As can be seen from the statements below, only $8,000 in cash was available at the end of 2001. Since the company reported a large net income for the year, and also issued both bonds and common stock, the sharp decline in cash is puzzling to Ms. Walker.

RUSCO PRODUCTS
Comparative Balance Sheet
July 31, 2001, and 2000

	2001	2000
Assets		
Current assets:		
Cash	$ 8,000	$ 21,000
Accounts receivable	120,000	80,000
Inventory	140,000	90,000
Prepaid expenses	5,000	9,000
Total current assets	273,000	200,000
Long-term investments	50,000	70,000
Plant and equipment	430,000	300,000
Less accumulated depreciation	60,000	50,000
Net plant and equipment	370,000	250,000
Total assets	$693,000	$520,000
Liabilities and Stockholders' Equity		
Current liabilities:		
Accounts payable	$123,000	$ 60,000
Accrued liabilities	8,000	17,000
Total current liabilities	131,000	77,000
Bonds payable	70,000	
Deferred income taxes	20,000	12,000
Stockholders' equity:		
Preferred stock	80,000	96,000
Common stock	286,000	250,000
Retained earnings	106,000	85,000
Total stockholders' equity	472,000	431,000
Total liabilities and stockholders' equity	$693,000	$520,000

"How Well Am I Doing?" Statement of Cash Flows

555

RUSCO PRODUCTS
Income Statement
For the Year Ended July 31, 2001

Sales		$500,000
Less cost of goods sold		300,000
Gross margin		200,000
Less operating expenses		158,000
Net operating income		42,000
Nonoperating items:		
Gain on sale of investments	$10,000	
Loss on sale of equipment	2,000	8,000
Income before taxes		50,000
Less income taxes		20,000
Net income		$ 30,000

The following additional information is available for the year 2001.

a. Dividends totaling $9,000 were declared and paid in cash.
b. Equipment was sold during the year for $8,000. The equipment had originally cost $20,000 and had accumulated depreciation of $10,000.
c. The decrease in the Preferred Stock account is the result of a conversion of preferred stock into an equal dollar amount of common stock.
d. Long-term investments that had cost $20,000 were sold during the year for $30,000.

Required:
1. Using the indirect method, compute the cash provided by operating activities for 2001.
2. Using the data from (1) above, and other data from the problem as needed, prepare a statement of cash flows for 2001.
3. Explain to the president the major reasons for the decline in the company's cash position.

PROBLEM 13–7 Prepare and Interpret a Statement of Cash Flows (Direct Method) (LO4)
(Appendix 13A) Refer to the financial statements for Rusco Products in Problem 13–6. Since the Cash account decreased so dramatically during 2001, the company's executive committee is anxious to see how the income statement would appear on a cash basis.

Required:
1. Using the direct method, adjust the company's income statement for 2001 to a cash basis.
2. Using the data from (1) above, and other data from the problem as needed, prepare a statement of cash flows for 2001.
3. Prepare a brief explanation for the executive committee setting forth the major reasons for the sharp decline in cash during the year.

PROBLEM 13–8 Worksheet; Prepare and Interpret Statement of Cash Flows (Indirect Method) (LO3)
"See, I told you things would work out," said Barry Kresmier, president of Lomax Company. "We expanded sales from $1.6 million to $2.0 million in 2001, nearly doubled our warehouse space, and ended the year with more cash in the bank than we started with. A few more years of expansion like this and we'll be the industry leaders."

"Yes, I'll admit our statements look pretty good," replied Sheri Colson, the company's vice president. "But we're doing business with a lot of companies we don't know much about and that worries me. I'll admit, though, that we're certainly moving a lot of merchandise; our inventory is actually down from last year."

A comparative balance sheet for Lomax Company containing data for the last two years follows:

CHECK FIGURE
(2) Net cash used for investing activities: $112,000

CHECK FIGURE
(2) Net cash used for investing activities: $570,000

LOMAX COMPANY
Comparative Balance Sheet
December 31, 2001, and 2000

	2001	2000
Assets		
Current assets:		
Cash	$ 42,000	$ 27,000
Marketable securities	19,000	13,000
Accounts receivable	710,000	530,000
Inventory	848,000	860,000
Prepaid expenses	10,000	5,000
Total current assets	1,629,000	1,435,000
Long-term investments	60,000	110,000
Loans to subsidiaries	130,000	80,000
Plant and equipment	3,170,000	2,600,000
Less accumulated depreciation	810,000	755,000
Net plant and equipment	2,360,000	1,845,000
Goodwill	84,000	90,000
Total assets	$4,263,000	$3,560,000
Liabilities and Stockholders' Equity		
Current liabilities:		
Accounts payable	$ 970,000	$ 670,000
Accrued liabilities	65,000	82,000
Total current liabilities	1,035,000	752,000
Long-term notes	820,000	600,000
Deferred income taxes	95,000	80,000
Total liabilities	1,950,000	1,432,000
Stockholders' equity:		
Common stock	1,740,000	1,650,000
Retained earnings	573,000	478,000
Total stockholders' equity	2,313,000	2,128,000
Total liabilities and stockholders' equity	$4,263,000	$3,560,000

The following additional information is available about the company's activities during 2001:

a. Cash dividends declared and paid to the common stockholders totaled $75,000.
b. Long-term notes with a value of $380,000 were repaid during the year.
c. Equipment was sold during the year for $70,000. The equipment had cost $130,000 and had $40,000 in accumulated depreciation on the date of sale.
d. Long-term investments were sold during the year for $110,000. These investments had cost $50,000 when purchased several years ago.
e. The company's income statement for 2001 follows:

Sales		$2,000,000
Less cost of goods sold		1,300,000
Gross margin		700,000
Less operating expenses		490,000
Net operating income		210,000
Nonoperating items:		
Gain on sale of investments	$60,000	
Loss on sale of equipment	20,000	40,000
Income before taxes		250,000
Less income taxes		80,000
Net income		$ 170,000

Required:
1. Prepare a worksheet like Exhibit 13–10 for Lomax Company.
2. Using the indirect method, prepare a statement of cash flows for the year 2001.
3. What problems relating to the company's activities are revealed by the statement of cash flows that you have prepared?

PROBLEM 13–9   Adjust Income Statement to Cash Basis (Direct Method) (LO4)

(Appendix 13A) Refer to the data for the Lomax Company in Problem 13–8. All of the long-term notes issued during 2001 are being held by Lomax's bank. The bank's management wants the income statement adjusted to a cash basis so that it can compare the cash basis statement to the accrual basis statement.

Required:
Use the direct method to convert Lomax Company's 2001 income statement to a cash basis.

CHECK FIGURE
Net cash provided by
operating activities:
$356,000

Building Your Skills

ANALYTICAL THINKING (LO3)

Oxident Products is the manufacturer of a vitamin supplement. The *changes* that have taken place in the company's balance sheet accounts as a result of the past year's activities follow:

CHECK FIGURE
Net cash used for investing
activities: $580,000

	Net Increase (Decrease)
Debit Balance Accounts	
Cash	$ (10,000)
Accounts Receivable	(81,000)
Inventory	230,000
Prepaid Expenses	(6,000)
Long-Term Loans to Subsidiaries	100,000
Long-Term Investments	(120,000)
Plant and Equipment	500,000
Net increase	$ 613,000

	Net Increase (Decrease)
Credit Balance Accounts	
Accumulated Depreciation	$ 90,000
Accounts Payable	(70,000)
Accrued Liabilities	35,000
Bonds Payable	400,000
Deferred Income Taxes	8,000
Preferred Stock	(180,000)
Common Stock	270,000
Retained Earnings	60,000
Net increase	$ 613,000

The following additional information is available about last year's activities:

a. The company sold equipment during the year for $40,000. The equipment had cost the company $100,000 when purchased and it had $70,000 in accumulated depreciation at the time of sale.
b. Net income for the year was $_____?_____ .
c. The balance in the Cash account at the beginning of the year was $52,000; the balance at the end of the year was $_____?_____ .
d. The company declared and paid $30,000 in cash dividends during the year.
e. Long-term investments that had cost $120,000 were sold during the year for $80,000.
f. The balances in the Plant and Equipment and Accumulated Depreciation accounts for the past year are given below:

	Ending	Beginning
Plant and Equipment	$3,200,000	$2,700,000
Accumulated Depreciation	1,500,000	1,410,000

g. If data are not given explaining the change in an account, make the most reasonable assumption as to the cause of the change.

Required:
Using the indirect method, prepare a statement of cash flows for the past year. Show all computations for items that appear on your statement.

COMMUNICATING IN PRACTICE   (LO3, LO4)
Use an online yellow pages directory such as www.comfind.com, or www.athand.com to find a company in your area that has a website on which it has an annual report, including a statement of cash flows. Make an appointment with the controller or chief financial officer of the company. Before your meeting, find out as much as you can about the organization's operations from its website.

Required:
After asking the following questions, write a brief memorandum to your instructor that summarizes the information obtained from the company's website and addresses what you found out during your interview.
1. Does the company use the direct method or the indirect method to determine the cash flows from operating activities when preparing its statement of cash flows? Why?
2. How is the information reported on the statement of cash flows used for decision-making purposes?

TAKING IT TO THE NET
As you know, the World Wide Web is a medium that is constantly evolving. Sites come and go and change without notice. To enable periodic update of site addresses, this problem has been posted to the textbook website (www.mhhe.com/folk1e). After accessing the site, enter the Student Center and select this chapter. Select and complete the Taking It to the Net problem.

"How Well Am I Doing?" Statement of Cash Flows

559

TEAMWORK IN ACTION (LO3)

With the economy in expansion, profits at America's large corporations are high, and cash flowing in is at record levels. Management must decide what to do with the growing pool of cash. Should the cash be plowed back into the business? Should it be used to buy back shares of stock? Should it be used to pay down the company's debt?

Required:

Your team should discuss the advantages and disadvantages (risks) of each of the alternatives discussed in each of the questions above. All team members should agree with and understand the answer and be prepared to report to the class. (Each teammate can assume responsibility for a different part of the presentation.)

Chapter Fourteen

"How Well Am I Doing?" Financial Statement Analysis

A Look Back

In Chapter 13 we showed how to construct the statement of cash flows, including the classification of various types of cash inflows and outflows. In addition we discussed the interpretation of the data found on that statement.

A Look at This Chapter

In Chapter 14 we focus on the analysis of financial statements to help forecast the financial health of a company. We discuss the use of trend data, comparisons with other organizations, and the analysis of fundamental financial ratios.

Chapter Outline

Limitations of Financial Statement Analysis

- Comparison of Financial Data
- The Need to Look beyond Ratios

Statements in Comparative and Common-Size Form

- Dollar and Percentage Changes on Statements
- Common-Size Statements

Ratio Analysis—The Common Stockholder

- Earnings per Share
- Price-Earnings Ratio
- Dividend Payout and Yield Ratios
- Return on Total Assets
- Return on Common Stockholders' Equity

- Financial Leverage
- Book Value per Share

Ratio Analysis—The Short-Term Creditor

- Working Capital
- Current Ratio
- Acid-Test (Quick) Ratio
- Accounts Receivable Turnover
- Inventory Turnover

Ratio Analysis—The Long-Term Creditor

- Times Interest Earned Ratio
- Debt-to-Equity Ratio

Summary of Ratios and Sources of Comparative Ratio Data

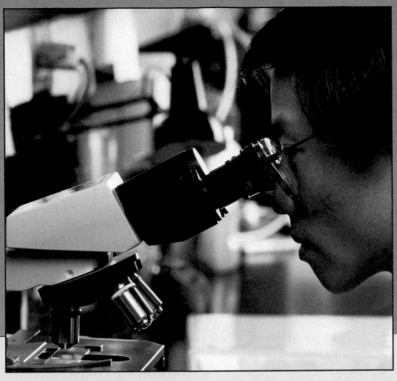

Decision Feature **Biotech Companies Go Out of Favor**

A venture capitalist will invest in a start-up company with the hope of recognizing a significant profit when the start-up company goes public by selling shares of its stock on the open market. During the 1980s and early 1990s, investments by venture capitalists in biotechnology companies helped fund the development of drugs used to treat a variety of diseases that were previously considered untreatable (e.g., cancer, kidney failure, heart attacks, arthritis, and the AIDS virus, among others). However, in 1997, a reallocation of funds took place in the venture capital market. Software vendors, health care service providers, and Internet-based businesses came into favor, and biotech companies went out of fashion. Instead of waiting for returns on biotech investments that took years to realize because of the length of time required to get drugs to market, venture capitalists opted for the quicker payoffs in other industries. Payoffs were especially rapid on investments in dot-com companies, which were managing to go public long before they reached profitability. By 1999, even biotech companies with experienced management teams and well-conceived development plans for a multitude of drugs were finding it difficult, if not impossible, to raise money.

Cynthia Robbins-Roth, the founding partner of Bio Venture Consultants, believes that the venture capitalists' decision-making model was flawed. Part of the problem is the tendency for investors to jump on board when a hot new fad (such as the dot-com one) surfaces. She emphasizes the need to separately analyze each company, rather than analyzing just one and then investing in all other similar companies. Robbins-Roth is also critical of the technical expertise of the analysts that were working for venture capital firms. College graduates with no exposure to the real world were hired to analyze biotech investments without any prior exposure to what it takes to develop, test, and market new drugs or manage a biotech company.

Robbins-Roth highlights the mounting need for new drugs as the population ages and the opportunities provided by recent leaps in biotechnology that will make possible the development of those drugs. She notes that venture capitalists are starting to talk about investing again in biotech companies. She hopes that the decision-making process for investments changes to encompass an understanding of the nature of the companies in this industry.

Source: Cynthia Robbins-Roth, "Seduced & Abandoned," *Forbes ASAP,* May 29, 2000, pp. 153–154.

Learning Objectives
After studying Chapter 14, you should be able to:

LO1 Prepare and interpret financial statements in comparative and common-size form.

LO2 Compute and interpret the financial ratios used to measure the well-being of the common stockholder.

LO3 Compute and interpret the financial ratios used to measure the well-being of the short-term creditor.

LO4 Compute and interpret the financial ratios used to measure the well-being of the long-term creditor.

All financial statements are essentially historical documents. They tell what *has happened* during a particular period of time. However, most users of financial statements are concerned about what *will happen* in the future. Stockholders are concerned with future earnings and dividends. Creditors are concerned with the company's future ability to repay its debts. Managers are concerned with the company's ability to finance future expansion. Despite the fact that financial statements are historical documents, they can still provide valuable information bearing on all of these concerns.

Financial statement analysis involves careful selection of data from financial statements for the primary purpose of forecasting the financial health of the company. This is accomplished by examining trends in key financial data, comparing financial data across companies, and analyzing key financial ratios. In this chapter, we consider some of the more important ratios and other analytical tools that financial analysts use.

Managers are also vitally concerned with the financial ratios discussed in this chapter. First, the ratios provide indicators of how well the company and its business units are performing. Some of these ratios would ordinarily be used in a balanced scorecard approach as discussed in Chapter 8. The specific ratios selected depend on the company's strategy. For example, a company that wants to emphasize responsiveness to customers may closely monitor the inventory turnover ratio discussed later in this chapter. Second, since managers must report to shareholders and may wish to raise funds from external sources, managers must pay attention to the financial ratios used by external investors to evaluate the company's investment potential and creditworthiness.

in business today Those AOL Disks You Received

During the late 1990s, investors seemed to eagerly embrace any dot-com company that was losing money. However, there was a time when investors were more cautious, and start-up companies were under a lot of pressure to report positive earnings. This was the case in the mid-1990s as America Online was building its base of online customers.

AOL recorded the costs that it incurred to advertise its online services and mail disks to millions of potential subscribers as assets. Accounting professors and stock analysts were critical of the practice; these costs did not meet the asset criteria. Finally, in 1996, the company agreed that the costs should instead be expensed as incurred and wrote off $385 million of assets that were on its balance sheet.

AOL would have reported losses rather than earnings during six separate quarters in 1994, 1995, and 1996 if the company had expensed the costs as they were incurred. Some wonder whether the millions of online customers who subscribed to AOL would have flocked to the company if it had been reporting losses at that time. They also wonder if AOL would have been able to pull off its $160 billion deal to acquire Time-Warner in June if it had not been so successful in signing up online customers during the mid-1990s.

The SEC ultimately charged that the company should have been expensing the costs as incurred. During May 2000, the agency levied a fine of $3.5 million against AOL. Even though the SEC's investigation took years to complete, analysts agree that it sends a message to Internet-based businesses. Stock analysts will be taking a closer look at accounting policies, and they can react more quickly than the SEC can.

Source: David Henry, "AOL Pays $3.5M to Settle SEC Case," *USA Today*, May 16, 2000, p. 3B. Copyright 2000, *USA Today*. Reprinted with permission.

Limitations of Financial Statement Analysis

Although financial statement analysis is a highly useful tool, it has two limitations that we must mention before proceeding any further. These two limitations involve the comparability of financial data between companies and the need to look beyond ratios.

Comparison of Financial Data

Comparisons of one company with another can provide valuable clues about the financial health of an organization. Unfortunately, differences in accounting methods between companies sometimes make it difficult to compare the companies' financial data. For example, if one firm values its inventories by the LIFO method and another firm by the average cost method, then direct comparisons of financial data such as inventory valuations and cost of goods sold between the two firms may be misleading. Sometimes enough data is presented in footnotes to the financial statements to restate data to a comparable basis. Otherwise, the analyst should keep in mind the lack of comparability of the data before drawing any definite conclusions. Nevertheless, even with this limitation in mind, comparisons of key ratios with other companies and with industry averages often suggest avenues for further investigation.

The Need to Look beyond Ratios

An inexperienced analyst may assume that ratios are sufficient in themselves as a basis for judgments about the future. Nothing could be further from the truth. Conclusions based on ratio analysis must be regarded as tentative. Ratios should not be viewed as an end, but rather they should be viewed as a *starting point,* as indicators of what to pursue in greater depth. They raise many questions, but they rarely answer any questions by themselves.

The Ongoing Effects of Y2K   *in business | today*

During April 2000, Compaq Computer announced that it had earned $325 million on revenues of $9.5 billion during the first quarter. The numbers met analysts' expectations. Even though its profits were 16% higher than those reported for the first quarter of 1999, Compaq's revenues increased only by 1%. Addressing the lackluster growth in revenues, management explained that the Y2K scare negatively impacted corporate computer sales during the first quarter of 2000.

Source: Adam Shell, "Market Watch—Y2K Lingering at Compaq," *USA Today,* April 26, 2000, p. 3B. Copyright 2000, *USA Today.* Reprinted with permission.

In addition to ratios, other sources of data should be analyzed in order to make judgments about the future of an organization. The analyst should look, for example, at industry trends, technological changes, changes in consumer tastes, changes in broad economic factors, and changes within the firm itself. A recent change in a key management position, for example, might provide a basis for optimism about the future, even though the past performance of the firm (as shown by its ratios) may have been mediocre.

Credit Analyst   *you | decide*

You work for a company that sells industrial products to businesses. Your company routinely sells products to customers on credit—expecting to be repaid within a specified period. A potential customer has asked for an extension of the payment terms on a very large sale to a later date than your company usually allows. You have been asked to determine the creditworthiness of this customer. You have been provided with a copy of the company's financial statements and accompanying footnotes that were included in the company's most recent annual report. What other information should you obtain before you begin your analysis?

Statements in Comparative and Common-Size Form

Concept 14–1

Few figures appearing on financial statements have much significance standing by themselves. It is the relationship of one figure to another and the amount and direction of change over time that are important in financial statement analysis. How does the analyst key in on significant relationships? How does the analyst dig out the important trends and changes in a company? Three analytical techniques are widely used:

1. Dollar and percentage changes on statements.
2. Common-size statements.
3. Ratios.

The first and second techniques are discussed in this section; the third technique is discussed in the remainder of the chapter. To illustrate these analytical techniques, we analyze the financial statements of Brickey Electronics, a producer of computer components.

Dollar and Percentage Changes on Statements

A good place to begin in financial statement analysis is to put statements in comparative form. This consists of little more than putting two or more years' data side by side. Statements cast in comparative form underscore movements and trends and may give the analyst valuable clues as to what to expect.

Examples of financial statements placed in comparative form are given in Exhibits 14–1 and 14–2. These statements of Brickey Electronics reveal the firm has been experiencing substantial growth. The data on these statements are used as a basis for discussion throughout the remainder of the chapter.

Horizontal Analysis   Comparison of two or more years' financial data is known as **horizontal analysis** or **trend analysis.** Horizontal analysis is facilitated by showing changes between years in both dollar *and* percentage form, as has been done in Exhibits 14–1 and 14–2. Showing changes in dollar form helps the analyst focus on key factors that have affected profitability or financial position. For example, observe in Exhibit 14–2 that sales for 2001 were up $4 million over 2000, but that this increase in sales was more than negated by a $4.5 million increase in cost of goods sold.

Showing changes between years in percentage form helps the analyst to gain *perspective* and to gain a feel for the *significance* of the changes that are taking place. A $1 million increase in sales is much more significant if the prior year's sales were $2 million than if the prior year's sales were $20 million. In the first situation, the increase would be 50%—undoubtedly a significant increase for any firm. In the second situation, the increase would be only 5%—perhaps just a reflection of normal growth.

Exhibit 14–1

BRICKEY ELECTRONICS
Comparative Balance Sheet
December 31, 2001, and 2000
(dollars in thousands)

	2001	2000	Increase (Decrease) Amount	Increase (Decrease) Percent
Assets				
Current assets:				
Cash	$ 1,200	$ 2,350	$(1,150)	(48.9)%*
Accounts receivable, net	6,000	4,000	2,000	50.0%
Inventory	8,000	10,000	(2,000)	(20.0)%
Prepaid expenses	300	120	180	150.0%
Total current assets	15,500	16,470	(970)	(5.9)%
Property and equipment:				
Land	4,000	4,000	–0–	–0–%
Buildings and equipment, net ..	12,000	8,500	3,500	41.2%
Total property and equipment	16,000	12,500	3,500	28.0%
Total assets	$31,500	$28,970	$ 2,530	8.7%
Liabilities and Stockholders' Equity				
Current liabilities:				
Accounts payable	$ 5,800	$ 4,000	$ 1,800	45.0%
Accrued payables	900	400	500	125.0%
Notes payable, short term	300	600	(300)	(50.0)%
Total current liabilities	7,000	5,000	2,000	40.0%
Long-term liabilities:				
Bonds payable, 8%	7,500	8,000	(500)	(6.3)%
Total liabilities	14,500	13,000	1,500	11.5%
Stockholders' equity:				
Preferred stock, $100 par, 6%, $100 liquidation value	2,000	2,000	–0–	–0–%
Common stock, $12 par	6,000	6,000	–0–	–0–%
Additional paid-in capital	1,000	1,000	–0–	–0–%
Total paid-in capital	9,000	9,000	–0–	–0–%
Retained earnings	8,000	6,970	1,030	14.8%
Total stockholders' equity	17,000	15,970	1,030	6.4%
Total liabilities and stockholders' equity	$31,500	$28,970	$ 2,530	8.7%

*Since we are measuring the amount of change between 2000 and 2001, the dollar amounts for 2000 become the base figures for expressing these changes in percentage form. For example, Cash decreased by $1,150 between 2000 and 2001. This decrease expressed in percentage form is computed as follows: $1,150 ÷ $2,350 = 48.9%. Other percentage figures in this exhibit and Exhibit 14–2 are computed in the same way.

Exhibit 14–2

			Increase (Decrease)	
BRICKEY ELECTRONICS **Comparative Income Statement and Reconciliation** **of Retained Earnings** **For the Years Ended December 31, 2001, and 2000** **(dollars in thousands)**				
	2001	**2000**	**Amount**	**Percent**
Sales	$52,000	$48,000	$4,000	8.3%
Cost of goods sold	36,000	31,500	4,500	14.3%
Gross margin	16,000	16,500	(500)	(3.0)%
Operating expenses:				
Selling expenses	7,000	6,500	500	7.7%
Administrative expenses	5,860	6,100	(240)	(3.9)%
Total operating expenses	12,860	12,600	260	2.1%
Net operating income	3,140	3,900	(760)	(19.5)%
Interest expense	640	700	(60)	(8.6)%
Net income before taxes	2,500	3,200	(700)	(21.9)%
Less income taxes (30%)	750	960	(210)	(21.9)%
Net income	1,750	2,240	$ (490)	(21.9)%
Dividends to preferred stockholders, $6 per share (see Exhibit 14–1)	120	120		
Net income remaining for common stockholders	1,630	2,120		
Dividends to common stockholders, $1.20 per share ..	600	600		
Net income added to retained earnings	1,030	1,520		
Retained earnings, beginning of year	6,970	5,450		
Retained earnings, end of year ...	$ 8,000	$ 6,970		

Trend Percentages Horizontal analysis of financial statements can also be carried out by computing *trend percentages*. **Trend percentages** state several years' financial data in terms of a base year. The base year equals 100%, with all other years stated as some percentage of this base. To illustrate, consider McDonald's Corporation, the largest global foodservice retailer, with more than 26,000 restaurants worldwide. McDonald's enjoyed tremendous growth during the 1990s, as evidenced by the following data:

	1999	1998	1997	1996	1995	1994	1993	1992	1991	1990	1989
Sales (millions)	$13,259	$12,421	$11,409	$10,687	$9,795	$8,321	$7,408	$7,133	$6,695	$6,640	$6,066
Net income (millions)	$ 1,948	$ 1,550	$ 1,642	$ 1,573	$1,427	$1,224	$1,083	$ 959	$ 860	$ 802	$ 727

By simply looking at these data, one can see that sales increased in every year. But how rapidly have sales been increasing, and have the increases in net income kept pace with the increases in sales? It is difficult to answer these questions by looking at the raw data alone. The increases in sales and the increases in net income can be put into better

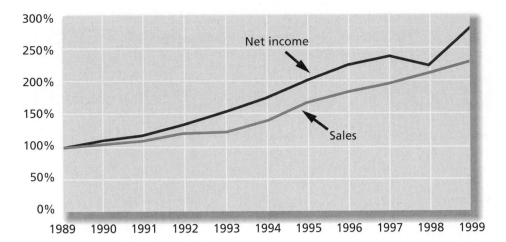

Exhibit 14–3
McDonald's Corporation
Trend Analysis of Sales and
Net Income

perspective by stating them in terms of trend percentages, with 1989 as the base year. These percentages (all rounded) are set forth below:

	1999	1998	1997	1996	1995	1994	1993	1992	1991	1990	1989
Sales*	219%	205%	188%	176%	161%	137%	122%	118%	110%	109%	100%
Net income	268%	213%	226%	216%	196%	168%	149%	132%	118%	110%	100%

*For 1990, $6,640 ÷ $6,066 = 109%; for 1991, $6,695 ÷ $6,066 = 110%, and so on.

The trend analysis is particularly striking when the data are plotted as in Exhibit 14–3. McDonald's sales growth was impressive throughout the entire 11-year period, but it was outpaced by even higher growth in the company's net income. A review of the company's income statement reveals that the dip in net income growth in 1998 was attributable, in part, to the $161.6 million that McDonald's spent to implement its "Made for You" program and a special charge of $160 million that related to a home office productivity initiative. Both amounts are separately disclosed on the company's income statement.

Common-Size Statements

Key changes and trends can also be highlighted by the use of *common-size statements.* A **common-size statement** is one that shows the items appearing on it in percentage form as well as in dollar form. Each item is stated as a percentage of some total of which that item is a part. The preparation of common-size statements is known as **vertical analysis.**

Common-size statements are particularly useful when comparing data from different companies. For example, in one year, Wendy's net income was about $110 million, whereas McDonald's was $1,427 million. This comparison is somewhat misleading because of the dramatically different sizes of the two companies. To put this in better perspective, the net income figures can be expressed as a percentage of the sales revenues of each company. Since Wendy's sales revenues were $1,746 million and McDonald's were $9,794 million, Wendy's net income as a percentage of sales was about 6.3% and McDonald's was about 14.6%. While the comparison still favors McDonald's, the contrast between the two companies has been placed on a more comparable basis.

The Balance Sheet   One application of the vertical analysis idea is to state the separate assets of a company as percentages of total assets. A common-size statement of this type is shown in Exhibit 14–4 for Brickey Electronics.

Notice from Exhibit 14–4 that placing all assets in common-size form clearly shows the relative importance of the current assets as compared to the noncurrent assets. It also shows that significant changes have taken place in the *composition* of the current assets over the last year. Notice, for example, that the receivables have increased in relative

Exhibit 14–4

			Common-Size Percentages	
BRICKEY ELECTRONICS **Common-Size Comparative Balance Sheet** **December 31, 2001, and 2000** **(dollars in thousands)**				
	2001	**2000**	**2001**	**2000**
Assets				
Current assets:				
Cash	$ 1,200	$ 2,350	3.8%*	8.1%
Accounts receivable, net	6,000	4,000	19.0%	13.8%
Inventory	8,000	10,000	25.4%	34.5%
Prepaid expenses	300	120	1.0%	0.4%
Total current assets	15,500	16,470	49.2%	56.9%
Property and equipment:				
Land	4,000	4,000	12.7%	13.8%
Buildings and equipment, net ...	12,000	8,500	38.1%	29.3%
Total property and equipment	16,000	12,500	50.8%	43.1%
Total assets	$31,500	$28,970	100.0%	100.0%
Liabilities and **Stockholders' Equity**				
Current liabilities:				
Accounts payable	$ 5,800	$ 4,000	18.4%	13.8%
Accrued payables	900	400	2.8%	1.4%
Notes payable, short term	300	600	1.0%	2.1%
Total current liabilities	7,000	5,000	22.2%	17.3%
Long-term liabilities:				
Bonds payable, 8%	7,500	8,000	23.8%	27.6%
Total liabilities	14,500	13,000	46.0%	44.9%
Stockholders' equity:				
Preferred stock, $100, 6%, $100 liquidation value	2,000	2,000	6.4%	6.9%
Common stock, $12 par	6,000	6,000	19.0%	20.7%
Additional paid-in capital	1,000	1,000	3.2%	3.5%
Total paid-in capital	9,000	9,000	28.6%	31.1%
Retained earnings	8,000	6,970	25.4%	24.0%
Total stockholders' equity	17,000	15,970	54.0%	55.1%
Total liabilities and stockholders' equity	$31,500	$28,970	100.0%	100.0%

*Each asset account on a common-size statement is expressed in terms of total assets, and each liability and equity account is expressed in terms of total liabilities and stockholders' equity. For example, the percentage figure above for Cash in 2001 is computed as follows: $1,200 ÷ $31,500 = 3.8%.

importance and that both cash and inventory have declined in relative importance. Judging from the sharp increase in receivables, the deterioration in the cash position may be a result of inability to collect from customers.

The Income Statement   Another application of the vertical analysis idea is to place all items on the income statement in percentage form in terms of sales. A common-size statement of this type is shown in Exhibit 14–5.

Exhibit 14–5

BRICKEY ELECTRONICS
Common-Size Comparative Income Statement
For the Years Ended December 31, 2001, and 2000
(dollars in thousands)

	2001	2000	Common-Size Percentages 2001	Common-Size Percentages 2000
Sales	$52,000	$48,000	100.0%	100.0%
Cost of goods sold	36,000	31,500	69.2%	65.6%
Gross margin	16,000	16,500	30.8%	34.4%
Operating expenses:				
Selling expenses	7,000	6,500	13.5%	13.5%
Administrative expenses	5,860	6,100	11.3%	12.7%
Total operating expenses	12,860	12,600	24.7%	26.2%
Net operating income	3,140	3,900	6.0%	8.1%
Interest expense	640	700	1.2%	1.5%
Net income before taxes	2,500	3,200	4.8%	6.7%
Income taxes (30%)	750	960	1.4%	2.0%
Net income	$ 1,750	$ 2,240	3.4%	4.7%

*The percentage figures for each year are expressed in terms of total sales for the year. For example, the percentage figure for cost of goods sold in 2001 is computed as follows:
$36,000 ÷ $52,000 = 69.2%

By placing all items on the income statement in common size in terms of sales, it is possible to see at a glance how each dollar of sales is distributed among the various costs, expenses, and profits. And by placing successive years' statements side by side, it is easy to spot interesting trends. For example, as shown in Exhibit 14–5, the cost of goods sold as a percentage of sales increased from 65.6% in 2000 to 69.2% in 2001. Or looking at this from a different viewpoint, the *gross margin percentage* declined from 34.4% in 2000 to 30.8% in 2001. Managers and investment analysts often pay close attention to the gross margin percentage since it is considered a broad gauge of profitability. The **gross margin percentage** is computed as follows:

$$\text{Gross margin percentage} = \frac{\text{Gross margin}}{\text{Sales}}$$

The gross margin percentage tends to be more stable for retailing companies than for other service companies and for manufacturers since the cost of goods sold in retailing excludes fixed costs. When fixed costs are included in the cost of goods sold figure, the gross margin percentage tends to increase and decrease with sales volume. With increases in sales volume, the fixed costs are spread across more units and the gross margin percentage improves.

While a higher gross margin percentage is generally considered to be better than a lower gross margin percentage, there are exceptions. Some companies purposely choose a strategy emphasizing low prices (and hence low gross margins). An increasing gross margin in such a company might be a sign that the company's strategy is not being effectively implemented.

Common-size statements are also very helpful in pointing out efficiencies and inefficiencies that might otherwise go unnoticed. To illustrate, in 2001, Brickey Electronics' selling expenses increased by $500,000 over 2000. A glance at the common-size income statement shows, however, that on a relative basis, selling expenses were no higher in 2001 than in 2000. In each year they represented 13.5% of sales.

Ratio Analysis—The Common Stockholder

Learning Objective 2

Compute and interpret the financial ratios used to measure the well-being of the common stockholder.

Concept 14–2

A number of financial ratios are used to assess how well the company is doing from the standpoint of the stockholders. These ratios naturally focus on net income, dividends, and stockholders' equities.

Earnings per Share

An investor buys a share of stock in the hope of realizing a return in the form of either dividends or future increases in the value of the stock. Since earnings form the basis for dividend payments, as well as the basis for future increases in the value of shares, investors are always interested in a company's reported *earnings per share*. Probably no single statistic is more widely quoted or relied on by investors than earnings per share, although it has some inherent limitations, as discussed below.

Earnings per share is computed by dividing net income available for common stockholders by the average number of common shares outstanding during the year. "Net income available for common stockholders" is net income less dividends paid to the owners of the company's preferred stock.[1]

$$\text{Earnings per share} = \frac{\text{Net income} - \text{Preferred dividends}}{\text{Average number of common shares outstanding}}$$

Using the data in Exhibits 14–1 and 14–2, we see that the earnings per share for Brickey Electronics for 2001 would be computed as follows:

$$\frac{\$1,750,000 - \$120,000}{(500,000 \text{ shares*} + 500,000 \text{ shares})/2} = \$3.26$$

*$6,000,000 ÷ 12 = 500,000 shares.

Price-Earnings Ratio

The relationship between the market price of a share of stock and the stock's current earnings per share is often quoted in terms of a **price-earnings ratio.** If we assume that the current market price for Brickey Electronics' stock is $40 per share, the company's price-earnings ratio would be computed as follows:

$$\text{Price-earnings ratio} = \frac{\text{Market price per share}}{\text{Earnings per share}}$$

$$\frac{\$40}{\$3.26} = 12.3$$

The price-earnings ratio is 12.3; that is, the stock is selling for about 12.3 times its current earnings per share.

The price-earnings ratio is widely used by investors as a general guideline in gauging stock values. A high price-earnings ratio means that investors are willing to pay a premium for the company's stock—presumably because the company is expected to have higher than average future earnings growth. Conversely, if investors believe a company's future earnings growth prospects are limited, the company's price-earnings ratio will be relatively low. For example, not long ago, the stock prices of some dot-com companies—particularly those with little or no earnings—were selling at levels that gave rise to

---

[1]Another complication can arise when a company has issued securities such as executive stock options or warrants that can be converted into shares of common stock. If these conversions were to take place, the same earnings would have to be distributed among a greater number of common shares. Therefore, a supplemental earnings per share figure, called diluted earnings per share, may have to be computed. Refer to a current intermediate financial accounting text for details.

unprecedented price-earnings ratios. However, these price-earnings ratios were unsustainable in the long run and the companies' stock prices eventually fell.

Dividend Payout and Yield Ratios

Investors hold shares in a company because they anticipate an attractive return. The return sought isn't always dividends. Many investors prefer not to receive dividends. Instead, they prefer to have the company retain all earnings and reinvest them internally in order to support growth. The stocks of companies that adopt this approach, loosely termed *growth stocks,* may enjoy rapid upward movement in market price. Other investors prefer to have a dependable, current source of income through regular dividend payments. Such investors seek out stocks with consistent dividend records and payout ratios.

The Dividend Payout Ratio   The **dividend payout ratio** gauges the portion of current earnings being paid out in dividends. Investors who seek growth in market price would like this ratio to be small, whereas investors who seek dividends prefer it to be large. This ratio is computed by relating dividends per share to earnings per share for common stock:

$$\text{Dividend payout ratio} = \frac{\text{Dividends per share}}{\text{Earnings per share}}$$

For Brickey Electronics, the dividend payout ratio for 2001 is computed as follows:

$$\frac{\$1.20 \text{ (see Exhibit 14–2)}}{\$3.26} = 36.8\%$$

There is no such thing as a "right" payout ratio, even though it should be noted that the ratio tends to be similar for companies within a particular industry. Industries with ample opportunities for growth at high rates of return on assets tend to have low payout ratios, whereas payout ratios tend to be high in industries with limited reinvestment opportunities.

The Dividend Yield Ratio   The **dividend yield ratio** is obtained by dividing the current dividends per share by the current market price per share:

$$\text{Dividend yield ratio} = \frac{\text{Dividends per share}}{\text{Market price per share}}$$

The market price for Brickey Electronics' stock is $40 per share so the dividend yield is computed as follows:

$$\frac{\$1.20}{\$40} = 3.0\%$$

The dividend yield ratio measures the rate of return (in the form of cash dividends only) that would be earned by an investor who buys the common stock at the current market price. A low dividend yield ratio is neither bad nor good by itself. As discussed above, a company may pay out very little dividends because it has ample opportunities for reinvesting funds within the company at high rates of return.

Return on Total Assets

Managers have both *financing* and *operating* responsibilities. Financing responsibilities relate to how one *obtains* the funds needed to provide for the assets in an organization. Operating responsibilities relate to how one *uses* the assets once they have been obtained. Both are vital to a well-managed firm. However, care must be taken not to confuse or mix the two when assessing the performance of a manager. That is, whether funds have been obtained from creditors or from stockholders should not be allowed to influence one's assessment of *how well* the assets have been employed since being received by the firm.

The **return on total assets** is a measure of operating performance that shows how well assets have been employed. It is defined as follows:

$$\text{Return on total assets} = \frac{\text{Net income} + \left[\text{Interest expense} \times (1 - \text{Tax rate})\right]}{\text{Average total assets}}$$

Adding interest expense back to net income results in an adjusted earnings figure that shows what earnings would have been if the assets had been acquired solely by selling shares of stock. With this adjustment, the return on total assets can be compared for companies with differing amounts of debt or over time for a single company that has changed its mix of debt and equity. Thus, the measurement of how well the assets have been employed is not influenced by how the assets were financed. Notice that the interest expense is placed on an after-tax basis by multiplying it by the factor $(1 - \text{Tax rate})$.

The return on total assets for Brickey Electronics for 2001 would be computed as follows (from Exhibits 14–1 and 14–2):

Net income	$ 1,750,000
Add back interest expense: $640,000 × (1 − 0.30)	448,000
Total (a)	$ 2,198,000
Assets, beginning of year	$28,970,000
Assets, end of year	31,500,000
Total	$60,470,000
Average total assets: $60,470,000 ÷ 2 (b)	$30,235,000
Return on total assets, (a) ÷ (b)	7.3%

Brickey Electronics earned a return of 7.3% on average assets employed over the last year.

Return on Common Stockholders' Equity

One of the primary reasons for operating a corporation is to generate income for the benefit of the common stockholders. One measure of a company's success in this regard is the **return on common stockholders' equity,** which divides the net income remaining for common stockholders by the average common stockholders' equity for the year. The formula is as follows:

$$\frac{\text{Return on common}}{\text{stockholders' equity}} = \frac{\text{Net income} - \text{Preferred dividends}}{\text{Average common stockholders' equity}}$$

where

$$\frac{\text{Average common}}{\text{stockholders' equity}} = \frac{\text{Average total stockholders' equity}}{- \text{Average preferred stock}}$$

For Brickey Electronics, the return on common stockholders' equity is 11.3% for 2001 as shown below:

Net income	$ 1,750,000
Deduct preferred dividends	120,000
Net income remaining for common stockholders (a)	$ 1,630,000
Average stockholders' equity	$16,485,000*
Deduct average preferred stock	2,000,000†
Average common stockholders' equity (b)	$14,485,000
Return on common stockholders' equity, (a) ÷ (b)	11.3%

*$15,970,000 + $17,000,000 = $32,970,000; $32,970,000 ÷ 2 = $16,485,000.
†$2,000,000 + $2,000,000 = $4,000,000; $4,000,000 ÷ 2 = $2,000,000.

Compare the return on common stockholders' equity above (11.3%) with the return on total assets computed in the preceding section (7.3%). Why is the return on common stockholders' equity so much higher? The answer lies in the principle of *financial leverage*. Financial leverage is discussed in the following paragraphs.

Financial Leverage

Financial leverage (often called *leverage* for short) involves acquiring assets with funds that have been obtained from creditors or from preferred stockholders at a fixed rate of return. If the assets in which the funds are invested are able to earn a rate of return *greater* than the fixed rate of return required by the funds' suppliers, then the company has **positive financial leverage** and the common stockholders benefit.

For example, suppose that CBS is able to earn an after-tax return of 12% on its broadcasting assets. If the company can borrow from creditors at a 10% interest rate to expand its assets, then the common stockholders can benefit from positive leverage. The borrowed funds invested in the business will earn an after-tax return of 12%, but the after-tax interest cost of the borrowed funds will be only 7% [10% interest rate $\times$ (1 − 0.30) = 7%]. The difference will go to the common stockholders.

We can see this concept in operation in the case of Brickey Electronics. Notice from Exhibit 14–1 that the company's bonds payable bear a fixed interest rate of 8%. The after-tax interest cost of these bonds is only 5.6% [8% interest rate $\times$ (1 − 0.30) = 5.6%]. The company's assets are generating an after-tax return of 7.3%, as we computed earlier. Since this return on assets is greater than the after-tax interest cost of the bonds, leverage is positive, and the difference accrues to the benefit of the common stockholders. This explains in part why the return on common stockholders' equity (11.3%) is greater than the return on total assets (7.3%).

Unfortunately, leverage is a two-edged sword. If assets are unable to earn a high enough rate to cover the interest costs of debt and preferred dividends (**negative financial leverage**), *the common stockholder suffers.*

The Impact of Income Taxes   Debt and preferred stock are not equally efficient in generating positive leverage. The reason is that interest on debt is tax deductible, whereas preferred dividends are not. This usually makes debt a much more effective source of positive leverage than preferred stock.

To illustrate this point, suppose that the Hospital Corporation of America is considering three ways of financing a $100 million expansion of its chain of hospitals:

1. $100 million from an issue of common stock.
2. $50 million from an issue of common stock, and $50 million from an issue of preferred stock bearing a dividend rate of 8%.
3. $50 million from an issue of common stock, and $50 million from an issue of bonds bearing an interest rate of 8%.

Assuming that the Hospital Corporation of America can earn an additional $15 million each year before interest and taxes as a result of the expansion, the operating results under each of the three alternatives are shown in Exhibit 14–6.

If the entire $100 million is raised from an issue of common stock, then the return to the common stockholders will be only 10.5%, as shown under alternative 1 in the exhibit. If half of the funds are raised from an issue of preferred stock, then the return to the common stockholders increases to 13%, due to the positive effects of leverage. However, if half of the funds are raised from an issue of bonds, then the return to the common stockholders jumps to 15.4%, as shown under alternative 3. Thus, long-term debt is much more efficient in generating positive leverage than is preferred stock. The reason is that the interest expense on long-term debt is tax deductible, whereas the dividends on preferred stock are not.

The Desirability of Leverage   Because of leverage, having some debt in the capital structure can substantially benefit the common stockholder. For this reason, most

Exhibit 14-6
Leverage from Preferred Stock and Long-Term Debt

	Alternatives: $100,000,000 Issue of Securities		
	Alternative 1: $100,000,000 Common Stock	Alternative 2: $50,000,000 Common Stock; $50,000,000 Preferred Stock	Alternative 3: $50,000,000 Common Stock; $50,000,000 Bonds
Earnings before interest and taxes	$ 15,000,000	$15,000,000	$15,000,000
Deduct interest expense (8% × $50,000,000)	—	—	4,000,000
Net income before taxes	15,000,000	15,000,000	11,000,000
Deduct income taxes (30%)	4,500,000	4,500,000	3,300,000
Net income	10,500,000	10,500,000	7,700,000
Deduct preferred dividends (8% × $50,000,000)	—	4,000,000	—
Net income remaining for common (a)	$ 10,500,000	$ 6,500,000	$ 7,700,000
Common stockholders' equity (b)	$100,000,000	$50,000,000	$50,000,000
Return on common stockholders' equity (a) ÷ (b)	10.5%	13.0%	15.4%

companies today try to maintain a level of debt that is considered to be normal within the industry. Many companies, such as commercial banks and other financial institutions, rely heavily on leverage to provide an attractive return on their common shares.

Book Value per Share

Another statistic frequently used in attempting to assess the well-being of the common stockholder is book value per share. The **book value per share** measures the amount that would be distributed to holders of each share of common stock if all assets were sold at their balance sheet carrying amounts (i.e., book values) and if all creditors were paid off. Thus, book value per share is based entirely on historical costs. The formula for computing it is as follows:

$$\text{Book value per share} = \frac{\text{Common stockholders' equity (Total stockholders' equity − Preferred stock)}}{\text{Number of common shares outstanding}}$$

Total stockholders' equity (see Exhibit 14–1)	$17,000,000
Deduct preferred stock (see Exhibit 14–1)	2,000,000
Common stockholders' equity	$15,000,000

The book value per share of Brickey Electronics' common stock is computed as follows:

$$\frac{\$15,000,000}{500,000 \text{ shares}} = \$30 \text{ per share}$$

If this book value is compared with the $40 market value of Brickey Electronics stock, then the stock appears to be somewhat overpriced. However, as we discussed earlier, market prices reflect expectations about future earnings and dividends, whereas book value largely reflects the results of events that occurred in the past. Ordinarily, the market value of a stock exceeds its book value. For example, in a recent year, Microsoft's common stock often traded at over 4 times its book value, and Coca-Cola's market value was over 17 times its book value.

To illustrate the computation and interpretation of financial ratios that are used to assess the company's performance from the standpoint of its stockholders, consider McDonald's Corporation. The data set forth below relate to the year ended December 31,

2001. (Averages were computed by adding together the beginning and end of year amounts reported on the balance sheet, and dividing the total by two.)

Net income	$1,948 million
Interest expense	$396 million
Tax rate	32.5%
Average total assets	$20,384 million
Preferred stock dividends	$0 million
Average common stockholders' equity	$9,552 million
Common stock dividends per share	$0.20
Earnings per share	$1.44
Market price per share—end-of-year	$40.3125
Book value per share—end-of-year	$5.80

$$\frac{\text{Return on}}{\text{total assets}} = \frac{\$1{,}948 + [\$396 \times (1 - 0.325)]}{\$20{,}384} = 10.9\%$$

$$\frac{\text{Return on common}}{\text{stockholders' equity}} = \frac{\$1{,}948 - \$0}{\$9{,}552} = 20.4\%$$

$$\text{Dividend payout ratio} = \frac{\$0.20}{\$1.44} = 13.9\%$$

$$\text{Dividend yield ratio} = \frac{\$0.20}{\$40.3125} = 0.50\%$$

The return on common stockholders' equity of 20.4% is higher than the return on total assets of 10.9%, and therefore the company has positive financial leverage. (About half of the company's financing is provided by creditors; the rest is provided by common and preferred stockholders.) According to the company's annual report, "Given McDonald's high returns on equity and assets and our global growth opportunities, management believes reinvesting a significant portion of earnings back into the business is prudent. Accordingly, our per share dividend is low. However, we have increased the per share dividend amount 25 times since our first dividend was paid in 1976. Additional dividend increases will be considered in the future." Indeed, only 13.9% of earnings are paid out in dividends. In relation to the stock price, this is a dividend yield of less than 1%. Finally, note that the market value per share is almost seven times as large as the book value per share. This premium over book value reflects the market's perception that McDonald's earnings will continue to grow in the future.

Ratio Analysis—The Short-Term Creditor

Short-term creditors, such as suppliers, want to be repaid on time. Therefore, they focus on the company's cash flows and on its working capital since these are the company's primary sources of cash in the short run.

Learning Objective 3
Compute and interpret the financial ratios used to measure the well-being of the short-term creditor.

Working Capital

The excess of current assets over current liabilities is known as **working capital.** The working capital for Brickey Electronics is computed below:

Working capital = Current assets − Current liabilities

	2001	2000
Current assets	$15,500,000	$16,470,000
Current liabilities	7,000,000	5,000,000
Working capital	$ 8,500,000	$11,470,000

The amount of working capital available to a firm is of considerable interest to short-term creditors, *since it represents assets financed from long-term capital sources that do not require near-term repayment.* Therefore, the greater the working capital, the greater is the cushion of protection available to short-term creditors and the greater is the assurance that short-term debts will be paid when due.

Although it is always comforting to short-term creditors to see a large working capital balance, a large balance by itself is no assurance that debts will be paid when due. Rather than being a sign of strength, a large working capital balance may simply mean that obsolete inventory is being accumulated. Therefore, to put the working capital figure into proper perspective, it must be supplemented with other analytical work. The following four ratios (the current ratio, the acid-test ratio, the accounts receivable turnover, and the inventory turnover) should all be used in connection with an analysis of working capital.

Current Ratio

The elements involved in the computation of working capital are frequently expressed in ratio form. A company's current assets divided by its current liabilities is known as the **current ratio:**

$$\text{Current ratio} = \frac{\text{Current assets}}{\text{Current liabilities}}$$

For Brickey Electronics, the current ratios for 2000 and 2001 would be computed as follows:

2001	2000
$\dfrac{\$15,500,000}{\$7,000,000} = 2.21 \text{ to } 1$	$\dfrac{\$16,470,000}{\$5,000,000} = 3.29 \text{ to } 1$

Although widely regarded as a measure of short-term debt-paying ability, the current ratio must be interpreted with great care. A *declining* ratio, as above, might be a sign of a deteriorating financial condition. On the other hand, it might be the result of eliminating obsolete inventories or other stagnant current assets. An *improving* ratio might be the result of an unwise stockpiling of inventory, or it might indicate an improving financial situation. In short, the current ratio is useful, but tricky to interpret. To avoid a blunder, the analyst must take a hard look at the individual assets and liabilities involved.

The general rule of thumb calls for a current ratio of 2 to 1. This rule is subject to many exceptions, depending on the industry and the firm involved. Some industries can operate quite successfully with a current ratio of slightly over 1 to 1. The adequacy of a current ratio depends heavily on the *composition* of the assets. For example, as we see in the table below, both Worthington Corporation and Greystone, Inc., have current ratios of 2 to 1. However, they are not in comparable financial condition. Greystone is likely to have difficulty meeting its current financial obligations, since almost all of its current assets consist of inventory rather than more liquid assets such as cash and accounts receivable.

	Worthington Corporation	Greystone, Inc.
Current assets:		
Cash	$ 25,000	$ 2,000
Accounts receivable, net	60,000	8,000
Inventory	85,000	160,000
Prepaid expenses	5,000	5,000
Total current assets (a)	$175,000	$175,000
Current liabilities (b)	$ 87,500	$ 87,500
Current ratio, (a) ÷ (b)	2 to 1	2 to 1

Acid-Test (Quick) Ratio

The **acid-test (quick) ratio** is a much more rigorous test of a company's ability to meet its short-term debts. Inventories and prepaid expenses are excluded from total current assets, leaving only the more liquid (or "quick") assets to be divided by current liabilities.

$$\text{Acid-test ratio} = \frac{\text{Cash + Marketable securities + Current receivables*}}{\text{Current liabilities}}$$

*Current receivables include both accounts receivable and any short-term notes receivable.

The acid-test ratio is designed to measure how well a company can meet its obligations without having to liquidate or depend too heavily on its inventory. Since inventory may be difficult to sell in times of economic stress, it is generally felt that to be properly protected, each dollar of liabilities should be backed by at least $1 of quick assets. Thus, an acid-test ratio of 1 to 1 is usually viewed as adequate.

The acid-test ratios for Brickey Electronics for 2000 and 2001 are computed below:

	2001	2000
Cash (see Exhibit 14–1)	$1,200,000	$2,350,000
Accounts receivable (see Exhibit 14–1)	6,000,000	4,000,000
Total quick assets (a)	$7,200,000	$6,350,000
Current liabilities (see Exhibit 14–1) (b)	$7,000,000	$5,000,000
Acid-test ratio, (a) ÷ (b)	1.03 to 1	1.27 to 1

Although Brickey Electronics has an acid-test ratio for 2001 that is within the acceptable range, an analyst might be concerned about several disquieting trends revealed in the company's balance sheet. Notice in Exhibit 14–1 that short-term debts are rising, while the cash position seems to be deteriorating. Perhaps the weakened cash position is a result of the greatly expanded volume of accounts receivable. One wonders why the accounts receivable have been allowed to increase so rapidly in so brief a time.

In short, as with the current ratio, the acid-test ratio should be interpreted with one eye on its basic components.

Accounts Receivable Turnover

The **accounts receivable turnover** is a rough measure of how many times a company's accounts receivable have been turned into cash during the year. It is frequently used in conjunction with an analysis of working capital, since a smooth flow from accounts receivable into cash is an important indicator of the "quality" of a company's working capital and is critical to the company's ability to operate. The accounts receivable turnover is computed by dividing sales on account (i.e., credit sales) by the average accounts receivable balance for the year.

$$\text{Accounts receivable turnover} = \frac{\text{Sales on account}}{\text{Average accounts receivable balance}}$$

Assuming that all sales for the year were on account, the accounts receivable turnover for Brickey Electronics for 2001 would be computed as follows:

$$\frac{\text{Sales on account}}{\text{Average accounts receivable balance}} = \frac{\$52,000,000}{\$5,000,000*} = 10.4 \text{ times}$$

*$4,000,000 + $6,000,000 = $10,000,000; $10,000,000 ÷ 2 = $5,000,000 average.

The turnover figure can then be divided into 365 to determine the average number of days being taken to collect an account (known as the **average collection period**).

$$\text{Average collection period} = \frac{365 \text{ days}}{\text{Accounts receivable turnover}}$$

The average collection period for Brickey Electronics for 2001 is computed as follows:

$$\frac{365}{10.4 \text{ times}} = 35 \text{ days}$$

This simply means that on average it takes 35 days to collect on a credit sale. Whether the average of 35 days taken to collect an account is good or bad depends on the credit terms Brickey Electronics is offering its customers. If the credit terms are 30 days, then a 35-day average collection period would usually be viewed as very good. Most customers will tend to withhold payment for as long as the credit terms will allow and may even go over a few days. This factor, added to ever-present problems with a few slow-paying customers, can cause the average collection period to exceed normal credit terms by a week or so and should not cause great alarm.

On the other hand, if the company's credit terms are 10 days, then a 35-day average collection period is worrisome. The long collection period may result from many old unpaid accounts of doubtful collectability, or it may be a result of poor day-to-day credit management. The firm may be making sales with inadequate credit checks on customers, or perhaps no follow-ups are being made on slow accounts.

Inventory Turnover

The **inventory turnover ratio** measures how many times a company's inventory has been sold and replaced during the year. It is computed by dividing the cost of goods sold by the average level of inventory on hand:

$$\text{Inventory turnover} = \frac{\text{Cost of goods sold}}{\text{Average inventory balance}}$$

The average inventory figure is the average of the beginning and ending inventory figures. Since Brickey Electronics has a beginning inventory of $10,000,000 and an ending inventory of $8,000,000, its average inventory for the year would be $9,000,000. The company's inventory turnover for 2001 would be computed as follows:

$$\frac{\text{Cost of goods sold}}{\text{Average inventory balance}} = \frac{\$36,000,000}{\$9,000,000} = 4 \text{ times}$$

The number of days being taken to sell the entire inventory one time (called the **average sale period**) can be computed by dividing 365 by the inventory turnover figure:

$$\text{Average sale period} = \frac{365 \text{ days}}{\text{Inventory turnover}}$$

$$\frac{365}{4 \text{ times}} = 91\tfrac{1}{4} \text{ days}$$

The average sale period varies from industry to industry. Grocery stores tend to turn their inventory over very quickly, perhaps as often as every 12 to 15 days. On the other hand, jewelry stores tend to turn their inventory over very slowly, perhaps only a couple of times each year.

If a firm has a turnover that is much slower than the average for its industry, then it may have obsolete goods on hand, or its inventory stocks may be needlessly high. Excessive inventories tie up funds that could be used elsewhere in operations. Managers sometimes argue that they must buy in very large quantities to take advantage of the best discounts being offered. But these discounts must be carefully weighed against the added costs of insurance, taxes, financing, and risks of obsolescence and deterioration that result from carrying added inventories.

Inventory turnover has been increasing in recent years as companies have adopted just-in-time (JIT) methods. Under JIT, inventories are purposely kept low, and thus a company utilizing JIT methods may have a very high inventory turnover as compared to other companies. Indeed, one of the goals of JIT is to increase inventory turnover by systematically reducing the amount of inventory on hand.

Vice President of Sales

Although its credit terms require payment within 30 days, your company's average collection period is 33 days. A major competitor has an average collection period of 27 days. You have been asked to explain why your company is not doing as well as the competitor. You have investigated your company's credit policies and procedures and have concluded that they are reasonable and adequate under the circumstances. What rationale would you consider to explain why (1) the average collection period of your company exceeds the credit terms, and (2) the average collection period of the company is higher than that of its competitor?

Ratio Analysis—The Long-Term Creditor

The position of long-term creditors differs from that of short-term creditors in that they are concerned with both the near-term *and* the long-term ability of a firm to meet its commitments. They are concerned with the near term since the interest they are entitled to is normally paid on a current basis. They are concerned with the long term since they want to be fully repaid on schedule.

> **Learning Objective 4**
> Compute and interpret the financial ratios used to measure the well-being of the long-term creditor.

Since the long-term creditor is usually faced with greater risks than the short-term creditor, firms are often required to agree to various restrictive covenants, or rules, for the long-term creditor's protection. Examples of such restrictive covenants include the maintenance of minimum working capital levels and restrictions on payment of dividends to common stockholders. Although these restrictive covenants are in widespread use, they are a poor second to adequate future *earnings* from the point of view of assessing protection and safety. Creditors do not want to go to court to collect their claims; they would much prefer staking the safety of their claims for interest and eventual repayment of principal on an orderly and consistent flow of funds from operations.

Times Interest Earned Ratio

The most common measure of the ability of a firm's operations to provide protection to the long-term creditor is the **times interest earned ratio.** It is computed by dividing earnings *before* interest expense and income taxes (i.e., net operating income) by the yearly interest charges that must be met:

$$\text{Times interest earned} = \frac{\text{Earnings before interest expense and income taxes}}{\text{Interest expense}}$$

For Brickey Electronics, the times interest earned ratio for 2001 would be computed as follows:

$$\frac{\$3,140,000}{\$640,000} = 4.9 \text{ times}$$

Earnings before income taxes must be used in the computation, since interest expense deductions come *before* income taxes are computed. Creditors have first claim on earnings. Only those earnings remaining after all interest charges have been provided for are subject to income taxes.

Generally, earnings are viewed as adequate to protect long-term creditors if the times interest earned ratio is 2 or more. Before making a final judgment, however, it would be necessary to look at a firm's long-run *trend* of earnings and evaluate how vulnerable the firm is to cyclical changes in the economy.

Debt-to-Equity Ratio

Long-term creditors are also concerned with keeping a reasonable balance between the portion of assets provided by creditors and the portion of assets provided by the stockholders of a firm. This balance is measured by the **debt-to-equity ratio:**

$$\text{Debt-to-equity ratio} = \frac{\text{Total liabilities}}{\text{Stockholders' equity}}$$

	2001	2000
Total liabilities (a)	$14,500,000	$13,000,000
Stockholders' equity (b)	$17,000,000	$15,970,000
Debt-to-equity ratio, (a) ÷ (b)	0.85 to 1	0.81 to 1

The debt-to-equity ratio indicates the amount of assets being provided by creditors for each dollar of assets being provided by the owners of a company. In 2000, creditors of Brickey Electronics were providing 81 cents of assets for each $1 of assets being provided by stockholders; the figure increased only slightly to 85 cents by 2001.

Creditors would like the debt-to-equity ratio to be relatively low. The lower the ratio, the greater the amount of assets being provided by the owners of a company and the greater is the buffer of protection to creditors. By contrast, common stockholders would like the ratio to be relatively high, since through leverage, common stockholders can benefit from the assets being provided by creditors.

In most industries, norms have developed over the years that serve as guides to firms in their decisions as to the "right" amount of debt to include in the capital structure. Different industries face different risks. For this reason, the level of debt that is appropriate for firms in one industry is not necessarily a guide to the level of debt that is appropriate for firms in a different industry.

in business today Transforming American Standard

Emmanuel Kampouris, the Egyptian-born CEO of American Standard, has transformed the manufacturer of bathroom fixtures, coolers, and truck parts into a lean competitor. The key to this transformation has been "demand flow technology"—a sort of just-in-time (JIT) on steroids. In addition to cutting inventories, the aim is to slash manufacturing time. The end result is the capability to respond to the customer faster, at lower cost, and with greater variety than before. At Home Depot, Standard's plumbing, heating, and air-conditioning goods now arrive within days—not months—of being ordered. Overall, the company has reduced its inventories by more than 50%—realizing hundreds of millions of dollars of savings. Inventory turnover has improved from less than 5 times to over 11 times, and working capital has declined from 8.6% of sales to 4.9%. The interest savings alone on the reduced inventories are over $60 million per year. Kampouris has also slashed the company's debt by nearly $1 billion—dropping the company's debt-to-equity ratio from 87.5% down to about 39%.

Source: "American Standard Wises Up," *Business Week*, November 18, 1996, p. 50; Shawn Tully, "American Standard: Prophet of Zero Working Capital," *Fortune*, June 13, 1994, pp. 113–114.

Summary of Ratios and Sources of Comparative Ratio Data

Exhibit 14–7 contains a summary of the ratios discussed in this chapter. The formula for each ratio and a summary comment on each ratio's significance are included in the exhibit.

Exhibit 14–8 contains a listing of published sources that provide comparative ratio data organized by industry. These sources are used extensively by managers, investors, and analysts in doing comparative analyses and in attempting to assess the well-being of companies. The World Wide Web also contains a wealth of financial and other data. A search engine such as Alta Vista, Yahoo, or Excite can be used to track down information on individual companies. Many companies have their own websites on which they post their latest financial reports and news of interest to potential investors. The *EDGAR* database

Exhibit 14–7
Summary of Ratios

Ratio	Formula	Significance
Gross margin percentage	Gross margin ÷ Sales	A broad measure of profitability
Earnings per share (of common stock)	(Net income − Preferred dividends) ÷ Average number of common shares outstanding	Tends to have an effect on the market price per share, as reflected in the price-earnings ratio
Price-earnings ratio	Market price per share ÷ Earnings per share	An index of whether a stock is relatively cheap or relatively expensive in relation to current earnings
Dividend payout ratio	Dividends per share ÷ Earnings per share	An index showing whether a company pays out most of its earnings in dividends or reinvests the earnings internally
Dividend yield ratio	Dividends per share ÷ Market price per share	Shows the return in terms of cash dividends being provided by a stock
Return on total assets	{Net income + [Interest expense × (1 − Tax rate)]} ÷ Average total assets	Measure of how well assets have been employed by management
Return on common stockholders' equity	(Net income − Preferred dividends) ÷ Average common stockholders' equity (Average total stockholders' equity − Average preferred stock)	When compared to the return on total assets, measures the extent to which financial leverage is working for or against common stockholders
Book value per share	Common stockholders' equity (Total stockholders' equity − Preferred stock) ÷ Number of common shares outstanding	Measures the amount that would be distributed to holders of common stock if all assets were sold at their balance sheet carrying amounts and if all creditors were paid off
Working capital	Current assets − Current liabilities	Measures the company's ability to repay current liabilities using only current assets
Current ratio	Current assets ÷ Current liabilities	Test of short-term debt-paying ability
Acid-test (quick) ratio	(Cash + Marketable securities + Current receivables) ÷ Current liabilities	Test of short-term debt-paying ability without having to rely on inventory
Accounts receivable turnover	Sales on account ÷ Average accounts receivable balance	A rough measure of how many times a company's accounts receivable have been turned into cash during the year
Average collection period (age of receivables)	365 days ÷ Accounts receivable turnover	Measure of the average number of days taken to collect an account receivable
Inventory turnover	Cost of goods sold ÷ Average inventory balance	Measure of how many times a company's inventory has been sold during the year
Average sale period (turnover in days)	365 days ÷ Inventory turnover	Measure of the average number of days taken to sell the inventory one time
Times interest earned	Earnings before interest expense and income taxes ÷ Interest expense	Measure of the company's ability to make interest payments
Debt-to-equity ratio	Total liabilities ÷ Stockholders' equity	Measure of the amount of assets being provided by creditors for each dollar of assets being provided by the stockholders

Exhibit 14–8
Published Sources of Financial Ratios

Source	Content
Almanac of Business and Industrial Financial Ratios. Prentice-Hall. Published annually.	An exhaustive source that contains common-size income statements and financial ratios by industry and by size of companies within each industry.
Annual Statement Studies. Robert Morris Associates. Published annually. See www.rmahq.org/Ann_Studies/assstudies.html for definitions and explanations of ratios and balance sheet and income statement data that are contained in the Annual Statement Studies.	A widely used publication that contains common-size statements and financial ratios on individual companies. The companies are arranged by industry.
Business & Company ASAP. Database that is updated continuously.	Exhaustive database of business articles in periodicals for both industry and company information. Many of the articles are available in full text. Directory listings for over 150,000 companies are also included in the database.
EDGAR. Securities and Exchange Commission. Website that is updated continuously. www.sec.gov	An exhaustive database accessible on the World Wide Web that contains reports filed by companies with the SEC. These reports can be downloaded.
EBSCOhost (Business Source Elite index). EBSCO Publishing. Database that is continuously updated.	Exhaustive database of business articles in periodicals useful for both industry and company information. Full text is included from nearly 970 journals; indexing and abstracts are offered for over 1,650 journals.
FreeEdgar. EDGAR Online, Inc. Website that is updated continuously. www.freeedgar.com	A site that allows you to search SEC filings. Financial information can be downloaded directly into Excel worksheets.
Hoover's Online. Hoovers, Inc. Website that is updated continuously. www.hoovers.com	A site that provides capsule profiles for 10,000 U.S. companies with links to company websites, annual reports, stock charts, news articles, and industry information.
Key Business Ratios. Dun & Bradstreet. Published annually.	Fourteen commonly used financial ratios are computed for over 800 major industry groupings.
Moody's Industrial Manual and Moody's Bank and Finance Manual. Dun & Bradstreet. Published annually.	An exhaustive source that contains financial ratios on all companies listed on the New York Stock Exchange, the American Stock Exchange, and regional American exchanges.
Standard & Poor's Industry Survey. Standard & Poor's. Published annually.	Various statistics, including some financial ratios, are given by industry and for leading companies within each industry grouping.

listed in Exhibit 14–8 is a particularly rich source of data. It contains copies of all reports filed by companies with the SEC since about 1995—including annual reports filed as form 10-K.

in business | *today* **More Information about Segments**

Comparisons of one company with others in its industry often help an analyst better interpret financial data about the company. As companies have become more diversified, it has become more difficult to select competitors for comparison.

The Financial Accounting Standards Board issued *SFAS No. 131* in response to analysts' demands for additional information about a company's segments. The Statement requires broader disclosure of segment information than previously reported under *SFAS No. 14* and may help to overcome some of the limitations otherwise inherent in comparing one company to another. For example, Wal-Mart did not report any segments under *SFAS No. 14;* but it now discloses information about three operating segments (its U.S.

discount stores, its U.S. warehouse membership-club stores, and its international operations) under *SFAS No. 131*. Likewise, IBM, which did not report any segments under the prior rules, now discloses information about seven different operating segments.

Critics of the new reporting standards note that the beneficiaries of the enhanced reporting requirements not only include investors and creditors, but also competitors, and worry that too much information is being provided.

Source: Joe Sanders, Sherman Alexander, and Stan Clark, "New Segment Reporting—Is It Working?" *Strategic Finance,* December 1999, p. 35.

Summary

LO1   Prepare and interpret financial statements in comparative and common-size form.
It is difficult to interpret raw data from financial statements without standardizing the data in some way so that it can be compared over time and across companies. For example, all of the financial data for a company can be expressed as a percentage of the data in some base year. This makes it easier to spot trends over time. To make it easier to compare companies, common-size financial statements are often used in which income statement data are expressed as a percentage of sales and balance sheet data are expressed as a percentage of total assets.

LO2   Compute and interpret the financial ratios used to measure the well-being of the common stockholder.
Common stockholders are most concerned with the company's earnings per share, price-earnings ratio, dividend payout and yield ratios, return on total assets, book value per share, and return on common stockholders' equity. Generally speaking, the higher these ratios, the better it is for common stockholders.

LO3   Compute and interpret the financial ratios used to measure the well-being of the short-term creditor.
Short-term creditors are most concerned with the company's ability to repay its debt in the near future. Consequently, these investors focus on the relation between current assets and current liabilities and the company's ability to generate cash. Specifically, short-term creditors monitor working capital, the current ratio, the acid-test (quick) ratio, accounts receivable turnover, and inventory turnover.

LO4   Compute and interpret the financial ratios used to measure the well-being of the long-term creditor.
Long-term creditors have many of the same concerns as short-term creditors, but also monitor the times interest earned ratio and the debt-to-equity ratio. These ratios indicate the company's ability to pay interest out of operations and how heavily the company is financially levered.

Guidance Answers to You Decide and Decision Maker

CREDIT ANALYST (p. 563)
You should request a copy of the entire annual report. Often, two other sections of the annual report, the president's letter and management's discussion and analysis, contain important information about the data set forth in the company's financial statements. If the company's financial statements are more than three or four months old, you will want to obtain copies of any quarterly reports or other forms that have been filed with the SEC since company's year-end. You might also visit the company's website and use a periodicals database (see Exhibit 14–8) to search for articles that contain pertinent information about the company. For a basis of comparison, you should also obtain industry information (again, see Exhibit 14–8) and information about close competitors.

VICE PRESIDENT OF SALES (p. 579)

An average collection period of 33 days means that on average it takes 33 days to collect on a credit sale. Whether the average of 33 days is acceptable or not depends on the credit terms that your company is offering to its customers. In this case, an average collection period of 33 days is good because the credit terms offered by your company are net 30 days. Why might the average collection period exceed the credit terms? Some customers may misjudge the amount of time that it takes mail to reach the company's offices. Certain customers may experience temporary cash shortages and delay payment for short periods of time. Others might be in the process of returning goods and have not paid for the goods that will be returned because they realize that a credit will be posted to their account. Still others may be in the process of resolving disputes regarding the goods that were shipped.

Turning to the competitor's average collection period of 27 days, it is possible that the competitor's credit terms are 25 days rather than 30 days. Or, the competitor might be offering sales discounts to its customers (e.g., 2/10, n/30) for paying early. You should recall from your financial accounting course that sales discounts are offered as an incentive to customers to motivate them to pay invoices well in advance of the due date. If enough customers take advantage of the sales discounts, the average collection period will drop below 30 days.

Review Problem: Selected Ratios and Financial Leverage

Starbucks Coffee Company is the leading retailer and roaster of specialty coffee in North America with over 1,000 stores offering freshly brewed coffee, pastries, and coffee beans. Data from recent financial statements are given below:

STARBUCKS COFFEE COMPANY
Comparative Balance Sheet
(dollars in thousands)

	End of Year	Beginning of Year
Assets		
Current assets:		
Cash	$126,215	$ 20,944
Marketable securities	103,221	41,507
Accounts receivable	17,621	9,852
Inventories	83,370	123,657
Other current assets	9,114	9,390
Total current assets	339,541	205,350
Property and equipment, net	369,477	244,728
Other assets	17,595	18,100
Total assets	$726,613	$468,178
Liabilities and Stockholders' Equity		
Current liabilities:		
Accounts payable	$ 38,034	$ 28,668
Short-term bank loans	16,241	13,138
Accrued payables	18,005	13,436
Other current liabilities	28,811	15,804
Total current liabilities	101,091	71,046
Long-term liabilities:		
Bonds payable	165,020	80,398
Other long-term liabilities	8,842	4,503
Total liabilities	274,953	155,947
Stockholders' equity:		
Preferred stock	–0–	–0–
Common stock and additional paid-in capital	361,309	265,679
Retained earnings	90,351	46,552
Total stockholders' equity	451,660	312,231
Total liabilities and stockholders' equity	$726,613	$468,178

Note: The effective interest rate on the bonds payable was about 5%.

STARBUCKS COFFEE COMPANY
Comparative Income Statement
(dollars in thousands)

	Current Year	Prior Year
Revenue	$696,481	$465,213
Cost of goods sold	335,800	211,279
Gross margin	360,681	253,934
Operating expenses:		
Store operating expenses	$210,693	$148,757
Other operating expenses	19,787	13,932
Depreciation and amortization	35,950	22,486
General and administrative expenses	37,258	28,643
Total operating expenses	303,688	213,818
Net operating income	56,993	40,116
Gain on sale of investment	9,218	–0–
Plus interest income	11,029	6,792
Less interest expense	8,739	3,765
Net income before taxes	68,501	43,143
Less income taxes (about 38.5%)	26,373	17,041
Net income	$ 42,128	$ 26,102

Required:

For the current year:

1. Compute the return on total assets.
2. Compute the return on common stockholders' equity.
3. Is Starbucks' financial leverage positive or negative? Explain.
4. Compute the current ratio.
5. Compute the acid-test (quick) ratio.
6. Compute the inventory turnover.
7. Compute the average sale period.
8. Compute the debt-to-equity ratio.

SOLUTION TO REVIEW PROBLEM

1. Return on total assets:

$$\text{Return on total assets} = \frac{\text{Net Income} + [\text{Interest expense} \times (1 - \text{Tax rate})]}{\text{Average total assets}}$$

$$\frac{\$42,128 + [\$8,739 \times (1 - 0.385)]}{(\$726,613 + \$468,178)/2} = 8.0\% \text{ (rounded)}$$

2. Return on common stockholders' equity:

$$\text{Return on common stockholders' equity} = \frac{\text{Net income} - \text{Preferred dividends}}{\text{Average common stockholders' equity}}$$

$$\frac{\$42,128 - \$0}{(\$451,660 + \$312,231)/2} = 11.0\% \text{ (rounded)}$$

3. The company has positive financial leverage, since the return on common stockholders' equity (11%) is greater than the return on total assets (8%). The positive financial leverage was obtained from current liabilities and the bonds payable. The interest rate on the bonds is substantially less than the return on total assets.

4. Current ratio:

$$\text{Current ratio} = \frac{\text{Current assets}}{\text{Current liabilities}}$$

$$\frac{\$339,541}{\$101,091} = 3.36 \text{ (rounded)}$$

5. Acid-test (quick) ratio:

$$\text{Acid-test ratio} = \frac{\text{Cash + Marketable securities + Current receivables}}{\text{Current liabilities}}$$

$$\frac{\$126,215 + \$103,221 + \$17,621}{\$101,091} = 2.44 \text{ (rounded)}$$

This acid-test ratio is quite high and provides Starbucks with the ability to fund rapid expansion.

6. Inventory turnover:

$$\text{Inventory turnover} = \frac{\text{Cost of goods sold}}{\text{Average inventory balance}}$$

$$\frac{\$335,800}{(\$83,370 + \$123,657)/2} = 3.24 \text{ (rounded)}$$

7. Average sale period:

$$\text{Average sale period} = \frac{365 \text{ days}}{\text{Inventory turnover}}$$

$$\frac{365 \text{ days}}{3.24} = 113 \text{ days (rounded)}$$

8. Debt-to-equity ratio:

$$\text{Debt-to-equity ratio} = \frac{\text{Total liabilities}}{\text{Stockholders' equity}}$$

$$\frac{\$274,953}{\$451,660} = 0.61 \text{ (rounded)}$$

Glossary

(Note: Definitions and formulas for all financial ratios are shown in Exhibit 14–7. These definitions and formulas are not repeated here.)

Common-size statements   A statement that shows the items appearing on it in percentage form as well as in dollar form. On the income statement, the percentages are based on total sales revenue; on the balance sheet, the percentages are based on total assets. (p. 567)

Financial leverage   Acquiring assets with funds that have been obtained from creditors or from preferred stockholders at a fixed rate of return. (p. 573)

Horizontal analysis   A side-by-side comparison of two or more years' financial statements. (p. 564)

Negative financial leverage   A situation in which the fixed return to a company's creditors and preferred stockholders is greater than the return on total assets. In this situation, the return on common stockholders' equity will be *less* than the return on total assets. (p. 573)

Positive financial leverage   A situation in which the fixed return to a company's creditors and preferred stockholders is less than the return on total assets. In this situation, the return on common stockholders' equity will be *greater* than the return on total assets. (p. 573)

Trend analysis   See *horizontal analysis*. (p. 564)

Trend percentages   The expression of several years' financial data in percentage form in terms of a base year. (p. 566)

Vertical analysis   The presentation of a company's financial statements in common-size form. (p. 567)

Questions

14–1   Distinguish between horizontal and vertical analysis of financial statement data.

14–2   What is the basic purpose for examining trends in a company's financial ratios and other data? What other kinds of comparisons might an analyst make?

14–3   Assume that two companies in the same industry have equal earnings. Why might these companies have different price-earnings ratios?

14–4   Armcor, Inc., is in a rapidly growing technological industry. Would you expect the company to have a high or low dividend payout ratio?

14–5   Distinguish between a manager's *financing* and *operating* responsibilities. Which of these responsibilities is the return on total assets ratio designed to measure?

14–6   What is meant by the dividend yield on a common stock investment?

14–7   What is meant by the term *financial leverage?*

"How Well Am I Doing?" Financial Statement Analysis

587

14–8   The president of a medium-size plastics company was recently quoted in a business journal as stating, "We haven't had a dollar of interest-paying debt in over 10 years. Not many companies can say that." As a stockholder in this firm, how would you feel about its policy of not taking on interest-paying debt?

14–9   Why is it more difficult to obtain positive financial leverage from preferred stock than from long-term debt?

14–10   If a stock's market value exceeds its book value, then the stock is overpriced. Do you agree? Explain.

14–11   Weaver Company experiences a great deal of seasonal variation in its business activities. The company's high point in business activity is in June; its low point is in January. During which month would you expect the current ratio to be highest?

14–12   A company seeking a line of credit at a bank was turned down. Among other things, the bank stated that the company's 2 to 1 current ratio was not adequate. Give reasons why a 2 to 1 current ratio might not be adequate.

Brief Exercises

BRIEF EXERCISE 14–1   Trend Percentages (LO1)

Rotorua Products, Ltd., of New Zealand markets agricultural products for the burgeoning Asian consumer market. The company's current assets, current liabilities, and sales have been reported as follows over the last five years (Year 5 is the most recent year):

	Year 5	Year 4	Year 3	Year 2	Year 1
Sales	$NZ2,250,000	$NZ2,160,000	$NZ2,070,000	$NZ1,980,000	$NZ1,800,000
Cash	$NZ 30,000	$NZ 40,000	$NZ 48,000	$NZ 65,000	$NZ 50,000
Accounts receivable, net	570,000	510,000	405,000	345,000	300,000
Inventory	750,000	720,000	690,000	660,000	600,000
Total current assets	$NZ1,350,000	$NZ1,270,000	$NZ1,143,000	$NZ1,070,000	$NZ 950,000
Current liabilities	$NZ 640,000	$NZ 580,000	$NZ 520,000	$NZ 440,000	$NZ 400,000

$NZ stands for New Zealand dollars.

Required:
1. Express all of the asset, liability, and sales data in trend percentages. (Show percentages for each item.) Use Year 1 as the base year and carry computations to one decimal place.
2. Comment on the results of your analysis.

BRIEF EXERCISE 14–2   Common-Size Income Statement (LO1)

A comparative income statement is given below for McKenzie Sales, Ltd., of Toronto:

McKENZIE SALES, LTD. Comparative Income Statement For the Years Ended June 30, 2001, and 2000		
	2001	2000
Sales	$8,000,000	$6,000,000
Less cost of goods sold	4,984,000	3,516,000
Gross margin	3,016,000	2,484,000
Less operating expenses:		
Selling expenses	1,480,000	1,092,000
Administrative expenses	712,000	618,000
Total expenses	2,192,000	1,710,000
Net operating income	824,000	774,000
Less interest expense	96,000	84,000
Net income before taxes	$ 728,000	$ 690,000

Members of the company's board of directors are surprised to see that net income increased by only $38,000 when sales increased by two million dollars.

Required:

1. Express each year's income statement in common-size percentages. Carry computations to one decimal place.
2. Comment briefly on the changes between the two years.

BRIEF EXERCISE 14–3　Financial Ratios for Common Stockholders (LO2)

Comparative financial statements for Weller Corporation for the fiscal year ending December 31 appear below. The company did not issue any new common or preferred stock during the year. A total of 800,000 shares of common stock were outstanding. The interest rate on the bond payable was 12.0%, the income tax rate was 40%, and the dividend per share of common stock was $0.25. The market value of the company's common stock at the end of the year was $18. All of the company's sales are on account.

WELLER CORPORATION
Comparative Balance Sheet
(dollars in thousands)

	2000	1999
Assets		
Current assets:		
Cash	$ 1,280	$ 1,560
Accounts receivable, net	12,300	9,100
Inventory	9,700	8,200
Prepaid expenses	1,800	2,100
Total current assets	25,080	20,960
Property and equipment:		
Land	6,000	6,000
Buildings and equipment, net	19,200	19,000
Total property and equipment	25,200	25,000
Total assets	$50,280	$45,960
Liabilities and Stockholders' Equity		
Current liabilities:		
Accounts payable	$ 9,500	$ 8,300
Accrued payables	600	700
Notes payable, short term	300	300
Total current liabilities	10,400	9,300
Long-term liabilities:		
Bonds payable	5,000	5,000
Total liabilities	15,400	14,300
Stockholders' equity:		
Preferred stock	2,000	2,000
Common stock	800	800
Additional paid-in capital	2,200	2,200
Total paid-in capital	5,000	5,000
Retained earnings	29,880	26,660
Total stockholders' equity	34,880	31,660
Total liabilities and stockholders' equity	$50,280	$45,960

WELLER CORPORATION
Comparative Income Statement and Reconciliation
(dollars in thousands)

	2000	1999
Sales	$79,000	$74,000
Cost of goods sold	52,000	48,000
Gross margin	27,000	26,000
Operating expenses:		
Selling expenses	8,500	8,000
Administrative expenses	12,000	11,000
Total operating expenses	20,500	19,000
Net operating income	6,500	7,000
Interest expense	600	600
Net income before taxes	5,900	6,400
Less income taxes	2,360	2,560
Net income	3,540	3,840
Dividends to preferred stockholders	120	400
Net income remaining for common stockholders	3,420	3,440
Dividends to common stockholders	200	200
Net income added to retained earnings	3,220	3,240
Retained earnings, beginning of year	26,660	23,420
Retained earnings, end of year	$29,880	$26,660

Required:
Compute the following financial ratios for common stockholders for the year 2000:

1. Gross margin percentage.
2. Earnings per share of common stock.
3. Price-earnings ratio.
4. Dividend payout ratio.
5. Dividend yield ratio.
6. Return on total assets.
7. Return on common stockholders' equity.
8. Book value per share.

BRIEF EXERCISE 14–4   Financial Ratios for Short-Term Creditors (LO3)
Refer to the data in Brief Exercise 14–3 for Weller Corporation.

Required:
Compute the following financial data for short-term creditors for the year 2000:

1. Working capital.
2. Current ratio.
3. Acid-test ratio.
4. Accounts receivable turnover. (Assume that all sales are on account.)
5. Average collection period.
6. Inventory turnover.
7. Average sale period.

BRIEF EXERCISE 14–5   Financial Ratios for Long-Term Creditors (LO4)
Refer to the data in Brief Exercise 14–3 for Weller Corporation.

Required:
Compute the following financial ratios for long-term creditors for the year 2000:
1. Times interest earned ratio.
2. Debt-to-equity ratio.

Exercises

EXERCISE 14–1   Selected Financial Ratios for Common Stockholders (LO2)

Selected financial data from the June 30 year-end statements of Safford Company are given below:

Total assets	$3,600,000
Long-term debt (12% interest rate)	500,000
Preferred stock, $100 par, 8%	900,000
Total stockholders' equity	2,400,000
Interest paid on long-term debt	60,000
Net income	280,000

Total assets at the beginning of the year were $3,000,000; total stockholders' equity was $2,200,000. There has been no change in the preferred stock during the year. The company's tax rate is 30%.

Required:

1. Compute the return on total assets.
2. Compute the return on common stockholders' equity.
3. Is financial leverage positive or negative? Explain.

EXERCISE 14–2   Selected Financial Data for Short-Term Creditors (LO3)

Norsk Optronics, ALS, of Bergen, Norway, had a current ratio of 2.5 to 1 on June 30 of the current year. On that date, the company's assets were:

Cash		Kr 90,000
Accounts receivable	Kr300,000	
Less allowance for doubtful accounts	40,000	260,000
Inventory		490,000
Prepaid expenses		10,000
Plant and equipment, net		800,000
Total assets		Kr1,650,000

The Norwegian currency is the krone, denoted here by the symbol Kr.

Required:

1. What was the company's working capital on June 30?
2. What was the company's acid-test (quick) ratio on June 30?
3. The company paid an account payable of Kr40,000 immediately after June 30.
   a. What effect did this transaction have on working capital? Show computations.
   b. What effect did this transaction have on the current ratio? Show computations.

EXERCISE 14–3   Selected Financial Ratios (LO2, LO3, LO4)

The financial statements for Castile Products, Inc., are given below:

CASTILE PRODUCTS, INC.
Balance Sheet
December 31

Assets

Current assets:	
Cash	$ 6,500
Accounts receivable, net	35,000
Merchandise inventory	70,000
Prepaid expenses	3,500
Total current assets	115,000
Property and equipment, net	185,000
Total assets	$300,000

Liabilities and Stockholders' Equity

Liabilities:		
Current liabilities		$ 50,000
Bonds payable, 10%		80,000
Total liabilities		130,000
Stockholders' equity:		
Common stock, $5 per value	$ 30,000	
Retained earnings	140,000	
Total stockholders' equity		170,000
Total liabilities and equity		$300,000

CASTILE PRODUCTS, INC.
Income Statement
For the Year Ended December 31

Sales	$420,000
Less cost of goods sold	292,500
Gross margin	127,500
Less operating expenses	89,500
Net operating income	38,000
Interest expense	8,000
Net income before taxes	30,000
Income taxes (30%)	9,000
Net income	$ 21,000

Account balances at the beginning of the year were: accounts receivable, $25,000; and inventory, $60,000. All sales were on account.

Required:
Compute financial ratios as follows:

1. Gross margin percentage.
2. Current ratio.
3. Acid-test (quick) ratio.
4. Debt-to-equity ratio.
5. Accounts receivable turnover in days.
6. Inventory turnover in days.
7. Times interest earned.
8. Book value per share.

EXERCISE 14–4 Selected Financial Ratios for Common Stockholders (LO2)
Refer to the financial statements for Castile Products, Inc., in Exercise 14–3. In addition to the data in these statements, assume that Castile Products, Inc., paid dividends of $2.10 per share during the year. Also assume that the company's common stock had a market price of $42 at the end of the year and there was no change in the number of outstanding shares of common stock during the year.

Required:
Compute financial ratios as follows:

1. Earnings per share.
2. Dividend payout ratio.
3. Dividend yield ratio.
4. Price-earnings ratio.

EXERCISE 14–5 Selected Financial Ratios for Common Stockholders (LO2)
Refer to the financial statements for Castile Products, Inc., in Exercise 14–3. Assets at the beginning of the year totaled $280,000, and the stockholders' equity totaled $161,600.

Required:

Compute the following:

1. Return on total assets.
2. Return on common stockholders' equity.
3. Was financial leverage positive or negative for the year? Explain.

Problems

CHECK FIGURE
(1e) Inventory turnover this year: 5.0 times
(1g) Times interest earned last year: 4.9 times

PROBLEM 14–1   Common-Size Statements and Financial Ratios for Creditors (LO1, LO3, LO4)

Paul Sabin organized Sabin Electronics 10 years ago in order to produce and sell several electronic devices on which he had secured patents. Although the company has been fairly profitable, it is now experiencing a severe cash shortage. For this reason, it is requesting a $500,000 long-term loan from Gulfport State Bank, $100,000 of which will be used to bolster the Cash account and $400,000 of which will be used to modernize certain key items of equipment. The company's financial statements for the two most recent years follow:

SABIN ELECTRONICS
Comparative Balance Sheet

	This Year	Last Year
Assets		
Current assets:		
Cash	$ 70,000	$ 150,000
Marketable securities	—	18,000
Accounts receivable, net	480,000	300,000
Inventory	950,000	600,000
Prepaid expenses	20,000	22,000
Total current assets	1,520,000	1,090,000
Plant and equipment, net	1,480,000	1,370,000
Total assets	$3,000,000	$2,460,000
Liabilities and Stockholders' Equity		
Liabilities:		
Current liabilities	$ 800,000	$ 430,000
Bonds payable, 12%	600,000	600,000
Total liabilities	1,400,000	1,030,000
Stockholders' equity:		
Preferred stock, $25 par, 8%	250,000	250,000
Common stock, $10 par	500,000	500,000
Retained earnings	850,000	680,000
Total stockholders' equity	1,600,000	1,430,000
Total liabilities and equity	$3,000,000	$2,460,000

SABIN ELECTRONICS
Comparative Income Statement

	This Year	Last Year
Sales	$5,000,000	$4,350,000
Less cost of goods sold	3,875,000	3,450,000
Gross margin	1,125,000	900,000
Less operating expenses	653,000	548,000
Net operating income	472,000	352,000
Less interest expense	72,000	72,000
Net income before taxes	400,000	280,000
Less income taxes (30%)	120,000	84,000
Net income	280,000	196,000

"How Well Am I Doing?" Financial Statement Analysis

593

Dividends paid:		
Preferred dividends	20,000	20,000
Common dividends	90,000	75,000
Total dividends paid	110,000	95,000
Net income retained	170,000	101,000
Retained earnings, beginning of year	680,000	579,000
Retained earnings, end of year	$ 850,000	$ 680,000

During the past year, the company introduced several new product lines and raised the selling prices on a number of old product lines in order to improve its profit margin. The company also hired a new sales manager, who has expanded sales into several new territories. Sales terms are 2/10, n/30. All sales are on account. Assume that the following ratios are typical of firms in the electronics industry:

Current ratio	2.5 to 1
Acid-test (quick) ratio	1.3 to 1
Average age of receivables	18 days
Inventory turnover in days	60 days
Debt-to-equity ratio	0.90 to 1
Times interest earned	6.0 times
Return on total assets	13%
Price-earnings ratio	12

Required:
1. To assist the Gulfport State Bank in making a decision about the loan, compute the following ratios for both this year and last year:
   a. The amount of working capital.
   b. The current ratio.
   c. The acid-test (quick) ratio.
   d. The average age of receivables. (The accounts receivable at the beginning of last year totaled $250,000.)
   e. The inventory turnover in days. (The inventory at the beginning of last year totaled $500,000.)
   f. The debt-to-equity ratio.
   g. The number of times interest was earned.
2. For both this year and last year:
   a. Present the balance sheet in common-size format.
   b. Present the income statement in common-size format down through net income.
3. Comment on the results of your analysis in (1) and (2) above and make a recommendation as to whether or not the loan should be approved.

PROBLEM 14–2 Financial Ratios for Common Stockholders (LO2)

Refer to the financial statements and other data in Problem 14–1. Assume that you are an account executive for a large brokerage house and that one of your clients has asked for a recommendation about the possible purchase of Sabin Electronics' stock. You are not acquainted with the stock and for this reason wish to do certain analytical work before making a recommendation.

Required:
1. You decide first to assess the well-being of the common stockholders. For both this year and last year, compute:
   a. The earnings per share. There has been no change in preferred or common stock over the last two years.
   b. The dividend yield ratio for common. The company's stock is currently selling for $40 per share; last year it sold for $36 per share.
   c. The dividend payout ratio for common.
   d. The price-earnings ratio. How do investors regard Sabin Electronics as compared to other firms in the industry? Explain.
   e. The book value per share of common. Does the difference between market value and book value suggest that the stock is overpriced? Explain.

CHECK FIGURE
(1a) EPS this year: $5.20
(1c) Dividend payout
     ratio last year: 42.6%

2. You decide next to assess the company's rate of return. Compute the following for both this year and last year:
   a. The return on total assets. (Total assets at the beginning of last year were $2,300,000.)
   b. The return on common equity. (Stockholders' equity at the beginning of last year was $1,329,000.)
   c. Is the company's financial leverage positive or negative? Explain.
3. Would you recommend that your client purchase shares of Sabin Electronics' stock? Explain.

CHECK FIGURE
(2) Return on common
     equity method A: 11.9%

PROBLEM 14–3   Effects of Financial Leverage (LO2)

Several investors are in the process of organizing a new company. The investors believe that $1,000,000 will be needed to finance the new company's operations, and they are considering three methods of raising this amount of money.

Method A: All $1,000,000 can be obtained through issue of common stock.

Method B: $500,000 can be obtained through issue of common stock and the other $500,000 can be obtained through issue of $100 par value, 8% preferred stock.

Method C: $500,000 can be obtained through issue of common stock, and the other $500,000 can be obtained through issue of bonds carrying an interest rate of 8%.

The investors organizing the new company are confident that it can earn $170,000 each year before interest and taxes. The tax rate will be 30%.

Required:

1. Assuming that the investors are correct in their earnings estimate, compute the net income that would go to the common stockholders under each of the three financing methods listed above.
2. Using the income data computed in (1) above, compute the return on common equity under each of the three methods.
3. Why do methods B and C provide a greater return on common equity than does method A? Why does method C provide a greater return on common equity than method B?

CHECK FIGURE
(1c) Acid-test ratio: 1.4 to 1

PROBLEM 14–4   Effects of Transactions on Financial Ratios (LO3)

Denna Company's working capital accounts at the beginning of the year are given below:

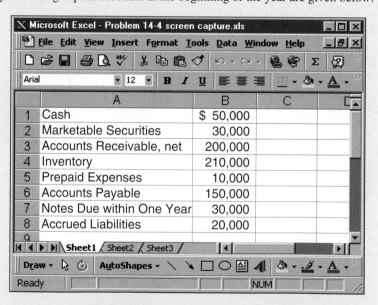

	A	B
1	Cash	$ 50,000
2	Marketable Securities	30,000
3	Accounts Receivable, net	200,000
4	Inventory	210,000
5	Prepaid Expenses	10,000
6	Accounts Payable	150,000
7	Notes Due within One Year	30,000
8	Accrued Liabilities	20,000

During the year, Denna Company completed the following transactions:

x. Paid a cash dividend previously declared, $12,000.
a. Issued additional shares of capital stock for cash, $100,000.
b. Sold inventory costing $50,000 for $80,000, on account.
c. Wrote off uncollectible accounts in the amount of $10,000. The company uses the allowance method of accounting for bad debts.
d. Declared a cash dividend, $15,000.
e. Paid accounts payable, $50,000.
f. Borrowed cash on a short-term note with the bank, $35,000.
g. Sold inventory costing $15,000 for $10,000 cash.

h. Purchased inventory on account, $60,000.
i. Paid off all short-term notes due, $30,000.
j. Purchased equipment for cash, $15,000.
k. Sold marketable securities costing $18,000 for cash, $15,000.
l. Collected cash on accounts receivable, $80,000.

Required:
1. Compute the following amounts and ratios as of the beginning of the year:
   a. Working capital.
   b. Current ratio.
   c. Acid-test (quick) ratio.
2. Indicate the effect of each of the transactions given above on working capital, the current ratio, and the acid-test (quick) ratio. Give the effect in terms of increase, decrease, or none. Item (x) is given below as an example of the format to use:

	The Effect on		
Transaction	**Working Capital**	**Current Ratio**	**Acid-Test Ratio**
(x) Paid a cash dividend previously declared	None	Increase	Increase

PROBLEM 14–5   Interpretation of Financial Ratios (LO1, LO2, LO3)

Paul Ward is interested in the stock of Pecunious Products, Inc. Before purchasing the stock, Mr. Ward would like to learn as much as possible about the company. However, all he has to go on is the current year's (Year 3) annual report, which contains no comparative data other than the summary of ratios given below:

	Year 3	Year 2	Year 1
Sales trend	128.0	115.0	100.0
Current ratio	2.5:1	2.3:1	2.2:1
Acid-test (quick) ratio..............	0.8:1	0.9:1	1.1:1
Accounts receivable turnover	9.4 times	10.6 times	12.5 times
Inventory turnover	6.5 times	7.2 times	8.0 times
Dividend yield	7.1%	6.5%	5.8%
Dividend payout ratio	40%	50%	60%
Return on total assets	12.5%	11.0%	9.5%
Return on common equity	14.0%	10.0%	7.8%
Dividends paid per share*	$1.50	$1.50	$1.50

*There have been no changes in common stock outstanding over the three-year period.

Mr. Ward would like answers to a number of questions about the trend of events in Pecunious Products, Inc., over the last three years. His questions are:

a. Is it becoming easier for the company to pay its bills as they come due?
b. Are customers paying their accounts at least as fast now as they were in Year 1?
c. Is the total of the accounts receivable increasing, decreasing, or remaining constant?
d. Is the level of inventory increasing, decreasing, or remaining constant?
e. Is the market price of the company's stock going up or down?
f. Is the amount of the earnings per share increasing or decreasing?
g. Is the price-earnings ratio going up or down?
h. Is the company employing financial leverage to the advantage of the common stockholders?

Required:
Answer each of Mr. Ward's questions using the data given above. In each case, explain how you arrived at your answer.

PROBLEM 14–6   Comprehensive Ratio Analysis (LO2, LO3, LO4)

You have just been hired as a loan officer at Slippery Rock State Bank. Your supervisor has given you a file containing a request from Lydex Company, a manufacturer of safety helmets, for a $3,000,000, five-year loan. Financial statement data on the company for the last two years follow:

LYDEX COMPANY
Comparative Balance Sheet

	This Year	Last Year
Assets		
Current assets:		
Cash	$ 960,000	$ 1,260,000
Marketable securities	–0–	300,000
Accounts receivable, net	2,700,000	1,800,000
Inventory	3,900,000	2,400,000
Prepaid expenses	240,000	180,000
Total current assets	7,800,000	5,940,000
Plant and equipment, net	9,300,000	8,940,000
Total assets	$17,100,000	$14,880,000
Liabilities and Stockholders' Equity		
Liabilities:		
Current liabilities	$ 3,900,000	$ 2,760,000
Note payable, 10%	3,600,000	3,000,000
Total liabilities	7,500,000	5,760,000
Stockholders' equity:		
Preferred stock, 8%, $30 par value	1,800,000	1,800,000
Common stock, $80 par value	6,000,000	6,000,000
Retained earnings	1,800,000	1,320,000
Total stockholders' equity	9,600,000	9,120,000
Total liabilities and stockholders' equity	$17,100,000	$14,880,000

LYDEX COMPANY
Comparative Income Statement

	This Year	Last Year
Sales (all on account)	$15,750,000	$12,480,000
Less cost of goods sold	12,600,000	9,900,000
Gross margin	3,150,000	2,580,000
Less operating expenses	1,590,000	1,560,000
Net operating income	1,560,000	1,020,000
Less interest expense	360,000	300,000
Net income before taxes	1,200,000	720,000
Less income taxes (30%)	360,000	216,000
Net income	840,000	504,000
Dividends paid:		
Preferred dividends	144,000	144,000
Common dividends	216,000	108,000
Total dividends paid	360,000	252,000
Net income retained	480,000	252,000
Retained earnings, beginning of year	1,320,000	1,068,000
Retained earnings, end of year	$ 1,800,000	$ 1,320,000

Helen McGuire, who just a year ago was appointed president of Lydex Company, argues that although the company has had a "spotty" record in the past, it has "turned the corner," as evidenced by a 25% jump in sales and by a greatly improved earnings picture between last year and this year. McGuire also points out that investors generally have recognized the improving situation at Lydex, as shown by the increase in market value of the company's common stock, which is currently selling for $72 per share (up from $40 per share last year). McGuire feels that with her leadership and with the modernized equipment that the $3,000,000 loan will permit the company to buy, profits will be even stronger in the future. McGuire has a reputation in the industry for being a good manager who runs a "tight" ship.

Not wanting to botch your first assignment, you decide to generate all the information that you can about the company. You determine that the following ratios are typical of firms in Lydex Company's industry:

Current ratio	2.3 to 1
Acid-test (quick) ratio	1.2 to 1
Average age of receivables	30 days
Inventory turnover	60 days
Return on assets	9.5%
Debt-to-equity ratio	0.65 to 1
Times interest earned	5.7
Price-earnings ratio	10

Required:

1. You decide first to assess the rate of return that the company is generating. Compute the following for both this year and last year:
   a. The return on total assets. (Total assets at the beginning of last year were $12,960,000.)
   b. The return on common equity. (Stockholders' equity at the beginning of last year totaled $9,048,000. There has been no change in preferred or common stock over the last two years.)
   c. Is the company's financial leverage positive or negative? Explain.
2. You decide next to assess the well-being of the common stockholders. For both this year and last year, compute:
   a. The earnings per share.
   b. The dividend yield ratio for common.
   c. The dividend payout ratio for common.
   d. The price-earnings ratio. How do investors regard Lydex Company as compared to other firms in the industry? Explain.
   e. The book value per share of common. Does the difference between market value per share and book value per share suggest that the stock at its current price is a bargain? Explain.
   f. The gross margin percentage.
3. You decide, finally, to assess creditor ratios to determine both short-term and long-term debt-paying ability. For both this year and last year, compute:
   a. Working capital.
   b. The current ratio.
   c. The acid-test ratio.
   d. The average age of receivables. (The accounts receivable at the beginning of last year totaled $1,560,000.)
   e. The inventory turnover. (The inventory at the beginning of last year totaled $1,920,000.) Also compute the number of days required to turn the inventory one time (use a 365-day year).
   f. The debt-to-equity ratio.
   g. The number of times interest was earned.
4. Evaluate the data computed in (1) to (3) above, and using any additional data provided in the problem, make a recommendation to your supervisor as to whether the loan should be approved.

PROBLEM 14–7   Common-Size Financial Statements (LO1)
Refer to the financial statement data for Lydex Company given in Problem 14–6.

Required:
For both this year and last year:
1. Present the balance sheet in common-size format.
2. Present the income statement in common-size format down through net income.
3. Comment on the results of your analysis.

PROBLEM 14–8   Effects of Transactions on Financial Ratios (LO2, LO3, LO4)
In the right-hand column below, certain financial ratios are listed. To the left of each ratio is a business transaction or event relating to the operating activities of Delta Company.

Business Transaction or Event	Ratio
1. The company declared a cash dividend.	Current ratio
2. The company sold inventory on account at cost.	Acid-test (quick) ratio
3. The company issued bonds with an interest rate of 8%. The company's return on assets is 10%.	Return on common stockholders' equity
4. The company's net income decreased by 10% between last year and this year. Long-term debt remained unchanged.	Times interest earned
5. A previously declared cash dividend was paid.	Current ratio
6. The market price of the company's common stock dropped from 24½ to 20. The dividend paid per share remained unchanged.	Dividend payout ratio
7. Obsolete inventory totaling $100,000 was written off as a loss.	Inventory turnover ratio
8. The company sold inventory for cash at a profit.	Debt-to-equity ratio
9. Changed customer credit terms from 2/10, n/30 to 2/15, n/30 to comply with a change in industry practice.	Accounts receivable turnover ratio
10. Issued a common stock dividend on common stock.	Book value per share
11. The market price of the company's common stock increased from 24½ to 30.	Book value per share
12. The company paid $40,000 on accounts payable.	Working capital
13. Issued a common stock dividend to common stockholders.	Earnings per share
14. Paid accounts payable.	Debt-to-equity ratio
15. Purchased inventory on open account.	Acid-test (quick) ratio
16. Wrote off an uncollectible account against the Allowance for Bad Debts.	Current ratio
17. The market price of the company's common stock increased from 24½ to 30. Earnings per share remained unchanged.	Price-earnings ratio
18. The market price of the company's common stock increased from 24½ to 30. The dividend paid per share remained unchanged.	Dividend yield ratio

Required:
Indicate the effect that each business transaction or event would have on the ratio listed opposite to it. State the effect in terms of increase, decrease, or no effect on the ratio involved, and give the reason for your choice of answer. In all cases, assume that the current assets exceed the current liabilities both before and after the event or transaction. Use the following format for your answers:

Effect on Ratio	Reason for Increase, Decrease, or No Effect
1.	
Etc.	

CHECK FIGURE
(1a) EPS this year: $4.65
(2a) Return on total assets
    last year: 14.0%

PROBLEM 14–9   Financial Ratios for Common Stockholders (LO2)
(Problems 14–10 and 14–11 delve more deeply into the data presented below. Each problem is independent.) Empire Labs, Inc., was organized several years ago to produce and market several new "miracle drugs." The company is small but growing, and you are considering the purchase of some of its common stock as an investment. The following data on the company are available for the past two years:

"How Well Am I Doing?" Financial Statement Analysis

599

EMPIRE LABS, INC.
Comparative Income Statement
For the Years Ended December 31

	This Year	Last Year
Sales	$20,000,000	$15,000,000
Less cost of goods sold	13,000,000	9,000,000
Gross margin	7,000,000	6,000,000
Less operating expenses	5,260,000	4,560,000
Net operating income	1,740,000	1,440,000
Less interest expense	240,000	240,000
Net income before taxes	1,500,000	1,200,000
Less income taxes (30%)	450,000	360,000
Net income	$ 1,050,000	$ 840,000

EMPIRE LABS, INC.
Comparative Retained Earnings Statement
For the Years Ended December 31

	This Year	Last Year
Retained earnings, January 1	$2,400,000	$1,960,000
Add net income (above)	1,050,000	840,000
Total	3,450,000	2,800,000
Deduct cash dividends paid:		
Preferred dividends	120,000	120,000
Common dividends	360,000	280,000
Total dividends paid	480,000	400,000
Retained earnings, December 31	$2,970,000	$2,400,000

EMPIRE LABS, INC.
Comparative Balance Sheet
December 31

	This Year	Last Year
Assets		
Current assets:		
Cash	$ 200,000	$ 400,000
Accounts receivable, net	1,500,000	800,000
Inventory	3,000,000	1,200,000
Prepaid expenses	100,000	100,000
Total current assets	4,800,000	2,500,000
Plant and equipment, net	5,170,000	5,400,000
Total assets	$9,970,000	$7,900,000

Liabilities and Stockholders' Equity		
Liabilities:		
Current liabilities	$2,500,000	$1,000,000
Bonds payable, 12%	2,000,000	2,000,000
Total liabilities	4,500,000	3,000,000
Stockholders' equity:		
Preferred stock, 8%, $10 par	1,500,000	1,500,000
Common stock, $5 par	1,000,000	1,000,000
Retained earnings	2,970,000	2,400,000
Total stockholders' equity	5,470,000	4,900,000
Total liabilities and stockholders' equity	$9,970,000	$7,900,000

After some research, you have determined that the following ratios are typical of firms in the pharmaceutical industry:

Dividend yield ratio	3%
Dividend payout ratio	40%
Price-earnings ratio	16
Return on total assets	13.5%
Return on common equity	20%

The company's common stock is currently selling for $60 per share. Last year the stock sold for $45 per share.

There has been no change in the preferred or common stock outstanding over the last three years.

Required:

1. In analyzing the company, you decide first to compute the earnings per share and related ratios. For both last year and this year, compute:
   a. The earnings per share.
   b. The dividend yield ratio.
   c. The dividend payout ratio.
   d. The price-earnings ratio.
   e. The book value per share of common stock.
   f. The gross margin percentage.
2. You decide next to determine the rate of return that the company is generating. For both last year and this year, compute:
   a. The return on total assets. (Total assets were $6,500,000 at the beginning of last year.)
   b. The return on common stockholders' equity. (Common stockholders' equity was $2,900,000 at the beginning of last year.)
   c. Is financial leverage positive or negative? Explain.
3. Based on your work in (1) and (2) above, does the company's common stock seem to be an attractive investment? Explain.

CHECK FIGURE
(1b) Current ratio this year:
     1.92 to 1
(1g) Debt-to-equity ratio
     last year: 0.61 to 1

PROBLEM 14–10 Financial Ratios for Creditors (LO3, LO4)

Refer to the data in Problem 14–9. Although Empire Labs, Inc., has been very profitable since it was organized several years ago, the company is beginning to experience some difficulty in paying its bills as they come due. Management has approached Security National Bank requesting a two-year, $500,000 loan to bolster the cash account.

Security National Bank has assigned you to evaluate the loan request. You have gathered the following data relating to firms in the pharmaceutical industry:

Current ratio	2.4 to 1
Acid-test (quick) ratio	1.2 to 1
Average age of receivables	16 days
Inventory turnover in days	40 days
Times interest earned	7 times
Debt-to-equity ratio	0.70 to 1

The following additional information is available on Empire Labs, Inc.:

a. All sales are on account.
b. At the beginning of last year, the accounts receivable balance was $600,000 and the inventory balance was $1,000,000.

Required:
1. Compute the following amounts and ratios for both last year and this year:
   a. The working capital.
   b. The current ratio.
   c. The acid-test ratio.
   d. The accounts receivable turnover in days.
   e. The inventory turnover in days.
   f. The times interest earned.
   g. The debt-to-equity ratio.
2. Comment on the results of your analysis in (1) above.
3. Would you recommend that the loan be approved? Explain.

PROBLEM 14–11   Common-Size Financial Statements (LO1)
Refer to the data in Problem 14–9. The president of Empire Labs, Inc., is deeply concerned. Sales increased by $5 million from last year to this year, yet the company's net income increased by only a small amount. Also, the company's operating expenses went up this year, even though a major effort was launched during the year to cut costs.

Required:
1. For both last year and this year, prepare the income statement and the balance sheet in common-size format. Round computations to one decimal place.
2. From your work in (1) above, explain to the president why the increase in profits was so small this year. Were any benefits realized from the company's cost-cutting efforts? Explain.

Building Your Skills

ANALYTICAL THINKING   (LO2, LO3, LO4)
Incomplete financial statements for Pepper Industries follow:

PEPPER INDUSTRIES Balance Sheet March 31	
Current assets:	
Cash	$?
Accounts receivable, net	?
Inventory	?
Total current assets	?
Plant and equipment, net	?
Total assets	$?
Liabilities:	
Current liabilities	$ 320,000
Bonds payable, 10%	?
Total liabilities	?
Stockholders' equity:	
Common stock, $5 par value	?
Retained earnings	?
Total stockholders' equity	?
Total liabilities and stockholders' equity	$?

PEPPER INDUSTRIES
Income Statement
For the Year Ended March 31

Sales	$4,200,000
Less cost of goods sold	?
Gross margin	?
Less operating expenses	?
Net operating income	?
Less interest expense	80,000
Net income before taxes	?
Less income taxes (30%)	?
Net income	$?

The following additional information is available about the company:

a. All sales during the year were on account.
b. There was no change in the number of shares of common stock outstanding during the year.
c. The interest expense on the income statement relates to the bonds payable; the amount of bonds outstanding did not change during the year.
d. Selected balances at the *beginning* of the current fiscal year were:

Accounts receivable	$ 270,000
Inventory	360,000
Total assets	1,800,000

e. Selected financial ratios computed from the statements above for the current year are:

Earnings per share	$2.30
Debt-to-equity ratio	0.875 to 1
Accounts receivable turnover	14.0 times
Current ratio	2.75 to 1
Return on total assets	18.0%
Times interest earned	6.75 times
Acid-test (quick) ratio	1.25 to 1
Inventory turnover	6.5 times

Required:
Compute the missing amounts on the company's financial statements. (Hint: What's the difference between the acid-test ratio and the current ratio?)

COMMUNICATING IN PRACTICE   (LO1, LO2, LO3, LO4)
Typically, the market price of shares of a company's stock takes a beating when the company announces that it has not met analysts' expectations. As a result, many companies are under a lot of pressure to meet analysts' revenue and earnings projections. Internet startups that have gone public fall into this category. To manage (that is, to inflate or smooth) earnings, managers sometimes record revenue that has not yet been earned by the company and/or delay the recognition of expenses that have been incurred.

   Some recent examples illustrate how companies have attempted to manage their earnings. On March 20, 2000, MicroStrategy announced that it was forced to restate its 1999 earnings; revenue from multiyear contracts had been recorded in the first year instead of being spread over the lives of the related contracts as required by GAAP. On April 3, 2000, Legato Systems Inc. announced that it had restated its earnings; $7 million of revenue had been improperly recorded because customers had been promised that they could return the products purchased. As further discussed in this chapter, America Online overstated its

net income during 1994, 1995, and 1996. In May 2000, upon completing its review of the company's accounting practices, the SEC levied a fine of $3.5 million against AOL. Just prior to the announcement of
the fine levied on AOL, Helane Morrison, head of the SEC's San Francisco office, reemphasized that the
investigation of misleading financial statements is a top priority for the agency. [Sources: Jeff Shuttle-
worth, "Investors Beware: Dot.Coms Often Use Accounting Tricks," *Business Journal Serving San Jose
& Silicon Valley,* April 14, 2000, p. 16; David Henry, "AOL Pays $3.5M to Settle SEC Case," *USA Today,*
May 16, 2000, p. 3B.]

Required:
Write a memorandum to your instructor that answers the following questions. Use headings to organize
the information presented in the memorandum. Include computations to support your answers, when appropriate.

1. Why would companies be tempted to manage earnings?
2. If the earnings that are reported by a company are misstated, how might this impact business decisions
   made about that company (such as the acquisition of the company by another business)?
3. What ethical issues, if any, arise when a company manages its earnings?
4. How would investors and financial analysts tend to view the financial statements of a company that
   has been known to manage its earnings in the past?

ETHICS CHALLENGE   (LO3, LO4)

Venice InLine, Inc., was founded by Russ Perez to produce a specialized in-line skate he had designed for
doing aerial tricks. Up to this point, Russ has financed the company from his own savings and from retained profits. However, Russ now faces a cash crisis. In the year just ended, an acute shortage of high-im-
pact roller bearings had developed just as the company was beginning production for the Christmas season.
Russ had been assured by the suppliers that the roller bearings would be delivered in time to make Christmas shipments, but the suppliers had been unable to fully deliver on this promise. As a consequence,
Venice InLine had large stocks of unfinished skates at the end of the year and had been unable to fill all of
the orders that had come in from retailers for the Christmas season. Consequently, sales were below expectations for the year, and Russ does not have enough cash to pay his creditors.

Well before the accounts payable were to become due, Russ visited a local bank and inquired about obtaining a loan. The loan officer at the bank assured Russ that there should not be any problem getting a loan
to pay off his accounts payable—providing that on his most recent financial statements the current ratio
was above 2.0, the acid-test ratio was above 1.0, and net operating income was at least four times the interest on the proposed loan. Russ promised to return later with a copy of his financial statements.

Russ would like to apply for a $80,000 six-month loan bearing an interest rate of 10% per year.

The unaudited financial reports of the company appear below:

VENICE INLINE, INC. Comparative Balance Sheet As of December 31 (dollars in thousands)		
	This Year	**Last Year**
Assets		
Current assets:		
Cash	$ 70	$150
Accounts receivable, net	50	40
Inventory	160	100
Prepaid expenses	10	12
Total current assets	290	302
Property and equipment	270	180
Total assets	$560	$482

Liabilities and Stockholders' Equity

Current liabilities:		
Accounts payable	$154	$ 90
Accrued payables	10	10
Total current liabilities	164	100
Long-term liabilities	—	—
Total liabilities	164	100
Stockholders' equity:		
Common stock and additional paid-in capital	100	100
Retained earnings	296	282
Total stockholders' equity	396	382
Total liabilities and stockholders' equity	$560	$482

VENICE INLINE, INC.
Income Statement
For the Year Ended December 31
(dollars in thousands)

	This Year
Sales (all on accounts)	$420
Cost of goods sold	290
Gross margin	130
Operating expenses:	
Selling expenses	42
Administrative expenses	68
Total operating expenses	110
Net operating income	20
Interest expense	—
Net income before taxes	20
Less income taxes (30%)	6
Net income	$ 14

Required:

1. Based on the above unaudited financial statements and the statement made by the loan officer, would the company qualify for the loan?

2. Last year Russ purchased and installed new, more efficient equipment to replace an older plastic injection molding machine. Russ had originally planned to sell the old machine but found that it is still needed whenever the plastic injection molding process is a bottleneck. When Russ discussed his cash flow problems with his brother-in-law, he suggested to Russ that the old machine be sold or at least reclassified as inventory on the balance sheet since it could be readily sold. At present, the machine is carried in the Property and Equipment account and could be sold for its net book value of $45,000. The bank does not require audited financial statements. What advice would you give to Russ concerning the machine?

TAKING IT TO THE NET

As you know, the World Wide Web is a medium that is constantly evolving. Sites come and go and change without notice. To enable periodic update of site addresses, this problem has been posted to the textbook website (www.mhhe.com/folk1e). After accessing the site, enter the Student Center and select this chapter. Select and complete the Taking It to the Net problem.

TEAMWORK IN ACTION (LO1, LO2, LO4)
Gauging the success of a company usually involves some assessment of the firm's earnings. When evaluating earnings, investors should consider the quality and sources of the company's earnings as well as their amount. In other words, the source of earnings is as important a consideration as the size of earnings.

Your team should discuss and then respond to the following questions. All team members should agree with and understand the answers (including the calculations supporting the answers) and be prepared to report in class. Each teammate can assume responsibility for a different part of the presentation.

Required:
1. Discuss the differences between operating profits and the bottom line—profits after all revenues and expenses.
2. Do you think a dollar of earnings coming from operations is any more or less valuable than a dollar of earnings generated from some other source below operating profits (e.g., one-time gains from selling assets or one-time write-offs for charges related to closing a plant)? Explain.
3. What is the concept of operating leverage? What is the relation between operating leverage and operating profits?
4. What is the concept of financial leverage? What is the relation between financial leverage and return on common stockholders' equity?

Photo Credits

Subject/Author Index